# HANDBOOK OF
# EUROPEAN HISTORY
## *1400–1600*

# HANDBOOK OF EUROPEAN HISTORY 1400–1600

*Late Middle Ages, Renaissance, and Reformation*

VOLUME I
STRUCTURES AND ASSERTIONS

*Edited by*

Thomas A. Brady, Jr. ❖ Heiko A. Oberman
James D. Tracy

WILLIAM B. EERDMANS PUBLISHING COMPANY
GRAND RAPIDS, MICHIGAN

© 1994 E. J. Brill, Leiden, the Netherlands

First published in the Netherlands 1994 by
E. J. Brill, Leiden

This edition published in the United States of America 1996
through special arrangement with Brill by
Wm. B. Eerdmans Publishing Co.
255 Jefferson Ave. S.E., Grand Rapids, Michigan 49503

Printed in the United States of America

02 01 00 99 98 97 96      7 6 5 4 3 2 1


Library of Congress Cataloging-in-Publication Data

Handbook of European history, 1400-1600: late Middle Ages,
Renaissance, and Reformation / edited by Thomas A. Brady, Jr.,
Heiko A. Oberman, James D. Tracy.
p.      cm.
Originally published: Leiden; New York: E. J. Brill, 1994-      .
Includes index.
Contents: v. 1. Structures [i.e.] Structures and assertions.
ISBN 0-8028-4194-5. — ISBN 0-8028-4195-3
1. Europe — History — 15th century. 2. Europe — History — 1492-1648.
I. Brady, Thomas A. II. Oberman, Heiko Augustinus. III. Tracy, James D.
D203.H36      1996
940.2 — dc20                          95-50652
                                        CIP

# CONTENTS

## VOLUME 1: STRUCTURES AND ASSERTIONS

# EDITORS' PREFACE

This is the first of two volumes of the *Handbook of European History,
1400-1600*, of which original conception came from the publishing firm of
E. J. Brill. The execution was put in the hands of three editors and a managing editor, whose collaboration has been harmonious, happy, and interesting.

The project's purpose is to present the current state of research in a field,
the shapes of which have been changing very rapidly during the past quarter-century, and to do this across as many fields and subjects as possible.
The volumes are meant very much to be introductions to the subjects and
aids to research, not summaries, though the mixture of narrative, analysis,
and historiographical commentary varies from author to author.

The publishers and editors felt that that the authors should be recruited
from among the best scholars active today, regardless of country and native language. Happily, almost without exception the editors' first choices
joined the project and produced the chapters assigned. In volume 1 they
represent ten different nationalities, eight countries of residence, and seven
native languages.

Inevitably, for some topics a top scholar was not available, so that vol.
1's coverage is less complete than desirable. Scandinavia and eastern Europe are lacking, though they will appear in volume 2; only one of the
countries of the British Isles is represented, and Portugal not at all. It
would have been desirable to have a comparative chapter on political institutions and a systematic survey of ecclesiastical institutions. In recom-
pense for the latter, vol. 2 will be devoted heavily to religious and ecclesiastical topics.

Each author was asked to keep the annotation to the essentials and to key
it, as much as possible, to the bibliographies, which are meant both to support the chapters and to provide selective introductions to the current literature on the topic. Inevitably, authors differed in their organization of
bibliographies, and the editors have not reduced them to a common plan.

Except for the writers of British English, whose text and notes are pre-

sented as written, the texts, notes of the chapters, and all the bibliographies, are presented in American English. This was made necessary, of
course, by the high percentage of translations. Otherwise, only glaring differences in format have been smoothed. The abbreviations in the notes follow, wherever possible, the comprehensive list in the *Theologische
Realenzyklopädie*. Following the Conclusion to this volume are a note on
money and monetary conversions and a list of European rulers for this period.

Scholarship, like all aspects of life, has joys and sorrows, and one of the
sorrows of this project was the death of our colleague, Volker Press, who
died at Tübingen on 15 October 1993.

The editors thank the firm of E. J. Brill in Leiden for its support of the
project. In particular, the publisher has produced a whole set of maps.

The editors also express their thanks to the *Handbook*'s managing editor,
Katherine G. Brady, who from her Berkeley headquarters has undertaken
the day-to-day work that made the production of this volume possible. All
of the practical work of coordination, scheduling, correspondence, translation, and editing was either done by her or ran through her hands.

Thomas A. Brady, Jr.
Heiko A. Oberman
James D. Tracy

# LIST OF ABBREVIATIONS

| | | |
|---|---|---|
| *ADH* | = | *Annales de démographie historique* |
| *AESC* | = | *Annales. Économies, Sociétés, Civilisations* |
| *AHR* | = | *American Historical Review* |
| *ARG* | = | *Archiv für Reformationsgeschichte* |
| *BIHR* | = | *Bulletin of the Institute of Historical Research* |
| *CEH* | = | *Central European History* |
| *EconHR* | = | *Economic History Review* |
| *EHR* | = | *English Historical Review* |
| *HAHR* | = | *Hispanic American Historical Review* |
| *HJ* | = | *Historisches Jahrbuch* |
| *HWJ* | = | *History Workshop Journal* |
| *JBS* | = | *Journal of British Studies* |
| *JEconH* | = | *Journal of Economic History* |
| *JEEH* | = | *Journal of European Economic History* |
| *JFH* | = | *Journal of Family History* |
| *JMH* | = | *Journal of Modern History* |
| *JRG* | = | *Jahrbuch für Regionalgeschichte* |
| *JSH* | = | *Journal of Social History* |
| *JWH* | = | *Journal of World History* |
| *PaP* | = | *Past and Present* |
| *PS* | = | *Population Studies* |
| *RBPH* | = | *Revue belge de philologie et d'histoire* |
| *REJ* | = | *Revue des études juives* |
| *RenQ* | = | *Renaissance Quarterly* |
| *RN* | = | *Revue du Nord* |
| *SCJ* | = | *Sixteenth Century Journal* |
| SFN | = | Spätmittelalter und Frühe Neuzeit. Tübinger Forschungen zur Geschichtswissenschaft |
| SHKBA | = | Schriftenreihe der Historischen Kommission bei der Bayerischen Akademie der Wissenschaften |
| SKRG | = | Schriften zur Kirchen- und Rechtsgeschichte |
| *SMRT* | = | *Studies in Medieval and Reformation Thought* |
| TRE | = | Theologische Realenzyklopädie |
| *TRS* | = | *Transactions of the Royal Historical Society* |
| VIEG | = | Veröffentlichungen des Instituts für Europäische Geschichte Mainz |
| VKLBW | = | Veröffentlichungen der Kommission für geschichtliche Landeskunde in Baden-Württemberg |
| *VSWG* | = | *Vierteljahrschrift für Sozial- und Wirtschaftsgeschichte* |
| WdF | = | Wege der Forschung |
| *ZAA* | = | *Zeitschrift für Agrargeschichte und Agrarsoziologie* |
| *ZBLG* | = | *Zeitschrift für bayerische Landesgeschichte* |
| *ZfG* | = | *Zeitschrift für Geschichtswissenschaft* |
| *ZGO* | = | *Zeitschrift für die Geschichte des Oberrheins* |
| *ZSRG* | = | *Zeitschrift der Savigny-Stiftung für Rechtsgeschichte* |
| *ZSSD* | = | *Zeitschrift für Stadtgeschichte, Stadtsoziologie und Denkmalpflege* |

# LIST OF MAPS

# LIST OF TABLES AND FIGURES

# INTRODUCTION: RENAISSANCE AND REFORMATION, LATE MIDDLE AGES AND EARLY MODERN ERA

## 1. "THE RENAISSANCE" AND "THE REFORMATION": TWO CLASSIC CONCEPTS

The pivotal role in European history of the two centuries between 1400 and 1600 has sometimes been questioned but rarely denied. Since the middle of the nineteenth century, two terms—"the Renaissance" and "the Reformation"—have commonly been employed to express the historians' sense of this role. Each term can claim roots in an era it helped to organize. Although "the Renaissance" is a nineteenth-century coinage, the notion behind it descends from the fourteenth century. "This was that Dante," wrote Giovanni Boccaccio, "who was first to open the way for the return of the Muses, banished from Italy. 'Twas he that revealed the glory of the Florentine idiom. 'Twas he that brought under the rule of due numbers every beauty of the vernacular speech. 'Twas he who may be truly said to have brought back dead poesy to life."[1] Rather older than "the Renaissance," "the Reformation" has long expressed the sense of momentous change that shrouded the religious schism of the sixteenth century. "Has there ever been a century," asked the Gallicized German humanist Johannes Sleidan, "in which such varied and wonderful occurrences have been compressed into the shortest space of time? What mighty changes have we experienced, as well in political as in ecclesiastical affairs!"[2]

By the mid-nineteenth century, "the Renaissance" and "the Reformation" became categories of periodization, designating not just events or series of events but great turning points in history. They became assertions about how to relate, as Ernst Troeltsch wrote, "the course of past events to the complex of effects which lies before us in the present."[3] The specific milieu of "the Renaissance" and "the Reformation" was the splendid century between Napoleon's fall and the Great War's onset, the age when a Protestant and national Europe struggled to overcome mentally a past which had been Catholic and universal. That is why, whatever their differences, in their prime "the Renaissance" and "the Reformation" bore closely related meanings of spiritual liberation from a "medieval" past that was asserted to have been backward, benighted, clerical, and Catholic.

The common emancipatory content of "the Renaissance" and "the Reformation" in their classic guise may be illustrated by formulations from just after the middle of the nineteenth century. In his *Civilisation of the Renaissance in Italy* (1860), Jacob Burckhardt, a Basel professor of art history, practically invented "the Renaissance" with these words:

> In the Middle Ages both sides of human consciousness—that which was turned within and that which was turned without—lay as though dreaming or half awake beneath a common veil. The veil was woven of faith, illusion, and childish prepossession, through which the world and history were seen clad in strange hues. Man was conscious of himself only as a member of a race, people, party, family, or corporation—only through some general category. It is in Italy that this veil dissolved first; there arose an *objective* treatment and consideration of the State and of all the things of this world, and at the same time the *subjective* side asserted itself with corresponding emphasis. Man became a spiritual *individual* and recognized himself as such. In the same way the Greek had once distinguished himself from the barbarian, and the Arab had felt himself an individual at a time when other Asiatics knew themselves only as members of a race.[4]

Although the emergence of this spiritual individualism "inevitably" made the Italians "the first-born among the sons of modern Europe," the blighting grasp of Rome and Spain on Burckhardt's Italy made the Protestant peoples of transalpine Europe the true heirs of "the Renaissance."

"The Reformation," unlike Burckhardt's Renaissance, did not have to be invented, for the emancipatory role of Protestantism was a commonplace of nineteenth-century Protestant historical belief. It was ready to hand, for example, when the Boston historian John Lothrop Motley addressed the New York Historical Society in December 1867 on the theme, "Historical Progress and American Democracy." Toward the end, he compared Luther's appearance on history's stage with the drilling of artesian wells in the western United States. Just as the shafts, he said,

> are sunk through the sod of the prairies, through the loam, through the gravel, through the hard-pan, which is almost granite, until at last, 1,000 or 1,500 feet beneath the surface, the hand of man reveals a deep and rapid river coursing through those solitary, sunless depths. ... And when the shaft has reached that imprisoned river, ... the waters, remembering the august source ... whence ages ago they fell, leap upwards to the light with terrible energy, rising in an instant far above the surface of the current to delight and refresh mankind. ... Such was

the upward movement out of intellectual thralldom which we call the
Reformation when the shaft of Luther struck the captive stream. ...[5]
The fruits of this irrigation, however, ripened not in Europe, plagued by
despotism and revolutions, but in the new and greater Europe across the
sea, the United States of America. Motley spoke—Bostonian to New
Yorkers—just thirty months after Appomattox.

There were differences, of course, between Burckhardt's and Motley's
choices of agents and settings for the great liberation from "dreaming" and
"intellectual thralldom." Burckhardt, who grew up in a world of established Christian churches, set his story of liberation in the European Athens—Florence—while Motley, who did not, set his story in the European
Jerusalem—Wittenberg. If their stories' settings differed, their meanings
did not, for "the Renaissance" and "the Reformation" carried the same
message of liberation from the Middle Ages, the church, and Catholicism.

The twentieth century has handled these classic ideas of "the Renaissance" and "the Reformation" very roughly, but even at their height of
popularity, they did not dispel other ideas about Europe's relationship to
its deeper past. One was the notion that transition between the Middle
Ages and modernity was very much more recent that Burckhardt's fourteenth or even Motley's sixteenth century. Such was the view of James
Bryce, an Ulster Scot from Belfast, who in his precocious 1860 book on the
Holy Roman Empire mused that the Empire was

> above all description or explanation; not that it is impossible to discover
> the beliefs which created and sustained it, but that the power of those
> beliefs cannot be adequately apprehended by men whose minds have
> been differently trained, and whose imaginations are fired by different
> ideals.
> ... Something more succeeding generations will know, who will judge
> the Middle Ages more fairly than we, still living in the midst of a
> reaction against all that is mediaeval, can hope to do, and to whom it
> will be given to see and understand new forms of political life, whose
> nature we cannot so much as conjecture.[6]

The Middle Ages, in Bryce's view, had ended only a few decades ago, and
its beliefs were not benighted but simply different from modern ones, so
much so that they were opaque to those who still stood very close in time
to that era.

The changes of sensibility after 1918 made the concepts of "the Renaissance" and "the Reformation" controversial, disputed, and ambiguous.
For one thing, the rise of economic and social history tended to carve the
boundary between modern and older Europe ever more deeply into the era

between 1750 and 1815. For another, the ebbing prestige of individualism and Christianity in European high culture undermined the concepts' explanatory power. This process, which has continued since 1945, can be illustrated by two recent and important biographies, whose authors share a desire to extricate their respective subjects from a much reduced role as mere "forerunners" of the modern era.

In his *John Calvin: a Sixteenth-Century Portrait* (1989), William J. Bouwsma asserts that "the Calvin we know is chiefly an artifact of later Calvinism." Far from being a systematic and forward-looking critic of the medieval past, the historical Calvin was in reality "two Calvins, coexisting uncomfortably within the same historical personage." He was, on the one hand, "a philosopher, rationalist and a schoolman in the high Scholastic tradition represented by Thomas Aquinas" and, on the other, "a rhetorician and humanist, a skeptical fiedeist in the manner of the followers of William of Ockham."[7] These attributes were "promiscuously jumbled together within the historical Calvin, much as they have been variously combined in the whole course of Western civilization." Here is no turning point, no break, no indication of any clear evolution or progress.

No less resolutely post-modern is *Luther: Man Between God and the Devil* (1989 [1982]) by Heiko A. Oberman. His Martin Luther is the heir to and harvester of medieval theologizing, especially in the Augustinian vein, which Luther liberated from its sacramental, hierarchical, and legal restraints by means of a transcendent, apocalyptic vision of the world and the human heart trapped "between God and the Devil." Oberman quashes the idea of Luther as the liberator of the modern world with the remark that "proclamation of man's total impotence on the eve of mans' greatest scientific discoveries and enduring cultural achievements could only eliminate Luther as a point of spiritual orientation in the tumult of modern times."[8] Luther is neither a turning point nor a revolutionary. Neither medieval nor modern, his worldview stands judgment on them both.

## 2. "LATE MIDDLE AGES" AND "EARLY MODERN ERA": DEPRESSION, STRUCTURAL CHANGE, TRANSITION, AND EXPANSION

Once "the Renaissance" and "the Reformation" are robbed of their explanatory power, what becomes of the centuries between 1400 and 1600? Do they slip quietly into the long sleep of what Emanuel Le Roy Ladurie has called "motionless history," rocked by the endless rhythms of the preindustrial age?[9] The most probable answer is that we can still have a Ren-

aissance and a Reformation—more accurately, Renaissances and Reformations—providing that we no longer force them to serve us as the turning
points from medieval to modern times. The concepts retain their value for
designating respectively the literate, classicizing, urban-based, culture of
the lay elites and the great upheaval in the Christian church. Today, one
speaks of Renaissance and Reformation as movements—the influence of
social history—but they are no longer grand categories of periodization.

Nowadays, the place of the old revolutionary shift from medieval to
modern has been taken by a gradual, fluctuating, highly contextualized
blending of "late medieval" with "early modern," the central phase of
which unfolds in the fifteenth and sixteenth century. The terminus a quo is
an event unknown to Burckhardt or the other nineteenth-century historians, the great depression of the fourteenth century; the terminus ad quem
is conventionally the end of the Religious Wars in the seventeenth century.
A focus on the fifteenth and sixteenth centuries, therefore, stakes out the
heart of this era and emphasizes its main characteristics rather than its becoming and its passing.

What characterizes the late medieval-to-early modern era? Three principal trends of twentieth-century historical research shape our picture.
First, there is the late medieval depression of economy and population and
the fifteenth-century recovery. Second, there is the rupture of Christendom—structured by the church with its parishes, monasteries, bishops,
and quasi-imperial papacy, its liturgy and its Latin, its monastic schools
and its universities, and its uniform goal of shaping life, deed, and
thought—and its supersession by the Europe of the national states. Third,
there is the founding of the first European seaborne empires in the wider
world, through which Europeans began to knit the world's regions and
peoples into a global, Europe-centered and -controlled network of production and exchange. Depression and recovery, Christendom and the states,
Europe and the empires—these are three profoundly important changes
specific to this era of late medieval-to-early modern transition.

### Depression and Recovery

The great dying off of the fourteenth century, the ensuing depression, and
the recovery after 1470 now dominate all accounts of late medieval Europe. Not so long ago, the catastrophic inception of this process appeared
as a nasty but brief tangle with the Black Death, chronicled in the
*Decamerone* of the same Giovanni Boccaccio who celebrated Dante's revival of poetry. Perhaps it required the terrible pessimism of the interwar
period to first appreciate that the fourteenth century—with its pestilences,

famines, and pogroms—was not a time of new spiritual birth but "an age of crisis."[10] If anything, the recovery, which, beginning around 1470 dominated Fernand Braudel's "long sixteenth century," seems more astonishing than either the cataclysmic collapse that preceded it or the gentler depression that set in during the 1620s. All general accounts of this era must now take into consideration the fact that most parts of Europe only recovered their pre-plague levels of population and production around 1530, and with some happy exceptions, they did not go much higher before new troubles began around 1570. This story has important implications, too, for a more general scheme of periodization, for this secular pattern of expansion and contraction can now be seen as part of a recurrent rhythm of growth and stagnation until the eighteenth century, when Malthusian checks on population were finally breached. From this vantage point, of course, James Bryce's sense of a "long Middle Ages" was quite justified.

### Christendom and the States

The current willingness to reflect on enduring structures in the past arises, perhaps, from the successive failures of each aspirant—science, communism, capitalism—to give a durable shape and values to modern civilization. In particular, there has been much recent reflection on the systemic aspects of the European state system and, reaching further back, on the large structures that preceded it. This means primarily the ecclesiastically structured civilization that called itself "Christendom," which was the primary way—naturally, after local identities—in which the ancestors of the Europeans spoke of themselves and their common features vis-a-vis the rest of the world, chiefly the Islamic world, until the sixteenth century.

The time has come, of which James Bryce spoke, when greater distance to the Middle Ages allows a freer judgment on that era. What to staunch defenders of the State once seemed like fantastic and pernicious pretensions in the ideology of the papal monarchy, for example, can now be seen as a theoretical statement about the near imperial role the papacy came to play. It can now be seen, for example, that the stupendous transformation of a fragmented, agrarian Europe into Latin Christendom, which came to rival and resemble its elder Islamic sibling, culminated between 1050 and 1250, when, under the Roman bishops' leadership the church struggled "against domination of the clergy by emperors, kings, and lords and for the establishment of the Church of Rome as an independent, corporate, political and legal entity, under the papacy."[11] Boniface VIII's full claim to direct papal authority over the world, framed in the bull "Unam Sanctam" in 1302, still seems, as it did to earlier generations, as the defense of a cause already lost. What is new, however, is an appreciation of the negative *consequences* of this entire development, chief of which must be the papacy's "very notable role in making a secular empire impossible," because "the church refused to serve as a second fiddle in an empire equivalent to those of China and Byzantium, and thus did not create a Caesaropapist doctrine in which a single emperor was elevated to semi-divine status."[12] The lack of military consolidation and political centralization on a very large scale made possible the bewildering blossoming of smaller units of governance, which in the very small form of the city-state reached the limits of its development by 1450 or so, but which on a larger scale, the "national" monarchy of Europe's western tier, produced an entity capable of consolidation, centralization, expansion, and endless disturbance of the world.

The political process of consolidation of fairly large monarchical states, equipped with at least the beginnings of a linguistically based patriotism has taken various names—notably "the new monarchies"—but it has always held pride of political place in accounts of the fifteenth and sixteenth centuries. Not for nothing does traditional national historiography divide medieval from modern at 1461 for France (accession of Louis XI), 1469 for Spain (marriage of Isabella and Ferdinand), 1485 for England (Tudor accession), and 1526 for Sweden (Vasa accession). What is new is the insight that this development depended on the prior enjoyment by Christendom's peoples of some elements of a common culture and relative pacification without the burdens of an immense military empire of the Roman sort. That the political symbols of the age were so heavily drawn from ancient Rome masked the utterly un-Roman character of Latin Christendom. Thomas Hobbes, though all unwittingly, thus had a point when he mused that "the Papacy is no other than the *ghost* of the deceased *Roman empire*, sitting crowned upon the grave thereof."[13] That was only half right, for what the papacy lacked was the character of a great military despotism of the Roman sort. The monarchies learned much of the art and instruments of governance from the papacy—law, bureaucracy, taxation, symbols, pageantry, and ideology—but not how to wage war. The union of these legacies with military power—the marriage of governance and war, sealed by finance—lay at the heart of the new process of state development between 1400 and 1600.[14] It took a double motion of fragmentation and consolidation, and sometimes the one was far more visible than the other. Already in 1399, for example, a French writer who sensed the movement of the times lamented the loss of unity: "The pagan world can exclaim, 'Christendom is finished,' one tongues hates another tongue, each nation its neighbour."[15]

*Europe and the Empires*

The third twentieth-century perspective is to look at the era from 1400 to 1600 as the beginnings of Europe's transformation of itself and the world by means of the merchant empires. The idea itself is quite old, going back at least to the birth year of the American Republic, when the Scottish philosopher Adam Smith wrote that "the discovery of America, and that of the passage to the East Indies by the Cape of Good Hope, are the two greatest events recorded in the history of mankind."[16] The years between 1400 and 1600 were Europe's "first imperial age," when the first seaborne empires were established and the work of building the world's trade into a Europe-centered global system began. Adam Smith caught this change, and his vision is preserved in several recent grand narratives of European history, most notably in the Marxist historians of the "world systems" school, who begin the history of capitalism with Europeans' unification of global trade between 1400 and 1600.[17] The subject attracts intense attention, of course, in our post-colonial age, even though study of its economic aspects—which attracted Adam Smith—has not yielded up a convincing account of the sources of European modernity. What it has done is to undermine the paradigmatic claims advanced by all forms of modernization theory and thereby to create new space for the exploration of religion and culture, both in the Christendom that was becoming Europe and in the zones of contacts with other peoples. In this space, however, the old concepts of "the Renaissance" and "the Reformation" prove to be least helpful, mainly because they were framed on a base that was socially too narrow and geographically too small. The larger perspectives common today tend to relativize and flatten the differences that used to be characterized as contrasts between "Middle Ages and Renaissance," "Middle Ages and Reformation," or "Renaissance and Reformation." Our perspective on the centuries from 1400 to 1600 is much longer than those of Jacob Burckhardt and John Lothrop Motley, and their perception of revolutionary changes in that age do not so much escape us as give way to a sense of deep, slow, and irreversible change, rooted below the intentional level. John Bossy, for example, has tried to capture such a change in his picture of how Christendom as a body of peoples was transformed into Christianity as a body of beliefs, and how "society" changed from "a state of companionship, fellowship or mutually recognised relation with one or more of one's fellow men" to "an objective collectivity exterior to its members and delimited from other such collectivities, ... an entity from which actual human contact had been evacuated."[18] It gives one pause to be reminded that Bossy is describing the same changes for which Motley employed the image of Martin Luther as a kind of metahistorical drill bit.

※ ※ ※

These softer contours of European events between 1400 and 1600 are the reason why Burckhardt's individualist princes and Motley's Luther seem to us typical not of the "modern" age, a phrase with which we identify our own era, but of the "early modern" one. Our acceptance of this term expresses a sense of distance from the era between 1400 and 1600, which our nineteenth-century predecessors did not have. Among them, only a prescient few sensed the depth and shape of the gulf that had already been carved between Middle Ages, Renaissance, and Reformation, on the one side, and their modern age, on the other. Now, at greater distance, most contemporary thinking about these matters holds that the breaking of the Malthusian barrier and the industrialization of Europe since 1750, rather than Dante and Luther, or Columbus and da Gama, form the "turning point" between the old order and the new.[19] The shift forward of "the turning point" to the eighteenth century has displaced the old pair, "the Renaissance" and "the Reformation," as the double-sided hinge of European development, but it has by no means robbed the centuries from 1400 to 1600 altogether of a pivotal role. They still mark boundaries between the world, say, of Thomas Aquinas and that, say, of Voltaire. "The Renaissance" still means the recovery, adaptation, and expansion of knowledge associated with the neo-classical revival, but it can no longer stand for Burckhardt's birth of modernity in the form of individualism. "The Reformation" still means the transformation and differentiation of western Christianity during the sixteenth century, but it can no longer stand for Motley's liberation of the world from priestcraft and superstition. Thus shorn of their former ideological freight, the concepts still retain distinct signatures as aspects of a world which was, at the same time, late medieval and early modern.

To relativize these old concepts is not to discard them, and, indeed, their relativization may be regarded, in the spirit of Burckhardt and Motley, as a kind of liberation. Freed from the great burden of being "the turning point" of European history, these centuries—late Middle Ages, Renaissance, Reformation, and early modern era—have become a conceptual bridge between the world of pre-modern Europe and the histories of most other parts of the world. This role, which the nineteenth-century historians could hardly have suspected, has lent the study of these centuries a remarkable energy in our time. In few other sectors of European historiography do social and cultural history coexist so fruitfully and, on the whole, happily, as they do for the centuries between 1400 and 1600.

To some, this promises enrichment; to others, merely confusion; and to yet others, loss and even danger. It is a situation of which the historian can, and should, make the best. The concepts of "the Renaissance" and "the Reformation" were hardened fruits of an idealist conception of history, which the rise of social history—Marxist and non-Marxist—struck down in the years after 1918. In the following decades, the centuries between 1400 and 1600 had to serve another tyranny, the story of Europe as economic development or "modernization." Now, that tyranny, too, has fallen, and if this change has left the subject in a state of disorder, well, "disorder" can be another name for "freedom."

# NOTES

1. *The Early Lives of Dante*, trans. P.H. Wicksteed (London, 1904), 10-11.
2. Quoted by A.G. Dickens, "Johannes Sleidan and Reformation History," in *Reformation Confomity and Dissent. Essays in Honour of Geoffrey Nuttall*, ed. R. Buick Knox (London, 1977), 21, from the preface to the Latin translation of Froissart.
3. Ernst Troeltsch, *Protestantism and Progress: The Significance of Protestantism for the Rise of the Modern World* (Philadelphia, 1986 [1912]), 17.
4. Jacob Burckhardt, *The Civilization of the Renaissance in Italy*, trans. S.G.C. Middlemore, ed. Irene Gordon (New York, 1960 [1860]), 121; and there, too, the quotes in the following sentence.
5. John Lothrop Motley, *Democracy: The Climax of Political Progress and the Destiny of Advanced Races. An Essay*, 2d ed. (Glasgow, 1869), 23.
6. James Bryce, *The Holy Roman Empire*, rev. ed. (New York, n.d. [1864]), 388.
7. William J. Bouwsma, *John Calvin: a Sixteenth-Century Protrait* (New York, 1989), 2, 230-31.
8. Heiko A. Oberman, *Luther: Man Between God and the Devil*, trans. Eileen Walliser-Schwarzbart (New Haven, 1989 [1982]), 219.
9. I allude to Emanuel Le Roy Ladurie, "History without Motion," in E. Le Roy Ladurie, *The Territory of the Historian*, trans. Ben Reynolds and Sîan Reynolds (Chicago, 1979).
10. Frantisek Graus, *Pest-Geissler-Judenmorde. Das 14. Jahrhundert als Krisenzeit*, Veröffentlichungen der Max-Planck-Gesellschaft für Geschichte, vol. 86 (Göttingen, 1987), 555.
11. Harold J. Berman, *Law and Revolution: The Formation of the Western Legal Tradition* (Cambridge, MA: 1983), 520; and there, too, is the following quote.
12. John A. Hall, *Powers and Liberties: The Causes and Consequences of the Rise of the West* (Berkeley and Los Angeles, 1985), 134-35.
13. Thomas Hobbes, *Leviathan or the Matter, Forme and Power of a Commonwealth, Ecclesiastical and Civil*, chap. 47 (edited by Michael Oakeshott [Oxford: 1960]: 457).
14. V. G. Kiernan, "State and Nation in Western Europe," *Past and Present*, no. 31 (July 1965): 20; Eric L. Jones, *The European Miracle* (Cambridge, 1981), 85, 89-90, 93-95, 104-24; Immanuel Wallerstein, *The Modern World-System*, vol. 1, *Capitalist Agriculture and the Origins of Europe* (New York, 1975), 15-18; Paul Kennedy, *The Rise and Fall of the Great Powers: Economic Change and Military Conflict from 1500 to 2000* (New York, 1987), 29.
15. Quoted by Denys Hay, *Europe: the Emergence of an Idea* (New York, 1966 [1957]), 76.

16. Quoted by André Gunder Frank, *World Accumulation, 1492-1789* (London, 1978), 25.
17. This is true, notably, of Wallerstein, *The Modern World-System*, vol. 1; and Eric R. Wolf, *Europe and the People Without History* (Berkeley and Los Angeles, 1982).
18. John Bossy, *Christianity in the West, 1400-1700* (Oxford, 1985), 170-71.
19. Most of the recent grand narratives of European history, both Marxist and non-Marxist, accept this periodization. Typical is Kriedte, *Peasants, Landlords and Capitalists*, 1: until the eighteenth century, "the economic system as a whole continued to be dominated by the feudal mode of production." Other important examples are Douglass C. North and Robert Paul Thomas, *The Rise of the Western World: a New Economic History* (Cambridge, 1973); Perry Anderson, *Lineages of the Absolutist State* (London, 1974); Jones, *The European Miracle*; Wolf, *Europe and the Peoples Without History*; T.H. Aston and C.H.E. Philpin, eds., *The Brenner Debate: Agrarian Class Structure and Economic Development in Pre-Industrial Europe* (Cambridge, 1985); R.J. Holton, *The Transition from Feudalism to Capitalism* (New York, 1985).

# Part 1.
# The Framework of Everyday Life:
## Structures

# POPULATION

Jan de Vries
(University of California, Berkeley)

In the tenth century a squirrel could have traveled from Paris to Moscow, jumping from tree to tree without ever touching ground. In 1936 Herbert Heaton used this intriguing image to convey the human emptiness of the wooded fastness that then was northern Europe. In Mediterranean Europe, by contrast, many centuries of dense, permanent settlement and urbanization made the environment less hospitable to a squirrel struck by wanderlust, but even there a population much thinned since Roman times had lost its grip on vast stretches of waste, marsh, and mountain.

Historians speak of Europe in the early fourteenth century as a "full" Europe, in which from the top of any church tower one could see several other steeples, each marking a concentration of population. Together, these human clusters had succeeded in forming a continuous settlement and a comprehensive appropriation of the land. From islands in a sea of waste and forest, the settlements had grown and multiplied during the "great age of clearing"; far into Eastern Europe, it was now the wastes and forests that formed islands in a sea of peasant settlement, knit together by thousands of cities and market towns. In this full Europe of some 75-80 million people the bubonic plague appeared in 1347, jumping from village to village and from town to town more rapidly than Heaton's tenth-century squirrel. By 1351 the infected fleas that disembarked at Marseille (via their host rats) from a ship that had sailed from the Black Sea port of Kaffa had transmitted the plague bacilla in a great counter-clockwise pattern of diffusion to France, England, Germany and back to Russia—and one-third of Europe's population had died.

Europe's demographic history long stood in the shadow of this dramatic event. For at least a century, and in many places for much longer, Europe had the aspect of a child wearing its parent's clothes: the church towers and cities, the cleared fields and craftsmen's tools all survived the Black Death intact, of course, but the people to inhabit, maintain, and use them were but a remnant of those who had created them. After this long and puzzling delay the population of Europe revived; in the course of the so-called "long sixteenth century" the population regained and then ex-

EUROPE ca.1500

Church Lands
x x   Lands of the Union of Calmar
Electorate of Brandenburg
Saxony (Electorate of Duchy)
Lands of the House of Habsburg
Bohemia and Hungary united under the same crown from 1490
Venetian Lands
Boundary of the Holy Roman Empire

EUROPE ca. 1500

ceeded its pre-plague levels, until once again, in the course of the first half of the seventeenth century, limits were reached bringing population growth to a halt. This great cycle of population—the fifteenth-century depression, the recovery and expansion of the long sixteenth century, and culminating in the crisis of the seventeenth century—is this chapter's subject. Our objective is to establish the size, rate of change, and distribution of Europe's population in this period (the population history) and to uncover the processes by which these changes occurred (the historical demography). But, before proceeding to these substantive matters we must first consider the sources and methods available to the historian wishing to study European populations in past time.

## 1. Sources and Methods

### Census-like Documents

Today, the most important source of information about populations and their characteristics is the census, a written enumeration of all inhabitants residing in a particular jurisdiction. Modern censuses, which repeat this exercise at regular intervals, go back no further than the French Revolutionary and Napoleonic period.[1] Before then we can turn to rare "stand-alone" censuses and to more numerous "census-like" documents, enumerations taken for purposes other than demographic and usually listing only a portion of a population.

Early censuses, usually taken in cities or urbanized territories, often provide a variety of details that administrators at the time found useful in order to regulate, tax, and conscript their populations. For example, the compilers of the 1701 census in the German city of Würzburg insisted on knowing everyone's birthplace, citizenship status, receipt of poor relief, and relation to the head of household in their zeal to expel from the city all those with weak claims to residence. The most extensive and certainly the most celebrated early census is the 1427-30 *catasto* of Florence, a detailed demographic and economic description of the more than 200,000 inhabitants of the Florentine state.[2] The *catasto*, though unusual in its scope and quality, does not stand alone. Northern Italian states pioneered in administering census enumerations, and although some are lost and others of disputed quality, they survive at scattered dates in the sixteenth and seventeenth centuries for Venice, Tuscany, Milan and several lesser polities.[3]

Most of the documents with a "census-like" character are nothing like these precocious Italian records: they were not intended for demographic purposes and made no effort to enumerate total populations. Fiscal records enumerated eligible tax payers; property tax records counted the number of hearths; military documents recorded men eligible for conscription; church documents listed communicants. The one thing all these examples have in common is the need for the historian to devise a method to convert the enumerated items into the desired result, usually a total population. Examples of such enumerations include the English Poll Tax of 1377, for which most persons over the age of 14 were eligible; a Castilian tax of 1588 that required the counting of *vecinos pecheros* (taxable inhabitants); Holland's *Informatie* of 1514, a survey of economic conditions that required parish priests to state the number of communicants; numerous sixteenth-century *dénombrements* in modern Belgium listing the number of hearths; and the *taille personnelle,* a property tax which in northern France attached to the person (hence the name) and required periodic enumerations of taxable individuals.[4]

A few of these enumerations were made with some frequency, revealing the general trends of population change, but only the lists of communicants offer totals at frequent, even annual, intervals. These parish-level documents exist for several countries, but only in Italy, where they are known as *stati d'anime* (lists of souls), are they numerous. Nearly all surviving lists date from after 1600. In 1614 Pope Paul V's *Rituale Romanum* sought to enforce the annual drafting of these documents, and gradually they became more detailed, as priests included information about the age and family membership of each communicant.

In principal, the *stati d'anime* fashion something like a system of civil registration, where each (communicant) individual can be tracked year-by-year, population totals can be followed, and migration identified. In practice, the attentiveness of most parish priests to this task left much to be desired. Things were different in Sweden, where the Lutheran clergy came to function as civil servants. Beginning in 1628 they were required to draw up annual registers of their parish populations, noting such things as literacy, state of religious instruction, and change of address. These *husförhörslängder* were imperfectly kept and preserved at first, but reforms in 1686 made more reliable a precocious practice which, when brought under the direct control of the state in 1749, formed the earliest reliable system of civil registration in Europe.

*Vital Events*

Enumerations of inhabitants (or some sub-set of inhabitants) offer important "snap shots" of the populations, and if they tell us more than simply
the number of residents, they can provide invaluable insights into the structure of the population: its age structure, marital status, sex ratio, etc. But
such measures of the *stock* of a population, especially if they are not frequently repeated, are of limited usefulness unless they can be supplemented
by information on the *flow* of vital events—births, marriages, and
deaths—over a substantial span of time. With a knowledge of these
events, it is possible to analyze how, and sometimes even why, the population changes in size and structure. The privileged position of Europe in the
historical study of demographic change is founded on the fact that the Roman Catholic and Protestant churches early became convinced of the utility of recording and preserving the religious events of baptism, marriage
celebration, and burial, which are close proxies for the vital events.[5]

The oldest "parish registers" date from the fourteenth-century Italy.
The Church was motivated to record marriages to enforce its prohibition
on the marriage of close relatives, but the earliest surviving records in most
places record baptisms, starting in 1314 in the dioceses of Arezzo, 1361 in
Udine, 1381 in Siena, and 1428 in Florence.[6] The earliest Swiss baptism
records date from 1481 (in the diocese of Constance) while in France the
only surviving pre-1500 records stem from four departments, all in the vi-
cinity of Nantes and Anger.

The Reformation provided a strong stimulus to what until then was a
slowly spreading practice. Notable landmarks in the regularization of parish registration are: Thomas Cromwell's 1538 ordinance requiring all
priests of the new Church of England to record all baptisms, marriages and
burials; Villers Cotterêts' (less effectual) order to the same effect in France
in 1539, the Council of Trent's 1563 decree that all Catholic clergy should
record baptisms and marriages, and, finally, the codification of these practices (with the addition of burials) in the *Rituale Romanum* of 1614. The
gap between theory and practice long remained large, but by 1600 the majority of French provinces included parishes in which these records were
not only produced but preserved; 37 percent of Swiss Catholic parishes
then were maintaining records of at least two types of events, as were a
majority of Protestant churches. In the Netherlands and in Central Europe
very few parish records reach back so far; rare is the parish register that
dates to before 1650.[7]

The earliest continuous series of baptisms, which all refer to urban
populations, reveal the irregular trends and severe short-term shocks to

which such populations were continually subject.[8] Although in the absence of burial and marriage data (which are usually less complete and less accurate) our ability to interpret these evocative series remains limited, the value of baptism series for long-term historical analysis can be enhanced when many such parish series are aggregated to represent the birth trends for a large territory. Since lengthy series of accurate parish records are not numerous, such territorial series can only be constructed by selecting a sample of parishes representative of the geographical, occupational, and cultural diversity of the territory and weighting them by the relative importance of these attributes. Figure 1 shows the constructed baptismal series for rural France and England. The annual fluctuations within such series remain substantial, of course, but the large variety of local experience represented by these series lend them a stability that permits one to infer long-term trends in total population change.

Such statements represent nothing more than a first step toward uncovering and understanding population history. When burial and marriage

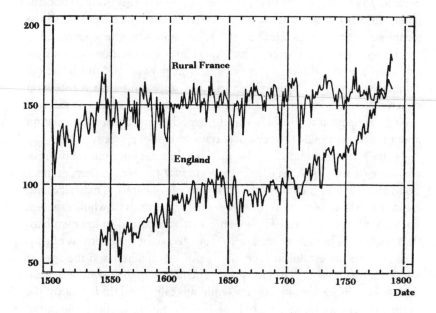

Figure 1. Indexes of the annual movement of baptisms in England and rural France.

*Source*:
Dupâquier (1988), vol. 2: 169.

series can be joined to the baptism series, it becomes possible to make much more penetrating inferences.  In their fundamental *Population History of England, 1541-1871*, Wrigley and Schofield calculate the annual totals of births, deaths, and marriages in England based on a technique called "back projection."[9]  This technique, and a related method called "inverse projection," starts from an end date when an accurate census provides information about the size of the population and its age distribution.  Then, working backward, this initial population is adjusted by adding deaths and subtracting births as far back as the time series reach.  In- and out-migration and uncertainties about ages of death introduce potential sources of error to this method, but it has been shown to be quite accurate when applied to large populations (where migration is a minor factor).[10]

Using back- and inverse-projection methods, the flows of events recorded in the parish registers can be coupled to an ongoing reconstruction of the total population and its age structure, permitting the calculation of birth rates, death rates, life expectancy, and marriage rates.  The revealed patterns of aggregate demographic behavior for England, which extend back to 1541, will be discussed in later sections of this essay.  Unfortunately, insufficient accuracy in mortality series has thus far prevented the technique from being used for pre-1650 populations in other countries.

The aggregative character of back- and inverse-projection methods offers insights into the average behavior of large populations, much like the summary results of a national census.  But since the parish registers on which these methods are based identify the baptized, buried, and married persons by name, it is possible to produce much more detailed information about the demographic behavior of specific groups of persons.

"Family reconstitution" is the method that exploits the nominative character of the parish registers.  Pioneered by the French demographer Louis Henry,[11] this method involves the linkage of baptism, marriage, and burial records in order to reconstitute the life histories of whole families.  For example, the linkage of a woman's marriage record to her own baptism establishes her age at marriage.  The linkage of the baptisms of children born to her establishes the number of her children and the ages at which she bears them.  The linkage of her children to their own burials establishes the incidence of infant and child mortality, and the linkage of the mother to her own burial (and of her husband to his) establishes the end of this conjugal family's existence and the number of years the wife was at risk of conceiving.  When a sufficient number of families can be reconstituted, they form a population for which fertility and other rates can be calculated as detailed and accurate as those available for modern populations.

Rates of illegitimate birth, pre-marital pregnancy, age-specific marital fertility and even evidence of family limitation practices are among the measurements of interest that can be generated by family reconstitution studies.

In order to reconstitute from the records of a single parish a family's demographic history from the birth of the man and woman who later marry until their deaths, it is obviously necessary that the persons involved spend their entire lives in the same community. One of the unexpected findings of these studies was that only a very small percentage of families living in Europe's pre-industrial villages could, in fact, be reconstituted fully. Migration, at least over short distances, was ubiquitous. Thus, the linkage of parish registers into reconstituted families proved to be akin to assembling a jigsaw puzzle in which the majority of pieces cannot be used at all. Such research is highly labor intensive, and for reasons of practicality most scholars have applied the technique to agricultural villages. Larger, urban communities, with their tens of thousands of vital events, high mobility, and many people with the same name have proved difficult to study.

Since Louis Henry's pioneering studies in the 1950s historical demographers have completed scores of village studies. An effort by Michael Flinn to summarize and analyze the findings of all family reconstitution studies completed as of 1979 identified over 130 parishes with studies for periods before 1750. They were spread through nearly every country in western and central Europe, but concentrated in France, which could then claim over half the total. Since then, many score more studies have been completed, including several major investigations of urban populations.[12]

The considerable power of nominative data linkage to reveal the secrets of past demographic behavior has an obvious appeal to the demographer, but it is also beguiling to the historian who can hope to proceed beyond the linkage of the parish register data to the linkage of the reconstituted family to other nominative documents that specify occupation, property ownership, place of origin, and tax liabilities. Demography has been described as a discipline "with a hard mathematical core and a softer socio-economic and biological rind,"[13] and in historical studies this "rind" is critical to the study's interpretive power.

*Special Populations and Other Sources*
The parish registers and the methodologies devised to exploit them have revolutionized historical demography in the past generation. But only a few exceptionally rich parish registers permit the application of the new methods to the sixteenth century, and none do so for earlier times. For these periods a useful alternative to parish register studies (also useful in

later periods) is the assembly of genealogical and biographical information about special populations. Instead of reconstituting families randomly (or, to be accurate, chosen for their failure to migrate), one can draw upon already existing genealogical information, which is usually available in abundance for populations that have a special reason to preserve such information: nobilities and urban patriciates. Indeed, genealogies formed the basis of Louis Henry's study of the Genevan bourgeoisie (1956), which extends back to the 1550s, and a study of the British peerage reaches back to the fifteenth century.[14] Several other studies of European noble and patrician populations begin around 1500,[15] and the so called "livres de raison"—compilations of edification and family history—allow small groups of urban bourgeois families in Italy and France to be studied in the fifteenth century.[16]

Genealogies permit the study of both fertility and mortality; biographical data—the life histories of persons (almost always men) inducted into a military order, serving in the clergy, or noted as artists—provide information only about adult mortality. A study of the Knights of the Golden Fleece, for example, begun as a Burgundian Order in 1430, could trace the mortality experience of its members from then through to the present day.[17]

Finally, we can note the usefulness of legal and notarial documents in tracking the incidence of mortality (as reflected by property transfers, wills, feudal payments) and the size and composition of families (in the lists of heirs in probate inventories). While these documents rarely cover an entire population, they are far more inclusive than the genealogies and biographies just mentioned.[18]

All of these sources have their drawbacks, which reside in the limited range of demographic experience that can be observed and/or the atypical behavior of the observable population. But, in conjunction with other information, these sources can be of considerable value in suggesting answers to the demographic questions we have for the fifteenth and sixteenth centuries, when the parish registers cannot yet come to our assistance.

## 2. RECONSTRUCTING EUROPE'S POPULATION HISTORY

### Population Size

A widely accepted estimate of the world's population sets it at 442 million on the eve of the Black Death (1340); this amounts to no more than 8 percent of world population in 1990.[19] Yet, if the necessarily rough estimates

of global population in the distant past are to be trusted, this represented a
considerable human achievement, since the world in the first millennium
of our era seems never to have exceeded the quarter billion mark. The medieval expansion whose culmination we observe in the population of 1340
was thus very nearly a global phenomenon. Europe's part in this great age
of expansion was, so to speak, only typical; its population of some 74 million inhabitants, 17 percent of the world total, is thought to have nearly
doubled in the preceding 300 years. In the years following 1340, however,
Europe's demographic experience was anything but typical, as bubonic
plague swept away roughly a third of the pre-plague population. By 1400
Europe's population stood at 52 million, not quite 14 percent of the
world's total, and it would remain in the 14-15 percent range for at least
the next three centuries. Odd as it may seem given Europe's decisive advance in these centuries, the challenge before us is to explain Europe's demographic mediocrity.

Before proceeding further, a word must be said about the boundaries of
this "Europe." Jean-Noël Biraben, whose estimates were cited above, used
the 1945-91 western boundary of the Soviet Union to define Europe, and
later in this chapter we will encounter an even more restricted Europe, mi-
nus the Balkan lands as well. These are "boundaries of convenience," not
of principle, but they do reflect the concentration of research on western
and central Europe and the belief, discussed more fully in the final section
of this chapter, that the generalizations made on the basis of current research have limited applicability, or none at all, in the Europe that lies east
of a line that runs from St. Petersburg to Trieste.

The chief feature of Europe's fifteenth-century population, whose explanation continues to challenge the historian, is its continuing stagnation.
The sharp and nearly universal decline occasioned by the Black Death led
not to recovery but to a prolonged era of unstable fluctuation around a
new, lower level. In England's county of Essex the annual listings of adult
males supplied by the Frankpledge, a requirement of manorial law, reveal
a fifteenth-century rural population standing at about one half its 1300
apogee,[20] and one showing no signs of recovery until after 1500. A variety
of sources reinforces this picture of collapse followed by stagnation, however much they disagree about the explanation;[21] in England as a whole,
the 3.7 million inhabitants of 1300 fell to perhaps 2.3, where it remained
throughout the fifteenth century.

Across the Channel, in the industrial and commercial heart of northern
Europe, matters were little different. In Flanders, Brabant, and Hainault
*dénombrements* form the basis of estimates of total population for the

southern Netherlands (modern Belgium) of 1.4 million in 1375 and, as a result of the political crisis ignited by the death of the last duke of Burgundy in 1477, an even lower population of 1.24 million in 1500.[22] Crossing the Alps to the economic heart of Mediterranean Europe does not change the picture. Herlihy and Klapisch-Zuber's masterful analysis of the 1427 Florentine *catasto* "shows us," in their words, "a population which has just dropped to a demographic floor, and would remain stable for another half-century."[23] The population of Florence and its hinterland (*contado*), stood at 128,000 in the year of the *catasto*, no more than that in 1470, and had crept up to only 137,000 by 1490.

There remain, of course, many areas where no direct evidence of fifteenth-century population trends is available. But the records of economic activity and of taxation sometimes suggest the direction of population change, as does topographical information. The *Wüstungen* (abandoned villages) of central Europe and the abandonment of marginal arable lands speak to a profound rural reorganization directly related to a long-term diminution of population.[24]

At some point in the late fifteenth century the forces holding down Europe's population gave way, inaugurating a long era of demographic expansion. This was a gradual matter in many areas, but it could also take on a sudden, explosive character. In England, for example, population growth was at best slow until around 1510, whereafter it nearly doubled in the next century. In the Netherlands, both north and south, the population grew by some 50 percent during the first 60 years of the sixteenth century, whereupon the Dutch Revolt and attendant mass migration disrupted profoundly the demographic patterns. The same explosive growth characterized Tuscany between 1490 and 1552, while southern Italy (the Kingdom of Naples) more than doubled in population between 1505 and 1595.

Population growth stands at the core of the "long sixteenth century," an era of heightened economic activity, price inflation, and overseas expansion. Not everywhere was that growth so rapid as in the examples just cited, but for Europe as a whole it was much more than a simple recovery from the fourteenth century collapse. Table 1 offers an overview of the available "national" population data. These data vary in quality, but suffice to make clear the substantial differences between the relatively slow sixteenth-century growth of the Mediterranean countries and the much faster growth of the north and western Europe.

A second important message of Table 1 is the demographic preponderance of France. Its sixteenth-century growth seems to have been brought

Table 1. European Populations 1500-1800 (in millions).

|  | 1500 | 1550 | 1600 | 1650 | 1700 | 1750 | 1800 |
|---|---|---|---|---|---|---|---|
| Scandinavia | 1.50 | 1.70 | 2.00 | 2.60 | 2.90 | 3.60 | 5.00 |
| England | 2.30 | 3.10 | 4.20 | 5.50 | 5.20 | 5.90 | 8.70 |
| Scotland | 0.80 | 0.90 | 1.00 | 1.00 | 1.20 | 1.30 | 1.60 |
| Ireland | 0.80 | 0.90 | 1.00 | 1.50 | 2.00 | 2.40 | 5.00 |
| Netherlands | 0.95 | 1.25 | 1.50 | 1.90 | 1.90 | 1.90 | 2.10 |
| Belgium | 1.25 | 1.65 | 1.30 | 1.75 | 1.90 | 2.30 | 2.90 |
| Germany | 12.00 | 14.00 | 16.00 | 12.00 | 15.00 | 17.00 | 24.50 |
| France | 16.40 | 19.00 | 20.00 | 20.50 | 22.00 | 25.50 | 27.30 |
| Switzerland | 0.60 | 0.75 | 0.90 | 1.00 | 1.20 | 1.30 | 1.70 |
| Italy | 10.50 | 11.40 | 13.10 | 11.30 | 13.30 | 15.30 | 17.80 |
| Spain | 6.80 | 7.40 | 8.10 | 7.10 | 7.50 | 8.90 | 10.50 |
| Portugal | 1.00 | 1.20 | 1.10 | 1.20 | 2.00 | 2.30 | 2.90 |
| Austria-Bohemia | 3.50 | 3.60 | 4.30 | 4.10 | 4.60 | 5.70 | 7.90 |
| Poland | 2.50 | 3.00 | 3.40 | 3.00 | 2.80 | 3.70 | 4.30 |
|  |  |  |  |  |  |  |  |
| North and West | 7.60 | 9.50 | 11.00 | 14.25 | 15.10 | 17.40 | 25.30 |
| Central | 29.00 | 33.75 | 36.90 | 33.50 | 38.20 | 43.80 | 53.50 |
| Mediterranean | 18.30 | 20.00 | 22.30 | 19.60 | 22.80 | 26.50 | 31.20 |
| Eastern | 6.00 | 6.60 | 7.70 | 7.10 | 7.40 | 9.40 | 12.20 |
|  |  |  |  |  |  |  |  |
| Total | 60.90 | 68.85 | 77.90 | 74.45 | 83.50 | 97.10 | 122.20 |

*Sources*: De Vries (1984), 36; Klep (1991), 505; Dupâquier (1988), vol. 2: 68.

to an early close, but the 19-22 million inhabitants of the period 1560-1750 always gave it something like a quarter of Europe's total population. No other European polity came close to this number of subjects and potential taxpayers.

Yet another important feature of Europe's population history revealed by Table 1 is the manner in which this era of expansion is brought to a close. The "long sixteenth century" is bounded by the "crisis of the seventeenth century," a reversal quite unlike the fourteenth-century crisis in that both its timing and its consequences varied greatly from country to country. In the Mediterranean region, famines in the 1590s, plague in 1599, and again in 1630 and 1649, and no shortage of misrule and disorder sent the populations of Italy and Spain into sharp reversal. In Central Europe, the Thirty Years' War brought demographic disaster beginning in 1618. Yet, it is precisely in this fateful half century that the "long sixteenth century" deserves its name in north and western Europe, where population growth continued until at least 1650. This North Sea-based region, whose total population in 1600 barely exceeded 50 percent of that in the Mediter-

ranean lands, possessed in excess of 75 percent of Mediterranean population by 1650.

Which is not to say that the North Sea lands were untouched by demographic reversals; they just came later. After the 1650s England's population declined by 300,000, and did not recover its earlier peak until 1730.
Holland's population also declined then, while that of the Dutch Republic
as a whole stagnated at best until deep into the eighteenth century. In the
Southern Netherlands the 1660s also introduced population reversals.[25] In
a complex phasing deeply implicated in the transferal of economic and political leadership from the Mediterranean to the North Sea, Europe's overall population growth slowed to a crawl in the seventeenth and early eighteenth centuries. In this era the important story resides in the *distribution* of
population—among regions, between city and country—rather than in its
overall rate of growth.

Finally, we can note the return of accelerated population growth to Europe sometime between 1730 and 1750. This new expansion era was all
but universal (only the Dutch Republic's population failed to participate
until after 1800), and it was a growth which would not abate until the
twentieth century, after having fueled, and been reinvigorated in turn, by a
world-transforming economic and political revolution.

Europe's population history defines a series of long-term waves of
growth and recession that take the approximate form of logistics: the long
medieval expansion followed by the Black Death and the fifteenth-century
depression, the long sixteenth century followed by the more illusive crisis
of the seventeenth century, and the eighteenth century expansion which led
to the construction of the industrial society which we moderns perhaps na-
ively believe has suspended the Malthusian rules that had governed the
earlier cycles.[26] These great cycles establish a periodization in European
history quite independent of the political and cultural periodizations that
long governed the telling of European history, and their demographic base
implies—but does not explain—a profound implication of demographic
movements with economic, political, and even cultural developments. The
elucidation of these connections was one of the chief objectives of the
"Annales School" of structural historians in the first three post-World War
II decades.[27]

*Population Distribution*

Europe's population history is expressed not only in aggregate terms, but
also in its internal distribution and redistribution. Some of the reasons for
regional differentials in natural increase will be discussed later in this chap-

ter. Here our concern is with redistributions that are the result of urbanization, rural depopulation, and international migration.

The "rise of the city" is a venerable theme of medieval history, and the
planting and development of thousands of urban settlements in the course
of the High Middle Ages directed a strategic part of that epoch's labor and
capital to the new centers of commerce, industry, and administration. By
1400 Europe's endowment of cities was nearly complete. Except at its
eastern and northern margins, few new urban foundations were planted
from then until the industrial age. By the fourteenth century these many
urban sites may well have housed some 7 or 8 percent of the total population: much more in Mediterranean Europe, much less in the north and
east.[28]

In the aftermath of the Black Death new factors emerged to buoy urbanization. The urban share of total population by 1500 had advanced
beyond the pre-plague level—reaching about 10 percent in Europe as a
whole—but the reason for this shift in favor of the cities had nothing to do
with the planting of new cities, nor with the absolute growth of the cities.
Rather, it was the result of a sharp drop of rural population. Though the
plague affected both urban and rural areas, with greater losses in the cities,
a conspicuous feature of the "fifteenth-century depression" was the earlier
and faster revival of the urban economies, such that by 1500 the aggregate
urban population had more than regained its pre-1347 size, while the rural
population was still at an early stage of recovery.[29]

What began as a recovery—but also as a reassertion of the urban preponderance of Italy in Renaissance Europe—continued in the sixteenth
century as a new type of urbanization, one that simultaneously raised the
urban share of Europe's population to new heights and directed the lion's
share of the new urban populations toward the largest cities. Given the demographic vigor of all of Europe, cities everywhere tended to grow, but urbanization was most spectacular in the larger cities of the Mediterranean.
By 1600 Italy and Iberia supported over 17 percent of their total population in cities of at least 5,000 inhabitants, while north of the Alps and Pyrenees the overall level did not much exceed 8 percent.

By 1600 changes were already afoot—convulsions, actually—which the
urban population data for the following century register rather like a seis-
mograph. The eclipse of the economies of the Inland Sea, the emergence of
the new center of Europe's economic and political strength in the north,
and the consolidation nearly everywhere of bureaucratic, national states
all reveal themselves in a new European urban system. The features of the
new urbanism were clear enough by the second half of the seventeenth cen-

tury, but let us take its measure a century later, in 1750, at the dawn of a new, very different urban epoch.

By 1750 Europe's urban population (always in cities of at least 5,000 inhabitants) had crept upward to 12.4 percent of the total. This is no striking advance over the level attained 400 years earlier. But now the internal distribution of these "city people" was very different: the Mediterranean lands' rate of urbanization had been steadily declining since 1600, while that of northern, and especially northwestern, Europe rose steadily. The Dutch Republic was 40 percent urban; England, 20 percent and climbing. Furthermore, nearly all net urban growth over the period 1600-1750 was for the account of Europe's largest cities. The population resident in very large cities, those with at least 40,000 inhabitants, were outnumbered by the residents of smaller cities (5 to 40 thousand) by 4 to 1 in 1500, and still by 2 to 1 in 1600. But by 1700 the 43 cities of at least 40,000 inhabitants contained nearly as many people as the 512 smaller cities; the capitals and great commercial centers dominated the urban hierarchies as never before.[30]

The economic and political forces driving this remarkable and profound form of urban growth are discussed in Chapter 4 of this volume. Here our interest is confined to the demographic processes by which this growth took place. There remains a great deal to learn about historical urban demography, since the modern techniques of parish register analysis were developed for, and long confined to, the study of rural communities. If we are not yet able to generalize with confidence about how urban populations differed from rural with respect to nuptiality and fertility, we can affirm that urban mortality generally exceeded levels common in less densely populated rural territories, and that this differential often placed cities in a situation of chronic inability to reproduce their own populations. That is, rates of natural increase were often negative. This was not inevitably true of small cities, but it was a conspicuous and often massive feature of large cities. As cities grew larger during the early modern period, the "urban graveyard" effect grew in strength, and rural-to-urban migration grew in scope both to sustain the growth of cities and to make good the urban surplus of deaths.[31]

The flows of rural-to-urban migration can rarely be observed directly, but models based on plausible assumptions suggest that the scope of this migration was such as to touch rural communities everywhere and to dominate the population histories of the growing districts that fell within the migratory fields of cities such as London, Paris, Amsterdam, Madrid, and Naples.[32] In most of these cities the majority of the residents were born elsewhere, and this was true even in periods when these cities did not grow in population. Since for every permanent migrant there were often many temporary migrants (rural people who live briefly in a city as servants, apprentices, or common laborers before returning to a village), the "other side of the coin" of cities filled with migrants was villages filled with people who had some direct experience with urban life. This urban influence upon rural society varied regionally, to be sure, being particularly strong in northern Italy and northwestern Europe. But everywhere rural folk, usually in their teens or twenties, made their way to nearby towns, and from there to larger cities, following well-trodden paths of structural migration. Young women were especially prominent in these migration flows, such that by the sixteenth century the European city typically housed more women than men—a characteristic that continues to this day.[33]

Europe's cities stood at the pinnacle of local and regional migration flows that formed complex but relatively stable patterns. Of the witnesses testifying before the church courts of Elizabethan Buckinghamshire, four of every five said they had moved at least once in their lives.[34] Yet, migration over truly long distances—crossing major cultural and national borders or oceans—remained quite exceptional and was often episodic, provoked by major political, religious, or economic forces. Thus, the project to reconstruct the population history of France was unable to find evidence for more than 600,000 emigrants from France in the entire period 1500-1800, nor more than 150,000 immigrants: an annual average of 2000 and 500, respectively. Only the Huguenot exodus, provoked by the revocation of the Edict of Nantes in 1685, stands as a demographically significant event at this level of analysis.

The paucity of international migration in this very large country did not typify all of Europe. In several important regions long-distance migration placed a heavy imprint on demographic life. Consider the Alpine cantons of Switzerland, the prime recruiting grounds for mercenary soldiers. Throughout the early modern period thousands of young men annually descended from their mountain homes to serve in foreign, especially French armies. Surely, most intended to return, but if we count as an "emigrant" anyone who dies abroad, regardless of his or her motive for leaving or intention to return, then the Swiss soldiers who died in foreign service or found other reasons not to return count as emigrants. The most recent, and most cautious, estimate places their number at 100,000 for the entire seventeenth century, about 1,000 per year.[35]

The Dutch Republic was one of the European states that regularly hired foreign troops; its own reserves of poor young men found employment at sea. One seaborne employer in particular, the Dutch East India Company, developed an insatiable appetite for their labor because of the enormous mortality experienced at sea and especially in the Tropics. Of the million men who embarked on Company ships in its two century history (1602-1795), it does not appear that more than one-third ever returned.[36] A few settled at the Cape or on Java, but most died in Asia while in Company service: an average of nearly 2500 per year in 1620-1700, and some 4400 per year in the eighteenth century. The seaborne and tropical mortality of the Portuguese, Spanish, and English cannot be charted with such precision, but they also had their effects. The later sixteenth-century demographic exhaustion of Castile—the recruitment ground for soldiers, New World settlers, and sailors—is often regarded as more a cause than a consequence of her political and economic crisis.[37] In England the population reconstruction carried out by Wrigley and Schofield yielded the unexpected result of a *net* emigration (after subtracting immigrants from such places as Scotland and Wales) of nearly 5,000 persons annually in 1541-1600 and over 7,000 annually in the seventeenth century. "Classic" emigrants—settlers in the New World—figured in this outflow, to be sure, but here, just as on the Continent, sailors and soldiers accounted for much of the total.[38]

All these examples of large-scale, long-distance movements of population involve "demographically expendable men," who were overwhelmingly young and single. In a society in which reproduction took place within the context of marriage their absence would have its effect, via a skewed sex-ratio, on the marriage market and hence on overall fertility. These long-term migration flows will have played a role in the relative decline of Alpine populations (these regions made up 53 percent of the Swiss population in 1500, but only 34 percent by 1700), and the post-1660 stagnation of both Dutch and English population. Pre-industrial migration remains an understudied topic in demographic, social, and economic history.

## 3. EARLY MODERN EUROPE: THE PARISH REGISTER ERA

### Mortality

The influence of Thomas Robert Malthus looms large over the study of early modern Europe. It is something of a commonplace to note that Malthus wrote his *First Essay on Population* (1798) at just the time that his analysis ceased to be generally valid. This statement directs our curiosity to those post-1798 developments that undermined the power of his "positive checks" to population growth; unfortunately, it also invites the uncritical acceptance of a pre-industrial Europe never far from the subsistence precipice—and from the mortality crises waiting just over the edge.

Parish register-based research on early modern mortality suffers from the fact that the burial registers are usually the least complete and least accurate of all. Moreover, the family reconstitution method designed to exploit the parish registers generates less information about mortality than about either fertility or nuptiality. As a consequence, modern research has been far more successful in casting doubt on old generalizations than in establishing a new understanding of mortality.

Among the very first achievements of parish register-based research was the charting of the great mortality crises that were thought to hold pre-industrial society in thrall. The *crises de subsistence* typically began with a severe harvest failure, presumably induced by the weather. The consequent food shortages drove prices up, which so reduced the population's intake of nutrients as to increase the incidence of death to a multiple of the normal level. If famine was not the proximate cause of death, widespread malnutrition gave every manner of disease and physical weakness the chance to do its work on the very young, the old, and the poor. During the months of crisis marriages were postponed, many persons fled the site of dearth in search of food and work, and fertility tended to fall. In the aftermath of the crisis came a wave of marriages, as the survivors found enhanced opportunities to establish new households (because of the pre-mature death of farmers, artisans, and others). In time, above-average fertility would at least partially restore the population loss caused by the initial mortality crisis. Such mortality crises punctuated the ordinary short-term volatility of the vital rates with a frequency that left few generations unaffected. Usually, the brunt of a crisis remained confined to one region, but the most severe of the *crises de subsistence*—such as 1555, 1597, 1630-32, 1693-94, 1709—brought economic and social dislocation to large parts of Europe.[39]

These mortality crises, once the centerpiece of any analysis of pre-industrial demography, now loom less large. This is not because they were not the dreadful events that contemporaries described and historians reconstructed, but because the search for an adequate explanation of their occurrence has led scholars away from the "crude Malthusianism" that underlay the initial understanding of pre-industrial mortality. Harvest failures did initiate many mortality crises, but statistical studies of the mortality-increasing impact of sharp rises in grain prices have found a relation-

ship that varies by country, and is highly unpredictable. English data for
the period 1548-1640 show that a sudden doubling of grain prices is associated with a 35 percent increase in mortality, but only a 10 percent increase in the following century (and an unexpected 13 percent *reduction* of
mortality in the period 1746-1834!).[40] More generally, only 22 percent of
the annual fluctuations in mortality could be "explained" by fluctuations
in prices in the 1548-1640 period, and progressively less in later periods. A
similar methodology applied to French experience found a stronger mortality effect than in England—a 50 percent increase in mortality when
prices doubled in the period 1670-1739—but here, too, the relationship re-
verses after 1740.[41] These results directed the attention of researchers to
other determinants of high mortality: epidemics, warfare, and social organization.

The unstable and varied response of mortality to sudden evidence of
scarcity appears to be a consequence of the generally stronger influence of
disease epidemics and the important influence of social organization in mediating or exacerbating the direct effects of harvest shortfalls. In short, the
"positive check" of Malthus proved to be much less immediate and automatic than he had proposed, while epidemiological factors exogenous to
the socio-economic system often overwhelmed the influence of the means
of subsistence.

These findings pertain to the explanation of short-term variations in
mortality. Their plausibility is reinforced by efforts undertaken to explain
long-term changes in the mortality level. The old view can be stated briefly
as follows: the disappearance of mortality crises caused the long-term
mortality rates to fall to a "base-line" level, ushering in the beginnings of
the demographic transition and accelerated population growth toward the
end of the eighteenth century. Standing behind this process were economic
improvements that increased the supply and improved the distribution of
foodstuffs.[42] This interpretation rested largely upon western Europe's
post-1740 mortality experience, when the frequency of mortality crises diminished and population growth accelerated. As, however, parish register
analyses for earlier times expanded the scope of our knowledge of long-
term trends in the death rate, the shortcomings of this view became evident.

Severe mortality crises had been common enough in the sixteenth century, but the long-term mortality level was then strikingly low. Calculations of life expectancy at birth, which incorporate a lifetime of mortality
risks, reveal higher life expectancy in the sixteenth and early seventeenth
century in England (averaging over 38 years) than would again be reached

until the 1870s. England suffered a substantial deterioration in the course of the seventeenth century, an experience which can also be documented for Geneva, and for which indirect evidence abounds for many areas, including non-European societies.[43] Ironically, death rates rose in a period that saw the final disappearance from Europe of the bubonic plague, whose episodic outbursts constituted the greatest disruptions to the economic and demographic systems from 1347 to 1667, when the last plague epidemic struck in northern Europe.[44]

Long-term variations in mortality tended to be exogenous, that is, they were influenced more by natural or biological factors than by social and economic ones. This argument should not be interpreted to mean that European societies were the helpless playthings of epidemiological forces. On the contrary, the weakness of the climate-harvest-mortality nexus stands as testimony to the considerable power of economic and social organization in many parts of Europe to diminish the impact of natural forces on material life. But these same societies stood powerless before infectious diseases, which had their own dynamic—their own history, so to speak. Indeed, the most systematic study of the influence of climate change on pre-industrial societies concludes that its biometeorological effects dominated its direct effects on food supply in shaping the course of the vital rates.[45]

The *trends* of pre-industrial mortality continue to resist easy explanation. What about its *structure*? Was there a distinctive pattern to the incidence of death? Perhaps the most elementary error to which the uninitiated is prone is to suppose that in a society where the average age at death is, say 35, this is also the typical (or modal) age at which persons died. It is true that today, when the average life lasts well over 70 years, the vast majority of persons actually die at advanced ages. But the pattern of death by age in the past, while broadly similar to today's, featured one important difference: a far higher level of infant mortality. For those who survived infancy and early childhood, the prospects were fair for living one's allotted three score and ten years. For example, life expectancy at birth in early eighteenth-century France stood at an abysmal 24 years, but those Frenchmen and women who survived to adulthood could expect, at age 25, an additional 31 years of life.[46]

It will be clear from this example that a very large portion of all births, usually over half, did not survive to adulthood. Infant mortality stood at large multiples of modern levels, and would show little tendency to fall until after 1870. The incidence of infant and child deaths was such that even couples conceiving child after child throughout their fertile years could not be assured of surviving adult heirs. In a typical stationary population, only 60 percent of married men would leave at their own deaths at least one surviving son; 20 percent would leave one or more surviving daughters, but no sons; 20 percent would leave no surviving children at all.[47]

This stubborn persistence of very high levels of infant death deep into the nineteenth century suggests the powerlessness of society to attend to the afflictions that threatened infants. But the matter is not so simple. In fact, the rates of infant mortality, while everywhere high by modern standards, differed enormously and persistently from region to region. In eighteenth-century Germany over 350 of every 1000 births did not survive its first year of life in several Bavarian villages, while in Waldeck and East Friesland these rates were well below 200 per 1000 births.[48] In Spain infant mortality was always far higher in Castile and Andalusia than along the northern and eastern coasts,[49] while in France rates of 191 per 1000 in the southwest, the most favored region, contrasted with 249 per 1000 in the northeast quadrant of the country and even higher levels in the towns.[50]

In none of these cases can the differing levels of infant mortality be linked closely to economic conditions. Indeed, where family reconstitution studies can distinguish the mortality experience of social classes the infant mortality of higher social classes, if anything, exceeds that of workers and farmers. The single most important direct factor in explaining the differing levels of pre-industrial mortality is breastfeeding customs—whether it is done and for how long. Since child mortality (deaths between ages 1 and 5) often follows the same pattern as infant mortality, the possibility exists that breastfeeding practices were closely connected to other dimensions of child rearing. It appears that culture was far more important than economics, medicine, or social class in determining whether 650 or 450 of every 1000 births would survive childhood.

If upper income groups did not succeed in protecting their infants from death, it will come as no surprise that their mortality rates at adult ages were also not usually lower than those of ordinary folks. Indeed, the expectation of life at birth among British peers was lower than for the population at large throughout the seventeenth century. Only after 1750 could the rich begin to buy longer life.[51]

If social class did not protect the privileged from the grim reaper, perhaps gender did. In the twentieth century mortality at all ages is higher for men than women, giving the latter an additional five to eight years of life, on average, in the industrialized countries. In the pre-industrial era these differentials were smaller, but as of the mid-eighteenth century they remained in favor of women, by 3.5 years in the case of Sweden and 1.9 years in France.[52] If high infant mortality hid an indirect, neglectful infanticide, it appears not to have been directed at a single sex; nor were the dangers of childbirth such as to cause female mortality to differ from that of males. Maternal mortality (deaths of mothers within 60 days of a birth) did not usually exceed 10 per 1000 births in England (1500-1749), Sweden (1750-1800), and Germany (eighteenth century).[53]

### Fertility

While mortality was highly volatile and substantially beyond the control of pre-industrial populations, fertility was long thought to constitute a far more predictable phenomenon. After all, human biology establishes firm parameters for reproduction, while the human behavior that could modify the reproductive result was firmly anchored in social, religious, legal, and economic structures which changed glacially, if at all. Fertility was thought to be stable precisely because it was believed to be beyond the *conscious* control of men and women within marriage, while outside of marriage it was very much within the conscious control of society. Do the findings of family reconstitution studies, whose greatest strength is the measurement of marital fertility, give us reason to re-evaluate these generalizations?

The findings, a sample of which are displayed in Table 2, certainly confirm the stable character of human biology: the *shape* of the marital fertility rate by age is everywhere the same. It is highest for the age group 20-24, whereafter it declines, gently at first and more rapidly at higher ages. The average age of mothers at their last birth did not stray very far from 40. But Table 2 also shows that the fertility *level* of these populations varied considerably, even though none of them show evidence of attempting to control fertility. That is, "natural fertility" was not uniformly high across pre-industrial Europe. A Flemish woman married at age 20 who survived with her husband to age 44 could expect to bear 10 children; women in southwestern France, under identical circumstances, would bear fewer than 8.[54] Irish and English Quakers—groups drawn from the same stock, sharing the same culture, and in the same economic positions—managed to exhibit substantially different fertility levels. From the perspective of modern society, where the children borne per woman is less than two, there may seem little to choose among these examples, yet the difference between seven and ten was very great, both for the demographic character of society and for the life course of women and their social and economic roles in society. How could natural fertility regimes vary so greatly?

JAN DE VRIES

**Table 2. Age-Specific Marital Fertility Rates.**

| Place | Period | 15-19 | 20-24 | 25-29 | 30-34 | 35-39 | 40-44 | 45-49 | TMFR |
|---|---|---|---|---|---|---|---|---|---|
| *England* | | | | | | | | | |
| 13 parishes | 1600-49 | 399 | 395 | 362 | 308 | 256 | 130 | 33 | 7.26 |
| 13 parishes | 1650-99 | 358 | 409 | 364 | 306 | 248 | 126 | 39 | 7.27 |
| *Quakers* | | | | | | | | | |
| British urban | 1650-99 | | 401 | 445 | 372 | 277 | 128 | | 8.12 |
| Rural | 1650-99 | | 385 | 371 | 327 | 249 | 154 | | 7.43 |
| Irish | 1650-99 | | 443 | 438 | 421 | 360 | 192 | | 9.27 |
| *Germany* | | | | | | | | | |
| Overall (14) | 1750-74 | 384 | 439 | 425 | 374 | 303 | 173 | 26 | 8.57 |
| Bavaria (3) | 1648-1849 | | 499 | 486 | 449 | 371 | 171 | 28 | 9.88 |
| East Frisia | 1662-1849 | | 449 | 376 | 322 | 250 | 118 | 17 | 7.58 |
| Waldeck (4) | 1662-1849 | | 433 | 399 | 361 | 287 | 166 | 23 | 8.23 |
| Giessen | 1631-80 | 415 | 424 | 420 | 353 | 297 | 168 | 36 | 8.31 |
| *Belgium* | | | | | | | | | |
| 11 parishes | pre-1750 | | 472 | 430 | 366 | 317 | 190 | | 8.88 |
| Flanders | | 442 | 494 | 453 | 413 | 338 | 196 | 24 | 9.47 |
| Nobles | | 304 | 441 | 386 | 304 | 212 | 97 | 13 | 7.20 |
| *Netherlands* | | | | | | | | | |
| Maasland | 1670-1819 | 490 | 528 | 482 | 386 | 276 | 118 | 12 | 8.95 |
| Duiven | 1666-1795 | 375 | 492 | 438 | 384 | 314 | 164 | 5 | 8.96 |
| *Switzerland* | | | | | | | | | |
| Overall | pre-1750 | | 509 | 463 | 398 | 321 | 164 | | 9.28 |
| Zürich | 1580-1649 | | 439 | 432 | 413 | 364 | 200 | | 9.24 |
| "well-to-do" | 1650-89 | | 476 | 419 | 387 | 278 | 143 | | 8.52 |
| *France* | | | | | | | | | |
| Overall (91) | 1720-39 | | 467 | 445 | 401 | 325 | 168 | | 9.03 |
| Northeast | 1670-1769 | | 515 | 458 | 405 | 323 | 158 | 13 | 9.30 |
| Southwest | 1720-69 | | 445 | 350 | 351 | 245 | 147 | 21 | 7.69 |
| *Florence* | 1400-1549 | 478 | 574 | 505 | 353 | 249 | 65 | 0 | 8.73 |

*TMFR = Total Marital Fertility Rate, the sum of age-specific marital fertility rates across ages 20-44

*Sources*
England: Wrigley and Schofield (1983); Quakers: Vann and Eversley (1992), 134; Germany, Bavaria: Knodel (1978); Waldeck, Giessen: Imhof (1975), vol. 1: 412; Flanders: Vandenbroeke (1976); Maasland: Noordam (1986), 151; Duiven: Schuurman (1979), 171; Zürich: Mattmüller (1987), vol. 2: 225; France: Flinn (1981), 103-7; Northeast France: Houdaille (1976); Southwest France: Henry (1972); Florence: Klapisch-Zuber (1988), 44.

There are four significant determinants of natural fertility: fecundability, post-partum non-susceptibility, sterility, and intrauterine mortality.[55]
The last of these, consisting primarily of miscarriages (but including abor-
tions), cannot be detected by family reconstitution studies. Sterility can be,
and while it varied from group to group, it was nowhere so widespread as
to have a major impact on total fertility. Indeed, since childbearing is a
major cause of (secondary) sterility, its chief impact was probably to keep
the fertility differences from being larger than they were.

This leaves the first two fertility determinants. Fecundability (the probability of conception in a given period) is determined by physiology and
the frequency of intercourse. While direct information about these determinants is almost always lacking, the fecundability of populations can be
compared by noting the speed of first conception after marriage (among
populations where pre-nuptial conceptions are excluded). These differ
ences were often substantial, but they turn out to have a much smaller effect on total fertility across the whole span of the childbearing period than
the remaining variable, the period of non-susceptibility following a birth.
The longer this period, the further apart successive births will be spaced
and, hence, the fewer births there will be within the childbearing period.
The major factor influencing the duration of non-susceptibility was
breastfeeding practices: the longer infants were suckled, the longer conception was delayed.

We have already been introduced to infant feeding practices as a determinant of infant mortality. It is certainly a gross simplification to state
that breastfeeding by itself explains whether a population would have low
fertility and low infant mortality—a "low pressure" demographic regime—or high fertility and high infant mortality—a "high pressure" regime.[56] The duration of breastfeeding must have been embedded in child
rearing practices more generally, and this, in turn, must have been deeply
implicated in the structure of households and the position of wives within
them. All of this deserves further study. We have here an instructive example of what is meant by the statement that historical demography is a
discipline with a hard mathematical core and a soft socio-economic rind.
The one is not simply a subordinate feature of the other; this kind of historical study depended on the interaction of its two component parts.

So far we have considered only marital fertility under conditions unaffected by family limitation measures. A major objective of the pioneers of
the family reconstitution technique was to determine whether European
populations acted consciously to limit the size of their families. After all,
since the nineteenth century "fertility transition" occurred substantially

without the benefit of modern birth control technologies, it would not have been physically impossible for similar family limitation practices to have been used earlier. And, if this is true, then uncovering the beginnings and diffusion of such practices would be very revealing of the "mentalité" of early modern European populations.

The detection of family limitation practices relies on a simple assumption: that couples limit the number of their offspring not by "spacing" (discussed above), but by "stopping." That is, once a desired family size is reached, the couple will take steps to avoid further conceptions. Such "parity-specific" behavior should reveal itself in family reconstitution studies by: 1) an earlier age at final childbearing; 2) a significantly longer interval between the penultimate and ultimate birth (because "stopping" measures are not without accidents); and 3) a lowered age-specific fertility concentrated in the higher age groups.

In Henry's family reconstitution of Geneva's burghers, he uncovered a substantial reduction of fertility beginning in the late-seventeenth century. Similar behavior can be detected after 1650 among upper income families in Zürich. The evidence for this is presented in Table 2. Fertility until age 34 was within 5 percent of the pre-1650 level, but at ages 35-39 it fell to 76 percent and at 40-44 to 72 percent of the pre-1650 level.[57] These high-status burgers obviously were not pressed to these measures by immanent poverty; rather, it appears that the maintenance of their high status in an economically constricted environment was sufficient to elicit this behavioral innovation.

Was "stopping" behavior limited to urban upper income groups? The most clear-cut examples remain those of the upper classes of Geneva, Zürich, and Rouen. But studies of the *total* populations of Geneva and Rouen reveal that the lower classes participated, in a more muted way, in the reduction of fertility from the very high levels that obtained until the mid-seventeenth century.[58] The more numerous village studies occasionally encounter prima facie evidence for family limitation practice. Wrigley detected a radical throttling back of fertility after 1650 in the Devonshire village of Colyton,[59] but the skeptical scrutiny of revisionists has called into question whether "parity-specific birth control" (i.e., conscious efforts to achieve a target family size) truly characterize these examples. It is now doubted that these practices were "of any significance in determining the overall patterns of marital fertility" in England.[60]

With few exceptions, fertility in pre-industrial Europe was "natural fertility," but this does not mean that it was a constant, even in the long run. Fertility varied considerably by region. But so far we have been looking at *theoretical* fertility. That is, the total fertility rates displayed in Table 2 refer to the number of births that *would have occurred* to women "at risk" throughout the age period 20 to 44. European societies, however, did not generally expose women to the risk, or obligation, of childbearing throughout this period. Childbearing was overwhelmingly confined to the conjugal state, and the institution of marriage came to be carefully controlled. Marriage, an eminently social institution, stood at the intersection of fertility regulation, economic prospects, political participation and social status in early modern Europe.

### Nuptiality: the "European Marriage Pattern"

John Hajnal opened a famous 1965 article on nuptiality with the provocative statement that "the marriage pattern of most of Europe . . . was, as far as we can tell, unique or almost unique in the world. There is no known example of a population of non-European civilization which has had a similar pattern."[61] The "European marriage pattern" he described was not unknown; it had been an important object of Malthus's attention in the later editions of his *Essay on the Principle of Population*. But Hajnal's article sought to place this long-term functional behavior pattern in its geographic and temporal context. West of a line drawn from St. Petersburg to Trieste—a line roughly dividing Latin from Orthodox Christianity—marriage was late, usually at an average age of between 23 and 27 years for women and higher for men; celibacy (i.e., remaining single) was widespread, usually above 10 percent of all men and women. These marriage characteristics were closely associated with the expectation that couples contemplating marriage would establish a separate household from either of their parents (neolocal marriage). The resulting conjugal family unit did not ordinarily include other resident kin (parents, siblings, uncles, or aunts of the husband and wife), but it did commonly supply or take into the household, at some point in the life-cycle of the family, non-kin in the form of servants, apprentices or lodgers. Jacques Dupâquier summarized the "unwritten rules" governing the families of traditional Europe this way: "One married couple to each home; no marriage without a home; no babies outside of marriage."[62]

The European marriage pattern and the conjugal family unit with exchange of servants did not occur in combination by coincidence. In Hajnal's opinion, bolstered by Peter Laslett's pioneering work on household size,[63] these were the interlocking, mutually reinforcing features of a demographic, social, and economic phenomenon of long standing, which made possible the adjustment of fertility to changing economic conditions.

Table 3. Mean Age at First Marriage in Selected European Populations.

| Place | Period | Women | Men |
|---|---|---|---|
| *England* | | | |
| 13 parishes | 1600-49 | 25.6 | 28.1 |
| | 1650-99 | 26.2 | 28.1 |
| | 1700-49 | 25.4 | 27.2 |
| British nobles | 1550 | 20.3 | 25.2 |
| | 1600 | 20.7 | 26.0 |
| | 1650 | 21.3 | 26.6 |
| | 1700 | 23.2 | 30.0 |
| | | | |
| *Netherlands* | | | |
| Duiven | 1711-50 | 28.5 | 29.7 |
| Maasland | 1650-99 | 26.7 | 26.8 |
| | 1700-49 | 25.9 | 28.2 |
| Amsterdam | 1626/27 | 24.5 | 25.7 |
| | 1676/77 | 26.5 | 27.7 |
| | 1726/27 | 27.2 | 27.8 |
| Zierikzee | 1500-49 | 25.3 | 30.6 |
| patriciate | 1550-99 | 24.2 | 28.9 |
| | 1600-49 | 26.0 | 31.4 |
| | 1650-99 | 25.0 | 30.6 |
| | | | |
| *Scandinavia* | | | |
| 6 parishes | pre-1750 | 26.7 | |
| | | | |
| *Germany* | | | |
| 14 parishes | 1700-49* | 24.1 | 26.7 |
| | | | |
| *France* | | | |
| Overall | 1675-99 | 24.7 | |
| | 1700-24 | 25.0 | |
| | 1725-49 | 25.6 | |
| Paris Basin | 1671-1720 | 24.5 | 26.6 |
| Pont-de-Vaux | 1600-28 | 21.6 | 24.7 |
| in Bresse | 1644-57 | 22.9 | 25.1 |
| Athis in Ile | 1595-1634 | 20.4 | 24.9 |
| de France | 1635-70 | 23.3 | 24.9 |
| 10 parishes | | | |
| near Athis | 1737-43 | 25.6 | 29.0 |
| Lorraine | 16th c. | 22.1 | 23.9 |
| | 17th c. | 24-28 | 26-30 |
| Rouen | 1650-72 | | |
| Notables | | 24.8 | 30.8 |
| Shopkeepers | | 26.0 | 28.5 |
| Artisans | | 24.9 | 27.2 |
| Laborers | | 25.6 | 26.1 |

| Place | Period | Women | Men |
|-------|--------|-------|-----|
| *Geneva* | 1550-99 | 20.1 | |
| bourgeoisie | 1600-49 | 22.1 | |
| | 1650-99 | 23.1 | |
| | 1700-49 | 24.8 | |
| *Italy* | | | |
| Florence | 1251-1475 | | 28.9 |
| City | 1427 | 18.0 | 30.0 |
| Countryside | 1427 | 18.4 | 25.6 |
| Altopascio | 1625-49 | 18.6 | |
| (Tuscany) | 1650-99 | 20.4 | |
| | 1700-49 | 21.9 | |

*Median age. Given the form of most distributions of age at first marriage, the median age will be slightly lower than the mean age.

*Sources:*
England: Wrigley and Schofield (1983), 162; British nobles: Hollingsworth (1964), 26-27; Duiven: Schuurman (1979), 163; Maasland: Noordam (1986), 106; Amsterdam: Van der Woude (1980), 156; Zierikzee patriciate: Schuurman (1979), 163; Scandinavia: Flinn (1981), 84; Germany: Knodel (1988), table 6.2; France overall: Henry and Houdaille (1978), 50, and (1979), 413; Paris Basin: Dupâquier (1988), 305; Pont-de-Vaux: Moriceau (1981), 487; Athis, 10 parishes near Athis: Dupâquier (1988), 305; Lorraine: Cabourdin (1980); Rouen: Bardet (1983), vol. 1: 255; Geneva: Henry (1956), 55; Florence: Herlihy (1985), 109, and Herlihy and Klapisch-Zuber (1985), 210; Altopascio: McArdle (1977).

In a word, it made possible the operation of Malthus's "preventive check" (whereby fertility was reduced to avoid economic disaster), thereby making unnecessary the intervention of the "positive check" (whereby overpopulation unleashed a rising mortality to restore balance to society).[64] The positive check long continued to reign supreme in (non-western) societies where marriage was nearly universal; where the marriage age, for women, was controlled more by biology than by economic circumstances; and where married couples were incorporated in existing households of parents or other relations.

Family reconstitution and other research offers abundant evidence that the European marriage mattern existed at least as far back as the seventeenth century. Table 3 offers an overview of average ages at first marriage. Data on the proportions never marrying are scarcer, but, here too, seventeenth-century studies show that women remaining unmarried throughout the childbearing years sometimes exceeded 20 percent of the total.[65] All-in-all, we possess a well-founded picture of a society where youth typically left their parental homes in the mid-teens but did not marry until the mid-twenties. A "stage of life" typically lasting nearly a decade was spent by both men and women "subsumed" in the households of non-kin, functioning as servants or apprentices—sexually mature but barred from regular sexual relations. To become a "full citizen" in the community depended upon gaining access to the married state, but the wait was long, and for a significant minority it lasted forever. Exploring the implications of this regime—psychological, economic, and social—has exposed a fruitful research terrain.[66]

While the broad contours of the European marriage pattern are generally accepted, several important questions, both demographic and historical, remain. Here we will consider briefly just three. First, did nuptiality actually vary enough to have a significant and timely effect on fertility? A necessarily related question is whether fertility, in fact, was substantially restricted to marriage? Obviously, the demographic significance of the European marriage pattern would be minor if illegitimacy was widespread. Second, did this regime really affect all of Europe to the St. Petersburg-Trieste line, or were there important differences *within* this vast territory? Third, when did it begin? Shortly before the seventeenth century, or much earlier?

*The European Marriage Pattern: Effects on Fertility?*
Figure 2 is designed to illustrate in an intuitive way how the potential fertility of a population could be reduced in the absence of deliberate family limitation practice.

If marriage were universal at age 15, the entire rectangle would constitute the "reproductive space" of society. This is never the case, if for no other reason than mortality, which causes the removal of some portion of the cohort of 15-year-old women (represented by the vertical height of figure 2). Curve A indicates the portion of this initial cohort of 15-year-olds that would be removed from reproduction over time, either by their own death or that of their husband. In the case of widowhood, some women could be returned to the "reproductive space" depending on the social acceptability of (prompt) remarriage.[67] Curve A' shows the compensating effect of remarriage on the disruptive force of adult mortality. High mortality reduced the number of children born to a cohort of women, but its impact was reduced by the obvious fact that mortality rises with age, while

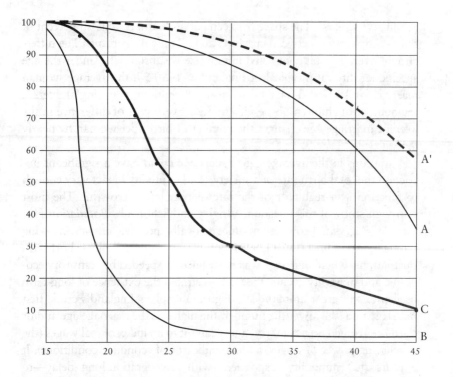

**Figure 2. Illustration of the effect of late marriage on the utilization of the "potential fertility" of a population of women.**

A.   The removal of women from childbearing through their own death or that of their husband.

A'.  The restoration of a portion of widowed women to childbearing via remarriage.

B.   The entry to childbearing via marriage of a population where marriage is nearly universal and is concentrated in the ages 15-20.

C.   The entry to childbearing of a "European Marriage Pattern" population. Based on the ages at first marriage in England, 1650-99, assuming 10 percent remain single at age 45.

fecundity—the likelihood of conceiving—is highest at the younger ages.

For this reason, a second factor—the age at first marriage—has a much greater impact on total realized fertility. Curve B traces the entry of the initial cohort of women into the married state under the assumptions that marriage is nearly universal and women marry between the ages of 15 and 20. Curve C is based on the actual experience of English women in the period 1650-99. The difference between Curves B and C represents the impact of the European marriage pattern in removing women from the "re-

productive space." The space between curves B and A' fills 73 percent of
the rectangle; that between curves C and A' only 48 percent. The difference in average total completed family size is substantial. Under the age
specific fertility rates typical of England in 1650-99, the average woman
marrying at 18 would have borne nearly 8 children; marrying at age 25,
the number of children borne falls to 5.2. Every year of difference in the
average marriage age changes the number of births per woman by nearly
0.4.[68]

Variations in the average age at marriage *could* have a significant impact on the total birth rate of a society. Did nuptiality in fact vary enough
to function as a regulator of the rate of population growth? The most
thorough study of this question, Wrigley and Schofield's *Population History of England*, provides an unequivocally positive answer, viewing
nuptiality as the linchpin of English population change. Besides short-term
fluctuations, where marriage was postponed or speeded by transitory economic and mortality events, they demonstrated the existence of long-term
oscillations of great amplitude.[69] Figure 3 displays England's crude first
marriage rate (the lower the number, the higher is the marriage age and/or
the more women do not marry) and relates it to an index of real wages (the
purchasing power of wages, a crude indicator of economic conditions). It
appears that nuptiality responded—with a generation-long delay—to
changes in the economy, and these changes were sufficient to throttle England's population growth down to zero in the late-seventeenth century,
and to generate rapid growth in the mid-sixteenth and late-eighteenth centuries.

The "strategy" of gradually revising marriage behavior to (yesterday's)
economic circumstances produced slow swings in fertility that enabled
early modern England to accommodate its numbers to its economic prospects. The country possessed a "low-pressure" demographic regime, one
dominated by nuptiality-driven fertility change, rather than a "high-pressure" system dominated by mortality. This is the prevailing view of pre-industrial England's demographic system. Since England would later develop the first industrial economy, a natural next question is whether her
demographic experience was typical of all areas subject to the European
marriage pattern, or *sui generis*.

Before turning to that question, two additional features of this
nuptiality-fertility nexus require a few words of discussion: celibacy and illegitimacy.

An unexpected result of modern research into nuptiality has been that
the percentage of the population remaining single was neither stable nor of

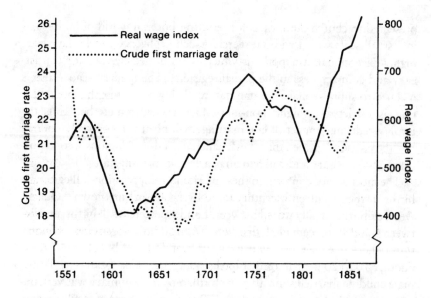

Figure 3. Real Wage Trends and the Crude First Marriage Rate in England. Both in 25-year moving averages.

Real Wage Rate: Construction wage rates deflated by an index of the cost of consumables.
Crude First Marriage Rate: Marriages per 1000 population, excluding re-marriages.

*Source:*
Wrigley (1985), 278.

marginal importance. It varied considerably over time and often in surprising ways. Instead of rising as the age at first marriage rose (restrictions causing both delay and denial of access to the married state), the percentage of persons never marrying sometimes rose when the marriage age fell, and vice versa.[70] Moreover, in England at least variations in celibacy exerted a larger impact on the overall birth rate than did variations in the age at first marriage. This highlights the need for demographic research that is more sensitive to social class than have been the aggregative studies—whether of whole countries or whole villages.

This is also the point at which to address the issue of illegitimacy. For, if non-marital fertility was high, or if it was systematically under-recorded in the parish baptism records, the argument made here for the central importance of marriage as a regulator of fertility would be called into question. The modern reader is inclined to doubt that illegitimate children would be presented to church authorities for baptism, but in a world of faith—and in a small-scale world without secrets—such negligence would have been highly exceptional, a hypothesis which is confirmed by tests for consistency and completeness in the parish registers. The modern reader also is inclined to suppose that, "human nature" being what it is, the more marriage is restricted the higher non-marital fertility will tend to be. Thus, the fertility-reducing impact of late marriage will be at least partially undone by "the passion between the sexes" which in Malthus' famous second postulate, "is necessary and will remain nearly in its present state."[71]

The facts do not conform to these modern presuppositions. Illegitimate births in the seventeenth century were by no means unknown. Out-of-wedlock births usually varied between 1 and 4 percent of all births, and between 4 and 10 percent of all *first births*.[72] In addition, pre-nuptial conception (where marriage occurs between conception and birth) could affect another 10 to 20 percent of first births. But, since most bearers of illegitimate children married soon after the birth, repeat illegitimacy was very uncommon. In 14 German parishes in 1700-49, 9.7 percent of fertile women bore children out of wedlock, but only 12.3 percent of that number (i.e. 1.2 percent of all fertile women) were repeaters. The "bastardy-prone" formed a very small sub-culture.[73]

All over Europe illegitimacy would become far more widespread in the course of the eighteenth century, but in the seventeenth century illegitimate births were actually becoming less common than before. Some interpret this as the result of a new (and temporary) sexual discipline imposed by the Reformation and Counterreformation churches.[74] This certainly cannot be dismissed out of hand, but any interpretation must take into account the fact that illegitimate fertility tended to move parallel to trends in nuptiality. That is, whatever stimulated earlier marriage and higher fertility, also stimulated a higher incidence of illegitimate births. Whatever restricted nuptiality in the seventeenth century also reduced the incidence of illegitimacy. In short, illegitimacy occurred in close relation to marriage; it rarely served as an alternative to it.

### The European Marriage Pattern: Universality?

An evident shortcoming of the European marriage pattern as an historical model is that it seems to have yielded different demographic results in various parts of the vast European space to which it is thought to apply. England after 1541 featured nuptiality behavior highly responsive to economic conditions that established a "low-pressure regime" of low fertility and low mortality. The frequent bouts of crisis mortality in France suggested the presence there of a "high-pressure regime," where mortality dominated the demographic system, and marriages were less sensitive to economic shocks. In fact, the economic sensitivity of marriage formation in France appears to have been fully as great as in England (at least after 1670, when French data are available to test this hypothesis).[75] But, the fact remains that the same European marriage pattern gave rise to substantially different levels of fertility and mortality, as descibed earlier in this chapter. And the further one penetrates Europe to the east and south, the more diversity of experience one can expect to uncover.

The search for solutions to this puzzle has focused primarily on the identification of different household structures, since Hajnal in 1965 linked the European marriage pattern to the nuclear, or conjugal, family.[76] Even if space allowed, no satisfactory summary can now be made of the varying ways in which household structure and demographic behavior interacted throughout Europe. Too much remains unclear. It may be fair to say that we must seek shelter in a provisional structure, one that will certainly be rebuilt, but in ways that are not yet certain. This provisional structure adds to the north-south "Hajnal Line" a less firmly drawn east-west line, running through France and central Europe and distinguishing a northern zone of small, nuclear families from a southern zone where "stem families" (where one son marries and assumes the headship of the parental household) were common. The new structure also requires a distinction between northwestern Europe—in truth, England and Holland—and the rest of northern Europe. Here the distinction is not so much formal household structure as the legal and, ultimately, cultural differences that made Europe's northwestern extremity especially individualistic.[77]

These distinctions have the virtue of focusing attention on how demography is embedded in legal-social-cultural structures of great durability. But, they also invite the making of ever more distinctions, dividing the common European house into many, many mansions. The suggestion that Mediterranean Europe possessed a distinctive demographic pattern recently has been shown to be untenable. In the Mediterranean lands a new line must be drawn, separating southern Italy from the north and southern Iberia from its north. In both cases, nuclear families dominated to the *south* of this line, while co-residential groups of complex structure were numerous to the north.[78] The drift of all this line-drawing, of course, is toward the resurrection and celebration of regional "ethnicities" and "cultures" for which contemporary Europe seems to have an inordinate fondness. Some movement in this direction nonetheless seems necessary in order to understand better how the various components of demographic behavior were integrated.

At present the enormous variety of local experience is rendered coherent by the intentionalist assumption "that societies strive to maintain equilibrium." It follows, then, that "any disequilibrium tends to generate a correcting or homeostatic response."[79] Essentially exogenous mortality fluctuations and shifts are the usual source of disequilibrium, while nuptiality and fertility are adjusted in ways that are closely linked to the household structures of society. This model of a self-equilibrating demographic system must not blind us to the fact that it could hope to offer partial compensation for, but could not wholly undo, the impact of mortality shifts. This always remained an exogenous force substantially beyond the power of European societies to tame, for the level of mortality was determined by infectious diseases much more than by food supplies, and the former possessed its own dynamic.

### The European Marriage Pattern: Old or New?

There remains the question of the European marriage pattern's antiquity. For a contemporary demographer the revelation that a basic family strategy could be shown to have prevailed in a large geographical zone from "at least" the seventeenth century through the post-World War II era suggests a wealth of interesting questions, not least about the relationship of this durable pattern to the demographic transition that disturbed nearly every other aspect of Western society in the nineteenth century. For the historian of early modern Europe, however, attention is inevitably directed toward the unsettled issue of its origins. Evidence consistent with the European marriage pattern extends back so long as the parish records are available (see Table 3), but some of the earliest evidence of age at first marriage hints at the possibility that marriage took place at much earlier ages before 1600. Hajnal's review of an eclectic mix of ancient and medieval evidence led him to hypothesize that the fifteenth and sixteenth centuries experienced a transition from an earlier marriage pattern, presumably more like the rest of the world, to the uniquely European regime of late marriage. Were this hypothesis to be sustained the Renaissance and Reformation era would acquire yet another foundation stone on which to support its claim to being the hearth of modernity. Moreover, even for historians uninterested in such mega-claims, the question retains a very practical value, for the interpretation of fifteenth-century demographic history (a statistical "dark age" compared to the era of parish registers) depends sensitively on whether we can use, or must reject, the behavioral models described above.

Recent research is by no means unanimous about Hajnal's hypothesis of a 1400-1600 transition to the European marriage pattern, but it tends to favor rejection. Not everyone follows Eric Jones's argument that Europeans have adhered to this demographic behavior since their days in the Teutonic forests,[80] but most scholars are inclined to stress continuity over regime change. The reasons for this, and its implications will become clear in this chapter's final section, which reviews historical demography before the parish register era.

## 4. HISTORICAL DEMOGRAPHY BEFORE THE PARISH REGISTERS

The focal point of most demographic interest in the fifteenth century is the long delay in the recovery of Europe's population from the Black Death. Since conventional Malthusian theory anticipates that a mortality crisis will be followed by a vigorous revival of population, fed by numerous and early marriages, the absence of any sustained revival for over a century stands as a puzzle—or, better put, an affront.

Most efforts to explain this phenomenon have not so much tried to solve the puzzle as remove the affront by positing the continued existence until deep in the fifteenth century of extremely high levels of mortality, sustained by recurring outbreaks of plague. An acerbic summation of this position was made by Sylvia Thrupp, when she dismissed the argument that the post-plague shortage of workers had created a "golden age of labor" (which should have increased fertility) with the observation that "if [the period from 1349 to the 1470s] was a golden age, it was the golden age of bacteria."[81]

This approach to the fifteenth century may be said to be agnostic with respect to the question of the early existence of the European marriage pattern: sheer survival in the face of the overwhelming presence of death required that marriage occur early and be widespread.[82] This position locates the beginning of effective controls on marriage in the "long sixteenth century" of rising population. At some point in this more benign mortality environment (some) Europeans begin to sense the need to limit fertility. The chief weakness of this argument is its total dependence on a belief in persisting, extraordinarily high mortality. Although there is abundant evidence of recurring plague epidemics and other mortality crises, such evidence also exists for the sixteenth century, when we know long-term mortality levels to have been low by later standards. Indeed, the knowledge that long-term death rates varied considerably after 1600, without ever forcing society to abandon its controls on nuptiality, invites doubt that the "high mortality" argument is adequate to explain either the long delay in post-plague recovery or the "suspension" of controls on marriage.

A second argument in support of the transition position turns to law, religion, and culture instead of observable demographic measurements. It argues, in effect, that "measurements" are of little use when the categories are not stable, and "marriage" did not mean in, say, 1400 what it would mean in the post-Reformation and post-Tridentine Europe.[83] Here we encounter another of the dimensions in which the hard core of demography leads us directly into its soft rind. While this specialized topic cannot be discussed *in extenso* here, we should pause long enough to observe that the very organization of the historical profession into specialized medievalists and early modernists tends toward the exaggeration of differences. Just as the latter focus on the sixteenth century as the birthplace of modern marriage, the former find many of the same features emerging in the eleventh and twelfth centuries.[84] Research spanning these two professional domains, such as that of R. M. Smith, tends to deflate the claims for a sixteenth-century discontinuity in the history of marriage and the family.[85]

It does not seem possible to develop a persuasive account of Europe's post-plague demographic history without confronting directly the issue of nuptiality and fertility. Easily the richest and fullest study of a fifteenth-century population is that of Tuscany, based on the *catasto* of 1427. Herlihy and Klapisch-Zuber's study, supplemented by evidence from other Renaissance Italian towns, reveals a demographic regime very different from the European marriage pattern. Nearly all women married, and they did so during their teens (average age: 18.0), and they married men more than ten years their seniors. The widowed men commonly remarried; the women but rarely, causing Florence to fill with widows. The overall marriage pattern is one in which the life courses of men and women differed fundamentally: while the women passed directly from their fathers to their husbands, and when widows were guarded by male relatives, the men lived long years in a single state as members of youth groups and confraternities in which involvement in prostitution and "life cycle homosexuality" featured prominently.[86] While Florence's urban society may have differed in many particulars from the countryside, in the matter of marriage age the rural patterns were similar. In rural Tuscany, in the Rhone valley of southern France, in Périgueux, and in the heretical Pyrenean village of Montaillou most women married in their teens.[87]

Herlihy felt confident that the relatively abundant Italian data were broadly representative of conditions elsewhere in Europe at the time: that 1427 Tuscany revealed a medieval marriage pattern much as Wrigley and Schofield's England revealed a modern pattern. The interpretation of this evidence requires a confrontation of an important issue in historical demography discussed above, namely, was there a common European demographic system or did it differ fundamentally by region? In this case the issue is put succinctly by asking whether the Tuscan families were "medieval" or "Mediterranean."[88]

Some local studies of English manors provide evidence for early marriage, offering support for the belief in a late medieval transition,[89] but this position has not gone unchallenged. Evidence allowing for a calculation of average marriage age is scare for northern Europe, but notarial and "census-like" records sometimes permit the estimation of the proportion of an adult population that is in the married state. In urban settings such as Coventry (England), Rheims (France) and Zierikzee (Netherlands), and in parts of rural England (based on poll-tax records) and Flanders (based on probate inventories), the marriage behavior seems to have been broadly consistent with the European marriage pattern. That is, while the age at first marriage at times may have been rather younger than in the seventeenth century, nuptiality showed variation over time, was not universal, and did not feature stark differences between the experiences of men and women.[90]

This evidence, fragmentary and imprecise, supports the view that before the sixteenth century, just as thereafter, demographic behavior was linked together in a loose, nuptiality-centered mechanism that sought to maintain equilibrium with the economic environment. For the seventeenth century and beyond our understanding of economic conditions is now sufficient to test and measure the relationships between demographic and economic variables. Such research has generated models in which the marriage-real wage nexus holds center stage. For earlier periods, however, especially the fifteenth century, such economic-demographic studies have achieved far less. The shortcomings of the quantitative data in this pre-parish register era account for a part of this weakness, but fully as important is the disagreement that long persisted about the essential characterization of Europe's fifteenth-century economy.

If the plague survivors were delivered from an over-populated Europe into a world of abundant land, high wages, and plentiful work—a golden age for labor—then restrictions on fertility and marriage would seem unnecessary, even irrational. The long delay in population recovery could then only be explained by extraordinary levels of mortality—which would give further impetus to a demographic regime of universal and early marriage.

If, however, the Black Death was no boon to the survivors but a great disequilibrating shock that brought depression to most sectors of the European economy, none of the above mentioned assumptions about demographic life would hold. If the low food prices (and consequently high real wages) encouraged farmers to take in servants rather than hire laborers, this could be no golden age for laborers—and the large number of servants would tend to delay marriage, just as it did in the late seventeenth century. If the fall in demand for grain caused the agricultural economy to shift toward the less labor-intensive livestock sector, young couples may have found they needed much more land than before to establish an economically viable household.[91] Economic factors such as these seem to help account for the rather low fertility suggested by English "churching" (postpartum purification) records,[92] and these plus high adult mortality help explain periodic reductions in fertility in rural Flanders after 1450.[93]

Clearly, a great deal remains to be learned about the historical demography of the fifteenth and sixteenth centuries. Just as for the better-charted centuries thereafter, the great challenge is to relate the particular to the general—the fragmentary and local data to models and concepts of broad applicability.

# NOTES

1. The first modern census, held by Spain in 1787 and named after the responsible government minister, the Conde de Floridablanca, predates the Revolution. Between 1790 (USA) and 1820, most western nations initiated census-taking programs that continued into this century (although a few countries, such as the Netherlands and Germany, have recently suspended this practice on privacy grounds).
2. Herlihy and Klapisch-Zuber (1978),
3. An old, but comprehensive and accessible source is Beloch (1937-61). See also, Comitato Italiano per lo Studio della Demografia Storica, *Le fonti della demografia storica in Italia* (Rome, 1971-72).
4. Arnoud (1956); Dupâquier (1979a); Russell (1948); Moliné-Bertrand (1985); Van der Woude (1982).
5. It is important to note that the events recorded in the parish registers are not exactly the same as the vital events of concern to the demographer. The difference between deaths and burials is chiefly a matter of accuracy; through neglect, not every dead body received a Christian burial, and many parish registers included only burials in the church yard, ignoring burials at pesthouses, hospitals, etc. In the case of births, the matter is more complex: the customary delay between birth and presentation at the baptismal font could vary from a day or two to many weeks, and the number of infant deaths in this interval could be substantial. In addition, stillbirths were generally not baptized, yet are important for demographic analysis of fertility.
6. Corsini (1971-72), 651-54. See also Cipolla (1991), 142-43.
7. Mols (1954), vol. 1:78-83; Corsini (1971-72); Dupâquier (1988), vol. 2:147-50; Mattmüller (1987), vol. 1: 149; Van der Woude (1980), 113-19.
8. Belletini (1980), 31-32 (Bologna, Parma, Florence, and Siena); Dupâquier (1988), 169 (France, England).
9. See Wrigley and Schofield (1981), pullout 1. On these methods, my account of which simplifies, perhaps to excess, see Oeppen (1993) and Lee (1994).
10. Lee (1973), (1981), and (1993); Oeppen (1993); Galloway (1993).
11. Henry (1956) and (1967); Henry and Gautier (1958).
12. Flinn (1981); Dupâquier (1988); Wrigley and Schofield (1983).
13. Schofield and Coleman (1986), 5.
14. Hollingsworth (1964).
15. Peller (1965); Litchfield (1969); Van Dijk and Roorda (1979).
16. Biget and Tricard (1981); Delmaire (1983); Klapisch-Zuber (1988).
17. Vandenbroucke (1985); see also De Vries (1991).
18. Thoen (1988); Fournial (1967); Higounet-Nadal (1978); Gottfried (1978); Razi (1980); Poos (1991).
19. Biraben (1979); Durand (1977).
20. Poos (1991), 106-09.

21. Russell (1948); Razi (1980); Gottfried (1978); Hatcher (1977).
22. Klep (1991).
23. Herlihy and Klapisch-Zuber (1985), 362.
24. Abel (1978), 80-91; Postan (1950).
25. Wrigley and Schofield (1981); Van der Woude (1980); Klep (1991).
26. An extreme articulation of the contrast between the traditional and modern worlds is provided in Le Roy Ladurie (1977).
27. While most of the French *Annalistes* were not themselves demographic historians, they leaned heavily on the demographic research in the construction of comprehensive regional histories. A classic example is Le Roy Ladurie (1966), especially its final chapter "La grande cycle agraire." In truth, this new historical movement fed from more sources of renewal than the French school alone. Major independent contributions include: Abel (1978 [1935]) and B. H. Slicher van Bath, *Agrarian History of Western Europe, 500-1850* (London, 1963 [1960]).
28. Bairoch (1988), 135-39; De Vries (1984), 40-43, 69-73.
29. Miskimin (1977), 20-24.
30. De Vries (1984), 76-77, 255-58.
31. The "urban graveyard" phenomenon has generated a substantial literature. See: Mols (1954-56); Sharlin (1978); Van der Woude, (1982); De Vries (1984), 175-97.
32. Wrigley (1967); De Vries (1984), 199-217.
33. Sex ratios below 100 (i.e., more women than men) seem to have been characteristic neither of medieval cities nor of eastern Europe and Russia until the nineteenth century. Seventeenth-century Berlin was full of soldiers, while Warsaw and Moscow long remained "male worlds" of estate owners and their retinues, often present in the city on a seasonal basis. Rome forms an exception to the rule for yet another reason, the massive presence of clergy. But, the towns of fifteenth century Tuscany also numbered more men than women, while the northern cities of Reims and Coventry already exhibited a surplus of women. R. M. Smith (1981b), 117-18; Mols (1954-56), vol. 2:183-99, draws together data from many sources.
34. Clark and Souden (1987), 29-34.
35. Dupâquier (1988), vol. 2:124-37.
36. Mattmüller (1987), vol. 1:317-32.
37. Elliott (1963), 290-95.
38. Wrigley and Schofield (1981), 219-28; for corrections and refinements, see Oeppen (1993), 252-54.
39. The initial, classic account of the pre-industrial mortality crisis is Meuvret (1946). Other major works include: Abel (1974); Lebrun (1980), 205-34; Andrew B. Appleby, "Grain Prices and Subsistence Crises in England and France, 1590-1740," *Journal of Economic History* 34 (1979): 868-88; V. Perez Moreda, *Las crisis de mortalidad en la España interior, siglos XVI-XIX* (Madrid, 1980); Massimo Livi-Bacci, *Population and Nutrition* (Cambridge, 1991).
40. Lee (1981); Galloway (1988). These results are the product of regression equations incorporating distributed lags. The dependent variable (crude death rates, in this case) are regressed against annual changes in the independent variable (prices). The dependent variable may respond to the effects of price fluctuations in earlier years as well as that occuring in the same year as the measured mortality. A distributed lag model seeks to capture the delayed effect of a given price fluctuation, in this case up to four years after the event.

41. Weir (1984a).
42. A more nuanced analysis, but one broadly consistent with this "old view," is presented in Flinn (1981), chaps. 4 and 6.
43. Schofield, Reher, and Bideau (1991).
44. Biraben (1975-76).
45. Galloway (1986), 20.
46. Blayo (1975).
47. Wrigley (1978).
48. Knodel (1988), 470.
49. Reher (1990), 110-11.
50. Dupâquier (1988), vol. 2:225.
51. Hollingsworth (1964), 56; Livi-Bacci (1991), 63-67.
52. Vallin (1991), 63-64.
53. Schofield (1986); Knodel (1988), 105-11.
54. The total marital fertility rate is simply the total of children that would be born to someone married from age 20 through 44, and subject to the age-specific fertility rates that characterize the entire population. This is a construction useful for comparative purposes, but it *does not* accurately describe the actual number of children that would in fact be born to a woman married throughout this period. The earlier one marries, the faster the age-specific fertility rate declines with age (primarily because of secondary sterility). Thus, at age 30-34, women married since age 20 will exhibit lower fertility than those who married at 25, which, in turn, will be lower than those married at age 30.
55. My analysis follows Henri Leridon, *Human Fertility: the Basic Components* (Chicago, 1977).
56. See Wrigley and Schofield (1981), 450-53, 478-80, and Weir (1984a) on high and low pressure regimes.
57. Mattmüller (1987), 1: 225.
58. Perrenoud (1990), 258-63; Bardet (1983), vol. 1:279.
59. Wrigley (1966), 82-109; for other evidence see Imhof (1975).
60. Wilson (1984), 240; see also Wrigley and Schofield (1983), 169-70.
61. Hajnal (1965), 130.
62. Dupâquier (1979b), 89.
63. Laslett (1965); Laslett and Wall (1972).
64. The Malthusian model is discussed in relation to the historical demography of early modern England in Wrigley and Schofield (1981), chap. 11.
65. Wrigley and Schofield (1981), 260.
66. A classic study is Laslett (1965); the economics of servanthood is explored in Kussmaul (1981); the sexual dimension of delayed marriage and its discontents attracted the curiosity of Edward Shorter, *The Making of the Modern family* (New York, 1975). On the intergenerational tensions that accompany this system see Berkner (1972).
67. The incidence of remarriage and the length of the "mourning" interval varied substantially by region, and by sex. Men generally remarried faster and more universally than women. See Knodel and Lynch (1985); Dupâquier, et al., eds., (1981).
68. In fact, matters are not quite so simple. See the systematic discussion by Knodel (1988).
69. See Wrigley (1985), 278, the table on real wage trends and marriage rates in England.

70. On this issue, see Weir (1984b); Schofield (1985).
71. Malthus (1970), 70.
72. Flinn (1981), 82.
73. Knodel (1981), table 8.4; Laslett (1980).
74. Flandrin (1976) and (1981).
75. Weir (1984a).
76. Since 1965 the study of household structure has been advanced by legal and anthropological research, yielding a more complex, more confusing picture of Europe west of the St. Petersburg-Trieste line.  Hajnal recently acknowledged this work, suggesting that the demographic structure he had identified applied fully only to northwestern Europe. Hajnal (1982), 450.
77. These distinctions are discussed by Macfarlane (1978); Laslett, Robin, and Wall (1983).  A more complex and more controversial system of European, and world, household categorization is found in Todd (1985).
78. See Benigno (1989); R. M. Smith, "The People of Tuscany and their families in the Fifteenth Century: Medieval or Mediterranean?" *JFH* 6 (1981b); Rowland (1987).
79. D. S. Smith (1977), 20.
80. Jones (1981), 11-14.
81. Chambers (1972), 22.
82. Hatcher (1977), 56-67; Russell (1948).
83. Flandrin (1981); Ozment (1983).
84. See Sheehan (1978); Herlihy and Klapisch-Zuber (1985); Van Hoecke and Welkenhuysen (1981).
85. R. M. Smith (1986).
86. Herlihy and Klapish-Zuber (1978), 414.
87. Le Roy Ladurie (1975); Higounet-Nadal (1978); Rossiaud (1976).
88. R. M. Smith (1981b).
89. Hanawalt (1986); Razi (1980).
90. Thoen (1988), part I; Hallam (1985); Poos (1991); R. M. Smith (1981a); Phythian Adams (1979); Desportes (1966).
91. A good introduction to the economic problems of the late-medieval economy is provided in Miskimin (1969).
92. Poos (1991).
93. Thoen (1988).

# BIBLIOGRAPHY

Abel, Wilhelm. *Agrarkrisen und Agrarkonjunktur. Ein Geschichte der Land- und Ernährungswirtschaft Mitteleuropas seit dem hohen Mittelalter.* 3d ed. Hamburg and Berlin, 1978 [1935].

Abel, Wilhelm. *Massenarmut und Hungerkrisen im vorindustriellen Europa.* Hamburg and Berlin 1974.

Appleby, Andrew. "Nutrition and Disease: the Case of London 1550-1750." *Journal of Interdisciplinary History* 6 (1975); 1-19.

Arnoud, M.-A. *Les dénombrements de foyers dans le comté de Hainault XIVe - XVIe siècle.* Brussels, 1956.

Bairoch, Paul. *Cities and Economic Development From the Dawn of History to the Present.* Chicago, 1988.

Bardet, J.-P. *Rouen au XVIIe et XVIIIe siècles: les mutations d'un espace social.* Paris 1983.

Belletini, A. "La démographie italienne au XVIe siècle: sources et possibilités de recherche." *ADH* (1980): 19-38.

Beloch, Karl Julius. *Bevölkerungsgeschichte Italiens.* 3 vols. Berlin, 1937-61.

Benigno, Francesco. "The Southern Italian Family in the Early Modern Period: a Discussion of Co-residential Patterns." *Continuity and Change* 4 (1989): 165-94.

Berkner, Lutz. "The Stem Family and Developmental Cycle of the Household: an Eighteenth-Century Austrian Example." *AHR* 76 (1972): 398-418.

Bideau, A. "Les mechanismes autoregulateurs de populations traditionnelle." *AESC* 38 (1983): 1040-57.

Biget, J.-L., and Tricard J. "Livres de raison de démographie familiale en Limousin au XVe siècle." *ADH* (1981): 321-63.

Biraben, Jean-Noël. "Essai sur l'évolution du nombre des hommes." *Population* 34 (1979): 13-25.

Biraben, Jean-Noël. *Les hommes et la peste en France et dans les pays européens et méditerranéens.* 2 vols. Paris, 1975-76.

Blayo, Yves. "La mortalité en France de 1740 à 1829." *Population* 30 (special issue 1975).

Bois, Guy. *Crise du féodalisme. Économie rurale et démographie en Normandie du début du 14e siècle au milieu de 16e siècle.* Paris, 1976.

Bonfield, L., R. M. Smith, and K. Wrightson, eds. *The World We Have Gained: Histories of Population and Social Structure.* Oxford, 1986.

Cabourdin, G. "Introduction aux problèmes de la démographie de la période 1500-1670." *ADH* (1980): 13-18.

Carbourdin, G. *Terres et hommes en Lorraine (1550-1635).* Nancy, 1977.

Chambers, J. D. *Population Economy and Society in Pre-Industrial England.* Oxford, 1972.

Cipolla, Carlo M. *Between Two Cultures: an Introduction to Economic History.* New York, 1991.

Clark, Peter, and David Souden, eds. *Migration and Society in Early Modern England.* London, 1988.

Corsini, Carlo A. "Nascite e matrimoni." In *Le fonti della demografia storica in Italia*, ed. by the Comitato Italiano per lo Studio della Demografia Storica. Rome 1971-72.

Croix, Alain. *Nantes et le pays Nantais au XVIe siècle: étude démographique.* Paris, 1974.

Delmaire, B. "Le livre de famille des Le Borgne (Arras 1347-1538). Contribution a la démographie historique médiévale." *RN* 65 (1983): 301-26.

Desportes, P. "La population du Reims au XVe siècle d'après un dénombrement de 1422." *Le moyen âge* 72 (1966): 463-509.

Dijk, H. van, and Roorda D. J. *Het patriciaat in Zierikzee tijdens de Republiek.* Rotterdam, 1979.

Dupâquier, Jacques, et al., eds. *Histoire de la population française.* Vol. 2, *De la Renaissance à 1789.* Paris, 1988.

Dupâquier, Jacques. "Population." In *New Cambridge Modern History*, vol. 13, ed. Peter Burke, 80-114. Cambridge, 1979.

Dupâquier, Jacques. *La population française aux XVIIe et XVIIIe siècles.* Paris, 1979.

Dupâquier, Jacques, E. Helin, Peter Laslett, Massimo Livi-Bacci, and S. Sogner, eds. *Marriage and Remarriage in Populations in the Past.* New York, 1981.

Durand, J. D. "Historical Estimates of World Population." *Population and Development Review* 32 (1977): 253-96.

Elliott, J. H. *Imperial Spain 1469-1716.* New York, 1963.

Flandrin, Jean-Louis. *Families in Former Times: Kinship Household and Sexuality.* Cambridge, 1976.

Flandrin, Jean-Louis. *Le sexe et l'occident. Évolution des attitudes et des comportements.* Paris, 1981.

Flinn, Michael *The European Demographic System, 1500-1820.* Baltimore, 1981.

Fournial, E. *Les villes et l'économie d'échange en Forez aux XIIIe et XIVe siècles.* Paris, 1967.

Galloway, Patrick R. "Basic Patterns in Annual Variations in Fertility, Nuptiality, Mortality, and Prices in Pre-Industrial Europe." *PS* 42 (1988): 275-303.

Galloway, Patrick R. "Long-Term Fluctuations in Climate and Population in the Preindustrial Era." *Population and Development Review* 1 (1986): 21-24.

Galloway, Patrick R. A Population Reconstruction of North Italy from 1650 to 1881 using Annual Inverse Projection with Comparisons to England, Sweden, Venice, Verona, Rome, and Stockholm. Unpublished paper, Department of Demography, University of California, Berkeley, 1993.

Glass, D. V., and D. E. C. Eversley, eds. *Population in History.* London, 1965.

Goody, Jack. *The Development of the Family and Marriage in Europe.* Cambridge, 1983.

Gottfried, R. S. *Epidemic Disease in Fifteenth Century England: the Medical Response and the Demographic Consequences.* Leicester, 1978.

Hajnal, John. "European Marriage Patterns in Perspective." In Glass and Eversley (1965), 101-43.

Hajnal, John. "Two Kinds of Pre-industrial Household Formation Systems." *Population Development Review* 8 (1982): 449-94.

Hallam, H. E. "Age at First Marriage and Age at Death in the Lincolnshire Fenland, 1254-1478." *PS* 39 (1985): 55-69.

Hanawalt, Barbara A. *The Ties that Bound: Peasant Families in Medieval England.* Oxford, 1986.

Hatcher, John. *Plague Population and the English Economy 1348-1530.* London, 1977.

Heaton, Herbert. *Economic History of Europe.* New York, 1936.

Henry, Louis. *Anciennes familles genevoises. Étude démographique: 16e-20e siècles.* Paris, 1956.

Henry, Louis. "Fécondité des mariages dans le quart sud-ouest de la France de 1720 à 1829." *AESC* 27 (1972): 612-39, 977-1023.

Henry, Louis. *Manuel de démographie historique.* Geneva, 1967.

Henry, Louis, and Etienne Gautier. *La population de Crulai, paroisse normande: étude historique.* Paris, 1958.

Henry, Louis, and J. Houdaille. "Célibat et âge au mariage au 18e et 19e siècles en France." *Population* 33 (1978) and 34 (1979).

Herlihy, David, and Christiane Klapisch-Zuber. *Les Toscans et leur familles. Une étude du catasto florentin de 1427.* Paris, 1978.

Herlihy, David, and Christiane Klapisch-Zuber. *Tuscans and Their Families.* New Haven, 1985.

Higounet-Nadal, A. *Périgueux aux XIVe et XVe siècles.* Bordeaux, 1978.

Hoecke, W. Van, and A. Welkenhuysen, eds. *Love and Marriage in the Twelfth Century.* Leuven, 1981.

Hollingsworth, T. H. "The Demography of the British Peerage." *PS* 18 (1964), Supplement 2.

Houdaille, J. "Fécondité des mariages dans le quart nord-est de la France de 1670 à 1829." *ADH* (1976): 341-92.

Imhof, Arthur E., ed. *Historische Demographie als Sozialgeschichte. Giessen und Umgebung vom 17. zum 19. Jahrhunderts.* Quellen und forschungen zur hessischen Geschichte, vol. 21. Darmstadt and Marburg, 1975.

Imhof, Arthur E. *Lebenserwartungen in Deutschland vom 17. bis 19 Jahrhundert.* Weinheim, 1990.

Jones, E. L. *The European Miracle: Environments, Economies, and Geopolitics in the History of Europe and Asia.* Cambridge, 1981.

Klapisch-Zuber, Christiane. "La fécondité des florentines (XIVe-XVIe siècles)." *ADH* (1980): 41-57.

Klep, P. M. M. "Population Estimates of Belgium by Province (1375-1831)." In *Historiens et Populations. Liber Amicorum Etienne Helin,* 485-507. Louvain-la-Neuve, 1991.

Knodel, John D. *Demographic Behavior in the Past: a Study of Fourteen German Village Populations in the Eighteenth and Nineteenth Centuries.* Cambridge, 1988.

Knodel, John D. "Natural Fertility in Pre-Industrial Germany." *PS* 32 (1978): 481-510.

Knodel, John D., and Katherine Lynch. "The Decline of Remarriage: Evidence from German Village Populations in the 18th and 19th Centuries." *JFH* 10 (1985): 34-59.

Kussmaul, A. *Servants in Husbandry in Early Modern England.* Cambridge, 1981.

Laslett, Peter. *The World We Have Lost.* London, 1965.

Laslett, Peter, Klara Oosterveen, and Richard M. Smith, eds. *Bastardy and its Comparative History.* London, 1980.

Laslett, Peter, J. Robin, and Richard Wall, eds. *Family Forms in Historic Europe.* Cambridge, 1983.

Laslett, Peter, and Richard Wall, eds. *Households and Family in Past Time.* Cambridge, 1972.

Le Roy Ladurie, Emanuel. *Montaillou village occitan de 1294 à 1324.* Paris, 1975.

Le Roy Ladurie, Emanuel. "Motionless History." *Social Science History* 1 (1977): 115-36.

Le Roy Ladurie, Emanuel. *Les Paysans de Languedoc.* 2 vols. Paris, 1966.

Lebrun, F. "Les crises démographiques en France au XVIIème et XVIIIème siècles." *AESC* 35 (1980): 205-34.

Lee, Ronald D. "Inverse Projection and Demographic Fluctuations: a Critical Assessment of New Methods." In *Old and New Methods in Historical Demography,* ed. David Reher and David Schofield, 7-28. Oxford, 1994.

Lee, Ronald D. "Population in Preindustrial England: An Econometric Analysis." *Quarterly Journal of Economics* 77 (1973): 581-607.

Lee, Ronald D. "Short-term Variation: Vital Rates Prices and Weather." In Wrigley and Schofield (1981), 356-401.

Leridon, Henri. *Human Fertility. The Basic Components.* Chicago 1977.

Litchfield, R. Burr "Demographic Characteristics of Florentine Patrician Families Sixteenth to Nineteenth Centuries." *JEconH* 29 (1969): 191-205.

Livi-Bacci, Massimo. *A Concise History of World Population.* Oxford, 1992.

Livi-Bacci, Massimo. *Population and Nutrition: an Essay on European Demographic History.* Cambridge, 1991.

Lorcin, M.-T. *Vivre et mourir en Lyonnais à la fin du moyen âge.* Lyons, 1981.

Lynch, Katherine A., and J. Willigan. *Sources and Methods of Historical Demography.* New York, 1982.

Macfarlane, Alan. *The Origins of English Individualism: the Family, Property and Social Transition.* Oxford, 1978.

Malthus, Thomas Robert. *An Essay on the Principle of Population.* Harmondsworth, 1970 [1798].

Mattmüller, Markus. *Bevölkerungsgeschichte der Schweiz.* 2 vols. Basel and Frankfurt am Main, 1987.

McArdle, Francis B. *Altopascio 1587-1784: a Study in Tuscan Rural Society.* Cambridge, 1977.

Meuvret, Jean. "Les crises de subsistance et la démographie de la France de l'Ancien Régime." *Population* 1 (1946): 643-50.

Miskimin, Harry A. *Economy of Early Renaissance Europe, 1300-1460.* Englewood Cliffs N. J., 1969.

Miskimin, Harry A. *Economy of Later Renaissance Europe, 1460-1600.* Cambridge, 1977.

Moliné-Bertrand, A. *Au siecle d'or. L'Espagne et ses hommes; la population du royaume de Castille au XVI siècle.* Paris, 1985.

Mols, Roger, S.J. *Introduction à la démographie historique des villes d'Europe du 14e au 18e siècle.* 3 vols. Leuven, 1954-56.

Moriceau, Jean-Marc "Mariages et foyers paysans aux XVIe et XVII siècles: l'example des campaganes du sud de Paris." *Revue d'histoire moderne et contemporaine* 28 (1981): 481-502.

Noordam, D. J. *Leven in Maasland. Een hoogontwikkelde plattelandssamenleving in de achttiende en het begin van de negentiende eeuw.* Hilversum 1986.

Oeppen, J. "Back Projection and Inverse Projection: Members of a Wider Class of Constrained Projection Models." *PS* 47 (1993): 245-267.

Ozment, Steven. *When Fathers Ruled: Family Life in Reformation Europe.* Cambridge, Mass., 1983.

Peller, S. "Births and Deaths among Europe's Ruling Families since 1500." In Glass and Eversley (1965).

Peréz Moréda, Vicente. *Las crisis de mortalidad en la España interior siglos XVI-XIX.* Madrid, 1980.

Perrenoud, Alfred. "Aspects of Fertility Decline in an Urban Setting: Rouen and Geneva." In *Urbanization in History: a Process of Dynamic Interactions,* ed. A. Van der Woude, Jan de Vries, and Hayami Akira, 241-63. Oxford, 1990.

Perrenoud, Alfred. *La Population de Genève du 16ème au début du 19ème siècle: Étude démographique.* Geneva, 1979.

Phythian Adams, C. *Desolation of a City: Coventry and the Urban Crisis of the Late Middle Ages.* Cambridge, 1979.

Poos, L. R. *A Rural Society after the Black Death: Essex 1350-1525.* Cambridge, 1991.

Postan, M. M. "Some Economic Evidence of Declining Population in the Later Middle Ages." *EconHR* 11 (1950).

Razi, Zvi. *Life Marriage and Death in a Medieval Parish. Economy Society and Demography in Halesowen, 1270-1400.* Cambridge, 1980.

Reher, David Sven. *Town and Country in Pre-industrial Spain: Cuenca, 1550-1870.* Cambridge, 1990.

Rossiaud, J. "Prostitution, jeunesse et société dans les villes du sud-est au XVe siècle." *AESC* 31 (1976): 289-325.

Rowland, R. "Sistemas matrimoniales en la peninsula iberica (siglos XVI-XX). Una perspectiva regional." In *Demografia histórica en España,* ed. Vicente Peréz Moréda and David S. Reher. Madrid, 1987.

Russell, Josiah C. *British Medieval Population.* Albuquerque, 1948.

Schofield, R. S. "Did the Mothers Really Die? Three Centuries of Maternal Mortality in 'The World We Have Lost.'" In Bonfield, Smith, and Wrightson (1986), 231-61.

Schofield, R. S. "English Marriage Patterns Revisited." *JFH* 10 (1985): 2-21.

Schofield, R. S. and D. Coleman. "Introduction: the State of Population Theory." In *The State of Population Theory: Forward from Malthus,* ed. R. Schofield and D. Coleman, 1-13. Oxford, 1986.

Schofield, R. S., David S. Reher, and A. Bideau, eds. *The Decline of Mortality in Europe*. Oxford, 1991.

Schuurman, Anton "De bevolking van Duiven 1665-1795. Een historisch-demograpfische studie." *A.A.G. Bijdragen* 22 (1979): 138-89.

Sharlin, Allan "Natural Decrease in Early Modern Cities: a Reconsideration." *PaP*, no. 79 (1978): 126-38.

Sheehan, M. "Choice of Marriage Partner in the Middle Ages: Development and Mode of Application of a Theory of Marriage." *Studies in Medieval and Renaissance History*, new ser. (1978): 13-33.

Smith, Daniel Scott "A Homeostatic Demographic Regime: Patterns in West European Family Reconstitution Studies." *Population Patterns in the Past*, ed. Ronald d. Lee, 19 51. New York, 1977.

Smith, Richard M. "Hypotheses sur la nuptialité en Angeterre aux XIIIe-XIVe siècles." *AESC* 38 (1983): 107-36.

Smith, Richard M. *Land, Kinship and Life Cycle*. London, 1981a.

Smith, Richard M. "Marriage Processes in the English Past: some continuities." In Bonfield, Smith, and Wrightson (1986), 43-99.

Smith, Richard M. "The People of Tuscany and their Families in the Fifteenth Century: Medieval or Mediterranean?" *JFH* 6 (1981b): 107-28

Souden, David. "Demographic Crisis and Europe in the 1590s." In *The European Crisis of the 1590s*, ed. Peter Clark, 231-43. London, 1985.

Thoen, E. *Landbouw en bevolking in Vlaanderen gedurende de late Middeleeuwen en het begin van de Moderne Tijden*. 2 vols. Ghent, 1988.

Todd, Emmanuel. *The Explanation of Ideology: Family Structure and Social Systems*. Oxford, 1985.

Vallin, Jacques. *La mortalité en Europe de 1720 à 1914: tendances a long terme et changements de structure par sexe et par âge*. Paris, 1991.

Vandenbroeke, Christiaan. "Het huwelijks- en voortplantingspatroon in Vlaanderen en Brabant (17de - 19de eeuw)." *Tijdschrift voor sociale geschiedenis* 2 (1976): 107-46.

Vandenbroucke, Jan P. "Survival and Expectation of Life from the 1400s to the Present: a Study of the Knighthood Order of the Golden Fleece." *American Journal of Epidemiology* 122 (1985): 1007-16.

Vann, Richard T., and D. E. C. Eversley D. E. C. *Friends in Life and Death: the British and Irish Quakers in the Demographic Transition*. Cambridge, 1992.

Vries, Jan de "Art History and Economic History." In *Art in History, History in Art*, ed. David Freedberg and Jan de Vries, 249-82. Santa Monica, Cal., 1991.

Vries, Jan de. *European Urbanization, 1500-1800*. London, 1984.

Weir, David R. "Life Under Pressure: France and England, 1670-1870." *JEconH* 44 (1984a): 27-47.

Weir, David R. "Rather Never than Late: Celibacy and Age at Marriage in English Cohort Fertility, 1541-1871." *JFH* 9 (1984b): 341-55.

Wilson, C. "Natural Fertility in Pre-Industrial England, 1600-1799." *PS* 38 (1984): 225-40.

Woude, A. M. van der "Demografische ontwikkeling van de Noordelijke Nederlanden van 1500-1800." In *Algemene Geschiedenis der Nederlanden*, vol. 5:102-68. Haarlem, 1980.

Woude, A. M. van der "Population Developments in the Northern Netherlands (1500-1800) and the Validity of the 'Urban Graveyard' Effect." *ADH* (1982): 55-75.

Wrigley, E. A. "Family Limitation in Pre-industrial England." *EconHR* 19 (1966): 82-109.

Wrigley, E. A. "Fertility Strategy for the Individual and the Group." In *Historical Studies of Changing Fertility*, ed. Charles Tilley, 35-54. Princeton, 1978.

Wrigley, E. A. "The Means to Marry: Population and Economy in Pre-Industrial England." *Quarterly Journal of Social Affairs* 1 (1985).

Wrigley, E. A. "A Simple Model of London's Importance in Changing English Society and Economy 1650-1750." *PaP*, no. 37 (1967): 44-70.

Wrigley, E. A., and R. S. Schofield. "English Population History from Family Reconstitu-
    tion: Summary Results, 1600-1799." *PS* 37 (1983).
Wrigley, E. A., and R. S. Schofield. *The Population of England 1541-1871. A Reconstruc-
    tion.* London, 1981.

# FAMILY, HOUSEHOLD, AND COMMUNITY

Merry E. Wiesner
(University of Wisconsin-Milwaukee)

## 1. FAMILY HISTORY, WOMEN'S HISTORY, GENDER HISTORY

Over the last thirty years, the family has emerged from virtual obscurity as a topic of historical research to become one with its own journal—the *Journal of Family History*, which began publication in 1976—and a steadily expanding number of studies and analyses. This is true for families in all time periods and all cultures, for some of the most interesting questions being asked by historians of the family may best be answered cross-culturally and comparatively. The central question is always this one: "Why did families develop the way that they did?" The most important outcome of all this research is the historicization of the family. We now recognize that the meaning of the word "family" and the delineation of who is a member of one's family have changed over time, and that the family is a socially-constructed unit, not a natural one.

This interest in the history of the family is related to the even more dramatic development of women's history during the same period. During the 1960s and 1970s, women's history and family history were often regarded by more traditional historians as largely the same thing, both somehow "private" and separate from the "public" political, intellectual, and economic history of men. Historians of women and those of the family both asserted that this equation was misleading, however, for women were as much a part of structures and events beyond the family as men were, and men just as much family members as women. The two fields have gradually grown increasingly distinct and have been joined in the last ten years by another area of research which grew out of studies of women and the family—the analysis of gender as a historical variable. Though it may seem self-evident to note that gender is as important a determinant of human experience as race and class, and that norms for appropriate masculine and feminine behavior have changed with time, these ideas have only begun to permeate historical studies during the past decade.

In many ways the study of the social construction of gender leads away from a focus on the family or women, because analysts of gender often focus on its symbolic uses—for example, the way in which ideas about gender hierarchies shaped people's thinking about other political and social relationships. Historians argue that those areas of history which have proved most resistant to the questions raised by historians of women and the family, such as political and intellectual history, are precisely those in which gender issues must be investigated most thoroughly. The history of the family has nevertheless benefitted in two important ways from the new interest in gender. First, analysts of gender stress that gender relations in all social and political institutions are linked both ideologically and politically to those within the family, making the family a key part in the way any society organizes its social relations of power. Family history, therefore, can not be considered simply a sub-field of social history, but must be integrated into all analyses of political, economic, or intellectual change. Second, gender analysis has led to the recognition that along with studying the family as a unit whose members had mutual interests, historians must also examine it as a group divided by gender and age. Focusing on gender as a category of analysis has thus deepened and complicated the external and internal history of the family. The mutual enrichment of family/women's/gender history has occurred in studies of all cultures and time periods, but especially for those investigating the late Middle Ages and early modern period, in particular because many of the earliest studies of the family focussed on this period. This was partly accidental, the result of the fact that many of the French historians associated with the *Annales* school and thus interested in the family and other slowly-changing "structures of everyday life" happened to be specialists in this period. It was also intentional, however, as French and other historians focussed on this period in a search for the "birth of the modern family." If this time was that of the beginning of the modern world in general (whether one saw this as the result of the development of capitalism, the intellectual changes of the Renaissance, the religious changes of the Reformation, the growth of the centralized nation-state, or a combination of these factors) shouldn't it also have heralded a new type of family?

## 2. ORIGINS: THE "DISCOVERY OF CHILDHOOD"

One of the first to argue that the capitalist age did produce a new type of family, was the French historian Philippe Ariès. He argued that in the Middle Ages the idea of childhood as a separate stage of life did not exist; children were dressed as little adults once they reached the age of six or seven, at which point they often left their own families to serve as apprentices or servants in the houses of strangers. Both daily life and special events brought together individuals of all ages and classes, with little idea that parents and children formed a distinct group or that there should be greater intimacy among them than among any other group. Ariès sees the beginnings of a change in the fifteenth century, as educational reformers and then middle-class parents called for a longer period of education for boys that was not simply vocational training, supporting this with new ideas about "the special nature of childhood and the moral and social importance of the systematic education of children in special institutions devised for that purpose." Ariès sees this "discovery of childhood" as a slow process spreading out from the middle classes to the upper classes only by the eighteenth century and the lower only by the nineteenth, if then. He notes that it resulted in a dramatic change in ideas about the family, for "the family ceased to be simply an institution for the transmission of a name and an estate—it assumed a moral and spiritual function, it moulded bodies and souls." Ariès sees the early modern family as a transitional one, for other institutions and groups remained important in the socialization of the young; not until the eighteenth century would "the family begin to hold society at a distance, to push it back beyond a steadily extending zone of private life."[1]

Ariès primarily focuses on ideas about the family, but other historians came to regard the transition from a "medieval" to "modern" family as a structural, as well as an ideological, change—from some type of larger family unit to a nuclear family. In this they built on much earlier ideas about family structure, notably those of Frédéric Le Play, a nineteenth-century French administrator and social reformer, who argued that the traditional family form in most of Europe had been either a large patriarchal household, in which all sons stayed within the household after marriage, or what he termed the "stem family [famille souche]," in which a single son inherited all family land. In this "stem family" only the inheriting son continued to live with his parents after he married; the other sons either sought their fortunes and wives away from the parental household or remained unmarried while continuing to live with their parents and married brother. Le Play's ideas did not come from quantitative analysis of French households in past time, but from his critique of the modern "unstable family" (his term), in which patriarchal authority is undermined by children's wage labor and free choice of spouses, and all children divide inheritance, leading to pauperization. He advocated a return to the "stem family" to prevent further social decay and ward off a threat of population loss.[2]

Though the ideological content of Le Play's ideas is clearly recognized now, his work directly influenced the structural analyses of the family that began several decades ago. Their authors, like Le Play, focussed on the co-resident domestic group, the household, as the most important unit in understanding the family. A good example of this kind of work Peter Laslett's *Household and Family in Past Time*, a series of essays comparing the "size and structure of the domestic group" in various parts of Europe, North America, and Japan.[3] Laslett's studies form part of the ongoing research of the Cambridge Group for the History of Population and Social Structure, a study group formed in the late 1960s to investigate historical demography. The Cambridge Group's focus on the household derives not only from Le Play, but also from the Group's recognition that "the household" is an easier unit to define than "the family," membership in which is not usually a matter of opinion. In the main, the early modern records that lent themselves to quantitative analysis also dealt with households. Le Play's ideas, however, have also shaped the Cambridge Group program in additional ways, for during the 1970s and 1980s many studies concentrated on discovering the kinship content of households and debating the prominence of the stem family or the existence of a link between family form and land ownership patterns.[4]

While Ariès was intentionally very loose in his chronology about the gradual change from the medieval family centered on the lineage or community to the modern family centered on its children, and while Laslett shied away from both precise chronology and the problematic term "family," Lawrence Stone in *The Family, Sex and Marriage in England 1500-1800* posited a distinct set of stages in the organization and conceptualization of the family as well as the household. During the three hundred years his work covers, Stone sees the family as evolving through a number of distinct stages: first, the "open lineage" (1450-1630), in which kin networks are very important and "the nuclear family had only weak boundaries to separate it from wider definitions of social space"; secondly, the "restricted patriarchal nuclear family" (1550-1700), in which the nuclear family headed by an authoritative father is the dominant type; thirdly, the "closed domestic nuclear family" (1640-1800), in which companionate marriage and affection for children begin to mitigate paternal authority, "accompanied by a further walling-off of the nuclear family from either interference or support from the kin, and a further withdrawal from the community." Stone, like Ariès, sees the bourgeois and lower-level nobility as leading these transitions, while the higher nobility and lower classes are slower to change. Like Ariès, he uses prescriptive and de-

scriptive discussions of education, childhood, and family life, and iconographic evidence, but also, like Laslett, he relies on demographic data regarding such factors as child mortality, age at first marriage, and illegitimacy rates to support his arguments.[5]

In many ways, nearly all of the research on the late medieval and early-
modern family since Ariès, Laslett, and Stone—particularly that in English
or French or focussing on western Europe in any language—builds on or
reacts to their theses. This is not to say that all newer research has been de-
rivative, but that especially the theses of Ariès and Stone were so sweeping
and made in such a general way (or interpreted in such a way) that more
recent investigators have felt obliged to take a stand on them. These more
recent studies can be roughly divided into two types, based on the type of
sources which each has favored—first, investigations into family structure
and composition based on demographic and legal sources, and second,
analyses of ideas about the family or changes in the actual emotional history of the family based on prescriptive and descriptive written sources.

## 3. Mapping Families: The Demographers at Work

Demographic data for the period before 1600 are very scanty, but in a few
unusual cases enormous amounts of information, which were gathered by
governments for specific purposes, have been mined very creatively for information about families. The most fruitful of these has been the
Florentine *catasto*, or census, of 1427-30, in which the city of Florence surveyed the age, sex, and wealth of all individuals living within the city and
its surrounding countryside. Based on this survey, unique in premodern
Europe, David Herlihy and Christiane Klapisch-Zuber have investigated
many aspects of Tuscan family life and discovered that household size varied tremendously from class to social class.[6] The households of the
wealthy were much larger, for wealthy women had more children than
poor ones as they married earlier and did not breast-feed their children;
wealthy households also often took in orphaned relatives and the teen-
aged members of poor households as servants and apprentices. Herlihy
and Klapisch-Zuber also found that the average age at first marriage
—17 for women and 30 for men—had enormous implications, both for
family dynamics, since a teen-aged girl much more likely to be submissive
to her husband's wishes than a mature woman, and also for the marriage
market, since there were always many more 17-year old women than
30-year old men, so that dowries were extremely high.

To their statistical analysis (and the Florentine *catasto* is available as a data-base for anyone wishing to do further study) Herlihy and Klapisch-Zuber have added consideration of other sources to paint a very full picture of Tuscan family life. Klapisch-Zuber in particular has emphasized the increasing importance of the patrilineage, with women viewed as temporary residents in their families of marriage, useful for the dowries they brought, but never considered true members of the family according to the Florentine men who kept detailed family record books called *ricordanze*.[7] Her assessment of the strength of the patrilineage and the power of husbands over their wives in Florence has been challenged by Thomas Kuehn in his analyses of legal cases involving inheritance, legal guardianship, and the *patria potestas*.[8] Stanley Chojnacki, using material from Venice, and Barbara Diefendorf, using material from Paris, have noted that the Florentine case may have been unusually bleak for women; in both of these cities, they stress, family ties remained bilateral, and both married women and widows retained economic and social power.[9]

Besides the Florentine *catasto*, the sources which have proved most fruitful for quantitative analysis of the family have been English. For the period before the sixteenth century, there are poll tax surveys, manorial court rolls, copyhold land transfers, and other documents, and beginning in about 1540, there are English parish registers which at least in theory record all baptisms, burials, and marriages. Beginning in the 1970s, the Cambridge Group, assisted by a large number of local volunteers, began to transcribe the parish registers into machine-readable form and use them and other sources to study the structure of the household, the relationship between the household and the larger kin group, the relationship between family structure and land ownership, and similar questions.[10] Many of these studies have now broadened beyond investigations of households at single points in time to involve family reconstitution. Family reconstitution is a method of determining the structure of households over a long time period by analyzing all available data—from the moment a family was formed through a marriage, to the births of its children, to the death of a spouse, then possibly remarriage, the deaths of children, the taking in of other family members such as grandmothers or cousins or non-family members such as servants or lodgers, and so on. This method, first used by French historians in the mid-1950s, has really been perfected over the last twenty years by the Cambridge Group. It is easy to see why this is complex and tedious for just one family, and why studies of this type are usually limited to a single family or village.[11] Despite their narrow focus, however, these single studies have provided a number of correctives to Stone's assertions about the increasing nuclearization of the family, or Le Play's about the relationship between family form and land ownership. In general, they tend to show that kin networks remained quite strong, even among the middle classes, throughout the early modern period, and that land ownership patterns were affected as much by the possibility of wage labor or subtenancy as by family structure.

Family reconstitution like that being done in England is simply not possible for the continent before 1600, because the long series of records it requires, such as the parish registers, don't exist. Quantitative structural studies are thus based on one-time population surveys, such as the Tuscan *catasto*, generally undertaken by cities or states in times of crisis to assess military preparedness or the need for food. The results of such surveys are thus not always representative of normal household arrangements and can give us no information about how households changed over time. They can, in fact, lead to misleading conclusions. A good example is the study by Karl Bücher in *Die Frauenfrage in Mittelalter*, who in 1910 deduced that late medieval cities had many more women than men and speculated that this might have been a factor in the widespread acceptance of urban mystical movements and must have led guilds to be more open to women's work than they were later.[12] The most important record of this "surplus of women" was the 1449 count of the population in Nuremberg, taken to assess the need for grain during a war with Archduke Albrecht of Brandenburg. The war had been going on already for six months when the count was taken, leading journeymen to avoid the city because they might be drafted into military service; therefore though the numbers are accurate, the generalizations Bücher drew from them about late medieval urban population structure are not. His notion of an urban "surplus of women" has been remarkably long-lived, particularly in German scholarship, and has led to somewhat misguided conclusions about family structure in late medieval cities. Only recently have its limitations been realized, and Bücher's numbers no longer used in longitudinal studies that extend into the modern period.[13] There is a great deal of family reconstitution and other types of longitudinal quantitative analysis now going on for the continent, but only for the period after 1600, once records similar to English parish registers appear in some places. Many of these studies are based not simply on population listings, but also on sources, such as wills, marriage contracts, godparent lists, guardianship documents, and court records, which show how individuals interacted with one another, and so give information about kin networks as well as household arrangements.[14]

## 4. BIRTH OF THE MODERN FAMILY?

Despite its limitations for the period before 1600, quantitative analysis of family structure for both England and the continent has yielded some unexpected results. One has been the realization that families often appear to have at least attempted to space the births of their children and used a variety of means to influence fertility. Some of these means—charms, amulets, religious incantations—were most likely physically ineffective, but others—*coitus interruptus* and prolonged lactation to limit fertility, wetnursing and a sort of "rhythm method" to enhance it—were, so that to speak of this as a time of "natural fertility" is incorrect.[15] Quantitative analysis has also been used in studies of the effects of the Protestant Reformation on family life, to test whether ideological change led to actual changes in behavior or family structure due to such things as the increased possibility of divorce.[16]

Perhaps the most important result of quantitative analysis has been the identification of a distinctive marriage pattern in northwestern Europe, which some historians see as unique in the pre-modern world. In northwestern Europe—the British Isles, Scandinavia, at least some parts of France, and western Germany—couples waited until their mid- or late twenties to marry, long beyond the age of sexual maturity, and then immediately set up an independent household; Le Play's stem family had largely disappeared already by the fourteenth century or even earlier, for few households had three generations under one roof. Husbands were likely to be only two or three years older than their wives at first marriage, as opposed to southern Europe where marriage was often between a man in his twenties or thirties and a much younger woman, or eastern Europe where it was between teenagers who lived with one set of parents for a long time. Though kin beyond the nuclear family were only to be found in a minority of households, non-related servants were quite common; service was, in fact, a normal stage of life for both men and women as they saved money for marriage. This northwestern European pattern seems to have resulted largely from the idea that couples should be economically independent before they married, so that both spouses needed to accumulate wages or receive an inheritance, which was often distributed only when parents died; Christianity's stress on the consent of both spouses as a requirement for marriage may have also contributed to preventing early marriage, though why it did not do so in southern and eastern Europe has not been explained.

The discovery of this marital pattern resulted largely from family reconstitution in England, though Laslett and others posited that it might be common throughout a large part of Europe. More recent studies of central Europe and parts of France have indicated that this is not so, for complex households continued to exist in many areas. Lutz Berkner has also pointed out that even a seemingly small percentage of complex households might mean that something akin to a stem or multi-generational patriarchal household was the ideal in a society; because life expectancies were short, the time during which three generations in any family were all alive together was brief.[17] Thus, at any one time, the percentage of multigenerational households was small, but nearly everyone lived in such a household at some point in their lives, and perhaps *thought* of such households as the norm. Berkner, Pierre Goubert, and Michael Anderson have been key figures in the critique of family reconstitution, questioning not only the geographical and social extent of the conclusions drawn from such data, but also more basic problems of meaning and theory.[18] Just because early modern records were structured according to households, did co-residence have the same meaning for family members that it does for us? (One indication that it did not is the fact that servants were very often relatives—cousins, nieces, nephews, or even sisters and brothers—yet are referred to as "servants" by the household head and the census taker. Are such households thus "extended families" or is this reading twentieth-century sentiments back into the past?) Could not similar household structures result from quite different social and economic forces, so that comparisons are misleading or meaningless? Isn't there a tendency, especially in wider family reconstitutions, to equate genealogy with kinship, that is, to assume that all genealogical ties had meaning to the people involved when in fact they may have made no difference at all?

The critique of family reconstitution has provoked a sharp counter-response by its practitioners and defenders, with both sides sometimes sinking into invective and quibbling. Given the tremendous problems of interpreting or establishing the typicality of all pre-1600 demographic data, it is a debate not likely to be resolved soon. The arguments have had some positive results, however, particularly in encouraging historians to go beyond simple descriptive family reconstitution to probing the reasons behind both change and continuities. Even if one can't determine exactly what was happening to household structure or kinship ties, it is possible to look at what *might* have affected people's attitudes and behavior.

## 5. THE SEARCH FOR CAUSES: LAW, ECONOMY, AND THE FAMILY

Law codes and legal structures have been one focus. James Brundage, for example, has surveyed both variations within and continuities throughout medieval canon law, stressing that "the medieval Church's doctrines concerning marriage and sex not only furnished antecedents from which modern law grew, but continue to exert a powerful influence on both law and practice."[19] Research on the effects of the Protestant Reformation on laws regarding marriage, sexuality, and legitimacy have certainly borne this out.[20] Municipal and state law codes have also been used as evidence of growing patrilineality in inheritance practices in Italy and France and growing patriarchalization of the language of power in Germany and England.[21] Reliance on prescriptive sources such as law codes has its limitations, however, and some of the best recent legal studies also include analyses of the actual effects of legal changes, using court records in tandem with law codes.[22]

Another focus in the search for explanations of changes in family structure has been the economy, and in particular during this period the changes associated with the rise of mercantile capitalism and proto-industrialization. In English-language scholarship this area of research has largely resulted from the feminist critique of Marxist analysis, which first noted that power relations are expressed in any society in patterns of reproduction as well as production, and then that the modern dichotomy of production/reproduction might not have much explanatory value in the early modern economy. What any society defines as "work" is socially constructed, changes over time, and is gender-related.[23] In some ways, all contemporary studies in this area build on Alice Clark's *Working Life of Women in the Seventeenth-Century*, first published in 1919.[24] Clark argued in essence that capitalism was bad for women because as the household workshop was gradually replaced by larger scale production, wages were increasingly paid to individuals rather than families; women were consistently paid less than men, often so little that they retired from paid work altogether if they were married and their husband's wages could support the family. Thus women were increasingly divided into middle-class wives whose work was not remunerated and thus not regarded as "work," and lower-class wives and single women who were badly paid and had no job security. Clark has been criticized in most recent studies for idealizing the pre-capitalist economy and giving women too great an independent role within it, but these studies also admit their debt to her for pioneering in questions about gender differences in economic change.[25]

More recent analysts of the connections between family structure, gender differences in work patterns, and economic developments have been much more guarded in their conclusions than Alice Clark was. They have pointed out that families varied widely in their response to similar economic conditions, and that seemingly small differences, such as whether sickles or scythes were used for harvest, might make tremendous differences as to which family members worked for the market and which for non-market subsistence.[26] They have, to use a term borrowed from literary analysis, "deconstructed" all of the variables, pointing out, for example, that economic change only rarely affected married women in the same way as single, or first-born sons in the same way as last-born, or rural residents who could walk to a large town the same way as those who could not. Even the terms "the market" or "the family economy" are false generalizations, for women often sold items they had gathered or produced to other women in a sort of secondary "market" without gaining the status accruing to men who sold goods in what we usually think of as "the market," and families often divided even horse stalls and grain bins into individual shares though they all lived together.

Though there were tremendous differences in families' responses to economic change from region to region, in all areas that have been studied so far the introduction of significant possibilities for wage labor altered family relationships and structure. Children no longer had to wait to inherit to marry, so were less dependent on their parents and often had more children themselves to maximize the family work force; the wife's wage-labor was often essential for family survival, so infants were cared for by wet-nurses if the wife could not combine labor and breast-feeding.[27]

It is wrong to over-emphasize such changes in the period before 1600, however, because in many parts of Europe, land remained a more important economic commodity than labor, so that inheritance practices continued to be the most important determinant of family structure and behavior.[28] Speaking strictly for the period before 1600, a more significant change than the introduction of wage-labor, and one which would have repercussion for family life in all classes, was the gradual conceptualization of male work as "production" or "work" and female as "reproduction" or "housekeeping."[29] This change in the meaning of work is partly the result of the rise of capitalism, as work became equated with participation in the market economy, but connections to the market do not fully explain the gender difference, for even tasks for which women were paid (taking in sewing and boarders, for example) came to be defined as "housekeeping" and therefore not work. Gender distinctions in the valuation of tasks which supported the family economy stemmed not only from economic changes, but also from intellectual and institutional developments such as the professionalization of many occupations, the Protestant notion that a woman's proper vocation was wife and mother, whereas a man's was his occupation, and the growing masculinization of guild notions of honor. In investigating family strategies for survival, it is clear that gender ideology as well as economic constraints must be taken into account.[30]

## 6. The Search for Causes: "the Whole House"

German-language scholarship on the connections between family structure and economic change in this period has a different focus than English-language because it has remained more closely linked to sociology and has generally not been informed by the work of women's historians. It has also been tremendously influenced by the idea of "the whole house" (*das ganze Haus*) first mentioned in the work of the nineteenth-century ethnographer Wilhelm Riehl and expanded since the 1950s by the historian Otto Brunner.[31] The "whole house" has great similarities to Le Play's stem family, in that it is a patriarchal household in which the interests of individual family members were subordinated to those of "the family" as a whole, and in which servants as well as the wife and children were dependent on the male head of household. Brunner argued that this "whole house" was the basic family form for rural residents into the nineteenth century, surviving the commercialization of agriculture and the early Industrial Revolution intact. Though his argument does not have the strong nostalgic longing for this kind of family found in Le Play and Riehl, it still is based partly on reading prescriptive literature as descriptive. The sources which lend themselves most readily to this are the guides for male heads of household published in Germany in the sixteenth and seventeenth centuries. This *Hausvaterliteratur*, containing practical and spiritual advice, was often written by Protestant pastors and is an extremely common literary genre in Germany, though not elsewhere in Europe where similar advice manuals were generally directed at women. It serves as an excellent source for ideas about the family, but cannot be used as descriptions of reality, a problem which has plagued other historians of the German family along with Brunner.

Very recent scholarship on German rural communities has pointed out that "the whole house" may have been as much a wishful dream of political and church authorities who wanted households to act in a more orderly and disciplined manner and obey the wishes of their male head as a description of actual power relationships and living arrangements.[32] Interestingly, much of this critique has come from English-language scholars, for even the very few German feminists or historians of women writing on the topic often use "the whole house" as an explanatory device. This all means that in German analysis of economic change during this period "the family" is regarded more often as an undifferentiated whole whose experience was shaped by class than as a unit divided by age and gender differences. The strength of the notion of "the whole house" in German historiography of family structure and relations combined with the strength of the notion of "individualism" in English historiography makes it difficult at times to judge whether there are significant differences in family form in England or western Europe as a whole when compared with central Europe, or whether such differences are largely a matter of perception.[33] Reliable answers will only come when the number of local studies of actual family relationships are sufficient to make comparative generalizations possible.

Though German historians and those from western Europe and the United States differ as to when the change to the "modern" family occurred, and no one agrees about the legal and economic causes and consequences of this change, most analysts of family structure share with Ariès the notion that the "modern" family is somehow distinct from the medieval. This conviction is less widespread in recent scholarship on the emotional and intellectual history of family, the second type of study we will investigate. Here, perhaps because of the strong statements by Ariès, Stone and others about the coldness of early-modern family life, the main emphasis has been demonstrating in what ways premodern families resemble modern ones.

## 7. CHILDHOOD, PARENTS, AND CHILDREN

The relationships between parents and children and the experience of childhood in general have been the object of a great deal of research, including, since 1973, a specialized journal, *The History of Childhood Quarterly*. This research has provided a corrective to the earlier view that children were raised harshly—a view derived largely from strict child-raising manuals—by using archival sources about the way children were actually treated. Shulamith Shahar and Linda Pollock have directly refuted the Ariès/Stone thesis about coldness toward children and the lack of a concept of childhood, Shahar ending her study in 1500 and Pollock beginning hers at that date.[34] They and other historians have discovered that many parents showed great affection for their children and were very disturbed when they died young; they tried to protect them with religious amulets and pilgrimages to special shrines, made toys for them and sang them lullabies. Even practices which to us may seem cruel, such as tight swaddling, were motivated by a concern for the child's safety and health at a time when most households had open fires, domestic animals wandered freely, and mothers and older siblings engaged in productive work which prevented them from continually watching a toddler.

Some recent studies have pointed out gender differences in the attitudes toward children, for misogynist attitudes and inheritance laws which favored males led early modern parents to favor the birth of sons over daughters. Jewish women prayed for sons, and German midwives were often rewarded with a higher payment for assisting in the birth of a boy. English women's letters sometimes apologize for the birth of daughters. Girls significantly outnumbered boys in most orphanages and foundling homes, as poor parents decided their sons would ultimately be more useful since they could earn higher wages; infants had a much poorer chance of survival in such institutions than among the population at large. Generalizations about early modern parents are also now being differentiated by gender, with innovative sources being used to explore the physical and emotional experience of mothers in pregnancy, childbirth, breast-feeding, and child rearing; despite great attention to it in the early modern period, fatherhood, as with so many other aspects of masculinity, is still waiting for its historians.[35]

## 8. Wives and Husbands: Conformity and Choice

Studies of parent/child relationships have also focused on the extent of parental or other kin involvement in spousal selection, seen as a key indicator of "individual" vs. "family" concerns. This has received particular attention in England, with historians presuming that the late age of marriage for women might also mean that they had a greater say in who they married. Miriam Slater and John Gillis have argued that kin networks and a woman's immediate family continued to play a major role.[36] Slater's evidence comes largely from the upper classes, where she finds complicated marriage strategies to cement family alliances; Gillis' comes from the lower-classes, where neighbors and public authorities also helped determine whether a couple would marry, the neighbors through pressuring courting couples and public authorities by simply prohibiting marriage between individuals regarded as too poor. Historians who have focussed on the middle classes assert that though couples may have received advice or even threats, they were largely free to marry who they wished.[37]

In some ways this debate sets up a false dichotomy because both sides tend to focus on cases in which there was clear and recorded conflict between individuals and family or community. As Miranda Chaytor has noted in regard to women's choices:

> What women may have wanted from marriage was often perfectly
> compatible with the interests of parents, kin and society as a whole.
> The love and attraction that they may have felt for a man were not
> unconnected to other emotions, their need for honor, status, and
> security. Women's sense of their sexual identity was constructed
> around their future function as wives and childbearers; their emotional
> and sexual needs were directed toward the roles which ensured their
> social prestige and economic security.[38]

Chaytor's comment is confirmed by the few studies of spousal choice outside of England, which point out that parents and children more often agreed than disagreed on spousal choice.[39] Throughout Europe, though twentieth-century notions of romantic love as a *necessary* prelude to marriage did not exist, romantic love within marriage was regarded as something positive. Some historians have seen this emphasis on affection and companionability within marriage as a product of the Protestant Reformation, though others have pointed out that it existed long before because of Christian ideas of free consent as the most important determinant of the validity of a marriage.[40]

## 9. WIVES AND HUSBANDS: MARRIAGE AND GENDER ROLES

The search for family affection in the past has not only focussed on relations between parents and children, but also on those between spouses. In this the key spark has been Edward Shorter's sweeping generalizations about the "cool formality... emotional isolation...lovelessness... and lack of affection [which] characterized most couples in traditional society," a society in which "a cow was worth much more than a wife." Shorter cheerfully admits that all his sources come from small parts of France for the period 1750-1850, and that even "this documentation will be closer to sub-audible taps than to the hammering down of irrefutable data," but these considerations in no way limit his conclusions.[41] Jean-Louis Flandrin does not see the same linear trend from affectionless to affectionate marriage, but agrees with Shorter that sentimental attachments within families were discouraged rather than encouraged in the pre-modern period; like Shorter, he bases his arguments on a wide range of often unconnected sources.[42] More cautious analysts have been pointing out counter-examples ever since Shorter and Flandrin's major studies were published—spouses becoming physically ill or mentally deranged because of the death of a spouse; spouses using affectionate language for each other in letters, wills and other public and private documents; spouses becoming depressed when they had to be apart; spouses caring for each other during illnesses.[43] The economic ties holding a family together, they have pointed out, might have actually worked to *increase* affection between spouses, rather than decrease it as Shorter and others have argued. Speedy remarriage might be an indicator that people are trying to replicate the happiness of their first union rather than a sign that a spouse was only valuable for the economic role she or he fulfilled.

A key issue in this debate about relations between spouses has been try-ing to assess the actual workings of the idea of the inferiority of women in early modern marriages. In terms of the realm of ideas alone, there is little disagreement. With very few exceptions, Catholics, Protestants (both magisterial and radical) and Jews, English, French, Italians and Germans, highly-educated humanists and illiterate street singers, all agreed that women should be subservient and that husbands should rule over their wives.[44] Indeed, there is no issue that early modern men—and apparently most women—agreed upon so completely. This notion was not only an intellectual construct, but shaped legal codes throughout Europe, with married women always under the legal control of their husbands, usually unable to transfer property or make contracts without his consent, and adult single women and widows often required to have a male guardian oversee their legal and financial affairs. Husbands were generally given the right—either explicitly or implicitly—to coerce or punish their wives physically, and courts rarely supported a wife's leaving her husband even for serious physical abuse. The inequality inherent in marriage has led some analysts to view all changes in the early modern period as having lit-tle impact on women; as Ian MacLean puts it: "Marriage is an immovable obstacle to any improvement in the theoretical or real status of woman in law, in theology, in moral and political philosophy."[45]

While MacLean sees little change in the period in terms of the ideal or actual relationship between spouses, other historians see significant developments. They are sharply divided, however, as to whether these developments led to more egalitarian marriages and a more positive view of women, or to more patriarchal marriages with increasing restrictions on women's independent actions. Those in the first camp, such as John Yost, Luise Schorn-Schütte, and Edmund Leites, point to the more positive valuation of marriage seen first in civic humanists and then trumpeted loudly by Protestants in their critique of clerical celibacy.[46] They note that, especially in Protestant areas, married people were no longer regarded as second-class Christians; the affirmation of "wife" as a proper vocation for women improved the status of most women. Along with their husbands, wives were held responsible for overseeing children and servants, and thus were viewed as co-rulers in the household. Those in the second camp, such as Lyndal Roper, Allison Coudert, and Susan Cahn, note that more positive views of marriage do not necessarily mean more positive views of women, and that the Reformation actually increased the power of the male head of household over his dependents, including his wife, by giving it a stronger religious sanction.[47] Women who were not married—and there were significant numbers of these, given the northwestern European pattern of late marriage—were increasingly suspect, a suspicion that may have been a factor in the witch persecutions. Both sides in this debate have ample evidence from both prescriptive literature and records of actual family life, and it is clear that more analyses with attention to class, regional, and religious differences are needed.

The difficulty of making generalizations about the effects of the Reformation on marriage and gender roles has led some historians to more localized investigations of specific aspects of family life. Recent studies which relate religious to familial change include ones which analyze how religious differences and the possibility of marriage to clergy shaped familial marriage strategies, how changes in religious ideas brought changes in the role of godparents, and how cities handled religious differences between spouses.[48] Studies which directly compare Protestant with Catholic experience, such as that of Miriam Chrisman which investigates how doctrinal differences shaped family identity in a French Catholic and English Puritan family, are particularly important for assessing the role of religious change[49] A few historians have also begun to analyze not only the way in which religious ideas and choices influenced the family, but also the ways in which property and marital strategies influenced religious affiliation.[50] We have long been aware that the family and dynastic connections of rul-

ing families influenced national and regional religious policy, but have only
recently begun to investigate how this worked for families much further
down the social scale than Henry VIII or Marguerite of Navarre.

Some recent studies of family relations have sought to integrate ideas
about gender hierarchies with those about other types of social and political hierarchies. These often build on the provocative essay by Natalie
Davis, "Women on Top," which explores the sexual symbolism in all early
modern descriptions of order and disorder.[51] Susan Amussen analyzes the
relationship between gender and class hierarchies in both political thought
and the behavior of people in Norfolk villages, and Sarah Hanley traces
the creation of what she terms the "family-state compact" in early modern
France through which the power of the state was strengthened by empow-
ering male family heads at the expense of women.[52] Attention to gender
and age hierarchies has also informed some of the most recent studies of
prominent or ruling families, such as that of Joel Rosenthal for fifteenth-
century England, though there are still many which view "family history"
in the same way that medieval chroniclers or traditional political historians
did, as dynastic succession through the male line with women playing a
role only when this line failed.[53] More perceptive analysts have begun to
trace gender differences in the views of lineage, realizing that though male
family members or male historians men might exclude women from the official patrilineage, women had their own ways of defining lineage and
carving out a position as a member of two lineages.[54]

At this point, the types of questions asked in the best of the new family
history, and the ones which should prove most interesting and fruitful for
future research, are ones which bring together demographic, economic,
political, and intellectual issues. To give just a few examples: Did the
"family/state compact," which has been detected in France, develop in
other centralizing states as well? If not, why not? How are family interests
and state interests integrated in areas of Europe which do not develop into
nation-states, such as the Empire, particularly, as Paula Fichtner has
pointed out, because many states of the Empire were very resistant to primogeniture?[55]


10. THE FAMILY AS THE CROSSROADS OF RELIGION AND SOCIETY

What happened when family aims came into conflict with religious ideas?
One area where this can be tested is remarriage for widows, which the
Catholic Church in theory frowned upon, particularly if the woman was

past childbearing age, but Protestants encouraged. Did religious differences have any actual impact on marriage patterns, or were family goals and the personal preference of the woman always more important?[56] Similar questions may also be asked about the relationship between the Reformation and dowries. Did Protestants, who favored marriage in theory, also favor lower dowries, as this would allow more people to marry? Could being of the correct faith make up for lack of a dowry? This may be an area where the actual effects of the Reformation are far less than the reformers hoped; Luther's endorsement of early marriage as a cure for lust appears to have had little effect on marriage patterns in Protestant areas, though religious differences are almost never explicitly considered in demographic analyses and perhaps need more attention. The interplay between religious and family values has clearly only begun to be investigated, with city and private archives still holding a wealth of untouched quantitative and qualitative material.

How did the variables of class and gender influence which genealogical ties would be meaningful for people? Andrejs Plakans has recently suggested that historians adopt the methods of anthropologists more than demographers and base their ideas of the importance of kinship more on actual records of interactions between related individuals than on genealogical ties discovered through family reconstitution.[57] Those supporting or criticizing Stone's ideas about the decreasing importance of kinship and the extended family have often done this, but they have been more successful in incorporating class differences than those based on gender. Only a few studies test the differences between agnatic and uterine kin ties in such things as children's names, the choice of godparents, the formation of family businesses or family charitable endowments. Is the increasing importance of the patrilineage which Christiane Klapisch-Zuber has so convincingly demonstrated in Renaissance Florence a particularly Italian development? Particularly Florentine? If not, what effects did it have elsewhere in Europe? If so, why didn't European men elsewhere pick this up the way they did Florentine artistic styles or business procedures?

Quantitative studies of family structure for the period after 1600 have revealed cycles of illegitimacy and premarital sex which have been attributed to changes in fertility levels, opportunities for wage labor for young people, breakdown in paternal and community control, the decreasing importance of church moral prescriptions, and an increasing desire for personal sexual gratification among young women.[58] Though the scarcity of demographic data before 1600 does not allow similar quantitative analyses, there are cycles in the concern of political authorities about illegitimacy and attempts to control it. How are these related to work opportunities? To ideas about female and male sexuality? To the control of or attitudes toward other types of sexuality perceived as deviant, such as homosexuality?[59]

If the family was becoming increasingly privatized and domesticated in this period—a position which Stone, Shorter, and Flandrin all maintain, and which has been less disputed by their critics than other of their conclusions—how did this alter political theories of the household as a state writ small? Of the state as a household writ large? What role did women of different social classes play in creating this new domestic ideal? How did it influence the way in which children were socialized into gender roles?


## 11. The Modern Family

The last thirty years of research on the early modern family, combined with more recent analysis of the social construction of gender, have, as you can see, led to much more complex sorts of questions rather than definitive answers. Most of these questions focus on the *meaning* of the family for its various members, an emphasis which is also evident in recent social history of other structures and institutions. Historians have not rejected the idea that there is as dramatic a change in family life during the early modern period as there is in religion, economics, or politics, but they have also accepted the notion that *the* modern family is as false a universal as *the* traditional family being championed by many modern American politicians. Diversity and variation have always been the hallmarks of the western family, whether in the sixteenth century or the twentieth.

# NOTES

1. Ariès (1962), 335, 412, 398.
2. Le Play (1855-78).
3. Laslett and Wall (1972).
4. See many of the essays in Laslett and Wall (1972); Wall, Robin, and Laslett (1983); Smith (1984).
5. Stone (1979), 69, 149.
6. Herlihy and Klapisch-Zuber (1985).
7. Klapisch-Zuber (1985).
8. Kuehn (1991).
9. Chojnacki, in Erler and Kowaleski (1988), 126-48; Diefendorf (1982).
10. The largest result of this project is Wrigley and Schofield (1981).
11. See, for examples, Raftis (1974); Laslett (1977), 50-101; Razi (1980).
12. Bücher (1910).
13. Wessoly (1980).
14. See Mitterauer (1973); several of the essays in Lee (1977); Dupaquier (1981); O'Neill (1987); Sabean (1990).
15. McLaren (1984); Ranum and Ranum (1972).
16. Safley (1984).
17. Berkner (1972).
18. Berkner (1972); Anderson (1980); Goubert (1977).
19. Brundage (1987), 617.
20. Ingram (1988).
21. Klapisch-Zuber (1985); Hanley (1989); Roper (1989); Zapalac (1990), 135-66; Amussen (1988).
22. Safley (1984); Kuehn (1991); Klapisch-Zuber (1985).
23. From the vast literature on this issue, see Hamilton (1978); Daley (1982); Hartmann (1981); Kelly (1984), 51-64.
24. Clark (1919 [1982]).
25. Amussen (1988); M. C. Howell (1986); Wiesner (1986); Cahn (1987).
26. Tilly and Scott (1978); Vanja (1987).
27. Tilly and Scott (1978); Medick (1976); Levine (1977); Grieco (1991).
28. Smith (1984); Goody, Thirsk, and Thompson (1976).
29. Roberts (1985); Roper (1985).
30. On the influence of non-economic factors on female and male patterns of work, see M. C. Howell, in Erler and Kowaleski (1988), 37-60; Wiesner (1989); Wiesner (1990); Bennett (1990).
31. Riehl (1855); Brunner (1968).
32. Sabean (1990); Robisheaux (1989).
33. For England, see esp. Macfarlane (1978) and (1986). For Germany and central Europe, see Mitterauer and Sieder (1982).
34. Shahar (1990); Pollock (1983).

35. Fildes (1990).
36. Slater (1984); Gillis (1985).
37. Macfarlane (1986); Pollock (1983); Mendelson (1987).
38. Chaytor (1980), 42.
39. Marshall (1987); Chojnacki (1985).
40. Hanawalt (1986); Houlbrooke (1984).
41. Shorter (1975), 55, 57.
42. Flandrin (1979).
43. Ozment (1983); MacDonald (1981).
44. For a survey of ideas about women, see Wiesner (1993), chap. 1.
45. MacLean (1980), 85.
46. Yost (1976); Leites (1983); Schorn-Schütte (1991).
47. Roper (1989); Cahn (1987); Coudert (1989).
48. Berlatsky (1978); Rublack (1979); Harris (1982); Bossy (1984).
49. Chrisman (1983).
50. Marshall (1987).
51. Davis (1975), 124-51.
52. Amussen (1988); Hanley (1989).
53. Rosenthal (1991).
54. Rosenthal (1991); Marshall (1987); Chojnacki, in Erler and Kowaleski (1988), 126-48.
55. Hanley (1989); Fichtner (1989).
56. Diefendorf (1982); Marshall [Wyntges] (1982); B. Todd (1985); Mirrer (1992).
57. Plakans (1984).
58. Laslett (1980).
59. See, e.g., Ruggiero (1985).

# BIBLIOGRAPHY

Note: This bibliography does not include studies of the portrayals of families in Renaissance literature or art, or works on women unless they contain significant discussions of family or kinship. If a collection of articles is cited, the individual articles contained within the collection are not.

Amussen, Susan. *An Ordered Society: Gender and Class in Early Modern England.* London, 1988.

Anderson, Michael. *Approaches to the History of the Western Family, 1500-1914.* London, 1980.

Ariès, Philippe. *Centuries of Childhood: a Social History of Family Life.* Trans. Robert Baldick. New York, 1962.

Ariès, Philippe, and André Bejin, eds. *Western Sexuality: Practice and Precept in Past and Present Times.* London, 1985.

Armengaud, André. *La famille et l'enfant en France et en Angleterre du XVIe au XVIIIe siècle: aspects démographiques.* Paris, 1975.

Barbagli, Marzio. *Sotto lo stesso tetto: mutamenti dela famiglia in Italia dal xv al xx secolo.* Bologna, 1984.

Bellomo, Manlio. *Problemi di diritto familiare nell'eta dei comuni: Beni paterni e "pars filii".* Milan, 1968.

Bennett, Judith. "Misogyny, Popular Culture and Women's Work." *HWJ* 31 (1990): 166-88.

Berkner, Lutz K. "The Stem Family and Developmental Cycle of the Household: an Eighteenth-Century Austrian Example." *AHR* 76 (1972): 398-418.

Berlatsky, Joel. "Marriage and Family in a Tudor Elite: Familial Patterns of Elizabethan Bishops." *JFH* 3 (1978): 6-22.

Bossy, John. "Godparenthood: the Fortunes of a Social Institution in Early Modern Christianity." In *Religion and Society in Early Modern Europe*, ed. Kaspar von Greyerz, 194-201. London, 1984.

Brooke, Christopher N. L. *The Medieval Idea of Marriage.* Oxford, 1989.

Brucker, Gene. *Giovanni and Lusanna: Love and Marriage in Renaissance Florence.* Berkeley and Los Angeles, 1986.

Brundage, James. *Law, Sex, and Christian Society in Medieval Europe.* Chicago, 1987.

Brunner, Otto. "Das 'ganze Haus' und alteuropäische 'Oekonomik.'" In Otto Brunner, *Neue Wege der Verfassungs- und Sozialgeschichte.* 2d ed. Göttingen, 1968.

Bücher, Karl. *Die Frauenfrage in Mittelalter.* Tübingen, 1910.

Bullard, Melissa Meriam. "Marriage Politics and the Family in Florence: the Strozzi-Medici Alliance of 1508." *AHR* 84 (1979): 668-87.

Burgière, André. "Pour une typologie des formes d'organisation domestique en l'Europe moderne (XVIe- XIXe siècles)." *AESC* 41 (1986): 639-56.

Cahn, Susan. *Industry of Devotion: the Transformation of Women's Work in England, 1500-1660.* London, 1987.

Chaytor, Miranda. "Household and Kinship: Ryton in the late 16th and early 17th Centuries." *HWJ* 10 (1980).

Chojnacki, Stanley. "Kinship Ties and Young Patricians in Fifteenth-Century Venice." *RenQ* 38 (1985): 240-70.

Chojnacki, Stanley, ed. "Recent Trends in Renaissance Studies: the Family, Marriage and Sex." *RenQ* 40 (1987): 660-761.

Chrisman, Miriam U. "Family and Religion in Two Noble Families: French Catholic and English Puritan." *JFH* 8 (1983): 190-210.

Clark, Alice. *Working Life of Women in the Seventeenth Century.* London, 1919. Reprint, 1982.

Cohen, Elisabeth S., and Thomas V. Cohen. "Camilla the Go-Between: The Politics of Gender in a Roman Household." *Continuity and Change* 4 (1989): 53-77.

Cohn, Samuel H., Jr. *Death and Property in Siena, 1205-1800: Strategies for the Afterlife.* Baltimore, 1988.

Coudert, Allison. "The Myth of the Improved Status of Protestant Women: The Case of Witchcraft." In *The Politics of Gender in Early Modern Europe*, ed. Jean R. Brink, et.al., 60-89. Kirksville, Mo., 1989.

Cressy, David. "Kinship and Kin Intervention in Early Modern England." *PaP*, no. 113 (1986): 38-69.

Daley, Patricia. "Unpaid Family Labor." *Monthly Labor Review* (October 1982): 1-6.

Davis, James C. *A Venetian Family and Its Fortune, 1500-1900: The Dona and the Conservation of Their Wealth.* Philadelphia, 1975.

Davis, Natalie Zemon. "Ghosts, Kin, and Progeny: Some Features of Family Life in Early Modern France." *Daedalus* 106 (1977): 87-114.

Davis, Natalie Zemon. *Society and Culture in Early Modern France.* Stanford, 1975.

Dekker, Rudolph M., and Lotte C. van de Pol. *The Tradition of Female Transvestism in Early Modern Europe.* New York, 1989.

Delumeau, Jean, and Daniel Roche, eds. *Histoire des peres et de la paternité.* Paris, 1990.

Diefendorf, Barbara B. *Paris City Councillors in the Sixteenth Century: the Politics of Patrimony.* Princeton, 1983.

Diefendorf, Barbara B. "Widowhood and Remarriage in Sixteenth Century Paris." *JFH*, 7 (1982): 379-95.

Dietrich, Hartwig. *Das protestantische Eherecht in Deutschland bis zur Mitte des 17. Jahrhunderts.* Jus ecclesiasticum, vol. 10. Munich, 1970.

Dugan, Eileen. "The Funeral Sermon as a Key to Familial Values in Early Modern Nördlingen." *SCJ* 20 (1989): 631-44.

Dupaquier, J., et al., eds. *Marriage and Remarriage in Populations of the Past.* New York, 1981.

Elshtain, Jean Bethke. *The Family in Political Thought.* Amherst, Mass., 1982.

Erler, Mary, and Maryanne Kowaleski, eds. *Women and Power in the Middle Ages.* Athens, Ga., 1988.

Fichtner, Paula Sutter. *Protestantism and Primogeniture in Early Modern Germany.* New Haven, 1989.

Fildes, Valerie, ed. *Women as Mothers in Pre-Industrial England.* London, 1990.

Flandrin, Jean-Louis. *Families in Former Times: Kinship, Household and Sexuality.* Trans. Richard Southern. Cambridge, 1979.

Forster, Robert, and Orest Ranum, eds. *Family and Society.* Baltimore, 1976.

Friedman, Alice T. *House and Household in Elizabethan England: Wollaton Hall and the Willoughby Family.* Chicago, 1989.

Gélis, Jacques. *History of Childbirth: Fertility, Pregnancy and Birth in Early Modern Europe.* Trans. Rosemary Morris. Boston, 1991.

Gillis, John. *For Better, for Worse: British Marriages 1600 to the Present.* Oxford, 1985.

Goody, Jack, ed. *The Character of Kinship.* Cambridge, 1973.

Goody, Jack. *The Development of the Family and Marriage in Europe.* Cambridge, 1983.

Goody, Jack. *Production and Reproduction: a Comparative Study of the Domestic Domain.* Cambridge, 1970.

Goody, Jack, Joan Thirsk, and E. P. Thompson. *Family and Inheritance: Rural Society in Western Europe, 1200-1800.* Cambridge, 1976.

Goubert, Pierre. "Family and Province: A Contribution to the Knowledge of Family Structures in Early Modern France." *JFH* 2 (1977): 179-95.

Grieco, Sara Matthews. "Breastfeeding, Wet Nursing and Infant Mortality in Europe (1400-1800)." In *Historical Perspectives on Breastfeeding*, 15-62. Florence, 1991.

Hajnal, J. "European Marriage Patterns in Perspective." In *Population in History: Essays in Historical Demography*, ed. D. V. Glass and D. E. C. Eversley, 101-43. Chicago, 1965.

Hamilton, Roberta. *The Liberation of Women: a Study of Patriarchy and Capitalism.* London, 1978.

Hanawalt, Barbara A. *The Ties that Bound: Peasant Families in Medieval England*. New York, 1986.

Hanley, Sarah. "Engendering the State: Family Formation and State Building in Early Modern France." *French Historical Studies* 16 (1989): 4-27.

Harris, Barbara. "Marriage 16th-Century Style: Elizabeth Stafford and the third Duke of Norfolk." *JSH* 15 (1982): 370-82.

Hartmann, Heide. "The Family as the Locus of Gender, Class and Political Struggle: The Example of Housework." *Signs* 6 (1981): 366-94.

Haverkamp, Alfred, ed. *Haus und Familie in der spätmittelalterlichen Stadt*. Städteforschung, series A, vol. 18. Cologne, 1984.

Helmholz, Richard. *Marriage Litigation in Medieval England*. Cambridge, 1974.

Herlihy, David. *Medieval Households*. Cambridge, Mass., 1985.

Herlihy, David, and Christiane Klapisch-Zuber. *Tuscans and Their Families: a Study of the Florentine Catasto of 1427*. New Haven, 1985.

Hoffer, Peter, and N. E. H. Hull. *Murdering Mothers: Infanticide in England and New England, 1558-1803*. New York University School of Law Series in Legal History, vol. 2. New York, 1981.

Houlbrooke, Ralph A. *The English Family 1450-1700*. London, 1984.

Howell, C. *Land, Family and Inheritance in Transition: Kibworth Harcourt*. Cambridge, 1983.

Howell, Martha C. *Women, Production and Patriarchy in Late Medieval Cities*. Chicago, 1986.

Hughes, Diane Owen. "From Brideprice to Dowry in Mediterranean Europe." *JFH* 3 (1978): 262-96.

Hughes, Diane Owen. "Representing the Family: Portraits and Purposes in Early Modern Italy." *Journal of Interdisciplinary History* 17 (1986): 7-38.

Hunt, David. *Parents and Children in History: the Psychology of Family Life in Early Modern France*. New York, 1970.

Ingram, Martin. *Church Courts, Sex and Marriage in England, 1570-1640*. Cambridge, 1988.

James, Mervyn Evans. *Family, Lineage and Civil Society: a Study of Society, Politics and Mentality in the Durham Region 1500-1640*. Oxford, 1974.

Kelly, Joan. *Women, History and Theory*. Chicago, 1984.

Kent, Francis William. *Household and Lineage in Renaissance Florence: the Family Life of the Capponi, Ginori and Rucellai*. Princeton, 1977.

King, Margaret L. *Women of the Renaissance*. Chicago, 1991.

Kirshner, Julius. *Pursuing Honor While Avoiding Sin: the Monte delle doti of Florence*. Milan, 1978.

Kirshner, Julius. "Wives' Claims Against Insolvent Husbands in Late Medieval Italy." In *Women of the Medieval World: Essays in Honor of John H. Mundy*, ed. Julius Kirschner and Suzanne Wemple, 256-304. London, 1985.

Klapisch-Zuber, Christiane. *La famiglia e le donne nel Rinascimento a Firenze*. Bari, 1988.

Klapisch-Zuber, Christiane. *Women, Family and Ritual in Renaissance Italy*. Trans. Lydia G. Cochrane. Chicago, 1985.

Kuehn, Thomas. *Law, Family and Women: Toward a Legal Anthropology of Renaissance Italy*. Chicago, 1991.

Laslett, Peter. *Family Life and Illicit Love in Earlier Generations*. Cambridge, 1977.

Laslett, Peter., et. al. *Bastardy and Its Comparative History: Studies in the History of Illegitimacy and Marital Non-Conformism in Britain, France, Germany, Sweden, North America, Jamaica and Japan*. Cambridge, Mass., 1980.

Laslett, Peter, and Richard Wall, eds. *Household and Family in Past Time*. Cambridge, 1972.

Lee, Ronald Demos, ed. *Population Patterns in the Past*. New York, 1977.

Lee, W. R. "Past Legacies and Future Prospects: Recent Research on the History of the Family in Germany." *JFH* 6 (1981): 156-76.

Leites, Edmund. "The Duty to Desire: Love, Friendship and Sexuality in Some Puritan Theories of Marriage." *JSH* 15 (1983): 383-408.

Le Play, Frédéric. *Les ouvriers européens. Etudes sur les travaux, la vie domestique et la condition morale des populations ouvrières de l'Europe.* 6 vols. Paris, 1855-78.

Levin, Eve. *Sex and Society in the World of the Orthodox Slavs, 900-1700.* Ithaca, N.Y., 1989.

Levine, David. *Family Formation in an Age of Nascent Capitalism.* London, 1977.

MacDonald, Michael. *Mystical Bedlam: Madness, Anxiety and Healing in Seventeenth-Century England.* Cambridge, 1981.

Macfarlane, Alan. *Marriage and Love in England: Modes of Reproduction 1300-1840.* London 1986.

Macfarlane, Alan. *The Origins of English Individualism: The Family, Property and Social Transition.* Oxford, 1978.

McLaren, Angus. *Reproductive Rituals: the Perception of Fertility in England from the 16th to the 19th Century.* London, 1984.

MacLean, Ian. *The Renaissance Notion of Woman.* Cambridge, 1980.

Marshall, Sherrin. *The Dutch Gentry, 1500-1650: Family, Faith and Fortune.* Contributions in Family Studies, vol. 11. New York and Westport, Ct., 1987.

Marshall [Wyntjes], Sherrin. "Survivors and Status: Widowhood and Family in the Early Modern Netherlands." *JFH* 7 (1982): 396-405.

Marshall [Wyntjes], Sherrin, ed. *Women in Reformation and Counter- Reformation Europe: Public and Private Worlds.* Bloomington, 1989.

Maschke, Erich. *Die Familie in der deutschen Stadt des späten Mittelalters.* Heidelberg, 1980.

Medick, Hans. "The Proto-industrial Family Economy: the Structural Function of the Household and Family during the Transition from Peasant Society to Industrial Capitalism." *Social History* 1 (1976): 291-315.

Medick, Hans, and David Warren Sabean, eds. *Interest and Emotion: Essays on the Study of Family and Kinship.* Cambridge, 1984.

Mendelson, Sara Heller. *The Mental World of Stuart Women: Three Studies.* Brighton, 1987.

Mertes, Kate. *The English Noble Household, 1250-1600.* London, 1988.

Mirrer, Louise, ed. *Upon My Husband's Death: Widows in the Literature and Histories of Medieval Europe.* Ann Arbor, 1992.

Mitterauer, Michael. *A History of Youth.* Oxford, 1992.

Mitterauer, Michael. "Zur Familienstruktur in ländlichen Gebieten Österreichs im 17. Jahrhundert." In *Beiträge zur Bevölkerungs- und Sozialgeschichte,* ed. Heimo Helczmanovski, 167-222. Vienna, 1973.

Mitterauer, Michael, and Reinhard Sieder. *The European Family: Patriarchy to Partnership from the Middle Ages to the Present.* Trans. Karla Oosterveen and Manfred Horzinger. Chicago, 1982.

Mousnier, Roland. *La Famille, l'enfant, et l'education en France et en Grande-Bretagne du XVIe au XVIIIe siècle.* 2 vols. Paris, 1975.

Muchembled, Robert. "Famille, amour, et mariage: Mentalités et comportements des nobles artésiens a l'époque de Philippe II." *Revue d'histoire moderne et contemporaine* 22 (1975): 233-61.

Nader, Helen. *The Mendoza Family in the Spanish Renaissance.* New Brunswick, N.J., 1979.

Noonan, John T. *Contraception: a History of Its Treatment by the Catholic Theologians and Canonists.* Cambridge, Mass., 1966.

O'Neill, Brian Juan. *Social Inequality in a Northern Portuguese Hamlet: Land, Late Marriage and Bastardy, 1870-1978.* Cambridge, 1987.

Outhwaite, R. B., ed. *Marriage and Society: Studies in the Social History of Marriage.* London, 1981.

Ozment, Steven. *When Fathers Ruled: Family Life in Reformation Europe.* Cambridge, Mass., 1983.

Perry, Mary Elizabeth. *Gender and Disorder in Early Modern Seville.* Princeton, 1990.

Plakans, Andrejs. *Kinship in the Past: an Anthropology of European Family Life 1500-1900.* London, 1984.

Pollock, Linda. *Forgotten Children: Parent-child Relations from 1500 to 1900.* Cambridge, 1983.

Raftis, J. A. *Warboys: Two Hundred Years in the Life of a Medieval English Village.* Toronto, 1974.

Ranum, Orest, and Patricia Ranum, eds. *Popular Attitudes toward Birth Control in Pre-industrial England and France.* New York, 1972.

Razi, Zvi. *Life, Death and Marriage in a Medieval Parish. Economy: Society and Demography in Halesowen, 1270-1400.* Cambridge, 1980.

Rebel, Hermann. *Peasant Classes: the Bureaucratization of Property and Family Relations Under Early Hapsburg Absolutism, 1511-1636.* Princeton, 1983.

Riehl, Wilhelm. *Die Naturgeschichte des Volks als Grundlage einer deutschen Social-Politik.* 3d ed. Vol. 3, *Die Familie.* Stuttgart and Augsburg, 1855.

Roberts, Michael. "'Words They are Women, and Deeds They are Men': Images of Work and Gender in Early Modern England." In *Women and Work in Preindustrial England,* ed. Linsey Charles and Lorna Duffin, 122-81. London, 1985.

Robisheaux, Thomas W. *Rural Society and the Search for Order in Early Modern Germany.* Cambridge, 1989.

Roper, Lyndal. *The Holy Household: Women and Morals in Reformation Augsburg.* Oxford, 1989.

Roper, Lyndal. "Housework and Livelihood: Towards the *Alltagsgeschichte* of Women." *German History* 2 (1985): 3-9.

Rosenberg, Charles, ed. *The Family in History.* Philadelphia, 1975.

Rosenthal, Joel. *Patriarchy and Families of Privilege in Fifteenth-Century England.* Philadelphia, 1991.

Rotberg, Robert I., and Theodore K. Rabb, eds. *The Family in History: Interdisciplinary Essays.* New York, 1971.

Rotberg, Robert I., and Theodore K. Rabb, eds. *Marriage and Fertility: Studies in Interdisciplinary History.* Princeton, 1980.

Rublack, Hans-Christoph. "Zur Sozialstruktur der protestantische Minderheit in der geistlichen Residenz Bamberg am Ende des 16. Jahrhunderts." In *The Urban Classes, the Nobility and the Reformation: Studies on the Social History of the Reformation in England and Germany,* ed. Wolfgang Mommsen, 140-46. Stuttgart, 1979.

Ruggiero, Guido. *Boundaries of Eros: Sex Crime and Sexuality in Renaissance Venice.* Oxford, 1985.

Rushton, Peter. "Property, Power and Family Networks: The Problem of Disputed Marriage in Early Modern England." *JFH* 11 (1986): 205-19.

Sabean, David Warren. *Property, Production and Family in Neckarhausen, 1700-1870.* Cambridge, 1990.

Safley, Thomas M. "Civic Morality and the Domestic Economy." In *The German People and the Reformation,* ed. R. Po-Chia Hsia, 173-90. Ithaca, N.Y., 1989.

Safley, Thomas M. *Let No Man Put Asunder: The Control of Marriage in the German Southwest. A Comparative Study, 1550-1600.* Kirksville, Mo., 1984.

Schorn-Schütte, Luise. "'Gefahrtin' und 'Mitregentin': Zur Sozialgeschichte der evangelischen Pfarrfrau in der Frühen Neuzeit." In *Wandel der Geschlechterbeziehungen zu Beginn der Neuzeit,* ed. Heide Wunder and Christina Vanja, 109-53. Frankfurt, 1991.

Schuler, Peter Johannes, ed. *Die Familie als sozialer und historischer Verband: Untersuchungen zum Spätmittelalter und zur frühen Neuzeit.* Sigmaringen, 1987.

Schwartz, Ingeborg. *Die Bedeutung der Sippe für die Öffentlichkeit der Eheschliessung im 15. und 16. Jahrhunderts.* Schriften zur Kirchen- und Rechtsgeschichte, vol. 13. Tübingen, 1959.

Shaffer, J. W. *Family and Farm: Agrarian Change and Household Organization in the Loire Valley, 1500-1900.* Albany, 1982.

Shahar, Shulamith. *Childhood in the Middle Ages*. London, 1990.

Shorter, Edward. *The Making of the Modern Family*. New York, 1975.

Slater, Miriam. *Family Life in the Seventeenth Century: the Verneys of Claydon House*. London, 1984.

Smith, Richard M. *Land, Kinship, and Life-Cycle*. Cambridge, 1984.

Soliday, Gerald, et. al. *History of Family and Kinship: a Select International Bibliography*. New York, 1980.

Sponsler, Lucy A. "The Status of Married Women under the Legal System of Spain." *Journal of Legal History* (1982): 125-52.

Stone, Lawrence. *The Family, Sex and Marriage in England 1500-1800*. Abridged ed. New York, 1979.

Stone, Lawrence. *Road to Divorce: England, 1530-1987*. Oxford, 1990.

Strocchia, Sharon T. "Death Rites and the Ritual Family in Renaissance Florence." In *Life and Death in Fifteenth-Century Florence*, ed. Marcel Tetel, Ronald G. Witt, and Rona Goffen, 120-45. Durham, 1989.

Tilly, Louise A., and Joan W. Scott. *Women, Work, and Family*. New York, 1978.

Todd, Barbara. "The Remarrying Widow: A Stereotype Reconsidered." In *Women in English Society 1500-1800*, ed. Mary Prior, 54-92. London, 1985.

Todd, Margo. *Christian Humanism and the Puritan Social Order*. Cambridge, 1987.

Trexler, Richard. "Infanticide in Florence: New Sources and First Results." *History of Childhood Quarterly* 1 (1973): 98-116.

Vanja, Christina. "Frauen im Dorf. Ihre Stellung unter besonderer Berücksichtigung landgräflich-hessischer Quellen des späten Mittelalters." *ZAA* 34 (1987): 147-151.

Wall, Richard, Jean Robin, and Peter Laslett, eds. *Family Forms in Historic Europe*. Cambridge, 1983.

Watt, Jeffrey. *The Making of Modern Marriage* (Ithaca, 1992).

Wessoly, Kurt. "Die weibliche Bevölkerungsanteil in spätmittelalterlichen und frühneuzeitlichen Städten und die Betätigung von Frauen im zünftigen Handwerk (insbesondere am Mittel- und Oberrhein)." *ZGO* 89 (1980): 69-117.

Wheaton, Robert, and Tamara K. Harevan, eds. *Family and Sexuality in French History*. Philadelphia, 1980.

Wiesner, Merry E. "Guilds, Male Bonding and Women's Work in Early Modern Germany." *Gender and History* 1 (1989): 125-37.

Wiesner, Merry E. "*Wandervogels* and Women: Journeymen's Concepts of Masculinity in Early Modern Germany." *JSH* 24 (1990): 767-82.

Wiesner, Merry E. *Women and Gender in Early Modern Europe*. Cambridge, 1993.

Wiesner, Merry E. *Working Women in Renaissance Germany*. New Brunswick, N.J., 1986.

Wiltenburg, Joy. *Disorderly Women and Female Power in the Street Literature of Early Modern England and Germany*. Charlottesville, 1992.

Wrightson, Keith. "Infanticide in European History." *Criminal Justice History* 3 (1982): 1-20.

Wrigley, E. A., and R. S. Schofield. *The Population History of England 1541-1871. A Reconstruction*. London, 1981.

Wormald, Jenny. "Bloodfeud, Kindred and Government in Early Modern Scotland." *PaP*, no. 87 (1980): 54-97.

Wunder, Heide. *Er ist die Sonn', sie ist der Mond: Frauen in der Frühen Neuzeit*. Munich, 1992.

Yost, John. "The Value of Married Life for the Social Order in the Early English Renaissance." *Societas* 6 (1976): 25-38.

Yver, Jean. *Egalité entre héritiers et exclusion des enfants dotés: essai de géographie coutumière*. Paris, 1966.

Zapalac, Kristin E. S. "*In His Image and Likeness*": Political Iconography and Religious Change in Regensburg, 1500-1600*. Ithaca, N.Y., 1990.

# THE WORLD OF THE VILLAGE

Thomas W. Robisheaux
(Duke University)

At the beginning of the fifteenth century the civilization of Europe drew most of its human and material resources from the countryside. Two centuries later Europe was no different. The long expansion of the sixteenth century—the steady growth in population and trade, overseas exploration and the development of the Renaissance monarchies—depended, in large part, on new resources set free in the village. Despite the rise of cities such as Venice, Florence, Antwerp, Seville, Amsterdam and London—all of them wealthy cities with far flung trading empires—the main engine of European economic development remained rural and agricultural. Renaissance aristocracies may have become more "civilized," to use the term of Norbert Elias, more courtly, certainly better educated and better suited for state service. The vast majority of nobles, however, were still no more than big men of the village, lords of the countryside. The lifeblood of the new monarchies—taxes and soldiers—also came largely from the countryside. If the city was the generator of this civilization, the place where energy concentrated and flowed out, as Fernand Braudel colorfully suggests, then indeed the village provided the civilization's main resources, its raw power.

Who inhabited the world of the village? Not long ago the answer was a simple and self-evident one: peasants. Daniel Thorner defines peasants as that mass of agriculturalists who fall somewhere between landlords and the landless poor.[1] Some scholars might stretch the definition at both ends, but generally peasants were thought to include settled agriculturalists of varying legal status who were always in some dependence on the society's elites. The unspoken assumption about the village then was that it was, by definition, a peasant community. Today this assumption no longer holds. The early modern village was a complex community, one that was no longer dependent on subsistence agriculture to the degree that it was in the Middle Ages. Its population defies simple definition. The classic peasant represented almost everywhere a dwindling portion of the population. By 1600 the classic village, if there was one, included far more women, cottagers, landless laborers, artisans, peddlers, and other dependent groups than settled heads of households living completely from the land.

The same might be said about the village as a community. The village was once thought to be a closed and corporate community, small in scale, relatively isolated from the outside world, a community easily defined by its lands and buildings. Today we realize that the world of the village was not bounded by markers, fields and woods, the landmarks that set off the peasant world physically from the communities around it. Villagers occupied many other worlds as well, worlds not seen with the eye but that were no less real: worlds of the spirit, the broader culture and other associations that reached far beyond the narrow confines of the village itself. Was the village a harmonious community? Sometimes. But rural communities were also fractious, unruly and ridden with conflict. By 1600 they were also increasingly complex and stratified, and also attuned to provincial and state authorities in novel ways.[2] The early modern village, in short, was far more open to the broader world than was ever suspected only a generation ago.

## 1. RURAL ECONOMY: DECLINE, RECOVERY, AND CRISIS

One measure of the new importance historians see in the village was its central role in shaping the early modern economy. In 1935 Wilhelm Abel, a German agrarian historian, discovered that population and agriculture moved in tandem through long cycles of advance and decline. The medieval cycle, he argued, began around 1000 and, after three centuries of almost uninterrupted advance, came to an end around 1350. In the period that followed, the period that concerns us in this essay, the agrarian economy recovered, advanced throughout the sixteenth century and reached its peak, depending on the region, sometime in the second quarter of the seventeenth century.[3]

Almost all modern views of the rural economy begin with this early modern agrarian cycle. How to explain the cycle, however, has given rise to considerable differences of opinion. Perhaps the dominant view of the cycle has come to be associated with the French *Annales* school and the theory of Emmanuel Le Roy Ladurie. He argues that Europe's peasant economies developed a rough equilibrium between population and resources from 1000 to 1720. Without a technological breakthrough, without an agricultural revolution, Malthusian constraints strangled growth. An inevitable contraction in population set in and, after a period of halting growth and crisis, agriculture would decline once again. The village economy, to put it bluntly, expanded in the fifteenth and sixteenth century but simply could not break through its Malthusian limits.[4]

The theory appears to account for the central feature of the early modern rural economy: the persistence of subsistence-oriented agriculture in most parts of France, Germany, Italy and Spain. But how can one account for the development of capitalist agriculture in England and the Low Countries at this same time? In these countries population declined and fell in the same long cycles as in France, Germany and Spain. Grain prices, rural wages and land rents were no different: they followed a similar curve. The same general conditions that led to stagnation in many parts of Europe, in other words, posed no serious obstacle to the development of capitalist agriculture in Northwest Europe. Population trends, while important, were obviously not the only driving mechanisms of the village economy. In an effective critique of the neo-Malthusian theory Robert Brenner has called attention to just this problem. He proposed in its place a Marxian argument: agrarian class structures must have determined rural economic development.[5] While Brenner's theory has its merits, its reductionism does not solve all of the problems involved in explaining rural economic development in the early modern period. Indeed the failure of neo-Malthusianism and the Brenner debate illustrate the fallacy of any simple explanations of agrarian development.

## Conditions of Production

One of the central issues in this debate, for example, involves agricultural productivity. One can easily be misled about the apparent backwardness of the peasant economy and its failure to innovate, for example, by defining agricultural productivity too narrowly. The argument of Le Roy Ladurie rests on the assumption that significant improvements in productivity only came at the time of the Agricultural Revolution. The agrarian advance after 1450, in other words, depended on the continued application of medieval farming techniques. Almost every study of seed-yield ratios—the comparison of seed sown to harvested yields—has certainly confirmed the impression that productivity, at least in cereals production, was low throughout the fifteenth and sixteenth centuries. Seed-yield ratios for most cereal crops fluctuated between 1:3 and 1:5 for most of Europe, i.e. harvests large enough for a farm to feed a peasant family and perhaps leave a small surplus. In bad years the surplus vanished.[6]

One must realize, however, that peasants were capable of slowly improving productivity before the Agricultural Revolution. A veritable "green revolution" could be brought about by applying the widely known and simple techniques first developed in late medieval Flanders. These techniques involved liberal fertilizing, planting high yield legumes and

other crops and altering the traditional field system. Using these techniques Flemish peasants developed a remarkably productive economy. Already in the fourteenth and fifteenth centuries seed-yield ratios in parts of
Flanders averaged between 1:7 and 1:11![7] The equilibrium between population, land and technology could be broken through, in other words, but
the breakthrough had less to do with technology than it did with capital investment, income distribution, market systems, crops and field systems.
The persistence of common field systems has also been cited as an obstacle
to rural economic development. To a certain extent they were. The common field systems evolved over the course of the medieval period and by
the fifteenth century they were sustained by village custom and law. And
yet one should not lose sight of the fact that village field systems also embodied a shrewd economic calculus. Peasants could not afford the risks,
the bold gambles, associated with merchant capitalism. The peasant's
punishment for failure was brutal: starvation. Hence the village evolved
laws and customs governing fields, work and crops that were risk-aversive.
They embodied not the principle of maximizing profit but the principle, indeed the imperative, of minimizing risk. Common fields secured villagers
access to the diverse resources of the community: they guaranteed an income and minimized the risk of crop failure. The scattering of fields served
the same purpose. By farming small strips of land scattered over the village
lands a peasant made up for any loss in one field by gains in another.[8]
Strains of barley, oats and rye were chosen not for their high yields but for
their proven hardiness and reliability. These old and tested field systems,
finely attuned to local conditions, were the backbone of the village
economy. But, as the enclosure movement in England suggests, villages
could also be prodded into abandoning them and adopting field systems
that would make capitalist agriculture possible.

Was the seigneurial system then an obstacle to investment and innovation? Many historians have answered this question, perhaps hastily, that it
was. Few studies, however, have examined the economy of the reformed
seigneury of the sixteenth century without bias. The great interest in the
peasant economy and capitalist agriculture has not yet been matched by an
equal interest in the seigneurial economy and its role in encouraging or dis-
couraging agrarian development. One reason for the failure to answer this
question successfully lies in the difficulty of grasping the arcane and complex world of feudal law and inheritance customs. One should therefore
be cautious about generalizing about the economic incentives built into
Europe's old property systems. Seigneurial property and traditional inheritance customs shared a common purpose: they did not secure individual

ownership so much as rights of usufruct and they almost always entailed obligations to maintain property in the corporate interests of family and community. They were therefore designed to secure access to land and resources in the interest of the family and household. This did not mean, however, that these property systems always discouraged investment and economic initiative. The fierce debates among modern scholars about the effects of the new share-cropping arrangements in late medieval and early modern Italy, the *mezzadria*, for example, suggest that generalizations cannot easily be made. Seigneurial burdens may indeed have been excessive in many places and even discouraged investment, but, in other times and places they might also provide the basis for surprisingly innovative developments.

Many of these debates about the rural economy tend to take place in a vacuum. They often fail to examine a given rural economy as part of a regional economic system. The few studies that do so have shown that local economic development depended in part on regional economic development. It is no accident that the most productive, efficient and market-oriented village economies after 1400 developed in regions with an expanding economic infrastructure: the Netherlands, the midlands and southern counties of England, the lower Rhineland and islands of intensive development around major cities like Paris, Barcelona and Milan. These regions developed the most advanced marketing systems, low cost transportation and effective public administration. The net effect was to stimulate agriculture. In regions where governments made no improvements in the local infrastructure, however, rural economic development stagnated and fell behind. Peasants had no incentives to produce for the market when goods circulated inefficiently and at high cost.

*Decline, 1400-1450*

While the debates may continue about whether population, class structures or other causes lay at the root of rural economic development one central fact has not been called into question: the agrarian cycle itself. Study after study since the 1950s has only confirmed the cycles of contraction and expansion that Wilhelm Abel pointed out long ago. In the following sections I will try to characterize the three phases of this great agrarian cycle.

The first of these phases, a late medieval contraction and decline in agriculture, can be detected as early as 1320. To some scholars the period between 1320 and 1450 has all of the characteristics of a long and deep crisis: falling population, falling prices for grain, high agricultural wages and declining rents. Was this a crisis of feudalism? While many scholars have argued for a general late medieval agrarian crisis, the case has never been persuasive for all of Europe.[9] The idea of a generalized crisis seems poorly suited to describe the slow, erratic and uneven changes set in motion between 1320 and 1450.[10] The agricultural economy certainly contracted and regional crises may have accelerated an overall decline. These changes, however, brought about as much prosperity and economic diversification as suffering and dislocation.

The decline in population and the corresponding economic adjustments did not occur all at one time. The initial pandemic of bubonic plague may have reduced the population by a third but it struck rural populations already weakened and, in many places, declining since 1320. The recurrence of plague every ten to twelve years further reduced the population, but only in stages and in conjunction with localized episodes of famine and war. One can only date lasting structural changes in the rural economy to the 1380s and 1390s, in fact, and even then the economic trends were diverse and uneven across Europe.

The economies of some regions were more seriously affected than others. The steepest decline in agriculture came in regions where the soils were already poor or marginal or where the burden of rents, dues and taxes was unusually heavy. Plague and famine were often of secondary importance in affecting the local economy in these areas. Migration to the towns emptied these communities of people as much as the plague or famine did. The population of the mountainous areas of Provence and Languedoc, for example, declined more rapidly than the settlements in the rich lowland river valleys. The pattern was the same in Germany. Many of the so-called "abandoned villages" of Germany were located in poorer regions such as the Harz Mountains and the Black Forest.[11] But some villages experienced no decline at all. In the most fertile agricultural belts and in areas with flexible local institutions and easy access to urban markets villages replaced population losses quickly. Indeed, some villages flourished in the new economic environment. The villages near London, for example, were by no means exceptional in their prosperity and stability.[12] Overall productivity probably improved as peasants abandoned marginal lands and concentrated production on the most fertile lands.

The effects of population losses were also mitigated by new market relationships with the towns. The towns and cities of Europe gained in population and wealth relative to the countryside and this new concentration of urban wealth and power frequently stimulated the development of economic production in the surrounding countryside. The villages in these green belts diversified their economies, turning to dairy farming, market gardening or the production of industrial crops like flax, woad, and hemp. Whether the changes worked to the benefit of the village economy or not, however, depended on local conditions. The staggering loss of population in the Tuscan countryside—declines of 40% to 60% were not uncommon by 1427—contributed to the economic dominance of Florence over many rural communities. That dominance, however, also brought benefits. The Tuscan rural economy received a fresh infusion of much needed capital from Florence as a result.[13]

One of the best ways to understand the difficulty of assessing these changes is to look at wage and price trends. At first glance the secular economic trends of this period—chronically low prices for grain, falling rents and higher wages—suggest that agriculture became less profitable. The decline in grain prices drove peasants and lords to abandon fields or allow them to revert to forests or wastes. At the least they took them out of grain production. Cereals production therefore declined in the late fourteenth century, thus undermining rural incomes dependent upon grain sales. While rural incomes contracted, wages increased. Ample evidence now suggests that rural wages had risen substantially by 1400 and that they remained high throughout the fifteenth century. The higher costs of labor further increased production costs on estates and farms, squeezed profits and encouraged landlords to abandon the direct cultivation of their estates.

Whether these adjustments actually led to a crisis in rural incomes, however, is open to debate. What importance did general market prices and overall wage trends have to most peasants? Most peasants produced for their own subsistence, not for the market, and so declines in prices did not automatically mean that rural incomes fell. In addition, for those farmers who did produce for the market, reduced incomes might be compensated for by expanding production, planting new cash crops or raising cattle. The latter enterprise not only required less labor but it also took advantage of the rising demand for meat in the late fourteenth century. Others supplemented income with wages. The conjuncture, in other words, may not have precipitated a crisis in incomes so much as it made rural incomes more diverse and complex.

Can one find evidence then of a crisis in seigneurial incomes? Several trends suggest that this was the case. The difficulty of mobilizing labor and the fall in grain prices encouraged many landlords to break up their estates and loosen seigneurial controls over the peasantry. Peasants fled estates heavily encumbered with servile obligations and the resulting scarcity of labor made it even more difficult for lords to farm out their lands directly. As a result manorial estates were broken up almost everywhere in western Europe; land was increasingly leased out in return for modest cash rents.

Serfdom declined as a result. Lords tried to reimpose servile obligations in some regions—the most notorious case being the revival of serfdom in southern Germany on the eve of the German Peasants' War—but in most areas serfdom was in irreversible decay by 1450. Already by the 1420s the English manorial system was largely broken up. By 1500 serfdom had disappeared entirely from England.[14] In France and Germany peasants pressed for more secure control over their lands in the form of heritable land tenures. By 1450 heritable land tenure and fixed and low customary rents were firmly established in the German West and remained largely unchanged until the nineteenth century.[15] Even in rural Tuscany one could make the case that the new share-cropping arrangements, the *mezzadria*, helped stabilize agriculture and only later worked to the detriment of the peasantry. These trends clearly favored peasants and laborers.

Whether they precipitated a general crisis in seigneurial incomes, however, is unclear. The evidence is mixed. Guy Bois makes the case, on the basis of a study of Normandy, that seigneurial incomes fell disastrously in the early fifteenth century.[16] But one should be cautious in generalizing about noble income from individual case studies. The lesser nobility may have had fewer resources to weather these changes than did the great aristocratic houses. In the absence of complete household account books generalizations are hazardous at best. The few complete account books that exist make it clear that seigneurial incomes were complex and not always tied directly to agricultural production. Incomes from rents, sales of agricultural products and other incomes from the land may have fallen after 1380, but these losses might have been offset by acquiring new lands, marriage alliances, and service to the crown.

Whether regions experienced a crisis or not, the low ratio of population to land and the decline in grain prices encouraged a new degree of economic diversification. Arable land was abandoned or transformed into pasture. The English Midlands turned increasingly to sheep-raising. Castile did as well, and its wool was exported to the Low Countries and Italy. Dutch peasants began to specialize in dairy-farming. Farther from urban areas—in parts of Provence, Hungary, Denmark and Poland—fields were turned to pastures, cattle raised and then shipped off to towns to meet the growing demand for meat as diets changed in the fifteenth century.[17] Subsistence agriculture may have still predominated in most areas, but some areas turned to specialized production and laid the foundations for a broader commercialized agriculture in the sixteenth century.

*Advance, 1450-1560*

When population and agriculture stabilized around 1450 a new phase of the agrarian cycle began: a broad advance that would shape the rural economy until the early and middle decades of the seventeenth century. Explaining the boom itself presents few problems. Population growth increased the demand for land and food supplies and this, in turn, encouraged producers to clear land that laid waste or to expand production in other ways. Where the difficulty arises is in understanding why some rural economies became more market oriented and why the boom slowed and problems mounted. Had the rural economy really begun to reach its limits by 1560? A number of exceptional studies for France have provided the clearest picture of the boom in its early stages. The broad foundations for an advance were clearly laid everywhere by 1450. By this time population had ceased to decline. Tithe receipts—a rough indicator of total grain production—reached bottom around 1420 and then expanded rapidly in the 1430s in the south and west of France. A sizable middling peasantry had formed and led the recovery, clearing new lands, repairing and enlarging old farms, employing laborers and producing small surpluses of grain to feed the growing population. In the Paris basin the recovery dated from the 1440s, but then the expansion took off rapidly. Overall in France the trend was for a rapid expansion to 1500, a break, and then a slower but steady expansion to 1560. Prices followed. The price of grain rose slowly after 1500, then steeply in the 1520s and 1550s. By 1560 overall prices of agricultural products had almost tripled compared to 1500.[18]

The picture for many parts of Spain, Italy, Germany, and Eastern Europe is not as complete, but scholars generally agree that population growth and an agrarian advance were European-wide trends by 1500. How to characterize the changes in these regions of traditional subsistence agriculture, however, is a difficult question. Did these regions simply fail to develop beyond a certain point? The evidence is incomplete and hard to interpret. One can find evidence that peasant agricultural productivity remained low, and this has been used to argue that the traditional village economy simply could not expand beyond a certain point. In one of the few quantitative studies of agricultural production for this period, Emmanuel Le Roy Ladurie and Joseph Goy argue, on the basis of tithe receipts, that overall agricultural production increased up to 1560 and then stagnated. The levelling off of tithe receipts, they suggest, resulted from the failure to break through the traditional limits on agricultural productivity.[19]

Studies of tithe receipts and cereals production, however important and

useful, can also be deceptive. Tithe receipts may not be an accurate guide
to agricultural productivity. They almost certainly cannot be equated with
overall economic productivity since they fail to take into account the increasingly complex nature of rural economies in the sixteenth century.
Even small adjustments could have lasting consequences. When the peasants of Tuscany diversified their economy even slightly—shifting from cereals cultivation to more production of wine, olives and silk—the regional
economy developed a flexibility it had lacked in the late Middle Ages.[20]
The same was true in other rural areas. In the valleys of the Loire and
Seine viticulture spread and provided many peasant households with supplemental cash incomes. Still other villages came to depend on incomes
from small-scale market gardening. The production of industrial crops
such as woad, hemp, mulberry trees, and flax provided still other sources
of income. Employment in rural industry rose. Some models of the peasant economy take this new diversification into account. One should therefore be cautious about equating overall economic productivity simply with
the production of cereals crops.

What lies behind some views of the rural economy is the assumption
that peasants could not make the transition to productive, market-oriented
agriculture. Marxists and neo-Malthusians alike share this bias, which has
especially influenced explanations of the development of capitalist agriculture in the sixteenth century. The history of English agriculture is often
seen as the model of how traditional subsistence-oriented peasant agriculture had to be transformed. The old obstacles to growth had to be swept
away: the middling peasantry, small family farms, customary land tenure
arrangements, and medieval common fields. In their place would have to
come large and efficiently managed farms, leased to innovative farmers
and worked by wagelaborers.[21] These efficient market-oriented enterprises came to dominate the English rural economy by the end of the seventeenth century.

But was this the *only* way to transform traditional peasant agriculture?
Looking closely at rural hinterlands of cities in Northwest Europe another
alternative can be seen: specialized peasant agriculture, a kind of peasant
capitalism. The innovative productive unit here was not the large consolidated farm but the medium-sized peasant household. In a model case
study Jan de Vries has shown how the Dutch commercial economy came
to depend upon the development of a highly intensive and specialized agriculture in Holland, Zeeland, and Friesland.[22] All of these regions were
dominated by the middling peasantry. Population growth was no obstacle
to the economic development of these regions: it stimulated the develop-

ment of specialized agriculture. One can find similar trends in what German economists call *Intensitätsinseln*, areas of intensive and market-oriented agricultural production around towns and cities. Several of these regions evolved during the agrarian advance: the Ile-de-France, the Po Valley around Milan, and the countryside of Catalonia near Barcelona.[23] The peasantry did not have to vanish and give way to innovative farmers and landlords in order for commercialized agriculture to develop.

One of the key factors in the development of commercial agriculture, whatever its form, was the availability of land. Not everywhere could peasants easily acquire new land since an open market in land was only beginning to appear in the sixteenth century. Not surprisingly the flexibility of rural economies in countries like England and the Low Countries resulted partly from the tendency to treat land like a commodity.[24] The trend was not limited to these regions alone. Even in areas dominated by seigneurial property one can detect a trend towards the monetization of transactions involving land and land rights. Scholars once ascribed a great deal of significance to the dissolution of monastic lands in encouraging the growth of this livelier market in land parcels and in the development of commercial agriculture in general. The obvious reference here was to England. Comparable studies of France, however, have shown that the sale of church lands itself did not necessarily encourage the development of commercial agriculture. During the Wars of Religion church lands changed hands on a massive scale but without significantly encouraging the rise of entrepreneurial agriculture.[25]

Where new land remained unavailable most peasants had to acquire land through inheritance. There seems to be little controversy among historians who have studied this problem about the woeful consequences of these practices in the sixteenth century. In areas of partible inheritance peasants progressively subdivided their lands, a process first observed in detail by Le Roy Ladurie for Languedoc.[26] The pattern of gradual impoverishment he discovered there seems to have been a universal one in many parts of France and Germany. The reform and codification of inheritance laws made the transactions more orderly, perhaps, but hardly stopped the erosion of peasant wealth in areas of partible inheritance.

What role did landlords play in shaping the rural economy during the boom? The blame that is heaped on "parasitic" landlords for deforming the rural economy is common enough in the literature, but, as was noted above, this judgment rarely flows from careful empirical studies of noble household economies in the sixteenth century. The stereotype of the nobility and the church—the two largest groups of landholders—as more interested in conspicuous consumption than in investment and rural economic development, however, has some basis in fact. In almost every corner of the countryside revenues from the land grew in the sixteenth century, first slowly up to the 1550s and 1560s, and then steeply and dramatically into the early seventeenth century.[27] The main sources of revenue, however, were not the old seigneurial dues. These often remained fixed and assumed a smaller portion of overall income from the land. Still, these seigneurial incomes often went into the building of stately chateaux and the ostentatious expenditures expected of Renaissance gentlemen and ladies.

The methods of raising these revenues, however, reveal the nobility's keen eye for improving incomes. How was this done? Where it was possible to do so some lords renegotiated land as short-term leaseholds. One can cite the obvious case of England in this regard, but leaseholds were also introduced in parts of France, Italy, and Germany. Others raised incomes by acquiring new land, reorganizing estates, revising rent books and estate administration, and managing incomes with a shrewd eye towards maximizing returns. This frequently involved managing forests more carefully, for example, and marketing lumber and firewood for cash incomes.[28] Innovative nobles also continued to develop diverse sources of income wherever possible: investments in urban properties, commerce, credit, rural industry, or state service.

What do these practices tell us about nobles' attitudes toward property and wealth? The subject has received scant attention. The fact that nobles were not capitalists and failed to invest in agricultural improvements may be a statement of the obvious but this hardly helps explain the meaning of material wealth and incomes to this elite. The odd position of Eastern European Junkers as they turned to the production of grain for export illustrates our difficulties in understanding this problem. The old picture of the sixteenth-century Junkers and their peasants has been considerably revised in recent years. It once was common to describe the rural economies of Eastern Europe as curiously "deformed" when nobles used their coercive political power to undermine the peasant economy, forcing villagers into a "second serfdom" and developing a "backward-looking" domainal economy. The Junkers, however, were neither so powerful nor the peasantry so oppressed as scholars once thought. They improved their estates, invested in agriculture and developed an export-oriented agriculture. And yet they paradoxically limited the burden on peasants and compromised long-term economic development in favor of short-term accommodation to peasant interests.[29]

Paradoxes like this one abound when one looks closely at the economic behavior of the nobility. Over the last thirty years A. V. Chayanov's theory of the peasant economy has made its way into the mainstream literature on the rural economy and, with adjustments, it has been instrumental in illuminating the dynamics of the peasant household economy. What is needed now is a theory of the noble economy. In some ways the noble household economy may have shown the same logic as that of the peasant household economy.[30] In an old work, now in disfavor, Otto Brunner once proposed the idea that rural nobles viewed the economy in terms of their own "household management."[31] If one looks through the household manuals of the sixteenth century, manuals becoming widely popular by the end of the century, one finds considerable evidence for this part of Brunner's argument. These manuals have no positive references to "markets" or "capital investment" or even "income" in the modern sense of the word. What one does find are admonitions to care for household dependents, maintain the household, and trade for maintenance and not for gain. What to a modern economist was "conspicuous consumption" and a curious or "irrational" lack of interest in investment was actually a calculus of investment in the household and the family, kin, and other people dependent on it.

### Mounting Crises, 1560-1600

All of the above problems in understanding the village economy become even more vexing when one turns to the closing decades of the sixteenth century. Expansion slowed after 1560 and, while it would continue in some areas into the early seventeenth century, signs of stagnation and crisis multiplied. The famines and epidemics of the 1570s were the worst of the century up to that time. By the 1590s population growth had stalled in some regions. After 1600 these crises would become even more serious, leading in some regions to a collapse in agricultural production, losses in population and a reversal of long-term secular trends.

Why did these economic troubles mount after 1560? And why did some regions fare better than others? Most current answers to these questions focus on the strains on the rural economy as the rural economy failed to improve and the population continued to grow. Population was simply outstripping the economy's ability to sustain it. But was it?

At first glance the neo-Malthusian argument provides a plausible answer to the question. Land was in short supply after 1560. Villagers still brought new lands under cultivation, but they tended to be marginal lands, lands where agricultural productivity was lower. Yields from these poor fields were low. Grain prices, reflecting both the limits of agricultural productivity and the population's pressures on food supplies, rose faster after 1560 than in the first half of the sixteenth century. The pressure of population also contributed to the skyrocketing rents of the late sixteenth century. Peasant incomes fell as landlords reaped windfall profits. All of these problems, the argument goes, contributed to the worsening subsistence crises. In regions of traditional peasant agriculture these were ominous signs of an economy no longer able to meet the minimal needs of villagers.

The classic case of this Malthusian dilemma was Spain. Villages in Castile and Valencia were starved of capital investments in the sixteenth century. Population, however, continued to grow. By the 1570s cereals production stagnated, peasant incomes declined, and debts to urban creditors mounted: all signs of an increasingly exhausted rural economy. By 1600 an irreversible decline had set in.[32] Southern and central Italy, one might add, were comparable and hardly better off.[33]

This neo-Malthusian view of the crises, however, has a number of shortcomings. The theory assumes that the subsistence crises of this period were caused by crises of production. On the contrary, many crises originated in the distribution system. In regions with a more developed infrastructure, the shortages of food were far less severe. The elaborate international grain trade that had developed in northwestern Europe, for example, cushioned the Netherlands from serious famines and food shortages. The trade had two consequences: it relieved local shortages of food and it made it possible for villages to continue to specialize in dairy farming, market gardening, and other specialized economic activities. The effect of market relationships was no less significant in the interior of Europe. Along the Upper Rhine many local village economies had become intricately tied together into a regional network of markets more elaborate than in the Middle Ages. Even as economic growth slowed the villages of this region continued to diversify into small craft production; the more complex rural economy cushioned them somewhat from the ups and downs of any single trade.[34] The story was wholly different in more underdeveloped parts of Spain, southern France, and southern Italy. In these areas, by contrast, the poorly developed market structures aggravated subsistence crises and further weakened the rural economy.

The ups and downs of food production and distribution were also not always the key to understanding subsistence crises. In areas of rural industry the troubles may have reflected cyclical problems of commerce and manufacturing. By the late sixteenth century rural industry had spread far more widely than in the late Middle Ages and often into regions of dense population growth and partible inheritance; the regions most vulnerable to

subsistence crises.[35]  In addition, many village economies had come to depend on local artisanal production on a much broader scale than the late
Middle Ages.  The economic troubles of these village economies often had
as much to do with commercial cycles as they did with the problems of traditional agriculture.

What is striking about the subsistence crises of the 1570s, 1580s, and
1590s is that they could have been much worse than they were.  Why?  In
contrast to the end of the medieval agrarian cycle in the early fourteenth
century, governments were more willing and able to distribute bread or
grain in times of shortage, to administer prices and regulate the markets.
This was usually done to head off public disorders or rebellion.  The English Poor Law provided at least a minimal cushion for the village poor and
made English villages less vulnerable to famine than was the case in other
areas.  But the English were not unusually progressive in this regard.  Small
German principalities broadened their care for the poor, making food
available, administering prices, and regulating market relationships in
ways that often relieved local shortages.[36]  Even in Italy city-states and rural lords developed policies that helped stave off disaster for the poor by
the 1590s.[37]  These policies may have been self-serving, but they made subsistence crises less severe than they otherwise would have been.


## 2. Social Structure: The Polarization of Village Life

The structure of the early modern village reflected the norms of a broader
society dominated by the nobility and based on rank and status. These
were not simply social norms imposed from above.  Rank, status, and hierarchy often counted as much to villagers as they did to nobles, townspeople, and the clergy.  Despite the ups and downs of the rural economy, these
norms remained intact.  Only in the late eighteenth and nineteenth centuries would they be seriously challenged.  Stability and continuity, however,
should not be confused with rigidity and inflexibility.  The old idea of the
early modern village as an immobile corporate community, closed off from
the outside world, has been modified significantly in recent years.  The village community was often a surprisingly mobile and, by the mid-sixteenth
century, increasingly stratified community, one with new and deeper ties
to the other villages and towns in its region.

*Mobility*

The decline in population and agriculture after 1320, for example, ushered in a new era of social mobility in the countryside. The overall patterns of mobility for the late Middle Ages and early modern period can never be completely reconstructed. Tax registers, parish registers, rentbooks, and court records tend to describe the lives of settled householders and not those who were on the move. In general, however, we know that for those who survived the epidemics, famines, and wars between 1320 and 1450, land and wealth was much easier to acquire than it once had been. Lords eased the restrictions on peasant movements and marriages. Towns offered new opportunities for rural immigrants. Around 1450 one finds telling evidence of how this mobility had transformed many villages. The names of ambitious, newly wealthy, and upwardly mobile "new men" frequently appear in village rentbooks. Some of them would slowly rise into the ranks of sizable land-holders. A few would even acquire titles and blend into the ranks of the lower gentry or nobility.

This late medieval mobility has been well known, if poorly documented, but one of the surprising recent discoveries involves mobility in the sixteenth century. The trends are more firmly established for the English countryside than for other parts of Europe, but they suggest that certain social groups in the village were more mobile than others. Below the settled householders of many English villages was a youthful population frequently on the move. Mobility was also closely associated with gender and occupation. Women often left the village of their birth not only to marry but also to work as farm servants and domestics. Young men often moved about as farm laborers, artisans and peddlers plying their trade from village to village. The slowing of the agricultural advance in the middle of the century and the hard times of the 1570s, 1580s, and 1590s seem to have been accompanied by a hardening of social boundaries and more difficulty in achieving upward mobility. Downward social mobility became more common. Those who were the most vulnerable included middling and smallholders and widows.[38]

Were English villagers unusually mobile? Perhaps. The enclosure movement and the development of consolidated farms often drove a number of smallholders and cottagers off the land and onto the roads. The complaints in Parliament about this were bitter and real. In the absence of comparable studies for France, Spain, and Germany, however, one cannot really know whether this high degree of mobility was unusual or not. Even the most casual look at the reports from the French, Italian, and German countryside in the 1570s, 1580s, and 1590s reveals a similar alarm about

vagrants and bandits. One of the distinctive features, then, of many villages by the 1590s was the presence of a mobile, newly impoverished
population of vagrants and landless laborers. At the top of the village hierarchy one also finds a great deal of mobility. A number of aristocratic
families died out or declined as a consequence of plague, war, and an inability to adjust to the new economic conditions in the fifteenth century.
Partly as a consequence of these and other changes the direct authority of
many rural nobles over the peasantry loosened and became more indirect.
By 1500 most of the manors were broken up, serfdom had declined, and
rents and dues were commuted for cash payments. And yet, most nobles
continued, despite the lure of court life and state service, to be directly involved in the affairs of the village through their dominance of landholding
and provincial and seigneurial institutions.

### Rural Lords

How to characterize this new era in lord-peasant relationships, is a puzzle.
The observation that nobles tended to "withdraw" from village life in the
sixteenth century, while true in an institutional or even a legal sense, does
not really help us to grasp the complexity of these relationships. One need
only turn the pages of the memoirs of Gilles de Gouberville, a petty nobleman from Normandy, to discover a man intimately involved in directing
the affairs of his estate, personally disciplining his peasants and servants,
and exuberantly participating in family and village celebrations.[39]

One illustration of this problem involves the "re-feudalization" of Eastern Europe, Austria, and Italy in the sixteenth century. Marxist scholars
use the term to refer to the tendency of nobles in these areas to tighten direct institutional and legal controls over their peasants, impose a heavier
burden of labor services, and develop a larger domainal economy.[40] While
the term may call attention to the new character of lord-peasant relationships the concept is a seriously misleading one. In most of these areas no
seigneurial or "feudal" institutions existed before the sixteenth century,
and so lords were hardly returning to an old and archaic way of dominating their peasants. In addition, the new lord-peasant relationships were
more complex, impersonal, and even bureaucratic than at any time in the
earlier history of seigneurialism. In Austria, for example, these relationships became heavily bureaucratized.[41] The concept of "refeudalization,"
in short, fails to capture the modern face of seigneurial authority in the sixteenth century.

*Outsider Elites*

Regardless of whether the local lord became more distant or more directly involved in disciplining his villagers one can see a general tendency for more outsiders to take up residence in the village. Older, outsider elites resident in the village since the Middle Ages also changed their role vis-a-vis other villagers. These groups—state and seigneurial officials, commercial middlemen, and reformed pastors and priests—tended to open the village to broader institutions of authority and the regional market economy. In contrast to traditional village elites, whose local standing derived from the control of the land, these groups derived authority, power, and prestige from relationships and contacts beyond the village. Their lives and relationships were part of a complex web of ties both within and beyond the village, and their loyalties, as a result, were ambiguous and exceedingly complex. Petty commercial elites, for example, became wealthy and respected contacts as the agrarian boom transformed the rural economy. In times of crisis, however, these shopkeepers, peddlers, millers, innkeepers, and artisans were blamed for unfair marketing practices, hoarding and high prices.[42]

The clergy played a similar role in mediating village relationships with the broader world. Here, too, conflicts were inevitable. The religious reforms of the sixteenth century created a rural parish clergy better trained and educated than in the late Middle Ages, but they found themselves under stricter controls from the church hierarchy. The rural parish became less autonomous and more subject to the discipline and control of the church than ever before. Relationships with the parish pastor, where they have been sensitively explored by scholars, have been shown to be fraught with ambiguity and difficulty as a result.[43] They were the eyes, ears, and arms of state-churches and opened the village to more effective state supervision.

*Peasants*

These elites were by no means alone in opening the village to broader influences. Behind the front of village solidarity lay an increasingly stratified village society, one frequently polarized between the wealthy and the poor. One of the striking trends by the middle of the sixteenth century was the emergence of wealthy peasant elites, substantial propertyholders and yeomen, many of whom tended to align themselves with the world beyond the village. One reason was strictly economic: the agrarian advance enabled substantial peasants and yeomen to prosper as land became scarce and grain prices soared. These farmers, tenant farmers and small entrepreneurs were therefore more likely to produce surpluses for the market and share in a commercial and cultural world beyond the village. Studies have shown them playing prominent roles in shaping the village culture of southern and eastern England, northern France, and parts of western Germany, and Switzerland.[44] Many of these substantial villagers, in addition, tended to sympathize with reformed religions or identify themselves with national elites and the cultural values of the broader society. If anyone inclined towards Puritanism, supported the Poor Law, and called for more moral discipline in the village, it was the English yeoman.[45]

This polarization of village life came at the expense of very specific groups: the middling peasantry and the village poor. In 1450 the middling peasantry was the backbone of village societies across Europe. By 1600 these peasants were reduced in number or had even vanished altogether. In Germany middling and smallholders may have often held their own in terms of numbers, but they declined as a percentage of the village population, as the numbers of cottagers, rural artisans and laborers steadily grew.[46] As peasants divided up their lands in Languedoc and the Ile-de-France, the number of middling peasants fell sharply by 1550. In Italy the decay of the middling and smallholder advanced even further, benefitting nobles, the bourgeoisie, and the clergy, and contributing to a social landscape marked by extremes of wealth and poverty. Between 1460 and 1480 the percentage of land in the hands of smallholders in Umbria fell from 40% to 25%. By the middle of the sixteenth century the small and independent peasant farmer had virtually disappeared from the countrysides surrounding Florence, Siena, Modena, Padua, and Parma.[47] In England many small husbandmen lost their lands to enclosures, engrossing, or rapidly rising rents. Those who held on did so by clinging to old freeholds and copyholds or cobbling together a livelihood from the diverse resources of the fens and woods.[48]

The polarization of social life is even more evident when one looks at the groups at the bottom of the social hierarchy: smallholders, cottagers, laborers and the landless poor. These groups have always been difficult to study. By any measure, however, rural poverty grew substantially in the sixteenth century. The rural poor defy easy categorization. They hardly formed a uniform class. Smallholders and cottagers might naturally be included in this group, but in some regions the village poor might also include peasants who specialized in certain types of agricultural production, such as viticulture. The spread of village manufactures and small crafts meant that many types of artisans—cobblers, tailors, barrelmakers, ropemakers, and carpenters, for example—might also be classed among the poor.

One trend that these groups shared with the village elites was an increasing dependency on relationships, influences, and institutions from beyond the village. The plight of the poor in the German County of Hohenlohe illustrates what was a problem common in many rural regions. Lacking the means to produce their own food the poor were sensitive to broader trends in wages and market prices. In times of crisis they were the first to feel the disruptive effects of high prices for bread and grain and tried to mobilize local institutions or the government to protect them.[49] Rural industry with its close ties to regional commerce reinforced this dependency on the market economy. Poor relief and charity, while organized in many regions on a broader and firmer institutional basis, stigmatized the poor more visibly than in the medieval period and accentuated the social distance to honorable villagers.

### Women

Where are the gaps in our understanding of the social structure of the village? Certainly the largest gap involves peasant women. What little we know about the lives of peasant women focuses narrowly on their reproductive roles. Women's roles and contributions to village social life, however, went far beyond giving birth, mothering, and tending the hearth. The emergence of a more ordered and stratified village society, in fact, depended upon the labor of women, the uses they made of their dowries, their attentiveness to the issues of honor and shame, and the ways that they shaped the social and moral order of the family and household. Partly because women formed such a central part of village life, they were also seen as symbols of order and disorder.[50] One aspect of the problem involves the growing number of prosecutions of women for illegitimacy, infanticide, and witchcraft after 1560.[51] In each of these categories women were singled out for discipline and punishment far more often than men. In England lawsuits for defamation frequently involved women, an indicator of how easily a woman's honor and reputation were damaged.[52] When these efforts to discipline village women overlapped or coincided with village customary beliefs and practices—as they did with charivaris—the result was less tolerance for disorderly women.

The trends were not solely in one direction, however, and women also assumed roles that involved them directly in shaping their own fortunes and those of their families. The importance of property and inheritance in peasant families meant that a woman's dowry was essential in assuming proprietorship of a farm or establishing an independent household. Customs varied greatly, but in some areas women exercised considerable control over their dowries while married or assumed pivotal roles in disposing of property as widows. A widow's decisions about remarriage and the disposal of the patrimony directly affected the fortunes of everyone with a claim to an inheritance. In areas where rural industry developed women almost always played a key part in the labor force. Silk production in Tuscany was largely women's work.[53] The concentration of property in the hands of village men, however, made women dependent on male kinsmen for much of their lives and they were therefore more vulnerable when it changed hands or the wealth was dissipated.[54]

## 3. THE VILLAGE COMMUNE IN A LARGER WORLD

Social and economic changes as sweeping as the ones we have discussed above had political consequences that reached far beyond the countryside. While progress in understanding the politics of the village has largely come from studies of peasant rebellions, the comments that follow focus on the underlying political movement that made rebellions possible: the rise to prominence of the village commune. Next to the peasant family and household and the seigneury, the commune assumed the largest role in structuring the public life of the community. For this reason scholars have looked to the commune for the most important evidence of the political attitudes of peasants. What political values did the commune instill in villagers? Was the communal tradition an alternative to seigneurial rule and the authoritarianism of the "new" monarchies of the late fifteenth and sixteenth centuries? Was the commune a democratic institution?

### The Communal Tradition

The most challenging answers to these questions come from studies of the Swiss and German village commune between 1400 and 1600. In this body of work the old stereotype of the peasant as passive, conservative, and backward-looking has been set aside in recent years. The work of Peter Blickle deserves special attention in this regard. Building on the work of an earlier generation of German scholars, Blickle has argued that the village commune rose to new prominence in the fifteenth and early sixteenth centuries. He also sees the communal tradition as a serious alternative to seigneurialism and the authoritarian power of the princes in parts of Switzerland and South Germany. The commune instilled proto-democratic or egalitarian political values in the peasantry. It embodied the ideals of the "common man." How was this achieved? The commune was governed by an assembly of propertyholding peasants experienced in governing the internal affairs of the community. The need to govern the rotation of crops, regulate agricultural work and manage communal resources inevitably instilled anti-seigneurial values in the villager.[55] The enthusiasm with which peasants embraced communal values not only in times of rebellion, but also during the Reformation points to the vitality of this political tradition by the early sixteenth century.[56]

Blickle's thesis has the merit of calling attention to the rise of communalism not just in Switzerland and Germany but almost everywhere in Europe in the wake of the upheavals of the late Middle Ages. Why? The institutions of seigneurialism—serfdom and manorial courts, for example—weakened, leaving villages with broader latitude in governing their internal affairs. By 1500 serfdom was fast becoming archaic and insignificant in most other parts of France and Germany. Many villages also broadened their control over communal resources as manors were broken up, and as lands fell vacant and then were claimed by the commune as common lands. In both France and Germany one finds countless examples of peasant communes successfully contesting lords for control of seigneurial lands between 1400 and 1500. With these common pastures, fields, woods and streams came the legal rights and jurisdictions over them.[57] The middling peasantry, as a larger, wealthier and more autonomous class by 1450, also provided a broad social base of support for communal institutions. Finally, some central authorities bolstered village autonomy as a way of trimming the powers of the local nobility. In France, for example, the Valois monarchs consistently broadened the royal jurisdictions and, in the process, undermined seigneurial courts. Lords were left with less power to contest peasant gains.[58]

One of the consequences of this scholarly interest in the communal tradition is a new appreciation for the breadth and complexity of village politics. What Blickle and other scholars have called attention to is the fact that seigneurial authority and even state authority rested to a large degree on the cooperation of villagers and a sharing of local power. Peasants held ideas about authority that implied a reciprocal relationship between lords and peasants, an exchange of loyalty for protection and support. Rebellions, while important, must be understood within a much broader field of politics at the local level. Passive resistance, bargaining, and litigation had perhaps as important a place in peasant politics by the late sixteenth century as did violent resistance. Rebellions broke out only when negotiation or litigation failed to defuse tensions; they were the last stage in a long and complicated process.[59] One sees these political principles at work in events

as seemingly different as the great French peasant rebellions of the sixteenth century and the quiet, tenacious resistance to taxes in the Holy Roman Empire. In parts of southern Germany peasants were even represented in territorial assemblies.[60]

### Crime, Violence, and Disorder

One can easily romanticize the communal tradition and see in the politics
of the village the lost virtues of the small, personal, and egalitarian community. By doing so, however, one would have to turn a blind eye to the dark
world of communal violence, factionalism, and crime. The world of village politics and violence is admittedly difficult to penetrate for the modern
researcher. The documents often fall silent about what lay behind the
petty disputes and feuds so common in the everyday world of the village.
And yet these disputes bound villagers together every bit as much as did
the moments of communal solidarity. One measure of communal discord
was the incidence of inter-personal violence and crime. The role of violence in the day-to-day life of the late medieval village may never be fully
understood. Studies such as M. T. Lorcin's work on the Lyonnais countryside are rare.[61] More studies exist for the sixteenth century, but by no
means enough. What are some of the patterns that have been found? In
England the evidence is contradictory and ambiguous. Records of crime
and communal violence become more voluminous around the middle of
the sixteenth century. Whether the actual incidence of crime increased, or
whether better records were kept, will never be known. Church and state
courts prosecuted crime more actively after 1550, but they may have simply taken over cases once prosecuted in manorial or seigneurial courts before this time. At the very least, fears of rural violence and disorder seem to
have grown by this time.[62]

The crimes that can be studied often reveal a surprising social dynamic
at work: the prominence of "moral crimes" and crimes against social
laws. Prosecutions for crimes like vagrancy and illegitimacy increased
steadily by the end of the sixteenth century. One of the surprising discoveries is that offenses against property, while perhaps the largest single category of crime, actually declined or, at least, were prosecuted less frequently by the late sixteenth and seventeenth century.[63] Was crime a
weapon of the weak and the poor against the powerful and the wealthy?
Sometimes. Even more unexpected, however, is the frequency with which
village elites resorted to violence against individuals below them in social
rank. Was this violence a way of reinforcing order, status and rank? Certainly the casual way that some nobles commented on the violent punish-

ments they meted out to inferiors suggests that this may have been the case.

One final category of violence deserves special mention: communal disorders and violence. The village was a moral community, after all, and, on occasion, certain social groups or members from the entire commune banded together in acts of violence or disorder to reinforce communal norms. In addition to the peasant rebellion, typically a communal defense against taxes in the sixteenth century, scholars have identified three other types of disorders. First, there were riots or disorders in defense of communal resources such as common fields, pastures, woods or waters. In England enclosure riots became common at the end of the fifteenth century and slowly came to an end only in the seventeenth century. Secondly, there were disorders in defense of community norms involving marriage, sex, and gender roles. The charivari and the local witch hunt—both of them more common after 1560—shared in common this defense of communal social norms. Thirdly, there were protests involving food shortages, prices and marketing practices. This type of communal disorder assumed more importance as market relationships broadened in the late sixteenth and seventeenth centuries.[64]

While it is important to understand the separate dynamics of these disorders one should also begin to see the common threads that united them. One can detect in many of these disorders, for example, a subtle shift towards the end of the sixteenth century. Communal solidarity became more difficult to sustain, as the social structure of the community became more complex, and as ties from beyond the community pulled villagers in conflicting directions. Wealthy tenant farmers were not the only ones to align themselves with elites, moral values, laws, and legal procedures from beyond the local community. Cottagers and smallholders on occasion did as well. To the degree that they did so the village tended to split and opened itself more readily to outside influences.

### Decline

Scholars commonly see the second and third quarters of the sixteenth century as a watershed for the rural commune. The commune provided the basis, the primary unit of political organization, in the German Peasants' War of 1525 and in the peasant rebellions that tested public authority in France in the middle of the century. By 1600 the autonomy of the commune seems to have been increasingly compromised. It is tempting to ascribe its "decline" to the rise of the modern state after this date, but, while one can discern a kernel of truth in this old cliche, the nature of the changes in the public life of the commune bear a more nuanced reading.

Some easy generalizations should first be set aside. Communal solidarity did not automatically wither in the face of expanded state power. The
process by which the early modern states insinuated themselves into communal institutions was exceedingly complex. No "rise and fall" model can
adequately describe the new nature of public power in the village as a result. When the French monarchy broadened its taxing authority in the sixteenth century, for example, it made the village a unit corporately responsible for assessing its own share of royal taxes. The village acquired new
stature, new responsibilities, indeed new authority and power over its inhabitants. In Germany the structures of the small states of the Holy Roman Empire were even more complicated. The state often drew in the village into administrative affairs as much as possible, making it a lower level
of state administration.[65] But this process also had the reciprocal effect of
opening the state to new pressures from below. In some cases petty princes
found that peasants could set strict limits to taxes, labor services, and other
burdens. Peasants in the Holy Roman Empire even had a sympathetic protector in the highest courts of appeals, the Imperial Aulic Court
(Reichshofrat) and Imperial Chamber Court (Reichskammergericht).[66]

The Reformation and the Counter Reformation also required decades
to transform old semi-autonomous parish organizations into more centrally administered units. In Catholic Europe parish organizations continued to overlap with and reinforce communal loyalties even well after the
introduction of Tridentine reforms. The reforms, in fact, seem to have had
an ambiguous initial effect on the village. Family and fraternal loyalties
may have been undermined, but the parish was reinforced and emerged as
even more central in the life of the village than it had been in the Middle
Ages. The parish priest remained a part of the community and supported
communal activities. Village elders continued to occupy parish offices and
administer and maintain church properties in the service of the local community. The church may have begun to bring religious confraternities, the
cults of the saints, pilgrimages, feasts, and festivals more strictly under
church supervision, but this did not mean that these institutions no longer
functioned as supports of communal identity.[67] Even in Protestant regions
the parish remained a central institution supporting the moral and religious order of the village community. In many ways the commune was as
central to the governance, stability, and social order of the village in 1600
as it had been in 1400.

The tenor of village communal life was nevertheless almost everywhere
changing by 1600. The growth in population, broader market relationships and the new demands of the state meant that many problems could

no longer be solved locally. The sheer scale of some of these problems—the reduction of the middling peasantry, the spread of rural poverty, the heavy new burdens of taxes and the alarming indebtedness of many communes—went far beyond the ability of any single village to cope with. It is no surprise then that villagers themselves sought out alliances with elites from beyond their communities, adopted the ideas of reform or even sided with provincial authorities in local conflicts. The village was not yet fully tamed by an overbearing centralized state—that would come later. But the village world was no longer so small, parochial, and isolated as it once had been.

# NOTES

1. Thorner (1968).
2. Sabean (1984).
3. Abel (1980).
4. Le Roy Ladurie (1974).
5. Brenner (1976).
6. Slicher van Bath (1963).
7. Slicher van Bath (1963), 175-78.
8. McCloskey (1975).
9. Bois (1976).
10. Hybel (1989).
11. Abel (1955).
12. McIntosh (1986).
13. Herlihy and Klapisch-Zuber (1985), 106-8.
14. Miller (1991).
15. Lütge (1963).
16. Bois (1976).
17. Miskimin (1975), 32-72.
18. Le Roy Ladurie (1987), 95-230.
19. Neveux (1980).
20. Brown (1982), 60-125.
21. Brenner (1976).
22. De Vries (1974).
23. Sella (1979).
24. Youings (1984), 154-77.
25. Le Roy Ladurie (1987), 239-52.
26. Le Roy Ladurie (1966).
27. Neveux, Jacquart, and Le Roy Ladurie (1975), 250-55.
28. Dewald (1987), 213-68.
29. Hagen (1985).
30. Chayanov (1966).
31. Brunner (1949).
32. Weisser (1976), 55-72.
33. Delumeau (1991), 95-115.
34. Scott (1987).
35. Kriedte (1983).
36. Bechtel (1952), 201-22.
37. Burke (1985).
38. Wrightson (1982), 40-44.
39. Le Roy Ladurie (1987), 199-230.
40. Heitz (1975).

41. Rebel (1983).
42. Robisheaux (1989), 162-67.
43. Sabean (1984).
44. Wrightson and Levine (1979); Jacquart (1974); Robisheaux (1989).
45. Wrightson (1982), 213-14.
46. Robisheaux (1989), 68-91.
47. Delumeau (1991), 96.
48. Wrightson (1982), 136-38.
49. Robisheaux (1989), 153-62.
50. Amussen (1988); Davis (1965), 124-51.
51. Monter (1987), 212-18.
52. Ingram (1987), 301-2.
53. Robisheaux (1989), 68-91.
54. Wiesner (1987).
55. Blickle (1981).
56. Blickle (1992).
57. Blickle (1979).
58. Neveux, Jacquart, and Le Roy Ladurie (1975), 135-38.
59. Blickle, et al., eds. (1980), 298-308.
60. Blickle (1973).
61. Lorcin (1968).
62. Sharpe (1984).
63. Sharpe (1984), 58-60.
64. Wrightson (1982), 173-79; Neveux, Jacquart, and Le Roy Ladurie (1975), 329-53.
65. Wunder (1986), 80-113.
66. Schulze (1980).
67. Neveux, Jacquart, and Le Roy Ladurie (1975), 278-300.

# BIBLIOGRAPHY

*General and Comparative*

Abel, Wilhelm. *Agricultural Fluctuations in Europe: From the Thirteenth to the Twentieth Centuries.* Trans. Olive Ordish. New York, 1980.

Abel, Wilhelm. *Massenarmut und Hungerkrisen im vorindustriellen Europa: Versuch einer Synopsis.* Hamburg, 1974.

Aston, T. H., and C. H. E. Philpin, eds. *The Brenner Debate: Agrarian Class Structure and Economic Development in Pre-Industrial Europe.* Cambridge, 1985.

Blum, Jerome. "The European Village as Community." *Agricultural History* 45 (1971): 157-78.

Boserup, Ester. *The Conditions of Agricultural Growth.* London, 1965.

Braudel, Fernand. *Civilisation matérielle, économie, et capitalisme, XVe-XVIIIe siècle.* 3 vols. Paris, 1979.

Brenner, Robert. "Agrarian Class Structure and Economic Development in Pre-Industrial Europe." *PaP*, no. 70 (1976): 30-75.

Burke, Peter. *Popular Culture in Early Modern Europe.* New York, 1978.

Chayanov, A. V. *The Theory of the Peasant Economy.* Homewood, Ill., 1966.

Duby, George. *Rural Economy and Country Life in the Medieval West.* Columbia, S.C., 1968.

Goody, Jack, Joan Thirsk, and E. P. Thompson, eds. *Family and Inheritance: Rural Society in Western Europe, 1200-1900.* Cambridge, 1976.

Kamen, Henry. *The Iron Century: Social Change in Europe, 1550-1660.* New York, 1971.

Kellenbenz, Hermann. "Rural Industries in the West from the End of the Middle Ages to the Eighteenth Century." In *Essays in European Economic History*, ed. Peter Earle, 45-88. Oxford, 1974.

Kriedte, Peter. *Peasants, Landlords and Merchant Capitalists: Europe and the World Economy, 1500-1800.* Cambridge, 1983.

Kriedte, Peter, Hans Medick, and Jürgen Schlumbohm. *Industrialization before Industrialization: Rural Industry in the Genesis of Capitalism.* Cambridge, 1981.

Le Roy Ladurie, Emmanuel. *Histoire du climat depuis l'an mil.* Paris, 1967.

Le Roy Ladurie, Emmanuel. "L'histoire immobile." *AESC* 29 (1974): 673-92.

Miskimin, Harry. *The Economy of Early Renaissance Europe, 1300-1460.* Cambridge, 1975.

Monter, William. "Protestant Wives, Catholic Saints, and the Devil's Handmaid: Women in the Age of Reformations." In Renate Bridenthal, Claudia Koonz, and Susan Stuard, eds. *Becoming Visible: Women in European History*, 203-19. 2d ed. Boston, 1987.

Parker, William N., and Eric Jones, eds. *European Peasants and their Markets: Essays in Agrarian Economic History.* Princeton, 1975.

Postan, M. M. *Essays on Medieval Agriculture and General Problems of the Medieval Economy.* Cambridge, 1973.

Postan, M. M., ed. *The Cambridge Economic History of Europe.* Vol. 1, *The Agrarian Life of the Middle Ages.* 2d ed. Cambridge, 1966.

Rich, E. E., and C. H. Wilson, eds. *The Cambridge Economic History of Europe.* Vol. 5, *The Economic Organization of Early Modern Europe.* Cambridge, 1978.

Rösener, Werner. *Bauern im Mittelalter.* Munich, 1985.

Shanin, Teodor. "The Nature and Logic of the Peasant Economy." *Journal of Peasant Studies* 1 (1973/74): 63-80, 186-206.
Slicher van Bath, B. H. *The Agrarian History of Western Europe A.D. 500-1850.* Trans. Olive Ordish. New York, 1963.
Thorner, Daniel. "Peasantry." *International Encyclopedia of the Social Sciences*, vol. 11: 503-11. New York, 1968.
Wallerstein, Immanuel. *The Modern World-System: Capitalist Agriculture and the Origins of the European World-Economy in the Sixteenth Century.* New York, 1974.
Wiesner, Merry. "Spinning Out Capital: Women's Work in the Early Modern Economy." In *Becoming Visible: Women in European History*, ed. Renate Bridenthal, Claudia Koonz, and Susan Stuard, 221-49. Boston, 1987.


*Central and Eastern Europe*
Abel, Wilhelm. *Geschichte der deutschen Landwirtschaft vom frühen Mittelalter bis zum 19. Jahrhundert.* Deutsche Agrargeschichte, vol. 2. Stuttgart, 1962.
Abel, Wilhelm. *Strukturen und Krisen der spätmittelalterlichen Wirtschaft.* Quellen und Forschungen zur Agrargeschichte, vol. 32. Stuttgart, 1980.
Abel, Wilhelm. *Die Wüstungen des ausgehenden Mittelalters.* 2d ed. Stuttgart, 1955.
Bader, Karl Siegfried. *Studien zur Rechtsgeschichte des mittelalterlichen Dorfes.* 3 vols. Vienna, 1957-73.
Bechtel, Heinrich. *Wirtschaftsgeschichte Deutschlands. Vom Beginn des 16. bis zum Ende des 18. Jahrhunderts.* Munich, 1952.
Blickle, Peter. *The Communal Reformation: the Quest for Salvation in Sixteenth-Century Germany.* Trans. Thomas Dunlap. Atlantic Highlands, N.J., 1992.
Blickle, Peter. *Deutsche Untertanen. Ein Widerspruch.* Munich, 1980.
Blickle, Peter. *Landschaften im Alten Reich: die staatliche Funktion des gemeinen Mannes in Oberdeutschland.* Munich, 1973.
Blickle, Peter. "Peasant Revolts in the German Empire in the Late Middle Ages." *Social History* 4 (1979): 223-39.
Blickle, Peter. *The Revolution of 1525: The German Peasants' War from a New Perspective.* Trans. Thomas A. Brady, Jr., and H. C. Erik Midelfort. Baltimore, 1981.
Blickle, Peter, et al., eds. *Aufruhr und Empörung? Studien zum bäuerlichen Widerstand in Alten Reich.* Munich, 1980.
Brunner, Otto. *Adeliges Landleben und europäischer Geist: Leben und Werk Wolf Helmhards von Hohberg 1612-1688.* Salzburg, 1949.
Franz, Günther. *Geschichte des deutschen Bauernstandes vom frühen Mittelalter bis zum 19. Jahrhundert.* Deutsche Agrargeschichte, vol. 4. Stuttgart, 1970.
Franz, Günther, ed. *Deutsches Bauerntum im Mittelalter.* WdF, vol. 16. Darmstadt, 1976.
Hagen, William W. "How Mighty the Junkers? Peasant Rents and Seigneurial Profits in Sixteenth-Century Brandenburg." *PaP*, no. 108 (1985): 80-116.
Hahn, Peter-Michael. *Fürstliche Territorialhoheit und lokale Adelsgewalt: Die herrschaftliche Durchdringung des ländlichen Raumes zwischen Elbe und Aller (1300-1700).* Veröffentlichungen der Historischen Kommission zu Berlin, vol. 72. Berlin, 1989.
Harnisch, Hartmut. "Klassenkämpfe der Bauern in der Mark Brandenburg zwischen frühbürgerlichen Revolution und Dreißigjährigem Krieg." *JRG* 5 (1975): 142-72.
Heitz, Gerhard. "Probleme des bäuerlichen Klassenkampfes im Spätfeudalismus." In *Der Bauer im Klassenkampf: Studien zur Geschichte des deutschen Bauernkrieges und der bäuerlichen Klassenkampfe im Spätfeudalismus*, ed. Gerhard Heitz, et al., 513-25. Berlin, 1975.
Hoffmann, Richard C. *Land, Liberties, and Lordship in a Late Medieval Countryside: Agrarian Structures and Change in the Duchy of Wroclaw.* Philadelphia, 1989.
Imhof, Arthur. *Verlorenen Welten: Alltagsbewältigung und unsere Vorfahren—und weshalb wir uns heute so schwer damit tun.* Munich, 1984.

Kiessling, Rolf. *Die Stadt und Ihr Land: Umlandpolitik, Bürgerbesitz und Wirt-schaftsgefüge in Ostschwaben vom 14. bis ins 16. Jahrhundert.* Vienna, 1989.
Kula, Witwold. *An Economic Theory of the Feudal System: Towards a Model of the Polish Economy, 1500-1800.* Trans. Lawrence Garner. London, 1976.
Lütge, Friedrich. *Geschichte der deutschen Agrarverfassung vom frühen Mittelatter bis zum 19. Jahrhundert.* Deutsche Agrargeschichte, vol. 3. Stuttgart, 1963.
Rebel, Hermann. *Peasant Classes: the Bureaucratization of Property and Family Relations Under Early Habsburg Absolutism 1511-1636.* Princeton, 1983.
Robisheaux, Thomas W. *Rural Society and the Search for Order in Early Modern Germany.* Cambridge, 1989.
Rössler, Helmut, ed. *Deutscher Adel.* 2 vols. Deutsche Führungsschichten in der Neuzeit, vols. 1-2. Darmstadt, 1965.
Saarbrucker Arbeitsgruppe. "Die spätmittelalterliche Leibeigenschaft in Oberschwaben." *ZAA* 22 (1974): 9-33.
Sabean, David. *Landbesitz und Gesellschaft am Vorabend des Bauernkrieges: Eine Studie der sozialen Verhältnisse im südlichen Oberschwaben in den Jahren vor 1525.* Quellen und Forschungen zur Agrargeschichte, vol. 26. Stuttgart, 1972.
Sabean, David. *Power in the Blood: Popular Culture and Village Discourse in Early Modern Germany.* Cambridge, 1984.
Schulze, Winfried. *Bäuerlicher Widerstand und feudale Herrschaft in der frühen Neuzeit.* Neuzeit im Aufbau, vol. 6. Stuttgart-Bad Cannstatt, 1980.
Schulze, Winfried. "Herrschaft und Widerstand in der Sicht des 'gemeinen Mannes' im 16./17. Jahrhundert." In *Vom Elend der Handarbeit*, ed. Hans Mommsen and Winfried Schulze, 182-98. Stuttgart, 1981.
Schulze, Winfried, ed. *Aufstände, Revolten, Prozesse: Beiträge zu Bäuerlichen Wider-standsbewegungen im frühneuzeitlichen Europa.* Geschichte und Gesellschaft. Bochumer Historische Studien, vol. 27. Stuttgart, 1983.
Scott, Tom. "Economic Conflict and Co-operation on the Upper Rhine, 1450-1600." In *Politics and Society in Reformation Europe: Essays for Sir Geoffrey Elton on his Sixty-Fifth Birthday*, ed. E. I. Kouri and Tom Scott, 210-31. London, 1987.
Scott, Tom. *Freiburg and the Breisgau: Town-Country Relations in the Age of the Refor-mation and Peasants' War.* Oxford, 1986.
Weiss, Eberhard. "Ergebnisse eines Vergleichs der grundherrschaftlichen Strukturen Deutschlands und Frankreichs vom 13. bis zum Ausgang des 18. Jahrhunderts." *VSWG* 57 (1970): 1-14.
Wunder, Heide. *Die Bäuerliche Gemeinde in Deutschland.* Göttingen, 1986.


*England*
Amussen, Susan Dwyer. *An Ordered Society: Gender and Class in Early Modern England.* London, 1988.
Appleby, Andrew B. *Famine in Tudor and Stuart England.* Stanford, 1978.
Clay, G. C. A. *Economic Expansion and Social Change: England 1500-1700.* Vol. 1, *People, Land and Towns.* Cambridge, 1984.
Hey, D. G. *An English Rural Community: Myddle under the Tudors and Stuarts.* Leicester, 1974.
Hilton, R.H. *The English Peasantry in the Later Middle Ages.* Oxford, 1975.
Hilton, R.H. *Medieval Peasant Movements and the English Rising of 1381.* London, 1973.
Hoskins, W. G. *The Midland Peasant: the Economic and Social History of a Leicestershire Village.* London, 1957.
Howell, Cicely. *Land, Family and Inheritance in Transition: Kibworth Harcourt, 1280-1700.* Cambridge, 1983.
Hybel, Nils. *Crisis or Change: the Concept of Crisis in the Light of Agrarian Structural Re-organization in Late Medieval England.* Copenhagen, 1989.
Ingram, Martin. *Church Courts, Sex and Marriage in England, 1570-1640.* Cambridge, 1987.

Ingram, Martin. "Ridings, Rough Music and the 'Reform of Popular Culture' in Early Modern England." *PaP*, no. 105 (1984): 79-113.

McCloskey, Donald N. "The Persistence of English Common Fields." In *European Peasants and their Markets: Essays in Agrarian Economic History*, ed. William N. Parker and Eric Jones, 3-22. Princeton, 1975.

Macfarlane, Alan. *The Origins of English Individualism: the Family, Property, and Social Transition.* London, 1978.

McFarlane, K. B. *The Nobility of Later Medieval England.* Oxford, 1973.

McIntosh, Marjorie Keniston. *Autonomy and Community: the Royal Manor of Havering, 1200-1500.* Cambridge, 1986.

McIntosh, Marjorie Keniston. *A Community Transformed: the Manor and Liberty of Havering, 1500-1620.* Cambridge, 1991.

Miller, Edward, ed. *The Agrarian History of England and Wales.* Vol. 3, *1348-1500.* Cambridge, 1991.

Sharpe, J. A. *Crime in Early Modern England, 1550-1750.* London, 1984.

Spufford, Margaret. *Contrasting Communities: English Villagers in the Sixteenth and Seventeenth Centuries.* London, 1974.

Stone, Lawrence. *The Crisis of the Aristocracy 1558-1641.* Oxford, 1965.

Tawney, R. H. *The Agrarian Problem in the Sixteenth Century.* New York, 1912.

Thirsk, Joan, ed. *The Agrarian History of England and Wales.* Vol. 4, *1500-1640.* Cambridge, 1967.

Walter, John, and Keith Wrightson. "Dearth and the Social Order in Early Modern England." *PaP*, no. 71 (1976): 22-42.

Wrightson, Keith. *English Society, 1580-1680.* New Brunswick, N.J., 1982.

Wrightson, Keith and David Levine. *Poverty and Piety in an English Village: Terling, 1525-1700.* New York, 1979.

Youings, Joyce. *Sixteenth-Century England.* Harmondsworth, 1984.


*France and the Low Countries*

Bercé, Yves-Marie. *Croquants et Nu-pieds: Les soulèvements paysans en France du XVIe au XIXe siècle.* Paris, 1974.

Bloch, Marc. *French Rural History: an Essay on its Basic Characteristics.* Trans. Janet Sondheimer. Berkeley and Los Angeles, 1966.

Bois, Guy. *Crise du féodalisme: économie rurale et démographie en Normandie orientale du début du XIVe siècle au milieu du XVIe siècle.* Cahiers de la fondation nationale des sciences politiques, no. 202. Paris, 1976.

Bottin, Jacques. *Seigneurs et paysans dan l'ouest de Caux (1540-1661).* Paris, 1983.

Boutruche, Robert. *La crise d'une société: seigneurs et paysans du Bordelais pendant la Guerre de Cent Ans.* Paris, 1947.

Cabourdin, Guy. *Terre et hommes en Lorraine (1550-1635): Toulois et comté de Vaudémont.* 2 vols. Nancy, 1977.

Charbonnier, Pierre. *Une autre France: la seigneurie rurale en Basse Auvergne du XIVe au XVIe siècle.* 2 vols. Clermont-Ferrand, 1980.

Contamine, Philippe, ed. *La noblesse au moyen age XIe-XVe siècles: Essais à la mémoire de Robert Boutruche.* Paris, 1976.

Croix, Alain. *Nantes et le pays nantais au XVIe siècle: Étude démographique.* Paris, 1974.

Davis, Natalie Zemon. *Society and Culture in Early Modern France.* Stanford, 1965.

Day, John. "Crise du féodalisme et conjoncture des prix à la fin du moyen âge." *AESC* 34 (1979): 305-18.

De Vries, Jan. *The Dutch Rural Economy in the Golden Age, 1500-1700.* New Haven, 1974.

Dewald, Jonathan. *Pont-St.-Pierre 1398-1789: Lordship, Community, and Capitalism in Early Modern France.* Berkeley and Los Angeles, 1987.

Fourquin, Guy. *Le campagnes de la région parisienne à la fin du moyen âge.* Paris, 1970.

Goldsmith, James L. "The Agrarian History of Preindustrial France: Where do we go from here?" *JEEH* 13 (1984): 175-99.

Goldsmith, James L. *Les Salers et les d'Escorailles: seigneurs de Haute Auvergne, 1500-1789.* Clermont-Ferrand, 1984.

Guenée, Bernard. *Tribunaux et gens de justice dans le bailliage de Senlis à la fin du moyen âge (vers 1380-vers 1550).* Paris, 1963.

Hoffman, Philip T. "The Economic Theory of Sharecropping in Early Modern France." *JEconH* 44 (1984), 309-19.

Jacquart, Jean. *La crise rurale en Ile-de-France 1550-1670.* Paris, 1974.

Le Roy Ladurie, Emmanuel. *The French Peasantry 1450-1660.* Trans. Alan Sheridan. Berkeley and Los Angeles, 1987.

Le Roy Ladurie, Emmanuel. *Montaillou, village occitan de 1294 à 1324.* Paris, 1975.

Le Roy Ladurie, Emmanuel. *Le paysans de Languedoc.* 2 vols. Paris, 1966.

Lorcin, Marie-Thérèse. *Les campagnes de la région lyonnaise aux XIVe et XVe siècles.* Lyon, 1974.

Lorcin, Marie-Thérèse. "Les paysans et la justice dans la région lyonnaise aux XIVe et XVe siècles." *Moyen âge* (1968): 269-300.

Major, J. Russell. "Noble Income, Inflation, and the Wars of Religion in France." *AHR* 86 (1981), 21-48.

Nicholas, David. *Town and Countryside: Social, Economic, and Political Tensions in Fourteenth-Century Flanders.* Bruges, 1971.

Neveux, Hugues. *Vie et déclin d'une structure économique: Les grains du Cambrésis (fin du XIVe-début du XVIIe siècle).* Civilisations et sociétés, no. 64. Paris, 1980.

Neveux, Hugues, Jean Jacquart, and Emmanuel Le Roy Ladurie. *Histoire de la France rurale.* Vol. 2, *L'âge classique des paysans 1340-1789.* Paris, 1975.

Sivery, G. *Structures agraires et vie rurale dans le Hainaut à la fin du moyen âge.* Lille, 1973.

Slicher van Bath, B. H. "The Rise of Intensive Husbandry in the Low Countries." In *Britain and the Netherlands,* ed. J. S. Bromley and E. H. Kossman, vol. 1:130-53. London, 1960.

Van der Wee, Herman, and E. van Cauwenberghe, eds. *Productivity of Land and Agricultural Innovation in the Low Countries.* Louvain, 1978.

Yver, Jean. *Egalité entre héritiers et exclusion des enfants dotés: essai de géographie coutumière.* Paris, 1966.


*Spain and Italy*
Aymard, A. "La transizione dal feudalesimo al capitalismo." *Storia d'Italia, Annali* 1 (1975), 133-92.

Brown, Judith. *In the Shadow of Florence: Provincial Society in Renaissance Pescia.* New York, 1982.

Burke, Peter. "Southern Italy in the 1590s: Hard Times or Crisis?" In *The European Crisis of the 1590s: Essays in Comparative History,* ed. Peter Clark, 177-90. London, 1985.

Delumeau, Jean. *L'Italie de la Renaissance á la fin du XVIIIe siècle.* 2d ed. Paris, 1991.

Delumeau, Jean. *Vie économique et sociale de Rome dans la seconde moitié du XVIe siècle.* 2 vols. Paris, 1957.

Galasso, Giuseppe. *Economia e società nella Calabria del '500.* Naples, 1967.

Ginzburg, Carlo. *The Cheese and the Worms: the Cosmos of a Sixteenth-Century Miller.* Trans. John A. Tedeschi and Anne Tedeschi. New York, 1980.

Herlihy, David. "Santa Maria Impruneta: A Rural Commune in the Late Middle Ages." In *Florentine Studies: Politics and Society in Renaissance Florence,* ed. Nicolai Rubinstein, 242-76. London, 1968.

Herlihy, David, and Christiane Klapisch-Zuber. *Tuscans and their Families: a Study of the Florentine Catasto of 1427.* New Haven, 1985.

McArdle, Frank. *Altopascio: a Study in Tuscan Rural Society, 1587-1784.* Cambridge, 1978.

Nader, Helen. "Noble Income in Sixteenth-Century Castile: The Case of the Marquises of Mondéjar." *EconHR,* 2d ser., 30 (1977): 412-28.

Reher, David Sven. *Town and Country in Pre-industrial Spain: Cuenca, 1550-1870*. Cambridge, 1990.

Salomon, Noël  *La campagne de nouvelle Castille à la fin du XVIe siècle, d'après les "Relaciones topgráficas"*. Paris, 1964.

Sella, Domenico. *Crisis and Continuity: The Economy of Spanish Lombardy in the Seventeenth Century*. Cambridge, Mass., 1979.

Vassberg, David E. *Land and Society in Golden Age Castile*. Cambridge, 1984.

Vassberg, David E.  "Peasant Communalism and Anti-communal Tendencies in Early Modern Castile." *Journal of Peasant Studies* 7 (1980): 477-91.

Vicens Vives, Jaime, with Jorge Nadal Oller. *An Economic History of Spain*. Trans. Frances M. López-Morillas. Princeton, 1969.

Vilar, Pierre. *La Catalogne dans l'Espagne moderne*. 3 vols. Paris, 1962.

Weisser, Michael R. *The Peasants of the Montes: the Roots of Rural Rebellion in Spain*. Chicago, 1976.

# ECONOMIC CYCLES AND STRUCTURAL CHANGES

Bartolomé Yun
(University of Valladolid)

The years 1400 and 1600—do these two century years frame a single destiny? The first one witnessed a Europe laboring under difficulties, enclosed in itself, but young and vital, about to open up to the world. It was a Europe with an unfavorable trade balance with Asia. The second century year, 1600, reveals a Europe still struggling with the same deficit vis-a-vis Asia. It was, however, a Europe aggressive as never before, quite unlike the Europe of Marco Polo, which had basked in the Great Khan's protection. It was also a Europe whose questing merchants in Asia no longer spoke Italian but Portuguese and Dutch, and who paid for Asian products with the sweat, transmuted into silver, of the Indians of Peru and New Spain.

## 1. TRANSFORMATIONS AND FLUCTUATIONS: FROM CRISIS TO RECOVERY

That this era played a central role in Europe's development, of this there can be no doubt. On its stage the Marxists framed their debate on the "transition from feudalism to capitalism," though beyond this their emphases diverge. While some Marxist scholars have talked about the internal disintegration of feudal society that began with the crisis of serfdom and would give birth to capitalism, others have preferred to focus on the prodigious development of the market that would undermine the economic basis of feudalism.[1]

Clearly, from the vantage point of the rest of the world, this era marked the birth of Europe, but it is by no means so clear just when or how this Europe overcame the plague and its ravages, the destruction and abandonment of the fields, the lack of coordination among fourteenth-century commercial networks—in a phrase, the damage done by the late medieval depression. Some historians, seeing the conditions prior to 1350 and the depression's effects on trade and the cities, have hypothesized about a "Renaissance depression," even though others, notably Carlo M. Cipolla, have adduced solid arguments to the contrary.[2] Still others have spoken of a new correlation between resources, available land, and population, which launched productive activity to new levels, surpassing those of the thirteenth century. On the other hand, Marxists explain this transition through changes in "relations of production" and variations in agrarian models of recovery according to the "social relations of property." In this view, the differences between western Europe and central and eastern Europe, where serfdom was just beginning to develop, date from the fifteenth century. Yet another view, which also emphasizes agrarian aspects, brings to the fore the combination of an increase in labor productivity on the small peasant holding with a decreasing rate of feudal extraction. Different yet, though still within the Marxist framework, is an interpretation which identifies the search for food, including wheat, the nobility's needs for increased incomes as the causes of an overseas expansion that would lead to a new, international division of labor. This change, in turn, would generate capitalist relations in international trade, which established a new path of development for the various regions in the world.[3] Yet, as historians nowadays acknowledge with increasing force, economic recovery from the late medieval depression depended fundamentally on an improvement in living standards among the survivors of the disasters of the fourteenth century, on their easier access to resources, on their capacity to escape the pressures of seigneurial rents that were too inelastic to follow the rapid pace of changes in peasant economies, and on the effects of the crisis on income distribution.[4]

### The Chief Rhythms of Change

Controversies and emphases apart, many things clearly did change between 1400 and 1600, and the old cliché, an "age of change," probably best summarizes the period. One fundamental change concerned the relationships among population, land, and subsistence. Population pressure on the available land had diminished after the Black Death, and although the lords fought energetically to reinstate old forms of peasant subjection, so as to maintain their supplies of labor, nevertheless traditional demesne farming and serfdom were disappearing.[5] In addition, wars and fiscal pressure forced a redrawing of the European commercial map. It is difficult to say how these changes should be evaluated. Are they sufficient to explain the recovery of European economic vitality during the post-depression era? The speediest changes occurred in international trade, especially in northern Europe and especially in the seaborne sector. In the cold northern seas, for example, the Hansa, taking advantage of England's troubles,[6] was developing a trade in bulky commodities for everyday use.

The sustained demand for such goods may ultimately be explained by the late and limited impact of the fourteenth-century disasters on the Baltic region and eastern Europe, as well as by the abundance of products low in labor intensity, such as wood, fur, honey, and—though for the moment of lesser importance—grain.[7] In England, textile production showed renewed vitality, partly because of protection through tariffs, while in Flanders and Brabant a complex symbiosis of town and countryside not only halted the collapse of the cities, but also, by maintaining the urban market, contributed to intensified agriculture and productive specialization in the countryside.[8]

*Patterns of Recovery: Trade*
The patterns of exchange between northern and southern Europe were also changing. While there was a crisis in Champagne, the old nexus of the north-south overland trade, the opening of Gibraltar created new links that, despite disruptions through war, connected the north with the Mediterranean. This new, seaborne connection between Italy and Flanders was supported by a dynamic hinterland, by an Andalusia in the process of resettlement, and by an expansive Portugal. All along this route, new fuel for seaborne trade appeared, such as Iberian and Bordeaux wines, salt from Ibiza, Basque iron, and, little by little, Castilian wool.

In Italy, meanwhile, the capacity to respond to the crisis was equally impressive. Venice and Genoa, their commerce with the east under pressure from Turkish expansion in Asia Minor and the Black Sea region, turned to fight one another, but they also divided up areas of influence and continued their previous searches for substitutes for Asian imports. The Genoese turned westward, to Sicily, Andalusia, and Valencia, where they promoted the cultivation of sugar, a product they had previously imported from Syria and Egypt. They also sought the gold that was brought from Africa by trans-Saharan traders; they financed the Castilian campaigns in the Canary Islands and Africa; they joined in the stubborn Atlantic expansion of both Portugal and Castile; and they tried to monopolize luxury products suited to the taste and palate of refined Renaissance society.[9] To the east, meanwhile, the Venetians adopted an even more aggressive policy. Responding to the Turkish advance, they reinforced their links with the Mamluk kingdom in Egypt and Syria, to which they exported more and more textiles, and diversified the market for spices in view of the fall in the price of pepper. They also tried to revitalize the overland trade with Germany by expanding control over their own hinterland, which controlled the southern approaches to the eastern Alps, and by improving access to

the Alpine passes. They also established ties with the gold and silver producing zones of Austria, Hungary, Serbia, and Bosnia.[10] Meanwhile, Florence witnessed an economic reconversion from the production of high
quality textiles to silk, luxury wool, and artistic production, all items requiring heavy capital investment.[11]

### Patterns of Recovery: Agriculture

At the same time, slower but no less interesting changes were taking place
in the European countryside. Was it a matter of an adjustment between
population and resources that promoted more efficient use of the best
land? This was doubtless one factor, though not sufficient in itself to produce the changes. The leasing, for example, of the former seigneurial demesne to the tenants in exchange for rents, often paid in coin, promoted
the formation of a peasant "aristocracy," which now held larger and more
diverse means of production. These "strong farmers," to use an Irish term,
stood in a good position to take advantage of the times by putting their resources to good use.

Did the rate of seigneurial extraction actually fall? The available data
demonstrate that it did, though it is also apparent that recovery depended,
too, on the development of fiscal systems and on qualitative changes in
rent composition, namely, the movement from natural to monetary rents.
This combination of changes forced the farmers to sell their surplus on the
market as a matter of course and to adapt, in small but decisive ways, their
crops to their need for cash to pay annual rents. As grain prices declined,
the need for cash generated greater diversity of production, always with a
view to the market. Barley grown for beer, for example, expanded in Germany and in many other regions. This happened with hops and grapes,
the latter especially around the port of Bordeaux. The same forces promoted cattle-raising for meat and milk in Germany and Denmark, while in
Italy, Aragon, and Castile, sheep-raising for wool generated the organization of local producers' unions. The production of woad expanded in
southern France and in Thuringia. Much of this change was fueled by urban demand, as in Brabant, where demand from the cities stimulated an intensive and highly commercialized agriculture.[12] Conversely, the same
changes explain the diffusion of industry into the countryside, for which
urban investors devised a new form of organization, the putting-out system. Changes in the structure of demand, high urban wages, and the organizational rigidities imposed by urban guilds all contributed to this process.

*Patterns of Recovery: Intensification of Markets*

The profusion of local and regional markets was both a result of, and a stimulus to, these changes. Some changes pre-dated the Black Death, such as the small fairs whose energy arose not from large-scale trade but from local sales. Some of the market centers thus established later grew prominent through the establishment of wider connections. Such was the case at Toulouse and Aix-en-Provence, which developed ties with Italy, and at Medina del Campo and Chalon-sur-Saône, whose fairs assumed the roles previously performed by those of Champagne. The same happened to the fairs of Brabant and Cologne, and also at Frankfurt am Main and Leipzig, the two cities through which, from the second quarter of the century, English textiles penetrated Germany.[13]

It is easy to see what these changes meant, at least in large terms. They meant intensification of markets, crop diversification, flexibility in making improvements, associations between agriculture and industry capable of mobilizing more peasant effort, and the development of processing activities without the necessity of a highly technical division of labor. These were activities that enlarged the spectrum of available resources and made the rural economy more resistant to the effects of bad harvests. Domestic consumption was still important, but a minimum development of commerce in a small population represented a considerable marginal stimulus to development. It is no surprise that peasants were familiar with money, though they saw it only at certain times of the year.[14]

*The Renaissance: an Age of Depression?*

Was this economy of the Renaissance era one of "depression" or "growth"? Fluctuations in the economic *conjuncture* varied, of course, with local circumstances. A clear case is presented by the Guadalquivir valley, where both tithes and population showed tendencies toward growth from 1430. The same may be said for the Douro valley. It was also logical that Seville grew, and that Lisbon did so as well. Nor is it surprising that, according to some estimates—or better, assumptions—the growth rates in Poland and Germany in 1450 were higher than those in the rest of Europe. Nor that from 1430 growth was visible in Toulouse or Aix-en-Provence. Brittany, whether neutral or allied to England, which controlled maritime trade in the Channel, also experienced an increase in commerce, and there were signs of take-off in some English textile zones. Genoese *conjuncture* exhibits fluctuations through 1433 but, following a period of stagnation, the years from 1444 to 1460 brought expansion. In many Italian cities, true, more capital was invested in land, a logical reaction to commercial instability, but it is also true that "the flight of capital" to the land did not undermine urban markets. The cities, after all, remained home both to artisans and to a nobility eager to consume a variety of products, and their combined consumption stimulated crop production and productivity.[15]

In some areas, on the other hand, agrarian production and population continued to decline or stagnate, as in Normandy up to 1450. English rural population did not show signs of recovery until 1470 and did not grow strongly until some decades later. Even textiles, a leading sector, witnessed important disruptions of its tendencies to growth. The dynamic commerce of Brittany was affected by the vicissitudes of war, while in Brabant and Flanders the unstable *conjuncture* did not change clearly until the end of the fifteenth century. The Genoese trade experienced a profound crisis in the 1460s, while some regions of the Iberian peninsula, like Catalonia, suffered a recession through the 1480s, partly because of internal problems, partly because of displacement by the Genoa-Mallorca-Valencia axis. The demographic decline in Florence is also understandable, as is the comparable decline in the urban populations between 1475 and 1500 of Flanders and Brabant, where the old draperies reached their low point in 1465, not least because of new zones of textile productions in the Netherlands.[16]

It is thus understandable that some historians speak of a "Renaissance depression," for it is difficult to say that these changes stimulated strong recovery in some regions, while in others the recovery was often weak and fragile. One can point to obstacles to recovery, of course, such as war, social disorder, and internal political strife, but the effects are difficult to document. War, for example, could and did stimulate *particular* economic sectors, such as German metallurgy and mining, or the drapery trade of Southwater in England. Fifteenth-century wars were nonetheless very negative forces for *general* growth, for both strategic and contextual reasons. During the first half of the century, the final stages of the Hundred Years War, and the raiding that accompanied it, made north-south trade very unstable. The wars' negative effects were felt even in Brittany, which witnessed a phase of commercial vigor in the fifteenth century, thanks to trade with England.[17] In Normandy the "alternating phases of depression and growth correspond to periods of conflict and peace."[18] Taxes on English wool exports and the Bullion Acts hurt the wool trade with the Low Countries, by now very dependent on English wool.[19] Once this conflict was over, the War of the Roses prolonged the difficulties for the English economy. In Castile, the civil war of 1464-74 brought disorder to a country undergoing economic expansion and also affected its connections with northern Europe. When Flanders was in an expansive phase, civil war in the 1480s and 1490s affected a zone particularly critical for the general recovery of the international economy, for Flanders exported not only its own production but also English textiles by way of the Rhine and through its overland trade with Germany. Examples could be multiplied of how the wars adversely affected trade and manufacturing.

The connection between war and economic growth can be taken a step further. Amid the economic expansion of the sixteenth century, war would continue to be a regular and even more destructive force, though its negative economic impact, however, lessened with the recovery. The key to this change lies perhaps in the fact that until 1460, wars struck in various ways a still fragile and very disarticulated international economy, in which some of the variables still operated quite timidly. While the fiscal systems of the various countries still lay in their infancy, these conflicts provoked monetary devaluation and manipulation, financial disorder, and uncertainty in the use of currency. Although these negative influences on the economy continued into the sixteenth century, during the fifteenth century they were especially harmful, because one of the society's chief problems was the means of payment. Fifteenth-century trade desperately needed sound money, which was in shorter supply than ever before. Devaluation promoted hoarding, because the very high intrinsic value of precious metal exceeded the exchange value of the coinage.[20]

War was not the sole cause of the monetary crisis. The needs of states unable to find ways to increase their revenues also contributed to monetary instability. The economic model already described, and the type of demand that it created, accentuated the problem. In Renaissance societies consumption was ostentatious, ostentation generated social prestige, and prestige brought power. Hence the increase in the marginal tendency toward the consumption of luxury products, Asian cloth, spices, silk, and pearls, all of which assured that, despite import substitution, Europe's balance-of-trade with Asia remained negative. Silver continued to flow from central Europe to Italy and thence to North Africa and Asia.

The discovery from time to time of new ore bodies helped to loosen the tension and increase liquidity, but their output was never sufficient to stem the dominant trend of rising value of metals and falling prices of goods. This challenge had a response, but it was not for the faint-hearted. It was to "create money," and all the instruments of the "commercial revolution" were deployed to this end. Checks, bills of exchange, endorsements, transfers involving debts contracted and later to be paid at a fair in a different money of account—all such devices enhanced the trading system's liquidity by allowing many transactions to be based on only one disbursement of cash. These instruments stimulated trade and favored credit, though not evenly or everywhere. Neither goods nor means of payment circulated in a single homogeneous world. There were circuits, and they were international, while in the national and local and more important, and where "black coin" (i.e., debased coins) was still accepted, these techniques were unknown. This is understandable, for their use required training, diffusion, and time, and they were not common everywhere even in the international realm. At certain levels, therefore, paper did not replace coin, and the supply of money depended on the fluctuating availability of metals, the small and spasmodic supply of precious metals meant that violent fluctuations of credit and crises were inevitable.[21] Thus, while the spread of instruments of credit increased the degree of articulation and interdependence among large economic spaces, it did so in an uneven and incomplete way, for transaction costs and uncertainties in economically strategic regions remained high. This seemed to be especially true in northern and in eastern Europe, largely because of the monetary flows toward the south. This meant that the regions that could potentially supply the rest of Europe with basic goods faced decisive problems of development, such as a chronic unfavorable balance-of-payments much like that between Europe and Asia.

It is easy to exaggerate the speed and extent of the structural changes in the European economy in the early phase of the recovery. Urban wages were rising, to be sure, but we must not exaggerate the positive effect on consumption from a variable that was only a portion of income. The multiplying effect of wage increases remained limited unless urban activities capable of generating a wide spread of wages (even with lower wages) were also developed, that is, unless more of the urban work force engaged their services for wages. In the countryside, the fall of agricultural prices provoked productive readjustments. Opportunities for peasants with a surplus, however, were limited by the growth of urban markets. Despite growth in rural wages, fiscal and seigneurial pressure could sometimes be disproportionate to income and, combined with poor harvests, could severely harm the lowest strata of the rural population. Although the amount of land per capita in the countryside was higher after the Black Death, its use was limited by property rights and by a system of land distribution that did not always encourage the most productive use of the land.

For these reasons, the fifteenth century was a century of poor people, and economic growth and demographic expansion were affected by local combinations of complex variables. The weakness of economic integration, too, meant that the recovery was necessarily unequal and fragile. Any local problem, such as poor harvests or commercial crises, could disrupt the process of economic recovery.

### Patterns of Growth, 1460-1500

Only from the 1460s—the dating is to be taken with caution—does general recovery become perceptible. One reason for recovery, surely, was the maturation of the changes already noted, but perhaps concrete circumstances impinge on these general trends as well. In other words, the recovery rested on a combination of structural elements, some of them quite traditional, which produced stimuli highly localized in time and space.

One new development was the increase in knowledge. The crisis of feudalism culminated in a long-term advance in the stock of knowledge that would erupt in the Renaissance. This improvement exerted a multiplying effect on the advances, mentioned above, in the sphere of means of payment and credit. In the Iberian countries, maritime experience contributed to the improvement in navigation methods, such as the use of the compass, the astrolabe, and navigational maps, and in marine engineering, notably the development of the caravel. Printing served as a vehicle for the transmission of advances and limited the continued propagation of errors in maps.[22] To this accumulation of knowledge we must add what was taking place in Germany, where capital generated in commerce and the increasing value of gold and silver made possible and profitable the application of mining techniques, some of them known long before. Now we can understand why it has been said that it was only at this moment that the West surpassed China in technical development. But it is worth remembering that necessity is the mother of invention.

In this era, too, the Europeans' standard of living was higher, and their diet more regular and diversified, than it had been during the fourteenth century. Wages, whether paid to English artisans or Florentine construction workers and domestic servants, reached their peak in the later fifteenth century.[23] Meanwhile, both the dynamism of trade and fear of social unrest promoted improved provisioning systems in many cities. These changes, in turn, generated higher incomes for peasants involved in transport, industry, and mining, for those who emigrated temporarily in search of a wage, and for those who brought unused land under cultivation. In some regions, it was not a greater volume of earnings, but a greater variety of them and a wider spectrum of available resources which provided domestic economies with greater elasticity and resistance. People ate more meat, drank more beer, or built better wooden houses, not only because of higher incomes (they were sometimes lower, too) or secondary activities, but also because of the availability of land, pastures, and marginal fields (sometimes abandoned by their legitimate owners) where those items could be produced or gathered.[24]

Is it therefore correct to say that seigneurial rents were falling at this time? Some evidence, notably from England and France, suggests that they were.[25] The picture is nonetheless incomplete, because in the fourteenth century new fiefs had been created to pay for services and to support both members of the aristocracy without hereditary rights to land and the increasingly important lesser nobility. The need to maintain the social and political system thus promoted an "extensive growth" of seigneurial income. Kings needed loyal nobles, who had to be compensated, and noble families had to make room for their collateral branches. Then, too, fiscal pressure from the state compounded that from the seigneurs, though both varied greatly with the country or territory. There is still a great deal to be learned about this subject. We need to ask, for example, whether these changes increased per capita payments by the peasants, though the known data suggest that the negative effects may have been less than expected, because these exactions fell upon a more diversified peasant income and a rising marginal productivity of labor. This meant that the creation of new fiefs did not abort the productive capacities of investment and hence the growth in population and overall production. On the other hand, many of these new seigneuries were less burdensome for the peasants than the older ones, because they were based on a high degree of labor productivity on the part of tenants, and some lords were very interested in promoting activities that enriched and diversified peasant income, because they benefitted as well. The lords of Castle Comble in England, for example, were pleased by the development of textiles, and those of Medina de Rioseco and Villalón in Castile promoted rural fairs and markets which, at the cost of a periodic franchise, increased their annual income through their multiplying effects on the economy and population.[26]

These widespread improvements in living conditions help to explain why in this era Europeans married somewhat earlier than before, and why the number of children per family increased from a rate of 1:1 between 1350 and 1410 to a rate of 1:4 between 1440 and 1510.[27] Despite economic fluctuations caused by oscillations in harvests, the elasticity of resources also led to a greater capacity to resist mortality in bad times. Even for England, where enclosures were beginning to affect peasant holdings, it is assumed today that the delay in demographic growth was caused by forces "exogenous" to the system, such as epidemics, rather than by "endogenous" or internal ones.[28]

More particular, because more localized, stimuli to growth also need to be examined. For example, a special role is often attributed to the discovery of the German silver deposits after 1460. New silver did not cause the growth, which had begun before the discoveries, but its steady flow made it possible to take advantage of the profound changes in the European economy and the development of the market. Moreover, the discoveries of silver occurred in a strategic area for economic expansion. A sort of "pre-revolution" of prices[29] hastened the influx of bulky merchandise from the north and the east through the corridors created over the decades. Large numbers of cattle from Galicia and Hungary were driven overland along the network of settlements established in previous years in central Europe.[30] The peasant economies, still agents of the productive process, grew stronger despite the lords' efforts to consolidate their own privileges and rights over the market.[31] The traffic of textiles from Flanders and England through the Rhine corridor was also reinforced, as well were the links through the Rhone valley and the fairs of Lyon and Geneva to the south of France and Catalonia, where the Germans sought woad and saffron. The old Venetian connections to the mainland also grew stronger and more regular, as the export of European textiles to Syria and Egypt increased. The growth in luxury imports—pepper, among others—in the opposite direction, therefore, did not worsen the monetary imbalance, thanks to the mining boom. The central European region certainly profited: German textile, iron, and copper industries expanded, and in Silesia and Bohemia trade with the east quickened.[32]

During this era, therefore, the old commercial network assumed new strength and regularity that affected both commercial and agrarian development. Energies incubated in Europe during decades of transformation were liberated, stimulating an overland traffic that promoted the growth of a dense network of villages, from Silesia to France and from the Alps to Denmark. This network in turn stimulated agrarian activity and led to a *system* of fairs around nuclei such as Lyon—which gained ground on Geneva—Nuremberg, Frankfurt, Vienna, and Krakow.[33] Some of these centers grew into important money markets, whose fairs were scheduled in coordination with one another, and which generated transfers and bills of exchange that regularized traffic and reduced transaction costs. Links established between newer markets and the older fairs of Brabant, Flanders, and later Iberia, began to draw the network's cords together.[34]

The end of the Hundred Years' War (1453) and the pacification of Castile (1474), which now cultivated closer relations with England and Burgundy, regularized the ties between both the Mediterranean and Atlantic trading economies and the north, particularly with the Low Countries and England. Portuguese and Atlantic products, Castilian wool, sugar, muscatel, salt, Vizcayan iron, and the wines from Oporto and Andalusia were exchanged on a more regular basis for art, textiles, and northern fish and fur.[35] In England the expansion of foreign trade began under Henry VII.[36] The exchange between north and south during the second half of the fifteenth century also stimulated the intermediate trading zones, such as ports of the Cantabrian Sea and the Bay of Biscay, Brittany, and Normandy. The Baltic trade and the east-west links did the same for intermediate continental zones, such as the Low Countries and the cattle-raising zones in Denmark and Schleswig-Holstein. This quickening trade, which exchanged luxury and bulk goods from the south for bulk goods from the north, brings the story to the year 1492 and the great leaps over the oceans to America and India.

### The Reality of General Economic Growth

There is no reason, therefore, to doubt the reality of general economic growth during the later fifteenth century. The new complexity of interrelated structural change and economic cycles becomes evident already during the fifteenth century. The main structural changes had their roots in a crisis of serfdom since the late thirteenth century, and they signalled the growing importance of market relations. These crises did not, however, become so intense as to shape the specific evolutions of the various countries and regions. We do not know, for example, whether the need for more land drove the Portuguese and Castilians out into the Atlantic, and although it can be shown that the Iberian expansion followed a series of poor harvests, the long-term stability of fifteenth-century grain prices in the Iberian kingdoms makes us cautious about connecting the Iberian expansion with a need for more wheat.[37] Some domestic facts, to be sure, such as the need for bullion and the consumption of goods of elastic demand, do indicate a pressure for expansion, but the converse is not true, for maritime expansion does not, on the whole, serve as the motor of economic recovery. The truth seems to be that the growth of *overland* trade, which resulted from deeper economic transformations, helped to form a positive context for international maritime trade. This overland commerce not only possessed a greater volume than it had in 1300, but also seemed to penetrate the local economies of thousands of Europeans to a much greater degree than ever before.

The significance of both the market and the availability of means of payment to the recovery was linked to social and economic changes. Contrary to the discussions among Marxist historians during the 1950s, mercantile development and the crisis of social relations did not interact in a single direction. What emerged from the crisis, rather, does not seem to have been a new kind of division of labor, not even in regions where serfdom gained terrain. In eastern Europe, for example, in 1500 serfdom was not yet important.

## 2. FROM GROWTH TO "CRISIS" IN THE SIXTEENTH CENTURY— TOWARD A POLARIZED ECONOMY?

The growth of population made itself felt during the phase of expansion. Between 1500 and 1600 European population increased from around 80 to around 100 million. In many areas, such as southern Europe, France, and Germany, the pace of growth was rapid until 1560. Cities grew even faster, and urbanization rates for 1600 were higher than in 1500. Production and population entered into an expansive spiral, which extended settlement in many regions. While *polders* were reclaimed from the sea in the Low Countries, for example, vast expanses of land were being settled in Russia, and in the Castilian and French countryside, forests receded before wheat. Following the intercyclical recession of the 1550s,[38] oceanic expansion provided spices and other products as well as more bulky goods (fur, indigo, cochineal). European capital stock and profits increased, though with different trajectories in different countries. In addition, the swelling river of American silver more than made good the German mines' exhaustion after 1530 and helped to maintain a regular monetary supply.[39]

During the sixteenth century, even more so than in the fifteenth, wars and their destruction affected economic development. Yet, even though larger wars required greater fiscal efforts, war's effects on expanding economies were not necessarily greater than before. In France, for example, it is estimated that fiscal pressure on agrarian production decreased from 1482 to 1547,[40] just as it did in Castile between 1520 and 1560. With more settled international circuits, mounting rural population and production, and a variety of trade corridors to choose from, the international commercial network had become more flexible, and the effects of conflicts in some areas could be compensated for by development in others.

*Rhythms of Sixteenth-Century Economies*

It is possible to delineate general phases in the economic history of sixteenth-century Europe. Until the 1530s, probably, there was growth in
every sense of the word. Despite increases in population, cities, and monetary circulation, prices reckoned in silver remained stable through the first
decades of the sixteenth century, because agrarian production increased
faster than the number of mouths to feed.[41] Moreover, the increase of
monetary stock during a moderate growth-phase of cereal prices activated
demands for non-primary consumption and industrial goods.

How should we interpret this economic growth? Advocates of the
quantity theory of money used to hold that the increasing amount of currency in circulation drove prices upward and generated a growth of profits, since wages did not rise in proportion.[42] Today, however, the matter
appears more complex. It has been noted that inflation was more accentuated in basic products, such as wheat, than in other commodities. Does
this rebut the quantitative theory of prices, or does it rather refine that
theory in the sense that the effects of an increase in monetary stock were
more pronounced where demand was least elastic, as in grain? It has been
also held that in Spain, the first stop for imported precious metals after
1520, inflation was more accentuated in relative terms in the first half of
the century, when the growth of monetary circulation had just begun, than
later, when bullion flowed more plentifully.[43] If one assumes, on the other
hand, a smaller initial stock of money, does it not follow that even slight
additions would have a relatively great impact on prices? In any case, did
the inflation not gain added impulses from population growth, from the
plowing of marginal fields placed under cultivation at higher costs, and
from urbanization itself, which implies a division of labor and faster monetary circulation?[44] Finally, so far as the accumulation of profits is concerned, it has been correctly stated that profits cannot be determined
through the analysis of prices and wages alone, for by this time profit had
other components ranging from colonial pillage to generalized speculation.[45]

*"World" Economy and Regional Economies*

A broader question concerns the relationship of the economic growth to
the formation of a world economy, divided between "core" and "periphery," in which capitalist relations fostered the spread of serfdom in eastern
Europe and the development of industry in northwestern Europe. Did this
system of production and exchange actually consist, as has been argued, of
a series of Western "world-economies" aligned on the axis Venice-Ant-

werp-Genoa-Amsterdam?[46] Even critics of these ideas have recognized the sixteenth-century tendencies toward concentration and polarization, and it is clear that the Antwerp-based commercial network produced very positive effects on the economy of the Low Countries and the regions linked to it, such as England, northern France, and Germany.

Antwerp's chance came during the Italian Wars, and the first Portuguese ships arrived shortly after 1500, laden with spices, pepper and gold. Their purveyors sought copper and silver, which the Fuggers and other firms brought from southern Germany, where an important center of manufacturing had arisen based on Augsburg and Nuremberg, thanks to the growth of metallurgy and fustian-weaving. At Antwerp, too, the English sold their draperies; Castilian wool, the type most useful in the new textiles, was concentrated; Hanseatic and other northern ships sold Baltic wood, wheat, and dried-and-salted fish; and cattle were brought from eastern and central Europe, Denmark, and northern Germany. Antwerp thus rose on a combination of luxury products and bulky commodities for everyday use.

From the 1530s onward, this new pattern was affected by many factors. As the German mines played out, and religious wars created instability, the international trading network adapted to the changes. Most importantly, American silver erupted onto the market, flowing abundantly by 1545, and becoming by 1560 a veritable flood. The Genoese were already active in Spanish trade and finance, and the Medina del Campo-Antwerp axis, speeded Spanish development and the expansion of cloth and luxury goods from Flanders, England, northern France in Castile. Meanwhile, demand for cereals, fish, fur, and wood from eastern Europe increased to the benefit of the Dutch, especially as in the later sixteenth century overland transportation became more difficult.

Despite the special roles of particular regions in the general European economy and the shifts in the pattern of urban trading centers, we must remember that each land and country also possessed its own potential for growth. For example, even as Portuguese competition and the Germans' shift to Antwerp damaged its pepper trade, Venice advanced in the rapidly growing wool industry.[47] The Genoese naval industry grew stronger, as did its commercial networks in both the Mediterranean basin and northern Europe. Raw materials obtained by the Genoese in Castile, and also from the circuits of the American economy by way of Seville, fed the industries of the area. At Florence, despite difficulties at the beginning of the century, and although the city did not regain its thirteenth-century levels, industrial and demographic growth mounted to a new peak in 1560. Italy accumulated capital and invested in more promising sectors.[48] This intensification of commercial links is especially perceptible at Lyon, the headquarters of Italian lenders to the king of France, where the silk and the printing industries developed vigorously.[49] In Germany, many local iron and textile industries were expanding, and the same is true for Bohemia, Silesia, and Moravia.

All over Europe, the structure of demand, conditioned both by a highly concentrated distribution of income and by the increase in commercial profits, stimulated the manufactures. The effects are clearest in the Low Countries, but they also can be seen in the high-quality cloth industry in Italy and at Toledo, Granada, Segovia, and Lyon, as well as in textile production at Rouen and other French centers. Local accumulation stimulated through the building of palaces, churches, and cathedrals, and it benefitted from the explosive growth of population in some cities, notably Seville, London, and Naples.

The larger picture clearly shows the plurality of economic nuclei and the importance of economic circuits independent of international economic relations. Indeed, it displays an economic system which operated much like a group of interconnected vessels, in which, as the water rises and falls in the system, no single vessel suffers a decline. It is difficult to summarize this growth solely from the perspective that sees the chief outcome as the economic dependency of some regions on others.[50] The crisis of 1557, for example, and the ensuing struggle in the Low Countries, which have been seen as a "turning point" in the construction of such a system of dependency,[51] in fact display a complex picture of consequences. Antwerp certainly faced new problems; English trade was also affected; and the export of Castilian wool to the north was reduced. But it is not accurate to speak of a general "peripheralization," that is, marginalization, of the Mediterranean countries, as a few examples will show. These were the golden years for Segovian textiles and for a Milanese economy developing under Spanish rule. Florence benefitted from Castilian wool flowing more easily. Venice continued the expansion of its textile manufactures and developed other sectors such as glass-making, printing and soap-making.[52]

Nor does the trade with eastern Europe fit the model of "peripheralization," in which the terms of trade are negative for countries producing raw materials. On the contrary, the price of the wheat exported by eastern Europeans increased faster than that of textiles they bought, giving them a quite positive balance-of-trade with western Europe.[53] From this, as from the Mediterranean experience, we may conclude that the key to any one area's performance lay not in international economic relation alone but also—perhaps even more—in the local economy that shaped each country's involvement in long-distance trade. Indeed, the relationship of economic dependency did not operate then as it does today, for during this era the Polish peasants multiplied their income three or four times, and internal trade appears to have been more important than the export trade.[54] In Poland, and also in Bohemia, the cities were also growing, and they continued to do so until the downturn of the late sixteenth and early seventeenth century.[55]

*Sixteenth-Century Agriculture: Rents and Intensification of Cultivation*
Questions of interpretation do not end here, for students of agrarian trends have tried to explain both the initial expansion and the problems that arose during the second half of the sixteenth century. Emmanuel Le Roy Ladurie, for example, has proposed a model of growth and crisis based on population increase and pressure for food production in agrarian economies with low technical development. In his view, the tension between population, on the one hand, and available land and resources, on the other, generated a Malthusian ceiling capable of reversing expansion once the seventeenth century was well advanced. Another, more refined model, which to some degree contradicts Le Roy Ladurie's, arises from Guy Bois' interpretation of the evolution of seigneurial rent: a decrease in the extraction rate would favor expansion, but it would end by creating the conditions for the crisis, since a decrease in the real value of the rights of landlords would bring a reaction from them precisely at the moment in which the marginal productivity of peasant holdings was decreasing.[56] A third explanation has been proposed by Robert Brenner, who argues that the concentration of property in England generated accumulation on a scale proper to a capitalist agriculture, that is, an agriculture capable of breaking the limits of the pre-industrial economies that persisted on the continent. The key, in his view, lay in the different regimes of property relations in the various countries.[57] Such general explanations have their critics, most of whom focus on their character as closed models with limited explanatory capacity for Europe as a whole.[58]

Can the realities of economic growth and decline possibly be fitted into such formulas? On the one hand, the stifling of expansion is visible everywhere. Whereas down to 1530 much of the agricultural growth arose from bringing abandoned land under the plow, by 1560 the expansion of cultivation was touching marginal lands of decreasing efficiency. On the other hand, we also have examples in which pressures of this kind were overcome by means of an intensification of labor which increased efficiency and diversified agriculture. This was the case in the Low Countries, where the importation of eastern wheat also promoted more specialized crops and more complex systems of rotation.[59] We know, too, that there was a progressive fall of wages, and that it brought, first, a reduction of costs in zones of large holdings, and later, serious problems in peasant economies that depended on wage labor, such as those of France and England. There remains, however, as Wilhelm Abel pointed out, a need for more careful study, given the complexity of wages, the frequency of payment in kind, and the fact that wages constituted but one portion of the family budget.[60]

Beyond all variations from region to region, we can see a pattern of low rents favoring expanded production during the early sixteenth century, giving way to higher rents and more risky expansion during the century's later decades. In England, for example, the extraction of income from the land increased faster than the price of wheat.[61] It is worth remembering, however, the elasticity of peasant holdings and the capacity of peasants to engage in transport, rural industry, and diverse complementary activities. In England, it seems, high rents precisely did not destroy the possibilities for productive and demographic growth.

The growing European trend toward wheat farming is no less clear and explainable, for high prices stimulated it on large holdings, and the need for food made it inevitable on small ones. In many areas, however, the cost of labor, the availability of capital for significant investments, and the market favored not grain but olives, woad, silk, and even such labor-intensive crops as grapes. And there were also zones such as Switzerland, where cattle raising expanded thanks to the availability of French wheat and the abundance of meadows.[62]

In England the correlation between large-scale enclosures and pasture and crop rotation, the harbingers of intensive capitalist agriculture, cannot be denied. The link, however, does not seem to have been a universal one, for it is absent in another area of concentration of property, the large estates of Andalusia, where exploitation systems remained extensive rather than intensive.[63] At the same time, important initiatives like sugar cane farming by the Duke of Gandia, or the investment by the Duke of Ferrara to promote the mulberry in Naples, cast doubts on the idea of a general disinvestment by a southern European nobility, who are often supposed to have been interested in rents alone rather than in profits.

### Regional Variation: a Dominant Theme

We must conclude, therefore, that European "agrarian systems" and the *conjunctures* they generated cannot be reduced to a single evolution.[64] The large-scale theories cited at the outset, therefore, may supply lines of analysis and models for contrasts, but they cannot be accepted as adequate explanations for all of Europe. Similar symptoms and trends developed, it is true, in different parts of Europe, but the reactions to them were diverse. The various forms of economic development must thus be seen products of more concrete factors and of historical contingencies. Among such factors, special emphasis should be given to institutions, to political structures, and to the role of each area in the whole system. A look at some examples will show how strikingly diverse were the regional variations of this process.

### Economic Diversity in Late Sixteenth-Century Europe

In Mediterranean Europe after about 1580, there were symptoms of fatigue in the predominantly extensive agriculture that had to feed overcrowded cities. The struggle for land and wheat—especially scarce when Venice lacked access to Turkish grain—soon appeared.[65] Industry also failed to respond positively to the difficulties of the period, for reasons which are not easy to fathom.

Castile presents the classic case of the struggle to overcome the forces that were promoting stagnation. In contemporary Castile, ecclesiastical institutions and the indebted aristocracy strove against the depreciation of some components of their income, often through quite traditional ways. Castile's service aristocracy had huge expenses that legitimated it socially and helped to support the king and to reproduce a social order. These were expenses covered by credit systems which, combined with entailments (*mayorazgos*) and royal pensions in recognition of services, kept noble families from ruin. Such conditions encouraged heads of lineages to pursue political advancement rather than to invest in production. Something similar happened with the large ecclesiastical properties, which grew large enough to be capable of strangling peasant economies in many regions. The state, burdened by great military expenditures, was also unable to break the social compromises on which it rested or to stem the urban oligarchies' rapid shift toward a rentier existence, and it therefore gradually lost much of its economic basis. The ill effects of this deterioration were felt by peasants cultivating common land auctioned by the Crown in 1580. They were also felt by artisans who paid taxes on basic goods—such as the *servicio de millones*. Castile's overall tax burden was not higher in proportion to the gross national product than those of other countries, but taxes of this kind increased the costs of manufacturing and made it difficult or impossible to enlarge the units of production. The central problem in the manufacturing sector was not only that wages were high, as Earl J. Hamilton pointed out long ago,[66] but that the lack of agrarian improvements and the concentration of taxes on the urban economies raised the prices of basic goods, thereby reducing both the demand for industrial products and the craftsmen's profit margins. This already unfavorable situation was worsened by the flight of merchant capital from industrial investment, which prevented its owners from taking advantage of rural poverty by developing a putting-out system similar to, say, that of northern Germany. Also, the inflation of the prices of Castilian grain, meat, wine, and oil did not bring a proportional rise in the peasants' margin of profit, because it masked both a drainage of income to the State as well as a concentration of land among rentier classes. From around 1580-90 the urban crisis exacerbated difficulties in the countryside by depriving many small producers of markets and by limiting their spectrum of resources. With such rigid productive and social structures, the great wave of silver imports between 1560 and 1600 did not inject dynamism into Castilian production. After 1600, when prices reckoned in silver stopped climbing, because of the cessation of urban growth and the demographic crisis—important components according to some critics of the quantitative theory[67]—profit expectations clouded over completely, and the tempo of production slowed in both agriculture and industry.

Italy resisted comparable forces better than Spain did, not least because of Genoese profits from the Iberian world and from the extraction of raw materials, which were increased by the second Atlantic cycle of expansion based on the development of the plantation economy. Naples was chastened by Habsburg fiscal pressure, and its industrial development was limited by that process, but northern Italy resisted decline more successfully. The production of luxury goods benefitted from income concentration and from the free-spending ways of baroque courts. Florentine and Venetian industries became models of reconversion to silk cloth, while Milan virtually monopolized the production of a super-luxury good, namely, rich golden brocades.[68] The specialized nature of these profitable activities, of course, limited its capacity to generate employment, especially when artisans wrapped themselves in their guild privileges, and mercantile savings, facing such obstacles, were turned to luxury spending rather than to investment. Italy did resist decline, and it is understandable that such resistance has been attributed to its trade rather than to its agriculture, whose profitability, at least in the south, had been diminishing since the late six-teenth century.[69] This prosperity was nevertheless the economic swan song of the Renaissance, and it pointed toward a bleaker Baroque era. North-ern European competition did contribute to Italy's eventual decline, but the key to Italy's fate lay in the development of the political and social structures that shaped its economies.[70]

Eastern Europe's most salient characteristic, the evolution toward serf-dom, is usually associated by the economic historians with the westward export of grain. The process was nonetheless very complex, and it varied according to regions. The export of cereals, considered in itself, grew a great deal, though the figures do not seem to be high with respect to pro-duction as a whole, and nowadays the importance of the internal market tends to loom larger than it formerly did.[71] It is also evident that the con-crete impact of the market on the productive structures was related to the high degree of political immunity and decision-making capacity, which the lords had achieved in the preceding phase. It was this juridical, political, and social context that allowed Polish nobles to monopolize privileges of the market, which in turn allowed them to control the country's main source of income and to enlarge their domains. In a similar way, the Hun-garian gentry was able to exercise preferential rights over the sale of the peasants' produce, with similar effects. Serfdom, then, was a direct conse-quence of this process, though it was imposed in individual territories in different ways and with different chronologies. In Russia, for example, the process took place much later, while in Bohemia it gathered force only in the second half of the seventeenth century.[72]

In the middle run, of course, the consequences for eastern European so-ciety were less drastic than they seem in the long view. The rise of the ex-port economies and serfdom did not mean the immediate ruin of local in-dustries or of the cities. Regions such as Bohemia, Moravia, and Silesia, apart from having mineral deposits, developed their export industries to-ward the east, becoming "a small west within" the east,[73] which also ex-plains the survival, except in Turkish-controlled Hungary, of relatively in-tact urban networks during the sixteenth century. The fragility of the cities seems to have rested on local antagonism to German merchants and on the political weakness of the burghers, and in the longer run it led to the de-cline of urbanization in both Poland and Bohemia by the end of the six-teenth century.[74]

Farther westward, in France, Germany, and Switzerland, we find a di-versity of situations not inconsistent with agrarian, mining, industrial, and demographic expansion. As in many other regions, in the Hurepeix and in

Languedoc the fragmentation of peasant property complemented the enlargement of both noble property and of a "bourgeoisie" that found in the "venality of offices" one of its chief areas for investment. Burdened by financial problems, the aristocracy increased pressure on rents, and its success helped to strangle peasant economies already in decline. All of this happened within a social system which had limited possibilities for economic development, and in which large-scale property did not reorient its operations to the market. Instead, the system encouraged forms of land transfer that favored a "peasant aristocracy" able to resist the pressure of market forces, but that would in the long run promote radical changes in forms of cultivation.[75]

These structures were tested during the Religious Wars. Among war's diverse effects, crucial trading corridors like that of the Rhone below Lyon, were burdened by tolls. War shattered some basic components of the expansion by pushing rural communities into debt, by forcing the sale of common land, and by increasing the expropriation of the peasantry. It also accelerated both the spread of sharecropping (*metayage*) and the dependence of the peasantry on the lords and the rural bourgeoisie.[76] Much of the energy and strength of peasant exploitation of lands, so important to the expansion of this zone between north and south, especially since 1460, was now diminished. There was also in this region no alternative agrarian model based on the enclosed large holding.

Unlike Spain, however, France possessed a powerful internal market based on many small nodules, which stimulated "economic creativity."[77] With an urban structure much less damaged by the fiscal system than Castile's was, many French peasants retained a high degree of elasticity in their operations, largely because of auxiliary activities promoted by the mercantile development, or cash-cropping for the cities. This was especially the case of that "peasant aristocracy" that had to pay higher taxes, but had the means and resources to do so. Given these circumstances, it is no surprise that once the French Religious Wars ended, tithe and baptism registers for many French regions began to show an upward tendency of population that would continue during the first decades of the seventeenth century. The Religious Wars dealt one more shock to a French agricultural economy that was hampered by major limitations even though it was supported by a model of commercial and urban development distinct from that of the Mediterranean, thanks in part to the process of diversification.[78]

In western Germany growth continued, despite the south's loss of economic leadership after the 1530's, until the first decades of the seventeenth century; in the north, growth rested on the strength of Baltic trade; and in the center, it accompanied the development of the linen industry that took advantage of the commercial network around Frankfurt, Leipzig, and Nuremberg. In western Germany, Denmark, and other areas, the demand of urban markets in the Low Countries also helped to stimulate profits.

The English case has been frequently presented as a counter-example to the general European trend. Revisions of property rights and enclosures, true, appear most vigorously there, though they were not uniquely English, and the same may be said for the formation of large properties. Nevertheless, the concentration of property that eroded communal practices in England was achieved by a "gentry" and an "aristocracy" which, despite public offices and royal patronage, could not deploy for the solution of its problems a bureaucratic and fiscal apparatus as well developed as those of France or Castile. In England occurred the crudest form of the struggle for economic efficiency to the detriment of social peace, as the English landlords developed a more efficient combination of cattle-raising and farming against a background of social mobility, and they gradually overcame the prevailing insecurity through investment and improvements in productivity, not only in agriculture, but also in mining and commerce.[79] In this dynamic context, the expansion of the urban market and the growth of London exerted, despite some maladjustments, a positive effect on the activities of both the largest proprietors and the most humble peasants, who were forced to resort to auxiliary activities as investment moved from the land to commerce and industry. The troubles of the peasant economy, because of demographic pressure and the increase in enclosures, meant a stimulus for industrial development. Although the concept of an "early Industrial Revolution," once advanced by John U. Neff, has given way to a more nuanced picture today, it is clear that the period from 1550 to 1650 witnessed important advances in England.[80] Among these we may highlight the development of rural industry and, in particular, of the "new draperies." Rural production implied lower wage costs, and it was less dependent on agricultural surpluses, because the division of labor between agriculture and industry was almost nonexistent. This picture differed dramatically from that of Italy or Spain, which would soon see their markets overstocked with light and cheap textiles, suitable for warm southern climates.

It is sometimes argued that efficiency in production and the establishment of the link between agriculture and industry were exclusively the consequences of large holdings, although this proposition has been criticized even for England, and the Low Countries constitutes a major counter-example. Commercial agriculture in the Low Countries had continued its progress and diversification to the extent required by demographic pressure and urban expansion and permitted by grain imports from the Baltic. More complicated crop rotations combined with mixed farming and the cultivation of forage crops, in part because in the Low Countries the communal regulation of agriculture was of limited importance.[81] Industrial development spread, thanks to the size of the market and to the region's central position in intercontinental-scale commercial networks. All of this promoted a diversification of activities and allowed an increase in wages, paralleling the rise in prices, without strangling profits and economic growth.[82] The rebellion against Spain and the independence of the northern Netherlands proved to be decisive in this situation, though to understand the revolt's importance we must turn back to the general context.

### The Later Sixteenth-Century: an Era of New Problems

It is clear that, despite regional variations, from the last quarter of the sixteenth century the whole European economy faced new problems. The combination of agrarian difficulties with epidemics put at risk what had been an expansive rhythm of the economy and demographic growth. It is no surprise that in many areas positive and negative population-control mechanisms were activated. The spectrum of available productive resources was diminished by the fiscal development of the State, by commercial problems, and by pressure from landlords. Peasant debt was greater, and crucial variables of living standard, such as meat consumption, seem to have decreased from fifteenth-century levels.[83] These changes also affected the market for commercial products. A wider disparity in income implied a steady demand for luxury products appropriate to baroque courts, such as silks, golden brocades, and art objects. This movement, as already noted, formed one of the keys to Italy's resistance to economic decline, but the same phenomenon, combined with wheat prices growing faster than those of industrial products, reduced the growth rate of the effective demand for more popular manufactured items, especially ordinary textiles. In these market conditions, and given the growing degree of international economic integration, those countries able to achieve faster adaptation and to defend their markets more efficiently, had possibilities for success, and the larger picture came to present a panorama quite different from that of polynuclear growth after 1450. The possibilities for success were dependent on many factors, including political and administrative structures, the availability of resources, the organization of production and—not least—the course of unforeseeable events and the denouement of international tensions.

It is accepted today that a key event in this process was the revolt of the Netherlands that began in the 1560s. The subsequent independence of the United Provinces in the north, even though it produced short-term economic revival in other areas, also fostered in the long term the formation of a more polarized model of growth. The conflict itself accelerated the process of "financial revolution" initiated in Holland, which ended by putting in the hands of such a state (or, in the words of Elliott, an "anti-state" by the standards of that time) a great amount of resources serving the mercantile interests that constituted the articulating nucleus of this society.[84] The religious conflict also generated a mainly Protestant emigration of many southern artisans and merchants, who, after stimulating the economy of some German areas, strengthened the economic basis of the United Provinces. By 1590 one can see converging in this area a variety of positive reactions to the challenges of the late sixteenth century: efficient and market-oriented agrarian structures; mercantile development, nurtured in the previous stage and now completed by a parallel development of finance and the public treasury; and the creation of an industrial base. This convergence configured an economic power more complex than those of the cities or city-states that had been predominant in the Low Countries in earlier times, and it did so at a time when other parts of the interconnected system proved incapable of solving a bundle of similar problems, despite the interaction among the system's parts.[85] This achievement formed the economic basis of the Dutch Golden Age in the seventeenth century.

During the same era the Hispano-Portuguese empire, by contrast, faced obstacles to its internal economic development, both in Spain and in Portugal (both kingdoms were under Habsburg rule from 1580 to 1640). It also faced the insufficiencies of a bureaucratic and colonial rule which had become a source of profit for bureaucrats and aristocrats alike, and whose operations illustrate the contemporary motto, "office as private profit [oficio como beneficio]."

The inland European zones between the Pyrenees and the Elbe had preserved a great deal of their economic potential, but they were at a comparative disadvantage for maintaining their mid-term growth, because of a position more displaced from the international routes which, with the development of the plantation economies, were turning more and more toward Europe's Atlantic margin. In addition, by 1590 the Dutch, now well established in the Mediterranean basin, began by stages to gain the upper hand in their struggle with the Hansa over control of the trade of the Baltic, where they had long been active.

England, too, was becoming a country with enormous potential, thanks to its agrarian, institutional, and social development. This led to conflicts but also to revolutions that would, in the long term, further liberate productive energies that would consolidate in the eighteenth century. Thus, in the overall economic picture, even though England and the Netherlands had blockages and other problems, it was in these two European countries that the different variables (prices, population, agrarian production, and the diffusion of more efficient techniques) showed the clearest expansive tendency during the first half of the seventeenth century.

### 3. EARLY MODERN ECONOMIES: PATTERNS AND CONCEPTS

Looking back from 1600, one can see that although many things had remained the same since 1400, others had changed, sometimes dramatically. For example, Europe continued to run a trade deficit with Asia despite the immense expansion of its Asian trade. This trade, though facilitated by military superiority, was still a matter of partnership rather than of commercial subordination of Asia to Europe. Entirely new, on the other hand, was the European trade with the Americas, where the control of raw materials gradually expanded the trade in bulky goods that would end by transforming the productive structures of both Europe and the Americas. Overall, this era saw the laying of bases for commercial relations and for a more intense international division of labor. This process achieved greater or lesser consolidation, depending on the degree of integration of internal markets in each region—a decisive and frequently overlooked element that explains the capacity of international trade for penetrating the social and economic web of different countries.

More importantly, an examination of the structural changes and economic fluctuations that did occur between 1400 and 1600 gives rise to questions that affect the validity of our indices of *conjuncture*, our conceptual frameworks, and our evaluation of the phases of crisis and recovery. From 1530 to 1580 there was a clear expansive rhythm for prices, population, and production, despite a decline in some areas of per capita wealth and of elasticity of resources. This situation seems to meet the criteria for what we consider today as "growth." Yet, the fact that an expansive phase also brought an increase in poverty and mendicancy challenges our tendency to assume an automatic connection between economic growth and social progress. The dichotomy of expansion and recession, with which we normally chart economic cycles today, does not seem to fit a situation such as that of fifteenth-century Europe, in which per capita wealth was high and technical advances were beginning to accumulate. We need not be surprised, on the other hand, that the fifteenth-century monetary shortage has been interpreted in contradictory ways, both as a symptom of crisis and as the sign of a expanding market's growing need for money. Finally, we must ask whether the questions have been posed correctly in debates which pit the international market against internal class relations to explain, for example, the growth of serfdom in eastern Europe during an age of general economic expansion. Indeed, might we not say that the real problem is to isolate for purposes of evaluation one single factor in a process which involves many factors?

Translated by Carlos Aguirre

# NOTES

1. See the discussion that followed Maurice Dobb, *Studies in the Development of Capitalism* (London, 1946), and the debate between Paul M. Sweezy, "A Critique," and Maurice Dobb, "A Reply," both in *Science and Society* 19 (1950).
2. Cipolla (1949); Lopez and Miskimin (1961/62); Cipolla, Lopez, and Miskimin (1964).
3. Summaries of the various Marxist positions can be found in Ashton and Philpin (1985). See also Wallerstein (1974), 42-43.
4. Dyer (1989); Hatcher (1977).
5. Rösener (1985), 255-76.
6. Dollinger (1970).
7. Topolski ((1981), 383-84.
8. Carus-Wilson (1959); Herman van der Wee, "Industrial Dynamics and the Process of Urbanization and De-urbanization in the Low Countries from the Late Middle Ages to the Eighteenth Century. A Synthesis," in van der Wee (1988), 323-26.
9. Heers (1961).
10. Herman van der Wee, "Structural Changes in European Long-Distance Trade, and Particularly in the Reexport Trade from South to North, 1350-1750," in Tracy (1990), 14-33; Spufford (1988), 441-43, 455, 459.
11. Goldthwaite (1980).
12. Abel (1980), 99-146.
13. Van der Wee (1963), vol. 2:314-16.
14. Spufford (1988), 334-35.
15. Recent work registering regional variations of the economic *conjuncture* is so extensive that we can only offer some titles as examples. See García de Cortázar (1988); Henryk Samsonowicz and Antoni Maczak, "Feudalism and Capitalism: A Balance of Changes in East-Central Europe," in Maczak, Samsonowicz, and Burke (1985), 6-23; Neveux and Jacquart (1975); Abel (1980); Heers (1961); Romano and Vivanti (1978); and Ruggiero Romano and Ugo Tucci, eds., *Economia naturale, economia monetaria* (Turin, 1983), in Romano (1978- ).
16. Bois (1976), 63-64, 117-22; Dyer (1989), 4-8; Britnell (1986); Heers (1961), 504-5; van der Wee, "Industrial dynamics," in van der Wee (1988), 316-26; Touchard (1967), 377-78; Carrère (1967); Vilar (1962), vol. 1:459-520; Goldthwaite (1980), 33.
17. Touchard (1967), 157-74.
18. Mollat (1952), 542.
19. Munro (1973).
20. See the overview in Spufford (1988), 289-362.
21. Day (1978).

22. Leo Bagrow, *History of Cartography*, rev. ed. by R. A. Skelton (Cambridge, Mass., 1964), 65ff.
23. For an interesting critical view see Dyer (1989), 211-33; Goldthwaite (1980), 317-50.
24. Dyer (1989), 109-87; Bennassar and Goy (1975).
25. Bois (1976), 356-60; Dyer (1989), 146-50; Neveux and Jacquart (1975), 82.
26. Carus Wilson (1959), 204; Yun (1987), 82-86.
27. Neveux and Jacquart (1975), 140.
28. Hatcher (1977), conclusion.
29. Braudel and Spooner (1967), 400-4.
30. Pach (1968), 309-11.
31. Topolski (1981), 379.
32. Pach (1968), 309.
33. Pach (1968), 310-11.
34. A recent synthesis in Herman van der Wee, "La banque européenne au moyen âge et pendant le temps modernes (1476-1789)," in van der Wee (1991), 134-70; Carande Thobar (1987), vol. 1:331-40.
35. Mollat (1952), 177-269, was able to verify this increase in trade from the excellent watchtower of Norman trade.
36. Ramsay (1953).
37. As is argued by Wallerstein (1974), 42.
38. Chaunu (1959), vol. 8, part 2,1:255-352.
39. For a general revision and synthesis, see Ward Barrett, "World Bullion Flows, 1450-1800," in Tracy (1990), 224-54.
40. Michel Morineau, "La conjoncture ou les cernes de la croissance," in Le Roy Ladurie and Morineau (1977), 979.
41. Braudel and Spooner (1967), fig. 19.
42. Hamilton (1934).
43. Nadal Oller (1959).
44. For a discussion that makes further bibliographical references unnecessary, see Miskimin (1977), 35-46.
45. Vilar (1956).
46. Braudel (1979), vol. 3:56-234.
47. Sella (1957), 30.
48. Ruíz Martín (1970), 84-99; Malanima (1982), 296-97.
49. Gascon (1971).
50. For a criticism along these lines, see Carla Rahn Phillips, "The Growth and Composition of Trade in the Iberian Empires, 1450-1750," in Tracy (1990), 34-101.
51. Wallerstein (1974), 181ff.
52. Domenico Sella and Franco Capra, *Il ducato de Milano. 1535 al 1796* (Torino, 1984), 107ff.; Ruíz Martín (1965), civ-cxx.
53. Pach (1968), 307.
54. The figure has been calculated by Wyczanski and is quoted by Topolski (1981), 394.
55. Maria Bogucka, "The Towns of East-Central Europe from the Fourteenth to Seventeenth Century," in Maczak, Samsonowicz, and Burke (1985), 97-108.
56. Le Roy Ladurie (1966), 633-54. Guy Bois' model has been applied to the sixteenth century, with interesting nuances, by Kriedte (1983).
57. Robert Brenner, "The Agrarian Roots of European Capitalism," in Aston and Philpin (1985), 213-327.

58. Aymard (1981), 426-35.
59. De Vries (1974).
60. Peter Bowden, "Agricultural Prices, Farm Profits, and Rents," in Thirsk (1967), 598-600; Neveux and Jacquart (1975), 152-53; and see Abel (1980), 197-203.
61. Kerridge (1953/54), 28.
62. Kellenbenz (1976), chap. 2.
63. The concentration of property in the case of France has been highlighted by Jacquart (1974), 106.
64. For the variety of situations, see Bennassar (1977), 449-92.
65. Braudel (1976), vol. 1:517-48.
66. Hamilton (1934).
67. See the discussion in Goldstone (1991).
68. The models of change can be seen, in a synthetic and up-to-date way, in the various studies on Italy put together in van der Wee (1988), 17-160.
69. Romano (1962), 480-531.
70. Cipolla (1952) and (1980).
71. Many of the contributions to Maczak, Samsonowicz, and Burke (1985) underline the diversity of eastern Europe. See, for examples, Leonid Zytkowitcz, "Trends of Agrarian Economy in Poland, Bohemia, and Hungary from the Middle of the Fifteenth to the Middle of the Seventeenth Century," 59-83, especially 66, on the rhythm of exports. According to Topolski (1981) 391, 395-96, based on Wyczanski's data, the export of Polish wheat does not exceed 2.5% of the total production.
72. Zytkowicz, "Trends of Agrarian Economy," in Maczak, Samsonowicz, and Burke (1985).73. Henryk Samsonowicz and Antoni Maczak, "Feudalism and Capitalism," in Maczak, Samsonowicz, and Burke (1985), 18.
74. Samsonowicz (1968), 173-84.
75. Kellenbenz (1976); Jacquart (1974), 755-56.
76. Philip Benedict, "Civil War and Natural Disaster in Northern France," in Clark (1985), 84-105.
77. Michel Morineau, "La conjoncture ou les cernes de la croissance," in Le Roy Ladurie and Morineau (1977), 892-95.
78. Jacquart (1974), 597-622; Le Roy Ladurie (1966), 427-52.
79. Stone (1965), 273-384.
80. See Clay (1984), 65-66.
81. De Vries (1974), 119-73.
82. Van der Wee (1978), 72.
83. Jacquart (1974), 623; Bennassar and Goy (1975), 427.
84. Tracy (1985). A short but suggestive comparison with Spain in John H. Elliott, "Yet Another Crisis?" in Clark (1985), 308-11.
85. Israel (1989), 1-79.

# BIBLIOGRAPHY

Abel, Wilhelm. *Agricultural Fluctuations in Europe from the Thirteenth to the Twentieth Century.* Trans. Olive Ordish. New York, 1980.

Aymard, Maurice. "L'Europe moderne: féodalité ou féodalités? (note critique)." *AESC* 36 (1981): 426-35.

Aston, Trevor H., and C. H. E. Philpin, eds. *The Brenner Debate: Agrarian Class Structure and Economic Development in Pre-Industrial Europe.* Cambridge, 1985.

Bennassar, Bartolomé. "L'Europe des Champagnes." In *Histoire économique et sociale de la France,* ed. Pierre Léon, vol. 1: *L'Ouverture du monde, XIVe-XVIe siècles.* Paris, 1977.

Bennassar, Bartolomé, and Joseph Goy. "Contribution à l'histoire de la consommation alimentaire du XIVe au XIX siècle." *AESC* 30 (1975): 402-30.

Bois, Guy. *Crise du féodalisme: économie rurale et démographie en Normandie orientale du début du XIVe siècle au milieu du XVIe siècle.* Cahiers de la fondation nationale des sciences politiques, no. 202. Paris, 1976.

Braudel, Fernand. *Civilisation matérielle, économie et capitalisme, XVe-XVIIIe siècle.* 3 vols. Paris, 1979.

Braudel, Fernand. *La Méditerranée et le Monde Méditerranéen à l'époque de Philippe II.* 3d ed. 2 vols. Paris, 1976.

Braudel, Fernand, and Frank Spooner. "Prices in Europe from 1450 to 1750." In *The Cambridge Economic History of Europe,* vol. 4: *The Economy of Expanding Europe in the Sixteenth and Seventeenth Centuries,* ed. E. E. Rich and C. H. Wilson, 378-486. Cambridge, 1967.

Britnell, R. H. *Growth and Decline in Colchester, 1300-1525.* Cambridge, 1986.

Carande Thobar, Ramón. *Carlos V y sus banqueros.* 2d ed. 3 vols. Barcelona, 1987.

Carrère, Claude. *Barcelone, centre économique à l'époque des difficultés, 1380-1462.* Paris, 1967.

Carus Wilson, E. H. "Evidences of Industrial Growth of Some Fifteenth-Century Manors." *EconHR,* 2d ser., 2 (1959): 190-205.

Chaunu, Pierre. *Seville et l'Atlantique (1504-1650).* 8 vols. Paris, 1959.

Cipolla, Carlo M. *Before the Industrial Revolution.* 2d ed. New York, 1980.

Cipolla, Carlo M. "The Decline of Italy: the Case of a Fully Matured Economy." *EconHR,* 2d ser., 2 (1952): 178-87.

Cipolla, Carlo M. "The Trends in Italian Economic History in the Later Middle Ages." *EconHR,* 2d ser., 2 (1949): 181-84.

Cipolla, Carlo M., Robert S. Lopez, and Harry A. Miskimin. "Economic Depression of the Renaissance?" *EconHR,* 2d ser., 16 (1964): 519-29.

Clark, Peter, ed. *The European Crisis of the 1590s. Essays in Comparative History.* London, 1985.

Clay, C. G. A. *Economic Expansion and Social Change: England, 1500-1700.* 2 vols. Cambridge, 1984.

Day, John. "The Great Bullion Famine of the Fifteenth Century." *PaP,* no. 79 (1978): 3-54.

De Vries, Jan. *The Dutch Rural Economy in the Golden Age, 1500-1700.* New Haven, 1974.

Dollinger, Philippe. *The German Hansa.* Stanford, 1970.

Duby, Georges, and Armand Wallon, eds. *Histoire de la France rurale.* 3 vols. Tours, 1975.

Dyer, Christopher. *Standards of Living in the Later Middle Ages: Social Change in England c. 1200-1520.* Cambridge, 1989.

García de Cortázar, Jose A. *La sociedad rural en la España medieval.* Madrid, 1988.

Gascon, Richard. *Grand commerce et vie urbaine au XVIe siècle: Lyon et ses marchands (environs de 1520-environs de 1580).* 2 vols. Paris, 1971.

Goldstone, Jack. "Monetary versus Velocity Interpretations of the 'Price Revolution': a Comment." *JEconH* 51 (1991): 176-81.

Goldthwaite, Richard A. *The Building of Renaissance Florence: an Economic and Social History.* Baltimore, 1980.

Hamilton, E. J. *American Treasure and the Price Revolution in Spain, 1501-1650.* Cambridge, Mass., 1934.

Hatcher, John. *Plague, Population and the English Economy, 1348-1530.* London, 1977.

Heers, Jacques. *Gênes au XVe siècle: activité économique et problèmes sociaux.* Paris, 1961.

Israel, Jonathan I. *The Dutch Primacy in World Trade, 1585-1740.* New York, 1989.

Jacquart, Jean. *La crise rurale en Ile-de-France, 1550-1670.* Paris, 1974.

Kellenbenz, Hermann. *The Rise of the European Economy. An Economic History of Continental Europe, 1500-1750.* London, 1976.

Kerridge, Eric. "The Movement of Rent, 1540-1640." *EconHR*, 2d ser., 6 (1953-54): 16-34.

Kriedte, Peter. *Peasants, Landlords, and Merchant Capitalists. Europe and the World Economy, 1500-1800.* Cambridge, 1983.

Le Roy Ladurie, Emmanuel. *Les paysannes de Languedoc.* 2 vols. Paris, 1966.

Le Roy Ladurie, Emmanuel, and Michel Morineau. *Histoire économique et sociale de la France.* Vol. 2, *Paysannerie et croissance.* Paris, 1977.

Lopez, Robert S., and Harry A. Miskimin. "The Economic Depression of the Renaissance." *EconHR*, 2d ser., 14 (1961-62): 408-26.

Maczak, Antoni, Henryk Samsonowicz, and Peter Burke. *East-Central Europe in Transition from the Fourteenth to the Seventeenth Century.* Cambridge, 1985.

Malanima, Paolo. *La decadenza di un'economia citadina: l'industria di Firenze nei secoli XVI-XVIII.* Bologna, 1982.

Miskimin, Harry A. *The Economy of Later Renaissance Europe, 1460-1600.* Cambridge, 1977.

Mollat, Michel. *Le commerce maritime normand à la fin du moyen âge.* Paris, 1952.

Munro, John. *Wool, Cloth and Gold: the Struggle for Bullion in the Anglo-Burgundian Trade, 1340-1478.* Brussels and Toronto, 1973.

Nadal Oller, Jordi. "La revolución de los precios españoles en el siglo XVI: estado actual de la cuestión." *Hispania* 19 (1959): 511-14.

Neveux, Hugues and Jean Jaquart. *L'âge classique.* In *Histoire de la France rurale*, ed. Georges Duby and Armand Wallon, vol. 2. Tours, 1975.

Pach, Z. P. "The Shifting of International Trade Routes in the 15th-17th Centuries." *Acta Historica Academiae Scientiarum Hungaricae* 14 (1968): 277-319.

Ramsey, P. "Overseas Trade of Henry VII: the evidence of Customs Accounts." *EconHR*, 2d ser., 6 (1953): 173-82.

Romano, Ruggiero, ed. *Storia d'Italia.* 9 vols. Turin, 1978- .

Romano, Ruggiero, ed. "Tra XVI e XVII secolo. Una crisi economica: 1619-1622." *Rivista di Storia di Italia* (1962).

Romano, Ruggiero, and Corrado Vivanti, eds. *Dal Feudalismo al Capitalismo.* Turin, 1978.

Rösener, Werner. *Bauern im Mittelalter.* Munich, 1985.

Ruíz Martín, Felipe. *Lettres marchandes échangées entre Florence et Medina del Campo.* Paris, 1965.

Ruíz Martín, Felipe. "Los hombres de negocios genoveses de España durante el siglo XVI." In *Fremde Kaufleute auf der iberischen Halbinsel*, ed. Hermann Kellenbenz, 84-99. Cologne and Vienna, 1970.

Samsonowicz, Henryk. "Les villes d'Europe Centrale à la fin du moyen âge." *AESC*, 21 (1968): 173-84.

Sella, Domenico. "Les mouvements longs de l'industrie lanière à Venice aux XVIe et XVIIe siècles," *AESC*, 12 (1957).

Spufford, Peter. *Money and its Use in Medieval Europe.* Cambridge, 1988.

Stone, Lawrence. *The Crisis of the Aristocracy, 1558-1641.* New York, 1965.

Thirsk, Joan. *The Agrarian History of England and Wales.* Vol. 4, *1500-1640.* Cambridge 1967.

Topolski, Jerzy "Continuity and Discontinuity in the Development of the Feudal System in Eastern Europe (Xth to XVIIrh centuries)." *JEEH* 2 (1981): 373-400.

Touchard, Henry. *Le commerce maritime breton à la fin du Moyen Age.* Paris, 1967.

Tracy, James D. *A Financial Revolution in the Habsburg Netherlands: "Renten" and "Renteniers" in the County of Holland, 1515-1566.* Berkeley and Los Angeles, 1985.

Tracy, James D., ed. *The Rise of Merchant Empires: Long-distance Trade in the Early Modern World, 1350-1750.* Cambridge, 1990.

Van der Wee, Herman. *The Growth of the Antwerp Market and the European Economy (Fourteenth-Sixteenth Centuries).* 3 vols. Louvain/Leuven, 1963.

Van der Wee, Herman. "Prices and Wages as Development Variables: A Comparison between England and the Southern Netherlands, 1400-1700." *Acta Historicae Neerlandica* 10 (1978): 58-78.

Van der Wee, Herman, ed. *The Rise and Decline of Urban Industries in Italy and the Low Countries (Late Middle Ages - Early Modern Times).* Louvain/Leuven, 1988.

Van der Wee, Herman. *La banque en occident.* Bruges, 1991.

Vilar, Pierre. "Problems of the Formation of Capitalism." *PaP*, no. 10 (1956): 15-38.

Vilar, Pierre. *La Catalogne dans l'Espagne moderne. Recherches sur les fondaments économiques des structures nationales.* 3 vols. Paris, 1962.

Wallerstein, Immanuel. *The Modern World-System, Capitalist Agriculture and The Origins of The European World-Economy in the Sixteenth Century.* 2 vols. New York, 1974.

Yun Casalilla, Bartolomé. *Sobre la transición al capitalismo en Castilla: economía y sociedad en Tierra del Campos (1500-1830).* Salamanca, 1987.

# PATTERNS OF TRADE, MONEY, AND CREDIT

John H. Munro
(University of Toronto)

The two most momentous developments in European commerce and finance between 1350 and 1600 were the creation of negotiable credit instruments and the shift in mercantile power from the Mediterranean to northwestern Europe, that is, from Italy to the Netherlands and England, which would dominate the European economy well into the industrial era. The two developments were very closely related; throughout the medieval and early modern era merchants controlled banking; and supremacy in international banking and finance was almost always the consequence of commercial hegemony, especially in long-distance trade. When Italian merchants were gaining that ascendancy, they were also creating the fundamental instruments of modern banking; and subsequently Netherlandish and English merchants, during their rise, perfected the techniques of negotiability and vastly expanded the commercial role of credit.

## 1. MONEY AND PRICES

Credit provides one of the exchange functions of money by effecting the acquisition of current goods in return for a written promise to make future payment. Thus the development of credit instruments and their role in international trade must be understood in terms of the changing European money supplies, which requires some understanding of price changes. The only two comprehensive sets of late medieval price data, from England and the Netherlands, reveal an oscillating pattern of inflations and deflations. They began with a long upward swing in prices during the thirteenth century, which ended abruptly just after the Great Famine of 1315-22 and was followed by a quarter-century of very severe deflation. This, in turn, ended just as abruptly with the Black Death in 1348, which was followed by another quarter-century of equally severe inflation that ended in the late 1370s (though prolonged in Flanders to 1390 by coinage debasements). Once more an almost equally stark deflation ensued and lasted until into the fifteenth century, though in northern Europe the resumption of inten-

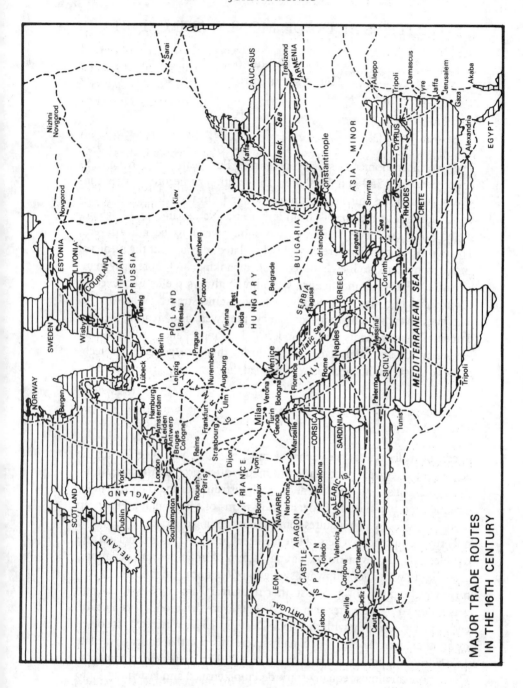

MAJOR TRADE ROUTES
IN THE 16TH CENTURY

sive warfare from the 1410s brought on another era of prolonged inflation. Then followed the most prolonged, if much less severe, era of general
deflation, from the late 1440s to about 1510/15, temporarily disrupted
during the 1480s and early 1490s by warfare and other "supply shocks."
The scattered price data for France, Italy, and Spain generally agree with
this pattern.[1]

Focusing on falling prices, many historians of the late medieval
economy have sought to explain them by the drastic depopulations. This
view is contradicted by both the quarter-century of severe inflation that
followed the Black Death and the subsequent fifteenth-century inflation
(1415-40), when population was still declining. Using a more sophisticated demographic model, Michael Postan argued that depopulation and
the consequent alteration in the land:labor ratio ultimately brought about
converse changes in *relative* prices: falling grain prices, with production
concentrated on lower-cost arable lands, and rising livestock and industrial prices, with a growing scarcity of labor and increased demand generated by higher real incomes.[2] Like others, however, Postan ignored the evidence for the post-Plague inflations and deflations, which contradict his
contention that the subsequent price-fall was limited to grains, for in all
these series the component price-indices for grains, livestock, and industrial goods generally rose and fell together during these cycles.

More credence should thus be given to monetary explanations for these
price movements. Indeed, before (and after) Postan, some historians argued that late medieval Europe had experienced a severe and deflationary
"bullion famine" caused by a combination of factors: 1) a drastic slump in
European silver mining; 2) a diminution of coinage stocks from "wear and
tear," shipwrecks and other losses; 3) a reduced inflow of gold from North
African trade; and 4) an ever growing bullion outflow in trade with the
East, as western Europe's appetite for costly luxuries grew.[3]

According to the Quantity Theory of Money, of course, a progressive
reduction in the stock of coined money should have meant a continuous
fall in the price-level. Some other factors are therefore required to explain
both the two post-1350 inflationary periods, when clearly there was no
"bullion famine," and the intervening and succeeding deflations. They
may be found by resorting to the modernized Fisher Identity (M.V = P.y, or
P = MV/y). First, any gradual decline in European money stocks (M) was
undoubtedly more than offset, after the Black Death, by a precipitous fall
in aggregate output and incomes (y—as *real net national income*), with
drastic disruptions of production and trade. At the same time, two related
factors evidently promoted a rapid growth in the *income velocity of money*

(V): dishoarding from extortionate taxation in financing warfare; and social trauma from the initial plagues that evidently induced rapid, hedonis-
tic spending of inherited cash balances.[4]  Finally extensive coinage debasements both expanded the effective stock of M and promoted a further rise
in V.  Thus all three variables, monetary and *real*, readily explain the post-
Plague inflations (rising P).

The subsequent deflation of the later fourteenth, early fifteenth centuries is probably more related to a drop in velocity (V) rather than to any accelerated reduction in money stocks (M).  Both international and regional
bullion flows were increasingly impeded by the secondary effects of late
medieval warfare: commercial blockades and embargoes, widespread, anarchic ravages from unruly soldiers, but especially the bullionist tendencies
of war-related fiscal measures.[5]  Virtually all princes, especially those exploiting their mints, banned both the export of bullion (including foreign
coin) and the import of suspect foreign coins.  The periodic economic re-
cessions also curbed coinage and income velocity, as widespread insecurity
and pessimism further discouraged spending and promoted hoarding.
Falling prices in turn encouraged more extensive hoarding by raising the
real value or purchasing power of coined money.  Many contemporary observers believed that "thesaurisation was the main cause of the bullion
famines" during the later fourteenth and early fifteenth centuries.[6]

In northern Europe this late medieval deflation was interrupted by the
final, most intense phase of the Hundred Years' War, after 1415, which
entailed drastic coinage debasements, heavy taxation, and evident
dishoarding (reflected in rising mint outputs).  But even before the final
French victory in 1453, northern mint outputs had plummeted, and deflation resumed.  This, its most prolonged phase, was finally terminated by
the sixteenth-century Price Revolution.

## 2. CREDIT AND CREDIT INSTRUMENTS

Many historians believe that the development of credit instruments during
the later Middle Ages should have counteracted these deflationary forces.
The two most important financial innovations, both Italian, were deposit-
and-transfer banking and foreign-exchange or bills-of-exchange banking.
They failed, however, to provide a sufficient remedy for periodic monetary
contractions in late medieval Europe, for the following reasons.  First,
these financial institutions appeared long before this era, which then experienced very few additional credit innovations to augment the effective

money supply. Second, bills of exchange and similar credit instruments could not do so because they were not negotiable before the end of this era; at best they could only affect velocity. Third, while many "bullionist" forces promoted a more widespread diffusion of credit, more powerful forces impeded its use. Fourth, with inadequate or too costly legal measures for enforcing debt repayments, credit transactions depended upon a personal trust that could be generated only by close relationships between relatively few merchants. Finally, credit instruments continued to depend on the use of coined money, and credit often expanded or contracted more than proportionally with changes in coin supplies.[7]

One relationship between coin and credit can be seen in the system of deposit and transfer banking that Lombard, Genoese, and Venetian money-changers had developed from the late twelfth century. Deposit banking came to operate on a fractional-reserve system of lending, by which individual bankers could lend out between one-half and two-thirds of cash deposits, holding the balance as a reserve. Furthermore, to conserve cash, they could make loans by the stroke of a pen, crediting such funds to the client's deposit account and permitting payments, on oral command, by book-transfers (later by checks). In theory, the banking system collectively could expand or contract the money supply by the reciprocal of the reserve ratio, operating through a chain of deposits, loans, expenditures, and redeposits. Late medieval banking, however, did not really have such expansionary powers, because it constituted such a very small segment of market-oriented monetary systems. Even in its Italian homeland, deposit banking was largely confined to the large urban commercial centers; and outside of Italy it spread only to regions dominated by Italian commerce, such as Catalonia and especially Flanders, where Bruges became the commercial and financial capital of northern Europe.[8] Even in Venice and Bruges, only about 10 percent of adult males maintained bank accounts, and in Spufford's view, "the vast majority of transactions" still required metallic coin.[9] Furthermore, during the fifteenth century, the Burgundian government of the Low Countries imposed many severe restrictions on banking and credit, as part of misguided policies to protect their coinage during periods of evident bullion scarcities. During the Burgundian monetary reform and unification in 1433-34, the regime curbed indigenous deposit-banking, and subsequently tried to prohibit it.[10]

An even greater force for credit restriction in late medieval Europe was the ecclesiastical ban on usury, defined as the exaction of any certain, predetermined charge for the use of money. From the end of the thirteenth century the Church revived and intensified its anti-usury campaign, which gained enough secular support during the next two centuries to become a significant impediment to financial capitalism. While merchants did devise various means of evading the ban, they all involved higher transaction costs, including death-bed restitutions by merchants fearing mortal peril to their souls.[11]

In such a hostile social climate, the credit institution that fared the best was the bill of exchange, or foreign-exchange banking, which the Italian merchants had developed at the Champagne Fairs. Fully evolved by the late thirteenth century, it was both a credit and a transfer instrument. It enabled merchants to invest in foreign trade by financing the export of goods between cities, and to remit funds abroad in order to pay for imports, redeem debts, or transmit taxes. The bills worked by means of a principal/agent system involving four parties: two principals in the city where the funds were advanced, and two agents effecting (re)payment in another city. In city A, the *deliverer* or *remitter* lent or advanced funds in the local currency to the *taker* or *drawer*, who in return "sold" him a bill of exchange (*cambium*), by which the *taker* "drew upon" his banker or agent in city B (the *accepter/payer*) for payment. By a simple letter, the *taker* instructed his foreign banker to debit his account and make, at some future date, the specified payment in B's currency at a specified exchange rate to the designated *payee*, who was the banking agent for the *deliverer/remitter*. The *payee* then arranged or "purchased" a return bill of exchange (*recambium*) to remit the proceeds to the original *deliverer* in city A.

Whether serving as a credit or transfer instrument, the bill of exchange provided considerable economies by allowing merchants to effect these transactions without having to accompany their goods or funds, and by obviating the very risky transport of specie, since payments were always made in the local currency. Besides reducing transaction costs, the bill of exchange also provided an important mechanism for accommodating the almost universal bans against bullion exports. According to Raymond De Roover and his followers, the bill of exchange was even more important in circumventing the equally universal usury prohibitions: it "disguised the loan-interest" in the two bills' exchange rates, which were raised above par in favor of the *deliverer*-lender. But canon lawyers, not so easily fooled, regarded the returns on such bills not as interest but as an uncertain and quite licit profit from sales of mercantile-bank balances—uncertain because of market fluctuations in exchange rates.[12] Furthermore the bill of exchange was a high-risk credit instrument, for it lacked any provisions for collateral, any official standing in the courts, and thus the legal protection bestowed upon creditors holding legitimate loan contracts (i.e., a non-usurious *mutuum* or *recognizance*).[13]

The use of late medieval bills of exchange was thus restricted to a very small coterie of wealthy merchant-bankers, chiefly Italian, who operated a closely knit, international network, and had full confidence in one another. No other ethnic or national group of merchants was able to construct a comparable network, with the potential exception of the Hanseatic Germans. Contrary to many assertions, Hanse merchants did make use of bills of exchange (between Bruges and Lübeck) as early as the 1290s; but after the formal creation of the Hanseatic League in 1370, its assemblies or "diets" imposed increasingly severe restrictions and even bans on such bills and other credit transactions (on the grounds that they promoted fraud and price instability).[14] During this same era, the English government also enacted legislation against bills-of-exchange and other credit instruments, banning or restricting their use not only for promoting fraud and usury but more especially for impeding the import of precious metals and disguising their export. Such measures only fostered the development of alternative credit instruments, especially *bills obligatory* (informal bonds, promissory notes) and helped to consolidate the Italian virtual monopoly on the formal bill of exchange and, therefore, Italian predominance in late medieval international trade.[15]

## 3. "LATE MEDIEVAL DEPRESSION" AND INTERNATIONAL TRADE

Any discussion of late medieval commerce must commence with the vexing issue of the so-called "Great Depression," a term still undefined in the economists' lexicon.[16] But since they define a recession as a continuous decline in aggregate output (real GNP) over six months, then "depression" as a recession of much greater magnitude could well apply to the late medieval economy. The fall of Europe's population by 40 percent certainly caused a very great, if less than proportional, drop in aggregate output over more than a century. Various data, however, reveal a pattern not of continuous slump but of cyclical movements of booms and slumps woven around a declining trend. The more suitable term, therefore, is "secular decline" or "economic contraction."

Since the fifteenth-century "depression" is examined by Bartolomé Yun elsewhere in this volume,[17] here we may concentrate on fourteenth-century trade. The Black Death and subsequent plagues were not the primary causes of the decline of international trade, which had begun at least a half-century earlier with the outbreak of warfare more widespread and more debilitating than at any time since the Carolingian era. The Anglo-French wars, Franco-Flemish wars, and Flemish civil wars (1293-1328), along with wars in Italy, fatally undermined the Champagne Fairs, which had provided the chief agency for north-south trade. Just as injurious were two sets of overlapping wars in the western Mediterranean: the Muslim-Christian wars in Spain and North Africa from 1291 to 1341 and the Angevin-Aragonese wars in Aragon-Catalonia, southern France, Sicily, Naples, and the Papal States between 1282 and 1302. The ferocious Guelf-Ghibelline wars (1313-43) then brought almost continuous foreign intervention in Italy by Catalan, French, German, and Hungarian armies, while from the 1330s disbanded mercenary soldiers pillaged Italy from north to south. Meanwhile, commerce in the eastern Mediterranean was similarly disrupted by the Genoese-Venetian naval wars (1291-99), the Mamluk conquest of Crusader Palestine (1291) and retaliatory papal bans against Muslim trade, Ottoman advances into the Byzantine Empire (from 1303), and during the 1330s anarchic warfare in the Mongol khanates from the Black Sea to Persia.[18] In the historical literature, all these wars, plus the subsequent Genoese-Venetian wars (1350-55, 1378-81), have been unfairly overshadowed by the better-known Hundred Years' War (1336-1453) between France and England, which also involved the Low Countries, Spain, and the German Empire.

Bartolomé Yun has rightly observed in his essay that "until 1460, wars struck in various ways a still fragile and disarticulated international economy." Their true impact can best be understood through the economic concept of *transaction costs*, a term embracing all direct and indirect costs in exchanging goods and services. Elastic enough to include transportation, distribution, and marketing costs, its more important components are "search and measurement" costs in acquiring vital market information and "protection costs" in negotiating and enforcing contracts, especially involving property rights. These components all involved very large fixed costs, so that the entire "transaction sector" was subject to considerable economies of scale (i.e., smaller markets meant higher unit costs).[19] The major costs of late medieval warfare should thus be seen in terms less of military campaigns than of the much more pervasive, enduring consequences of retaliatory trade embargoes, piracy, brigandage, civil strife, and fiscal measures to finance both aggression and defense, plus related monetary measures, such as coinage debasements and the aforesaid bullionist controls.

The importance of such war-related transaction costs can also be seen, albeit implicitly, in the model of international trade that Herman Van der Wee has employed to explain fluctuations in the European economy from the thirteenth to eighteenth centuries.[20]  Somewhat paradoxically, he contends that medieval economic growth and prosperity had fundamentally depended upon the vitality of overland continental trade routes, especially those linking the Low Countries and Italy.  During the fourteenth century, chronic warfare and general insecurity along those routes led to a disproportionate contraction in commerce, which in turn reduced the demand for transport and commercial services, labor, manufactures, foodstuffs and other goods.  Declining consumption in turn reduced investment and aggregate incomes by a reverse multiplier-accelerator effect.  Beginning with the arterial routes via the Champagne fairs, the economic contraction spread via tributary routes into numerous regional trade networks servicing thousands of towns and villages throughout the continental hinterland. Continental overland trade did not disappear, to be sure, and sometimes even recovered its vitality during lulls in warfare.  But it became more oriented towards periodic regional fairs (as noted by Yun), while more and more of the longer-distance trade was diverted to the new sea routes to northwestern Europe; indeed, from the 1320s the Italians developed new sea-routes to northwestern Europe precisely because of these disruptions to overland trade and the Champagne fairs.  Such trade diversions further concentrated wealth and income flows into fewer and fewer hands, principally those Italian, German, and Netherlandish towns based on maritime trade.  Their impressive gains, however, did not offset the much greater aggregate economic decline of Europe's continental hinterlands from the early fourteenth to mid-fifteenth centuries.

Furthermore, even if maritime routes did gain a greater share of long-distance commerce, late medieval shipping also found itself subjected to rising transport, protection, and other transaction costs.  As Katele has argued, the fourteenth century marked "a watershed in the history of naval plundering."[21]  The chief response was much bigger ships armed with more sophisticated weapons:  larger complements of specialized crossbowmen, steel-plated body armour even for other sailors, naval artillery, from the 1330s, and more mobile small-arms.  The consequence was more complicated and far more costly naval construction, whether in traditional galleys or the new northern-style square-rigged cogs, and thus far higher freight rates.  The Venetians found their most effective defense in the heavily-armed three-masted great-galley, a speedy hybrid military and commercial vessel that became the exclusive carrier of precious cargoes.[22]

Rising transaction costs had a particularly striking impact upon western European textile industries, which supplied by far the most important manufactured commodities for long-distance trade.  During the twelfth and thirteenth centuries, when such costs were relatively low, surprisingly low for overland transport, the major northern textile producers in France, the Low Countries, and the Rhineland, along with newer textile centers in Italy and Catalonia, had exported a wide variety of textiles across Europe and throughout the Mediterranean basin. The predominant exports, both by aggregate volume and evidently by value, were cheaper and lighter textiles: worsteds, mixed woolen-worsted serges, coarse woolens, linens, and fustians (mixed linen-cottons).[23]  For two reasons, the densely populated Mediterranean basin, including the adjacent Near East, provided the most important market for such textiles: its markets were by far the largest, most concentrated, and thus efficient in terms of scale economies and transaction costs; and many of those markets lay in warm zones that favored the lighter textiles.

By the early fourteenth century, most northern producers of cheap, light textiles found themselves unable to survive in the now saturated but disrupted Mediterranean markets. Not only did they face the greatest rise in transport and transaction costs, but they were also unable to compensate by raising prices, because the homogenous nature of their products had made them "price-takers," whose virtually indistinguishable cheap textiles—says, biffes, stanforts, etc.—could not be sold above the market price.[24]  When costs rose above these prices, they had to surrender Mediterranean markets to regional producers, who enjoyed a comparative advantage in lower transaction costs. Those drapers who were not content merely to rely upon their own local markets then chose to re-orient production to more expensive, luxury-quality woolens. Transaction costs for the latter represented a much lower proportion of the final price, which, furthermore, these drapers could now more easily determine as "price-makers," who competed by distinguishing their woolens from rival products through superior quality and reputation.

Initially the most successful were a relatively small number of urban Flemish and Brabantine draperies, especially those that had long produced luxury woolens, who were joined by newer northern draperies in Normandy (Rouen), England (West Country, East Anglia) and Holland (Leiden). Most produced for export markets in the colder climes of northern Europe, especially in the still stable Baltic zone. Some Flemish and Brabantine luxury woolens also retained their Mediterranean markets, though ultimately they were outsold by imitation or less expensive grades of luxury woolens exported by the rising Flemish *nouvelles draperies*. In the Mediterranean, northern woolens faced strong competition from Italian and Catalan draperies, which had also reoriented production to better quality woolens; of these, the most luxurious were Florentine.[25] Many Mediterranean regions with cold winters favored this shift to heavier woolens, especially the plateau regions of Ottoman Anatolia and Persia but also the North African desert.

During this same era, various economic and social factors may also have favored luxury consumption. The fourteenth-century economic dislocations seem to have widened, not narrowed, the gap between the few rich and the many poor. The periodic war-inspired, debasement-induced inflations effectively transferred incomes from the lower to upper strata of society, while extortionate taxation bore most heavily on the lower strata of society. The much-vaunted rise in real incomes for wage-earners did not begin until the deflationary era of the very late fourteenth century; but even when their incomes peaked in the mid-fifteenth century they still did not provide much of a market for luxury textiles, certainly not compared to wealthy merchants, aristocrats, and the upper clergy.[26] Finally, as Yun has observed, "in Renaissance societies consumption was ostentatious, ostentation generated social prestige, and prestige brought power."

## 4. ITALIANS AND CATALANS IN MEDITERRANEAN TRADE

Italian commercial and financial supremacy during the later Middle Ages depended not only on the structural economic changes that favored both maritime and luxury trades, but also on relations with the Mamluk Levant, the prime source of oriental luxury goods.[27] During the early fourteenth century, papal and secular bans on Mamluk trade had forced the Italians to seek alternative sources of those goods, chiefly in Black Sea and Lesser Armenian (Cilician) ports. By the 1340s, however, civil wars in the Mongol khanates had seriously disrupted the Central Asian overland routes leading to those ports, diverting more and more trade to the Indian Ocean and Red Sea routes. The latter terminated at Alexandria in Mamluk Egypt, and in 1344-45 the Italians overcame strong papal objections to resume full commercial relations there.

Economic and political conditions did not then favor expansion in Levantine trade, for from the outset the Italians faced exploitation at the hands of the Mamluk karimis cartel, stiff fees for papal licenses, and strong competition from the Catalans. Then, in 1348 the Black Death struck the Mamluk Levant with great ferocity, and from 1350 to 1355 Venice and Genoa fought another destructive naval war. When the papacy renewed its ban on the Mamluk trade (1359), and the Genoese and Catalans joined

Peter I of Cyprus's crusade against Mamluk ports and shipping (1361), Venice skillfully stayed neutral and in 1370 secured a treaty with the Mamluks that permitted them to develop an expanding trade in Syrian cotton. Threatened with defeat at Genoese hands in the War of Chioggia, Venice rebounded in 1381 to win a surprising, crushing victory. Finally, in the 1390s more peaceful conditions brought new prosperity to the Levantine trade with Egypt and Syria.

Venice prospered, while its rivals declined. By the mid-fifteenth century Venice had gained supremacy in Mediterranean trade and became Europe's wealthiest city.[28]  Meanwhile, the Genoese and the Catalans damaged their own trade by raids against the Mamluks, the Ottomans, other Muslims, and each other, and the extremely aggressive Catalans lost ground during the Catalonian civil wars (1462-78), which seriously disrupted Catalan Levantine shipping and hastened the decline of the Catalan industrial mainstay, woolen textiles.  Genoa certainly fared no better. Wracked by internal strife between 1413 and 1453, the city's ambition to dominate western Mediterranean commerce was thwarted not only by Catalans but also by Provençals.  In the eastern Mediterranean, where the Genoese had chosen to rely on a very geographically dispersed and insecure trading network, their trade with the remnants of a now impoverished Byzantine Empire steadily declined, while that with Kaffa and Tana in the Black Sea suffered under constant Tartar attacks.  Though trade with the rising Ottoman Empire was more promising, it meant dealing with a potential enemy who granted few trading concessions and permitted pirate attacks on Genoese shipping in the Aegean.  Finally, in the all-important trade with northwestern Europe, Genoa suffered much greater injury from the Hundred Years' war, especially during the post-Agincourt phase (1415-53), than Venice did.  Not only did heavily armed Venetian galleys provide better protection in corsair-infested shipping lanes, but the Venetians also directed more and more of their European trade to the much safer Alpine routes into South Germany, a relatively peaceful region whose economy had been expanding from the early fifteenth century.

Venice's greatest source of prosperity was its share of Levantine trade, which grew from 40 percent around 1400 to almost 65 percent by the 1450s.  Venice benefited especially from continued peace with the Mamluks, which was threatened only once, when Sultan Barsby attempted to monopolize the all-important spice trade (1426-38) that eventually accounted for 60 percent of Venetian expenditures in the Levant. Venice not only thwarted this Mamluk policy but further gained from Barsby's destruction of the *karimis* spice cartel. With both obstacles eliminated, spice prices fell by almost 50 percent by the 1450s and remained low until 1498, the year of the first Portuguese expedition to India. The slump probably reflected not so much a prolonged depression and monetary deflation in the Mamluk economy, as some historians have believed, but excess supply and inelastic European demand. Thus consumption of pepper, ginger, cinnamon, cloves, and sugar undoubtedly grew in the fifteenth century, but not in proportion to the fall in prices.[29]

Spices were not, as often stated, a necessity for preserving foods, not when salt was far more effective, more readily available, and much cheaper. Spices were still a far too costly luxury for most people, even for skilled artisans, despite falling relative prices and rising real-wage incomes. For the aristocracy, however, savoring a radical change in late medieval cuisine, such spices provided a highly desirable diversion from a generally bland diet and perhaps also an affordable symbol of prestige. Their demand may thus well have been relatively inelastic, yet quite sufficient to continue making the spice trade by far the most lucrative sector of international trade.

The Venetian's second most valuable Levantine commodity, Syrian cotton, was doubtless more mundane, but it possessed considerable industrial importance. Since the twelfth century, Italian (chiefly Lombard) textile manufacturers had been producing linen-cotton fustians, a very popular, cheap, light fabric. From the early fourteenth century this industry suffered a slow but irredeemable decline, facing the same difficulties that afflicted other cheap textile industries. In the 1370s, when warfare disrupted the supply of Lombard fustians, various South German towns—Ravensburg, Regensburg, Constance, Basel, Augsburg, and Ulm—converted their domestic linen crafts into a rival and far more successful fustians industry, providing one of the major springs of South German economic growth. For their cotton, they depended almost entirely on the exchange of German silver and copper with Venice by way of the Brenner Pass, and by the early fifteenth century rising demand was promoting large increases in Syrian cotton cultivation.[30]

Textiles, naturally, constituted Venice's most important export item of exchange for Levantine spices and cotton, and with the fourteenth-century shift to medium-priced and costly woolens, the chief suppliers were the Mediterranean draperies—Tuscan, Lombard, Catalan, and Provençal. Only from the 1420s did English broadcloths begin to assert a new northern presence in Levantine markets as medium-quality but generally lower-priced woolens than those from the Flemish nouvelles draperies.[31]

Although Ashtor believed that Venice had taken advantage of industrial decline in Mamluk Egypt and Syria to expand its export trade with the Levant, it is difficult to see how this depressed region, which also experienced severe depopulation, provided any growing markets for the West during the fifteenth century.[32] Indeed, all the evidence indicates that no more than 35 to 40 percent of the total European expenditures on Levantine goods were financed by sales of western export goods, chiefly textiles, glassware, soap, paper, copper, salt, grains, olive oil, and dried fruits. The remaining 65 percent had to be covered by exporting bullion and specie, chiefly silver, which Ashtor estimates at 660,000 Venetian ducats (equal to 27,768 kg. silver or 2,314 kg. gold) annually by the 1490s.[33] This flow of silver to the Levant was particularly important for the expansion of South German commerce, which can best be understood by first examining contemporary changes in the Baltic and the Low Countries.

## 5. The Baltic Zone: the German Hanse and Holland

Hanseatic German trade in the Baltic Sea posed in three respects a lesser, northern counterpoint to Italian commerce in the Mediterranean: first, the eastern Baltic supplied a few luxury items for export—Russian and Livonian furs (sable, marten, beaver), amber, and wax; second, woolen textiles were the most important western European export to the Baltic; and third, western Europe's growing imbalance of payments with the Baltic had to be covered by silver shipments.[34]

Baltic maritime commerce differed, on the other hand, from Mediterranean trade by its much greater reliance on high-bulk, low-valued cargoes in foodstuffs and industrial raw materials. Indeed, by the early modern era, the Baltic zone had become western Europe's primary source of imported grains (Prussian rye, barley), forest products, naval stores (flax, hemp, pitch), copper, and iron. During the later Middle Ages, three other Baltic exports rivalled them in aggregate values: beer, salt, and herring. Beer exports (from Baltic barley) had gained a strong stimulus in the mid-fourteenth century from the introduction of hop-brewing, which greatly improved taste, stability, and portability. An even more important Baltic export was salt, the universal preservative, the main source of which, the rock-salt of Lüneburg, was monopolized by nearby Lübeck. In the late fourteenth century, however, growing depletion of these salt beds led German and then seafaring towns from Holland-Zeeland to exploit another, more abundant source, in France's Bay of Bourgneuf; and in the fifteenth century Bay Salt imports rivalled woolen textiles in aggregate value. Salt

was vital for curing in the herring industry; and salt and Baltic herring together had provided the late medieval German Hanse with their chief commercial mainstay. Salt-cured herring was a very abundant, relatively
cheap, and highly nutritious food, which could be shipped over long-dis-
tances and stored for long periods without much degradation.[35]

Lübeck dominated not only the salt trade but also the Baltic herring
fisheries, principally by controlling the nearby spawning grounds at
Skania, just off the Dano-Swedish coast, and the chief access routes
between the Baltic and North Seas. These factors made Lübeck the natural
leader of the Hanseatic League, when it was formally created, following
the Hanse-Danish war of 1367-70. It was actually a loose confederation
of four regional town-leagues: the Wendish League in the western Baltic,
led by Lübeck in alliance with Hamburg and Bremen; the Livonian League
in the eastern Baltic, led by Riga; the adjacent Prussian League, dominated
by Danzig and the Teutonic Order; and the Cologne-led Rhenish League,
dominating trade routes into southern Germany and Central Europe. Together they controlled four major trading factories or *kontors* abroad: the
London Steelyard for English trade; the Peterhof in Novgorod, the eastern
terminus of Hanse trade routes, for the Russian fur-amber-wax trade;
Bergen, dominating both the Norwegian and Icelandic fisheries and trade;
and Bruges, by far the most important *kontor*, serving the largest and
wealthiest market in Northwestern Europe, and the primary source of
woolen cloths.

During the fourteenth century, both the principal Hanse markets and
their supply of quality woolens lay in the Flemish and Brabantine towns of
the southern Low Countries. From the 1360s, however, the seafaring
towns of Holland and Zeeland, directly to the north, had begun to embark
upon a commercial expansion that would, by the sixteenth century, gain
them economic ascendancy over both their southern neighbors and the
Hanse. The wellsprings of the Northern Netherlands' growth, as Jan de
Vries has cogently argued, lay in the fact that their livestock-raising
economy was far more successful in resisting feudal-manorial encroach-
ments than were grain-based economies (e.g., in the English Midlands).
Pastoral economies, moreover, much more readily turned to commerce to
acquire other necessary foodstuffs.[36] For these towns, whose inland water-
ways provided much easier access by ship than by horse, this meant maritime trade, supplemented by coastal fisheries, and many of their ships
came to be employed by the Hanse as supplemental carriers of Baltic cargoes between Hamburg and Bruges. Furthermore, many of the Holland-
Zeeland towns, led by Amsterdam, had joined the Hanse in their war

against Denmark (1367-70), though very shortly thereafter, these North Sea allies became dangerous enemies by invading Hanse commercial preserves within the Baltic itself.

These Netherlanders were not the first invaders, for English merchant ships had been sailing directly into the Baltic, from the 1360s, through the Kattegat-Danish Sund.[37] This dual invasion came at a bad time for the Hanse, just when their markets were seriously contracting, and provided the Hanseatic League with its prime raison d'être: monopoly and protectionism. Lübeck, concerned about the transit trade between the Baltic and North Seas, more than other Hanse towns saw the greater threat from the Holland-Zeeland towns, whose seamen, unlike the English, offered their ships as common carriers on terms very appealing to the Prussian and Livonian towns. They also paid cash for furs, timber, grain, and naval stores and marketed their own woolen goods—Leiden woolens were almost as fine as Flemish ones—in the Prussian towns, evading the Hanseatic *kontor*-staple at Bruges and thereby further angering Lübeck. Furthermore, North Holland towns also became powerful competitors in the beer and salt trades.[38]

The Holland-Zeeland towns gained by far their most important victory in the herring trades, based on their development of a large fishing craft which could spend a week or more in the vastly larger herring grounds far out in the North Sea. This was the buss (*buis*), a 140-ton flat-bottomed boat with three sets of sails, which carried not only the supplies for and catch from a week's fishing, but also sufficient salt for on-board curing, a related innovation made necessary by the longer periods spent at sea. On-board salt-curing improved quality (aroma, taste) not only by its very immediacy, but also by its rapidity, which first by accident and then by design left intact appendices (*pyloric caecae*) containing a very fast-acting chemical preservative, *trypsin*. Demand for salt drew more and more ships from Holland-Zeeland to the Bay of Bourgneuf, where, with shorter distances, they could acquire salt more cheaply than the Baltic Germans could. Thus the Hollanders' victory in herring was the product of both superior quality and lower cost, especially through greater scale economies.[39]

Herring, like salt, soon became a major import into the Baltic zone, after the sudden disappearance of herring from the Skania spawning grounds, by the 1430s.[40] The most likely explanation is overfishing at Skania as an ill-advised German response to North Sea competition, not declining salinity in a colder Baltic. Nevertheless, the greater salinity of the North Sea, warmed by the Gulf Stream, did sustain a far more plentiful supply of plankton, which produced much larger herring. Not for two centuries would anyone challenge Holland's supremacy in the herring fisheries, which the States General later (1606) called "the chiefest mine of the Netherlands." The Dutch then controlled over half the European market in herring, with annual sales of over 200 million, whose value exceeded aggregate revenues from all English exports. Both the herring and salt trades vastly expanded the range of Holland's maritime commerce and promoted a great expansion in its ship-building industry and thus a need to acquire Baltic timber and naval stores.[41]

As early as the 1430s, the Hollanders' invasion of the Baltic had provoked a decisive war with Lübeck's Wendish League. While Holland secured an alliance with Denmark, the Prussian and Livonian towns remained neutral, thereby revealing the fatal flaw of the Hanseatic League: disunity from regional self-interest, especially by those profiting from shipping and trade with North Holland towns. Isolated and beaten by 1441, Lübeck reluctantly signed the Treaty of Copenhagen, which granted the Hollanders full trading rights in the Baltic, which they quickly exploited.[42] For the Hanse now turned to face a seemingly greater threat, from England.

### 6. ENGLISH COMMERCIAL EXPANSION & CONFLICTS WITH THE HANSE

English penetration of the Baltic was based upon cloth exports, which would also prove crucial for their subsequent commercial expansion. By the later fourteenth century, England's woolen industry had acquired competitive advantages that should have been decisive: in producing lower-cost cloths woven from abundant home-grown wools whose peerless quality faced no rivals before the much later improvement in Spanish merino wools. A voracious continental demand had long made wool England's most lucrative export; and, when the Hundred Years' War began, the crown took advantage of this dependence by levying exorbitant export duties—up to 50 percent of mean-wool prices by the 1390s. It also established a cartel of wool-dealers, the Calais Staple Company (1363), to pass this tax burden on to foreign buyers, chiefly Netherlandish luxury draperies, for whom English wools now represented 70 percent of total production costs. English clothiers, on the other hand, acquired these wools tax-free and their exports were taxed only 3 percent (from 1347), to give them a cost advantage of 25-35 percent.[43]

Less important were other cost advantages derived from a rural location: freedom from urban taxes and guild controls, lower wages, and mechanical fulling (displacing traditional foot-fulling). In fact, however, about half of cloth-making for export still took place in towns, which also used fulling-mills; and lower rural wages reflected not just cheaper food but also the inferior productivity of part-time farm workers. In the rural West Country, however, "undershot" fulling-mills on fast-flowing upland streams probably did provide substantial savings on *value-added* production costs, up to 20 percent.[44]

These English advantages make puzzling the survival of the traditional urban draperies in the Low Countries (Flanders, Brabant, Holland) until the mid-fifteenth century. The fundamental explanation lies in those structural economic changes favoring luxury textiles, for without them these urban draperies could not have so long maintained their almost exclusive reliance on such heavily taxed English wools. Furthermore, the *specific* rather than *ad valorem* (proportional) nature of the wool duties encouraged these draperies to purchase only the finest wools, for which their tax burden was thus relatively lighter. These draperies produced extremely expensive woolens (more than double the price of English broadcloths) and shunned mechanical fulling for fear that it would fatally impair their reputation for luxury quality. They collectively chose, therefore, survival for a small number of producers, based upon a narrow if stable market, and surrendered the lower, broader ranges of European markets for quality textiles to other competitors—except the Flemish market. From 1359, the Flemish drapery towns, enjoying greater powers than those of Brabant and Holland, had resolutely enforced a ban on all English woolens within their county.[45]

That Flemish ban undoubtedly influenced the diversion of English cloth exports into the less promising Baltic zone during the later fourteenth century. English merchants focused upon Prussia, establishing a merchant colony in Danzig during the mid-1370s, and shortly thereafter the Flemish civil war and then Hanseatic embargoes (1379-92) allowed them to expand Baltic sales of their woolens. They did so at the expense of Prussian merchants, bypassing the Hanse staple-towns, and they petitioned Parliament to make Hanse privileges in England conditional on reciprocal rights for the English at Danzig. Other Hanse towns, concerned about their English trade, urged a compromise, which the Prussians reluctantly accepted in a treaty signed by the Teutonic Grand Master in 1410.[46] The English victory was a hollow one, for by then war, piracy, and economic contraction had sent England's Baltic trade into a prolonged slump. The Prussian towns shared in the Teutonic Order's terrible defeat in 1410 at the hands of Polish and Lithuanian armies, while Lübeck became embroiled in naval wars with first Holland and then England, whose piratical attacks on Lübeck's Bay Fleets made it now appear the more ominous threat. Then, in the 1450s and 1460s, the English further undermined their Baltic prospects by quarreling with Denmark over Scandinavian and Icelandic fisheries and trade.[47]

Well before this point, however, the English had secured two alternative, more promising outlets in the nearby Low Countries. Since the 1380s, English merchants had been selling cloths at Middelburg in Zeeland, which doubtless benefited from England's Baltic tribulations, and in 1421 the London based Merchants Adventurer Company set up residence in Antwerp to exploit the newly expanding Brabant Fairs as its principal continental base for English cloth exports.[48] This most important breakthrough for the English cloth trade had far more to do with these fairs and the revival of overland continental trade routes than with any difficulties in Baltic maritime trade.

### 7. THE RISE OF ANTWERP: ENGLISH CLOTH AND GERMAN MERCHANTS

During the first half of the fifteenth century, the most important foreign customers for English woolens at the Brabant Fairs of Antwerp and Bergen-op-Zoom were merchants from Cologne and other Rhenish Hanse towns, whose commerce was then stimulating a renewed growth in overland trade between the Low Countries and Italy. This revival of continental trade, preceding developments in maritime trade, converted the Brabant Fairs from a regional market in foodstuffs (Rhenish and Alsatian wines, German and Netherlander beer, salt, herrings, French grains) into a truly international entrepôt that would dominate northern Europe from the mid-fifteenth to mid-sixteenth centuries.[49] These new overland trade flows followed more easterly routes, away from the Hundred Years' War; and the Rhine, now the chief commercial highway to the south, brought Rhenish merchants together at the Frankfurt Fairs with South Germans, who dominated the trans-Alpine trade with Venice and Lombardy. This whole expansion, indeed, took its rise from a precocious economic and demographic recovery in southern Germany and northern Italy, which also stimulated the growth of fairs at Besançon, Geneva, Chalon-sur-Saône, and Lyons—none of which yet rivalled those of Frankfurt and Brabant.

Ultimately, Antwerp's commercial supremacy rested on a tripod of English woolens, South German metals, and Portuguese-Asian spices, but the first and strongest leg was English cloth, most of which was dyed and dressed in Antwerp itself or adjacent towns. The English cloth trade developed unevenly from an initial boom between 1420 and the 1440s, followed by three decades of serious setbacks connected with the final phase of the Hundred Years' War, another demographic slump, and a commercial recession.[50] The English government exacerbated these setbacks by bullionist measures, which, however, finally benefited the English cloth trade by severely damaging the Flemish and Brabantine urban draperies. In 1429, responding to falling mint outputs, blamed on Burgundian coinage debasements, the English crown imposed the now infamous Partition and Bullion Ordinances, which by 1433 allowed a small clique of merchants to dominate the Calais Staple. In return, they were required to raise wool prices and to exact immediate, full payment in good English coin, with no credit permitted. A Burgundian retaliatory ban on all English cloth imports (1434) led to open warfare between England and Burgundy (1436-39), once firm allies against the French. The ensuing peace treaty, however, failed to resolve the economic conflicts, and by 1478, when the hated Calais bullion laws were repealed, both the English wool trade and most Netherlandish urban draperies had suffered irreparable damage.[51] The drapers, petty entrepreneurs, had long required credit from the Calais Staple to buy wool, and the bullion ordinances forced them to resort to moneylenders, thereby raising costs and prices to punitive levels.

Between the 1420s and the 1470s, the Staple's wool sales fell 44 percent; but that was less than the drop in output from the traditional Flemish-Brabantine draperies, because some other customers had responded more effectively to these adverse conditions.[52] The more resilient of the now numerous *nouvelles draperies* had done so by mixing at least some English wools with cheaper yet much improved Spanish merino wools, which most traditional draperies continued to disdain, lest their reputation for luxury quality be impaired. Most would not use them until long after the English cloth trade and the *nouvelles draperies* had supplanted them on the Antwerp market.[53] In the traditional sector, only Leiden's drapery prospered for most of the century, while still relying solely on English wools, principally because its cloth sales depended not on foreign merchants but on Holland's own merchant marine, which was then making rapid gains in Baltic markets. After 1500, however, Leiden's drapery would also steadily lose ground to the now irresistible English cloth trade.[54]

The English cloth trade owed both its recovery from the mid-fifteenth-century slump and its final victory to an equally dramatic expansion in South German trade, the second leg of Antwerp's commercial tripod. The roots of South German commercial expansion lay in previously noted developments in Levantine trade, in which Venice exchanged German silver and copper for Syrian cotton, which supported South Germany's new fustian industries. Far more important, however, in propelling South German commerce and finance to hegemony over the revitalized transcontinental trade with the Low Countries was the Central European boom in copper and silver.

The mining boom began in the 1460s during northern Europe's most severe phase of monetary contraction. Whatever the chief cause, reduced monetary stocks or reduced flows, the result was the closure of many mints and a prolonged deflation, which in turn enhanced the real value (purchasing power) of silver.[55] This in turn sparked a technological revolution in both mining and smelting that increased the output of silver and copper five- or six-fold by the 1520s. The first stage was an innovation in mechanical engineering. New drainage pumps and adits (downward-slanted tunnels) eliminated the perennial problem of flooded mine shafts in mountainous Central Europe. Then came an even more important innovation in chemical engineering: the *Seigerhütten* process, using a lead smelting catalyst to separate previously inseparable silver and copper. The copper thus extracted from this region's vast ore deposits also had considerable value as the chief ingredient in making bronze artillery, which had already played a major role in ending the Hundred Years War.[56]

Virtually the entire era of the Central European mining boom, from the 1460s to the 1520s, coincided with the rise, expansion, and first apogee of both the English cloth trade and the Antwerp market. Initially, despite the growth of Rhineland-South German trade, the Brabant Fairs had to compete with Venice, Danzig, and Lübeck as markets for these metals; but thanks to two coincidental acts of coinage debasements in the 1460s—one English and one Burgundian, both partly inspired by bullion scarcities—Antwerp soon gained an overwhelming command of the trade in South German metals. The English debasement of 1464-65 reduced exchange rates on the pound sterling at Antwerp by almost 25 percent, thus making English cloth an even more attractive return cargo for Rhenish and South German merchants, while the Burgundian debasement of 1466 (silver by 13 percent, gold by 4 percent) turned a strongly pro-gold into an even more strongly pro-silver mint ratio, attracting a far greater share of the South German silver flows to the new Antwerp mint.[57]

These monetary changes touched off an explosion of English cloth exports. From 1460-69 to 1490-99 London-based exports, principally to the Brabant Fairs, more than doubled to account for almost 70 percent of the

English total, prompting a Burgundian observer to compare such cloths to an "tremendous invasion of the sea [*inundacionis maris immensis*]."[58] Nothing succeeds like success. Exchanges of English broadcloths for South German silver and copper, along with the concurrent expansion in the Brabant Fairs, attracted merchants from all over Europe, and finally the Portuguese with their Asian spices, who completed the tripod on which Antwerp's commercial-financial hegemony rested for the next half century.

## 8. PORTUGAL: TRADE WITH AFRICA, ASIA, AND BRAZIL

Portugal, like South Germany, was a traditional "backwater" whose commerce began to grow in the late fourteenth century. Political unification under the Aviz dynasty, ensuring independence from Castile (1385), and an English alliance (1386) spurred Portugal's trade with England and Flanders in her few but important resources: wine, olive oil, citrus fruits, cork, Bay salt, and salted fish. Within thirty-five years Portugal would inaugurate European overseas expansion, a story told elsewhere in this volume.[59] Neither there nor here, regrettably, can justice be done to the revolutionary changes in ship design that made that overseas expansion possible: the two-or three-masted caravel, with triangular Arabic lateen sails; and then the much larger, heavily-armed, full-rigged carrack, combining the two square-rigged sails of northern cogs, for power, with the caravel's lateen sail in the rear or mizzen-mast, for manoeuverability.[60] Here space permits only a discussion of the commercial patterns that arose from the Portuguese and then Spanish maritime explorations, conquests, and colonizations in Africa, Asia, and the Americas.

The Portuguese trade with West Africa and the Atlantic Islands was based chiefly upon gold, slaves, sugar, *malaguetta* pepper, and ivory, in roughly that order of importance. From the very beginning in the 1440s, the Portuguese acquired these commodities, even slaves, not by conquest but through peaceful trade, selling European textiles, copper and bronze goods, and horses in well organized West African markets. Slaves may have been Portugal's earliest African acquisitions, and undoubtedly slave labor became absolutely vital in developing sugar plantations in Madeira, the Azores, and the African islands of Fernando Po, Principé, and Sâo Tomé (also serving as slave entrepôts). For almost a century, however, gold led all other African exports in value. Of the two precious metals, gold had become the scarcer in mid-fifteenth century Europe (as the bimetallic ratio rose from 10:1 to 12:1), and the initial influx of African gold may have helped relieve European monetary scarcity even before the Central European silver mining boom got underway. African gold was not, however, a Portuguese "discovery," nor did they ever gain direct access to its principal sources, in the upper reaches of the Senegal (Bambuk), Niger (Mali), and Volta (Lobi) rivers systems, whence gold had for centuries flowed (possibly in diminished amounts after the 1370s) across the trans-Saharan routes to North African ports. By the late 1400s, the Portuguese gained much more West African gold, evidently at the expense of the trans-Saharan routes, and between 1470 and 1500 they shipped about 17 metric tons of African gold, plus another 19 tons by 1550 (with a peak flow in the 1520s).[61]

Well before then, Asian spices had surpassed African gold to dominate Portuguese overseas trade. The component values were similar to those of the fifteenth-century Venetian spice trade: pepper from Malabar and Sumatra typically accounted for 85 percent (producing profits from 90 percent to 150 percent); ginger, for 6 percent; cinnamon, for 2 percent; and all other spices combined (cloves, mace, nutmeg), for 6 percent.[62] Almost from the first, in 1501, the Portuguese had established their official European spice staple at Antwerp, where they sought not only international distribution and financial facilities but also the two most important commodities to be exchanged for Asian spices: South German silver and copper (supplemented by African gold). Both copper and silver were much scarcer in Asia, where they commanded a purchasing power two to three times higher than in Europe.[63]

Most historians agree that the Portuguese only briefly, if ever, monopolized the Asian spice trades, despite a superiority in naval artillery, because of chronic shortages in shipping, manpower, and commercial capital. In the eastern Indian Ocean, they failed to prevent the rise of Atjeh (Aceh) in northern Sumatra, whose merchants were exporting as many spices as the Portuguese by the 1580s; and in the western zone, they could not prevent Asian rivals from delivering spices toward Egyptian and Syrian ports (under Ottoman control from 1517) by both the Persian Gulf and the Red Sea. They thus failed to prevent the Venetians from regaining over half of the European spice trade by the 1550s.[64]

Portugal nevertheless did not suffer any absolute impairment in her Asian commerce during the sixteenth century. In the 1590s, on the eve of the combined Dutch and English invasions of the Indies, Portuguese export tonnages to Asia were 14 percent higher and import tonnages 7 percent higher (67 percent higher in the 1580s) than they had been in 1501-

20.  While the Portuguese *share* of the spice trade had fallen, its total volume had about doubled, reflecting the formation of a far larger European market based on sustained population growth during most of the sixteenth century.  Furthermore, from the 1570s the Portuguese increased both their intra-Asian commerce, especially with China and Japan, and export volumes in Asian cotton textiles and dyestuffs, which in 1600 accounted for 19 percent of their European sales.  At that time, the Asian trades still ranked first in state revenues, with a 26 percent share, followed by 17 percent for their African commerce, and 14 percent for the Atlantic-American trades.[65]

Though third in rank, the Atlantic-American trades were by then the most rapidly expanding, primarily because of Brazil.  Commercial exports had begun with brazilwood, the costly red dyestuff after which this American colony was named, previously obtained from tropical East Indian trees (genus *Caesalpinia*).  From the 1530s a more active colonization (to evict the French from this trade) brought many settlers from the Atlantic islands and led to a rapid development of sugar plantations worked by African slave labor.  By 1610 some 130 sugar plantations and 210 mills were producing about 13,800 metric tons of sugar annually, of which about 60 percent (8,050 metric tons), producing over 90 percent of Brazil's export revenues, was shipped to Portugal.[66]  In converting an expensive luxury good into a cheap, mass-consumption commodity, Eric Hobsbawm once argued, the creation of sugar plantation economies constituted an essential feature of the shift from "Old to New Colonialism," which he dated from the 1660s.[67]  In truth, the Portuguese had created such an economy more than a century earlier, establishing the very pattern that the Spanish, French, and English would follow in the Americas.

## 9. SPAIN IN THE NEW WORLD: COCHINEAL, SUGAR, AND SILVER

The first commercial export (from 1523) from the new Spanish colonies in the Americas was also a red dyestuff:  Mexican cochineal (*grana cochinilla*), which became a much more abundant, cheaper, but even more effective substitute for the world's most luxurious dyestuff, scarlet *kermes* (also known as *grana* or *grain*).  By the 1590s cochineal exports were worth about 125 million maravedis (about 295,000 florins), or about 42 percent of the aggregate value of the non-bullion commodity exports from the Spanish Americas.  Much less important in the 1590s, if by no means negligible, were sugar exports, chiefly from the Caribbean islands, whose value then amounted to 40 million maravedis (94,250 florins), in volume less than 5 percent of contemporary Brazilian sugar exports.[68]

Silver, of course, was by far the most valuable American export in the 1590s. Until the 1530s gold had accounted for virtually all of the recorded treasure imports at Seville; and silver became predominant only with the nearly simultaneous discovery in 1545-46 of two vast deposits at Potosí, in the Vice-Royalty of Peru (in modern Bolivia) and at Zacatecas in northern New Spain (modern Mexico). Subsequently, from the 1560s, the mercury amalgamation process allowed the Spanish to engage in large-scale smelting at low cost, especially at Potosí, whose production more than tripled to a decennial mean of 184,830 kg. in the 1590s. That was also the peak decade for (official) bullion imports at Seville with an annual mean of 270,763 kg. of silver and 1,945 kg. of gold, together worth 3,133.44 million maravedis (7.38 million florins). The second most important producer, at Zacatecas, achieved its peak output three decades later, in the 1620s, but at a much lower level, with a decennial mean of 50,105 kg. By that time, furthermore, a much higher proportion of a diminishing output was being retained for colonial economic development, while a small but significant Mexican share (from 5 to 21 percent) was being diverted across the Pacific in trade with the Spanish Philippines and China.[69]

Europe did not retain all, nor even most, of imported American silver, whose most important role, especially when Europe's own output of precious metals began to decline, was to generate a vast expansion in world trade. In West European trade with the Baltic, the Levant and Asia, from the sixteenth to eighteenth centuries, precious metals always commanded a far greater value than all other exports combined, financing 65 to 85 percent of imports.[70] But too often historians have ignored the role of these metals in generating European trade with the Americas themselves. According to Pierre and Huguette Chaunu, Spanish exports to the Americas, including a wide variety of European textiles, almost doubled from the 1560s to the 1590s, from 450 million maravedis to about 850 million maravedis (2.0 million gold florins); and Spain's trade with the Americas was much greater in value (or so they contend) than the foreign trade conducted by any other European rival—Venetian, Dutch, English, or Portuguese.[71]

## 10. The "Price Revolution": money and credit

For historians of past generations, the primary importance of the influx of silver from Spanish America was to generate the European Price Revolution, a century of sustained inflation (to the 1640s) with a five-or six-fold rise in regional price levels, following a long era of falling or stable prices.[72] More recently, however, this monetary explanation for the Price Revolution has been rejected by historians who contend, quite correctly, that inflation had begun at least twenty years before any major silver shipments reached Spain.[73] Other monetary factors, however, can explain the origins of the European inflation. First and foremost, the Central European mining boom had already expanded silver output more than five-fold by the mid-1520s, when it was annually producing about 90,000 kg., an amount unmatched by American silver imports before the 1560s. Second, before the American influx began, the Portuguese had imported about 36,000-40,000 kg. of African gold, worth about 520,000 kg. of silver. Third, drastic coinage debasements continued to afflict western Europe, if sporadically and regionally, and in England they were the major source of inflation during the 1540s and 1550s. Fourth, from the early sixteenth century, Europe experienced a veritable explosion in credit that rapidly expanded both money supplies and their income velocities.

And yet American silver inflows from the 1540s certainly did aggravate and prolong the European-wide inflation well into the seventeenth century, spreading through trade and war from Spain to other European countries, especially to support Spanish military campaigns in Italy, France, Germany, and the Netherlands.[74] Though some historians still assert that England received no Spanish bullion, the mint accounts document a quite different story, particularly after its Great Debasement (1542-52). The surviving Tower Mint Melting Books (for 1561-99) indicate that 78 percent of its silver came from Spain and most of the rest from the Netherlands (and indirectly from Spanish sources).[75] Moreover, while 75 percent of total coinages struck from 1470 to 1520 (with a mean annual value of £45,775) was in gold, thereafter, from 1520 to 1600, 75 percent of total coinages struck (with a mean annual value of £141,891) was in silver— over 90 percent in the 1590s. Furthermore, in 1575-99, with no coinage changes, 4.87 times more silver was coined than in 1500-24: 287,644 kg. vs. 59,090 kg. Similarly dramatic increases in silver minting can also be found in the southern Netherlands. During the quarter-century 1550-74, their mints struck 5.88 times more silver than in 1500-24—280,955 kg. vs. 47,789 kg.—while even in the ensuing war-torn Revolt era of 1575-99, they struck 144,398 kg. or 3.02 times as much silver as in 1500-24.[76]

Despite such monetary evidence, the most popular explanation for the Price Revolution remains "population growth," an undeniable phenomenon of this entire era.[77] The demographic model, however, as argued above, can explain only *relative price changes*, or different rates of price changes for specific commodities with differing supply and demand elasticities. Indeed, from 1510-19 to 1630-39 the rise in English grain prices (+670 percent), with inelastic supply, was much steeper than those for livestock products (+355 percent) or industrial goods (+204 percent). The demographic model cannot explain, however, why virtually all prices and the composite English price index rose (by 490 percent),[78] nor how population growth itself could produce an "inflationary increase in aggregate demand" without a commensurate expansion in the volume of money payments.

Population growth may nonetheless have promoted an expansion in money payments by inducing a rising income velocity of money, which may have become a more powerful inflationary agent than increased coin stocks. Recently, Jack Goldstone has propounded this view in a complex model of "financial-exchange networks" combining demographic growth, rapid urbanization, a spread of fully monetized market economies, and greater use of credit. In a more comprehensible version of this model, Peter Lindert contends that population growth, by increasing the ratio of dependent children to adults and raising relative food prices, thus diminishing real household incomes, reduced the demand for idle cash balances, induced dishoarding, and so increased the income-velocity of money.[79]

A combined increase in both monetary *stocks* and *flows* can thus explain the Price Revolution through the modernized income version of the Fisher Identity: $MV = Py$ or $P = MV/y$, where y again represents real net national income or aggregate output of goods and services. On the right side of the second equation, both the real variable (y) and the two monetary variables (M) and (V) were rising from ca. 1510 to ca. 1640. But when the growth in aggregate money payments (M x V) finally outstripped the growth in real y, the consequence was necessarily a rise in P, i.e. inflation. In an economy that remained strongly agrarian or land-based, with inadequate technological changes, real national income y could not have kept pace with rapidly growing money payments, as rising population finally used up most of the readily available land and natural resources, producing diminishing returns and rising marginal costs.

Another powerful force in expanding the volume of money payments in sixteenth-century Europe was an exponential increase in private and public credit, which had been made possible, in part, by legal changes that had permitted credit instruments to become negotiable. Paradoxically, supposedly "backward" England was the first northern country to provide such legal sanctions in 1437, when London's law-merchant Mayor's Court ruled that the bearer presenting a bill for collection on its maturity had as much right to payment as the original payee in the bill. Subsequently, in 1499 and 1502, Lübeck's civic court issued a similar verdict on bearer bills. So did Antwerp's court in a 1507 *turba* involving English cloth merchants, and Habsburg edicts of 1537 and 1541 extended these legal provisions on debt assignments and bearer bills to establish full negotiability throughout the Netherlands. In 1541 the Habsburg government also legalized interest payments on loans, up to 12 percent, which removed a major impediment to discounting negotiable bills (since the amount so discounted before maturity had represented "usury," as foregone interest).[80]

At the very same time provincial governments in the Habsburg Netherlands were also engaging in short-term borrowing through "letters obligatory" (promissory notes) that had also become fully negotiable bearer bills. Ultimately far more important in public finance throughout western Europe was the now negotiable *rente* or *censo*, an annuity with medieval origins in both private and municipal credit. By the former (*bail à rente*) a private landholder sold his claim to some specific real-estate income (*cens*) in return for fixed annual cash payments, often as a hereditary annuity. By the latter (*constitution de rente*), a creditor provided a debtor, often a municipal or state government, with a lump sum of money in return for a fixed lifetime annuity (*rente viagère*), or one that included his heirs (*rente heritable*), or "in perpetuity;" and governments made annuity payments from their excise (*accijnzen*) or other taxes. While debtors (i.e., governments) could redeem or buy back these *rentes*, the creditor, who could not compel redemption, might regain his principal (with profit or loss) by selling his *rente* to some third party, who then received the annuity. Such negotiability had been facilitated by papal bulls (1425, 1455) that found *rente* contracts to be exempt from the usury laws and thus fully licit.

The Netherlands provided sixteenth-century Europe's fastest growing market for such *rentes*, private and public, domestic and foreign, especially Antwerp itself, after the establishment of its *Bourse* in 1531. Much of this extensive financial activity, which also included all kinds of short-term floating debt, was conducted by the leading South German merchant-banking houses—the Fuggers, Welsers, Höchstetters, Herwarts, Imhofs, and Tuchers—whose success in organizing these markets is reflected in a steep decline in both *rente* yields and interest rates on public loans from the late fifteenth to mid-sixteenth centuries. Many of these bankers, especially the Fuggers, had also become heavily engaged in both papal and Spanish finances, employing similar annuities.[81]

Indeed, nowhere was an expansion in public credit more dramatic than in Habsburg Spain, commencing in 1515 with Charles V's issue of new *juros*, as heritable/redeemable annuities yielding 3 to 7 percent. Since foreigners could hold or sell these *juros*, they proved to be immensely popular throughout Europe. By the 1550s annuity payments were consuming over 50 percent of public revenues, and by 1600 the aggregate value of *juros* issued had risen from 5 to 83 million ducats (375 maravedis/ducat). Equally important was the role that syndicates of South German bankers performed in managing royal *asiento* contracts: advancing short-term funds to the crown by purchasing its bills of exchange that were usually drawn upon the Antwerp market. The *asientos* were backed by the crown's share of bullion imports, and the very arrival of silver fleets often promoted a vast expansion in state credit. In 1557, however, the South German merchant bankers encountered financial disaster when Philip II suspended all short-term financial claims, converting them into 5 percent perpetual *juros*. In ruining the South German bankers this Spanish default also terminated "the supremacy of the Antwerp market over Habsburg official finances." A similar bankruptcy by France's Henry II the next year led to the ruin of rival Florentine bankers and the Lyons financial fairs. The beneficiaries of these two great disasters were the Genoese merchant-bankers, who then dominated Spanish and European public finances for the rest of the century, much more successfully than the South Germans before them. As Van der Wee so aptly concluded, "the age of the Fuggers and the Genoese [to 1619] was one of spectacular growth of public finances;"[82] and their inflationary role in the Price Revolution has never been given its proper due.

Though Europe had envied Spain for its vast wealth in American silver, this wealth bore the seeds of ruin for the Spanish Habsburg empire. It provided an intoxicating stimulus for widespread chronic warfare and ruinous public finances that ultimately drained Spain of vital economic resources, and the inflationary impact of both bullion flows and ballooning credit retarded rather than stimulated economic, especially industrial, development. Ultimately, those who gained the most from the Price Revolution were Holland and England, whose rise to commercial-financial pre-eminence was first facilitated by the downfalls of the South Germans, Spain, and the Antwerp market.

## 11. FROM ANTWERP TO AMSTERDAM: THE HEGEMONY OF HOLLAND

Well before the Spanish and German financial crises of 1557-58, Antwerp had suffered two key blows to her commercial tripod. First, the flow of South German silver and copper lessened, as the Central European mines began to encounter diminishing returns, falling outputs, and rising costs, which made their silver uncompetitive when American bullion began to arrive at Seville. Moreover, Venice, with the strong revival in its spice trade, was diverting more of those metals to the Mediterranean. The second blow fell in 1548, when Portugal responded to these events by transferring her spice staple from Antwerp to Lisbon, closer to both the cheaper silver and the major spice markets in the Mediterranean.[83]

Until the mid-century, however, Antwerp continued to enjoy a substantial prosperity chiefly based on a boom in the textile trades, foreign and domestic (including silk-finishing, fine linens, fashionable clothing, embroideries, cambrics, and tapestries).[84] Though the southern Netherlands had lost their supremacy in luxury woolens, they had gained a new industrial pre-eminence in less costly cloths. The no-longer-new *nouvelles draperies* based on Spanish wool had just reached their peak; and a multitude of urban *sayetteries*, led by Hondschoote, were becoming the major textile industries, with much cheaper, lighter semi-worsted fabrics. Once again, as in the thirteenth century, conditions in the Mediterranean for these cheap, light textiles had become more advantageous than they had been during the intervening late medieval era. The sixteenth-century Mediterranean basin in particular experienced a rapid demographic, commercial, and urban expansion that widened and deepened concentrated markets to provide greater scale economies and lower transaction costs. Furthermore, though warfare still loomed large, notably the Franco-Imperial and Ottoman wars, it was far more organized, no longer breeding the chronic, widespread, and debilitating anarchy of the later Middle Ages. Indeed, security generally prevailed along the vital transcontinental routes between the Netherlands and Italy through which passed almost all the trade in these cheap textiles to reach their major markets in the Mediterranean basin.[85] Economies of scale and reduced transaction costs were also promoted by numerous innovations and the spread of improvements in commercial organization, credit, and transport. To those already discussed should be added printed commodity-price and exchange rate "currents," large-scale warehousing facilities, merchandising by "commission" houses, and embryonic joint-stock companies. For overland transport, the new Hesse carts and postal services generally made the continental routes speedier and more reliable than Atlantic shipping routes.[86] In the Mediterranean the increasing use of carracks and improved navigation had already cut maritime freight rates by 25 percent.[87]

Even more important than the light says for the Antwerp market, especially for the finishing and re-export trades, were Italian silks and English woolens, which in 1560 accounted for 22 percent and 18 percent of total imports respectively (55 percent for all textile products).[88] By then the English cloth trade had already passed its peak, with a 36 percent surge in exports during the 1540s, partly fuelled by the 83 percent devaluation of the pound sterling during the Great Debasement. The consequent reductions in cloth prices on the Antwerp market were nonetheless short-lived, because these debasements, unlike those of 1464-65, aggravated an internal inflation that quickly drove up costs. In 1552 the crown abruptly ended the debasements with a 77 percent revaluation that produced a brutal rise in exchange rates and thus in cloth prices on the now glutted Antwerp market. London's cloth exports quickly plummeted 36 percent (from 132,767 to 84,969 broadcloths).[89] Any recovery from the 1550s slump was prevented by Habsburg trade bans in 1563-65, then rebellion and Alva's brutal repression after 1566, by new trade bans in 1568, by an open military revolt from Holland and Zeeland in 1572, and by the Spanish Fury at Antwerp in 1576. These events pushed the English to seek safer continental outlets, at Emden, Middelburg, Stade, and Hamburg.[90] When Antwerp fell to Parma's armies in 1585, few English merchants were left.

By this stage in the Netherlands' Revolt, Amsterdam, which lay protected by its inland location on the Zuider Zee, by the Maas and Rhine river barriers, and by Dutch sea-power, had gained decisive ascendancy over Antwerp, reinforced by a permanent Dutch blockade of the Scheldt's estuary. Into the new Republic of the United Provinces (from 1579), and especially into Amsterdam itself, bearing much human and financial capital, flocked mainly Protestant refugee merchants, bankers, and artisans. Among the latter were those who transplanted various forms of semi-worsted crafts to Leiden and Haarlem as a flourishing *nieuwe draperie*. The revolt also led to Dutch aggression in the Asian spice trades. Long engaged in the wine and salt trades with Portugal, Holland's merchant marine had added spices after the Portuguese transferred their staple to Lisbon in 1548. When, however, Portugal became part of the Spanish empire in 1580, the Dutch were cut off from Lisbon, while Mediterranean warfare with the Turks was disrupting the alternative spice-trade routes. Thus the Dutch, inspired by a volatile mix of Calvinism and nationalism, and in a

race with the English, strove to reach the East Indies first and dislodge their
enemy from the very source of the spices. Their success after 1600, which
gave them a greater power over the spice trade than the Portuguese or
Venetians had ever enjoyed, lies beyond the scope of this study.

The significance of Dutch expansion outside Europe should nonetheless
not be exaggerated, for even in the seventeenth century the true heart of the
Dutch commercial empire remained where it had been born, in the Baltic.
Indeed, at their very commencement in 1497, the Danish Sund tolls already indicate a predominance of ships from North Holland towns;[91] and
by 1557, when these records become more inclusive and continuous, the
volume of their shipping had increased another 77 percent to account for
almost 60 percent of inbound voyages. Lübeck had already conceded their
supremacy (Treaty of Speyer, 1544); and, apart from a steep plunge in the
early 1570s, when naval resources were diverted to fight the Spanish,
Dutch shipping and their share of total Baltic traffic continued to rise,
reaching 69 percent at the onset of the Thirty Years' War in 1618.[92]

These shipping data also indicate how Holland had benefited so
strongly from the economic forces of the Price Revolution. A combination
of demographic and commercial expansion, rapid European urbanization,
growth in overseas shipping, and the modernized military structures of
Renaissance states had driven up the *relative* prices of the chief commodities shipped from the Baltic: grains, lumber, naval stores, copper and iron.
If western Europe's steady growth in Baltic imports aggravated its balance
of payments deficit, the North Holland towns, by dominating the carrying
trades and related financial services, managed to acquire sufficient Spanish
American silver to settle those deficits with the Baltic. The most valuable
import from the Baltic, until the early seventeenth century, was grain
(ranking third in value at Antwerp ca. 1560);[93] but even more important
for Holland's commercial power were Baltic naval stores and timber, so vital to its rapidly growing shipbuilding industry, especially when timber
had become so scarce and expensive in Mediterranean shipyards.[94]

Holland's continued domination of the Baltic trades also came to rest
upon superior naval technology, represented by an all-purpose cargo boat,
the "flute" [*fluitschip*]. Slowly evolving through the sixteenth century, the
flute was a large carrack built for Baltic bulk goods, but its combination of
square and lateen sails made it much faster than similar sized cogs. Its
most important and novel feature was the lack of cannons, which allowed
smaller crews, greater speed, more usable cargo space, and construction
from cheap Baltic pine rather than the costly oak required for cannon-
bearing ships. Ships of other nations, relatively more dependent on luxury

trades, dared not dispense with cannon, while the Dutch, having calculated that the flute's advantages outweighed any risks from piracy, devoted this specialized ship to the Baltic bulk trades. Furthermore, the growing volume of shipping that arose from mastery of the Baltic, along with the flute's simplicity of design and standardized parts, allowed Holland's shipyards to engage in even lower-cost, mass-production techniques and produce ships for about 60 percent of rival shipyards' prices. This cost reduction, along with crews smaller by two-thirds and superior commercial organization, resulted in freight rates only half that charged by their competitors.[95]

The English and other rivals thus faced a classic "vicious circle." They could not build or operate cargo ships as cheaply as the Dutch, and so could not compete in the Baltic-North Sea trades, nor could they afford to adopt the flute's specialized design or dispense with cannons. For the English, the resolution of this problem lay in securing their own comparative advantage in those seas where the Dutch could not use unarmed flutes and where the English could exercise superior naval power, especially in the Mediterranean, the Caribbean, and the Indian Ocean.

## 12. English Commercial Expansion and the Decline of Antwerp and Venice

English overseas commercial expansion really began in the mid-sixteenth century with Antwerp's crises, which forced the English to sever their centuries-old umbilical cord to the nearby Netherlands. The slump of the 1550s revealed just how easily a glut could occur when 90 percent of English exports, chiefly woolens, went to just one port, Antwerp, which also supplied most of England's continental imports. Seeking commercial diversification through many other continental ports, especially Hamburg, brought the London Merchants Adventurers into conflict with the German Hanse, who were still major cloth exporters. The crown, now financially indebted to the Adventurers, soon came to their aid by limiting Hanse cloth exports to the Netherlands (1555); by abolishing their preferential duties (1558); and finally by expelling the League itself (1598).[96]

In 1555, furthermore, the crown also chartered the Muscovy Company, the first of several new overseas trading ventures, to market woolens in Russia and Persia. It was also the first joint-stock company, whose sales of stock or ownership shares to hundreds of investors provided the vastly greater sums of capital required for such long-distance, long-term trading ventures than could small partnerships and family firms (such as those within the Merchants Adventurer organization). The Muscovy Company nonetheless never really prospered against superior Dutch competition, though it did survive into the seventeenth century. The Merchants Adventurer were responsible for the next major overseas trading company, the Eastland Company (est. 1579) with headquarters in the Prussian city of Elbing (near Danzig) to sell woolens in the eastern Baltic in exchange for grain and naval stores. The only new overseas trading company not to use joint-stock, it was not much more successful in competing with the Dutch, whose ships still outnumbered the English by about 13:1.[97]

The third new trading company, the Levant Company (est. 1581), marked England's first major entry into Mediterranean commerce, where it soon posed a major threat to the Venetians and even to the Dutch. Though founded to take advantage of Turkish conflicts with Venice, the English company was careful to engage in Turkish trade only after the Christian powers' crushing naval victory at Lepanto (1571). When western naval artillery had proved so decisive, the Turks now wanted not a European ally but a secure supply of arms, munitions, lead, tin, and bronze.

Ottoman Anatolia, with its cold winters, also needed an alternative supply of good quality woolens, having become so dependent on the Venetian cloth industry, which had gained its current pre-eminence after the Italian wars (1494-1557) had severely disrupted both Lombard and Tuscan production. Initially, the Levant Company marketed only cheap kerseys, but from the 1590s its sales of fine Suffolk broadcloths rapidly superseded kerseys and displaced most other woolens, especially those from the Venetian industry, which then plunged into irredeemable ruin. Although most historians have blamed the Italian industrial defeat upon their rigid guild structures, high urban taxes, and wages, there is no compelling evidence that English cloth production, now as much dependent upon merino wools (for "Spanish Medleys") as the Italian, was any cheaper. The English victory may have just been the product of growing commercial ties between the Ottomans and the Levant Company.[98]

English merchants proved even more successful in finding Mediterranean markets for the cheap, coarse, light semi-worsted fabrics—much like Flemish says—from the New Draperies of East Anglia. Indeed, this English industry owed its birth partly to an influx of Flemish Protestant refugees during the 1560s. At the same time, current agrarian enclosures favored these new draperies over the old through changes in both farm-management and sheep-breeding, chiefly for urban meat markets, which also produced heavier, coarser, long-stapled fleeces. By the 1640s, the New

Draperies, supported by a comparative advantage in wool supplies, innovative urban entrepreneurs, and aggressive marketing abroad, had come to dominate European markets. Well over half their cloth exports, now surpassing those of the Old Draperies, went to Spain, Italy, and the Levant.[99]

Perhaps the most important component of English success in Mediterranean trade was naval superiority. Powerful, heavily-gunned, and very swift carracks, especially those of the Levant Company (400-600 tons), were virtually impervious to attacks by pirates and Muslim corsairs. Though more costly to operate than Venetian or Dutch ships, they gained a competitive edge through lower insurance premiums, so that "the Mediterranean was the first, and for a long time, the only region where English ships took a large part in the carrying trade between foreign countries."[100]

Finally, the Levant Company also supplied many eastern products: raw and spun silk, Syrian cotton (for England's own nascent cotton-fustian industry, another New Drapery), olive oil, dyestuffs, and spices. This trade fueled interest in the Asian spice trade, and merchants from the Levant Company helped to found the East India Company (est. 1600), which, along with its Dutch counterpart, ended forever Venice's historic role in that trade. This story, however, lies beyond the chronological limit of this study. The English East India company did not surpass its parent, the Levant Company, until the 1660s, and in its early years it was too weak in capital, military power, and commercial organization to compete with the Dutch company. In the 1620s, the Dutch drove the English from the Indonesian archipelago, forcing them to concentrate on the then less promising Indian subcontinent. Yet, by the 1660s the Indian and intra-Asian commerce had become much more valuable than the East Indies spice trades, especially because England gained a lucrative re-export trade in printed cotton muslins and calicoes, tea, and dyestuffs, with far broader, more elastic markets.

Indeed, in both East and West, the 1660s were a watershed inaugurating a new economic era for England. In the New World, the sugar plantations of the Caribbean, the tobacco plantations of Virginia, and rapidly growing colonial settlements throughout the Americas would make this region England's most important foreign market by the 1790s (taking almost 60 percent of exports), especially when warfare disrupted continental European trade. In retrospect, the crucial Dutch failure lay in not developing its North American colonies, by exploiting instead a fur-trade economy that inhibited settlement. With a population less than half that of Connecticut, the New Netherlands colony along the Hudson was cruelly hemmed in and easily captured in 1664, during the second Anglo-Dutch war. Its chief port, Nieuw Amsterdam, was then renamed New York.

# NOTES

1. Munro (1979a), (1981), (1984), (1988a), and in Richards (1983); Herlihy (1966); Hamilton (1936); Braudel and Spooner (1967).
2. Postan (1951), (1972), (1987); Hatcher (1977).
3. See Miskimin (1964), (1975), (1983); Day (1978), (1987); Spufford (1988), 339-95; Munro (1979a), (1984), and in Richards (1983); M. North (1990), 115-28.
4. Miskimin (1975), 25-32, 81-111, 132-50.
5. Contamine (1984); Munro (1973), (1979b), (1981); Feavearyear (1963), 32-36.
6. Spufford (1988), 346-47.
7. See Spooner (1972); Spufford (1988), 345-49; Nightingale (1990).
8. De Roover (1948), (1954), (1963a); Goldthwaite (1985), (1987); Spallanzani (1978); Mueller (1979); James Murray, in Aerts and Munro (1990), 24-31.
9. Spufford (1986).
10. De Roover (1948), 130-33, 338-42; Van der Wee (1963), vol. 2:105-9, 333-40, 355-58, (1977), 302-3, 362.
11. Noonan (1957); De Roover (1955), (1963b); LeGoff (1979), (1988); Galassi (1992).
12. De Roover (1953), (1954), (1963a), (1963b), (1968); Munro (1979b); Spufford (1986).
13. Postan (1930), (1951); Nightingale (1990).
14. Dollinger (1970), 204-09, 417-18; Michael North, in Puncuh and Felloni (1991), 809-26.
15. Munro (1973), (1979b), (1991a).
16. Lopez (1987); Lopez, Miskimin, and Cipolla (1964); Lopez, Miskimin, and Udovitch (1970); Miskimin (1975); Postan (1987); Day (1987); Reed (1979).
17. See chap. 4 in this volume.
18. Munro (1991b), 121-30; Ashtor (1983), 1-80; Kedar (1976); Dufourcq (1966).
19. North and Thomas (1973), 79-85, 89, 93-94, 134-38; Reed (1973); D. North (1981), (1984), (1985), (1991).
20. Van der Wee and Peeters (1970); Van der Wee (1990).
21. Katele (1988).
22. Katele (1988); Lane (1934), 6-26, 36-46, 129-34, (1973), 120-34; Cipolla (1965), 75-79; Dufourcq (1966), 534-42; Lewis and Runyan (1985), 121-28; Unger (1980b), 176-82. (1981), 238-48.
23. Krueger (1987); Chorley (1987); Mazzaoui (1972), (1981); Manuel Riu, in Harte and Ponting (1983), 205-59; Munro (1991b), 110-19. On transport, see Postan (1987), 182-204; Russell Menard, in Tracy (1991), 228-75; Masschaele (1993).
24. See Hideotshi Hoshino, in Harte and Ponting (1983), 184-204, here at 185; John Munro, in Aerts and Munro (1990), 41-52.

25. Hoshino (1980), (1983); Cipolla (1949-50); Manuel Riu, in Harte and Ponting (1983); Ashtor (1988); Munro (1991b).
26. Herlihy (1966), 180-97; Perroy (1955); North and Thomas (1973), 78-79; Munro (1991b), 139-43. See also Dyer (1989), 188-233; and the appendix on coinage.
27. See Ashtor (1975), (1976a), (1976b), (1983); Lopez (1987); Van der Wee (1990).
28. For the following see Lane (1973); Ashtor (1976a), (1983), (1988); Van der Wee (1990); Heers (1961); Carrère (1967); Braudel (1984), 116-38.
29. Ashtor (1975), (1983), 200-512; Lane (1940), (1968). But see also Wake (1979); coinage appendix.
30. Ashtor (1975), 573-612, (1983), 95-102, 200-2, 254-62, 476-79; Mazzaoui (1981), 129-53; Hermann Kellenbenz, in Harte and Ponting (1983), 259-76; Stromer (1978).
31. Ashtor (1988); Fryde (1976); Hidetoshi Hoshino, in Harte and Ponting (1983); Hoshino and Mazzaoui (1985-86); Munro (1991b), 116-20, 130-38.
32. Ashtor (1976a), (1983); Lopez, Miskimin, and Udovitch (1970); Jere Bachrach, in Richards (1983), 159-82.
33. Ashtor (1983), 476-79, 510-12; but lower estimates in Ashtor (1975), 610-11.
34. Dollinger (1970); Postan (1933), (1987); Attman (1981); Lloyd (1991).
35. Unger (1980b); Dollinger (1970), 210-59. See appendix on coinage.
36. De Vries (1973), (1974).
37. Kampen (Zuyder Zee) had been the first to do so, in 1251. Unger (1980b); Lloyd (1991), 48-49.
38. T. S. Jansma, in Spallanzani (1976), 51-56; De Boer (1978); Dollinger (1970), 210-59, 281-310; Unger (1992).
39. Unger (1978), (1980b).
40. Van der Wee (1963), vol. 1:277-86.
41. Unger (1980b); Braudel (1984), vol. 3:177-195.
42. Jansma (1960); Malowist (1972); Dollinger (1970), 299-301.
43. Munro (1977), 231-32, 254-6, Tables 13.1-2, (1978), (1979b); Lloyd (1977), 144-224.
44. Munro (1988); Bridbury (1982), 16-26, 47-85, with somewhat different views.
45. Munro (1977); Nicholas (1992), 273-85, 378-80.
46. Lloyd (1991), 50-126; Postan (1933).
47. Lloyd (1991), 109-234; Postan (1933); Ammann (1954).
48. Carus-Wilson (1933); Davis (1976); Van Houtte (1940); Munro (1973), 65-92.
49. Van der Wee (1963), vol. 2:9-88.
50. Van Houtte (1940), (1952); Postan (1933); H. L. Gray, in Power and Postan (1933), 1-38; Van der Wee (1963), vol. 2:37-80; Munro (1973), 127-80, (1979b).
51. Munro (1973), (1979a); Power (1933); Lloyd (1977); Nicholas (1992), 378-80.
52. Industrial indices, with declines up to 70 percent, in Munro (1973), (1977), (1979b), (1983); Raymond Van Uytven, in Spallanzani (1976), 85-97; and data on wool exports in Carus-Wilson and Coleman (1963).
53. Munro (1973), (1977), (1991b).
54. Malowist (1972); Munro (1979a), (1991b).

55. Munro (1984), (1988), (1991a); Day (1978); Spufford (1970), 106-29, (1988), 339-68.

56. Nef (1941), (1987), 735-39; Braunstein (1983); Munro (1991a); M. North (1990); Spufford (1988), 349-55, 365.

57. Van der Wee (1963), vol. 2:80-84; Munro (1973), 155-86, 198-200, (1984), (1991a).

58. Rising to a decennial mean of 39,409 broadcloths.   Carus-Wilson and Coleman (1963), 95-110; Munro (1973), 182; (1983).

59. In chap. 4 by Wolfgang Reinhard.  See Boxer (1969); Godhino (1969); Braudel (1984), 138-43.

60. Unger (1973), (1980b), (1981); Boxer (1969).

61. Day (1978), 36-39; Spufford (1988), 368-70; Bovill (1968), 98-206; Boxer (1969); Malowist (1970); Elbl (1992); Ralph Austen in Tracy (1990), 311-41; Ward Barrett, in Tracy (1990), 224-54, here at 247, table 7.5; Godhino (1969); Braudel (1972-73), vol. 1:463-75, who does not believe that the trans-Saharan flow was diminished.

62. Wake (1979), 381-95; Subrahmanyan and Thomaz (1991), 309-10; Van der Wee (1990); Pearson (1991), 77-78. See also the coinage appendix.

63. Van Houtte (1952); Van der Wee (1963), vol. 2:124-40, (1981), (1990); Boxer (1969).

64. Lane (1973), 284-96; Wake (1979); Steensgaard (1974); Musgrave (1981); Braudel (1972-73), vol. 1:543-70.

65. Subrahmanyam and Thomaz (1991); Duncan (1986); Godhino (1969). See also the coinage appendix.

66. José de Andrade Arruda Jobson, in Tracy (1990), 360-420; Schwartz (1986); Boxer (1969); Godhino (1969); Mauro (1983)—whose figures do not agree with each other.

67. Hobsbawm (1954), (1960). See also the coinage appendix.

68. Carla Rahn Phillips, in Tracy (1990), 34-101; Lee (1951).

69. Hamilton (1934); Brading and Cross (1972); Harry Cross, in Richards (1983), 397-424; John TePaske, in Richards (1983), 424-46; Bakewell (1972); Adam Szaszdi, in Kellenbenz (1981), 151-223; Pieper (1990), (1993).

70. F. S. Gaastra, in Richards (1983), 447-76; Chaudhuri (1968), (1984); Attman (1981), (1986); Parker (1974).

71. Chaunu and Chaunu (1955-59), (1977); Carla Rahn Phillips, in Tracy (1990), 34-101; MacLeod (1984).

72. Van der Wee (1963), vol. 1, (1978); Phelps Brown and Hopkins (1956); Munro (1991a).

73. See essays in Ramsey (1971); Burke (1972); Outhwaite (1982).

74. Officially Seville received about 17,000 metric tons of American silver from ca. 1520 to 1660 (Hamilton, 1934).  Parker (1974), 529, estimates that ca. 1600 western Europe was losing about 80,000 kg./yr. in external trade, while acquiring about 240,000 kg./yr. from European mines and the Americas (which should be almost 300,000 kg./yr., for which the references in note 69).

75. Challis (1975), (1978); and see Outhwaite (1982).

76. Munro (1991a), appendices.

77. About a 83% increase in England, 1540-1640.  Wrigley and Schofield (1989), 528-9.  See also Outhwaite (1982); Ramsey (1971); Brenner (1961-62).

78. Phelps Brown and Hopkins (1956); Van der Wee (1978).

79. Goldstone (1984), (1991); Lindert (1985); but see also Bordo (1986), 373-74.

80. John Munro, in Puncuh and Felloni (1991), 29-62; M. North in Puncuh and Felloni (1991), 809-26; Van der Wee (1963), vol. 2:333-68), (1967), (1977), (1991), (1993). England legalized interest up to 10% in 1545 (repealed 1552, re-enacted 1571).

81. Van der Wee (1967), (1977), (1991); Parker (1974); Tracy (1985).

82. Van der Wee (1977), 375-76. See also Van der Wee (1967), (1991); Spooner (1972); Parker (1974).

83. Van Houtte (1952), (1961); Van der Wee (1963), vol. 2:144-65, (1993); Braudel (1984), 147-50.

84. Van der Wee (1963), vol. 1:166-208, (1993); Coornaert (1950), (1961); Soly and Thijs (1979); Alfons Thijs, in Aerts and Munro (1990), 76-86; Thijs (1987); Robert DuPlessis, in Aerts and Munro (1990), 66-75; Brulez (1968); Braudel (1984), 150-54.

85. Van der Wee (1963), vol. 2:177-94; Van der Wee and Peeters (1970); Edler (1936), (1936-37); Brulez (1959); Endrei (1974).

86. Van der Wee (1963), vol. 2:325-64, (1977), 290-357, (1991), (1993); Edler (1936), (1936-37); McCusker and Gravesteijn (1991).

87. Lane (1934), 45-46, 262, (1973), 378-84; Unger (1980b), 183-95.

88. Brulez (1968), based on Ludovico Guicciardini, *Description de la cité d'Anvers, 1560*, trans. François de Belleforest (Antwerp, 1920), composed in 1560 and published in 1582.

89. Fisher (1940); Carus-Wilson and Coleman (1963); for a different view, see Gould (1970), 133-60.

90. Fisher (1940); Lloyd (1991), 292-362; Baumann (1990).

91. Christensen (1941), 42-44: 71 percent, but incomplete, excluding many German ships.

92. Van Houtte (1977), 193-94; Christensen (1941), 43-44, 85-99, 346, 444-47. See also Israel (1989); Bogucka (1973); Braudel (1984), 202-11.

93. Brulez (1968).

94. Lane (1933), (1934), (1973), 378-84; Usher (1932); Unger (1980a), (1981).

95. Barbour (1930); Unger (1973), (1980b), 251-82; Jaap Bruijn, in Tracy (1990), 174-94; Van Beylen (1970).

96. Lloyd (1991), 293-362; Dollinger (1970), 330-70.

97. Davis (1973); Willan (1953), (1956); Hinton (1959); Christensen (1941), 444-45.

98. Davis (1961), (1973); Ramsay (1982); Sella (1957), (1959); Cipolla (1959); Pullan (1964); Braudel (1972-73), vol. 2:1088-1105, 1188-1203.

99. Bowden (1962), 1-76; Allison (1961); Coleman (1969); Kerridge (1985); Priestley (1990); Pilgrim (1959-60).

100. Davis (1961), 128-30, (1962); Tenenti (1967); Braudel (1972-73), vol. 1:295-312, 606-43, and vol. 2:865-891.

# BIBLIOGRAPHY

[Editors' Note: The entries for each author are arranged in chronological, not alphabetical, order.]

Aerts, Erik, and John Munro, eds. *Textiles of the Low Countries in European Economic History*. Proceedings of the Tenth International Economic History Congress, Studies in Social and Economic History, vol. 19. Leuven, 1990.

Allison, K. J. "The Norfolk Worsted Industry in the Sixteenth and Seventeenth Centuries, 2: the New Draperies." *Yorkshire Bulletin of Economic and Social Research* 13 (1961): 61-77.

Ammann, Hektor. "Deutschland und die Tuchindustrie Nordwesteuropas im Mittelalter." *Hansisches Geschichtsblätter* 72 (1954): 1-63.

Ashtor, Eliyahu. "The Volume of Levantine Trade in the Later Middle Ages (1370-1498)." *JEEH* 4 (1975): 573-612.

Ashtor, Eliyahu. *A Social and Economic History of the Near East in the Middle Ages*. London, 1976a.

Ashtor, Eliyahu. "Observations on Venetian Trade in the Levant in the XIVth Century." *JEEH* 5 (1976b): 533-86.

Ashtor, Eliyahu. *The Levant Trade in the Later Middle Ages*. Princeton, 1983.

Ashtor, Eliyahu. "Catalan Cloth on the Late Medieval Mediterranean Markets." *JEEH* 17 (1988): 227-57.

Attman, Artur. *The Bullion Flow Between Europe and the East, 1000-1750*. Goteborg, 1981.

Attman, Artur. *American Bullion in the European World Trade, 1600-1800*. Goteborg, 1986.

Bakewell, P. J. *Silver Mining and Society in Colonial Mexico: Zacatecas, 1546-1700*. Cambridge, 1972.

Barbour, Violet. "Dutch and English Merchant Shipping in the Seventeenth Century." *EconHR*, 1st ser. 2 (1930).
Reprinted in Carus-Wilson (1962), vol. 1:227-53.

Baumann, Wolf-Rüdiger. *The Merchants Adventurers and the Continental Cloth Trade (1560s-1620s)*. Berlin and New York, 1990.

Bogucka, Maria. "Amsterdam and the Baltic in the First Half of the Seventeenth Century." *EconHR*, 2nd Ser. 26 (1973): 433-47.

Bordo, Michael. "Explorations in Monetary History: A Survey of the Literature." *Explorations in Economic History*, 23 (1986): 339-415.

Bovill, E. W. *The Golden Trade of the Moors*. 2d ed. London, 1968.

Bowden, Peter. *The Wool Trade in Tudor and Stuart England*. London, 1962.

Boxer, C. R. *The Portuguese Seaborne Empire, 1415-1825*. London, 1969.

Brading, D. A., and Harry Cross. "Colonial Silver Mining: Mexico and Peru," and "Estimated Minimum Spanish-American Bullion Production, 1571-1700." *HAHR* 52 (1972): 545-79.

Braudel, Fernand. *The Mediterranean and the Mediterranean World in the Age of Philip II*. Trans. Sían Reynolds. 2 vols. London and New York, 1972-73.

Braudel, Fernand. *Civilization and Capitalism, 15th-18th Centuries*. Vol. 3, *The Perspective of the World*. Trans. Sían Reynolds. New York, 1984.

Braudel, Fernand, and Frank Spooner. "Prices in Europe from 1450 to 1750." In *Cambridge Economic History of Europe*, vol. 4, ed. E. E. Rich, 374-486. Cambridge, 1967.

Braunstein, Philippe. "Innovations in Mining and Metal Production in Europe in the Late Middle Ages." *JEEH* 12 (1983): 573-91.

Brenner, Y. S. "The Inflation of Prices in Early Sixteenth-Century England." *EconHR*, 2nd ser., 14 (1961-62).
    Reprinted in Ramsey (1971), 69-90.

Bridbury, A. R. *Medieval English Clothmaking: an Economic Survey*. London, 1982.

Brulez, Wilfrid. "L'exportation des Pays-Bas vers l'Italie par voie de terre au milieu de XVIe siècle." *AESC* 14 (1959): 461-91.

Brulez, Wilfred. "Le commerce international des Pays-Bas au XVIe siècle: essai d'appreciation quantitative." *RBPH* 46 (1968): 1205-21.
    Reprinted as "The International Trade of the Low Countries in the Sixteenth Century." *Acta Historiae Neerlandicae* 4 (1970).

Burke, Peter, ed. *Economy and Society in Early-Modern Europe: Essays from Annales*. London, 1972.

Carrère, Claude. *Barcelone: centre économique à l'époque des difficultés, 1380-1462*. Paris, 1967.

Carus-Wilson, E. M. "The Origins and Early Development of the Merchant Adventurers' Organization of London." *EconHR*, 1st ser., 4 (1933).
    Reprinted in E. M. Carus-Wilson, *Medieval Merchant Venturers: Collected Studies*, 143-82. London, 1954.

Carus-Wilson, E. M., ed. *Essays in Economic History*. 3 vols, London, 1954-62.

Carus-Wilson, E. M., and Olive Coleman. *England's Export Trade, 1275-1547*. Oxford, 1963.

Challis, Christopher. "Spanish Bullion and Monetary Inflation in England in the Later Sixteenth Century." *JEEH* 4 (1975): 381-92.

Challis, Christopher. *The Tudor Coinage*. Manchester, 1978.

Chaudhuri, K. N. "Treasure and Trade Balances: the East India Company's Export Trade." *EconHR*, 2nd ser. 21 (1968): 480-502.

Chaudhuri, K. N. "Circuits monétaires internationaux, prix comparées et spécialisation économique, 1500-1750." In *Études d'histoire monétaire, XIIe - XIXe siècles*, ed. John Day, 49-68. Lille, 1984.

Chaunu, Huguette, and Pierre Chaunu. *Séville et l'Atlantique, 1504-1640*. 8 vols. Paris, 1955-59.

Chaunu, Pierre, and Huguette Chaunu. *Séville et l'Amérique: aux XVIe et XVIIe siècles*. Paris, 1977.

Chorley, Patrick. "The Cloth Exports of Flanders and Northern France During the Thirteenth Century: a Luxury Trade?" *EconHR*, 2nd ser. 40 (1987): 349-79.

Christensen, Aksel. *Dutch Trade to the Baltic About 1600: Studies in the Sound Toll Registers and Dutch Shipping Records*. Copenhagen, 1941.

Cipolla, Carlo M. "Revisions in Economic History, XII: Trends in Italian Economic History in the Later Middle Ages." *EconHR*, 2nd ser. 2 (1949-50): 181-84.

Cipolla, Carlo M. "Il declino economico dell'Italia." *Storia dell'economia italiana*, ed. Carlo M. Cipolla, vol. 1. Turin, 1959.
    Translated as "The Economic Decline of Italy," in Pullan (1968), 127-45.

Cipolla, Carlo M. *Guns, Sails, and Empires: Technological Innovation and the Early Phases of European Expansion 1400-1700*. New York, 1965.

Coleman, Donald. "An Innovation and its Diffusion: the 'New Draperies'." *EconHR*, 2nd ser. 12 (1969): 417-29.

Contamine, Philippe. *War in the Middle Ages*. Trans. Michael Jones. Oxford, 1984.

Coornaert, Emile. "Draperies rurales, draperies urbaines: l'evolution de l'industrie flamande au moyen âge et au XVI siècle." *RBPH* 28 (1950): 60-96.

Coornaert, Emile. *Les français et le commerce international à Anvers, fin du XVe-XVIe siècle*. 2 vols. Paris, 1961.

Davis, Ralph. "English Foreign Trade, 1660-1700." *EconHR*, 2nd ser., 7 (1954): 150-66.
    Reprinted in Carus-Wilson (1962), vol. 2:227-56.

Davis, Ralph. "England and the Mediterranean, 1570-1670." In *Essays in the Economic and Social History of Tudor and Stuart England*, ed. F. J. Fisher, 117-37. London, 1961.

Davis, Ralph. *English Overseas Trade, 1500-1700.* London, 1973.

Davis, Ralph. "The Rise of Antwerp and Its English Connection, 1405-1510." In *Trade, Government and Economy in Pre-Industrial England*, ed. D. C. Coleman and A. H. John, 2-20. London, 1976.

Day, John. "The Great Bullion Famine of the Fifteenth Century", *PaP*, no. 79 (May 1978), 1-54.

Day, John. "Crisis and Trends in the Later Middle Ages." In Day (1987), 185-224.

Day, John. *The Medieval Market Economy.* Oxford, 1987.

De Boer, Dick. *Graaf en grafiek: sociale en economische ontwikkelingen in het middeleeuwse "Noordholland" tussen 1345 en 1415.* Leiden, 1978.

De Roover, Raymond. *Money, Banking and Credit in Mediaeval Bruges: Italian Merchant-Bankers, Lombards, and Money Changers: A Study in the Origins of Banking.* Cambridge, Mass., 1948.

De Roover, Raymond. *L'evolution de la lettre de change, XIVe-XVIIIe siècles.* Paris, 1953.

De Roover, Raymond. "New Interpretations of the History of Banking." *JWH* 2 (1954): 38-76.
Reprinted in De Roover (1974), 200-38.

De Roover, Raymond. "Scholastic Economics: Survival and Lasting Influence from the Sixteenth Century to Adam Smith." *Quarterly Journal of Economics*, 69 (1955): 161-90.
Reprinted in De Roover (1974).

De Roover, Raymond. *The Rise and Decline of the Medici Bank, 1397-1494.* Cambridge, Mass. 1963a.

De Roover, Raymond. "The Scholastic Attitude toward Trade and Entrepreneurship." *Explorations in Entrepreneurial History*, 2nd ser. 1 (1963b): 76-87.
Reprinted in De Roover (1974), 336-45.

De Roover, Raymond. *The Bruges Money Market Around 1400.* Brussels, 1968.

De Roover, Raymond. *Business, Banking, and Economic Thought in late Medieval and Early Modern Europe: Selected Studies of Raymond de Roover.* Ed. Julius Kirschner. Chicago, 1974.

De Vries, Jan. "On the Modernity of the Dutch Republic." *JEconH* 33 (1973): 191-202.

De Vries, Jan. *The Dutch Rural Economy in the Golden Age, 1500-1700.* New Haven, 1974.

Dollinger, Philippe. *The German Hansa.* Trans./ed. D. S. Ault and S. H. Steinberg. London, 1970.

Dufourcq, Charles-Emmanuel. *L'Espagne catalane et le Maghrib aux XIIIe et XIVe siècles: de la bataille de Las Navas de Tolosa (1212) à l'avènement du sultan mérinide Abou-l-Hasan (1331).* Paris, 1966.

Duncan, T. B. "Navigation between Portugal and Asia in the Sixteenth and Seventeenth Centuries." In *Asia and the West: Encounters and Exchanges from the Age of Explorations: Essay in Honor of Donald F. Lach*, ed. C.. Pullapilly and E. J. Van Kley, 3-25. Notre Dame, 1986.

Dyer, Christopher. *Standards of Living in the Later Middle Ages: Social Change in England c. 1200-1520.* Cambridge, 1989.

Edler, Florence. "Le commerce d'exportation des sayes d'Hondschoote vers Italie d'après la correspondance d'une firme anversoise, entre 1538 et 1544." *RN* 22 (1936): 249-65.

Edler, Florence. "Winchcombe Kerseys in Antwerp (1538-44)." *EconHR*, 1st ser. 7 (1936-37): 57-62.

Elbl, Ivana. "Cross-Cultural Trade and Diplomacy: Portuguese Relations with West Africa, 1441-1521." *JWH* 3 (1992): 165-204.

Endrei, Walter. "English Kerseys in Eastern Europe with Special Reference to Hungary." *Textile History* 5 (1974): 90-99.

Feavearyear, Albert. *The Pound Sterling: a History of English Money.* 2d ed. rev. by E. V. Morgan. London, 1963.

Fisher, F. J. "Commercial Trends and Policy in Sixteenth-Century England." *EconHR,* 1st ser. 10 (1940).
    Reprinted in Carus-Wilson (1962), vol. 1:152-72.

Fryde, E. B. "The English Cloth Industry and the Trade with the Mediterranean, c. 1370-c. 1530." In Spallanzani (1976), 343-67.
    Reprinted in E. B. Fryde, *Studies in Medieval Trade and Finance* (London, 1983).

Galassi, Francesco. "Buying a Passport to Heaven: Usury, Restitution, and the Merchants of Medieval Genoa." *Religion* 22 (1992): 313-26.

Godhino, Vitorino Magalhâes. *L'économie de l'empire portugais aux XVe et XVIe siècles.* Paris, 1969.

Goldstone, Jack. "Urbanization and Inflation: Lessons from the English Price Revolution of the Sixteenth and Seventeenth Centuries." *American Journal of Sociology* 89 (1984): 1122-60.

Goldstone, Jack. "Monetary Versus Velocity Interpretations of the 'Price Revolution': A Comment." *JEconH* 51 (March 1991): 176-81.

Goldthwaite, Richard. "Local Banking in Renaissance Florence." *JEEH* 14 (1985): 5-55.

Goldthwaite, Richard. "The Medici Bank and the World of Florentine Capitalism." *PaP,* no. 114 (Feb. 1987). 3 31.

Gould, J. D. *The Great Debasement: Currency and the Economy in Mid-Tudor England.* Oxford, 1970.

Hamilton, Earl. *American Treasure and the Price Revolution in Spain, 1501-1650.* Cambridge, Mass., 1934.

Hamilton, Earl. *Money, Prices, and Wages in Valencia, Aragon, and Navarre, 1351-1500.* Cambridge, Mass., 1936.

Harte, Negley B., and K. G. Ponting, eds. *Cloth and Clothing in Medieval Europe: Essays in Memory of Professor E. M. Carus-Wilson.* London, 1983.

Hatcher, John. *Plague, Population and the English Economy, 1348-1500.* London, 1977.

Heers, Jacques. *Gênes au XVe siècle: activité économique et problèmes sociaux.* Paris, 1961.

Herlihy, David. *Medieval and Renaissance Pistoia: the Social History of an Italian Town, 1200-1430.* New Haven, 1966.

Hinton, R. K. *The Eastland Trade and the Common Weal.* London, 1959.

Hobsbawm, Eric. "The General Crisis of the European Economy in the 17th Century." *PaP,* no. 5 (May 1954): 33-53; no. 6 (November 1954), 44-65.
    Reprinted as "The Crisis of the Seventeenth Century." In *Crisis in Europe, 1560-1660: Essays from Past and Present,* ed. Trevor Aston, 5-58. London, 1965.

Hobsbawm, Eric. "The Seventeenth Century in the Development of Capitalism." *Science and Society* 24 (1960): 97-112.

Hoshino, Hidetoshi. *L'arte della lana in Firenze nel basso medioevo:il commercio della lana e il mercato dei panni fiorentini nei secoli XIII-XV.* Florence, 1980.

Hoshino, Hidetoshi, and Maureen Mazzaoui. "Ottoman Markets for Florentine Woolen Cloth in the Late Fifteenth Century." *International Journal of Turkish Studies* 3 (1985-86): 17-31.

Israel, Jonathan. *Dutch Primacy in World Trade, 1585-1740.* Oxford, 1989.

Jansma, T. S. "Philippe la Bon et la guerre hollando-wende, 1438-1441." *RN* 42 (1960): 5-18.

Katele, Irene B. "Piracy and the Venetian State: the Dilemma of Maritime Defense in the Fourteenth Century." *Speculum* 63 (1988): 865-89.

Kedar, Benjamin. *Merchants in Crisis: Genoese and Venetian Men of Affairs and the Fourteenth-Century Depression.* New Haven, 1976.

Kellenbenz, Hermann, ed. *Precious Metals in the Age of Expansion.* Stuttgart, 1981.

Kerridge, Eric. *Textile Manufactures in Early Modern England.* Manchester, 1985.

Krueger, Hilmar. "The Genoese Exportation of Northern Cloths to Mediterranean Ports, Twelfth Century." *RBPH* 65 (1987): 722-50.

Lane, Frederic. "Venetian Shipping During the Commercial Revolution." *AHR* 38 (1933): 219-39.
   Reprinted in Lane (1966), 3-24.
Lane, Frederic C. *Venetian Ships and Shipbuilders of the Renaissance*. Baltimore, 1934.
Lane, Frederic C. "The Mediterranean Spice Trade: Its Revival in the Sixteenth Century." *AHR* 45 (1940): 581-90.
   Reprinted in Lane (1966), 23-34.
Lane, Frederic C. *Venice and History: The Collected Papers of Frederic C. Lane*. Baltimore, 1966.
Lane, Frederic C. "Pepper Prices Before Da Gama." *JEconH* 28 (1968): 590-97.
Lane, Frederic C. *Venice: A Maritime Republic*. Baltimore, 1973.
Le Goff, Jacques. "The Usurer and Purgatory." In *The Dawn of Modern Banking*, ed. by the Center for Medieval and Renaissance Studies, UCLA, 25-52. New Haven, 1979.
Le Goff, Jacques. *Your Money or Your Life: Economy and Religion in the Middle Ages*. Trans. Patricia Ranum. New York, 1988.
Lee, R. L. "American Cochineal in European Commerce, 1526-1625." *JMH* 23 (1951): 205-24.
Lewis, Archibald, and Timothy Runyan. *European Naval and Maritime History, 300-1500*. Bloomington, 1985.
Lindert, Peter. "English Population, Wages, and Prices: 1541 -1913." *Journal of Interdisciplinary History* 15 (1985): 609-34.
Lloyd, T. H. *The English Wool Trade in the Middle Ages*. Cambridge, 1977.
Lloyd, T. H. *England and the German Hanse, 1157-1611: A Study of Their Trade and Commercial Diplomacy*. Cambridge, 1991.
Lopez, Robert. "The Trade of Medieval Europe: the South." In *Cambridge Economic History of Europe*, vol. 2, 2d ed. by M. M. Postan and Edward Miller, 306-473. Cambridge, 1987 [1952].
Lopez, Robert, and Harry A. Miskimin. "The Economic Depression of the Renaissance." *EconHR*, 2nd ser. 14 (1962): 408-26.
Lopez, Robert, Harry A. Miskimin, and Carlo M. Cipolla. "Economic Depression of the Renaissance: Rejoinder and Reply." *EconHR*, 2nd ser. 16 (1964): 519-29.
Lopez, Robert S., Harry Miskimin, and A. L. Udovitch. "England to Egypt, 1350-1500: Long-Term Trends and Long-Distance Trade." In *Studies in the Economic History of the Middle East*, ed. M. A. Cook, 93-128. London, 1970.
   Reprinted in Miskimin (1989), no. VIII.
MacLeod, Murdo. "Spain and America: The Atlantic Trade, 1492-1720." In *The Cambridge History of Latin America*, vol. 1. Cambridge, 1984.
Malowist, Marian. "Quelques observations sur le commerce de l'or dans le Soudan occidentale au moyen âge." *AESC* 25 (1970): 1630-36.
Malowist, Marian. "L'expansion économique des Hollandais dans le bassin de la Baltique aux XIVe et XVe siècles." In Marian Malowist, *Croissance et regression en Europe, XIVe-XVIIe siècles*, 91-138. Cahiers des Annales, no. 34. Paris, 1972 [1954].
Masschaele, James. "Transport Costs in Medieval England." *EconHR*, 2nd ser., 46 (1993): 266-79.
Mauro, Frédéric. *Le Portugal, le Brésil, et l'Atlantique au XVIIe siècle, 1570-1670: Étude économique*. Paris, 1983.
Mayhew, Nicholas. "Numismatic Evidence and Falling Prices in the Fourteenth Century." *EconHR*, 2nd ser. 27 (1974): 1-15.
Mazzaoui, Maureen F. "The Cotton Industry of Northern Italy in the Late Middle Ages, 1150-1450." *JEconH* 32 (1972): 262-86.
Mazzaoui, Maureen F. *The Italian Cotton Industry in the Later Middle Ages, 1100-1600*. Cambridge, 1981.
McCusker, John, and Cora Gravesteijn. *The Beginnings of Commercial and Financial Journalism: The Commodity Price Currents, Exchange Rate Currents, and Money Currents of Early Modern Europe*. Amsterdam, 1991.

Miskimin, Harry A. "Monetary Movements and Market Structures: Forces for Contraction in 14th and 15th Century England." *Journal of Economic History* 24 (1964): 470-90.
   Reprinted in Miskimin (1989), no. VII.
Miskimin, Harry A. *The Economy of Early Renaissance Europe, 1300-1460.* Cambridge, 1975 [1969].
Miskimin, Harry A. "Money and Money Movements in France and England at the End of the Middle Ages." In Richards (1983), 79-96.
   Reprinted in Miskimin (1989), no. XI.
Miskimin, Harry A. *Cash, Credit, and Crisis in Europe, 1300-1600.* London, 1989.
Mueller, Reinhold. "The Role of Bank Money in Venice, 1300-1500," *Studi Veneziani*, new ser., 3 (1979): 47-96.
Munro, John H. *Wool, Cloth, and Gold: the Struggle for Bullion in Anglo-Burgundian Trade, ca. 1340-1478.* Brussels and Toronto, 1973.
Munro, John H. "Industrial Protectionism in Medieval Flanders: Urban or National?" In *The Medieval City*, ed. Harry A. Miskimin, David Herlihy, and Avrom Udovitch, 229-68. New Haven, 1977.
Munro, John H. "Wool Price Schedules and the Qualities of English Wools in the Later Middle Ages." *Textile History* 9 (1978): 118-69.
Munro, John H. "Monetary Contraction and Industrial Change in the Late-Medieval Low Countries, 1335-1500." *Coinage in the Low Countries (880-1500)*, ed. Nicholas Mayhew, 95-161. Oxford, 1979a.
Munro, John H. "Bullionism and the Bill of Exchange in England, 1272-1663: a Study in Monetary Management and Popular Prejudice." In *The Dawn of Modern Banking*, ed. by the Center for Medieval and Renaissance Studies, UCLA, 169-239. New Haven, 1979b.
   Reprinted in Munro (1992), no. IV.
Munro, John H. "Mint Policies, Ratios, and Outputs in England and the Low Countries, 1330-1420", *Numismatic Chronicle* 141 (1981): 71-116.
   Reprinted in Munro (1992), no. V.
Munro, John H. "Economic Depression and the Arts in the Fifteenth-Century Low Countries." *Renaissance and Reformation*, 19 (1983): 235-50.
Munro, John H. "Mint Outputs, Money, and Prices in Late-Medieval England and the Low Countries." In *Münzprägung, Geldumlauf und Wechselkurse/ Minting, Monetary Circulation and Exchange Rates*, ed. Eddy Van Cauwenberghe and Franz Irsigler, 31-122. Trierer Historische Forschungen, vol. 7. Trier, 1984.
Munro, John H. "Deflation and the Petty Coinage Problem in the Late-Medieval Economy: The Case of Flanders, 1334-1484." *Explorations in Economic History* 25 (1988): 387-423.
   Reprinted in Munro (1992).
Munro, John H. "The Central European Mining Boom, Mint Outputs, and Prices in the Low Countries and England, 1450-1550." In *Money, Coins, and Commerce: Essays in the Monetary History of Asia and Europe from Antiquity to Modern Times*, ed. Eddy Van Cauwenberghe, 119-83. Leuven, 1991a.
Munro, John H. "Industrial Transformations in the North-West European Textile Trades, c. 1290-c. 1340: Economic Progress or Economic Crisis?" *Before the Black Death: Studies in the 'Crisis' of the Early Fourteenth Century*, ed. Bruce M. S. Campbell, 110-48. Manchester, 1991b.
Munro, John H. *Bullion Flows and Monetary Policies in England and the Low Countries, 1350-1500.* London, 1992.
Musgrave, Peter. "The Economics of Uncertainty: The Structural Revolution in the Spice Trade, 1480-1640." In *Shipping, Trade, and Commerce: Essays in Memory of Ralph Davis*, ed. P. L. Cottrell and D. H. Aldcroft. Leicester, 1981.
Nef, John U. "Silver Production in Central Europe, 1450-1618", *Journal of Political Economy* 49 (1941): 575-91.

Nef, John U. "Mining and Metallurgy in Medieval Civilization." In *Cambridge Economic History of Europe*, vol. 2, 2d ed. by M. M. Postan and Edward Miller, 696-734. Cambridge, 1987 [1952].

Nicholas, David, *Medieval Flanders*. London and New York, 1992.

Nightingale, Pamela. "Monetary Contraction and Mercantile Credit in Later Medieval England." *EconHR*, 2nd ser. 43 (1990): 560-75.

Noonan, John. *The Scholastic Analysis of Usury*. Cambridge, Mass. 1957.

North, Douglass C. *Structure and Change in Economic History*. New York, 1981.

North, Douglass C. "Government and the Cost of Exchange in History." *JEconH* 44 (1984): 255-64.

North, Douglass C. "Transaction Costs in History." *JEEH* 14 (1985): 557-76.

North, Douglass C. "Institutions, Transaction Costs, and the Rise of Merchant Empires." In Tracy (1991), 22-40.

North, Douglass C., and Robert P. Thomas. *The Rise of the Western World: A New Economic History*. Cambridge, 1973.

North, Michael. *Geldumlauf und Wirtschaftskonjunktur im südlichen Ostseeraum an der Wende zur Neuzeit (1440-1570)*. Kieler Historische Studien vol. 35. Sigmaringen, 1990.

North, Michael. "Bullion Transfer from Western Europe to the Baltic and to Asia, 1550-1750: A Comparison." *Money, Coins, and Commerce: Essays in the Monetary History of Asia and Europe from Antiquity to Modern Times*, ed. in Eddy Van Cauwenberghe, 185-96. Leuven, 1991.

Outhwaite, R. B. *Inflation in Tudor and Early Stuart England*. 2d ed. London, 1982 [1969].

Parker, Geoffrey. "The Emergence of Modern Finance in Europe, 1500-1750." In *Fontana Economic History of Europe*, ed. Carlo M. Cipolla, vol. 2:527-94. Glasgow, 1974.

Pearson, Michael N.. "Merchants and States." In Tracy (1991), 41-116.

Perroy, Edouard. "Wage Labour in France in the Later Middle Ages." *EconHR*, 2nd ser., 7 (1955).
      Reprinted in *Change in Medieval Society: Europe North of the Alps, 1050-1500*, ed. Sylvia Thrupp, 237-48. New York, 1964.

Phelps Brown, E. H., and Sheila V. Hopkins. "Seven Centuries of the Prices of Consumables Compared with Builders' Wage-Rates." *Economica*, 23 (Nov. 1956).
      Reprinted in E. H. Phelps Brown and Sheila V. Hopkins, *A Perspective of Wages and Prices* (London, 1981).

Pieper, Renate. "The Volume of African and American Exports of Precious Metals and its Effects in Europe, 1500-1800." In *The European Discovery of the World and its Economic Effects on Pre-Industrial Society, 1500-1800: Papers of the Tenth International Economic History Congress*, ed. Hans Pohl, ed., 97-121. Stuttgart, 1990.

Pieper, Renate. "American Silver Production and West European Money Supply in the Sixteenth and Seventeenth Century." In *Economic Effects of the European Expansion, 1492-1824*, ed. José Casas Pardo, 77-98. Stuttgart, 1993. Special issue of *Beiträge zur Wirtschafts- und Sozialgeschichte* 51 (1992).

Pilgrim, J. E. "The Rise of the 'New Draperies' in Essex." *University of Birmingham Historical Journal* 7 (1959-60): 36-59.

Postan, Michael M. "Private Financial Instruments in Medieval England." *VSWG* 22 (1930).
      Reprinted in Michael M. Postan, *Medieval Trade and Finance*, 28-64. Cambridge, 1973.

Postan, Michael M. "The Economic and Political Relations of England with the Hanse from 1400 to 1475." In Power and Postan (1933), 91-154.

Postan, Michael M. *The Medieval Economy and Society: an Economic History of Britain, 1100-1500*. Cambridge, 1972.

Postan, Michael M. "The Economic Foundations of Medieval Society." *Jahrbücher für Nationalökonomie und Statistik* 161 (1951).
      Reprinted in M. M. Postan, *Essays on Medieval Agriculture and General Problems of the Medieval Economy*, 3-28. Cambridge, 1973.

Postan, Michael M. "The Trade of Medieval Europe: the North." In *Cambridge Economic History of Europe*, vol. 2, 2d ed. by M. M. Postan and Edward Miller, 240-66. Cambridge, 1987 [1952].

Power, Eileen. "The Wool Trade in the Fifteenth Century." In Power and Postan (1933), 39-90.

Power, Eileen, and M. M. Postan, eds. *Studies in English Trade in the Fifteenth Century.* London, 1933.

Priestley, Ursula. *The Fabric of Stuffs: The Norwich Textile Industry from 1565.* Norwich, 1990.

Pullan, Brian. "Wage Earners in the Venetian Economy, 1550-1630." *EconHR*, 2nd ser., 16 (1964).
    Reprinted in Pullan (1968), 146-74.

Pullan, Brian, ed. *Crisis and Change in the Venetian Economy in the Sixteenth and Seventeenth Centuries.* London, 1968.

Puncuh, Dino, and Giuseppe Felloni, eds. *Banchi pubblici, banchi privati e monti di pietà nell'Europa preindustriale: Amministrazione, tecniche operative e ruoli economici.* 2 vols. Genoa, 1991.

Ramsay, George. *The English Woollen Industry, 1500-1750.* London, 1982.

Ramsey, Peter, ed. *The Price Revolution in Sixteenth-Century England.* London, 1971.

Reed, Clyde. "Transactions Costs and Differential Growth in Seventeenth Century Western Europe." *JEconH* 33 (1973): 177-90.

Reed, Clyde. "Price Movements, Balance of Payments, Bullion Flows, and Unemployment in the Fourteenth and Fifteenth Centuries." *JEEH* 8 (1979): 479-87.

Richards, John F., ed. *Precious Metals in the Later Medieval and Early Modern Worlds.* Durham, N.C., 1983.

Schwartz, Stuart. *Sugar Plantations in the Formation of Brazilian Society: Bahia, 1550-1835.* Cambridge, 1986.

Sella, Domenico. "Les mouvements longs de l'industrie lainière à Venise." *AESC* 12 (1957).
    Revised as "The Rise and Fall of the Venetian Woollen Industry." In Pullan (1968), 106-26.

Sella, Domenico. "Il declino dell'emporio realtino." In *La civiltà veneziana nell'età barocca*, ed. G.C. Sansoni. Venice, 1959.
    Revised as "Crisis and Transformation in Venetian Trade," in Pullan (1968), 88-105.

Soly, Hugo, and Alfons Thijs. "Nijverheid in de Zuidelijke Nederlanden." *Algemene geschiedenis der Nederlanden*, vol. 6:27-57. Haarlem, 1979.

Spallanzani, Marco, ed. *Produzione, commercio, e consumo dei panni di lana nei secoli XII-XVIII.* Florence, 1976.

Spallanzani, Marco. "A Note on Florentine Banking in the Renaissance: Orders of Payment and Cheques." *JEEH* 7 (1978): 145-68.

Spooner, Frank. *The International Economy and Monetary Movements in France, 1493-1725.* Cambridge, Mass. 1972.

Spufford, Peter. *Monetary Problems and Policies in the Burgundian Netherlands, 1433-1496.* Leiden, 1970.

Spufford, Peter. *Handbook of Medieval Exchange.* London, 1986.

Spufford, Peter. *Money and Its Use in Medieval Europe.* Cambridge, 1988.

Steensgaard, Niels. *The Asian Trade Revolution of the Seventeenth Century: The East India Companies and the Decline of the Caravan Trade.* London, 1974.

Stromer, Wolfgang von. *Die Gründung der Baumwollindustrie im Mitteleuropa: Wirtschaftspolitik im Spätmittelalter.* Stuttgart, 1978.

Subrahmanyam, Sanjay, and Luis Filipe F. R. Thomaz. "Evolution of Empire: The Portuguese in the Indian Ocean during the Sixteenth Century." In Tracy (1991), 298-332.

Tenenti, Alberto. *Piracy and the Decline of Venice, 1580-1615.* Trans. Janet and Brian Pullan. London, 1967 [1961].

Thijs, Alfons. *Van 'werkwinkel' tot 'fabriek': de textielnijverheid te Antwerpen, einde 15de-begin 19de eeuw.* Brussels, 1987.

Tracy, James D. *A Financial Revolution in the Habsburg Netherlands: Renten and Renteniers in the County of Holland, 1515-1565.* Berkeley and Los Angeles, 1985.

Tracy, James D., ed. *The Rise of Merchant Empires: Long-Distance Trade in the Early Modern World, 1350-1750* Cambridge, 1990.

Tracy, James D., ed. *The Political Economy of Merchant Empires: State Power and World Trade, 1350-1750.* Cambridge, 1991.

Unger, Richard. "Dutch Ship Design in the Fifteenth and Sixteenth Centuries." *Viator* 4 (1973): 387-412.

Unger, Richard. "The Netherlands Herring Fishery in the Late Middle Ages: The False Legend of Willem Beukelszoon of Biervliet." *Viator* 9 (1978): 335-56.

Unger, Richard. "Dutch Herring, Technology, and International Trade in the Seventeenth Century." *JEconH* 40 (1980a): 253-79.

Unger, Richard. *The Ship in the Medieval Economy, 600-1600.* London and Montreal, 1980b.

Unger, Richard. "Warships and Cargo Ships in Medieval Europe." *Technology and Culture* 22 (1981): 233-52.

Unger, Richard. "Technical Change in the Brewing Industry in Germany, the Low Countries and England in the Late Middle Ages." *JEEH* 21 (1992): 281-313.

Usher, A. P. "Spanish Ships and Shipping in the Sixteenth and Seventeenth Centuries." In *Facts and Factors in Economic History*, 189-213. Cambridge, Mass. 1932.

Van Beylen, Jan. *Schepen van de Nederlanden van de late middeleeuwen tot het einde de 17e eeuw.* Amsterdam, 1970.

Van der Wee, Herman. *The Growth of the Antwerp Market and the European Economy, 14th to 16th Centuries.* 3 vols. The Hague, 1963.

Van der Wee, Herman. "Anvers et les innovations de la technique financière aux XVIe et XVII siècle." *AESC* 22 (1967): 1067-89.

Van der Wee, Herman. "Monetary, Credit, and Banking Systems." In *Cambridge Economic History of Europe*, vol. 5, ed. by E. E. Rich and Charles Wilson, 290-393. Cambridge, 1977.

Van der Wee, Herman. "Prices and Wages as Development Variables: A Comparison between England and the Southern Netherlands, 1400-1700." *Acta Historiae Neerlandicae* 10 (1978): 58-78.

Van der Wee, Herman. "World Production and Trade in Gold, Silver, and Copper in the Low Countries, 1450-1700." In Kellenbenz (1981), 79-86.

Van der Wee, Herman. "Industrial Dynamics and the Process of Urbanization and De-Urbanization in the Low Countries from the Late Middle Ages to the Eighteenth Century: A Synthesis." In *The Rise and Decline of Urban Industries in Italy and in the Low Countries: Late Middle Ages-Early Modern Times*, ed. Herman Van der Wee, 307-81. Leuven, 1988.

Van der Wee, Herman. "Structural Changes in European Long-Distance Trade, and Particularly in the Re-export Trade from South to North, 1350-1750." In Tracy (1990), 14-33.

Van der Wee, Herman. "The Medieval and Early-Modern Origins of European Banking." In Puncuh and Felloni (1991), 1157-73.

Van der Wee, Herman, and Jan Materné. "Antwerp as a World Market in the Sixteenth and Seventeenth Centuries." In *Antwerp: Story of a Metropolis, 16th-17th Century*, ed. J. Van der Stock, 19-31. Ghent, 1993.

Van der Wee, Herman, and Theo Peeters. "Un modèle dynamique de croissance interseculaire du commerce mondiale, XIIe-XVIIIe siècles." *AESC* 15 (1970): 100-28.

Van Houtte, J. A. "La genèse du grande marché international d'Anvers à la fin du moyen âge." *RBPH* 19 (1940): 87-126.

Van Houtte, J. A. "Bruges et Anvers: marchés 'nationaux' ou 'internationaux' du XIVe au XVIe siècle?" *RN* 24 (1952): 89-108.

Van Houtte, J. A. "Anvers aux XVe et XVIe siècle." *AESC* 16 (1961): 248-78.

Van Houtte, J. A. *An Economic History of the Low Countries, 800-1800.* London, 1977.

Wake, C. H. H. "The Changing Pattern of Europe's Pepper and Spice Imports, ca. 1400-1700." *JEEH* 8 (1979): 361-403.

Willan, T. S. *The Muscovy Merchants of 1555.* Manchester, 1953.
Willan, T. S. *The Early History of the Russia Company, 1553-1603.* Manchester, 1956.
Wrigley, E. A., and R. S. Schofield. *The Population History of England, 1541-1871: a Reconstruction.* 2d ed. Cambridge, 1989 [1980].

# URBAN COMMUNITIES: THE RULERS AND THE RULED

Steven Rowan

(University of Missouri-St. Louis)

By 1400 the urban structure of Europe was already dense and fully articulated. It was characterized by immense variety in civic institutions within the towns and by complex relationship without, both with the rural hinterlands and with the higher governing authorities.[1] Towns came in all sizes, and they served a variety of functions: mercantile, military, administrative, and artisanal. Every town lived in an agrarian setting, often with some agriculture, such as market gardening and winegrowing, within the town itself. In some regions towns were rather sharply distinguished from the surrounding countryside, as in northern Germany, while in others towns ruled their hinterlands, as in South Germany, Switzerland, and, above all in Italy. In such urban landscapes, some towns became autonomous to the point of being city-states, while in other regions, notably in England, France, and the Spanish kingdoms, they were dominated by royal administrations.

Europe in 1400 wallowed in the middle of a century-long demographic slump, which had begun with the coming of bubonic plague around 1350 and would not end until after 1450. The attendant reshuffling of population and resources tended to raise wages and depress prices for food and other goods, though in such a way as to favor towns and urban manufactures over the countryside and agriculture. On the land there occurred a marked shift away from a combination of monoculture of grain with manufacturing of luxury goods toward a pattern of regional agricultural specialization and the manufacture of consumer goods for those of middling income. Subsequently, the period from around 1450 through the end of the sixteenth century witnessed a secular rise in population which would only cease at some point in the seventeenth century. This "long sixteenth century" was marked by a poorer bargaining position of wage-earners, rewarding those who controlled land and other resources. The turning point between the two phases came in the fifteenth century, which also saw the onset of altered interregional relationships arising from specialization. Such tendencies transformed, for example, East Central Europe into a virtual colonial appendage of the European heartland, supplying raw materials in exchange for finished goods. This shift, in turn, altered the pattern of urbanization in East Central Europe by stunting small urban centers in favor of large entrepôts, such as Danzig/Gdansk. In all parts of sixteenth-century Europe, provincial and national governments sought aggressively to tax and regulate urban activities with the aim of integrating them into larger patrimonial or bureaucratic states.

## 1. The Cities in a World of Larger States

Urban communities as a whole were more typified by size than by the possession or lack of formal legal autonomy, doubly so, since very few towns of the era enjoyed true independence. Even the German Imperial and "free" cities were embedded in the larger legal and political structures of the Holy Roman Empire, which could and did intervene in internal civic matters when occasion permitted. Size and economic strength were the basic characteristics of any urban community. A town's political integration into a region could be accomplished in any one of several ways, depending on the concrete historical context. Towns were a necessary economic element of feudal and post-feudal European society, to which they provided marketing, manufacture and a social compliment to a noble-dominated rural hinterland.[2] Still, the pre-modern European town was not so much a modern society in embryo as an integral part of a specifically late medieval/ early modern social order.

The range of autonomy enjoyed by urban governments varied dramatically during this era. Few of them enjoyed more than functional internal autonomy, and truly independent city-states were *ipso facto* exceptional. This point can be illustrated by looking at some major zones of urbanization.

### Italy

In Italy, despite the theoretical sovereignty of the Empire, from the twelfth century the communes ruled themselves as autonomous republics, extending their rule over their subject hinterlands (*contadi*), which might include villages, castles and even once-independent towns.[3] The *contado* supplied immigrants to the ruling town in keeping with economic relations, but residents of the hinterland were definitely subjects rather than citizens. The strain of competition between cities led to a steady reduction of the number of Italian autonomous towns in the course of the fourteenth and fifteenth centuries, and those which survived often became subject to the *signoria* of princes.  By the beginning of the fifteenth century, there appeared a tendency for individual political bosses to take over political leadership through the manipulation of increasingly complex civic electoral systems—for example, by the Medici family at Florence.  During the sixteenth century most Italian towns became parts of true principalities, a process which was greatly accelerated by the Italian Wars between the Valois and Habsburg dynasties.[4]

### The Empire

In the Empire the late fourteenth century had seen the ultimate failure of urban efforts to band together in leagues against the lords who had restricted their expansion and independence.[5]  Most German towns were at least in principle proprietary and subordinated to the more or less substantial control of town lords.  By the later fifteenth century the princes were nonetheless rarely able to intervene in the cities' internal affairs, because they lacked sufficiently powerful bureaucratic governments.  The German urban communities that had once belonged to the old royal domain (*Krongut*) of the Empire could claim to be Imperial cities (*Reichsstädte*), though they continued to be subject to taxation and alienation by sale or mortgage by the emperor.  Former episcopal towns which had won autonomy enjoyed the distinct status of "free cities [*Freie Städte*]."  These functionally autonomous towns were of all sizes and degrees of economic viability, and they did not constitute a separate category of town except in terms of their legal status.  Imperial and free cities participated in a subordinate way in the Imperial Diet (*Reichstag*), as well as in such mixed associations as the Swabian League (est. 1488) under Habsburg leadership and the Empire's administrative districts called "Circles [*Reichskreise*]" (est. 1500).  Proprietary towns in Germany and the Low Countries often played major roles as estates in provincial diets (*Landstände*), often representing the entire non-noble spectrum to the exclusion of the peasantry.  Only in the Swiss Confederation did self-governing towns, such as Zürich, Basel, and Bern, share control of the assembly (*Tagsatzung*) with peasant federations.[6]  The Hanseatic League, an association of merchant towns in northern Germany bordering the North Sea and the Baltic, declined after the mid-fifteenth century in the face of aggressive territorial states and mercantile competition from the Low Countries, though it would preserve its formal organization into the seventeenth century.[7]  The Hansa represented the trading interests of northern German merchants in the convoy trade from Russia to the Bay of Biscay, and it also guaranteed merchant domination in member towns against artisan pressure.

Fifteenth-century German towns often lived in a state of antagonism with their feudal and rural neighbors, so that law and popular attitude saw a dramatic dichotomy between the town and the "open land [*platte Land*]".[8] Towns had long endeavored to assert direct control over at least a limited area beyond their walls, enforcing economic discipline within a specified distance (*Bannmeil*).[9] Though few German towns ever conquered their hinterlands to the extent that was common in Italy, and though they rarely administered areas as large as found in Spain—due to the concentration of non-mercantile landowners within their walls—most did have a subject teritory or *Herrschaft*. These territories are best known in the case of such Imperial cities as Nuremberg or Ulm, but proprietary towns also obtained subject territories by purchase or the imposition of their will on neighboring noble proprietors. Beyond the area ruled directly, the town could use its military and political power to impose restrictions on the building of alternative roads or the erection of competing markets. In times of crisis, such as during the Peasants' War, constitutional niceties were overlooked by urban militias trying to suppress peasant conspiracies in the countryside.

### France

In France the recovery of the monarchy from the Hundred Years' War led to a steady diminution of urban autonomy through the cooptation of municipal leadership into the royal administrative system. This process deprived the mercantile element of its continuity and weight.[10] Paris in particular was kept under the thumb of royal institutions.[11] Town leagues revived in importance during the Wars of Religion, mainly because of their prominent roles in the Catholic League and in associations of Protestant towns. The latter were permitted by the Edict of Nantes to maintain their armament even after the conclusion of peace.[12] In more orderly times, merchants tended to be coopted into the expanding officialdom, and urban resources were absorbed either through the purchase of offices or through communal purchase of new offices posted for sale by the royal government, so as to prevent the dilution of the incomes enjoyed by those who already held the offices.

### The Iberian Kingdoms

Towns in Castile and other kingdoms of the Iberian peninsula ruled over extensive hinterlands which placed them in perpetual conflict with aggressive nobles or such royally-sponsored corporations as the sheep-raiser's association called the *mesta*.[13] Spanish towns often housed the landowning classes for whole regions as well as artisans and merchants. Through much of the fifteenth century, urban militias and town-supported regional peace-keeping forces (the *hermandad*, similar to the forces supporting the *Landfriede* in Germany) preserved the importance of towns, which included noble, landowning and mercantile elements in their own leaderships. Basic conflicts of interest between the towns and encroaching noble latifundists led eventually to the most radical European confrontation between towns and the feudal order in the entire period, the *comuñero* revolt in 1520-21. In that revolt, a league of towns led by a *junta* attacked seigneurial enemies as well as a corrupt royal administration. Members of religious orders, particularly Dominicans, provided intellectual support for the communes' cause. The revolt culminated in urban defeat and led only to marginal reforms of the royal administration, which tended to identify with the seigneurial nobles rather than with the towns. Theologians such as Francisco Vitoria continued to argue on behalf of limited and responsible royal powers over local urban governments even after the end of the uprising.

### The British Kingdoms

The towns were cowed by powerful royal governments in the kingdoms of England and Scotland, and much of the official record of the period is filled with declarations of decay and decline, at least in part a tactic to avoid taxation.[14] During the fifteenth-century the English royal administration began to pay more attention to the towns, both because they probably contained a larger proportion of the kingdom's wealth than ever before, and because the growth of the cloth industry probably distributed that wealth more widely than in earlier times, when prosperity had depended on the export of wool rather than of woollen cloth. London continued to be a disproportionately large town, in which much of the mercantile activity of the country was concentrated, and in a suburb of which, Westiminster, the royal government sat. Although there had been a disturbing alliance between the "commons" of towns, including London, and the rebellious peasants in 1381, the main trend of English urban life in the fifteenth and sixteenth centuries involved the consolidation of oligarchical rule of municipal corporations.[15]

## 2. Political Structures

*Constitutions*

Formal urban constitutions, sometimes summarized in charters but just as often lacking explicit documentation, had developed gradually since the twelfth century. The thirteenth and fourteenth centuries witnessed a deliberate alteration of town governments to accommodate self-conscious political groups, particularly non-noble merchants and artisans organized in guilds. The oldest urban constitutions had normally formed around a town lord's courts of law, on which members had once served for life and to which members were either appointed by a town lord or coopted by the other members. The only broader body which could be consulted in necessity was the mass of the citizenry itself, which was often formally gathered once a year to renew oaths of loyalty. The chief constitutional changes during the thirteenth and fourteenth centuries were alterations of the composition and tenure of the old urban court, sometimes making the membership subject to some sort of election. Often a second council was created, the members of which were drawn from a broader constituency, and representatives of guilds sometimes came to participate in the council's work. It was common for each new group to install a chief officer to represent them in executive or military functions, though the older urban elites often managed to take over the office after a decent interval.

Each wave of constitutional change commonly left vestiges of the earlier constitution intact. In Germany, for example, the traditionally noble chief justice of the old court (*Schultheiß*) persisted alongside the *Bürgermeister* who had represented merchant-inspired reforms, joined eventually by an *Ammeister* or *Obristzunftmeister* representing guildsmen's political aspirations. In Italy, the separate organization of the Guelph Party sometimes survived as a vestige of earlier political struggles. Political reforms often left more lasting marks in the redesign of committee structure controlling finances, markets and public facilities.[16] A guild coup in 1389 at Freiburg im Breisgau was soon reversed by the Habsburg town lord, for instance, but the centralization of the fiscal administration in the hands of the *Kaufhausherren* was preserved, along with other administrative changes as permanent features of the communal government. In Florence, though the greatest prestige accrued to the *Gonfaloniere di Giustizia* and the priors of the *signoria*, committees such as the Eight for Justice (*Otto di Guardia*) and the Ten for Liberty and War (*Dieci di Libertà e Guerra*) had continuous traditions of their own.[17]

In proprietary and subordinate towns, the organically developed consti-

tutions of the High Middle Ages seldom survived past the middle years of
the sixteenth century, when political crisis often led to radical redesigning
of existing institutions.[18]  Princely governments came to be uncomfortable
with guild representatives, since they were not regarded as sufficiently
wealthy or "sad" (sober) to lend urban administration dignity.  Although
princes sometimes sided with artisans as a pretext to upset local monopolies of power to their own advantage, they preferred governments which
embodied the values of wealth and stability.  Many urban communities,
including economic "boom-towns" of the sixteenth century (Nuremberg,
Lyon) were able to function without political guilds, though they often organized crafts on an *ad hoc* basis through special legislation to serve public
interests.[19]

### Symbols of Authority and Social Order

The ideological framework for rulership and community was more often
articulated in ceremony and symbol than in explicit treatises, though the
increase in the number of political officers with legal training made ideological expression more explicit.[20]  Civic pageants marked the movement
of the year, some of them quite clearly political (the *Schwörtag* of Switzerland and South Germany) and some flamboyantly allegorical (the *joyeuse
entrée* in the Low Countries or the Lord Mayor's Show in London).  The
religious basis of most civic festivals helped to reinforce a notion of the urban community as a divinely-sanctioned unity, and this was intensified in
the later Middle Ages by the rise of Corpus Christi festivals.[21]  That holiday
became the particular setting for civic processions and plays stressing the
identity of the town with the community of God and the operation of the
salvation drama on earth.

In most cases the lordly origins of the authority of urban institutions
was preserved as a source of ceremonial legitimacy long after it ceased to
reflect political reality, such as in the Swiss Confederation and the United
Netherlands, where the sanction of a monarch was proclaimed even after
that ruler's actual control had been rendered void.[22]

Sumptuary and dress regulations, which institutionalized the prejudices
or values of the dominant political community, used proto-mercantilist arguments to justify regulating the visible signs of social status and reinforcing at least the visible symbols of the moral regime.  These went along with
regulations of conduct enforced by criminal statute, but most control over
day-to-day acts was exerted by communal institutions such as guilds or by
community pressure.  Those who violated the norms of moral conduct
were subject to ritual ridicule, and the right to lampoon or shame with im-

punity (*das Schmährecht*) was one of the most important sanctions against a debtor or malefactor permitted by local law-courts. Other municipal penalties, such as display in the stocks or mild floggings, were more attacks on self-esteem than they were inflictions of pain, but they were regarded with all the more dread.

### Formal Urban Political Theory

The urban settings and presumptions of Greek and Roman political theory led the scholastic writers to propagate an ethical doctrine of politics which was imbued with implications for urban communities.[23] On the whole, however, urban communes and corporations tended not to win ideological support in formal thought. It was chiefly in Italy, and particularly in Florence, Milan or Venice, that a consciously republican ideology was developed to service the self-governing urban regime. In Florence the discipline of "politics," an ethical science of rulership, was gradually replaced in the sixteenth century by a more cynical concept of "statecraft," reflecting the shift from self-governing commune to a Medici dukedom administered through a bureaucracy.[24]

## 3. ADMINISTRATION

Administration or rulership in urban communities was divided among political officers or magistrates (such as councillors, commissioners), technically-trained functionaries (chancery personnel, jurists), and artisanal or menial servants (beadles, gatekeepers, guards).[25] In the course of the sixteenth century, the center of municipal power shifted from magistrates to functionaries, a municipal version of the triumph of bureaucracy in territorial states.[26]

### Officers

Pre-modern governments relied extensively on voluntary, essentially uncompensated service by persons who were well-off enough to afford the leisured time needed to pursue public business. Communities felt empowered to call on such persons for service, often penalizing them when an assigned office was declined. This practice entailed selection from the upper percentiles of the community, though wealth did not automatically lead to frequent selection. In smaller towns, in fact, this "elite" could draw members as low as the fiftieth percentile of the permanent residents. The service of such political officers could be seen as a variation of the principle by which ordinary residents were obligated to help collect taxes, stand watch or serve in the military levy.

Since the urban levy usually prescribed a certain level of armament to be provided by the individual resident, the forces were hierarchically organized in parallel to the wealth-structure of the commune. In the course of the sixteenth century, towns tended to finance a standing force for garrison duty, or even for the night watch and gate guard. This *miles perpetuus* (as it was called in humanist Latin in Germany) was then only supplemented by the citizenry in case of emergency. Princely administrations of course preferred to raise their own forces with tax money provided by the towns, since such forces were less politically dangerous.

Magistrates ranged in rank from political leaders, sought after and showered with ceremonial honors, to panels administering markets, walls or such charitable institutions as orphanages and lazarhouses. Executive officers such as mayors retained ceremonial precedent, but their powers were usually restricted to their representing the municipal corporation's collective will. Although the political leadership might discuss questions of policy among themselves (usually in secret), they presented a united front to outside authorities. The political leadership could be chosen by appointment from higher authorities, by cooptation, election by a broader constituency (a greater council or the assembled citizenry) or even by lot. Once elected, they often were rotated in office, though some magistrates might develop such expertise in a particular area as to remain in office for decades. Even a small community needed to call on the service of dozens of such officers year in and year out.

Even without explicit constitutional restriction, magistracies within an urban community were reserved to an elite. The oldest tradition in European towns had been to distribute such offices to nobles, ministerials and landowners, and merchants had been the first "bourgeois" group to assert a presence on the municipal court and administrative boards (the "council" by whatever name). The merchants often organized themselves in a mercantile guild, and this guild sometimes came to monopolize political leadership. Mercantile families used various strategies to appropriate to themselves the prestige of the older noble-ministerial elites for themselves, sometimes even obtaining recognition of noble status. The model of republican Rome suggested the generic term of "patrician" for those who had come to monopolize or dominate municipal office, though each community used its own terminology and its own mode of defining this elite. The historically more proper term of "meliores" or "optimates" (in Florence the *ottimati*) was used of those who controlled urban offices as early as the eleventh century, so that it is proper to speak of a "meliorate" or "optimate."

Political dominance of urban government and society by practicing merchants declined in the course of the sixteenth century, but irregularly according to region. There was a tendency for an increasing number of the leading persons in the commune to have professional training, whether they were participants in the political institutions of the town or not. In the greater cities of Europe (Paris, London), these professionals were often attached to princely governments, and nobles drawn to princely courts also participated in urban communities, even if they were immune to the duty to take up office.

### The Rise of the Functionaries

Functionaries began by 1400 as facilitators of municipal corporations and by 1600 had become the virtual masters of their communities, providing a continuity and competence which the formal urban constitutions lacked. Municipalities employed clerks from a very early date, often retaining local friars or other clerics, then professional secular scribes, and finally academically-trained jurists. Although they relied on the support of political officers, they molded that support themselves, and in time some functionaries might become guildsmen, citizens or even high municipal officers. The transition from medieval scribe to professional administrator had been completed by 1550. The town clerk became the core of an urban administration, in which capacity he might receive the title of chancellor or chamberlain. From this perch, he kept the correspondence and minutes of the council, hoarded its corporate memory in charters, and composed manifestos, tracts and chronicles glorifying the community and its policies. In the Reformation, the town clerk was often the engineer and ideologist of religious and institutional reorganization (an example is Lazarus Spengler of Nuremberg). Functionaries were often the first in particular towns to use the ideological tactics of humanism (a movement often lodged in law schools rather than in the arts faculties of universities) to promote civic institutions, but they could usually rely on sympathetic members of the council and other established officeholders.

In late-medieval Germany, town councils through their functionaries came to conceive of themselves as a sovereign government (*Obrigkeit*) when dealing with residents, who were equated with subjects. In the Reformation crisis, the perception of the town as a commonwealth existing under special divine sanction was conjured up to justify the establishment of a locally-controlled ecclesiastical polity and the expropriation of clerical institutions for more worthy educational and charitable purposes.

The secrecy in which the executive council of a commune pursued most of its activities enveloped the knowledge of past charters and privileges as well as the ongoing correspondence and acts of the council. Since there was rarely any central accounting system or anything approaching a single public budget, the actual state of the urban finances was often a secret even to those attempting to administer them. These *arcana civitatis* justified a coterie of councillors and administrators in seeing themselves as a sovereign corporation over against and separated from the mass of the community. In some cases Lutheran urban councils even asserted their right to call on the unquestioning obedience of residents under the authority of Romans 13. Urban opposition had to dispute such claims specifically and in detail, showing that they had to be taken seriously.

### The Coup of the Academic Jurists

The academically-trained jurist had been in existence even longer than the town clerk. In Italy the office of *podestà*, in principle an alien professional who served a limited term as a judge, opened the way for the spread of academic jurisprudence in municipal courts, particularly since the *podestà* had to stand review by syndics for decisions made during his term. Despite this model, however, learned jurists made only gradual inroads as judges into lawcourts in much of Europe, particularly where the preservation of traditional legal systems placed a premium on lay judges. It often took considerable time to organize customary legal systems into terms comprehensible to trained jurists, and longer still to make these terms incomprehensible to those without academic training, but both stages were eventually passed. The training and special mobility of learned jurists made them particularly avid to demand substantial salaries, enriched with fees and tips to provide a considerable income.

Modernization of courts in the fifteenth and sixteenth century entailed making the law applied more consistent and explicit, if only to prevent appeal to higher jurisdictions. Larger or older towns sometimes received appeals for communities thought to be in their "legal family" through appeal in the usual sense or through *Rechtszug*, which was the duty to instruct other courts concerning the proper law. Such associations of legal systems influenced the preservation of legal peculiarities even in the course of procedural modernization. Legal reform might take the form of reform legislation in keeping with academic jurisprudence, or it might even take the form of wholesale codification of civil or criminal law (normally called "reformations" of law) composed by the leading academic jurists of the time. These codes often retained characteristics of the older substantive law while adopting the forms of Roman law (which was the *ius commune* of most of Europe), either directly from Roman law or via canon law. In the *Constitutio criminalis Carolina*, adopted as the model for criminal procedure in the Empire in 1532, inquisitorial procedure was introduced, and the older adversarial Germanic procedure was reduced to a ceremonial role at the time of sentencing and execution.[27] The effect of this reform was to encourage the hiring of Latinate jurists, even if the vernacular continued to be used in the court. One mark of the advance of the "reception" of Roman law was the advent of the *consilium*, a legal opinion purchased from a jurist to define a difficult case. At first this opinion would be in the vernacular or perhaps bilingual, but in time it would be wholly in Latin and useless to someone without schooling. As a rule, secret procedure replaced open courts, and written procedure replaced the use of oral formulas. In England, local urban courts tended to preserve such archaic legal forms as oath-helpers (London's Hustings Court), as much of the important business passed to Common Law and prerogative courts in royal hands. Spanish urban courts were suffering a similar loss of vitality in the later sixteenth century, since intense litigiousness and currency devaluation encouraged appeals to royal courts.

Judicial training was also seen increasingly as the best preparation for positions in administration, even if these offices were not specifically judicial in form or procedure. In Spain, an increasing number of municipal positions were reserved for the educated (*letrados*), which conversely led to pressure to increase the size and number of degree-granting institutions. As the sixteenth century progressed, there was a general European trend for degreed office-holders to be drawn by preference from regional families, rather than from a larger "national" or international pool. Although trained immigrants always played a role in towns, the odds were stacked against them in practice by the later sixteenth century.

### Other Functionaries: Menials

Every large municipal government employed a spectrum of other professionals, most notably physicians and surgeons, employed or retained to advise the municipality on sanitation or to provide care to residents. Architects, armament experts and engineers managed special projects for town governments. The rapid evolution of military architecture in the sixteenth century combined with continued fear of internal warfare as well as the threat of Turkish attack to force many communities to reconstruct their wall systems on a new, more expensive basis.

Menial servants employed by the municipality covered all those routine

or artisanal undertakings which could not be contracted to private craftsmen or covered by unpaid citizens serving in rotation. These ranged from
ceremonial beadles, criers and watchmen through staffs of masons or carpenters to keep public buildings in repair, to the gravediggers, executioners
and disposers of dead animals. These officers were often paid small salaries or piecework wages, but they were also often given gifts of livery, food
and firewood at certain times of the year.

## 4. URBAN SOCIETY: CITIZENS, RESIDENTS AND MARGINALS

### Elites

Municipal "rulers" in the sixteenth century were not yet entirely separated
from the society, the "ruled," and any consideration of government requires an understanding of the economic order, social order and the vocabulary of political life in a concrete context.[28] Further, no matter what
the formal constitution, it must be interpreted in terms of how individuals
and families entered the community, persisted, perished or departed.[29] The
ability of urban elites to reproduce their number or recruit new members
decided whether their tradition flourished or waned.[30] Vital statistics of
towns in this period shows that most urban centers usually were sink-
holes of population, failing in most cases to replace their own numbers.
Further, a close examination of communities with the appearance of stability usually shows that the bulk of families of craft masters seldom lasted
longer than three or perhaps four generations within a single community.
Towns of intermediate size appear to have sent members on to larger communities, while they drew well-endowed recruits from smaller towns and
from the countryside. Further, despite the economic and social policies of
guild-dominated communities which would seem to shield them from all
risk, the actual fortunes of members of the middling urban classes were extremely precarious. Crises of market and money, endemic to the sixteenth
century, could always upset the well-being of the householder core of the
artisan community and plunge them into genuine poverty.[31]

In the fourteenth century, merchants had been seriously challenged by a
more diverse range of artisans, usually grouped in guilds.[32] In some communities, guildsmen did not so much seize power as assume it after political control over depressed communities had been abandoned by a dwindling or departing mercantile elite. Guilds encompassed a broad range of
the mercantile and artisan population, though leadership continued to go
to wealthier members either through election of the membership or ap-

pointment by the council.[33] None of these elements—nobles, merchants or craft guilds—had ceased to be factors in urban life in the sixteenth century.

Even the lordly "patrician" houses which provided members of high political bodies pursued marriage strategies which placed their survival at risk over the long term, since they restricted and delayed the marriages of a very few males and dedicated many male and female members to celibacy. Just as land-based fortunes were occasionally invested in trade, so also mercantile fortunes were often reinvested in land as the family's wealth "matured." Some families in the urban meliorate persisted over centuries, though their total number suffered continual attrition which required the elites to recruit new members in each generation. In some cases, former mercantile families left the bourgeois world altogether through the purchase of education or noble status for their progeny.[34]

### Households

The core of the premodern town could be said to be the household, whether restricted to a single nuclear family or constituting an artificial family (such as a convent, a hospital, or the agency of an outside religious house). In Italy, the later Middle Ages saw the redesigning of urban fortresses of great families so as to accommodate nuclear families rather than extended households. Although some urban fortresses survive in Italian towns (as they also survived in Regensburg), they were in the fifteenth century already monuments to a past in which an urban nobility had played a larger role. Concern about preserving the household core of the community expressed itself both in efforts to prevent clerical corporations from buying up the housing stock in the depressed market of the fifteenth century in Germany, and in Italy in the charitable provision of dowries for worthy young women (*Monte delle Doti*).

For most people the household was the setting for work as well as living, and sometimes of retail sale as well.[35] In the population slump of the later Middle Ages, however, there was a tendency for servants or journeymen, who would once have lived as subordinates in larger houses, to take lodgings of their own. The large number of abandoned houses in the depopulated towns made places for these dependents to reside, which tended to increase horizontal segregation according to wealth. The old pattern of residential integration of rich, middling, and poor nevertheless survived in the most Renaissance towns. Outlying areas, such as suburbs, tended to be more homogeneous and poorer than the town centers, and sometimes there grew up a "ring" of wealthier homes around a core occupied by institutional buildings and declining communal households.

*Marginal Groups*

Alongside the journeymen and apprentices of the craft world, there existed a mass of servants and other subordinate workers, both male and female, as well as large numbers of seamstresses, spinsters and other persons performing low-paid work outside of the ordinary artisan household structure.[36] The marginal population of the sixteenth century town included large numbers of this working poor, who were often the special targets of welfare officials.[37] When they were not being supported by charitable donations or tax abatements, they were the objects of hostility to the point of public ridicule and periodic expulsion. The late fifteenth and the sixteenth century witnessed a transition from the provision of charity for the spiritual benefit of the giver to the provision of aid to maintain and neutralize the deserving poor. These subsidized poor were made subject to a special regimen to limit their numbers and assure their continued worthiness (and political harmlessness). They consisted largely of elderly or female dependent workers and disabled persons, though institutions such as the *Fuggerei* in Augsburg supported pious poor families in exchange for prayer.

Despite militant efforts, there remained a residue of marginal persons including criminals and vagabonds, as well as practitioners of trades regarded as degrading if legal such as prostitution. Substantial persons practicing degrading activities (brothel keepers, bawds, torturers and executioners) were subject to special levies in time of war or emergency in which they were assessed on their property in excess of others, since they often escaped ordinary taxation as outside the usual resident body. In times of public emergency they were also subject to ritual abuse by mobs, exemplary punishment and even expulsion to cleanse the community of perceived guilt in the eyes of God.

Slavery had been a factor in southern-European urban society before the fourteenth century, though slaves were usually to be found as domestic servants rather than as craft workers. These slaves were often drawn from impoverished regions of the Balkans, though they also consisted of the full spectrum of nationalities subject to the Mediterranean slave trade which moved indifferently between Muslim and Christian states, with major entrepôts in Genoa and Barcelona. Female slaves were used in industrial undertakings, but more often as personal servants or concubines, and slaves from exotic countries were sought as a status symbols. Since it was always a pious work to emancipate slaves, they soon contributed to the growth of the wage-earning population of towns and countryside. Outside of Italy and Spain, however, slavery played a diminishing role in European towns, and a fluid free market for wage-labor, both male and female, predominated.

*Jews*

Where they had not been expelled from whole nations (particularly Spain in 1492), Jews usually resided by special arrangement, often segregated away from the centers of large towns or even outside urban areas altogether.[38] Jewish communities were increasingly isolated and marginalized in the later Middle Ages, when they were systematically excluded from crafts dominated by Christian guilds or normal markets. Even such supposedly safe Jewish trades as pawn-broking were attacked in Italy and Germany by such clerical demagogues as John of Capistrano, who advocated the establishment of a public pawnshop (*mons pietatis*) to provide small-scale loans to the poor in the place of Jewish lenders. Attacks on individual Jews or whole communities might take place at any time when the population was agitated, whatever the cause. The period just before the Reformation crisis, a time of intense agitation in Germany, saw mob-action against Jewish presence as part of a religious revival, most notably in Regensburg in 1519. The Reformation crisis itself, which upset the traditional protections enjoyed by all immunities, led to the destruction of Jewish property and the expulsion of Jews in many communities which were in the process of adopting the Lutheran faith. Urban governments tended to oppose attacks on Jews because they were seen as the most vulnerable and exposed end of the propertied class, and assaults on Jews often were a prelude to attacks on clergy and even lay propertied elites. The result of this concern by urban authorities was that they tended to cooperate to quash anti-Jewish rumors, most significantly the "Blood Accusation" that Jewish communes kidnapped and bled Christian children. It is significant that this vicious rumor was successfully opposed by most authorities at a same time when they were unwilling to act against similar accusations of witchcraft against isolated women. The reason would appear to be that governments continued to value the presence of Jews, if only as an easy target for taxation. Attacks on Jewish residency by theologians (Martin Bucer, Martin Luther, Johannes Eck) in the Reformation era were especially strident because they fell on the deaf ears of princes and urban administrations.

When they resided in towns, Jews were increasingly gathered into true separate settlements (*ghetto*; *Judenviertel, Judenstadt*) with synagogues, cemeteries, *mikvot* (ritual baths) and council houses of their own. As servants of the Emperor in Germany, Jews paid special taxes and were subject to the surveillance of Imperial courts, though towns where they resided often purchased Jewish oversight from the Emperor. Jews called before Christian courts were allowed to swear special oaths, and they were allowed to settle most disputes within their community by arbitration. In Germany, Jews made frequent use of Imperially-chartered courts to collect debts, overriding local venues. Although the rabbi held a special position in the community, a secular leader could be designated by the Jewish community, and in emergencies Jewish communities from a region or even a whole kingdom could choose a representative to speak on their behalf (most notably Josel of Rosheim in Reformation Germany). In those communities where Jewish residency was not permitted, they were often admitted only on special occasions or with the escort of a beadle. *Judenherbergen* (Jews' inns) were often situated outside the walls of the town for Jews in transit.

### Outburghers

The community of the ruled extended even beyond the area directly controlled by the town: despite repeated prohibitions, towns bestowed or sold residents' rights to persons residing beyond its borders, creating a halo of outburghers (*Ausbürger*; *Pfahlbürger*) defining the economic aura of particular urban centers in Germany and the Netherlands. Outburghers were often made immune to taxation by princes, and their access to urban markets helped to combat the endemic devolution of markets and artisan skills into rural communities under noble patronage. They were protected by the town's political and military force, which was still capable of cowing individual members of the feudality when princely government was weak.[39]

### Ecclesiastical and Feudal Immunities

The urban community, even if nominally autonomous, was riddled with ecclesiastical and feudal or princely immunities, which often had whole neighborhoods under their sway.[40] Bishops' closes often covered considerable portions of such towns as Worcester or Trier, complete with sanctuaries to which fugitives could flee. Universities were self-governing communities numbering thousands of persons scattered across towns and subject to removal when a strike was called. As property-holding, privileged institutions, universities often regulated particular crafts (copying, bookselling), oversaw services which concerned students (rents and food), and even exploited monopolies as sources of income (such as a postal system in Paris).

There were considerable populations in premodern cities who could neither be said to rule or to be ruled: they were exempt from direct municipal control. Before the Reformation crisis, this category would have included the clergy, both secular and regular, who enjoyed something akin to extraterritoriality. Both before and after the Reformation, there were many secular immunities, sometimes amounting to buildings or even whole streets, which did not answer to the communal government or its agents. After the Peace of Augsburg in 1555, Catholics were granted permission to hold services in selected churches in German Imperial cities (such as the cathedral in Frankfurt am Main), creating a class of residents without active political rights but protected by the Imperial administration.

Maintaining religious facilities was a central concern in medieval municipalities, and the fifteenth century saw an intensification of efforts by urban governments to curb the size and power of ecclesiastical immunities, whether wielded by the secular or regular clergy. Towns had long controlled the construction of the principal churches (*Dombauhütte; l'oeuvre de Nôtre-Dame*) and often managed the parish clergy through its endowment, limiting the power of local priests to amass livings within the urban jurisdiction. The Great Schism, which weakened the leverage of the papacy, when some dioceses in Germany had parallel Avignonese and Roman hierarchies, gave burghers ample opportunities to intervene in ecclesiastical matters, particularly to restrict scandalous behavior by clerics.

Ecclesiastical institutions which existed in the middle of the urban community often represented old religious movements whose era of spiritual flourishing was past; they had few inmates but massive endowments. Commanderies of crusading orders also had a strong urban presence, as did the friaries of the mendicant orders, and all persisted as privileged corporations resented by residents as well as civic governments. Movements with enthusiastic burgher support, such as the Carthusians, enjoyed a building boom in the fifteenth century and into the sixteenth century. Burghers also protected such religious communities of women and men as beguines or the Brethren of the Common Life from attack by ecclesiastical authorities. In the later Middle Ages, there is a tendency for most rural religious houses to elevate the stewardships they had always maintained in nearby towns into virtual permanent residences for the abbot. These residences continued to enjoy the immunities which the stewardships had originally received as a matter of course, but they brought a new higher clergy into the community in a manner which often led to friction.

Since charitable institutions such as schools, hospitals, lazarhouses, orphanages and pest-houses were clerical institutions often controlled by town governments, municipal and clerical competence faded into one another. The increased mortality of the fourteenth century precipitated many communities to adopt local forms of *mortmain* legislation to prevent the loss of taxable property to ecclesiastical institutions, particularly monasteries. The Observant reform within the Franciscan Order was particularly important in setting a precedent for reappropriating the endowment of regular institutions. Disputes of a doctrinal nature, such as the immaculist/maculist dispute between the Franciscans and Dominicans, mobilized popular opinion to the extent of street-riots and show-trials. Efforts by monasteries or their agencies within communities to avoid paying taxes or fees, particularly in times of public emergency or war, gave an opportunity for town councils to call for popular campaigns painting religious houses as bad corporate citizens. One interim resolution of that problem was to require the religious houses to name the urban government or one of its members as its business manager (*Schaffner*).

## 5. GUILDS

### Guilds as Urban Structures

The bulk of the population in most urban communities participated in political and economic life through guilds.[41] Guilds might be viewed "from above" as political constituencies, as units in the urban militia or as instruments of social education and control through their various guildhalls. Some communities preferred geographical wards or districts as constituencies of the common population, in which case craft guilds played a more modest role. Efforts to substitute wards for guilds as a principle of social organization often had the conscious purpose of shoring up an oligarchical urban administration (this was the case in London in the later fourteenth century, and in many German communities). Persons of wealth and prestige could be expected to be elected from every ward, while that was not always the case with guilds. If guilds were abolished, as occasionally happened, the property and functions of the guilds had to be redistributed to new institutions.

### Guilds as Economic Units

As units of artisanal activity, political guilds often harbored many crafts which might have associated organically, or which had been compounded together for the convenience of the urban government.[42] Viewed "from below," guilds sometimes also functioned as religious fraternities and drinking societies (which is the root meaning of the word "guild"), though such associations might exist apart from or alongside political guilds. Full membership in a political guild was normally extended only to masters or sometimes their spouses, and the trend in the fifteenth century was to place explicit bars against the illegitimate or those with a dishonorable past.[43]

## Women and Guilds

Women were members of some craft associations in their own right, but they tended to be subordinated in those guilds erected for political purposes.[44] Depending on local circumstances, some autonomous handicrafts were practiced by women alone, such as the Italian manufacture of silk purses or the making of lace in Flanders.[45] Some of these female crafts were practiced by women living in religious communities, such as beguinages. In most political guilds in the sixteenth century, women participated chiefly through their husbands, and they often retained only a second-class membership when they were widowed. Widows were sometimes expected to marry someone who could carry on the business. Closer inspection of records often shows women dominating the sale of goods in particular markets or such important activities as the brewing of ale or beer.

## Guilds and the Public Good

In the sixteenth century, there was a tendency for public authorities to require competency tests of outsiders wishing to enter guilds, which in time led to certification of a completed apprenticeship or a formal masterpiece. The introduction of such restrictions was gradual and reluctant, a sign of the maturity of a technologically stable craft, and the prime mover was often the urban government acting in response to consumer complaints about the poor quality of goods. Although individual guilds always sought their own economic advantage, the urban government—even one dominated by guildsmen—regarded obvious self-interest with suspicion. The normative standard for town councils was public utility, and rules were intended to benefit consumers rather than producers. When a guild was found to violate the government's perception of its public trust, whether in price, quality or performance of public duties, it was by no means unusual even for a guild-dominated government to discipline whole guilds. Tactics which could be applied by governments included fining members individually or as a group, revoking their right to practice, even expelling them and inviting new masters to take up the trade in their place. Guilds themselves had little leverage in the face of such practices, since they could not rely on broad public support from other guilds. In the context of our period, guilds were highly successful at rationing positions in static trades or during periods of economic stagnation, but they were placed under often intolerable strain in times of prosperity or when there was rapid technological change.

Some crafts required capital equipment which transcended the capacities of an individual master's household, so that groups of masters would pool their resources to purchase common equipment (such as tanning vats), or a true factory-scale enterprise dependent on merchant-generated capital arose. Tanners or butchers often shared facilities and equipment either rented from the government or owned by the guild. Paper-making and printing both entailed large facilities and extensive market risk, and the position of "master" was restricted to a manager of a shop which included many wage workers. Printers themselves tended to become dependent on contracts from separate publishers (the German for "publisher," "*Verleger*," is also the term for the organizer of the putting-out system). Regional or national markets for the products of such manufactures placed workers under a severe price-pressure which forced adoption of technological innovations and intense work-discipline. All of these factors meant that local authorities and guilds had only a limited ability to control the conditions of labor, since production could always be moved to the countryside or to other jurisdictions by capital investors if price-relations permitted.

Restriction of the ranks of the masters in the course of the period meant that poor journeymen without local links had little chance in principle to become masters, though in practice the low replacement rate of artisan masters presented more opportunities than would appear from guild charters. Brotherhoods of journeymen, sometimes associated as confraternities and organized even across whole regions, sought to act as a medium of mutual support and information for the relatively fluid and usually unmarried journeyman class. The decline of the artificially-extended household of the artisan master meant that many journeymen lived outside the home, sometimes in housing owned or rented by the brotherhood. Travelling journeymen used the brotherhood as a hiring hall to find work, or as a place to rest before continuing their *Wanderjahre* or *tour de France*. Although urban and princely governments viewed such brotherhoods with suspicion, the journeymen's associations served such a useful function in housing and assisting their members that they usually found a niche. When there was a dispute, journeymen often were permitted to explain their reasons for brief work-stoppages against particular masters or the shunning of members who violated discipline. Journeymen's associations occasionally would orchestrate job actions across entire regions, distressing urban and princely governments. Journeymen often managed to obtain cooperation from masters and governments in restricting wage-earners in established crafts to particular nationalities, particularly in border regions. In France in the sixteenth century, many regionally-organized brotherhoods of itinerant crafts (mercers, chapmen) were recognized by the royal government in order to make them amenable to control.

There were often some guilds with full standing which were relatively impoverished and lacked a solid core of substantial masters. In large communities (such as London), a small number of greater crafts with a luxury or mercantile orientation controlled great offices, leaving the others as "lesser misteries" (literally "lesser crafts").[46] Towns of modest size were seldom so clearly hierarchical, so that representatives of relatively rudimentary crafts had at least some seats on urban councils. Such lesser crafts often included the gardeners' or vintners' guilds in Germany, who were both agrarian townsmen (*Ackerbürger*) and collectivities of other dependent activities, such as porters. In some cases, membership in such guilds was granted to any person establishing residence who did not have a guilded craft. Still, efforts to create guilds of persons who were routinely subordinate wage-workers, such as the Florentine Ciompi, proved short-lived.

Many communities required those residents who were not rentiers to join guilds, and guild membership was often tantamount to full-fledged residency. Formal citizenship or "the freedom of the town," which bestowed the right to stand for election to public office, usually required many years of residency and the ownership of a certain amount of landed property subject to taxation. In many urban communities in the later Middle Ages, citizenship lost its independent importance, so that it often was bought only after a resident had been elected to an office requiring citizenship, and often at a reduced price. A resident was distinguished from someone from outside the community, who did not enjoy routine access to the market and other facilities of the town.

### Entrepreneurship and Capitalism

In the fifteenth century, even the most powerful urban administration was unable to prevent the concentration of economic and political power outside its jurisdiction through the creation of regionally-based trading companies (The Great Ravensburg Trading Company in South Germany) or banks and mercantile investment firms (such as the Augsburg family companies of the Fugger or Welser) which could control whole industries, such as mining, through their cooperation with princely administrations. Urban representatives sought to use estate institutions such as the Imperial Diet to limit the amount of capital such firms could possess, but to little avail. These large companies further attracted investments in fixed-rate bonds which diverted money from funding the communal debt of individual towns, and competition from large-scale capital enterprises had the potential of robbing master craftsmen of their independence.

## 6. Urban Political Conflict

### Traditions of Conflict and Resolution

Political conflicts in towns rarely had the character of clear class-struggles, since they usually proceeded as disputes between members of a propertied elite of rentiers, shopowners and merchants. Despite this consideration, the rise of craft guilds in the fourteenth century did constitute a considerable broadening of the political estate in terms of levels of wealth and sheer numbers. This "democratic" trend would only be reversed in the middle or at the end of the sixteenth century, as princely states tended to try to restore mercantile or even old noble elites. Such disputes occasionally provided pretexts for princely intervention through the imposition of audits or even a revised constitution. Even such functionally independent entities as Imperial cities could be subject to Imperial commissions as a result of citizen complaints or appeals.[47]

Internal urban conflict usually arose over questions of accountability for management of taxation and other public affairs.[48] Although the first advent of guildsmen to governments defined an era of "guild struggles," similar conflicts were a perennial feature of urban life through the eighteenth century, never completely resolved until the end of the Old Regime.[49] Although guilds were the most usual way of organizing the community below the level of the council, they were neither inevitable nor always satisfactory in a crisis. In times when hostility to the council crystallized, the "commons" or "commune" (as distinguished from the government, however defined) would find expression in self-selected speakers outside the guild structure.

Taxation was obviously a matter of central controversy in the late-medieval community, since the propertied persons preferred to collect customs and excises on consumption from the mass of the population, or poll taxes which did not pay attention to personal wealth. The mass of the population, on the other hand, viewed taxes on wealth (*Vermögen*) as fair and desirable. Even when an urban oligarchy conceded a tax on net wealth, it usually kept assessment solidly in its own hands, and combined a wealth tax with a graduated poll tax for those who had only their labor to support them. Direct taxes from outside on urban populations were fought bitterly by town administrations, who preferred to avoid a direct assessment of the wealth and status of individuals within their walls. The efforts to establish a direct Imperial tax at the end of the fifteenth century, the "common penny," proved abortive due to communal reluctance to collect the tax or pass the assessments on to higher authorities.

One important link between the wealthy and the town government was through the purchase of annuities and the provisions of loans, often forced, to fund the urban debt (the *Monte commune* in Florence). The dramatic decline in urban populations in the later fourteenth century often left depressed urban communities with debts out of all proportion with their current economic ability, and they often coped with the situation by requiring individual citizens to guarantee public debts personally. This frequently discouraged the immigration of wealthy persons into communes, or encouraged residents to withdraw and take their wealth elsewhere. Princely governments also maneuvered to tap the loans of wealthy town-dwellers, and in emergencies communes would make disadvantageous loan agreements (such as perpetual obligations denominated in gold) which might require the decree of a Church court to reverse. Those excluded from political control generally viewed the granting of annuities as a potential abuse by political insiders at the expense of the commune, and efforts were commonly made to restrict the right to grant them without public declaration or vote.

In all communities, whether ruled by townsmen or princes, the supply of food was an overriding interest, leading to efforts to buy grain in times of low prices and store it for times of shortage. *Kornspeicher* were found in all German communities, and the papal administration spent vast sums to guarantee the grain supply of Rome, which was called the *annona* in conscious reference to ancient precedent. Merchant exchanges often concentrated all market, customs, staple and supply operations into one place, called *Kaufhäuser* in Germany.

### The Reformation and the Cities

Perhaps the best documented broad movement of urban conflict in this era arose from the religious Reformation of the sixteenth century. Formally, to be sure, reforms were introduced—or rejected—in such a way as to preserve the control of the reigning group, as embodied in the smaller town council. Still, such a matter of great public concern aroused great interest and sparked debates and even conflicts well beyond the limits of the legal community of full-fledged, adult, male citizens.[50]

The social dimension of the urban Reformation has been a subject of intense dispute, because confrontations over changes in worship, the social integration of the clergy, and the expropriation of clerical propertyholders were major political questions, which often pitted reluctant town councils against enthusiasts lodged largely outside the council or even outside the commune altogether.[51] Further, outsiders demanding change might call up support from unenfranchised groups as shock-troops, leading briefly to riot, iconoclasm, and general disorder. It has been argued, particularly for Strasbourg, Basel and other southern communes, that the ruling classes ended up appeasing their opposition by sacrificing a portion of the Catholic cult and institutions they had controlled to preserve at least a part of their own control over the community.[52] In any case, the council was often cautious, responding to attacks rather than leading the critique of the older Catholic order, even when this critique was a logical extension of earlier municipal policies toward clerical institutions.[53] Many communities which did not commit themselves to the Reformation still asserted control over local religious institutions in the sixteenth century.[54]

The urban Reformation was precipitated by genuine religious conversions on the part of concerned laymen and clergy, and it often produced profound transformations of the ways in which people lived and worshipped.[55] Just as often, the Reformation also provided an opportunity for many town governments to integrate the clergy into the community as citizens and to transfer much of the ecclesiastic endowment to institutions which already existed for educational, charitable or social purposes.[56] Although the religious change was dramatic, the policies of reappropriation followed by town councils usually had a history, resulting in a reallocation of wealth in keeping with prejudices already well-established.[57] In those communities where this transfer was carried out by higher authorities (as in England), municipalities and local elites often were frustrated in their efforts to control the plunder or to see it was used to communal purposes.[58] In Germany, inmates of regular religious institutions were sometimes granted pensions which permitted them to live out their lives, sometimes in the same institution to which they had originally committed themselves.

The first wave of the urban Reformation saw Lutheran convictions predominate, particularly in the German North and Franconia, while subsequent urban religious conversions in Swabia and the Alemannic regions tended to be in the Reformed tradition of Zwingli, Bucer or, later, John Calvin. It has been argued that Lutheranism tended to appeal to the distress of isolated individuals in the first phase of religious agitation, while the consciously communal doctrine of the Reformed appealed to the political traditions of Upper Germany.[59] A further wave of council-precipitated reforms swept towns Imperial cities in Alsace and elsewhere in the later sixteenth century.[60] Princely-controlled towns tended to be able to isolate reformers and prevent permanent change if the prince was not contemplating a territorial change of religion for his own reason, and the result was often the emigration of those adamantly favoring an alternative faith (such as Protestants from Constance after its annexation by the Habsburgs), though in some Imperial free cities the legal enforcement of parity in magistracies forced modes of accommodation.[61] Displaced ecclesiastics, such as bishops and cathedral chapters, found new residences in Catholic communities far from their original titular locations. In this they were only continuing a tradition which went back to the era of the first communal movements, when bishops and chapters were frequently forced to leave town to prevent chronic friction with burghers (so that the archbishop of Cologne came to reside normally in Bonn and the bishop of Basel in Porrentruy). Anabaptists were seldom explicitly tolerated in towns, though Strasbourg and some other towns overlooked nonconformity unless prevoked.

The wars associated with the Reformation in sixteenth-century Germany and France lent towns increased significance as fortresses and sources of manpower and money, and the Protestant leagues gave special prominence to individual leaders of urban communities, such as Jacob Sturm of Strasbourg.

✄ ✄ ✄

The decline of independence on the part of towns in the period 1400-1600 did not mean an end to urban institutions or the social groups which had their being through them. Towns continued to provide the setting in which much of the economic vitality of Europe was realized.

# NOTES

1. Ehbrecht (1979); Haase (1969-73); Stoob (1978); Miskimin, Herlihy, and Udovitch (1977); Duby (1980) and (1981); Ryerson (1989).
2. Czok (1968); Berthold, Engel, and Laube (1973).
3. Lestocquoy (1952); Waley (1969). The best general study is Martines (1979).
4. Epstein (1991).
5. Heinig (1983).
6. Poyer (1978); Friedrichs (1981)
7. Dollinger (1970).
8. Brady (1985); Erich Maschke, "Deutsche Städte am Ausgang des Mittelalters," in Rausch (1974), 1-44.
9. Raiser (1969).
10. Petit-Dutaillis (1947); Chevalier (1982); Hilton (1992).
11. Llewelyn Thompson (1991).
12. Garrison-Estèbe (1980); Benedict (1981) and (1989).
13. Sáncho de Soprani (1959); Ruano (1961); Gutiérrez Nieto (1973); Haliczer (1981).
14. Tait (1936); Reynolds (1977); Hilton (1992).
15. Platt (1976).
16. Brown (1982).
17. Brucker (1969).
18. Dyer (1973); Zimmerman and Weissman (1989).
19. Strauss (1966).
20. Schmidt (1958); Menke (1959-60).
21. Fradenburg (1991).
22. Blockmans (1987); Nicholas (1992).
23. Black (1992); Viroli (1992); Rublack (1984). For the social context of urban humanist political ideas, the classic study is by Martines (1972a).
24. Skinner (1978), vol. 1.
25. Demandt, Dieter. "Stadtverfassung in spätmittelalterlichem Kitzingen," in Demandt and Rublack (1978), 9-34.
26. The process occurred early and strongly in Italy. See Litchfield (1986); Reinhardt (1991).
27. Strauss (1986).
28. Ehbrecht (1974); Bátori (1975); Brady (1978a); Martines (1972a); Thomson (1988).
29. Ellermeyer (1980).
30. Kent (1977).
31. Friedrichs (1975) and (1979); Bátori and Weyrauch (1982).
32. Hildebrandt (1974).
33. Maschke (1959).

34. Brady (1978a).
35. Maschke (1972); Hughes (1975); Herlihy and Klapisch-Zuber (1985); Bohmbach (1973).
36. Geremek (1987); Maschke (1967).
37. Fischer (1979).
38. Stow (1992); Kriegel (1979); Haverkamp (1981); Foa (1992).
39. Czok (1979); Kümmel (1980-82); Edwards (1982); Scott (1986).
40. Kiessling (1971); Heitzenröder (1982).
41. Thrupp (1965); Epstein (1991); Mackenney (1987); Füglister (1981).
42. Swanson (1988).
43. Schulz (1985).
44. Howell (1986); Hanawalt (1986).
45. Händler-Lachmann (1980); Herlihy (1990).
46. Thrupp (1948).
47. Rotz (1985).
48. Rotz (1976); Friedrichs (1978).
49. Martines (1972b).
50. Moeller (1975) and (1987).
51. Greyerz (1985); Rublack (1987).
52. Moeller (1964) and in Mommsen (1979); Brady (1978b) and (1987).
53. Demandt and Rublack (1978); Mörke (1983).
54. Scribner (1976); Blickle (1985) and (1992); Hsia (1987).
55. Chrisman (1972); Bornert (1981).
56. Fischer (1979); Abray (1985).
57. Demandt and Rublack (1978); Demandt (1980); Naujoks (1958).
58. Comparisons can be made from the studies in Mommsen (1979).
59. Moeller (1964); Brecht (1980).
60. Greyerz (1980).
61. Rublack (1978).

# BIBLIOGRAPHY

*General*
Czok, Karl. "Zur Stellung der Stadt in der deutschen Geschichte." *JRG* 3 (1968): 9-33.
Duby, Georges, general editor. *Histoire de la France urbaine.* Vol. 2, *La ville médiévale des Carolingiens à la Renaissance,* ed. Jacques Le Goff (Paris, 1980); vol. 3, *La ville classique de la Renaissance aux Révolutions,* ed. Emmanuel Le Roy Ladurie (Paris, 1981).
Ehbrecht, Wilfried, ed. *Voraussetzungen und Methoden geschichtlicher Städteforschung.* StF, series A, vol. 7. Cologne and Vienna, 1979,
Haase, Carl, ed. *Die Stadt des Mittelalters.* 3 vols. WdF, vols. 243-45. Darmstadt, 1969-73.
Laube, Adolf. "Die Stellung des Bürgertums in der deutschen Feudalgesellschaft bis zur Mitte des 16. Jahrhunderts." *ZfG* 21 (1973): 196-217.
Miskimin, Harry A., David Herlihy, and A. L. Udovitch, eds. *The Medieval City.* New Haven, Conn., 1977.
Ryerson, Kathryn L. "Urbanism, Western European." In *Dictionary of the Middle Ages,* ed. Joseph R. Strayer, vol. 12: 311-20. New York, 1989.
Stoob, Heinz, ed. *Altständisches Bürgertum.* 2 vols. WdF, vols. 352-53. Darmstadt, 1978.


*Cities and States*
Benedict, Philip, ed. *Cities and Social Change in Early Modern France.* London, 1989.
Benedict, Philip. *Rouen During the Wars of Religion.* Cambridge, 1981.
Berthold, Brigitte, Evamaria Engel, and Adolf Laube. "Die Stellung des Bürgertums in der deutschen Feudalgesellschaft bis zur Mitte des 16. Jahrhunderts." *ZfG* 21 (1973): 196-217.
Brady, Thomas A., Jr. *Turning Swiss: Cities and Empire, 1450-1550.* Cambridge Studies in Early Modern History. Cambridge, 1985.
Chevalier, Bernard. *Les bonnes villes de France du XIVe au XVIe siècle.* Paris, 1982.
Dollinger, Philippe. *The German Hansa.* Stanford, 1970.
Epstein, Steven R. "Cities, Regions and the late Medieval Crisis: Sicily and Tuscany Compared." *PaP,* no. 130 (February, 1991): 3-50.
Friedrichs, Christopher R. "The Swiss and German City-States." In *The City-State in Five Cultures,* ed. Robert Griffith and Carol Thomas, 109-42. Santa Barbara, Ca., 1981.
Garrison-Estèbe, Jeannine. *Les protestants du Midi, 1559-1598.* Toulouse, 1980.
Gutiérrez Nieto, Juan Ignacio. *Las communidades como movimiento antiseñorial (La formación del bando realista en la guerra civil castellana de 1520-1521).* Barcelona, 1973.
Haliczer, Stephen. *The Communeros of Castile: the Forging of a Revolution, 1475-1521.* Madison, Wisc., 1981.
Heinig, Paul-Joachim. *Reichsstädte, Freie Städte und Königtum 1389-1450: ein Beitrag zur deutschen Verfassungsgeschichte.* VIEG, vol. 108. Wiesbaden, 1983.
Hilton, Rodney H. *English and French Towns in Feudal Society: a Comparative Study.* Cambridge, 1992.
Lestocquoy, Jean. *Les villes de Flandre et l'Italie sous le gouvernement des patriciens, XIe-XVe siècles.* Paris, 1952.

Llewelyn Thompson, Guy. *Paris and Its People Under English Rule: the Anglo-Burgundian Regime, 1420-1436.* Oxford, 1991.

Martines, Lauro. *Power and Imagination: City-States in Renaissance Italy.* New York, 1979.

Petit-Dutaillis, Charles. *Les communes françaises.* Paris, 1947.

Peyer, Hans Conrad. *Verfassungsgeschichte der alten Schweiz.* Zurich, 1978.

Platt, Colin. *The Medieval English Town.* London, 1976.

Raiser, Elisabeth. *Städtische Territorialpolitik im Mittelalter. Eine vergleichende Untersuchung ihrer verschiedenen Formen am Beispiel Lübecks und Zürichs.* Historische Studien, vol. 406. Lübeck and Hamburg, 1969.

Rausch, Wilhelm, ed. *Die Stadt am Ausgang des Mittelalters.* Beiträge zur Geschichte der Städte Mitteleuropas, vol. 3. Linz, 1974.

Reynolds, Susan. *An Introduction to the History of English Medieval Towns.* Oxford, 1977.

Rotz, Rhiman A. "German Towns." In *Dictionary of the Middle Ages*, ed. Joseph R. Strayer, vol. 5: 457-71.

Ruano, Benito. *Toledo en el siglo XV.* Madrid, 1961.

Sáncho de Soprani, H. *Historia social de Jerez de la Frontera al fin de la edad media.* 3 vols. Jerez, 1959.

Tait, James. *The Medieval English Borough.* Manchester, 1936.

Waley, Daniel P. *The Italian City-Republics.* New York, 1969.

*Political Structures*

Black, Antony. *Guilds and Civil Society in European Political Thought from the Twelfth Century to the Present.* Ithaca, N.Y., 1984.

Black, Antony. *Political Thought in Europe, 1250-1450.* Cambridge, 1992.

Blockmans, Wim P. "Stadt, Region und Staat, ein Dreieckverhältnis. Der Kasus der Niederlande im 15. Jahrhundert." In *Europa 1500. Integrationsprozesse im Widerstreit: Staaten, Personenverbände, Christenheit*, ed. Ferdinand Seibt and Winfried Eberhard, 211-26. Stuttgart, 1987.

Brown, Judith. *In the Shadow of Florence: Provincial Society in Renaissance Pescia.* Oxford, 1982.

Brucker, Gene. *Renaissance Florence.* New York, 1969.

Dyer, Alan D. *The City of Worcester in the Sixteenth Century.* Leicester, 1973.

Fradenburg, Louise Olga. *City, Marriage, Tournament: Arts of Rule in Late Medieval Scotland.* Madison, Wisc., 1991.

Martines, Lauro. *The Social World of the Florentine Humanists, 1390-1460.* Princeton, 1972a.

Menke, Johannes B. "Geschichtsschreibung und Politik in deutschen Städten des Spätmittelalters." *Jahrbuch des kölnischen Geschichtsvereins* 33 (1958): 1-84; 34/35 (1959-60): 85-194.

Nicholas, David. *Medieval Flanders.* Harlow, Essex, 1992.

Rublack, Hans-Christoph. "Political and Social Norms in Urban Communities in the Holy Roman Empire." In Peter Blickle, Hans-Christoph Rublack, and Winfried Schulze, *Religion, Politics and Social Protest: Three Studies in Early Modern Germany*, ed. Kaspar von Greyerz, 24-60. London, 1984).

Schmidt, Heinrich. *Die deutsche Städtechroniken als Spiegel des bürgerlichen Selbstverständnisses im Spätmittelalter.* SHKBA, vol. 3. Göttingen, 1958.

Skinner, Quentin. *Foundations of Modern Political Thought.* 2 vols. Cambridge, 1978.

Strauss, Gerald. *Nuremberg in the Sixteenth Century.* New York, 1966.

Viroli, Maurizio. *From Politics to Reason of State: the Acquisition and Transformation of the Language of Politics, 1250-1600.* Cambridge, 1992.

Zimmerman, Susan, and Ronald F. E. Weissman, eds. *Urban Life in the Renaissance.* Newark, Del., 1989.

*Adminstration*
Fischer, Thomas. *Städtische Armut und Armenfürsorge im 15. und 16. Jahrhundert.* Göttingen, 1979.
Litchfield, R. Burr. *Emergence of a Bureaucracy: the Florentine Patricians, 1530-1790.* Princeton, 1986.
Reinhardt, Volker. *Überleben in der frühmodernen Stadt. Annona und Getreideversorgung in Rom 1563-1797.* Bibliothek des Deutschen Historischen Instituts in Rom, vol. 72. Tübingen, 1991.
Strauss, Gerald. *Law, Resistance, and the State: the Opposition to Roman Law in Reformation Germany.* Princeton, 1986.

*Urban Society: Citizens, Residents, and Marginals*
Bátori, Ingrid. "Das Patriziat der deutschen Stadt." *ZSSD* 2 (1975): 1-30.
Bátori, Ingrid, and Erdmann Weyrauch. *Die bürgerliche Elite der Stadt Kitzingen: Studien zur Sozial-und Wirtschaftsgeschichte einer landesherrlichen Stadt im 16. Jahrhundert.* SFN, vol. 11. Stuttgart, 1982.
Bohmbach, Jürgen. *Die Sozialstruktur Braunschweigs um 1400.* Brunswick, 1973.
Brady, Thomas A., Jr. "Patricians, Nobles, Merchants: Internal Tensions and Solidarities in South German Urban Ruling Classes at the Close of the Middle Ages." In *Social Groups and Religious Ideas in the 16th Century,* ed. Miriam U. Chrisman and Otto Gründler, 38-45, 159-64. Studies in Medieval Culture, vol. 13. Kalamazoo, Mich., 1978a.
Czok, Karl. "Die Vorstädte. Ihre Stellung in den Stadt-Land-Beziehungen." In *Gewerbliche Produktion und Stadt-Land Beziehungen,* ed. Konrad Fritze, Eckhard Müller-Mertens, and Johannes Schildhauer, 127-35. Abhandlungen zur Handels- und Sozialgeschichte, vol. 18. Weimar, 1979.
Edwards, John. *Christian Córdoba: the City and Its Region in the late Middle Ages.* Cambridge, 1982.
Ehbrecht, Wilfried. "Zu Ordnung und Selbstverständnis städtischer Gesellschaft im späten Mittelalter." *BDLG* 110 (1974): 83-103.
Ellermeyer, Jürgen. "Schichtung und Sozialstruktur in spätmittelalterlichen Städten. Zur Verwendbarkeit sozialwissenschaftlicher Kategorien in historischer Forschung." *Geschichte und Gesellschaft* 6 (1980): 125-49.
Foa, Anna. *Ebrei in Europa dalla peste nera all'emancipazione.* Rome and Bari, 1992.
Friedrichs, Christopher R. "Capitalism, Mobility, and Class Formation in the Early Modern German City." *PaP,* no. 60 (November, 1975): 24-49.
Friedrichs, Christopher R. *Urban Society in an Age of War: Nördlingen, 1580-1720.* Princeton, 1979.
Geremek, Bronislaw. *The Margins of Society in Late Medieval Paris.* Trans. Jean Birrell. Cambridge, 1987.
Haverkamp, Alfred, ed. *Zur Geschichte der Juden in Deutschland des späten Mittelalters und der frühen Neuzeit.* Stuttgart, 1981.
Heitzenröder, Wolfram. *Reichsstädte und Kirche in der Wetterau. Der Einfluss des städtischen Rats auf die geistlichen Institute vor der Reformation.* Studien zur Frankfurter Geschichte, vol. 16. Frankfurt am Main, 1982.
Herlihy, David, and Christiane Klapisch-Zuber. *Tuscans and their Families: a Study of the Florentine Catasto of 1427.* New Haven, 1985.
Hildebrandt, Reinhard. "Rat contra Bürgerschaft." *ZSSD* 1 (1974): 221-41.
Howell, Martha C. *Women, Production and Patriarchy in Late Medieval Cities.* Chicago, 1986.
Hughes, Diane Owen. "Urban Growth and Family Structure in Medieval Genoa." *PaP,* no. 66 (1975): 3-28.
Kent, Francis William. *Household and Lineage in Renaissance Florence: The Family Life of the Capponi, Ginori, and Rucellai.* Princeton, 1977.
Kiessling, Rolf. *Bürgerliche Gesellschaft und Kirche in Augsburg im Spätmittelalter: ein Beitrag zur Strukturanalyse der oberdeutschen Reichsstadt.* Abhandlungen zur Geschichte der Stadt Augsburg, vol. 19. Augsburg, 1971.

Kriegel, Maurice. *Les juifs à la fin du moyen âge*. Paris, 1979.
Kümmel, Julianne. *Bäuerliche Gesellschaft und städtische Herrschaft im Spätmittelalter. Zum Verhältnis von Stadt und Land im Fall Basel/Waldburg 1300-1535*. 2 vols. Constance and Paris, 1980-82.
Martines, Lauro, ed. *Violence and Civil Disorder in Italian Cities, 1200-1500*. Berkeley and Los Angeles, 1972b.
Maschke, Erich. Mittelschichten in deutschen Städten des Mittelalters." In *Städtische Mittelschichten*, ed. Erich Maschke and Jürgen Sydow, 1-31. VKLBW, series B, vol. 69. Stuttgart, 1972.
Maschke, Erich. "Die Unterschichten der mittelalterlichen Städte Deutschlands." In *Gesellschaftlichen Unterschichten in den südwestdeutschen Städten*, ed. Erich Maschke and Jürgen Sydow, 1-74. VKLBW, series B, vol. 41 Stuttgart, 1967.
Maschke, Erich. "Verfassung und soziale Kräfte in der deutschen Stadt des Spätmittelalters vornehmlich in Oberdeutschland." *VSWG* 46 (1959): 289-349, 433-76.
Scott, Tom. *Freiburg and the Breisgau: Town-Country Relations in the Age of Reformation and Peasants' War*. Oxford, 1986.
Stow, Kenneth. *An Alienated Minority: the Jews of Medieval Latin Europe*. Cambridge, Mass., 1992.
Thomson, John A. F. *Towns and Townspeople in the Fifteenth Century*. Wolfboro, N.H., 1988.

*Guilds*
Epstein, Steven R. *Wage Labor and Guilds in Medieval Europe*. Chapel Hill, N.C., 1991.
Füglister, Hans. *Handwerksregiment. Untersuchungen und Materialien zur sozialen und politischen Struktur der Stadt Basel in der ersten Hälfte des 16. Jahrhunderts*. Basler Beiträge zur Geschichtswissenschaft, vol. 143. Basel and Frankfurt am Main, 1981.
Hanawalt, Barbara, ed. *Women and Work in Preindustrial Europe*. Bloomington, Ind., 1986.
Händler-Lachmann, Barbara. "Die Berufstätigkeit der Frau in den deutschen Städten des Spätmittelalters und der beginnenden Neuzeit." *Hessisches Jahrbuch für Landesgeschichte* 30 (1980): 131-75.
Herlihy, David. *Opera muliebra: Women and Work in Medieval Europe*. New York, 1990.
Mackenney, Richard. *Tradesmen and Traders: the World of the Guilds in Venice and Europe, c. 1250-c. 1650*. Totowa, N.J., 1987.
Schulz, Knut. *Handwerkgesellen und Lohnarbeiter. Untersuchungen zur oberrheinischen und oberdeutschen Stadtgeschichte des 14. bis 17. Jahrhunderts*. Sigmaringen, 1985.
Swanson, Heather. "The Illusion of Economic Structure: Craft Guilds in Late Medieval English Towns." *PaP*, no. 121 (November 1988): 29-48.
Thrupp, Sylvia. "The Gilds." In *The Cambridge Economic History of Europe*, ed. M. M. Postan, E. E. Rich, Edward Miller, vol. 3, *Economic Organization and Policies in the Middle Ages*, 430-71. Cambridge, 1965.
Thrupp, Sylvia. *The Merchant Class of Medieval London*. Ann Arbor, 1948.

*Urban Political Conflict*
Abray, Lorna Jane. *The People's Reformation: Magistrates, Clergy and Commons in Strasbourg, 1500-1598*. New Haven, 1985.
Blickle, Peter. *The Communal Reformation: The Quest for Salvation in Reformation Germany*. Trans. Thomas Dunlap. Studies in German Histories. Atlantic Highlands, N.J., 1992.
Blickle, Peter. *Gemeindereformation: die Menschen des 16. Jahrhundert auf dem Weg zum Heil*. Munich, 1985.
Bornert, René. *La réforme protestante de culte à Strasbourg au xvie siècle (1523-1598): approche sociologique et interprétation théologique*. SMRT, vol. 28. Leiden, 1981.
Brady, Thomas A., Jr. "From the Sacral Community to the Common Man: Reflections on German Reformation Studies." *CEH* 20 (1987): 229-45.

Brady, Thomas A., Jr. *Ruling Class, Regime and Religious Reform at Strasbourg, 1520-1555.* SMRT, vol. 32. Leiden, 1978b.

Brecht, Martin. "Luthertum als politische und soziale Kraft in den Städten." In *Kirche und gesellschaftliche Wandel in deutschen und niederländischen Städten der werdenden Neuzeit,* ed. Franz Petri, 1-21. StF, series A, vol. 10. Cologne and Vienna, 1980.

Chrisman, Miriam U. "Women and the Reformation in Strasbourg 1490-1530." *ARG* 63 (1972): 143-52.

Demandt, Dieter. "Konflikte um die geistlichen Standesprivilegien im spätmittelalterlichen Colmar." In *Städtische Gesellschaft und Reformation,* ed. Ingrid Bátori, 136-54. SFN, vol. 12. Stuttgart, 1980.

Demandt, Dieter, and Hans-Christoph Rublack. *Stadt und Kirche in Kitzingen: Darstellung und Quellen zu Spätmittelalter und Reformation.* SFN, vol. 10. Stuttgart, 1978.

Friedrichs, Christopher R. "Citizens or Subjects: Urban Conflict in Early Modern Germany." In *Social Groups and Religious Ideas in the 16th Century,* ed. Miriam U. Chrisman and Otto Gründler, 46-58, 164-69. Studies in Medieval Culture, 13. Kalamazoo, Mich., 1978.

Greyerz, Kaspar von. *The Late City Reformation in Germany: the Case of Colmar, 1522-1628.* Wiesbaden, 1980.

Greyerz, Kaspar von. "Stadt und Reformation. Stand und Aufgaben der Forschung." *ARG* 76 (1985). 6 63.

Hsia, R. Po-chia. "The Myth of the Commune: Recent Historiography on City and Reformation in Germany." *CEH* 20 (1987): 203-15.

Moeller, Bernd. *Imperial Cities and the Reformation: Three Essays.* Translated by H. C. Erik Midelfort and Mark U. Edwards, Jr. Philadelphia, 1975.

Moeller, Bernd. "Die Kirche in der evangelischen freien Städten Oberdeutschlands im Zeitalter der Reformation." *ZGO* 112 (1964): 147-62.

Moeller, Bernd. *Reichsstadt und Reformation.* New ed. Berlin: Evangelische Verlagsanstalt, 1987 [1962].

Mommsen, Wolfgang, ed. *Stadtbürgertum und Adel in der Reformation: Studien zur Sozialgeschichte der Reformation in England und Deutschland.* Veröffentlichungen des Deutschen Historischen Instituts in London, vol. 5. Stuttgart, 1979.

Mörke, Olaf. *Rat und Bürger in der Reformation: Soziale Gruppen und kirchliche Wandel in den welfischen Handelstädten Lüneburg, Braunschweig und Göttingen.* Veröffentlichungen des Instituts für Historische Landesforschung der Universität Göttingen, vol. 19. Hildesheim, 1983.

Naujoks, Eberhard. *Obrigkeitsgedanke, Zunftverfassung und Reformation. Studien zur Geschichte von Ulm, Esslingen, und Schwäbisch Gmünd.* Stuttgart, 1958.

Rotz, Rhiman A. "Investigating Urban Uprisings (with examples from Hanseatic Towns, 1374-1416)." In *Order and Innovation in the Middle Ages,* ed. William C. Jordan, Bruce McNab, and Teofilo F. Ruiz, 215-23, 483-94. Princeton, 1976.

Rotz, Rhiman A. "'Social Struggles' or the Price of Power? German Urban Uprisings in the Late Middle Ages." *ARG* 76 (1985): 64-95.

Rublack, Hans-Christoph. *Gescheiterte Reformation. Frühreformatorische und protestantische Bewegungen in süd- und westdeutschen geistlichen Residenzen.* SFN, vol. 4. Stuttgart, 1978.

Rublack, Hans-Christoph. "Is There a "New History" of the Urban Reformation?" In *Politics and Society in Reformation Europe,* ed. E. I. Kouri and Tom Scott, 121-41. New York, 1987.

Scribner, R. W. "Why was there no Reformation in Cologne?" *BIHR* 49 (1976): 217-41.

# ELEMENTS OF POPULAR BELIEF*

Robert W. Scribner
(University of Cambridge)

'Popular belief' has been perhaps the most significant growth area in historical studies of late-medieval and early modern Europe over the past decade. The bookshelves of a university academic teaching this subject would have contained perhaps half a dozen major works on it at the beginning of the 1980s. A decade later that number would have been well over a hundred, comprised largely of basic teaching books rather than those of interest only to a specialist researcher. The growth in interest has developed from four directions: studies of medieval religion, heavily influenced by the *Annales* school; Reformation studies exploring the origins, nature and progress of religious reform; anthropological history; and studies of popular culture which focus on phenomena such as rituals and festivals, enriched by the more recent variant in this field, the study of daily life and material culture.

It is advisable to begin with some definitions, and to identify some associated problems for discussion. 'Popular belief' is a controversial term because of the ambiguity of the word 'popular', although it should cause no more than passing difficulty if we use it inclusively to mean the belief of the population in the broadest sense. 'Belief' is less problematic, despite some sceptical voices who claim that we will never know about the belief of the past. 'Popular belief' involves attention to four broad areas: the mentality of past populations, their cosmology, their experience of daily life and their unspoken assumptions about the nature and meaning of life in this world and the next. Some of these areas may seem scarcely susceptible of historical exploration, although the methodologies adopted by historians of popular belief have become increasingly sophisticated and have helped to illuminate many of them in ways previously unconsidered. In the essay that follows, I shall concentrate on a small number of key issues crucial for our understanding of popular belief: the material or 'inner-worldly' basis of belief; the 'other world' and the supernatural; official and unofficial religion; social stratification and belief; gender and belief; and power and belief. The emphasis throughout will fall on elements of continuity from the fifteenth to the seventeenth century, without losing sight of the considerable changes wrought by the Reformation. In the concluding section patterns of change over the period as a whole will be briefly discussed.

## 1. THIS WORLD: THE MATERIAL BASIS[1]

### Belief and the 'material' world

It is an inescapable fact that the material world plays a part in shaping popular belief, if for no other reason than that people interact with their environment wherever they attempt to render it understandable and to conform it to their spiritual purposes. Thus, distinct forms and expressions of belief and culture are discernible in arable and pasturage areas, areas of viticulture, and maritime or upland regions. This is not to suggest any crude form of determinism, but simply to remark that the environment provides one kind of conditioning factor. David Underdown called attention to such features in distinguishing between the 'chalk' and the 'cheese' cultures in seventeenth century Wiltshire. His analysis was based on John Aubrey's observation about the different temperaments and activities that seemed to characterize open-field arable villages or villages with highly developed arrangements for common pasture (the 'chalk' areas), compared to the 'cheese' country comprised of wood-pasture communities. In the former, a game such as football was favoured because it seemed an appropriate game for communities with the strong habits of cooperation that grew up in areas of common pasture or shared open fields. The wood-pasture communities, where there was a stronger sense of the individual were more inclined to individualistic sports such as stoolball.[1]

The same interaction of culture, belief and environment is observable in continental Europe, for example, in areas of developed grazing and pasturage, especially alpine regions, where herdsmen and shepherds are vital for the local economy. Here we find a localised popular culture with its own distinctive customs, such as trick-or-treat customs at New Year or Carnival. Important festivals and religious celebrations are linked to the key points of the pastoralist's year, such as the first driving out of cattle from their stalls after winter. These regions have their own distinctive autumnal feasts, with special fast days for the renewal of contracts such as St Bartholomew's Day (the patron saint of butchers), while the most characteristic festival is the Shepherd's Dance. Distinctive patron saints found in these regions are Wendelin and Wolfgang for shepherds; George and Leonhard for herdsmen. Lonely occupations carried out close to nature produced a pattern of characteristic beliefs about shepherds and herdsmen:

they encountered directly the world of spirits, fairies, elves; they knew
about rare herbs and their healing or poisonous qualities. Thus, in some
areas they took over the function of popular healing that was otherwise assigned to the midwife or sexton. They were held to dabble in magic, especially weather magic, and consequently shepherds and herdsmen were in
some areas classed as outsiders and suspected of malificent magic. There
also grew up an entire pattern of folklore concerned with the punishments
visited upon negligent shepherds or herdsmen. Their characteristic material culture was based on horn and wood, carved in the long hours watching flocks or herds, a skill which was also applied to the carving of amulets.
The herdsman's stock or staff carved into human and animal forms contributed to the belief in their magical powers.[2]

The interaction of the material world and popular belief is even more
marked in the links between religious belief and seasonal rhythms of production and reproduction. The importance of the rhythms of the agricultural year for the ordering of rituals and customs has often been remarked,
not merely the cycles of the four seasons, but especially the transitions
between seasons, sometimes with small ritual cycles marking the turning
point from one season to the next. The transitional cycle from winter to
spring serves as a good example. It begins on January 20 (the feast of Sts
Fabian and Sebastian), a day on which it is believed that new sap is rising
in trees, so that no new wood should be cut thereafter. The feast of St
Agnes on January 21 sees new lambs being blessed as symbol of new
spring life. After the feast of St Vincent (January 22) no vine is cut to prevent 'bleeding' of the sap. The Conversion of St Paul (January 25) is a day
of weather prophecy, telling how the weather will be in the spring. The
feast of St Bridget (a saint who had her eyes put out) on February 1 is a
feast of new light, as is the quintessential feast of new light, Candlemas on
the following day. St Blasius' Day on February 3 is concerned with protection for cattle and animals, while bread blessed on St Agatha's Day (February 5) provides protection against human and animal ills as well as against
fire. St Dorothea's Day (February 6) ensures protection against frost on
tender new plants, and St Valentine's Day (February 14) is a feast of spring
mating, as well as of new light. The feast of St Peter's Chair (February 22)
is the last day for gathering in dead wood for spring and summer tinder, as
well as a means of protection for cattle fodder.[3]

The rationale behind such beliefs has much to do with the fragility of
human existence, with the persistent problems of a low-growth pre-modern economy of precarious subsistence, shortness of life, sickness caused by
poor diet and hygiene, and ever-present epidemics and plagues. There was

also human inability to deal with natural disasters, especially those threatening fragile crops – hail, floods, storms, great frosts, severe cold or
drought.[4] Hence the prevalence of rituals of propitiation, as well as the importance of rituals of purification and cleansing, understandable enough
given the enormous threats to health believed to be caused by mists, nox-
ious 'miasmas' and foul smells. Such a culture placed great importance on
the purifying nature of the 'fragrant', herbs, spices and other natural rem-
edies.[5] Arthur Imhof has illuminated the mental constraints of this kind of
existence with his depiction of the 'many small worlds' inhabited by the
farmer Johannes Hooss (1670-1755) of Leimbach in Hesse. Hooss' small
world was constituted by the experience of isolation and fragmentation in
a constricted small-scale society, underlining the importance of family, kin,
community, corporations and other collective bodies as forms of belonging.[6] The material conditions of existence shaped expressions of social and
religious life.

### The Supernatural in the Natural

Much of the physical and moral effort of early modern people was directed
at simply coping. Some reassurance was offered by the commonplace belief that the supernatural world, a world more powerful and potent than
mere human agency, was continually present within the material world.
Indeed, 'mere' humans were offered a substantial consolation in that they
were held to straddle the two modes of being. Not only were humans
placed near the top of the great chain of being, a hierarchy of material creation that rose from insentient objects over sentient beings to those with in-
telligence and the capacity for moral action, but humans also partook of
the non-material world in their created nature, being composed of spirit as
well as matter. Indeed, the composition of a pre-modern person was quite
complex and far from a simplistic dualism of body and soul. Some followed a Pauline tripartite division of the person, as expressed by Rachel
Speght in 1621: 'Both man and woman of three parts consist, which Paul
doth bodie, soule and spirit call'. The soul represented the immortal part
of the person, and the spirit something akin to the modern notion of the
psyche or the mind.[7] Thus, it required no great mental leap to understand
the human person as a microcosm of the large-scale pattern of creation,
nor that she or he should experience the 'sacred' within the 'profane'. The
entire world, human and non-human, material and non-material, was regarded as an expression of the power of the Creator. This enabled belief in
the 'moralised universe', the notion that moral disorder could be reflected
in disorder in the material and social world. Belief in and attention to
signs, omens and portents was a consequence of such belief.[8]

Such presuppositions enable us to understand two characteristic features of the pre-modern mentality, sacramentalism and magic. Sacramentalism was the belief that the sacred, non-material world could be present in, and experienced through, the profane and the material. Underlying such a view was a complex semiology most effectively summarised by Augustine, who saw the entire world as a complex sign system, through which one gained access to the supernatural world by the signifying power of the natural. Sacramental action embodied this relationship par excellence, in that what was signified by ritual actions performed in this world was held to be supernaturally efficacious. 'Magic' stood close to this notion of the sacramental, since it too relied on the notion that ritual actions performed in the natural world could be efficacious. In the case of magic, however, the primary effects were inner-worldly, while the primary effects of sacramental action were other worldly.[9] Finally, we should be aware of the interpenetration of sacred and secular events, or put another way, of the inseparability of sacred and profane time. Sacred time, sacred events could enter the flow of merely human time, so that it was no contradiction for a historical observer to imagine him- or herself as present in sacred events such as the birth of Christ, the Crucifixion, the sufferings of the Virgin or the deeds of a saint.[10]

If we have difficulty apprehending this complex interweaving of material and non-material worlds, it is because our twentieth-century mentality is used to separating these two realms of experience. Certainly, there were those even in late-medieval Europe who had begun to split one from the other, to claim that the supernatural world was so far beyond human comprehension that mere humans could come to no understanding of it in and through the natural. Indeed, many were especially offended by the ways in which the supernatural was increasingly represented as immanent in the natural world, and regarded this as a form of materialism. It remains an open question whether many late-medieval expressions of sacramentalism were not forms of crypto-materialism, that is, the workings of the supernatural were understood in ways sufficiently crude to constitute an undermining of their supernatural status. The most eminent example of this tendency can be found in the miller Mennochio, whose understanding of the nature of creation was expressed in terms of the action of worms causing fermentation in cheese, a purely natural and materialist process.[11]

## 2. THE 'OTHER WORLD' AND THE SUPERNATURAL

It is difficult for people of the late twentieth century to conceptualise the intensity with which our pre-modern forebears perceived the 'other world' and the supernatural. The reality of the supernatural was something not merely apprehended in and through the natural world; rather it was understood as more tangible, more 'real' than the evanescence of 'this world', of created matter. This is the recurrent message of the images of death that permeated late-medieval culture, the material world of the flesh is infinitely corruptible, while only the world of the spirit has lasting reality. Thus, St Bridget of Sweden experienced a vision of hell in which the suffering soul – corpulent, putrefying, stinking and horribly deformed – had a corporeal reality that is horrifying in its concreteness.[12] Similarly, a tale of a woman who accidentally stumbled on the Mass of the Holy Souls at midnight in her village church reveals the potent reality of those who have passed into the 'other world'. Realising her mistake in the moment that her presence was perceived by the spirits of the dead, she fled the church, pursued by the howling souls. The cloak that she dropped in the churchyard in her hasty flight was found the next morning, torn in shreds, one of which was laid on each grave in the churchyard.[13] Many other tales and visions of this kind indicate some salient features of the 'other world'. It was a world of enormous potency, full of power to help or harm; encountering it, especially in unregulated and protected ways, involved enormous dangers; and it was full of the terrors of the unknown, from the anger of unquiet souls through to the terrors of the demonic, the Devil and the horrors of Hell. The 'other world' was also enormously complex in the beings who inhabited it: the entire range of 'supernatural' beings – God and his elaborate hierarchy of angels; the Devil, his demons and a vast universe of evil spirits; and a vast host of 'holy persons' – Mary, the Apostles and the Christian saints. To it also belonged the souls of the damned and the souls in Purgatory, as well as the 'revenant dead' and ambivalent groups such as the Wild Horde. There were also such strange beings as the will o' the wisp, fiery men and phantom horsemen, and residues of pre-Christian belief in creatures such as elves, fairies and sprites.[14]

Most pre-modern people lived comfortably with the continual presence of the 'other world', aware that it could be benign or harmful, depending on circumstances. Three matters caused concern, however: the Devil, the dead and the liminal. The Devil was the greatest source of ambivalence: on the one hand he was regarded as an over-familiar figure of fun and jest, on the other as a cause of fear, terror and loathing. He was taken most seriously because of his role as Tempter, luring the sinner into eternal damnation and the vivid torments of hell, and there was no more terrifying image that than of the sinner carried off bodily to hell. An equal cause for concern was his power to take possession of a person against his or her will, and the horrifying and disruptive reality of demonic possession was a continual problem for pre-modern people – including Protestants, who seemed just as defenceless as Catholics against such satanic intrusions. A good deal of protective magic, as well as recourse to the protective power of holy persons such as saints, was involved in countering the wiles of the Devil. His power was especially harmful because of his apparent ability to work material effects in the world and, more importantly, because of his ability to work on the human mind or psyche. Almost all sacramental forms and rituals involved protection against *Teufelsgespenst*, the psychological tricks of the Devil. The Reformation made little difference to this essential problem; indeed, in many ways it may have rendered its followers more defenceless through the abolition of traditional ritual and intercessionary forms of dealing with the diabolical.[15]

The dead were a special category of the 'other world' who demanded and received continual attention in popular belief. In the Catholic world, a major cause for concern was, of course, the souls in purgatory, a group who remained in intimate contact with the living through the belief that purgatory was localised, the suffering souls actually being understood as present in one's village or even house. No less a problem were the untimely dead, the unshriven snatched away to their eternal fate without an opportunity to repent of their sins. Such persons were the origin of the ghosts and poltergeists who continued to plague the living until they were released by an act of mercy. Curiously, despite removing belief in purgatory and so dramatically reorientating attitudes to the dead, Protestantism was unable to abolish belief in the presence of the untimely dead, and ghosts and poltergeists plagued Protestants and Catholic with confessional indifference. No less common to both confessions was the problem of the 'revenant dead', the recently deceased who came seeking a companion to take with them into the 'other world'. This could be either a mother who had died in childbirth, who came to seek her child or even a mother who had died without being churched; or it could be a dead person for whom the rites of separation had been imperfectly or inadequately performed. The central European belief in *Nachzehren*, that the dead came back seeking either their worldly goods or a companion from the world of the living, was a constant feature of both Catholic and Protestant popular belief right through to the twentieth century, and was closely related to the perform-

ance of rituals of separation from, and reconciliation with, the dead, something that was far from weakened by the Protestant abolition of purgatory.
Ariès has written about the 'tame death' and the different ways in which
the act of death was managed in late-medieval and early modern Europe.
More important, however, was the relationship with the dead after the act
of dying was completed.[16]

By its very nature, the supernatural and the 'other world' was unpredictable, even capricious in the ways in which it could irrupt into the world of
the natural, but there were regular points of contact between the two
worlds at which those living in this world could attempt some form of
management of relations between the two. These were most marked in
liminal areas, especially at boundaries which provided ontological points
of contact. Eaves, the threshold, fences, crossroads, were all liminal points
of leakage or seepage which enabled the supernatural to enter this world.
There were also liminal events and dates, such as All Souls and the surrounding days such as Halloween, on which souls were briefly released
from purgatory. A complex pattern of rituals and customs dealt with such
liminal points, and if nothing else mitigated the dangers of contact between
the natural world and the supernatural world of sacred power.[17] Recent
research has also made us aware of the continuing importance of persons
able to mediate between the world of the living and the world of the dead,
the figure of the shaman, who survived in various guises in northern and
central Europe.[18] Important for the nature and development of popular
belief were the ways in which official and institutional religious channels
dealt with such concerns and problems, with manifestations of the sacred
in general as well as with the demonic.

## 3. RELIGION, OFFICIAL AND UNOFFICIAL

Nothing illustrates the disparities and tensions between official and unofficial religion more than the frequent epiphanies of the sacred that occurred
in apparitions. Perhaps the best-known in late medieval Germany was the
apparition of the Virgin to Hans Boheim, the piper of Niklashausen,
whose attempt to propagate the message of his vision precipitated a mass
pilgrimage and a near-rebellion. Common features of such apparitions
are: the initially informal nature of the vision; the link of the apparition to
a prophetic message that makes it a matter of public concern and so brings
it to the attention of ecclesiastical and secular authorities; the spontaneity
of a mass upsurge of interest, which is followed by official attempts to con-

trol popular enthusiasm and ultimately to routinize it. Gradually a 'myth of origin' develops around the precipitating events, sometimes associated with a folklore through which the events pass into popular cultural tradition. In this latter stage, the creation of myth and folklore may also involve official intervention and promotion of the original apparition. The same pattern recurs, whether we are dealing with apparitions of the Virgin, host miracles (especially those linked to the blood libel against the Jews) or other miraculous interventions of the sacred which might lead to a pilgrimage cult. It is even found in cases such as the pilgrimage to the Beautiful Virgin of Regensburg, where the entire cult was undoubtedly promoted by the local city authorities for purposes of gain.[19]

Why should we focus on the polarity 'official-unofficial', rather than on other notions such as 'elite-popular'? The pair of concepts does at least call attention to an important historical phenomenon, namely, that many religious manifestations did emerge through non-institutional channels, often in opposition to, sometimes in creative tension with, ecclesiastical and secular authorities. The processes though which informal and spontaneous religious events were prohibited, modified, regulated or institutionalized, tells us a great deal about the development and dynamics of popular belief, not least about the ways in which a dual process of appropriation went on, with spontaneous and unofficial manifestations being appropriated to official religion, while official aspects of religion and cult were often reworked in many unofficial and officially disapproved ways. The terms 'official' and 'unofficial' should, therefore, be understood in terms not of a polarity, but as a continual dialectic.[20] We can better understand the relationship through a few examples which reveal the dialectic at work. I have chosen for comment the liturgy, devotion to the saints, popular drama, and confraternities.

The history of the late-medieval liturgy is full of examples of popular initiatives which developed on the fringes of the approved liturgy, but which were later routinized by being formally incorporated into the regular liturgical structure. John Bossy has called our attention to the importance of the kiss of peace and the commemoration of the living and the dead in the Mass (in the latter case, including the names of enemies placed on the list of the commemorated dead as a form of malice). More strikingly, there were the dramatic performances that became part of the liturgical cycle, such as the procession of Christ on the Palm-ass, the deposition of Christ in the grave on Good Friday, the opening of the Easter tomb, the drawing up of the figure of Christ on a rainbow at the Ascension and the showering of wafers and pentecostal fire at Pentecost. All of these elements may have developed from popular demand for the liturgy to be made more dramatic and participatory, and were certainly encouraged for their educational functions, as a way of making the mysteries of these great feast days more accessible to the theologically unlearned. Indeed, they were even preserved in some Lutheran territories for the same pedagogic purpose. Whatever the official intention, the mere existence of such ceremonies enabled a penumbra of unofficial belief to grow up around them, whether in the form of the enormous devotion directed at the Palm-ass, the scapegoat ceremony of 'expelling Judas' on Maundy Thursday, the levity associated with Easter laughter and the 'race to the tomb' on Easter Day, or the overtones of fertility magic often linked to the showering of wafers, water and fire at Pentecost. The dialectic of official and unofficial was only ruptured by the action of radical Protestants, who held that the only way of eradicating 'abuses' of such ceremonies was to abolish them completely.[21]

The cult of saints provides even more striking examples of the dialectic at work. At the most obvious level, we can point to those local holy persons revered as saints despite official disapproval, even indeed attempts to annihilate their memory by dishonour or infamy. Thus, Thomas Müntzer's remains were revered as holy for some years after his execution, as were those of other 'Christian preachers' condemned for their role in the Peasants' War. In some cases, such unofficial reverence developed into a tolerated cult, such as that of the 'holy greyhound' discussed by Jean-Claude Schmitt. Some saints from the early days of Germanic Christianity, such as Wolfgang, Wendelin and Leonhard, became important official territorial patron saints, while accumulating in popular devotion a complex structure of popular beliefs about their protective and magical powers.[22] The most elaborate interweaving of official and unofficial elements can be found in the late-medieval cult of the Virgin, and by extension the cult of St Anne, phenomena whose features we have only recently begun to explore.[23] 'Unofficial' elements here could range from the indecorous depictions of the lactating Virgin, or the representations of the Virgin which opened up to reveal the Trinity inside (giving rise to the popular view that the Virgin was the mother of the Trinity), through to curiosity about Christ's siblings in the 'holy kinship', and about Christ's sexuality.[24]

Popular drama in the form of religious plays, passion plays or carnival festivities provides an insight of a different kind into the complexity of the dialectic. In almost all these cases, it is clear that such dramatic performances were far from 'popular' in the sense of spontaneously unofficial. The organisation and staging of these dramas was invariably under official, corporate control, very often by the social elites who appropriated them as expressions of their status in the community. Yet they were undeniably 'popular' in the sense of mass participation, either in the form of a substantial audience or as actors in the pageants or staged scenes. Indeed, in some towns, the participants in these plays would have included almost all of the adult population. It is, however, also the case that such dramatic performances could get out of control, for example, if a small group decided to express irreverence or anticlerical sentiments, deviations for which the culprits were invariably punished. We have now abandoned romantic notions about carnival as an expression of popular justice and about rituals of rebellion and inversion. Most commentators would nowadays emphasise the ways in which these were officially allowed as a form of safety-valve. Indeed, in one distinctive interpretation, the excess of carnival was encouraged as a religious pedagogic device to drive home to the people their inherent inclination to vices of excess in order to turn them more effectively to the purifying asceticism of Lent. Yet as the work of Bakhtin reminds us, there was always an inherent possibility of unofficial subversion of authority and hierarchy through the alternative potential of the 'culture of laughter'. Carnival exemplified the complex and subtle dialectic between the official and the unofficial.[25]

Finally, we can mention confraternities, very often in recent years taken as manifestations of popular religious initiative, as a means of constructing a meaningful religious life alongside more formal manifestations such as the parish. These bodies were certainly an expression of sociability among peer groups of different kinds, whether locally in a parish or occupationally in a guild, or simply among those with a shared interest in a common form of devotion, as in Rosary or Corpus Christi confraternities. They provided a form of mutual assurance linking their living with their dead members, creating a solidarity of prayer and collective intercession, while offering a form of pious sociability that created a sense of social belonging. Yet they were never far from some kind of official control. If they were not subject to the guiding hand of a parish priest, they would be no less controlled by a guild or subject to the regulatory eye of municipal authorities. They often mirrored local social stratification, and were not infrequently dominated by social elites. Whatever their 'unofficial' elements, they were invariably and quickly incorporated into official and institutionalized structures, even those newer forms which might have arisen as spontaneous expression of religious or confessional feeling.[26]

In all these instances, we can see how 'popular belief' can both arise spontaneously 'from below', but it can also be officially constructed 'from

above' and offered to the people at large for acceptance. What arises spontaneously can be appropriated officially, while officially created norms and
practices can be internalised to the point where they may appear unofficial.
Popular belief always has the potential to subvert, to supplement and even
to replace the 'official' with the 'unofficial', although it may also endure a
form of toleration and assimilation which allows it permanency because it
is considered harmless, or not worth the effort to eradicate. It is worth
noting that the same dialectic can be found in Protestantism, despite its attempts to break down the problematic nexus of 'official and unofficial' by
simply abolishing unacceptable manifestations of religious devotion.[27] In
the ebb and flow of this dialectic much depends on issues of power and social location, points to be taken up below.

## 4. SOCIAL STRATIFICATION AND BELIEF

The issue of how popular belief is related to social structure is contentious
but inescapable. We can see this from a tale about the intercessory role of
the Virgin, which recurs in various forms but with essentially the same
message. A man who has always been devoted to the Virgin unexpectedly
dies in a state of mortal sin. Appearing before Christ as judge, he is about
to be sentenced to the torments of hell when the Virgin intercedes on his
behalf. Since the sinner has always been so devoted to the Mother of God,
she begs her son to pardon him as an act of grace to her, whereupon the
sinner is spared condemnation.[28] Although not at first apparent, the tale
reflects a number of assumptions about late-medieval social structure and
customs. It mirrors the relationship of patronage and clientage, through
which a client offers allegiance and receives in return protection from his
or her patron. Alternatively, the feudal relationship embodying homage
and allegiance in return for grace and protection is also recalled in tales
where the devotee takes a vow of devotion to the Virgin. Equally, the Virgin fulfills the social role of the noblewoman, who by virtue of her rank intercedes for convicted felons to have their punishment mitigated, a common feature of criminal justice even in sixteenth century Germany.
Clearly, the relationship of devotees to the Virgin has here been constructed in terms of familiar social relationships and common assumptions
about social structure.

   Similar observations could be made about the social forms through
which late-medieval religion was imagined. The heavenly hierarchy
seemed to mirror the feudal hierarchy, with God as king and Christ as

prince, surrounded by vassals from whom he expected homage and fealty. The Devil appeared as a rival king, determined to subject as many souls as possible to serfdom. From the perspective of peasant religion, God was understood as a 'peasants' God', entering into a contractual relationship in which the peasants swore their allegiance as long as God fulfilled his obligation to see to their material well-being. Lionel Rothkrug discerned a comparable assimilation of religious ideas to social presuppositions, by pointing to the cult of an imperial Virgin fostered by an essentially aristocratic society.[29] The notion that the Reformation produced a form of 'bourgeois' religion, that is, religion suited to the social life and presuppositions of townsfolk, has a long progeny, whether in a marxian form or in the weberian form of 'elective affinity' (the notion that people choose the form of religion that best accords with their social circumstances).[30] Following Lanternari, we could also speak of some religious phenomena in our period as belonging to the 'religions of the dispossessed', by which he meant the appeal of certain millennialist and chiliastic religious forms to those with no stake in a given society. Finally, the recent notion of 'communal Reformation', in which the high value placed on communal experience, communal collective life and endeavour is said to have influenced the forms of religious reformation in sixteenth century Germany and Switzerland reflects the same nexus between social circumstances and religious forms or expressions.[31]

   There seems no doubt that the relationships with holy persons were imagined in terms of known social relationships. The image of God was constructed in terms of a feudal ruler, lawgiver and judge, presiding over a feudal court in which the saints played the part of clients. Human relationships with the saints as intermediaries were undoubtedly relationships of clientage, and embodied notions of contract, homage and sworn allegiance. Indeed, thanks to recent sociological studies of sainthood, we are well aware of how sainthood was socially constructed in numerous ways. We find both the construction of real, historical holy persons as saints and the creation of imaginary saints in order to meet the needs of their devotees. Local saints were a result of local needs, while the process of recognition and canonization that invested local holy figures with wider significance was primarily a matter of promotion and agitation, what we might call the 'politics of the holy'. This has led Delooz to argue that saints were not saints on their own behalf, but for other people. The sociology of sainthood was also a socially selective process – those declared to be saints and so recognized by the official church have a very typical social profile: they were predominantly bishops, members of religious orders, kings and noblewomen. Indeed, in the case of some royal saints, the achievement of sainthood was part of a conscious political strategy, the conferral of saint-hood within a royal family reflecting glory and prestige on the dynasty as a whole, and so strengthening political legitimacy.[32] This process of dynastic hagiography, promoting a dynasty through glorification and apotheosis of its members, continued in more complex form in the early modern period, especially in the age of absolutism in which the ideas of sacral kinship and divine right were fostered to provide authority and legitimation for emer-gent dynasties. This was a process from which Protestant dynasties were not exempt. The pretension to social elevation through association with the sacred can be found not merely in such examples as the family of the Emperor Maximilian I being represented as the Holy Kinship, but even in burgher circles. In Dürer's Paumgärtner altarpiece, the two sons of the Paumgärtner family are depicted as the aristocratic saints George and Hubertus, an overt statement of social ambition.[33]

Given that saints were essentially role models for imitation, it is curious that the vast majority were typically aristocratic males. There were few commoner saints and even fewer women, so that the example of St Zita of Lucca stands out as a double exception that proves the rule, here a servant girl who stole from her master in order to feed the poor (and was, with some irony, the patron saint of servant girls). This was decidedly not an example that a strongly hierarchical society would have wished to multi-ply. More noticeable in the socially conditioned development of represen-tations of holy personages is what we might call the 'bourgeoisification of the Holy Family', which was increasingly represented as a burgher family of moderate means (a striking contrast with the imperial Virgin, who was patently queen of heaven and earth). The representation of holy person-ages thus tended in the direction of social conservatism, presenting an ide-alised social image that appeared to legitimate the status quo. The legiti-mation of social dissidence and dissent devolved upon more pronouncedly outside figures – prophets, hermits, wandering holy persons and social ren-egades such as St Francis.[34]

## 5. GENDER AND BELIEF

The gender specific nature of sainthood indicates the importance of gender for our understanding of patterns of popular belief. Recent research on gender in late-medieval and early modern Europe has now made us very aware of complex but basic differences in the nature of female and male piety. We could crudely illustrate the basic contrast with two examples, that of the fourteenth century visionary Margarethe Ebner, who developed a relationship of surrogate motherhood with a doll of the infant Jesus, and that of the adolescent Bernardino of Siena, whose devotion to a particular image of the Virgin above one of the city gates bore all the characteristics of male teenage infatuation, to the extent that his devout cousin Tobia feared that he was involved in some carnal relationship.[35]

This comparison can be filled out more completely in a general description of what is now virtually conventional wisdom about gender differences in medieval religion. The later Middle Ages, from the late twelfth to the mid-fourteenth century, witnessed a proliferation of opportunities for women to participate in specialised religious roles or behaviour. There was an increase in the numbers of convents, especially Cistercian, and there emerged a number of quasi-monastic religious possibilities in beguinages or orders of tertiaries which enabled women to pursue holy lives of poverty and self-denial without complete withdrawal from the secular world. The increased activity of women in popular piety is reflected in the number of women called as witnesses in canonization proceedings, well over half of all witnesses in the later middle ages. There was a noticeable rise in the number of women canonized, from ten per cent in the eleventh century to around twenty-eight per cent in the fifteenth. If women remained vastly underrepresented in this role-call of approved saints, outweighed by the numbers of saintly bishops and members of male religious orders, they really came into their own among the lay people canonized, accounting for seventy-one per cent of lay persons canonized in the fourteenth century. A similar, if more subtle trend is discernible in hagiographies. In the thirteenth century, brief lives of male saints outnumbered those of women, although longer lives were more equally balanced. In the fourteenth century, brief lives of the saints were still devoted mainly to male holy figures, but the longer lives were now predominantly about female saints. In the fifteenth century the gender balance was 'restored', indicating either that female piety was flourishing in the later Middle Ages as never before or that there was greater interest in it or in its promotion.[36]

It is also possible to point to significant differences between female and male spirituality: mysticism was far more prominent in female religiosity, and paramystical phenomena such as trances, levitations, stigmata and miraculous fasting were more common for women. Women's spiritual standing was more likely to be founded on charismatic authority rather than a result of their institutional status, and this charisma was especially acquired by visions. Female piety was also characterised by its penitential asceticism, especially that involving self-inflicted suffering. In the later Middle Ages women account for around eighteen per cent of all canonised saints, but of those whose saintly reputations were based on patient suffering of illness, women constituted fifty-three per cent. Female religious writing was more affective than the male equivalent, and we can also mention the close links between female piety and literacy discerned by some scholars. Certain devotions were also more favoured by women, especially those connected with an emphasis on Christ's humanity or those to do with the Eucharist, the body of Christ.[37]

Male piety presents a contrasting picture which underlines the gender specific nature of late-medieval religion. The great majority of canonized saints were male, their ranks swollen by members of (predominantly male) religious orders. Male piety was often associated with extraordinary attention to prayer, and while males could also display profound reverence for the Eucharist, their emphasis fell on seeing rather than on more tactile experience such as tasting. Male eucharistic piety was very much integrated into liturgical piety, undoubtedly through grounding in forms of monastic piety, with its close links to formal liturgy. The Mass was the centre of devotion for males, who because of their exclusive ability to celebrate it were able to participate more fully in this central liturgical act. Thus, women were more likely to experience visions relating to the reception of communion, while those of men were more linked to the act of consecration. Visions of the Infant Jesus were common to both men and women, although there was a marked male sentimentality related to the liturgical Eucharist, while women thought more of the intimacy of union between the hungering soul and its eucharistic food.[38]

Such gender differences also extended to the devotional uses of art, which was used more often in male than in female piety and with different functions. Women would seek empathetic identification with Christ or the Virgin, and experienced a fluid boundary between meditations and visions. Men had a more objective relationship, standing before a statue or painting as a source of power or as a surrogate for the real person, rather than approaching it as a direct experience of another individual. Kieckhefer posits as a characteristic of male piety in general that it emphasised more the objective favours available from a miracle-working image, rather than using the image as a means for inward transformation.[39]

The use made of reading in piety also is heavily gendered, as was mentioned above. Women's piety was connected to literacy in that female saints were more likely to be depicted with books. Reading was associated with interior, meditative piety, while the lives of male saints emphasized outward conduct rather than inward disposition. We may need to be cautious about the interpretation here, since much of the evidence depends not on actual examples of reading habits, but on iconographic evidence in which books may appear more for their symbolic value as signs of learning rather than as a reflection of real social practice. It is certain, however, that male piety was more linked to pedagogy and public instruction, undoubtedly determined by the preaching roles ascribed exclusively to men. In many ways, male piety was also more varied than female, doubtless because of the wider opportunities socially available, and there was nothing comparable to the female preoccupation with food, which Caroline Walker Bynum has claimed is the central motif above all others of medieval female piety. Were women marginalised and confined to a 'private' religious sphere, as was once thought? This assumption has now been challenged, suggesting that some of the preoccupations of feminist research in the 1980s, especially that with women's powerlessness, may have distorted understanding of the phenomenon. Caroline Walker Bynum sees women as wielding a potent influence on late-medieval religion, especially by what she calls a 'feminization of religious language'.[40]

Yet the task of discerning in more precise detail just how gender worked its way through the broadest manifestations of popular religion is rather more complicated than this brief sketch may have suggested. Three examples reveal the complexity. First, we may take devotion to images of Christ. We can point to a focus of late-medieval interest in the humanity of Christ and his redemptive suffering, an interest which could be said to lead to stronger emphasis on intimacy and personal encounter, perhaps fostered by growing habits of private reading and the use of the printed devotional image. This may have appealed strongly to pious women, but we find the same emphasis in many male figures, including Geiler von Keysersberg and Luther. The interest in the suffering body of Christ could also manifest itself in the curiosity about Christ's sexuality, unmistakably documented by Leo Steinberg. We can point to an allied sexualization of the male 'devout gaze', which was accompanied by an analogous 'sexualization of the female devout gaze', both remarked by Zwingli.[41]

Images of the Virgin provide a second complex example. The Virgin could be perceived as a theological sign, for example, as symbol of the Church or as the apocalyptic woman of Revelations 12, 1-2. There was the cult of the imperial Virgin as queen of heaven, undoubtedly a male-oriented cult not too far removed from the 'chivalric Virgin', the idealised female figure worshipped by a male devotee. It would be interesting to ask how far such a cult may have contributed to an explicit sexualization of devotion. There was the image of the Virgin as symbol of succour, appearing to male ascetics such as St Onophrius or St Bernhard. We can also point to the rise of an image of the domesticated, bourgeois Virgin, the Virgin of the nuclear family, depicted in a cosy domestic interior, familiar to the world of late-medieval townsfolk. There was the Virgin as personal patron, even as family intimate, shown in a panel painting such as Holbein the Younger's depiction of 'The Virgin and Child with the Family of Basel Mayor Jacob Meyer' (1528/9). There is also the Virgin as an image of idealised virginity, discerned by Margaret Miles, as well as the Virgin as scarcely disguised whore, as seen in Jean Fouquet's infamous 'Madonna with the Red Angels' of ca 1450. What is most intriguing about all these diverse images of the Virgin is that they reveal that the Virgin was a figure whose cult appealed to both men and women, but in decidedly gender specific ways.[42]

The third example reveals the same complexity, the cult of St Anne, the mother of the Virgin. St Anne was a constructed saint, her biography based not on New Testament sources, but on a developing apocryphal and popular tradition. She is traceable from the early church, but her cult reaches its peaks at the end of the fifteenth and the beginning of the sixteenth century. This cult has recently been cited to refute the notion that women's religious concerns and experiences were always marginal to dominant male culture, and to challenge the existence of any public/private dichotomy in the pre-modern period. Anne's significance is that she represents matriarchy, since it is she, rather than her husband Joachim, who is shown in all representations as the founding parent of the Holy Family. Jesus was therefore the product of a matrilineal descent system, rather than of the patrilineal system found in the Gospels. In this sense the cult of St Anne was perhaps genuinely 'popular' in that it expressed 'unofficial' belief which only gradually forced itself onto the attention of the ecclesiastical hierarchy. However, this cult too was many-sided: in the image of the Holy Kinship, it presented an idealized notion of the extended family as the true Christian community. St Anne represented a female figure available for both male and female uses: in her capacity as patron saint of barren women, she could speak to female desires for motherhood, but also represent male ideas of lineage and dynasty. Like all cults of saints, the figure of St Anne could also be appropriated for many other, especially political purposes, as she was for republican imagery in Florence in the fourteenth and fifteenth centuries. Pamela Sheingorn has called attention to significant secular changes in the associated image of the 'Holy Kinship', which around 1400 focussed on motherhood and positive relationships between women, but by the sixteenth century, had become an image championing fatherhood through increased emphasis on the role of Joseph and the isolation of women in the nuclear family.[43]

Such examples suggest that gender-specific piety was changing significantly on the eve of the Reformation, and there is no shortage of possible hypotheses about the nature of the changes. Was there a more explicit 'sexualisation of piety', linked to new or reemphasised views on female sexuality as dangerously voracious? Was there a rise of distinctively bourgeois views of piety, focussing on the intimacy of the nuclear family? (This latter hypothesis perhaps ought to be approached with caution if it is not to be too dependent on dubious assumptions about the 'rise of the nuclear family'.) Was there a reaction against a male-dominated objectifying tendency in popular devotion and a turning towards a further 'feminization' of religion in the sense defined by Caroline Walker Bynum? Luther's notions of inwardness and his close attachment to the humanity of Christ may owe much to such 'feminizing' elements, and may themselves have developed from his own self-confessed and powerful attachment to both the Virgin and St Anne. There is much work to be done here in one of the more exciting and fruitful fields of research, even before we turn to the question of how far the Reformation and Counter-Reformation made a significant difference to gendered ideas of piety, a point we shall return to in the concluding section.

### 6. POWER AND BELIEF

It should be evident by now that a great deal of popular belief (and a great deal of popular culture) has to do with human attempts to appropriate and apply supernatural power. Sometimes this is done by the powerless, but supernatural power can also be useful to the powerful, who seek to exploit it to buttress their own position. Certainly, in the period under discussion supernatural power is always involved in purely secular power struggles, even at the most mundane social level. The point is exemplified in the experience of a Protestant pastor, Georg Christoph Zimmermann, working in a Franconian village at the end of the seventeenth century. The village swineherd had injured the leg of a pig in his care; the owner, fearful that his pig would die, demanded compensation, which the swineherd refused to pay. Instead he proposed taking the pig to a nearby village where the herdsman knew how to apply the art of sympathetic magical healing. This was done by binding up a chair leg, with appropriate magical blessings, on

a Friday at the tolling of the evening bells. The owner was reluctant to accept this solution, possibly because of the inconvenience involved – the
other village was an hour's journey away – and the dispute was brought to
a meeting of the village commune. There it was decided that the owner
should try the magical remedy himself, binding up the chair leg at the
specified time in a dark place. Zimmermann was a pastor who had waged
a constant campaign against popular magic, and he promptly ordered the
owner to ignore this solution, an intervention which set the entire commune into uproar (the pastor labelled it 'rebellion'). They told their pastor
that he had no power of command in their community and if the owner
did not want to use such means, it would be his own fault if a pig died. The
outcome is not recorded, but the nature of the power struggle is clear.[44]

The desire to appropriate supernatural power was related to the belief
in sacred power as the sustaining force of creation, although it also had its
ambivalent, destructive side. This was especially evident in instances
where it was wielded punitively, exemplified in reports of supernatural
punishments visited upon public perjurers, who had limbs or visages cor-
rupted or blackened in consequence of divine wrath.[45] The power of the
demonic seemed no less present and was even more available to human be-
hest. I shall not recapitulate what has been said above when discussing the
nature of the supernatural, except to reiterate that power was diffused
throughout the supernatural hierarchy without diminution of its force,
that it could intervene in, and radically change, this-worldly affairs, affecting material existence, individual destinies and social relations. It is an interesting speculation whether the understanding of supernatural power
was constructed in the image of inner-worldly power, but this seems to me
to be a misleading parallel. Inner-worldly power is a complex matter in
any period, involving the notions of power as 'potential' (embodied in the
words *potens, Macht, Kraft, pouvoir*) as well as the notion of force and
violence (*vis, Gewalt*). The Middle Ages also knew a concept of power as
an innate ability or 'virtue' (*virtus, Kraft*). Power is also a relational matter, a question of dominance and superiority (in German: *Herrschaft,
Oberkeit* or *Obrigkeit*). However, these mere concepts will have little
meaning unless we also understand that secular power in the pre-modern
period was puny by modern terms, because it was so often diffused and
dispersed, albeit perhaps no less effective and humiliating when experienced by the individual. However, the tendency of secular power to
weaken through diffusion, true both of absolute and of feudal rule, was
matched by the ability of supernatural power to retain its full strength
when diffused.

Hence there arose attempts to appropriate supernatural power in the service of this-worldly power, not least the desire for supernatural legitimation. Charismatic authority thus took on an inherent force which is scarcely captured by modern sociological understanding of the term. The importance attached to the 'mandate of heaven', sacred kingship and royal saints all flowed from this fact, as well as the continual recourse to supernatural power by the powerless. The significant point here is that supernatural power was capable of overwhelming the diffused nature of secular power because of the latter's very puniness. The mobilising possibilities inherent in exceptional manifestations of supernatural power – miraculous visions or prophecies – were well understood by powerholders and power-brokers throughout the period, if only in order to preclude the powerless making full use of them. Thus, whenever we find power being contested throughout our period, whether in large-scale confrontations or in small-scale, mundane 'power-plays', we also find supernatural power being invoked and wielded.

The complexity of these power plays we can see in another incident cited by Georg Christoph Zimmermann, when one of his parishioners, a miller, suspected a woman day-labourer of theft of his property. The miller turned to divination reinforced by punitive magic, taking an axe from the suspect's house and burying it in an anthill, doubtless with appropriate incantations. The suspect immediately became so ill that the pastor was called to give absolution and communion as preparation for death. However, on hearing of the woman's condition the miller repented of his deed, went to her house to beg forgiveness and removed the stolen axe from the anthill, whereupon she recovered, to the bafflement of the pastor. This example shows the classic binary nature of power plays, albeit here someone socially more eminent is using supernatural power against a social inferior in order to protect his property. It also reveals the frequent helplessness experienced by the professional gatekeepers of supernatural power, the clergy.[46]

Power-plays involving supernatural power could be quite varied and complex. They could be inter-personal, inter-communal or involve factional strife within a given community. They could involve contests against a local power hierarchy, squeezing middlemen such as pastors, local officials or judges between the millstones of local opinion and superior authority; they could also involve power struggles within and between elites, often issues of competence or relative status. The complex power struggles that occurred in the Württemberg town of Urach in 1529 exemplify the conflicts with ruling elites aroused by charges of witchcraft, while the long-running conflict that erupted in the north German town of Burg in the years 1617-1621, also around the issues of witchcraft, reveals the way that factional strife could be mobilized by a question of supernatural power. Even secular inter-personal disputes could easily involve the sacred, shown by a further case drawn from Zimmermann's pastoral experience, involving a woman with two lease cows which had ceased giving milk. The woman complained to the (female) owner of the cows, who convinced her that the cows had been bewitched and that she could discover the agent of the bewitchment by means of magical divination. She was to purchase a mirror on a Friday and hang it in her cattle-stall, whereupon she would see revealed in it the face of the culprit. The woman did as she was told and thought she discerned the face of her neighbour. She imparted this to her husband, who then commented upon it to the neighbour's husband. The accused neighbour ran into the woman's house to refute the accusation and the two women came to blows, as did the two husbands who ran to their aid. Here the conflict precipitated by the appropriate of supernatural power was not binary but more like a chain reaction, with an economic grievance being deflected by the owner of the cows via a magical remedy, which then set off a chain of personal ill-will.[47]

One of the most interesting features of the period under discussion is the possibility that the Reformation, by its rejection of a sacramentalised world, set limits to the intrusion of sacred power into the inner-worldly realm. There were certainly many commentators who rejoiced in the repudiation of 'superstition' and believed that the struggle to overcome human misappropriation of supernatural power had been decisively won, although the persistence of witchcraft beliefs and obsession with the power of the devil seem to show that this as too optimistic an assessment. The problem of popular magic and of a weakly, rather than strongly sacramental universe remained to plague the attempts of Protestant reformers to reorientate the beliefs of ordinary people about the importance of supernatural power.[48] This points to our last theme, the question of long-term changes in popular belief.

## 7. PATTERNS OF CHANGE

Throughout the discussion above little has been said about the issue of change over the long-time span covered by this essay, although the theme has been alluded to several times in connection with the Reformation. It was once held that the Reformation produced a radical fracture in the structure of belief systems in early modern Europe, making this age of religious reform an epochal turning point in the history of European belief and culture. Many historians are now less convinced of the accuracy of this traditional picture. Increasingly, radical religious reform is seen to have been confined to literate and urban elites, while the process of reception of the Reformation in the population at large appears as a protracted affair spread over several generations.[49] There is no doubt about the radical impulse of Reformation thought, with its repudiation of purgatory, the cult of the saints, relics, pilgrimages, and numerous other popular practices associated with belief in the salvific value of good works. This entailed a dramatic reorientation in attitudes towards the dead, religious worship and religious knowledge, as well as an attack on the notion of a sacramental world. The last was perhaps the most important mental shift, since it involved denial of the belief that one could come to any knowledge of the supernatural world by the signifying power of the natural. The supernatural could still intervene in the natural world, but the traffic was irredeemably one-way. This left, in its most radical applications, no space for sacred time, persons, places or things, only an inner-worldly realm of purely human action in which acts of piety had no transcendental efficacy.

This is not the place to recount the complex story of the impact of the Reformation in its many manifestations and varieties. However, it seems likely that the picture of the Reformation as a sudden mass conversion to these new ideas is no longer tenable. The majority of the population of Reformation Europe probably received the new ideas as 'involuntary Protestants', for whom such radical changes were brought about by state action. This is not to underestimate the endeavour of those fervent believers in the new ideas who set about propagating them with missionary zeal and dedication, nor to deny the possibility of straightforward conversions to the new beliefs and repudiation of the old.[50] However, reform through state action did lead to a dramatic change in the *availability* of older religious forms and practices. Sacred places and objects were destroyed (the entire Reformation process can be seen as a massive destruction of symbolic capital), sacred persons, especially the saints, denigrated and demythologised, significant religious communities uprooted or dissolved. All of this upheaval presented ordinary people with problems of how to respond, whether with acquiescence, resistance, adaptation or strategies of survival. The issue is largely one of generations and generational change, since any 'reformation from above' had to last long enough for a new generation to grow up with no direct knowledge of the old religion, while those who retained its memory had to die out – a matter perhaps of seventy or eighty years. Thus, questions of the long-term impact of reform have often focussed on education and other forms of state action. This has produced several broad-meshed interpretations around notions such as 'christianisation', 'acculturation', 'social disciplining' and 'confessionalisation', whose central tenets have yet to be rigorously tested at any level other than that of official intention.[51] Popular belief has yet to be explored, either to demonstrate how far the old was effectively uprooted rather than merely suppressed, or how far new forms of 'reformed' popular belief replaced them. Preliminary studies have shown that the changes made at the level of availability may not have penetrated as far or as fast into the popular religious mentality as was once assumed. The sacramental world was not abolished but replaced by a weakly sacramentalised one, and as an important indicator of this fact, magic remained an ineradicable problem. The importance of ritual action in religious practice was diminished or redirected rather than eradicated. The dead continued to play a part in the world of the living, especially where rites of separation were inadequate or incomplete, and the liminal boundaries between the natural and the supernatural played a potent part in popular belief. All this suggests that there was a good deal of syncretism between old forms of popular religion and the new.[52] It is for this reason that this essay has concentrated on continuity rather than rupture in the elements of popular belief, while many of the problems it has sought to raise, for example, those of gender and power, cross the confessional boundaries established by Reformation and Counter-Reformation. We might usefully linger for a moment on the issue of gender to show how complex are the questions to be asked.

If we ask whether the reformations of the sixteenth century radically changed the religious situation of women, it is difficult to give a direct answer. Women's religious opportunities were undoubtedly narrowed by the Protestant Reformation, especially the religious space allowed to single women. The abolition of female religious institutions such as convents, which offered the possibility of living an independent celibate life devoted to prayer and charitable works, disappeared along with all those religious role models embodied in the female saints, who were no longer available as powerful intercessors for the alleviation of female ailments and the difficulties of childbirth. The only religious status available to women was that of the dutiful wife or daughter in the patriarchal household, the only role model that of the pastor's wife. Women were subjected to a new moralism which emphasized the need to discipline all disorderly elements. Whether the Protestant focus on Christ as sole saviour was capable of producing a female-oriented piety comparable to that mapped for the later middle ages by Caroline Walker Bynum remains an open question. The resurgence of, or reemphasis on, misogyny which saw a stigmatization of the female role in popular magical practice meant that the major way in which women were held to have contact with the supernatural world was as witches. Women were certainly not entirely relegated to purely passive domestic roles, and both Catholic and Protestant Reformations saw the emergence of new forms of female activity in new Catholic religious orders and in Protestant female prophets and visionaries. Both of these manifestations of female religious activity entailed appropriation of male teaching and preaching functions, although both were effectively marginalized by those wielding power in church and state, who regarded them as 'dangerous beliefs'. On the other hand, as Sherrin Marshall has pointed out, the enhanced role of charitable institutions may have helped legitimize activist roles for women; although modelled on familial patterns, at least they brought women into the public arena, and so to the attention of the historian. However, female piety and the devotional lives of women remain little understood, so that it is impossible to discern their role in post-Reformation popular belief in any detail comparable to our knowledge about medieval women.[53] It is an important agenda for future research.

# NOTES

\*   Research for this article was undertaken while the author was British Academy Marc Fitch Research Reader at Cambridge University. He expresses his gratitude for the time free from teaching and administrative duties.

1. Underdown (1985), esp. ch. 4: 'Regional Cultures', here at 75.
2. Beitl (1974), 372-73.
3. Scribner (1987), 4-5.
4. Most extensively stated by Muchembled (1985), 14-42; and in wider context by Delumeau (1990), 9-185.
5. For a comprehensive overview of such rituals see Muir (1995). See also Vigarello (1988), 7-8 on disease, plague and hygiene; Corbin (1986), 1-21 on the scientific basis of these views into the eighteenth century.
6. Imhof (1984), esp. 27-90.
7. Cited in Wiesner (1993), Preface; a challenge to the common assumption of a body-soul dualism in Bynum (1991), 222-35. See also Gurevich (1985), esp. 295-311 on 'human personality'.
8. Gurevich (1988), 42-91 on macrocosm and microcosm. On omens, signs, portents most recently Niccoli (1990), 33-35.
9. On the sacramental and magic, Gurevich (1988), 81-91, although he does not use the former term.
10. Gurevich (1988), 146; on medieval notions of time, Gurevich (1985), 93-151; and in more detail Borst (1994).
11. Ginzburg (1980). Gurevich (1988), who speaks of a 'materialization of the pretersensual', sees as a distinctive aspect of medieval popular belief 'a general orientation towards the close, concrete and visually perceptible', 140.
12. Camporesi (1990), 18-19.
13. Enoch Widmann, 'Chronk der Stadt Hof', *Hohenzollerische Forschungen* 2 (1893): 113-14. On the fragility and permeability of the body, see Vigarello (1988), 14.
14. Dinzelbacher (1981); Bächthold-Stäubli (1987), vol. 3, 473-87; Camporesi (1990), 24-89; Gurevich (1988), 176-210. Many of these themes also touched upon in Gurevich (1992), esp. 50-89.
15. The most recent survey on the Devil in the Middle Ages is Link (1995); see also Russell (1984); Gurevich (1992), 116-20; Walker (1981).
16. Now classic surveys on death and purgatory are Aries (1981) and Le Goff (1984). Gurevich (1992), 65-89 makes important corrections to Aries' picture. On the 'revenant dead', the pioneering work by Barber (1988); on Catholic and Protestant continuity, Scribner (1990a), 334-40.
17. Scribner (1992b), 821-41.
18. Ginzburg (1983) and (1990); Klaniczay (1990), 129-50.
19. On Hans Boheim most recently, Wunderli (1992); on apparitions and pil-

grimages, Christian (1981). See also Zika (1988); Hsia (1988); and Stahl (1968), 1-281.

20. On these categories Vrijhof and Waardenburg (1979).

21. On the Mass, see Bossy (1985), 64-72; on liturgy and popular drama, Simon (1991); Gibson (1989).

22. Schmitt (1983); Beitl (1974), 507-8, 960, 983.

23. Röckelein, Opitz and Bauer (1990); Ashley and Scheingorn (1990).

24. For indecorous depictions of the 'lactating Virgin', see Freedberg (1989), 290, 324; Schuster (1983), 254; Bynum (1991), 217 for the *Vierge ouvrante*. See also Miles (1986), 193-208.

25. The most recent overview of Carnival which discusses these themes is Schindler (1992), 121-74.

26. On confraternities, see Black (1989); Flynn (1989); Verdon and Henderson (1990).

27. Scribner (1990a).

28. These *exempla* are found in Johannes Herolt's *Promptuarium Discipuli de Miraculis Beatae Mariae Virginis* (1435-40), which was frequently republished throughout the fifteenth and sixteenth centuries; see Herolt (1928), 18, 71, 75-76, 78, 98-99.

29. Rothkrug (1980), 15-36. On the *Bauerngott*, Scribner, (1987), 13; on concordance of heavenly and earthly hierarchies, Gurevich (1985), 70-71.

30. On Weber's notion of 'elective affinity' (*Wahlverwandschaft*), see the succinct discussion in Hill (1973), 104-9, 131-32. The concept is too frequently overlooked in discussion of the Reformation or else garbled into the notion that religious ideas shaped forms of economic development, as in Cameron (1991), 302.

31. Lanternari (1963); see also the extensive discussion in Bak and Benecke (1984). On communalism, see Blickle (1992).

32. Klaniczay (1990), 111-28; Weinstein and Bell (1982), 194-238; Delooz (1983), 189-216, here at 194.

33. Ullmann (1985), Figures 72 (Dürer's Paumgärtner altarpiece), 155 (Bernhard Striegel's depiction of Maximilian I's family). For the aristocratic pretensions of Nuremberg patricians, see Strauss (1966), 82.

34. On St Zita, see Shahar (1983), 203; on 'bourgeoisification of the Holy Family', Scheingorn, (1990), 193; Brandenberg (1987), 120. See also the discussion in Weinstein and Bell (1982), 206-13.

35. On Margarethe Ebner, see Rublack, (1995); on St Bernadino, Kieckhefer (1991), 300.

36. On female witnesses and female canonizations, see Bynum (1991), 60; on hagiographies, Kieckhefer (1991), 302.

37. Bynum (1991), 60; Kieckhefer (1991), 302.

38. Kieckhefer (1991), 295, 298. See also Bell (1985); Bynum (1987).

39. Kieckhefer (1991), 299-300.

40. On reading and piety, see Kieckhefer (1991), 302-3; see also Bell (1988), 149-87; on 'feminization of religious language', Bynum (1982), 2, 135-46.

41. See Steinberg (1983), and the critique by Bynum (1991), 79-117; on the sexualization of the 'devout gaze', Scribner (1992a), 309-36.

42. Scribner (1992a), 316; for the images mentioned, Ullmann (1985), figures 71, 121, 196, 216. For the Fouquet painting, allegedly bearing the features of a royal mistress, Agnes Sorel, see Huizinga (1955), 160, who spoke of its 'air of decadent impiety'; for the debate on the picture, Lombardi (1983), 125-35.

43. On St Anne, see Scheingorn (1990), 193; Brandenberg (1987), 120. On St Anne and republicanism, see Crum and Wilkens (1990).
44. Georg Christoph Zimmermann, *Den in vielen Stücken allzuabergläubigen Christen hat ein viel Jahre lang unter denselbigen vor dem Herrn lehrender Diener gottes bey genauer Observation sehen und kennen lernen* (Frankfurt and Leipzig, 1721), 155-57.
45. See the newssheet published in Nuremberg in 1580, *Warhafftige und erschockliche Geschichte dreyer Maineidiger Personen*, reproduced in Strauss (1975), 425.
46. Zimmermann, *Den in vielen Stücken allzuabergläubigen Christen* (1721), 26-28.
47. Ibid., 191-93. On Urach, see Scribner (1987) 257-76; on Burg, Scribner (1990b); Sabean (1984) for the notion of 'power plays', as well as for the importance of enmity; see also Briggs (1989), 83-105.
48. See Scribner (1993).
49. The studies on England by Collinson (1988) and Duffy (1992) attesting the slow progress of religious reformation can be matched by findings for Germany, see Scribner (1990a and 1990b).
50. For the most recent surveys, see Cameron (1991); Pettegree, (1992); Scribner, Porter and Teich (1994).
51. For these processes, see Hsia (1989); Schilling (1992), 205-45. The best recent case studies have dealt with the Counter-Reformation: Gentilcore (1991); Forster (1992). But see Dixon (1993) for an excellent Reformation study.
52. See Scribner (1990a, 1992b and 1993) for preliminary thoughts on these themes.
53. On these themes, see Marshall (1989), the comment at 5; Rapley (1990); Roper (1989); Crawford (1993), esp. 98-115 on 'dangerous beliefs'; an effective summary in Wiesner (1993), ch. 6.

# BIBLIOGRAPHY

Ariès, Philippe. *The Hour of Our Death.* Trans. Helen Weaver. London, 1981.

Ashley, Kathleen, and Pamela Sheingorn, eds. *Interpreting Cultural Symbols: St Anne in Late Medieval Society.* Athens, Ga., and London, 1990.

Bächthold-Stäubli, Hans, ed. *Handwörterbuch des deutschen Aberglaubens.* Vol. 3. Berlin, 1987.

Bak, Janos M., and Gerhard Benecke, eds. *Religion and Rural Revolt.* Manchester, 1984.

Barber, Paul. *Vampires, Burial and Death: Folklore and Reality.* New Haven, 1988.

Beitl, Richard, ed. *Wörterbuch der deutschen Volkskunde.* Stuttgart, 1974.

Bell, Rudolph M. *Holy Anorexia.* Chicago and London, 1985.

Bell, Susan Groag. "Medieval Women Book Owners: Arbiters of Lay Piety and Ambassadors of Culture." In *Women and Power in the Middle Ages,* ed. Mary Erler and Maryanne Kowaleski. Athens, Ga., 1988.

Black, Christopher R. *Italian Confraternities in the Sixteenth Century.* Cambridge, 1989.

Blickle, Peter *Communal Reformation: the Quest for Salvation in Sixteenth-Century Germany.* Trans. Thomas Dunlap. Atlantic Highlands, N.J., 1992.

Borst, Arno. *The Ordering of Time: From Ancient Computus to the Modern Computer.* Oxford, 1994 (forthcoming).

Bossy, John. *Christianity in the West 1400-1700.* Oxford, 1985.

Brandenberg, Tom. "St Anne and her Family. The Veneration of St. Anne in Connection with Concepts of Marriage and the Family in the Early Modern Period," In *Saints and She-devils: Images of Women in the Fifteenth and Sixteenth Centuries,* ed. Lene Dresen-Coenders. London, 1987.

Briggs, Robin. "Ill-will and magical power in Lorraine Witchcraft." In *Communities of Belief: Cultural and Social Tensions in Early Modern France.* Oxford, 1989.

Bynum, Caroline Walker. *Fragmentation and Redemption: Essays on Gender and the Human Body in Medieval Religion.* New York, 1991.

Bynum, Caroline Walker. *Holy Feast and Holy Fast: the Religious Significance of Food to Medieval Women.* Berkeley and Los Angeles, 1987.

Bynum, Caroline Walker. *Jesus as Mother: Studies in the Spirituality of the High Middle Ages.* Berkeley and Los Angeles, 1982.

Cameron, Euan. *The European Reformation.* Oxford, 1991.

Camporesi, Piero. *The Fear of Hell: Images of Damnation and Salvation in Early Modern Europe.* Trans. Lucinda Byatt. Oxford, 1990.

Christian, William A. *Apparitions in Late Medieval and Renaissance Spain.* Princeton, 1981.

Collinson, Patrick. *The Birthpangs of Protestant England.* New York, 1988.

Corbin, Alain. *The Foul and Fragrant: Odor and the French Social Imagination.* Leamington Spa, Hamburg, and New York, 1986.

Crawford, Patricia. *Women and Religion in England 1500-1720.* London, 1993.

Crum, Roger J., and David G. Wilkens. "In the Defence of Florentine Republicanism: St Anne and Florentine Art 1343-1575." In Ashley and Scheingorn (1990), 131-68.

Delooz, Pierre. "Towards a Sociological Study of Canonized Sainthood in the Catholic Church." In *Saints and their Cults: Studies in Religious Sociology, Folklore and History,* ed. Stephen Wilson. Cambridge, 1983.

Delumeau, Jean. *Sin and Fear: the Emergence of a Western Guilt Culture 13th-18th Centuries.* Trans. Eric Nicholson. New York, 1990.

Dinzelbacher, Peter. *Vision und Visionsliteratur im Mitterlalter.* Stuttgart, 1981.

Dixon, C. Scott. The Reformation in the Parishes: Attempts to Implement Religious Change in Brandenburg Ansbach-Kulmbach 1528-1603. Ph.D. Dissertation, University of Cambridge, 1993.

Duffy, Eamon. *The Stripping of the Altars: Traditional Religion in England 1400-1580.* New Haven and London, 1992.

Flynn, Maureen. *Sacred Charity: Confraternities and Social Welfare in Spain 1400-1700.* Ithaca, 1989.

Forster, Marc. *The Counter-Reformation in the Villages: Religion and Reform in the Bishopric of Speyer 1560-1720.* Ithaca, 1992.

Freedberg, David. *The Power of Images: Studies in the History and Theory of Response.* Chicago and London, 1989.

Gentilcore, David. *From Bishop to Witch: the System of the Sacred in Early Modern Terra d'Otranto.* Manchester, 1991.

Gibson, Gail McMurray. *The Theatre of Devotion. East Anglian Drama and Society in the Late Middle Ages.* Chicago and London, 1989.

Ginzburg, Carlo. *The Cheese and the Worms: the Cosmos of a Sixteenth Century Miller.* Trans. John Tedeschi and Anne Tedeschi. London, 1980.

Ginzburg, Carlo. *Ecstasies: Deciphering the Witches' Sabbath.* Trans. Raymond Rosenthal. London, 1990.

Ginzburg, Carlo. *The Night Battles: Witchcraft and Agrarian Cults in the Sixteenth and Seventeenth Centuries.* Trans. John Tedeschi and Anne Tedeschi. London, 1983.

Gurevich, Aron. *Categories of Medieval Culture.* Trans. G. L. Campbell. London, 1985.

Gurevich, Aron. *Historical Anthropology of the Middle Ages.* Oxford, 1992.

Gurevich, Aron. *Medieval Popular Culture. Problems of Belief and Perception.* Trans. J. M. Bak and P. A. Hollingworth. Cambridge, 1988.

Herolt, Johannes. *Miracles of the Blessed Virgin Mary.* Trans. C. C. Swinton Bland. London, 1928.

Hill, Michael. *A Sociology of Religion.* London, 1973.

Hsia, R. Po-chia. *The Myth of Ritual Murder: Jews and Magic in Reformation Germany.* New Haven, 1988.

Hsia, R. Po-chia. *Social Discipline in the Reformation: Central Europe 1550-1750.* London, 1989.

Huizinga, Johann. *The Waning of the Middle Ages.* Harmondsworth, 1955.

Imhof, Arthur E. *Die verlorenen Welten: Alltagsbewältigung durch unsere Vorfahren.* Munich, 1984.

Kieckhefer, Richard. "Holiness and the Culture of Devotion: Remarks on Some Late Medieval Male Saints." In *Images of Sainthood in Medieval Europe,* ed. Renate Blumenfeld-Kosinksi and Timea Szell. Ithaca, 1991.

Klaniczay, Gabor. *The Uses of Supernatural Power: the Transformation of Popular Religion in Medieval and Early-Modern Europe.* Oxford, 1990.

Lanternari, Vittorio. *Religions of the Oppressed.* New York, 1963.

Le Goff, Jacques. *The Birth of Purgatory.* Chicago, 1984.

Link, Luther. *The Devil: a Name without a Face.* London, 1995 (forthcoming).

Lombardi, Sandro. *Jean Fouqet.* Florence, 1983.

Marshall, Sherrin, ed. *Women in Reformation and Counter-Reformation Europe: Private and Public Worlds.* Bloomington, 1989.

Miles, Margaret R. "The Virgin's One Bare Breast: Female Nudity and Religious Meaning in Tuscan and Early Renaissance Culture." In *The Female Body in Western Culture,* ed. Susan Rubin Suleiman. Cambridge, Mass., 1986.

Muchembled, Robert. *Popular Culture and Elite Culture in France 1400-1700.* Trans. Lydia Cochrane. Baton Rouge and London, 1985.

Muir, Edward. *Ritual in Early Modern Europe.* Cambridge, 1995 (forthcoming).

Niccoli, Ottavia. *Prophecy and People in Renaissance Italy.* Trans. Lydia G. Cochrane. Princeton, 1990.

Pettegree, Andrew, ed. *The Early Reformation in Europe.* Cambridge, 1992.

Rapley, Elizabeth. *The Dévote: Women and Church in Seventeenth-Century France.* Montreal and Toronto, 1990.

Röckelein, Hedwig, Claudia Opitz, and Dieter R. Bauer, eds. *Maria—Abbild oder Vorbild? Zur Sozialgeschichte mittelalterlicher Marienverehrung.* Tübingen, 1990.

Roper, Lyndal. *The Holy Household: Women and Morals in Reformation Augsburg.* Oxford, 1989.

Rothkrug, Lionel. "Religious Practices and Collective Perspectives: Hidden Homologies in the Renaissance and Reformation." *Historical Reflections* 7 (1980).

Rubin, Miri. *Corpus Christi: the Eucharist in Late Medieval Culture.* Cambridge, 1991.

Rublack, Ulinka. "Female Spirituality and the Infant Jesus in Late-Medieval German Convents." In *Popular Religion in Germany and Central Europe 1300-1800*, ed. Bob Scribner and Trevor R. Johnson. London, 1995 (forthcoming).

Russell, Jeffrey Burton. *Lucifer: the Devil in the Middle Ages.* Ithaca and London, 1984.

Sabean, David. *Power in the Blood. Village Discourse in Early Modern Germany.* Cambridge, 1984.

Schilling, Heinz. *Religion, Political Culture and the Emergence of Early Modern Society.* Leiden, 1992.

Schindler, Norbert. "Karneval, Kirche und verkehrte Welt. Zur Funktion der Lachkultur im 16. Jahrhundert." In *Widerspenstige Leute. Studien zur Volkskultur in der frühen Neuzeit*, 121-74. Frankfurt, 1992.

Schmitt, Jean-Claude. *The Holy Greyhound: Guinefort, Healer of Children since the Thirteenth Century*, trans. Martin Thom. Cambridge, 1983.

Schuster, Peter-Klaus. "Verbotene Bilder." In *Luther und die Folgen für die Kunst*, ed. Werner Hofmann. Munich, 1983.

Scribner, Robert W. "The Impact of the Reformation on Daily Life." In *Mensch und Objekt im Mitterlalter und der frühen Neuzeit. Leben—Alltag—Kultur*, Sitzungsberichte der Österreichischen Akademie der Wissenschaften, Phil.-hist. Klasse, no. 568:315-43. Vienna, 1990a.

Scribner, Robert W. *Popular Culture and Popular Movements in Reformation Germany.* London and Ronceverte, 1987.

Scribner, Robert W. "The Reformation, Popular Magic and the 'Disenchantment of the World.'" *Journal of Interdisciplinary History* 23 (1993): 475-94.

Scribner, Robert W. "Symbolising boundaries: defining social space in early modern Germany." In *Symbole des Alltags—Alltag der Symbole. Festschrift für Harry Kühnel zum 65. Geburtstag*, ed. Gertrud Blaschitz, 821-41. Graz, 1992b.

Scribner, Robert W. "Vom Sakralbild zur sinnlichen Schau. Sinnliche Wahrnehmung und das Visuelle bei der Objektivierung des Frauenkörpers in Deutschland im 16. Jahrhundert." In *Gepeinigt, begehrt, vergessen. Symbolik und Sozialbezug des Körpers im Späten Mittelalter und in der frühen Neuzeit*, ed. Klaus Schreiner and Norbert Schnitzler, 309-36. Munich, 1992a.

Scribner, Robert W. "Witchcraft and Judgement in Reformation Germany." *History Today*, April, 12-19, 1990b.

Scribner, Robert, Roy Porter, and Mikulas Teich, eds. *The Reformation in National Context.* Cambridge, 1994 (forthcoming).

Shahar, Shulamith. *The Fourth Estate: a History of Women in the Middle Ages.* London, 1983.

Sheingorn, Pamela. "Appropriating the Holy Kinship: Gender and Family History." In Ashley and Scheingorn (1990), 169-98.

Simon, Eckehard, ed. *The Theatre of Medieval Europe.* Cambridge, 1991.

Stahl, Gerlind. "Die Walfahrt zur Schönen Maria in Regensburg." In *Beiträge zur Geschichte des Bistums Regensburg*, ed. Georg Schwaiger, vol. 2:1-281. Regensburg, 1968.

Steinberg, Leo. *The Sexuality of Christ in Renaissance Art and Modern Oblivion.* London, 1983.

Strauss, Gerald. *Nuremberg in the Sixteenth Century.* New York, 1966.

Strauss, Walter L., ed. *The German Single-leaf Woodcut 1550-1600.* Vol. 1. New York, 1975.

Ullmann, Ernst, ed. *Geschichte der deutschen Kunst 1470-1559.* Vol. 1. Leipzig, 1985.

Underdown, David. *Revel, Riot and Rebellion. Popular Politics and Culture in England 1603-1660.* Oxford, 1985.

Verdon, Timothy, and John Henderson, eds. *Christianity and the Renaissance. Image and Religious Imagination in the Quattrocento.* Syracuse, 1990.

Vigarello, Georges. *Concepts of Cleanliness: Changing Attitudes in France since the Middle Ages.* Trans. Jean Birrell. Cambridge, 1988.

Vrijhof, Pieter H., and Jacques Waardenburg, eds. *Official and Popular Religion: Analysis of a Theme for Religious Studies.* The Hague, 1979.

Walker, D. P. *Unclean Spirits. Possession and Exorcism in France and England in the late Sixteenth and Early Seventeenth Centuries.* London, 1981.

Weinstein, Donald, and Rudolph M. Bell. *Saints and Society. The Two Worlds of Western Christendom, 1000-1700.* Chicago, 1982.

Wiesner, Merry E. *Women and Gender in Early Modern Europe.* Cambridge, 1993.

Wunderli, Richard. *Peasant Fires. The Drummer of Niklashausen.* Bloomington, 1992.

Zika, Charles. "Hosts, Processions and Miracles: Controlling the Sacred in Fifteenth-century Germany." *PaP* 118 (1988): 25-64.

# ALIENS WITHIN: THE JEWS AND ANTIJUDAISM[1]

Robert Bonfil
(Hebrew University, Jerusalem)

## 1. Jews in Christian Society

During the Middle Ages, the Jews were the only group with absolutely no political power to whom Christians accorded the right of theoretical and practical dissent. In this sense, they were not considered in the same light as Muslims, who were also tolerated on Christian soil, but who, unlike the Jews, could count on the effective protection of strong Muslim states which contained large Christian minorities. Nor were Jews considered on the same terms as heretical Christians, tolerance of whom was considered unthinkable. This coexistence of Jews and Christians in Europe was the result of a complex process of continuous adaptation that is difficult to interpret. In a world which saw in corporal punishment a legitimate means of education, and which had the diffusion of Christianity as one of its ideals, it was only natural that coercive persuasion of dissenters would constitute the norm. So far as the Jews were concerned, it was understood that such persuasion could—or rather should—make use of all available means to achieve its goal, including seduction, discussion, or even violent pressure. As a rule, however, such efforts were supposed to stop at the threshold of coercion, and exceptions to this rule were very rare. Enough such extraordinary cases existed, however, to reveal the contradictory nature of Christian attitudes toward the Jews, the logic of which is not easy to grasp.

## 2. Jews in Christian Europe: Expulsion and Re-admission

The fact that Jews were tolerated in Christendom cannot be adequately explained by looking at theoretical formulations, such as the Augustinian justification of tolerance of the Jews as witnesses to Christian truth. Nor was it merely an inertial persistence of Roman legal traditions, for which the pragmatic policies of Pope Gregory I "the Great" might provide the classic paradigm. Recently, careful quantitative researches make less plausible than before the idea that toleration can be traced to the fiscal oppor-

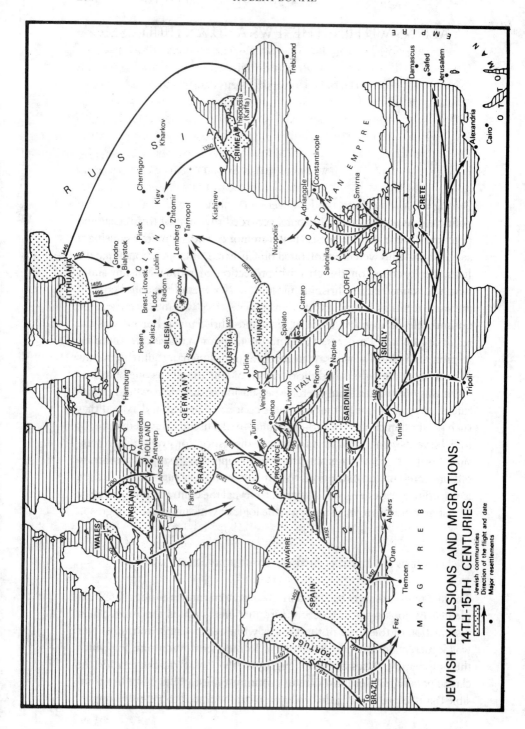

JEWISH EXPULSIONS AND MIGRATIONS,
14TH-15TH CENTURIES

▦ Jewish communities
→ Direction of the flight and date
• Major resettlements

tunism of Christian rulers, who supposedly tolerated Jews out of plain greediness, only to be rid of them the moment they could afford to do so. However unattractive it may be to historians seeking empirically verifiable explanations, in this case it is hard not to formulate an explanation which assumes the existence of some hidden mechanism inherent in the psychology of Christian religiosity as a determining factor in shaping the destiny of the Jews. The fact that antisemitism did not disappear in countries where there were no Jews at all, may indicate that Christians, more than reacting to the presence of real Jews, considered Jews and Judaism as a necessary part of their Christian endeavor to define their own cultural and religious identity.

For the Jews, who lacked political power, the terms of the problem were reversed. For them, the fundamental question was: why tenaciously (or obstinately, as the Christians put it) persist in refusing to be baptized and integrated into Christian society which, at least until the beginning of our period, declared its unreserved readiness to accept them? Yet, so far as the Jews are concerned, it may be easier to understand the religious psychology responsible for their choice. Educated to believe he possessed the truth, a Jew's passage into the camp of "the Other" amounted to abandoning Truth for Falsehood—unless, of course, the truth of "the Other" had somehow made inroads into his heart and mind. In such cases, however, it was persistence in Judaism that amounted to abandoning Truth for Falsehood, and conversion prevailed. Although it is reasonable to assume that socio-economic pressures constituted an important incentive to being baptized, the history of the Jews includes many cases of conversions that took place in the wake of religious illumination, whose sincerity the historian has no a priori right to doubt. There are several famous examples. Among those that come to mind for our period are Pablo de Santa Maria, Hieronymus de Sancta Fide, and Profiat Duran the Ephodi in Spain; Flavius Mithridates, Alessandro Franceschini and Domenico Gerosolimitano in Italy; and in the German-speaking area, Anthonius Margaritha and Johannes Pfefferkorn, Reuchlin's antagonist in the controversy over whether the Talmud ought to be destroyed.

The psychological dynamic that led to religious conversion, of course, was certainly not an exclusive characteristic of the Jews. True, during the Middle Ages, cases of conversion to Christianity far outnumbered the number of Christians who converted to Judaism. However, this was probably due to the total disparity in the amount of self-abnegation needed to cross the Rubicon in one direction rather than another, for a Jew's conversion to Christianity meant embarking on a road that, while paved with the

travails of separation from one's biological and cultural roots, did not involve risking one's fate. On the contrary, this road promised a radical improvement in social status, to the point where it became formulaic to accuse neophytes of opportunism. Converting to Judaism was, by contrast,
a very different matter. In addition to the anguish of being separated from
one's roots and accepting the lot of the disinherited, a convert to Judaism
ran the danger of being condemned to death as a heretic. And still, there
was no shortage of Christians who converted to Judaism.

The phenomenon of conversion thus seems mutatis mutandis to exhibit
a kind of perfect symmetry. From our perspective, it represents the most
convincing proof that, in defining their respective identities, Jews and
Christians saw themselves mirrored in one another. Sometimes (more often among Jews, and more rarely among Christians), "the Other's" reflection in the mirror proved so irresistibly attractive that one was persuaded
to renounce one's difference in order to be united once and for all with the
object of that reflection. In general, however, such reflections tended to
heighten people's perceptions of their own distinction, both in terms of difference and in terms of superiority. For Christians, this perception could
occasionally turn into a feeling of triumphant exclusivity, which by definition tended to exclude "the Other" from Christendom. Such was the tendency that prevailed in western Europe during the first half of the period
under review. For the Jews, political and military powerlessness constituted an advantage in these terms: they never had the means to translate
their own feelings of superiority into persecution of "the Other." Their incapacity in this respect had technological, not ideological, grounds. This
much was admitted, albeit unhappily, by the *Kuzari* of Judah Ha-Levi
(twelfth century), the Jewish sage to whom the king of the Kazars had objected that "given the chance, you, too, would massacre your enemies"
(*Kuzari*, I, 114).[2]

Seen in this perspective, both the history of the Jews' exclusion from
Christendom and the various patterns of their settlement within its bounds
should be interpreted as reflecting both the changes in the cultural and religious identities of Christian and Jewish communities and their translations
of these identities into practices of everyday life. From this point of view,
the time frame adopted by this volume seems particularly well-suited to
helping us reflect on the problem. Symmetrically divided in two by the
fateful year of 1492, the period consists of two phases, which stand in an
inverted relationship to one another. The first, which is presaged by the
Jews' expulsion from England in 1290, signals the conclusion of a gradual
process of exclusion of the Jews in western Europe. The new phase, ush-

ered in by the virulent anti-Jewish revolts of 1391 in Spain, and by the
Jews' definitive expulsion from the domains subject to French rule (1394),
ended with their expulsion from the Castile in 1492, and with the forced
conversions they endured in Portugal in 1497—in short, with the definitive
end of the Jewish presence in Europe's western tier. The second phase, after 1492, signals the start of a reversal in the process of exclusion, as Jews
were gradually reintroduced into the West, hastening the path to regenera-
tion from the painful experience of the wars of religion.

The most important problem for the scholar of this period is thus to locate the causes of this reversal of treatment and fortunes and to identify the
forces that triggered it precisely around 1500. Since we are dealing here
with a radical change, it seems logical to include the phenomenon that
seems prima facie to have been the absolute novelty of the age: the "New
Christians" and their impact on both Jews' and Christians' perceptions of
their own religious and socio-cultural identities. This approach requires
that we begin with a concise review of the demography and geography of
Jewish settlement during this era.

### 3. THE DIASPORA IN CHRISTENDOM: PATTERNS OF
### JEWISH POPULATION AND SETTLEMENT

The levels of Jewish populations in fifteenth-century Christendom is very
much an open question, and an emotionally charged one as well. High
population estimates may in fact stem from more or less conscious apologetic tendencies among Jewish historians, who are bent on maximizing the
tragic dimension of the expulsions. Low estimates may instead be the result of the opposite tendencies among non-Jewish historians, bent on minimizing this dimension. The documentation for European demography in
this era is not particularly generous, and it is even poorer for Jewish demography, for which the sources normally used by historical demographers are either useless or nonexistent.

At the beginning of the fifteenth century, the majority of European Jews
lived in the Iberian peninsula and the islands ruled by the crown of
Aragon, especially Sicily and Sardinia; in the southern regions of France
not subject to the king's rule, especially those belonging to the pope; in the
German-speaking regions of the Holy Roman Empire; and in Italy. A
lesser number lived in the countries of eastern Europe. The Jewish population of the entire Iberian peninsula on the eve of the 1492 expulsion can be
reasonably estimated at around 80,000 persons. It is impossible to calcu-

late precisely, however, how many Jews lived in Iberia on the eve of the anti-Jewish riots of 1391, which led to the wave of conversions that gave rise to the phenomenon of the *conversos* or "New Christians." In this case, however, the lack of quantitative data is partly made good by the agreement of Jewish and Christian sources that the scale of this phenomenon was indeed considerable. In Sicily during this same period, there were approximately 35,000 Jews; in Sardinia there were many fewer Jews, or in any case not more than a few thousand. Italy accounted for another approximately 35,000 people, who were scattered among the various states of the peninsula. In numbers, therefore, Italy was second to Spain and its annexed regions. In the German-speaking regions, the anti-Jewish revolts that followed the spread of the Black Death pushed down the Jewish population to a few thousand souls, while the Jews of Poland barely reached 10-11,000 people. Compared to the overall population of these places, the Jews were thus decidedly negligible in number. Everywhere, the Jews were but a miniscule minority.

The forced removal of most Jews from western Europe toward the end of the fifteenth century began the eastward movement of the geographical center of Jewish settlement. While a very considerable number of Jews left Christendom once and for all to settle in Muslim states, especially in the Ottoman Empire, Jewish settlements in eastern Europe registered an extraordinarily rapid and persistent increase. It was so great that toward the end of the sixteenth century, the number of Polish Jews had already reached approximately 100,000, rising to 170,000 toward the middle of the seventeenth century, and 500,000 toward the middle of the eighteenth. Eastern Europe in these generations experienced the spread of Jewish settlement similar to what had happened in western Europe between the eleventh century and the Spanish Reconquest, reaching its peak in the twelfth and thirteenth centuries. Thus, while eastern Europe was witnessing rapid demographic expansion, the regions of the Christian west where Jews were still tolerated were condemned to what appeared to be a near stagnation.

This change led to Italy's loss of its central importance for the greater Jewish world. The series of expulsions from Italian states in the sixteenth century prove that the tendency to exclude Jews from Christendom did not end with the exodus from the Iberian peninsula. Jews were first expelled from the Spanish kingdom of Naples in 1541. Then came the Papal States, except for the cities of Rome and Ancona: first expelled in 1569, Jews were only gradually allowed to return to the lands under papal rule at the end of the century. Finally, the Jews of the duchy of Milan, which also lay under Spanish rule, were also forced to leave in 1597. Gradually, however, the tendency to expel Jews waned during the second half of the six-teenth century, by which time Jewish settlement was reduced to parts of central and northern Italy: the Veneto, the area around Mantua, which in those days included the Monferrat; the dominions of the House of Este (Modena, Parma, and Ferrara); and some parts of Piedmont and Tuscany. Despite Italy's demotion to a country of secondary importance in the world map of Judaism, the Jewish population nevertheless assumed an im-portance decidedly out of proportion with its numerical size, which re-mained steady at about 35-40,000 people. Indeed, during the sixteenth century Italy became a real frontier region between the places in Europe where Jews were allowed and those that condemned them to the difficult paths of illegality and dissimulation. Italy was thus to play a mediating role in the process of readmission of the Jews to the west, a subject to which we will return below.

## 4. THE DEVIL'S MONEYLENDERS: CHRISTIAN VIEWS OF THE JEWS

The ambivalent Christian attitude toward the "Jewish Question" was re-flected in all aspects of Christian images of Jewry, as well as in Jews' per-ceptions of their own condition. This in turn affected all concrete expres-sions of daily life. The ambivalence was most visible in the distortion and lack of proportion underlying the very perception of the Jewish physical presence in Christendom, for, very often, the reality of the Jewish condi-tion appeared incompatible with the conditions that Christians considered appropriate for the Jews. In fact, the concrete presence of the Jew often challenged this fundamental axiom of the Christian mentality.

By this time, Jews almost everywhere were concentrated exclusively in urban areas. Various factors were responsible for the process that led to this state of affairs. Partly it resulted from Christian hostility, which mani-fested itself in an accumulation of restrictions on Jews which made it ex-tremely difficult for the Jews to remain in agriculture. Partly, too, it re-sulted from the natural preference of minorities for urban environments, where a group life is more easily led. To these reasons we can add the con-vergence of two more factors: on the one hand, the tendency on the part of minorities to specialize in exploiting the weak points of the socio-economic fabric of the majority; and, on the other, the gradual stiffening of Catholic doctrine with regard to what was defined as "usury."

Despite the fact that they were continuously employed in a great variety of occupations, by now Jews almost everywhere were associated with the practice of money-lending.  Although not confined to moneylending as pawnbrokers to the poor, for a number of reasons, money-lending was one of the activities most widely practiced by the Jews.  It was extremely lucrative and easily undertaken with little capital.  It could be practiced without having to forgo other activities, and did not require an excessive show of scruples toward people with whom one quite often was not particularly sympathetic.  It was looked upon with favor by Christian rulers who, by assigning the Jews the hated function of exploiting the poverty of their Christian subjects, made them the focus of the discontent that would otherwise be aimed at the Christian ruling classes.  Moreover, moneylending was an activity easy to tax.  The inevitable consequence of this convergence of factors was that the Jews naturally inclined to deal in money, particularly as lenders, so much so that these occupations shaped the stereotypical image of the Jew living in Christendom.  "Usurer" and "Jew" ultimately became synonymous terms in current usage, to the point that it is sometimes hard to decide whether Christian sources used the term to indicate a real Jew or as a pejorative adjective for a Christian.

The fact that Jews were concentrated in urban environments, which in medieval times were generally very small, and were engaged in an activity that rendered them particularly odious, meant that their presence was far more keenly felt than might be expected judging from their actual numbers.  The sense of otherness that Christians felt toward Jews thus included a considerable component of a sense of "absurdity."  The medieval mentality associated wealth with power and domination and poverty with weakness and subordination, so that it became customary to contrast the wealth of Jews to the poverty of the Christians who did business with them.  Thus, the physical presence of the Jew among Christians came quite often to be felt as an absurd inversion of the natural order of things.

Jews were generally characterized as being extraordinarily at variance with the general socio-cultural consensus.  Among other things, this attribution was accentuated by the cumulative effect of Christian symbolism, as well as by a xenophobic element, which was rendered especially acute thanks to a medieval mentality that conceived of difference in terms of deviance.  Jews' daily behavior also heightened this sense of estrangement, especially when it came to their religious rites, which to Christian eyes smacked of the Satanic.  The Jew was seen as the spiritual heir of his ancestors' "deicidal" mentality.  As such, the Jew remained a living symbol of diabolical opposition to the divinity of Christ, and of all that a good Christian might be expected to reject.  The Devil was an important part of man's vision of the world in this period.  In more than one way, the Jew constituted concrete, living proof of his existence.

His obstinacy in refusing Christ was irrefutable proof of the Jew's having been blinded by the Devil. The "fact" that he grew rich in an activity that Christian orthodoxy continued to prohibit was proof of the temptation to which the good Lord subjected the Christian. The popular imagination easily translated what it saw as the strange nature of daily Jewish rituals into typical aspects of a diabolical ritual. Given the Christian mentality, the Jew thus came to be associated with the very qualities that the popular imagination associated with the Devil: sexual intemperance, which Christians viewed in far more obsessive terms in this period than they had in the previous one; deception in the midst of danger; the temptation to sin, which could reach extraordinary heights in times when heresy was particularly widespread; and, above all, unlimited power, a source of danger and eventual harm to all Christians.

If Christians had coherently translated their traditional cultural ideas and symbols into practice, they would doubtless have expelled the Jews from Christendom long before the end of the fifteenth century. Instead, the incontrovertible fact is that they did not. We will probably never know how many of the literary expressions that went into making hostile depictions of the Jews were merely rhetorical and made no real difference. It is equally hard to measure the cumulative effect of this body of symbols and imaginary portrayals on the formation of Christian attitudes toward Jews or the extent to which it was actually translated into daily practice and legal dispositions. It is not simply a question of choosing between what Salo W. Baron scornfully defined a "lachrymose conception of Jewish history" and its opposite.[3] The historian's tendency to dramatize, or, alternatively, to reappraise this aspect of history inevitably leads to some distortion. This in turn influences his account of the definition of Christian religious and cultural identity and its bearing on the fate of the Jews. Naturally, the danger of distortion increases when the historian succumbs to the temptation to put his narrative at the service of a cherished ideology. The historians can only warn the reader and invite him to beware that any story, including this one, may conceal a camouflaged, ideological message.

## 5. THE BLOOD LIBEL AND THE ESCALATION OF CHRISTIAN ANTIJUDAISM

If generalizing is a legitimate application of the historical method, an overall consideration of the events that ushered in this period, as well as those of the entire fifteenth century, would seem to suggest that it was in this era that the logic of the Christian negative representation of the Jew reached a state of maturity, as did its application in terms of persecution and exclusion. We have already referred to the fact that this period opened with the virulent anti-Jewish riots that erupted in 1391. In many ways, these riots can be seen as the prelude to the Jews' definitive expulsion from the Spanish kingdoms in 1492 and to the forced conversions in Portugal in 1497—events which signalled the Jews' total exclusion from western Europe. One cannot deny the importance of socio-economic factors in catalyzing the popular uprisings of the end of the fourteenth century. Still, there is no doubt that a decisive share of the responsibility for these uprisings can be attributed to the idea that the common people who took part in these uprisings had of the Jews. This included their idea of the Jews' function in Christian society and their relationship to those in power, plus the need to subvert this relationship. Subversion was seen as a first step in a necessary process of social therapy aimed at a society that many considered ill and urgently in need of reform. Similarly, one cannot underestimate the importance of itinerant friars, especially Franciscans, whose sermons helped incite rituals of popular violence. Particularly notable in this regard was Vincent Ferrer, who played a leading role in the riots of 1391 in Spain. Entire communities were swept away during these events: thousands of panicked Jews found refuge at the baptismal font, while hundreds of families opted for exile.

The sermons of itinerant friars often crossed national boundaries: such was the case, for example, of Giovanni da Capistrano, who started in Italy, and travelled to Austria, Germany, and as far as Poland. Friars famous for their missionary ardor, but who did not leave Italy, were no less important internationally, notably Bernardino of Siena and Bernardino of Feltre. There is no doubt as to their responsibility in causing popular anti-Jewish reaction wherever they preached in Italy. For instance, the accusation of ritual murder lodged against the Jews of Trent in 1475 must very probably be seen in the context of Bernardino of Feltre's sermons, for in a Lenten sermon delivered in Trent that same year he mentioned that "he had sometimes heard it said that the Jews drink the blood of Christians at Eastertide."[4] The accusation against the Jews of Trent, following which the entire Jewish community of that town was exterminated, was one of many accusations of its kind recorded during this period. Contrary to one current view, the phenomenon was hardly restricted to the German-speaking area: more than a dozen cases of this kind were recorded in Italy in the second half of the fifteenth century. Nor was there any lack of such cases in Spain: in 1468 a Jew from Sepúlveda was accused of crucifying a Christian woman on Good Friday. In 1490-91 a trial was carried out before the Tribunal of the Inquisition, in the course of which a number of relapsed *conversos* were accused of crucifying a Christian child (the famous Holy Child of La Guardia).

The contribution of Christian indoctrination to the popular imagination was doubtless the source of the proliferation of accusations of ritual murder, which became especially numerous in the fifteenth century. The accusations of ritual murder present perhaps the most eloquent evidence of the contradiction between the trend fostered by the systematic indoctrination of preachers, priests and Catholic educators of every sort, and the stated policy of the rulers.

Christendom's supreme authorities, popes and emperors, repeatedly condemned the spread of accusations of ritual murder and insisted that they were baseless. Those who did so in our period include the Emperor Charles V (1544) and Popes Martin V (1422), Nicholas V (1447), and Paul III (1540). Yet, from the very first medieval example of the blood libel at Norwich in 1144, the spread of these accusations shows how the Christian imagination saw ritual murder as a kind of repetition of the crucifixion, an anti-sacrament, and thus as a indicative expression of the Jews' diabolical nature.

It was possible to imagine, for example, that Jews at Eastertide cooked their unleavened Passover bread (*matzot*) with Christian blood, or that they mixed this blood with the wine they drank in the ritual ceremony of Passover night—a transparent negative transposition of the sacrament of the Eucharist. Jews were also imagined drinking Christian blood to eliminate the smell associated with their diabolical nature, or using it to prepare medicinal ointments to cure the wounds of circumcision, or to prepare magic philters of various kinds. These were all ways of focusing attention on the ritual of affiliation to Judaism (anti-baptism), or on the stereotype of the Jew as sorcerer. Just as in the popular riots, there is no doubt that in accusations of ritual murder political and socio-economic factors played a role, such as opposition to the ruler, defined as a "defender of the murderous Jews."[5] Another possible motive was the desire to transform the remains of a dead Christian into an object of popular devotion, thereby increasing the "touristic" attraction of the sanctuary where they were deposited. It is also clear that no small part of the responsibility for such accusations should be attributed to the irrational religiosity of individual Christians who helped make such accusations public. None of these factors, however, could have been effective in the absence of an underlying mental structure essentially disposed to taking an idea of the Jews, and elevating it to a key position in its more general socio-economic and political discourse.

Among the accusations of ritual murder, the Trent affair of 1475 deserves our special attention. Unlike other cases of this type of anti-Jewish
myth, the Holy See was instead inclined to pay some attention to this one.
An investigation was opened, following which, many years later, Simon—
the child the Jews were accused of killing—was canonized. The cult of the
little St. Simon of Trent was not abolished by the Church until 1965. The
case is noteworthy, however, not just because of the Holy See's unusual
position on the matter, but also because it was the first time the newly invented printing press was used in a campaign to spread anti-Jewish myths.
By now, pamphlets and broadsides depicting the martyr, and illustrated
pamphlets describing the details of the martyrdom with morbid delight,
were capable of making an impression on public opinion without any help
from the sermons of itinerant friars. Just how extraordinary the impact of
the Trent affair was can be inferred from the fact that it was the object of
an entire series of figurative works painted in Lombard churches, almost
all of which belonged to the Franciscan order. The myth of the ritual murder of Trent was thus presented time and again to every Christian who entered those churches for reflection or prayer, alongside all the other sacred
iconographic themes that inspired the Christian mentality.

## 6. The Devil's Christians: Jewish Views of Christians

The Jews' condition of absolute subordination naturally precluded the
possibility of overtly venting their views about Christians and Christianity.
Yet, such views, which drew on the concepts and symbols of their own cultural and religious tradition, were no less radically anti-Christian than
Christians views were anti-Jewish. To the Jews, Christians were simply
idolatrous—unlike Muslims, with whom they shared an idea of the unity
of God and a rejection of the cults of images and statues. The idea of a
"dead" God was especially repellent to them, as was the Christian cult of
relics, which conveyed to them a sense of intimate association of Christian
ritual with impurity (Lev. 21:1-16; Num. 19:11-22), by definition antithetical to sacredness. In the course of the fifteenth century the conviction
began to take hold among Spanish Cabalists that while the soul of the Jew
sprang from the divine Essence, the soul of the non-Jew instead had a satanic origin—an idea which complemented perfectly the widespread notion of the diabolical nature of the Jew.

Affirmations to the contrary were extraordinarily rare and without
practical effect, such as those of Menahem Ha-Mei'ri (fourteenth century)

who theorized a certain fundamental affinity with the Christians, whom he also regarded as "people of religion." The times were still not ripe to neutralize the cumulative effect of a centuries-old literary polemics, and in particular, of a liturgy which abounded in references to the essential antithetical nature of the religion of "the Other," as well as in commemorations of martyrs who died refusing to "let themselves be sprinkled by the stinking water" of baptism.[6]

## 7. Confrontations: Jewish-Christian Debates

The mutually antithetical perceptions of the two religious and socio-cultural identities are, understandably enough, very clearly reflected in records of the disputations that actually took place between Jews and Christians, as well as in the very rich apologetical literature of both groups. The relative rarity of such disputations is probably to be explained by the Jews' reluctance to expose themselves to the danger of an open confrontation, for there is no lack of evidence attesting to the panic provoked by the prospect of an invitation to a public disputation. The goal of such invitations was to stage a propagandistic spectacle, designed to shore up Christians' certainty in their own faith and to demonstrate the intellectual superiority of the Christian disputants, without losing sight of the possibility that a spectacular defeat on the part of the Jewish contender could lead to mass conversions. Jews who had recently converted to Christianity excelled at this type of challenge, which placed their knowledge of Judaism at the service of their newly adopted faith.

The most notable example of this type of event in the period under review is the disputation of Tortosa (1413-14). Noticeably weakened by the consequences of the tragic events of 1391, the Jewish participants proved unable to engage in a consistent line of argumentation and defense. Their failure caused an extra-ordinary wave of mass conversions. This, in turn, contributed to a notable increase in the number of Christian neophytes, known also as "New Christians" or *conversos*, or by the pejorative epithet of *marranos* (a term which in Spanish means pig and which, for reasons which continue to arouse speculation, was associated not only with the *conversos* but also with heretics in general, or with Jews who did not convert).

Many converts, no doubt, arrived at such an extreme decision from a heart-felt conviction that triumphant Christianity was effectively in the right. Others doubtless harbored all sorts of mental reservations. A heated debate continues to rage over the actual nature of the majority of the *conversos'* perception of their religious identity. What does seem certain, however, is that for the first time in history, there appeared a variety of religious outlooks in which Judaism and Christianity were tightly interwoven. In the climate of extreme and virulent hostility that characterized the last decade of the fourteenth century, a continuum of Judeo-Christian religious perceptions thus paradoxically provided a bridge between the most extreme forms of Jewish and Christian orthodoxy. The crucial role this new socio-cultural and religious entity, as we shall see, was to play in reversing the historical drift in relations between Jews and Christians in western Europe.

The obstacles of a pragmatic and psychological nature that induced Jews to avoid openly facing Christians in disputations, were naturally much less of a barrier to the production of polemical writings for "internal use." In this sector the production of anti-Christian literature forms an absolute parallel to its anti-Jewish counterpart, which in this period joined an already long list of earlier works in the genre of *"adversus judaeos."* Like all literary expressions, works on both sides of the Judeo-Christian polemic reflect the tendencies and cultural interests of the age. Thus, the works produced by both sides during this period may be seen to betray a renewed interest in the Bible and in the textual traditions of "the Other," part of a more general interest in humanistic studies and possibly also in the Protestant Reformation, as well as of a gradual decrease in the previous era's interest in arguments of a philosophical nature. It is nevertheless difficult to decide just how much, and what part of this stereotypical literary production—so dull to analyze in depth—actually reflected the spirit of the times, and whether such reflection should rather be attributed to the conditioning of modern scholars, who approach these works with a predisposition toward finding what they seek.

## 8. THE STATUS OF JEWS IN CHRISTENDOM

Judeo-Christian disputations were not the only area in which mutually antithetical perceptions of the two religious and socio-cultural identities gained voice. Such perceptions also inevitably influenced the entire structure of relations between the two groups. A detailed treatment of this matter would necessarily have to examine an almost infinite variety of local situations in which these general elements found concrete expressions through their interplay with local political and socio-economic realities.

The following factors need to be considered in this analysis, though not necessarily in this order: the complicated play of interests and forces among leaders at various levels and those excluded from holding power; the complex law of demand and supply that emerged from concrete situations in which Jews might be considered more or less useful to Christian society or its rulers, or might themselves rate one place of residence as more attractive than another; the infinite variety of idiosyncrasies on the part of decision-makers, and the infinite variety of ways in which they assimilated the message handed down by their religious and cultural traditions; more generally, the degree to which ideologies affected concrete processes of decision-making; the amount of energy needed to offset the inertia inherent in concrete situations, and to bring about radical change; and, finally, the possible interference of foreign policy considerations.

In cases where a decision was made not to expel the Jews from Christian lands, the exercise of Christian power was expressed by applying the principle of toleration in a variety of practical ways, combining it with marginalization, discrimination, and even outright segregation. The special status of the Jews thus presents an infinite number of local variations, of which the terminology used in legislative records provides only an incomplete idea. The subordination of the Jews was legally expressed in the adoption of the term *servi camerae*, the meaning of which has become the subject of a vast literature. Christian rulers' reference to the *servitus* of the Jews can be interpreted as a simple rhetorical device for affirming their authority. It can also be read as a programmatic declaration of their responsibility toward Jews in the sense of protection owed a servant by his lord. Then again, it can be seen as a claim to exclusive sovereignty in fiscal matters, or as imposing a ban on moving to a state governed by another political authority.

There are no references, however, to the *servitus* of Jews in documents where Jews' legal status is precisely defined in terms of detailed privileges (charters), such as the so-called *condotte* (residence permits valid for a fixed period) granted by the Italian states. In all records of this type it is clear that, given the need to define precisely Christians' and Jews' reciprocal terms of obligation, Jews appear to be on a level of virtual equality with Christian "contracting parties." It is in the minutiae of these privileges' paragraphs that the patient researcher can hope to detect reflections of trends and changes in overall climate. For example, in the various *condotte* granted to immigrant Jews in Italian cities undergoing full-swing expansion between the end of the thirteenth and the first decades of the fourteenth centuries, not only is the *servitus* of the Jews not mentioned, but

Jews are actually defined as "real citizens [*cives originarii*]." While the fif-
teenth- and sixteenth-century *condotte* also contain no references to Jewish *servitus*, by then care was taken to consider them "as though they were
citizens [*sicut cives*]," without granting them the rights of citizens. By contrast, in records concerning the Jews in Sicily, where the Jews had lived
since time immemorial and where relations were not regulated by the regime of the *condotte*, the term *servitus* is commonly used.

   However they may have been regarded, Jews were always excluded
from exercising the positive rights of active citizenship. This exclusion, to
be sure, did not apply exclusively to them and was thus far less abnormal
than may seem to the modern viewer. The situation nevertheless conferred
a greater degree of estrangement from the local social and political fabric
on the Jews than it did on others. This degree of estrangement was convenient for Christian rulers, and was considered auspicious and even cultivated by the Jews themselves. Christians, for whom such foreignness fit
their more general idea of the Jews, found it convenient, because it released
them from many of the responsibilities generally incurred by those in
power in exchange for a grant of more or less autonomy or self-government. This practice, which had the obvious result of liberating local magistrates from the burden of dealing with matters concerning Jews, especially
in cases of marriage law, also allowed them to use the leaders of Jewish
communities to levy taxes imposed on Jews. From this point of view, Jews
came to constitute a kind of city within a city—both legally and, with the
growth of the ghettos, physically—and a state within a state. Accustomed
as they were to every sort of limitation on the sovereignty of princes, medieval Europeans did not object to this state of affairs and hence did not
share in the objections of the Roman legislators of antiquity or the future
rulers of absolutist states to such restrictions. The only objection of some
substance came from Christian theology, as codified in the *Summa
Theologica* of St. Thomas Aquinas, according to whom a prince who authorized the exercise of Jewish jurisdiction in his territory implicitly recognized the validity of sentences pronounced in accordance with the Old Testament and therefore with a law which all good Christians should instead
consider to be abrogated once and for all.

   In this realm, as in others, the application of theory followed the normal
course of interplay with the exercise of secular power. In the Papal States,
Jewish judicial autonomy was denied until the unification of Italy (1871).
The other Italian states granted Jewish communities various forms of more
or less broad autonomy, depending on the extent of Church influence on
individual rulers. The Republic of Venice, in many ways the most modern

of these states, may have been the only one to display extraordinary sensitivity with regard both to the exercise of its own sovereignty and to the dangers posed to such sovereignty by legal concessions of autonomy for the Jews, independently of the state's own view of itself as a Catholic state. Outside Italy, sovereigns were far less sensitive to this theological principle.

## 9. The Organization of Jewish Communities

For Jews the desire to organize themselves as cities within cities or states within states was justified by their perception of themselves as outsiders vis-à-vis the political and socio-economic fabric of Christian cities. Given, however, that Jewish communities depended on Christian authorities to exercise power over their own members, aspirations toward autonomy and self-government could only be realized to a limited degree and in a form tolerated by those governments. Jewish communities drew the elements necessary for their own organizational self-definition from two main sources. The first was the positive consequence of their sense of estrangement from the institutional frameworks of the places they inhabited—the awareness of belonging to the Jewish people, from which they derived the principle of observance of Jewish law in all matters. This self-consciousness applied not only to religious ritual, but also to the rules that expressed the community's sovereignty through the regulation of most details of daily life. The Jews drew inspiration from the models presented by Christian cities, but only insofar as these did not seem to threaten perceptions of their own Jewish identity. In the field of community organization, as in the other areas we have considered so far, defining a Jewish identity involved both a rejection of the local setting and a sui generis adherence to it. As usual, favoring either of these factors can lead to considerable distortion. The reader should thus exercise extreme caution in evaluating the various elements of this story, in order not to be led into thinking of Jewish communities as either absolutely averse to, or as entirely adapted to, different local settings.

The Jews' sense of their duty to follow Jewish law led them to adopt a priori the fundamental texts of the Jewish tradition, which provided the constituent laws for group organization. First among these was the Talmud, which for Jews of this period may roughly be compared in authority to the Roman law codes in ancient Rome. Then there were the various codifications of Talmudic law: the *Mishneh Torah* (*Code of Maimonides*) from the twelfth century, which was the precursor of this literary genre; the

*Arba'ah Turim* (*Four Columns*) of the Spaniard of German origin Jacob ben Asher, who was inspired by the structure of late thirteenth-century law code called the *Siete Partidas* of Alfonso X "the Wise" of Castile; and the *Shulhan 'Arukh* (*Prepared Table*) by Josef Caro (first printed edition, Venice, 1533), which addressed and summarized all preceding codifications and became and remains to this day one of the fundamental works of Jewish law. Finally, there are the collections of rabbinical *Responsa*, which in their various forms constituted the equivalent of the legal precedents formulated in the *consilia* of Christian jurists. Alongside these sources stood the ordinances (*takkanot*) of various kinds, which were comparable to various municipal and regional bodies of legislation and could take on a universalized character only in exceptional cases. One famous example of a universalized ordinance concerns the ruling against involuntary divorce, which is traditionally attributed to R. Gershom, the tenth-century writer known as *Me'or ha-Golah* (*Light of the Exile*). It contains the prohibition against marrying more than one woman.

Local settings provided institutional models for Jewish community organization. The first and most important communal institution was the General Assembly, made up of people with voting rights, i.e., people who paid taxes. In it we may discern an equivalent to the assemblies of medieval communes, in which citizens (*cives*), at least in principle, had a chance to express their political will. In theory, the General Assembly was the sovereign body of communal government, and it exercised the right to sanction the communal ordinances that corresponded to civic legislation. In practice, the community identified itself with the General Assembly, which organized subordinate bodies, which received executive powers from it and grew in complexity and number, depending on the size and practical needs of the population. Smaller communities limited themselves to nominating a couple of *parnassim* (plural of *parnas*) or leaders, who sufficed to fulfill administrative functions and represent the community to the local authorities. Larger communities developed a body of executive structures organized according to more or less hierarchical systems and generally modelled after local urban non-Jewish structures. At Venice, for example, the Jews' Great Council (*Va'ad Gadol*) compared to the corresponding Venetian civic institution or, even better, to the Serenissima's Senate. We also find there a Small Council (*Va'ad katan*), comparable to the Venetian *Collegio*, that is, to the executive committee of the Senate or, even better, to the Council of the Ten. Last of all, we find the *parnassim*, somehow reminiscent of the Venetian *savi*, who were elected magistrates responsible for specially delegated tasks.

Jewish communities also appointed special commissions for particular functions, such as helping the poor or maintaining the synagogue, cemetery and other community institutions. In their Registers (*Pinkessim*, plural of *Pinkas*) these commissions scrupulously noted the texts of the decisions made by the Assembly or by its delegated bodies, whose executive powers were unfailingly defined. At Verona, for example, the General Assembly of the Jewish community instituted a Council of Eleven members, whose decisions had to be unanimous or, failing that, had to receive a majority of seven votes, and who could not spend sums that exceeded the ad hoc limits set by the General Assembly. On this point it is worth noting that the sixteenth-century *Registers* of the Italian Jewish communities appear to be the oldest documents of their kind to be passed down to us intact. The register of Verona, perhaps the oldest of all, contains rulings that were adopted beginning in 1539. Various local contexts also helped shape operational models for electing leaders, with systems that tended both to guarantee the "democratic," that is, popular, nature of elections and to prolong the staying power of restricted oligarchies made up of richer and more influential members.

The exercise of community power was also fraught with a basic ambivalence, not unlike the one we noted above in discussing the nature of Jews' estrangement from local settings. On the one hand, despite its prestige, the exercise of power was not lucrative and sometimes could even be onerous, and the *parnassim* were often held personally responsible for their acts. In cases where they did not previously obtain a decree of immunity, they had to guarantee communal debts incurred with their own private assets, as when, for example, they decided that there was need to anticipate revenues in order to liberate imprisoned co-religionists. Thus it was both preferable and virtually indispensable that leaders be among the richest members of the community. Then, too, in addition to the prestige one could enjoy and flaunt within one's group, membership in a ruling group also brought undoubted socio-economic and political advantages both within and outside the group. Community leaders were responsible for choosing systems of taxation and for deciding the amount of taxes to impose, a power which enabled them to privilege their own interests, even if they would never admit to doing so. The same leaders were also the community's representatives to Christian governors, something they naturally could exploit not only for the good of the group, but for their own personal gain as well, sometimes even at the expense of the community. Records pertaining to the Jews in Sicily, for example, present various cases of notables who, having won from the viceroy complete exemption from communal taxes, oversaw the unequal assessment of the taxes on the non-privileged members of their own community. Cases of this sort can be found just about anywhere.

The communal leaders' mediating role between Jewish community and Christian power had another important implication. The Jewish exercise of communal power followed and depended on a Christian model, which influenced it and provided it with the necessary instruments of coercion. Even so, what may in similar fashion, though improperly, be called the Jewish aristocracy, modelled itself on its Christian counterpart. Recognition from powerful Christians provided the Jewish aristocracy with the legitimacy necessary to claim a preeminent position within the Jewish community. In other words, the Jewish community was called upon to provide its aristocrats with the social recognition they could not obtain in Christian society, which rejected them. This phenomenon, well-known to sociologists of minorities, is one more aspect of the paradoxical and contradictory nature of the Jewish condition. To obtain true social recognition within one's group, one had first to obtain a measure of protective recognition from powerful individuals in the very society from which one felt, and was, excluded. In other words, the kind of mediation needed to attain social recognition in a society whose very raison d'être lay in separating out "the Other," tended to annul that same separatist tendency.

Privileged notables naturally claimed the exclusive right to fulfill this mediating function by virtue of their social prominence or their meritorious ancestry, an attitude which closely reflected the paternalistic mentality of the times. So did the fact that most members of the Jewish community saw no reason to object to this arrangement. An honor bestowed on their leaders was an honor bestowed on the entire group! There was nevertheless no dearth of cases of violent criticism, the most notable example of which involved Spanish Jewish courtiers, who were accused of flagging orthodoxy and extreme assimilation to the uses and customs of the court milieu.

## 10. "Man of Knowledge": The Rabbi as Jewish Teacher

Accusations of failure in observing tradition lodged against the Jewish notables, who maintained close relations with non-Jewish rulers and aristocrats, raise several questions about authority and legitimacy within the Jewish community. How was orthodoxy perceived at the community level? What was the relation between those who exercised communal power and the official representatives of what, in orthodox terms, was considered to be traditional knowledge, that is, the rabbis?

In truth, it is not easy to precisely define the function of the rabbi in traditional Jewish society. On an etymological level, the term reveals a constant connection between the meaning of knowledge and the meaning of power. Indeed, it appears that since ancient times, the Hebrew term *rav*, customarily rendered as "rabbi," has been associated both with the possession of some particular type of skill and knowledge and with the idea of superiority and authority, of domination and power. Intimately tied to the idea of size and force, the latter meaning seems in fact to have predated that of skill and knowledge. It is often used in this sense in the Hebrew Bible, where it appears again and again (just as it does other ancient Semitic languages), while the term's association with skill and learning is, by contrast, very rare. In any case, the two ideas, that of authority/domination and that of knowledge/skill, are indissolubly linked in post-Biblical and Talmudic terminology. Talmudic language, while it more or less preserves the various Biblical meanings of the terms that concern us here, nevertheless clearly defines the rabbinate (*rabbanuth*) in terms of the exercise of authority and power. The connection between the two meanings stems from the typically ancient and medieval paternalistic conception of the relation between the rabbi—master of learning—and the scholar. By the fifteenth century, the period under consideration here, a union between knowledge and power has taken place in the vocabulary and mentality of Jews and found its way into local settings, such as those provided by relations between academies of study (*yeshivoth*, plural of *yeshivah*) and Jewish communal institutions.

The history of the rabbinate is bound up with the history of the Jewish community, and it reflects the immense variety of ways in which Jews defined their public and private behavior. This definition was a function of the ethos of Jewish religious and cultural tradition, of which, by consensus, men of knowledge were the legitimate depositaries and interpreters. From this point of view, it seems impossible to refer to the rabbinate as a specific profession (i.e., that of people appointed to carry out specific functions within the community, such as officiating at events of public worship and supervising rites related to marriage, divorce and other matters). So much so that it seems equally impossible to think of the rabbinate only in terms of a fixed field of academic knowledge.

By the fifteenth century the problem of how to define institutionally who was authorized to consider himself a "man of knowledge" had been adequately resolved. Two different types of approaches were by now well established in the Iberian region and the Italo-Germanic areas respectively. The procedure adopted by the communities of the Italo-Germanic area, better known than the Iberian practice, amounted to a form of rabbinical ordination. This same form was ultimately adopted with only a few changes by the entire Jewish diaspora, including the Iberian exiles, who did not know it until the era of the expulsion. The Hebrew term for this rabbinical ordination was *semikhah*, which literally means "laying on of hands [*impositio manuum*]." The rite vaguely recalls, on the one hand, the ordination of Catholic priests, and it suggests, on the other, the conferring of the university doctoral degree. The similarity did not escape the Spanish Jews, who simply took it to mean that the procedure followed in Italo-Germanic regions should be rejected by its Christian, hence spoiled, origin. Isaac Abravanel, illustrious minister of the kings of Portugal and Spain and a scholar of extremely high stature, scorned the Italian Jews, saying that they "had copied the Christians who are in the habit of making doctors."[7] Whatever the truth of this malevolent observation, our attention should be given precisely the possibility of juxtaposing the institution of rabbinical ordination with the act of conferring of the doctorate.

The comparison between rabbinical ordination and the conferring of the doctorate, both of which reached the peak of their institutional definition in the course of the fifteenth century, is far richer in meaning than it may at first seem. There are some striking analogies: the two kinds of men of knowledge, rabbis and doctors, share the same tendency to concentrate control of prerogatives in the academic world and to project into the surrounding society, thus translating an academic into a social hierarchy. Rabbis and doctors alike claimed, by virtue of their academic titles, privileges relating to their status, function, or socio-economic standing. Jewish society, like other societies, while it displayed its reluctance to abdicate its right to control, did not object to recognizing of the importance of knowledge for the proper functioning of society in general and the exercise of power in particular. The larger Christian society experienced the same kind of uncertainty and tension about who has the authority to authorize the founding of a *studium* (which term designated in Latin the *yeshivah* as well as the university) and the same model of compromise and "division of labor" between the two realms of learning, academic and non-academic. The social dignity of the doctorate corresponded in every way to the social dignity accorded the holder of the rabbinical title—in daily and extraordinary ceremonial protocol, in grants of exemptions from taxes (even though, by force of circumstance, such grants often failed to be respected), and in acknowledgment of exclusive rights to carry out certain administrative and judiciary functions that we might call "professional," though we must not exaggerate the weight of the financial rewards such privileges entailed.

The analogy between rabbinate and doctorate is even more marked when we consider the extraordinary concordance between rabbinical and university certifications. The two types of documents share the same structure and sometimes even the same terminology: a preamble praising the science that elevates and ennobles the person who, following arduous labors, has managed to take possession of it, a fact concretely represented by the conferral of the diploma; a more or less detailed presentation of the intellectual and moral qualities of the candidate, followed by a declaration stating that he is worthy of so great an honor; a formal declaration to the effect that the candidate is awarded the title of doctor or rabbi; a detailed list of the prerogatives and privileges he will henceforth be privy to; and finally the granting of the insignia that attest to his new status. The ceremonial conferring rabbinical degrees did not include, however, the academic ritual of conferring a cap, a book, and a ring. Instead, the latter part of this ceremony took on an eminently metaphorical shape: a symbolic "rod" was "handed over" to the candidate, representing the power to punish transgressors with excommunication, and a gown symbolic of rabbinical status was donned. Although all the sources relating to this analogy come from sixteenth-century Italy, we may with confidence extrapolate to cover the whole of the Italo-Germanic area, especially if we keep in mind Italy's model importance in the history of European Jewry during this era.

The differences between the doctoral and rabbinical degrees were no less important than their similarities. The doctoral degree qualified its holder to fulfill duties that were limited almost exclusively to the university and the profession: these comprised the rights "to lecture, to instruct, and to attain and hold the professorial chair [*legendi, doctorandi, cathedram magistram ascendendi illamque regendi*]," as well as "to give public instruction [*publice esercendi*]." The rabbinical degree, by contrast, qualified its holder to perform duties, such as legal consultations, which were almost always performed outside the *yeshivah*, in the midst of society. In addition, the rabbinical diploma granted other qualifications: to assume leadership of the *yeshivah* and to ordain others; to preach in public (or, better, to impose one's preaching on the public); and to decide what was permissible and what was not (not only with regard to ritual, but in moral matters as well), to excommunicate anyone who deserved it (meaning at the sole discretion of the rabbi). Underlying the uncontested exercise of all these duties was the assumption that the rabbi's ability to fulfil his role would be enough to eliminate any sort of difficulty, and that society would be unconditionally prepared to assign the rabbis as much power as they were prepared to exercise. In practice, this was precisely the crucial point of tension between rabbis who aspired to unconditional authority, and the community—what could, though imprecisely, be described as tension between rabbis and the community's "lay leaders." The public's well documented desire to control, or even to check, rabbis' claims expressed its own awareness of the need to respect the legitimate holders of the knowledge considered essential to their own cultural definition.

## 11. "MAN OF AUTHORITY": THE RABBI IN THE JEWISH COMMUNITY

That rabbis were "necessary" to the successful development of community life was fundamental to Jewish group identity. The primary reason for this lay in a basic idea of the Talmudic tradition, which held as indispensable to Jewish law the presence of a "man of authority [*adam hashuv*, literally: 'a man who counts'],ic who could wield what we might anachronistically call "constitutional" authority over current legislation, i.e., the promulgation of ordinances. This might more aptly be termed "para-legislative" activity, for Jewish communities considered legislation as such, the making of new laws, to be an impossibility. The law was God's word as contained in the Bible and interpreted by the Talmudic sages. In addition to declaring the absolute sovereignty of the urban communities, whose legal character was conceived as being of an essentially associative nature, a famous Talmudic text invalidated all ordinances that did not meet with the prior approval of the "man of authority," should such a man be present.[8] In the fluid conditions of medieval times, a "man of authority" was anyone whom public opinion recognized as such. Until proven otherwise, rabbis were just such people.

A second reason for the importance of rabbis lay in their skill in matters concerning Jewish law. Communities needed them as legal and ritual consultants, and above all as judges, in places where Christian authorities did not prevent communities from exercising judicial autonomy. Finally, one very important reason rabbis were essential to the development of community life lay in the fact that excommunication was practically the only coercive measure available to rulers when and where individuals' own sense of self-discipline was insufficient to settle potential controversies. Because it was so intimately tied to the sphere of doctrine and the sacred, excommunication was of fundamental relevance to the legitimate depositaries of doctrinal knowledge, the rabbis. They, in turn, were the only ones suited to "manage" an instrument capable of causing such terrible effects in the afterworld. Therefore, issuing excommunications was the exclusive prerogative of the rabbis. Such a prerogative was vitally important for community organization, for without it communities could not effectively coerce their own members.

The figure of the rabbi should thus be evaluated in terms not only of the importance that society attached to traditional knowledge, but also of the way this knowledge was applied in activities such as preaching, ritual and legal consulting, administering justice and imposing ordinances. Just as important were the varying degrees of autonomy granted Jewish communities by non-Jews and the different ways such autonomy was conceptualized and carried out in different settings. Such settings, in turn, naturally reflected the contexts of a variety of non-Jewish political and legal systems. All these factors were of crucial importance in the evolution of the rabbinate. Moreover, we should also take into consideration the particular significance of perceptions of the magic and the divine, without which the institution of excommunication would have been largely ineffectual.

The rabbi thus appears, on the one hand, as an intellectual in Jewish society, a member of a coterie of initiates, a possessor of sacred knowledge, and in this sense also a priest. This latter term is to be understood not in the Christian sense, as a man possessing sacramental powers, but in the earliest Muslim sense of the term *imam*, a man of law, the legitimate interpreter of Holy Law and thus a consultant to whoever exercised public authority. The rabbi also increasingly claimed exclusive jurisdiction over the legal functions necessary to the physical perpetuation of the Jewish community and the organization of community life. In fact, he pretended to the right to exercise of authority and power by virtue of being the only legitimate master of the Law. The figure of the rabbi thus came to combine the idea of the *dominus* and the *magister*, the teacher and the lord, with that of the *sacerdos* and the *doctor legis hebraicae*, the priest and the expert in Jewish law, but also with that of the judge (*judex*). We should take all this, however, as more often the expression of an ideal than a description of its application, and it may, in the last analysis, have remained more imaginary than real.

It is no wonder that the Christian world's first perceptions of the complex figure of the rabbi were from earliest times charged with uncertainty, as even the earliest testimonials show. The rabbi, in fact, was assigned various names in Latin and vernacular documents: he was *magister* or *doctor* (or even more explicitly, sometimes *doctor legis hebraicae*), *Juden-*

*bischof*, or *Hochmeister der Juden*. The most common solution to this ambiguity, and one which is still in use, was to carry the appropriately transliterated Hebrew term over into medieval Latin and various other vernaculars, thereby complementing the incorrect Latin or vulgar translation—*doctores legis hebraicae seu rabini*.

We need not dwell here on the various ways that rabbis were included in communal organization. In the Iberian peninsula until the very end, an extremely clear distinction was maintained between rabbis as men of learning and rabbis as officers in the community, such as judges, notaries, preachers, and educators. In these communities, both the absolute preeminence of "men of knowledge" and the absolute sovereignty of communities were guaranteed by a rigid separation between the sphere of communal organization and that of the academies of learning. The most renowned heads of the academies were considered by informal public consensus to be the most qualified experts in Jewish law, such that both rabbis who acted as functionaries of the community and "lay" community leaders could turn to them in moments of doubt. They were nonetheless unable to impose their authority on communities that did not already accept it by freely seeking out their advice. In short, they functioned as a sort of high constitutional court, whose authority was guaranteed mostly by virtue of their prestige. In the Italo-Germanic regions the academy instead came to be integrated into the community in such a way that rabbis became a part of the community's institutional structures. This led to the nomination of official rabbis of Jewish communities. In theory, these rabbis were granted absolute preeminence, but in practice they had to come to terms with the notables who nominated them. In the final analysis, the proper functioning of this arrangement required a balance between the rabbis' ideal aspirations and their practical realization. This required the communal leaders, in turn, to strike a balance between their own recognition of their theoretical subordination to rabbinical authority, and their determination not to relinquish their own rights to control this authority. So far as the self-government of communities is concerned, the history of the union between knowledge, on the one hand, and power and authority, on the other, is the history of the various ways in which such balances were struck in different local settings.

## 12. Jewish Culture

A rigid definition of the texts of traditional Hebrew learning, such as we have provided above, can lead to a serious distortion, for it might leave an impression of a complete break between Jewish and non-Jewish local culture, as though they were two worlds living in watertight compartments, linked at most by channels of communication held open by marginal and deviant elements. In fact, matters were quite different. Relations of inter-dependence between Jewish and non-Jewish local culture were of a very different nature than might be expected of two opposite camps separated by an impassable barrier.

Jews were in fact both an integral part of local life and members of a world that was alien to local life. Yet, despite the barriers that separated them, Jews and non-Jews constituted what might be called a single cultural context, for the Jews both inhabited the local culture and were strangers in it. The analogy between the rabbinical "ordination [*ordinatio*]" and the academic doctorate illustrates the fact the exclusion of Jews from local life, based on the definition of their religious and cultural identity, was by no means absolute. A look at Jewish culture—defined in the narrower sense of intellectual activity and literary production—can improve our understanding of the meaning and limits of that exclusion.

The first thing to consider on this point is linguistic awareness. There is no doubt that Jews knew the languages of the countries they lived in. If not, how could they have communicated with the world around them? It also seems certain that they used local languages in speaking to one another. Just as certain, too, is that before the late sixteenth century the only educated language of communication and cultural expression for Jews living in Christian Europe was Hebrew. All correspondence between Jews was conducted in Hebrew, and so were all acts of a legal nature that concerned the Jewish community (excepting those that, for whatever reason, needed to be brought to the attention of a Christian magistracy). The same can be said for all community records. The books that Jews kept in their libraries and the works they read and studied were almost exclusively in Hebrew. This is confirmed by a quantitative analysis of the books owned by Jews and examined by the local Inquisition at Mantua in Italy toward the end of the sixteenth century, 98% of the which were in Hebrew. Works on liturgy, biblical exegesis, ritual, and the Talmud were in Hebrew, as were almost all literary works of other kinds. Rare exceptions, discussed below, confirm this rule. Jewish culture, therefore, circumscribed within the Jewish space, a fact which emphasizes the Jewish separation from local life. So does the fact that Jewish intellectuals, almost all of them rabbis, generally were in close correspondence with their colleagues in other places. In other words, throughout the Christian Middle Ages and later, in the period we are studying here, *la république des lettres juives* was characterized by a universality comparable to Christian scholars' *la république des lettres latines*, only much more intensely felt.

There is, of course, another, less obvious side to the story of Jewish culture, for a close examination of Hebrew literary production reveals a multiplicity of connections to corresponding works of non-Hebrew literature. One can find affinities in form and content, not to mention translations or even crude imitations. As noted above, even a work of ritual codification like the *Arba'ah Turim* by Jacob ben Asher displays an affinity to the *Siete Partidas* of King Alfonso the Wise of Castile. The phenomenon of similarity is clearest in the fields of literature and, in a particularly intense way, philosophy, which until the last decades of our era comprised virtually all branches of scientific knowledge. So, for example, Moses Rieti composed his *Migdash Me'at* (*Small Sanctuary*), modelled on Dante's *Divina Commedia*; Judah Messer Leon wrote *Nophet Tsufim* (*The Book of the Honeycomb's Flow*), a treatise on Hebrew rhetoric based on the *Rhetorica ad Herennium* and Averroës' paraphrase of Aristotle's *Poetics*; and David Gans composed *Zemah David* (*The Sprout of David*), which drew heavily from contemporary German chronicles.

The fact that the principal representatives of Jewish culture of the age were indeed rabbis, or persons who held a stable position in the center of Jewish society's cultural establishment, obviously excludes the possibility that all these works might be expressions of marginal cultural deviance. Further, reading them dispels all doubt that their authors were conscious of sharing ideas, mentalities and even cultural content with the Christian society in which they lived. In the final analysis, what these men did was to transfer and translate ideas and contents from an external into an internal cultural space, perceiving and presenting the whole as a genuine creation of Jewish culture intended for Jews. Located at the top of the socio-cultural pyramid, when it came to culture the Jewish literati assumed the same mediating role between external and internal space that we encountered earlier in our discussion of ruling notables in Jewish communities. Given the barrier that separated the two cultures—a barrier most concretely expressed by linguistic difference—the literati arrogated the right to cross over it, to explore the external, and to decide what to import and how to elaborate or censor such imports. By exercising a possessive form of control over Jewish culture, these literati also ensured the existence of vital channels of communication between inside and outside worlds.

## 13. The End of Coexistence

The most notable consequence of the forced separation of most Jews from the western European lands was that most Jewish people found themselves concentrated in regions that were decidedly more distant from the centers of western cultural evolution. In this sense, one might say that for the Jewish people, 1492 symbolizes the end of an age of cultural coexistence with the Christian world based on a medieval model that had been tested over the course of some ten centuries. This separation was, however, neither total nor definitive. It was not total, because substantial groups of *conversos* were left behind by the exiles who left for the Orient. Even baptism had not succeeded in erasing their affiliation to Judaism. Nor was the separation total, since in Italy and in some regions of the Empire north of the Alps, some Jewish communities were still permitted to live according to a traditional, medieval model of coexistence.

In the sixteenth century, the model of separation took on its most rigidly oppressive form, so far as the Jews were concerned. In the first place, even in Italy the states in which Jews were still tolerated were drastically reduced in number. It was in this period that the practice of segregating Jews into ghettos began to be systematically adopted. There was nothing new about this practice. It had already been adopted before in various other places in Christian western Europe, out of deference to the discriminatory dispositions of the Fourth Lateran Council (1215), which in many ways inspired the policies vis-à-vis Jews that were drawn up in the sixteenth century. The first ghetto was instituted in Venice in 1516. Sadly slated for notoriety, this institution probably got its name from the Venetian neighborhood to which Jews were confined, i.e., *ghetto*, or foundry, so named because the foundries of Venice's military industry were located there. The introduction of the ghetto signalled a positive departure from the Serenissima's traditional policies toward the Jews, for previously the republic had repeatedly prohibited Jews from maintaining stable residence in the city of Venice. The Jews now forced to live in the ghetto were the same ones who had been granted temporary permission to enter the city as refugees during the War of the League of Cambrai (1509). Paradoxically, this restrictive disposition thus signalled a reversal of the traditional Venetian policy of maintaining the city *Judenrein*, that is, free of Jews.

Jews' segregation into separate neighborhoods was subsequently championed by Pope Paul IV in a bull known by the words of its programmatic preamble, "*Cum nimis absurdum.*"[9] Taking up the phrasing and basic thrust of the sections concerning Jews of the resolutions of the IV Lateran

Council, the Pope reiterated that "it is profoundly absurd and unbearable that the Jews, who are subordinated through their own fault to perpetual servitude, should show the Christians ingratitude, and, with the excuse that Christian mercy welcomes them by permitting them to live among Christians, they should repay the favor with scorn, aiming to dominate those they instead should serve." "On the contrary," he insisted, "considering that the Church tolerates Jews in order that they may bear witness to true Christian faith," in expectation of the day when they will recognize their errors and accept the light of the Catholic religion, "they must appear as servants of Christians, who are in truth free men in Jesus Christ and in God." The Jews were to be condemned to a life of confinement in neighborhoods where they would be isolated from Christians; they could not own real estate and had to immediately sell any they owned; and were required to wear a yellow sign as a badge of infamy. They would also be required to strictly abide by the old prohibition against having Christian wet-nurses or servants, as well as the prohibition against allowing poor Christians to address them with the title of "Sir." They could not work in public on Sundays or during Christian holydays; they were forbidden to do business (except in used objects, the famous "rag trade [*strazzaria*]"), dispense medical cures to Christians, or engage in relations with them. Nor could Jews play, eat, converse or bathe with Christians. Loans, too, were to be more carefully regulated and "moralized," to prevent any swindles on the part of the Jews. The Jews would in turn be required to keep account books in Italian, calculate months as being thirty days long, and so forth. In the last decades of the sixteenth century and over the course of the seventeenth century, the pope's initiative was imitated by various Italian states that had continued to tolerate the presence of Jews. Yet, despite its character of odious discrimination, the institution of the ghetto nonetheless paradoxically signalled the end of a tendency to exclude the Jews from western Europe, and opened a phase of reintegration. From this perspective, the mental disposition with which Christians approached Jews began to undergo a reversal.

That such a reversal began to take place cannot be understood without reference to the *conversos'* contribution to this trend. Most important in this regard were the Portuguese *conversos*, many of whom established themselves in various western European localities following Portugal's institution of the Inquisition. In places where it was forbidden to openly practice Judaism, as in France, these *conversos* naturally settled as Christians. However, in Italy, where it was not forbidden to practice Judaism, the Portuguese *conversos* were able to openly return to Judaism, and join existing Jewish communities. Thus, in this difficult situation, Italy was called upon to play a role of extraordinary importance in the reintegration of Jews into the western socio-economic fabric. The spread of mercantilism no doubt catalyzed this process. Not only did it favor the physical resettlement of the new arrivals, but it also favored a radical transformation in the way Christians represented Jews, and in the way Jews perceived themselves.

The newly arrived *conversos* were in fact merchants and entrepreneurs with strong business ties, which in general were strengthened by family connections that linked them to the most important cities of the Mediterranean basin. For this reason, rulers regarded them very differently than they did other Jews. The Jews showed that they were capable of making a real contribution to local economies, and that they could favor the development of commerce. Rulers thus preferred to integrate them into local economies rather than to employ them at the margins of society, where they carried out the detested task of moneylending to the poor. This was a radical change, in that it replaced the stereotype of the Jew as usurer and exploiter of Christian society with the idea of the useful Jew who could be integrated into this society—on condition, naturally, that he not subvert it. Various Italian states closed an eye to the fact that many of the newly arrived Jews who openly declared their faith and joined Jewish communities, were in reality relapsed *conversos*. In some cases the opinion even took hold that forced baptisms had no value even according to canon law, and that therefore a return to Judaism was permissible. In any case, this was the basic thrust of pontifical policy before the advent of Paul IV, who when it came to this particular point, nullified the decisions of his predecessors and condemned any *converso* on whom he managed to lay hands. Such was the case at Ancona (1556), which became internationally known.

In the mercantilistic world of the second half of the sixteenth century and beyond, the spectrum of religious perceptions of Judaism and Christianity that originated in the phenomenon of the *conversos* helped create a real bridge between Judaism and Christianity. The *conversos* present us with an extraordinary variety of religious perceptions, to which the generic label of "Marrano," sometimes used to describe their faith, does little justice. Their religious behavior ranged from the most rigidly orthodox Catholicism, to the most deeply felt return to Judaism. They cannot be comprehended, however, as a variety of individuals isolated from one another, for men and women of differing religious loyalties nevertheless maintained close links of family and business. A *converso* who returned to Judaism in Italy might well be the brother of another who remained a Christian in Ibe-

rian lands. The Christian brother might in turn handle the duties of a
Catholic clergyman while being closely related to other *conversos* in the
West, who pretended to be Christians, as well as to orthodox Jews who
had emigrated to the Ottoman Empire upon being expelled from Spain. In
this period, the complex weaving together of family and business ties produced an entirely new phenomenon: the perception of belonging to a
socio-cultural group defined by factors other than religious loyalty. Defining themselves as belonging to the Portuguese and Spanish "nation
[*nacâo*]," for the first time in history these men and women advanced the
possibility of belonging to a nation, even as they professed different religions, and expressed that sense of belonging in different institutional ways.
For example, in Amsterdam there was founded a confraternity called
*Santa Companhia de dotar orfans e donzelas pobres*, which was modelled
on the *Hebra de casar horphaos* of Venice.[10] In awarding dowries to poor
girls it gave absolute precedence to a girl from the *nacâo*, no matter where
she lived, over a Jewish girl living in the town of the confraternity itself.
Naturally, this phenomenon should be seen in the broader context of the
transformations in this field that took place in Europe under the impact of
Protestant victories. It should be underlined, however, that, so far as the
Jews were concerned, the wars of religion were not necessary for this phenomenon to emerge, even if, post factum, tensions of varying intensity
were hardly lacking for them either. In this case, the lack of political and
military power paradoxically worked in favor of the Jews.

The problem of the Inquisition's responsibility for, or contribution to,
as the case may be, preserving the *conversos*' spirit of resistance to Christianity and their attraction to Judaism, is still a matter of great controversy,
though the polarized interpretations, so much in vogue a few decades or so
ago, are giving way to make room for more nuanced formulations. Almost everyone now concedes that not all those who were persecuted by the
Inquisition were Judaizers, and that a very large number of *conversos*
adopted the Christian religion without any reservations. It is also accepted
that the existence of a very wide variety of religious perceptions was not
merely the result of opportunistic choices, with people merely trading mass
attendance for a good business network. Today, the spiritual world of the
*conversos* seems extraordinarily expressive, and is all the more compelling
from our modern point of view in that it raises questions about the very
nature of religious experience in settings where individuals are free to make
choices.

In this context, efforts have recently been made to focus on the contribution of the *conversos* to restructuring perceptions of the Jewish identity

on the eve of the modern era. Indeed, many of those who expressed their unequivocal desire to abandon Christianity and return to Judaism, ended up halfway between the two faiths. Once outside Christianity, the religion in which they had been raised since infancy, they could not fully embrace Judaism. The obstacle to their complete integration was not so much their ignorance of the details of Jewish religious practice and thought, which they worked hard to make up for in every way. The major obstacle was instead their Christian background. Having accepted Christianity into their lives, they were no longer capable of completely repudiating it, even if only as an extraordinarily strong dialectical element that helped define their vision of the world. Whoever had tasted Christianity's fundamental concepts and symbols found it difficult to forgo the better things that Christianity seemed to offer over Judaism. Raised with an essentially spiritual conception of religious practice, for example, the *conversos* could find rigid adherence to the detailed routines of Jewish formal teaching to be problematic. What is more, they could also serve to introduce typically Christian ideas and cultural expressions, to which they felt no instinctive aversion, into Jewish life. Here, too, the *conversos'* contribution was essentially to encourage a reconsideration and consequent reformulation of Jewish attitudes toward Christians and Christianity.

For reasons already noted, the new bridge between Judaism and Christianity was first and most completely established in sixteenth-century Italy. Here, Spanish and Portuguese Jews, many of them *conversos*, instituted the first separate communities that were later to be universally called "Sephardic" communities (e.g., "Spanish," from *Sefarad* = Spain). Their founders were inspired by the models provided by Italian Jewish communities, more than by Iberian tradition, which they only dimly understood, despite many efforts to do so with the help of teachers and books imported from the Islamic lands, where their Spanish brothers had established themselves in the wake of the expulsion. During the next century, the communities founded by the Sephardim in Italy were to serve as models for all the communities founded in western Europe by *conversos* who went back to Judaism, notably at Amsterdam, Hamburg, and London. In this respects, as in others, Italy played a mediating role between east and west that extended far beyond the level of economics and commerce. This role was further developed thanks to Italian printshops, which were used by oriental scholars during this period to print works intended for Jewish markets in both east and west. It was at Ferrara that the first printing press to produce Portuguese and Spanish works (1553-55) went into operation for a few years. These works were principally intended for the Jewish re-educa-

tion of *conversos* living in the Christian west. They are, however, merely
the most visible aspects of the phenomenon, and a more detailed study
could easily reveal many others.

In conclusion, we can say that the process of reintegration begun in the
second half of the sixteenth century did not merely represent a gradual
physical return of Jews to the regions from which they earlier had been
driven. It also produced a total restructuring of Christians' and Jews'
awareness of one another. In this sense, it may be fitting to say that this
process is not yet at an end, and that only in the twentieth century has it entered an accelerated phase.

Translated by Krystyna von Henneberg

# NOTES

1. The translator thanks Professor Richard A. Webster of Berkeley, California, for his generous assistance.
2. English in Judah Hallevi, *The Book of Kuzari*, trans. Hartwig Hirschfeld (New York, 1946), 69.
3. Salo W. Baron, "Emphases in Jewish History," *Jewish Social Studies* 1 (1939): 1-38, here at 37; reprinted in his *History and Jewish Historians* (Philadelphia, 1964), 65-89, here at 88.
4. Quoted by Léon Poliakov, *Les banchieri juifs et le Saint-Siège du XIIIe au XVIIe siècle* (Paris-The Hague, 1965), 205-6.
5. For cases, see R. Po-chia Hsia, *The Myth of Ritual Murder: Jews and Magic in Reformation Germany* (New Haven, 1988).
6. Anna Sapir Abulafia, "Invectives Against Christianity in the Hebrew Chronicles," in *Crusade and Settlement*, ed. Peter W. Edbury (Cambridge, 1985), 66-72, here at 71 note 7. The chronicles are translated into English by Shlomo Eidelberg, ed., *The Jews and the Crusaders: the Hebrew Chronicles of the First and Second Crusades* (Madison, Wisc., 1977), 22-23, though the original Hebrew should be consulted.
7. Isaac Abravanel, *Nahalath Avoth* (*Commentary to the Mishnah. Avoth*), I, 1.
8. *TB* (=*Babylonian Talmud*) Baba Bathra 8.
9. The bull is printed in *Magnum bullarium Romanum: bullarum, privilegiorum ac diplomatum Romanorum Pontificum amplissima collectio* (Graz, 1964-66), vol. 4, part 1: 321-22.
10. There was a similar confraternity in Lisbon, the Santa Casa de Misericordia, founded in 1499, possibly on a Genoese (ultimately a Florentine) model.

# BIBLIOGRAPHY

Note: The numbers key the bibliography's sections to those of the text.

1.

The general work with broadest view on the history of the Jews in Europe is currently that by Salo W. Baron, *A Social and Religious History of the Jews*, 2d ed. rev., vols. 9-17: *The Late Middle Ages and the Era of European Expansion, 1200-1650* (New York, 1965-80). This work, written by the greatest contemporary historian of Judaism, should be used with some caution, because its overall approach prevents one from grasping with sufficient clarity the changes that took place over time in various local contexts. More synthetic are the chapters devoted to our period by Haim Hillel Ben-Sasson, *A History of the Jewish People* (Cambridge, Mass., 1976), of which the original edition in Hebrew was published in 1969. A very recently published work is by Kenneth Stow, *An Alienated Minority: the Jews of Medieval Latin Europe* (Cambridge, Mass., 1992). Centered precisely on our period are recent works by Maurice Kriegel, *Les juifs à la fin du moyen âge* (Paris, 1979), and by Anna Foa, *Ebrei in Europa dalla peste nera all'emancipazione* (Rome and Bari, 1992). There is no shortage of excellent works on single countries. On the Jews in Spain, Fritz (Yitzhak) Baer's *A History of the Jews in Christian Spain* (Philadelphia, 1961) remains indispensable. The first edition of this work appeared in Hebrew in 1945. The following are also worth consulting: Luis Suárez Fernández, *Judíos españoles en la Edad Media* (Madrid, 1980); Benjamin R. Gampel, *The Last Jews on Iberian Soil: Navarrese Jewry 1479-1498* (Berkeley and Los Angeles, 1989); Miguel Angel Motis Dolader, *Los judíos aragoneses en la baja edad media (1283-1479)*, in *Historia de Aragon* vol. 6 (Zaragoza, 1987): 149-84; Asunción Blasco Martínez, "Los judíos del reino de Aragón: Balance de los estudios realizados y perspectivas," in *I Colloqui d'historia dels jueus a la Cornia d'Aragon* (Lleida, 1991), 13-97. On Portugal, see Maria José Pimenta Ferro Tavarez, *Os judeus em Portugal no seculo XV*, 2 vols (Lisbon, 1982-84). On Italy, see Moses Avigdor Shulvass, *The Jews in the World of the Renaissance* (Leiden, 1973), of which the original edition in Hebrew was published in 1955; Cecil Roth, *The Jews in the Renaissance* (Philadelphia, 1959), which deals, however, only with cultural history; the parts devoted to our period in the works of Cecil Roth, *The History of the Jews in Italy* (Philadelphia, 1946), 103-288; and Attilio Milano, *The History of the Jews of Italy* (Torino, 1963), 109-211. Finally Roberto [Robert] Bonfil, *Gli ebrei in Italia nell'epoca del Rinascimento* (Florence, 1991), an English translation by Anthony Oldcoru, *Jewish Life in the Renaissance* (Berkeley and Los Angeles, 1994). For the Germanic region the best overall narrative to be published recently is included in volume 9 of the work cited above by Salo W. Baron, while the best bibliographical list is *Germania Judaica*, vol. 1- (Tübingen, 1963- ). For Poland, see Bernard D. Weinryb, *The Jews of Poland: a Social and Economic History of the Jewish Community in Poland from 1100 to 1800* (Philadelphia, 1973). Documentary collections that are especially noteworthy for their breadth include, on Spain in general, Fritz Baer, *Die Juden im christlichen Spanien: Urkunden und Regesten*, 2 vols. (Berlin, 1929-36), reprinted with bibliographic addenda by Haim Beinart, 1970. Currently in press are the volumes of the *Hispania Judaica* edited by the Hebrew University of Jerusalem, of which the first four volumes have already appeared (1988-93). On the Kingdom of Aragon, see J. Régné, *History of the Jews in Aragon* (updated edition edited by Yom Tov Assis, Jerusalem, 1978). On Portugal, the second volume of the work cited above by M.-J. Pimenta Ferro Tavarez. On Sicily, Bartolomeo Lagumina and Giuseppe Lagumina, *Codice diplomatico dei giudei di Sicilia*, 3 vols. (Palermo, 1984-85; reprinted, 1992). On the various regions of Italy, the

*Fontes ad Res Judaicas Spectantes: a Documentary History of the Jews of Italy*, ed. Shlomo Simonsohn, of which, until now, four volumes devoted to the Duchy of Milan and three volumes to Piedmont have appeared.

On the papacy and the Jews, see Shlomo Simonsohn, *The Apostolic See and the Jews*, 8 vols. (Toronto, 1988-91). On Poland, a work worth singling out is the recently published collection in Hebrew of Shmuel Arthur Cygielman, *The Jews of Poland and Lithuania until 1648: Prolegomena and Annotated Sources* (Jerusalem, 1991); and see also Kenneth R. Stow, *Catholic and Papal Jewry Policy, 1555-1593* (New York, 1977). On trials of judaizers in Spain, see Haim Beinart, *Records of the Trials of the Spanish Inquisition in Ciudad Real*, 4 vols. (Jerusalem, 1974-85); Pier Cesare Ioly Zorattini, *Processi del Santo Uffizio di Venezia contro ebrei e giudaizzanti* (Florence, 1980-91), of which 9 volumes covering the period 1548-1632 have appeared to date.

## 2.

By now, there is an enormous bibliography on the problematic of Christian attitudes toward Jews and in particular on Christian anti-Semitism. We will limit ourselves to citing Léon Poliakov, *Histoire de l'Antisémitisme* (Paris, 1955); Heiko A. Oberman, *The Roots of Antisemitism in the Age of the Renaissance and Reformation*, trans. James Porter (Philadelphia, 1984); David Berger, *History and Hate: the Dimensions of Antisemitism* (Philadelphia and New York and Jerusalem, 1986); Gavin I. Langmuir, *Toward a Definition of Antisemitism* (Berkeley and Los Angeles, 1990) and *History, Religion and Antisemitism* (Berkeley and Los Angeles, 1990); Robert S. Wistrich, *Antisemitism: the Longest Hatred* (London, 1991). Aside from works that focus on Christian missions, which are not strictly pertinent to our topic, there are no synthetic general works on religious conversion. See Bernhard Blumenkranz, "Jüdische und Christliche Konvertiten im jüdisch-christlichen Religionsgespräch des Mittelalters," in *Miscellanea Medievalia*, vol. 4 (1986): 64-282; the introduction by Todd M. Endelman to the volume edited by him, *Jewish Apostasy in the Modern World* (New York and London, 1987). In the same volume, see the essay by Jeremy Cohen, "The Mentality of a Medieval Jewish Apostate: Peter Alfonsi, Hermann of Cologne, and Pablo Christiani," 20-47. On Jews who converted to Christianity in Spain, see the aforementioned work by Fritz Baer (note 1). For the Germanic area, Gustav Hamman, "Konversionen deutscher und ungarischer Juden in der frühen Reformationszeit," *ZBLG* 39 (1970): 207-37. For Italy, see Renata Segre, "Neophytes during the Italian Counter-Reformation: Identities and Biographies," in *Proceedings of the Sixth World Congress of Jewish Studies*, vol. 2 (Jerusalem, 1975):131-42; and more generally, the studies in *Ebrei e cristiani nell'Italia medievale e moderna: conversioni, scambi, contrasti: Atti del VI Congresso internazionale dell'Associazione italiana per lo studio del Giudaismo (Aisg), San Miniato, 4-6 November 1986* (Rome, 1988). On the anti-Jewish riots of 1391 see section (5) below.

## 3.

For the demographic history of the Jews in Europe, see the general observations by Salo W. Baron, "Reflections on Ancient and Medieval Jewish Historical Demography," in L. A. Feldman, ed., *Ancient and Medieval Jewish History: Essays* (New Brunswick, N.J., 1972), 10-22, 373-80. Also useful in this regard is Sergio Della Pergola, "Aspetti e problemi della demografia degli ebrei nell'epoca preindustriale: gli ebrei e Venezia, secoli XIV-XVIII," in *Atti del Convegno internazionale organizzato dell'Istituto di storia della società dello stato veneziano della Fondazione Giorgio Cini, Venezia 5-10 giugno 1983*, ed. Gaetano Cozzi (Milan, 1987), 201-10. A lively debate has recently sprung up concerning the number of Jews living in Spain on the eve of the expulsion. See the data concisely compiled by M. Kriegel, "Les Juifs à la fin du Moyen Age," cited above, 72-77; and Henry Kamen, "The Mediterranean and the Expulsion of the Jews in 1492," *PaP*, no. 119 (1988): 30-55. On the Jews of Sicily on the eve of the expulsion, see Attilio Milano, "La consistenza numerica degli ebrei di Sicilia al momento della loro cacciata," *Rassegna Mensile di Israel* 20 (1954): 16-24; Eliyahu Ashtor, "La fin du judaisme sicilien," *REJ* 142 (1983): 323-47.

4.

For the gradual concentration of the Jews in urban centers and for their professional stratification, see the more general works cited above. On the question of usury and the Jews, the literature is enormous. We will mention only a few titles: Benjamin Nelson, *The Idea of Usury: From Tribal Brotherhood to Universal Otherhood*, 2d ed. (Chicago, 1969); John T. Noonan, *The Scholastic Analysis of Usury* (Cambridge, Mass., 1957); Raymond De Roover, "New Interpretations of the History of Banking," *JWH* 2 (1954): 38-76 (reprinted in: Raymond de Roover, *Business, Banking and Economic Thought in Late Medieval and Early Modern Europe: Selected Studies*, ed. Julius Kirshner [Chicago, 1974]: 200-38); Siegfried Stein, "The Development of the Jewish Law of Interest from the Biblical Period to the Expulsion of the Jews from England," *Historia Judaica* 17 (1955): 3-40; id., "Interest Taken by Jews from Gentiles," *Journal of Semitic Studies* 1 (1956): 141-56; Léon Poliakov, *Les banchieri juifs et le Saint-Siège du XIIIe au XVIIe siècle* (Paris, 1965). Also useful, especially for its recent bibliography, is Giacomo Todeschini, *La ricchezza degli ebrei: merci e denaro nella riflessione ebraica e nella definizione cristiana dell'usura alla fine del Medioevo*, Biblioteca degli "Studi medievali," vol. 15 (Spoleto, 1989). On the alien and diabolical nature of the Jew, see Joshua Trachtenberg, *The Devil and the Jews* (New Haven, 1943; reprinted, Philadelphia, 1983); Freddy Raphael, "Le juif et le diable dans la civilisation de l'Occident," *Social Compass* 19 (1972): 549-66; Robert [Roberto] Bonfil, "The Devil and the Jews in the Christian Consciousness of the Middle Ages," in Shmuel Almog, ed., *Antisemitism through the Ages* (Oxford, 1988), 91-98.

5.

On the anti-Jewish riots of 1391, see Philippe Wolff, "The 1391 Pogrom in Spain—Social Crisis or Not?" *PaP*, no. 50 (1971), 4-18; Angus McKay, "Popular Movements and Pogroms in Fifteenth Century Castille," *PaP*, no. 55 (1972): 33-67; Natalie Zemon Davis, "The Rites of Violence," in *Society and Culture in Early Modern France* (Stanford, 1975), 152-87. On the expulsion from Spain, our bibliography has been extraordinarily enriched in these last few years, particularly with the 500th anniversary that took place in 1992. In addition to the chapters on the topic in the more general works cited above, we will mention only a few works: Stephen Haliczer, "The Castilian Urban Patriciate and the Jewish Expulsions of 1480-1492," *AHR* 78 (1973): 38-58; Maurice Kriegel, "La prise d'une decision: l'expulsion des Juifs d'Espagne en 1492," *Revue Historique* 260 (1978): 49-90; Haim Beinart, *"La Inquisición española y la expulsión de los Judíos de Andalucía,"* in *Andalucía y sus Judíos* (Córdoba, 1986), 51-81; Miguel Angel Motis Dolader, *La expulsión de los judíos del reino de Aragón*, 2 vols. (Zaragoza, 1990). Also see the essays collected in Haim Beinart, ed., *The Sephardi Legacy* (Jerusalem, 1992), and those in the special issue on the topic of the periodical *Judaism* (vol. 41, 1992: *The Expulsion from Spain: a Symposium*). On Fra Vincente Ferrer, see Francisca Vendrell Gallostra, "La actividad proselitista de San Vicente Ferrer durante el reino de Fernando I de Aragón," *Sefarad* XIII (1953): 87-104. On John of Capistrano, see J. Hofer, *Johannes von Capestrano. Ein Leben in Kampf um di Reform der Kirche* (Innsbruck, 1936). On the Franciscan preachers in Italy in general, see Robert Bonfil, *Jewish Life in Renaissance Italy*, cited above, 21-30. On Bernardino of Siena, see Iris Origo, *The World of San Bernardino* (London, 1963). On Bernardino da Feltre, the following should be consulted with extreme caution: Vittorino Meneghin, *Bernardino da Feltre e i monti di pietà* (Vicenza, 1974). On accusations of ritual murder in general one can usefully, but cautiously, consult: Ronnie Po-Chia Hsia, *The Myth of Ritual Murder: Jews and Magic in Reformation Germany* (New Haven and London, 1988). Very useful, even if about a period that predates the one treated here, are the essays collected by Gavin I. Langmuir in the fourth part of the aforementioned *Toward a Definition of*

*Antisemitism.* On the Trent affair, see Anna Esposito and Diego Quaglioni, *Processi contro gli ebrei di Trento (1475-1478),* vol. 1: *I process del 1475* (Padua, 1990), who cites the earlier literature.

6.

Leaving aside the antisemitic literature, for which this type of material naturally supplies a bevy of motives to foment hatred against the Jews, very little has been written on Jewish attitudes toward Christianity. A useful repertoire of pertinent liturgical sources can be found in Leopold Zunz, *Die synagogale Poesie des Mittelalters* (Frankfurt am Main, 1920. Reprint, 1927), 465-70. On the exceptional position of Menahem Ha-Meiri, see Jacob Katz, *Exclusiveness and Tolerance* (Oxford, 1961), 114-28. See also David Novak, *Jewish-Christian Dialogue: a Jewish Justification* (New York and Oxford, 1989), 26-72. On the memory of martyrs, above all the victims of the age of the Crusades, see Robert Chazan, *European Jewry and the First Crusade* (Berkeley and Los Angeles, 1987), 148-68.

7.

On the Judeo-Christian polemic there is by now a boundless literature which, however, favors certain periods predating ours. One of the most recent collection of essays on the topic is Jeremy Cohen, ed., *Essential Papers on Judaism and Christianity in Conflict: From Late Antiquity to the Reformation* (New York, 1991). We can also add: Frank Talmage, ed., *Disputation and Dialogue* (New York, 1975). On the disputation of Tortosa one could also consult with caution: Antonio Pacios López, *La disputa de Tortosa* (Madrid, 1957), 2 vols. The bibliography on the Inquisition and the *Conversos* is also especially voluminous. On the Inquisition we can cite, among the most recent summaries: Henry Kamen, *Inquisition and Society in Spain in the Sixteenth and Seventeenth Centuries* (London, 1985); Edward Peters, *Inquisition* (New York and London, 1988); Bartolomé Bennassar, *L'Inquisition espagnole* (Paris, 1979). On the *Conversos,* Cecil Roth, *A History of the Marranos* (Philadelphia, 1932); Haim Beinart, *Conversos on Trial: the Inquisition in Ciudad Real* (Jerusalem, 1981); id., "La Inquisición española y la expulsión de los Judíos de Andalucía," in *Andalucía y sus Judíos* (Córdoba, 1986), 51-81; Benzion Netanyahu, *The Marranos of Spain from the Late Twelfth to the Early Sixteenth Century According to Contemporary Hebrew Sources,* (New York, 1966); id., "On the Historical Meaning of the Hebrew Sources Related to the Marranos (A Reply to Critics)," in Josep Sola-Sole, et al., eds., *Hispania Judaica* I (1980): 79-102; I. S. Révah, "Les Marranes," *REJ* 108 (1959-60): 29-77; Antonio José Saraiva, *Inquisição e Cristãos-Novos,* 2d ed. (Lisbon, 1985); Yosef Hayim Yerushalmi, *From Spanish Court to Italian Ghetto: Isaac Cardoso—a Study on Seventeenth Century Marranism and Jewish Apologetics* (Seattle and London, 1981 [first edition 1971], 1-50; Gerard Nahon, "Les Marranes espagnols et portugais et les communautés juives issues du marranisme dans l'historiographie récente (1960-75)," *REJ* 136 (1977): 367-97.

8.

On the *servitus camerae,* see the chapters on the matter in volumes IX and XI of the work by Salo W. Baron, *A Social and Religious History of the Jews,* cited above, and the essays reprinted by Gavin I. Langmuir in part 3 of the previously cited *Toward a Definition of Antisemitism.* On the Italian *condotte,* and more generally on the problem posed for Christian authorities by the autonomy of Jewish communities, see Robert Bonfil, *Jewish Life in Renaissance Italy,* chapters 1 and 6. On the Sicilian documentation, Bartolomeo Lagumina and Giuseppe Lagumina, *Codice diplomatico dei giudei di Sicilia,* 3 vols. (Palermo, 1984-85; reprinted, 1992), passim.

9.

On self-government among Jewish communities, see Louis Finkelstein, *Jewish Self-Government in the Middle Ages* (New York, 1964); Salo W. Baron, *The Jewish Community: Its History and Structure to the American Revolution*, 3 vols. (Philadelphia, 1942). On the phenomenon of Jewish courtiers and the criticisms lodged against them on the part of Jewish society in Spain, see Haim Beinart, "Hispano Jewish Society," in H. H. Ben Sasson and Shmuel Ettinger, eds., *Jewish Society through the Ages* (New York, 1969), 220-38.

10.

On the rabbinate in general see Robert [Roberto] Bonfil, "Le savoir et le pouvoir: pour une histoire du rabbinat à l'époque pré-moderne," in Shmuel Trigano, ed., *La société juive à travers les ages* (Paris, 1992), 115-95; id., *Rabbis and Jewish Communities in Renaissance Italy* (Oxford, 1990). On the affinity between universities and rabbinical academies, see Roberto [Robert] Bonfil, "Accademie rabbiniche e presenza ebraica nelle università," in Gian Paolo Brizzi and Jacques Verger, eds., *Le università dell'Europa dal Rinascimento alle riforme religiose* (Milan, 1991), 131-51.

11.

On rabbis and the institutional frameworks of communities, see Baer, *A History of the Jews in Christian Spain*, cited above, passim; id., *The Jewish Community*, cited above, passim; Bonfil, *Rabbis and Jewish Communities*, cited above, 101-269.

12.

There is no work which provides an overview of Jewish culture for this period. Some very useful works are: Israel Zinberg, *A History of Jewish Literature*, trans./ed. Bernard Martin (New York, 1975-78). On the Arba'ah Turim of Jacob ben Asher and the Siete Partidas of Alfonso the Wise, see Ephraim Urbach, "Methods of Codification: The Tur," *American Academy for Jewish Research Jubilee Volume* (Jerusalem, 1980), Hebrew Section, 1-14. Judah Messer Leon's book on rhetoric is available in English as *The Book of Honeycomb's Flow*, ed./trans. Isaac Rabinowitz (Ithaca, N.Y., 1983). On this work, see Robert [Roberto] Bonfil, "The Book of the Honeycomb's Flow by Judah Messer Leon—the Rhetorical Dimension of Jewish Humanism in Fifteenth-Century Italy," in *The Frank Talmage Memorial Volume*, vol. 2 (=Jewish History 6, nos. 1-2 [1992]), 21-33.

13.

On the Jews in the era of mercantilism, see Jonathan I. Israel, *European Jewry in the Age of Mercantilism 1550-1750* (Oxford, 1985). On the contribution of the *Conversos* to restructuring reciprocal relations between Jews and Christians at the dawn of the modern era, see the very important recent work of Yosef Kaplan, *From Christianity to Judaism: the Story of Isaac Orobio de Castro* (Oxford, 1989). See also Brian Pullan, *The Jews of Europe and the Inquisition of Venice, 1550-1670* (Oxford, 1983); and, finally, the various essays collected in Haim Beinart, ed., *The Sephardi Legacy* (Jerusalem, 1992).

# Part 2.
## Politics, Power, and Authority:
## Assertions

# THE CHURCH IN THE FIFTEENTH CENTURY

John Van Engen
(University of Notre Dame)

## 1. The Western Schism and New Beginnings

Pope Gregory XI died unexpectedly on 27 March 1378, fourteen months after making his way from Avignon through war-torn Italy to Rome. Seven successive popes had resided in the city on the Rhone. Freed from Roman urban politics but wholly dependent for income and influence on the inventiveness of their court, they had deployed the full resources of monarchical government: they reserved for themselves appointment to all the major benefices in Christendom, extended the papacy's courts routinely into the jurisdictional affairs of bishops and abbots, reaped income from clerical appointments and legal decisions by way of an enhanced chamber, and staffed their court with some 600 people.[1] In Rome, sixteen cardinals, seven of Limousin origin, gathered in conclave. In the midst of riots and threats they elected, as a compromise candidate, the archbishop of Bari (Urban VI), a native of Angevin Naples and acting head of the chancery. Within three months discontent over his election, person, and governance swelled to the breaking point. First came talk of a council, then repudiation of his election, and finally in September a new conclave outside Rome to elect Cardinal Robert of Geneva, who became pope as Clement VII. When neither yielded, and the new pope and his cardinals failed to take Rome, Clement withdrew to Avignon, where the machinery of papal government was still in full operation. For the next thirty-seven years Latin Christendom knew two—for a time, three—"obediences," each allied with kings and princes, each enthroned with symbols of sacred authority, each claiming to hold the keys to the kingdom of heaven.

This unresolved double-election, the first significant papal schism in two hundred years, proved only the most remarkable and public in a series of unexpected turns that marked the decade between 1375 and 1385. Julian of Norwich experienced the first of her divine "showings" about 1372. Between 1374 and 1380 Catherine of Siena wrote some 400 letters prophetically exhorting and denouncing her fellow Christians, not least the male hierarchy.[2] Across Europe, independent of the schism, professed

religious broke ranks within their orders—Benedictines at Monte Oliveto
in 1378 and at Kastl in 1380, canons regular at the Lateran in 1382,
Franciscans at Foligno in 1368, Dominicans at Rome in 1380, Augustinian
friars at Rome in 1385—to set up houses they called "observant."[3]  About
1375 Geert Grote turned away from the world of clerical ambition to take
up preaching repentance, and before his death of plague in 1384 had
formed the core communities of the Brothers and Sisters of the Common
Life along with the Windesheim Congregation—the heart of the *devotio
moderna*.[4]  About that same year, 1375, Pierre d'Ailly completed a *Sentences* commentary which exercised great influence upon university faculties following the *via moderna*; as chancellor at Paris (1389), he assumed
the role of a theological master committed to the practical and political reform of Christendom—a role taken up after him by Jean Gerson, who also
wrote pastoral and devotional works in French.[5]  Such a master at Oxford,
John Wycliffe, wrote nearly all his works in Latin between 1376 and 1384,
his critical discourses on the church and Scripture in 1378, his attack on
transubstantiation in 1379; first the Lollards, teaching and writing in the
English vernacular, and then John Hus, preaching in Czech, took inspiration from his work.[6]  Already in 1378 and 1379 two other masters had
produced the earliest of numerous treatises advocating reform in the
church, Conrad of Gelnhausen his "Epistola brevis" and Henry of
Langenstein his "Consilium pacis."  Petrarch and Boccaccio died in 1374
and 1375 respectively, and the new learning they fostered reached the papal court by 1450.

## 2. THE HISTORIANS, THE CHURCH, AND THE PROBLEM OF REFORM

The historian of the late medieval church, faced with so many new beginnings in one decade, must make crucial decisions about narrative: how is a
reader to move coherently from these surprising turns in the 1370s to the
no less surprising outbreak of Reformation in 1517 or the convocation of
Trent in 1545?  How is an author to avoid setting up his story in such a
way as to make its end implicit in its beginning, thus obviating the freedom
of human beings and the conjuncture of historical circumstance, casting
the whole fifteenth century as some kind of prologue to the main event?
How, not least, is an author to improve upon several fine overviews written during the last years?[7]  Some historians have opted for the long view,
beginning well back in the Middle Ages and emphasizing all that became
characteristic and problematic in later medieval Christendom, while others

have fixed upon the sixteenth-century explosions, religious, cultural, or so-cial, and traced their fuses back to the supposed points of ignition.[8]  Either way, reading forward or backward to the fifteenth century, the result favors metaphors of decline, some, such as Huizinga's influential "autum-nal harvest," more resplendent than others.[9]  Reading the people in terms of religious psychology has suggested metaphors of extreme desire or ex-treme anxiety, people driven by a "hunger for the divine" or again as "anxious" for "liberation" from spiritual and material "burdens."[10] Reading the social forces of the fifteenth-century church as aligned mainly between two opposing groups, clergy and laity, a lettered elite and an un-lettered people, masks all the intriguing and complex inter-relations be-tween religion and society.[11]  Reading fifteenth-century life and learning, by contrast, as "renaissance"—a reading with as long and distinguished a career as that of "decline" or "harvest"—has yielded an entirely different story, at odds with or indifferent to precisely those features of interest to church historians.[12]

The "reading" of the fifteenth-century church is not only a matter of lens, of which framing questions or dispositions of mind are brought to bear upon the narrative.  It is no less fundamentally a matter of what gets read.  The historian faces here a dilemma of selection, for there are not only rich archival deposits and thousands of extant manuscripts, the envy of early medievalists, but printed books appear in ever increasing numbers after 1470.  For historians of the fifteenth-century church the most com-mon temptation is to reduce everything to "reform"—for which there is no single genre of sources.  Such an approach may rather misconstrue com-plex conflictual circumstances or blur literary intentions.  Treatises and let-ters advocating reform in the years between 1378 and 1517 have yet to be systematically catalogued.  Such treatises represented a variety of genres or sub-genres with many different occasions, purposes, audiences, and liter-ary forms, all subsumed in most historical accounts under a general cry for "reformation [reformacio]" with reform agendas for the cardinals or cu-ria, programs for observance within orders, legal or theological critique of specific ills such as simony, devout discourse on contested notions like pov-erty, and so on.  Only a complete mapping of such treatises would give shape to the landscape of ecclesiastical and religious reform (not to forget civic and legal reform) between 1378 and 1517 by specifying issues, au-thors, audiences and literary genres with reliable indications of literary dif-fusion and reception.  Better known, and more intensively surveyed, are the acts and deliberations of councils held between 1414 and 1517.[13]  Be-cause "reformation" was also at issue in those councils, historians are

tempted to homogenize calls for reform into a single, ever larger stream
emptying into the sixteenth century. In truth, as debates at the councils of
Constance and Basel made painfully clear, this term masked multiple, often opposing, interests, conceptions, and intentions, to be reconstructed in
all their particularity.

The most obvious way to particularize is to plunge into the whole range
of local archival materials: legal and economic records of given churches,
houses, or orders; records of political and legal interaction with local authorities, especially city councils or regional princes; and in the Vatican
such massive records as the Datary's *supplicationes* or the archive of the
*sacra poenitentiaria*. Careful research at this level can produce results so
peculiar to local situations or to the limits imposed by a given genre (for
example, economic or legal transactions) as to fall outside the usual grand
narrative, or to be linked up only in concluding or overarching reflections.
But this detailed work, resembling in style that of the early modern historians, remains essential for a fuller understanding of fifteenth-century
churches.

To get beyond the peculiarities of reform advocacy or the particularities
of local archives, historians have turned to conceptual sources to disclose
the "ordinary" or the "normative" in ecclesiastical and religious life. For a
generation they have searched out the works of late medieval schoolmen,
both their lectures and their finished works, reading theologians on matters of belief, canonists on matters of polity and ecclesiology.[14] With the
expansion of universities in the later fourteenth century, especially across
central Europe, the influence of schoolmen with Aristotelian habits of
mind reached into nearly every region; with growth in numbers came variety in thought, revealing "ways" or "schools" but no single late medieval
mind.

Historians have also begun to focus more attention on the wealth of devotional literature generated inside and outside the religious orders. Paradigmatic is the spread of the fifteenth-century "best-seller," *The Imitation
of Christ*, 700 manuscripts and numerous editions in less than a century,
this only the most spectacular of many possible examples.[15] Here the lines
of transmission and diffusion, given increased translation activity (*The
Imitation of Christ* appeared in Middle Dutch as early as in Latin), proved
more fluid than those set by an institutionalized university or a Latin cur-
riculum: works written for monks or friars found their way into the hands
of secular priests or learned masters or (in translation) lay men and
women. The same is true of hagiography, written for a particular cult or
house but transmitted, in Latin or in the vernacular, to a far wider audi-

ence, or indeed re-cycled, as in John Gielemans' compilations for the Low Countries or Osbern Bokenham's English translation of female hagiography, *A Legend of Holy Women.*

Works of still another sort, between the learned and the devotional, were pastoral in nature: handbooks for confession, guides to teaching the Creed, the Commandments, the Vices and Virtues,[16] prescriptions concerning the sacraments, innumerable sermons (not gathered for the later Middle Ages). Also at the level of pastoral activity are the synodal statutes that were to govern diocesan life (essentially normative in character),[17] records of pastoral visitations (more evaluative, though sometimes "executive" in nature, according to Binz), and bishops' registers (mostly in England). "Mirrors of Christians" originated earlier, but in the later fifteenth century spread widely in the vernacular, and contain the core of later catechisms.[18] Legal rather than pastoral in character are inquisition records, most from earlier generations, but a wealth of new materials appeared at the end of the fifteenth century in Spain.[19] Beyond written materials generated by and for the church are the sculpted and painted representations, so essential to the church's work, which survive in large numbers from the fifteenth century.

Since this *Handbook* contains a number of chapters on special topics related to the church—popular religion, the Jews, theologians and canonists, and ideas of reform—this chapter's task must be to present the fifteenth-century church as a whole and to emphasize tendencies which transcend any single genre of sources. The generalizations suggested here, these larger social and cultural patterns, must be tested against the evidence for particular fifteenth-century churches, communities, preachers, or thinkers. Those tendencies were, I will argue, five in number: an age-old forbearance with plural traditions, a drive towards increased participation, a tendency toward regionalization, a "vulgarization [Fr., *vulgarisation*]" or popularization of the church's work, and a self-conscious struggle to re-define the boundaries of the spiritual and the material.

### 3. A Mature Church: the Variety of Expressions and Accommodations

The most striking feature of the fifteenth-century European church was its forbearance with a complex variety of institutional and personal expressions that its sixteenth-century heirs would not allow. This came with the church's age, a longevity no modern institution can match, and with the lack of any effective instrument to compel uniformity or centralization, whatever the ideals and ambitions of reformers and prelates. By the Council of Florence in 1437-38, when the Byzantine emperor begged for union and support, European Christendom had achieved its greatest extent, pushing northeast into the Baltic lands and southwest into Iberia, but falling back in the southeast before the Muslim Turks, and with no clear vision as yet of the New World. Fifteenth-century Europe was long past its age of formation, seven or eight centuries earlier, when kings and monks had to strive to put in place basic Christian institutions with the force of arms and holiness. Yet, most of the monasteries, cathedrals, and parishes first founded 700 years earlier still existed and to varying degrees still dominated the local ecclesiastical landscape, thus, to take Benedictine examples, Boniface's church at Fulda, or St. Emmeran's in Regensburg or St. Gall. The church buildings might be updated, enlarged in the modern "gothic" or "French" style, as were forms of public worship, property-holding or library-building; but medieval churchmen took the foundations for granted, including idiosyncratic and privileged patterns of worship or property-holding or legal representation peculiar to each church or region.

Fifteenth-century Europe was, moreover, well past that formative age two or three centuries earlier, when popes, bishops, friars, and schoolmen had joined forces to spread a net of law and institutions, of preaching and teaching, across Christendom. By the opening of the Council of Constance in 1414, the mendicant houses that dominated religious life in European cities and the papal decretals that governed church affairs were nearly 200 years old. The cry in the fifteenth century was not to found mendicant houses or to gather papal decretals but to restrict mendicant privileges, to force stricter observance, to cut through the thicket of papal legislation—without fundamentally calling into question what had been put into place in the thirteenth century. For fifteenth-century Europeans the imprint of all these accumulated initiatives made itself manifest in the particularities of local practice, the ancient and privileged Benedictine house on the edge of town, the canons' quarter in the city, the parish patronized by a certain family, the friar's church, and processions to local shrines on certain days. Each element of medieval religious foundation and privilege accumulated over eight centuries, some older, some newer, continued to co-exist in the fifteenth-century church, each jostling alongside the other. To complicate the picture, the early humanists first began to peel back the layers, to expose origins and foundations. Lorenzo Valla, for example, exposed the "Donation of Constantine" wrote critically about the nature of the religious life.

Patterns persisted in the fifteenth century from each successive age of medieval Christendom: kings, princes, and founders still expected to oversee their churches, as they had since the beginning; popes, bishops, friars, and schoolmen still expected to set down the guidelines for church life, as they had since at least the twelfth century; parishioners expected to have their babies baptized at the local font, their children married at the church porch, their parents buried in the churchyard; priests expected to preside, laying claim to legal and monetary arrangements to which the people may or may not have agreed. People also pursued practices now labeled popular or folkloric, then tolerated as customary, which, though hard to verify without engaging in circular argumentation, some ascribe to the oldest layer of all, persisting pre-Christian rituals and world views.

There was of course change: churches, privileges, or practices coming into and going out of existence in ways and degrees difficult for historians to document on the grand scale, to be worked out patiently on the local level. But fifteenth-century churchmen consciously repudiated little of what they had inherited. Humanist scribes, ironically, attempting to recover the Roman hand, appropriated the Carolingian hand. In matters of ritual and ethical practice fifteenth-century Christians thought of theirs as inherited custom, the way things were suitably done in their church or locale. In social and political relations with lords, burghers, and villagers, churchmen thought of theirs as inherited privileges, a bundle of distinct rights defended by accumulating written privileges or concessions. In law and theology the educated thought in terms of the inherited authorities, always to be interpreted, rarely or never to be set aside entirely. The law that governed the church's institutional life had been collected from earlier traditions in 1140, corrected by new papal rulings gathered in 1234, updated in 1298 and 1322, and was still being read by way of thirteenth-century glosses and commentaries digested in fourteenth-century collections— available at the end of this period in print. So too churchmen read the Bible by way of the Ordinary Gloss, compiled from the Fathers in the early twelfth century, with Hugh of St. Cher's gloss of the 1220s for the more advanced, and Nicholas of Lyra's of the 1330s for the more up-to-date— these works handsomely printed in the later fifteenth century. Similarly, the prayers of the church, codified in layers stretching back to late antiquity, gained new elements with each age or order, from the elevation of the host in the later twelfth to the all-important feast of Corpus Christi in the later thirteenth, with the stations of the cross spreading from Franciscian into parish churches after 1342 and the rosary spreading from Dominican into Carthusian and lay practice in the fifteenth.

There was as yet no uniform pattern of prayer or practice imposed upon all European Christians. "Reformation," reducing all this to some desired norm or authority, meant purging inherited practices, privileges, or authorities. Few were prepared to undertake anything so contrary to their own interests and customs, so foreign to the age-old tradition of multiple accommodation. This pattern of accommodation, albeit grudging at times, partially accounts for juxtapositions in the fifteenth-century church that tend to get slighted in partisan accounts. Printed books took their place in cabinets and on shelves alongside handwritten books, laboriously copied out into the 1520s. Humanists, for all the harsh exchange of words, were accommodated alongside Aristotelian schoolmen, sometimes in the same court, household, or patronage system, eventually within the same institutions, exceptionally in the same person's thought—notably in Pico della Mirandola, their works copied from time to time in the same manuscript miscellany.[20] Observant religious rarely managed to reform existing orders or houses; they coexisted, often uneasily, as individual houses or a reforming network (eventually "congregations") within the larger whole. Reformers, so-called on the basis of a given treatise or stance, cooperated with princes, prelates, curial officials, or lawyers on other matters opponents judged corrupt. Exceptional individuals who ranged across several of these traditions or communities—a Nicholas of Cusa or Sylvius Aeneas Piccolomini (Pope Pius II)—presumed and lived in multiple ecclesiastical worlds.

## 4. The Drive for Participation: Councils and Conciliarism

Within this complex of inherited and still changing traditions and privileges, the issue for fifteenth-century Europeans was not how to found or organize the Christian church, as in ages past, but how to participate in and influence this multi-layered institution. The evidence points to a seeming paradox: people took the church for granted, its practices and structures so much a matter of inheritance and basic identity that they could wear them lightly for years at a time or treat them mockingly at set times in plays or at carnival. Yet people also increasingly sought ways to participate, means to make some part of its blessings or privileges their own, battling for their place in a ritual procession, for familial gain in a church, for sacred relics or a holy hermit in their locale. At the level of religious life this is supremely evident in the phenomenon I treat below as "vulgarization." Participation here means political engagement, broadly con-

strued—not to be misconstrued as democratic, though in urban or conciliar settings more people were striving for greater involvement.

The fifteenth-century church remained decidedly rural, and in the countryside evidence for participation is hardest to document. The English
have found it in churchwardens and their account books, concerned with
the upkeep of the church fabric and with the lay church (the nave in particular); the office may have originated in the thirteenth century, but the
books survive in numbers only from the fifteenth.[21] In central Europe historians have focused upon the right to elect—or at least to influence the
election of—local pastors, with the greatest gains in newly settled villages
or in more independent towns, especially in what became Switzerland.[22]
Urban historians, often with one eye on the Reformation, have documented the ever more active intervention of patrician authorities in the
work and life of city churches.[23]

This striving to gain influence presupposed, at times accentuated or reaffirmed, hierarchical or oligarchical forms of power. But it could also assume revolutionary proportions, a determination not to leave the church
to prelates, orders, or princes. The Brothers and Sisters of the Common
Life were accused initially of imitating religious orders, seeking to appropriate their privileges. Lollards were denounced by king, bishops, and religious orders for usurping such clerical roles as preaching and teaching and
for claiming that only those in a state of grace could manage church properties and incomes.[24] The Hussites took their church—like the chalice—literally into their own hands and defended it with arms, with their own extremists adopting ever more communal modes of life.[25] In the village of
Niklashausen (1476) and the city of Florence (1490s) a pilgrimage and a
penitential revival blended participatory and charismatic features to bring
on communal revolt.[26]

Of this drive towards participation the tone-setting event, or premiere
manifestation, was in some sense the general council. It, too, was an inherited structure, adapted in the fifteenth century for new forms of deepened
involvement in the church's deliberative and administrative work. Councils conceived as grand public forums offered the maximum opportunity
for involvement.[27] Here all parties, political, ecclesiastical, or intellectual,
could meet and bargain, enjoying that freedom of movement and expression which contemporaries associated mainly with universities and urban
communes, not with papal or royal courts. So real was this to participants
that some conciliar thinkers argued by analogy from the political process
at universities or in urban communities. Cardinal Zabarella, the key figure
in the drafting of "Haec sancta," likened the church to a corporate body or

commune in which the head executes on behalf of the body or citizens. In 1435 the Benedictine Escobar repeated these arguments and further likened the church to a *res publica* and its affairs to the *res communis* of a realm, drawing on the civil law tradition of power residing in the people and conferred by delegation or for execution upon the head.[28] At a key moment in the story of Basel, the Imperial Diet held in Frankfurt during the summer of 1442, the greatest canonist of his era, also a Benedictine, Nicholas de Tudeschi or Panormitanus, vigorously defended the continued legitimacy of the council, and ascribed to it, as representative of the whole church, what Bartolus had ascribed in civil law to a sovereign city, the power to make statutes and exercise jurisdiction—matters even some conciliarists had reserved ultimately for the papal office.[29]

The scandal of the schism had affected all Christendom, and to the south German city of Constance there came, eventually, thousands to help end it. Ulrich of Richental, betraying the taste of his age for titles and personalities, summarized the total attendance (never all at once) as 2 popes, the king, 5 patriarchs, 33 cardinals, 47 archbishops, 145 bishops, 93 suffragan bishops, 132 abbots, 155 priors, 5,000 spiritual lords, 39 dukes, 32 princes, 141 counts, 71 barons, 1,500 knights, 24 auditors and secretaries, 37 scholars, 217 doctors of theology, 361 doctors of both laws, 171 doctors of medicine, 1,500 masters, 5,300 simple priests and scholars, several apothecaries, 72 goldsmiths, 1,400 merchants, 700 prostitutes, 824 envoys—with both the mix and the proportions of social and ecclesiastical estates significant, even if the numbers are suspect. Each came with attendants, a total of 72,460 people according to Ulrich,[30] out of an estimated European population of some fifty million. These people gathered in forty-five official sessions, heard hundreds of sermons,[31] participated in countless deliberations, and exchanged freely—or in tense dispute—their notions about the state of the church and the means to effect reformations.

From Constance (1414-18) through Basel (1431-47) to the Fifth Lateran (1512-17), councils cast their shadows over the fifteenth-century church[32] until Trent (1545) and the Imperial Diet of Augsburg (1550-51) definitively repudiated—in quite different ways—an interim settlement by a council as a means to resolve religious schism. At the Council of Constance (1414-18) all the new beginnings of the previous generation first appeared on a public stage as contending forces in the church:[33] the Council Fathers ended the schism, approved the Brothers and Sisters of the Common Life, condemned Wycliffe and the Lollards, burned Hus, allowed princes to pursue their interests, secured places for university masters in the church's deliberations, facilitated contacts among humanists and observant religious, and generated pamphlets about how to resolve the inherited structural and spiritual problems. Down to the 1540's European Christians, to overstate the point, lived in the shadow of the Council, or rather of subsequent councils and their aftermaths, of political threats to convoke councils, of conciliar ideology with calls for structural and religious reform—of demands for participation, however class-, group-, or tradition-bound that proved in practice.

Pope John XXIII, who convoked the council, came at the end of October 1414 expecting confirmation as heir to the cardinals from both sides who had gathered at the Council of Pisa (1409); he fled in disguise when the council pressured him to resign, was captured and deposed by the council for some seventy crimes. From the beginning, however, it was not the pope or even the cardinals, as at Pisa five years earlier, but the German king Sigismund, properly titled the King of Rome or emperor-elect, who had maneuvered all three parties and their political backers into support of the council and then held it together when the pope attempted to scuttle it. With the pope's flight leadership went over to the university masters and cardinals. Two days after John XXIII's departure, on the eve of Palm Sunday (23 March 1415) Jean Gerson preached a dramatic sermon ("Ambulate dum lucem habetis") on the legitimacy and continuing authority of the council. The council fathers argued straight through Holy Week, and on the Friday after Easter (April 5), in their fifth general session, approved the decree "Haec sancta," which was to become the magna charta of conciliarists.[34] In its core formulations, and especially in the documents attending it, this decree aimed to preserve the council, together with its efforts for union and reform, at a time when the flight of its convoker and presider had put all at risk. In its first clause the council also claimed to be legitimately gathered in the Holy Spirit, to represent the church militant on earth, to have its power directly from Christ, and to be owed obedience in matters of faith, union, and reformation by all, even a pope if there were one.

In practice council fathers proceeded with due recognition of papal claims. In July proxies for the pope of the Roman obedience, Gregory XII, were allowed officially to convoke the council and then to resign in his name. The pope of the Avignon obedience, Benedict XIII, never conceded, despite losing his political support from the Aragonese crown, and it required two years and a lengthy trial, with ninety charges, to secure deposition, something the pope never recognized. The election of a new pope, following lengthy arguments, transpired (10-11 November 1417) through a combination of voting by cardinals (the traditional form) and by nations (the conciliar form). The new pope was elected only after approved reform decrees were promulgated, but before the really difficult work of structural reform was undertaken; that awaited a pope. Yet one month prior to the election of Martin V the fathers solemnly issued the decree "Frequens" on 9 October 1417, mandating that councils be held at established intervals (5, 7, then 10 years) and at pre-established places in given "nations," all this as a means of limiting/regulating the papal right of convocation, rooting out error, pursuing reformation, and forestalling future schisms. That is to say, ambiguity and tension between a drive for conciliar involvement and an expectation of papal leadership gripped the council fathers already at Constance, and permeated the late medieval outlook after 1414, never wholly disappearing before 1545. The constellation of political forces had much to do with the viability of councils, whatever the arguments of reformers, masters, or churchmen; the Council of Trent, it is worth recalling, was convoked only under imperial duress.

Beginning at Lyon II and including Vienne (1317) bishops had voted "in nations," meaning, it seems, approximate geographical units, or "parts of Christendom," as Ockham and the council fathers sometimes put it.[35] More importantly, university masters had long since habituated themselves to doing their work "by nations." At Constance the difficulty, made manifest immediately after the first public session, was both to achieve workable units, thereby to promote the work of union and reform, and to include all the many parties beyond bishops who took an active interest: the university masters in particular, but also the abbots, the procurators of absent bishops and princes, even simple priests. D'Ailly led the fight with a memo called "Ad obviandum."[36] The "English" and the "German" nations soon agreed; the "French," divided within, were persuaded by Sigismund; and so together in the second session they overcame the opposition of the "Italian" nation. Henceforth the presiding representative of each nation would deliver that nation's vote in public sessions, a victory, so it was proclaimed, for union. It made possible a conciliar role for the university masters, a practice which had been established at Pisa five years earlier, and secured participation, too, for abbots, procurators, and princes. The organization into "nations [nationes]," as in the universities, allowed each party to have its say, while allowing the achievement of coherent majorities in the council's public assemblies.

The decree "Frequens" was subsequently upheld only under duress, though the council that met at Basel in 1431 began by reaffirming it. As that council's deliberations dragged on through the 1430s, tensions between council fathers and the pope sharpened steadily, leading the pope to call his own council at Ferrara-Florence (1437-38), important for its agreement with the Greek church, and the fathers at Basel in 1439 to declare their own supremacy and Pope Eugene IV deposed. Basel came to represent the drive for participation in its extreme form: in its ideological claims for conciliar supremacy, in its practical allowance for the participation of many lesser churchmen in its deliberations, even its election finally of a layman (the duke of Turin) as pope.[37]

The collapse of Basel in the later 1440's and Pius II's attempt to forbid appeals from pope to council ("Execrabilis," 1460) marked one moment in the see-saw struggle over order and power in the church; it was not the end of conciliar thought or action. In the 1490's the Observant Dominican friar Savonarola appealed to the greatest princes of Europe for a council; in 1507 Michelangelo the artist called for a general council; in 1511 an anti-papal coalition led by the French king attempted to stage a council in Pisa; in 1512 the pope responded by calling his own general council (Lateran V) which churned out reform proposals for five years; in 1518 the Observant Augustinian Hermit friar Martin Luther appealed from the pope to a future general council; right down to Pope Paul's reluctant convocation of Trent.

Two generations of vigorous public debate about how Christ conferred authority upon his church, from the 1380's to the 1430's, did not suddenly come to a halt when the pope returned to Rome. On the contrary, the issue of conciliar authority became embedded in public consciousness—and that for several reasons. It rested upon deeper traditions locating ecclesiastical authority in the assembled secular clergy and recognizing the council as the ultimate authority in cases of erring popes.[38] After the 1430's the discussion settled into theological faculties and became inscribed in legal commentaries.[39] The key questions remained live: who called a council? Under what circumstances could someone other than the pope convoke a general council of the church? How did Christ confer his authority, on all the faithful, all priests, all consecrated bishops, or uniquely on his vicar in Rome? When are appeals permitted from pope to council or council to pope? What is then the exact relationship between pope and council? Papal monarchy acquired strong defenders such as Torrequemada, unlike the first conciliar period. Increasingly an assumption of papal leadership prevailed except among a few radical conciliarists. Yet the whole range of conciliar opinion remained in play to the early sixteenth century. Even papalists like Cardinal Jacobazzi favored the call in "Frequens" for regular general councils, without holding that the pope was bound by the decisions of a general council. Indeed several popes, including Julius II and Leo

X, were forced to oblige themselves to the calling of a council to secure election, though both resisted—Julius successfully—making good on their promises. Many historians have argued that secular constitutionalism in the later medieval and early modern periods derived much of its conceptual apparatus from the arguments and practice of these fifteenth-century churchmen.[40]

## 5. REGIONAL CHURCHES, NATIONAL CHURCHES: THE LOCALIZATION OF GOVERNANCE

The third general characteristic of the fifteenth-century church was its tendency toward regionalization, increased local oversight. The point, a commonplace in the historical literature, is most often made with respect to the strength of "national" churches—sometimes with remarks on the weakness of a "German" church. The papacy, weakened first by schism and then by councils, bargained away its privileges in order to gain support. A deal struck with the crown of Aragon in 1443, for instance, certainly contributed to a situation that left fifteenth-century popes with little power to intervene in Spanish affairs. But the evidence cited most often, the Pragmatic Sanction at Bourges in 1438 or an ever more independent "English church [*ecclesia anglicana*]," must not be overstated. Centralization had always been more of a dream than a reality, though under the lawyer-popes of the early thirteenth century or the fiscal and personnel regime of Avignon that dream edged closer to reality. After the schism, and partly owing to it, local lay leaders, kings, princes, or burghers, reasserted their enduring interest in oversight and intervention, less as a matter of principle than as a way of pursuing countless details of law, personnel, and income. The point was not to ignore Rome; in England bureaucratic contact increased in volume during the fifteenth century, as it probably did in German regions; nor was it to establish "national" churches.[41] The locus of interest was rather the "region," whatever the relevant unit, town, principality, or royal court, and the focus of interest was to claim or re-claim lay oversight, insofar as these regional authorities were not blocked by ecclesiastical law and lands.

This "regionalization" of the church was not inherently good or bad. In towns burgher leaders were anxious to see no more land and tax revenue alienated to the church, no more errant clergymen exempt from prosecution, just as kings had always aimed to oversee appointments to major posts. But these local lay powers were also anxious to have churchmen perform their religious duties and religious houses uphold their reputations—more so, it often seemed to townsmen or princes, than were prelates with oversight responsibilities. Princes and patrons proved more, not less, willing to support churches wherein their will for its organization and reform was heard and acted upon.[42] Great princes regularly founded new observant houses or Carthusian houses in this period when established houses functioned beyond the reach of reform or outside the scope of political intervention.

The paradoxical element in this trend toward regional churches is Rome itself. The restoration papacy of the later fifteenth century self-consciously built a capitol, with the library, the court bureaucracy, the pomp and circumstance, the architecture, and the patronage that entailed. Christians from across Europe directed their business and their prayers toward Rome, as massive records in the Vatican attest. Despite the reality of regional churches, the assumption of an overarching international order persisted, of appeals and requests carried to Rome, of bargains struck with curial officials. The paradox is that the papacy itself, as a political entity with churches under its immediate control, largely assumed the form of an Italian regional principate in the later fifteenth century, with all the attendant familial and dynastic politics, a luxurious court life sustained as well by cardinals, a desperate need for funds. Income accrued from the sale of offices and the holding of plural benefices, loans demanded of papal bankers, new rents and taxes imposed on reconquered Italian lands, and the income of alum mines. That is to say, the papacy oppressed the church, both in central Italy and at its international court, in just the ways churchmen charged regional laymen with doing.

## 6. Appropriations: the Shapes of Popular Participation

Beyond greater local participation and regional oversight, effected within the general context of multiple pre-existing and sometimes untouchable traditions and rights, the fifteenth-century church also attested to what might be called a "vulgarization" of its message. Fifteenth-century altar paintings, large and vivid, with innumerable pieces extant still in local museums and churches, represent what is meant here by the term "vulgarization." The central mysteries of the Christian faith, especially the incarnation and the crucifixion, are depicted large as life, with semi-realistic townscapes and landscapes in the background and the holy figures surrounded by a crowd of contemporary folk in all their finery. Like the life-size *sacra representazione* in Italy, this represents both a vulgarization of the sacred mysteries and a popular appropriation of them. The mysteries have become so commonplace as to be depicted taking place among contemporaries and so personally appropriated as to make such depictions desirable. This is not to say that everyone had, after eight centuries, become an enthusiastic supporter of the church. Bernardino of Siena could speak of people who never set foot in a church, and a very low level of religious practice has been shown for parts of Flanders.[43] But the church's message was achieving unparalleled degrees of inculcation at all levels, bringing with it—causally or concomitantly—inflation in everything the church represented from the spiritual to the material.

Indulgences are a good example. What was offered first in the eleventh century for extraordinary acts such as crusading, then more commonly for charitable activities such as building bridges and churches, became in the fourteenth and fifteenth centuries attached to nearly every altar or religious act, generating extensive legal discussion over kinds of indulgences and the jurisdiction of prelates. This same pattern obtained everywhere: what had been extraordinary or privileged became increasingly ordinary, with an accompanying demand for more—in the case of indulgences an explicit extension after 1476 into the realm of purgatory. Traditionally scholars have pointed to the heaping up of relics. At the more ordinary level, the stations of the cross, once the privilege of the pilgrim to Jerusalem, after 1342 the special concern of Franciscans, in the fifteenth century entered parish churches as a religious exercise, with images to make real what the pilgrim experienced in Jerusalem on Good Friday.

Intercession of the deity was central, ever more by way of the Mass. With the spread of chantry priests and chapels, bound to confraternities, guilds, and families, smaller groups or individuals within society made sure that daily intercession went on in their behalf, not just among the privileged in monasteries and convents as earlier, but in their own parishes, chapels and homes.[44] The prayers assigned to hours of the day, mentally associated with bells sounding abroad at regular intervals, made their way out of the cloister by way of books of hours, thousands produced during the fifteenth century in both serviceable and deluxe editions, in Latin and in the vernacular. Geert Grote's translation of the hours into Middle Dutch about 1380 spread far more widely than any other work associated with the Brothers and Sisters of the Common Life.[45] The saints loomed large in intercession and continued to populate the spiritual universe of the European peoples. Already in the 1260's a Genoese Dominican, Jacobus da Voragine, had rendered their stories, including modern saints such as

Elizabeth, more accessible to preachers in the compendium known as the "Golden Legend [*Legenda Aurea*]." The fourteenth and fifteenth centuries witnessed the translation of this preacher's work into the people's language, eight times into Middle High German and Middle Dutch alone.[46] While the number of officially recognized new saints declined, becoming the preserve of orders, the number of persons newly recognized locally, even in their own lifetime, increased, generating in late fifteenth-century Italy the "living saints [*sancti vivi*]" associated with various towns.[47] Not just saints' lives: for those who could read, devotional works in the vernacular became available in ever greater numbers, first in manuscript and then in print, based at times on spiritual "greats" such as Bernard and Anselm, often simple exercises linking human psychology to Jesus's passion and the divine virtues, occasionally even written to imitate the conventions and pretentions of profane literature.[48] Even the Bible, probably still associated mostly with schoolmen and priests, continued to be translated into the vernacular languages, despite the fears of churchmen and the challenge posed by Lollards and Hussites. Perhaps the most effective vehicle of all, at least within towns, was the sermon, and nearly all the great new preaching was associated with Observant religious: Vincent Ferrer, Bernardino of Siena, and John of Capistrano,[49] to mention only three crucial figures. Beyond chantries, books of hours, lives of saints, translated Bibles, vernacular devotional works, and sermons, it was probably the spread of images that most affected people, from pilgrimage medals to paintings for parish altars, from shrine statues to the "Bible of the Poor" with its typology of the Old and the New Testaments. With the invention of the sculpted image known today as the "pietà," women, and then men, set out to claim as their own the heart of Christian faith as experienced by the Mother of God.

The mix between popular demand and clerical supervision is nearly impossible to disentangle. All this certainly brought new tension between the Latinate elite and the vernacular peoples[50]—though theoretical pronouncements must be tempered by indications of actual practice. Lay people well understood that they were appropriating for themselves—hence my "vulgarization"—texts, images, and exercises that had been largely the preserve of privileged clergymen and religious. Clerics in turn understood that fiscal, juridical, and intellectual privileges were at stake but also that their own task was to inculcate Christian practice. Although critical voices, especially from Dominicans, were not wanting, these forms of Christian practice were gaining acceptance as authentic, that is, as subject to critique for excesses and abuses but not as fundamentally unsound.

They made it increasingly possible for fifteenth-century people to understand themselves as appropriating and spreading abroad the church's
ancient heritage of Christian practice and teaching.


## 7. The Body of Christ

A setting of plural and competing privileges, combined with enhanced
drives to participate in church life, to oversee the church locally, to appropriate church practices—all this raised new questions about a most sensitive point in Christian religion, the union of the flesh with the Word, the
material with the spiritual, the church militant as the mystic body of
Christ. During the high Middle Ages an incarnational vision had flourished: theology absorbed the ancient arts and philosophy, canon law provided the church of Christ with a full legal and institutional mechanism,
the mendicants represented the true Christian life as combining service
(teaching, preaching, confessing) with contemplation, and Francis, the embodiment of Christ and his suffering, became the prototypical saint. During the fourteenth century, the extremes emerged, the fiscality of the papacy on the material side, the quest for a direct experience of God on the
spiritual. Fifteenth-century Christians, in general, witnessed fewer extreme
manifestations, but they tested and attempted to realign the boundaries between the material and the spiritual, the underlying issue in much fifteenth-
century talk about reform and the true spiritual life.

The fundamental point of intersection, with the gravest consequences
for church life concerned the conception of church office: was it primarily
a spiritual charge or a material benefit?[51] Without the underpinnings of
material support, so all but the spiritual Franciscans agreed, the church's
ministrations would disappear. But how, when everyone belonged to the
church and it offered both a major form of social advancement and a ready
source of income, could the spiritual purpose be made to govern the material benefit? Nearly every fifteenth-century reformer took up this problem
in one form or another, beginning with the early reform proposals of
Dietrich of Niem, and not one finally had a workable answer. Each saw
the problem as most manifest in someone else, reforming bishops and masters in the excesses of the curia and the cardinals, popes and prelates in the
prestations of lay founders and money-starved princes, secular bishops in
the parochial incorporations and pastoral activities of the professed, secular prelates in the demands for advancement from the university masters.
Each had a good reason why appointment to church office should be reserved to them, each a claim on the incomes of a given parish.

Closely related, and equally unstudied for the most part, is the understanding of simony in the later Middle Ages, of the nexus between material payment and spiritual grace. It underlay the understanding of stole fees, which priests required to support themselves and people necessarily paid to obtain the grace of baptism, marriage, and burial. The fifteenth century also saw a new round of discussion about the fees and gifts expected, though officially forbidden, upon entry into a religious house, as evident in an unedited work ascribed to Theodore of Münster (Dietrich Kolde, also author of an influential "mirror" written in Low German). Gerson explicitly defended as not simoniac the trappings of office which prelates required to sustain the dignity of their high offices.

The central element of fifteenth-century religious life was an almost unquenchable fascination with the Passion of Christ, with its personal appropriation, material and spiritual, by whatever means possible, written or imaged. This extended to problematic forms of expression that treated Christ as materially present, from the miraculous blood of Wilsnack, disputed by Henry Toke, accepted by the pope and the people, to ever more frequent attacks upon Jews as living "killers of Christ."

Re-configuring the nexus between the spiritual and the material is one way to understand the Observant movement, one of the truly important new phenomena in the fifteenth-century church. Each order produced leaders and houses that insisted upon returning to the strict observance of the rule, which is to say, their spiritual purposes, and purging away the rest, much of it precisely material in character, separate living stipends, luxurious clothing, private rooms, and so on. Nearly every important leader, from San Bernadino to John Capistrano, Savonarola and Martin Luther, came out of an Observant formation; and the only new religious groups, the Windesheim Congregation, the Brothers and the Sisters of the Common Life, the Celestines, saw themselves as allied with the Observants. Indeed a common literature—the *Imitation of Christ*, Gerson's devotional teachings, Suso's *Horologium*—spread through these houses across Europe. Essential to it was the systematic cultivation of the spiritual, the rigorous restraining of the fleshly and the material. Under Cardinal Ximenes in Spain, with royal support, this spirit initiated the reform of a "national" church.

❊ ❊ ❊

Throughout the fifteenth century, in sum, church-related activities increased, generating more layers, not less, more lay founders and protectors, more chapels, more universities, more canon lawyers, more friar preachers, more relics and shrines, more local devotions, with the ensuing tensions or conflicts over opposing privileges and expectations spreading to more locales. The broad trends were these: complex inherited structures centuries-old, both institutional and cultural, presumed, fought over, adapted; an intensified drive to participate, to have a say in the work and privileges of the church, to appropriate church traditions for one's self, family, parish, or city; a consequent assertion of or struggle for control and responsibility at regional levels by king, burghers, patron, or parishioners; an accompanying "vulgarisation" or popular appropriation of the medieval religious inheritance at ever deeper levels with ever more local and vernacular adaptations; and an impulse to re-explore the age-old nexus between the spiritual and the material, the spirit and the flesh, indigenous to a religion that held at once to a Creator God and an Incarnate Lord, a church triumphant and a church militant, a natural law and a revealed word.

After about 1540 things changed decisively, as participation gave way to central authority, and "vulgarization" and regional forms to more uniform programs of reform. Once both humanists and reformers insisted upon a return to paradigmatic sources, once all parties in all churches agreed to some greater or lesser purge of past practices, once all churches (and governments) set as their goal a "reformed" uniformity, once firmer central control became the accepted means: thereafter the world of the fifteenth-century church was doomed, violently overthrown by the most radical of humanist and protestant reformers, forced into new and tighter patterns by more traditional reformers.

# NOTES

1. On the court at Avignon, basic is Bernard Guillemain, *La cour pontificale d'Avignon, 1309-76: Étude d'une société* (Paris, 1962); and now *Aux origines de l'état moderne: Le fonctionnement administratif de la papauté d'Avignon* (Rome, 1990).
2. Suzanne Noffke, trans., *The Letters of St. Catherine of Siena*, vol. 1 (Binghamton, 1988), with bibliography and introduction.
3. Elm (1989), 3-19; and Kaspar Elm, "Verfall und Erneuerung des Ordenswesens im Spätmittelalter: Forschungen und Forschungsaufgaben," in *Untersuchungen zu Kloster und Stift* (Göttingen, 1980), 189-238. Among individual studies, see Katherine Walsh, "The Observance: Sources for a History of the Observant Reform Movement in the Order of Augustinian Friars in the Fourteenth and Fifteenth Centuries," *Rivista di storia della chiesa in Italia* 31 (1977): 40-67.
4. Essential access to the sources is provided by Wilhelm Kohl, Ernest Persoons, and Anton G. Weiler, ed., *Monasticon Windeshemense*, 3 vols. (Brussels 1977-80); Wolfgang Leesch, Ernest Persoons, and Anton G. Weiler, *Monasticon fratrum vitae communis*, 2 vols. (Brussels, 1977-79). For interpretation, see Post (1968), Van Engen (1988), and idem, "A Brabantine Perspective on the Origins of the Modern Devotion: The First Book of Petrus Impens's *Compendium decursus temporum monasterii christifere Bethleemetice puerpere*," in *Serta Devota in memoriam Guillelmi Lourdaux* (Louvain, 1992), 3-78.
5. Francis W. Oakley, *The Political Thought of Pierre d'Ailly: the Voluntarist Tradition* (New Haven, 1964); Catherine Brown, *Pastor and Laity in the Theology of Jean Gerson* (Cambridge, 1987); and Christoph Burger, *Aedificatio, Fructus, Utilitas: Johannes Gerson als Professor der Theologie und Kanzler der Universität Paris* (Tübingen, 1986).
6. Hudson (1988); Kaminisky (1967); Smahel (1985); and Paul de Vooght, *L'Hérésie de Jean Huss*, 2d ed. (Louvain, 1975).
7. The best are Oakley (1979); Duggan (1978); Bossy (1985); and Cameron (1991). Significant for their scope and bibliographies are Delaruelle, Labande, and Ourliac (1962-64); Fink and Iserloh, in Jedin and Dolan (1970); Rapp (1980); and Moeller (1966).
8. The long view is best represented by Oakley (1979). The first attempt to trace the "fuses" of sixteenth-century explosions was C. H. Ullmann's *Reformers before the Reformation* (Edinburgh 1855). It is essentially the method of Moeller (1965) and Ozment (1980)—a textbook example, with the medieval materials serving mainly propaedeutic functions. The best modern re-thinking of this method is furnished by Oberman (1981a) and (1981b).
9. Huizinga (1924). Hay (1977) and Swanson (1989) have resisted the allure of either the "decline" or the "autumnal" metaphors.
10. The "hunger for the divine" is the starting point of Oakley (1979), "anxiety" and "liberation" of Ozment (1975) and (1980)—both ultimately indebted to Bernd Moeller. For a critique of this position, see Duggan (1978) and (1984).

11. This is the position defended by Hans-Jürgen Goertz, "'What a tangeled and tenuous mess the clergy is!' Clerical Anticlericalism in the Reformation Period," in Dykema and Oberman (1993), 499-520.

12. For new beginnings here, see Timothy Verdon, *Christianity and the Renaissance* (Syracuse, 1990); and John D'Amico, *Renaissance Humanism and Papal Rome: Humanists and Churchmen on the Eve of the Reformation* (Baltimore, 1983).

13. The fundamental collections of material are Finke (1896-1928); Haller (1896-1936). See Meuthen (1985), and A. P. J. Meijknecht, "Le concile de Bâle: aperçu général sur les sources," *Revue d'histoire écclésiastique* 65 (1970), 465-73.

14. The methods respectively of Oberman (1981a) and (1983), and of Tierney (1955) and (1972) and Nörr (1964).

15. See, for example, Berndt Hamm, *Frömmigkeitstheologie am Anfang des 16. Jahrhunderts: Studien zu Johannes von Paltz und seinem Umkreis* (Tübingen, 1982). For possible connections between devotional movements and the spread of printed books, see Richard Rouse, "Backgrounds to Print: Aspects of the Manuscript Book in Northern Europe of the Fifteenth Century," now in Mary A. and Richard H. Rouse, *Authentic Witnesses: Approaches to Medieval Texts and Manuscripts* (Notre Dame, 1991), 449-66.

16. See Morton Bloomfield, et. al., *Incipits of Latin Works on the Virtues and Vices, 1100-1500 A.D.* (Cambridge, Mass., 1979). See also Tentler (1977); Binz (1973).

17. See, for example, Richard Trexler, *Synodal Law in Florence and Fiesole, 1306-1518* (Vatican City, 1971).

18. One exemplary study for the Dutch-speaking lands is Petronella Bange, *Spiegels der christenen: Zelfreflectie en ideaalbild in laat-middeleeuwse moralistisch-didactische traktaten* (Nijmegen, 1986).

19. For the relative scarcity of fifteenth-century inquisitorial sources, see, for instance, Dietrich Kurze, ed., *Quellen zur Ketzergeschichte Brandenburgs und Pommerns* (Berlin, 1975). Spanish materials are mostly taken up in sixteenth-century accounts.

20. In this same vein, the argument of Kaspar Elm, "Die Franzikanerobservanz als Bildungsreform," in Boockmann, Moeller, and Stackmann (1989), 201-13; and John O'Malley, *Praise and Blame in Renaissance Rome: Rhetoric, Doctrine, and Reform in the Sacred Orators of the Papal Court, c. 1450-1521* (Durham, 1979).

21. Charles Drew, *Early Parochial Organization in England: The Origins of the Office of Churchwarden*, St. Anthony's Hall Publications, vol. 7 (Oxford, 1954).

22. Dietrich Kurze, *Pfarrerwahlen im Mittelalter: Ein Beitrag zur Geshichte der Gemeinde and des Niederkirchenwesens* (Cologne, 1966); Peter Blickle, "Antiklerikalismus um den Vierwaldstättersee 1300-1500: Von der Kritik der Macht der Kirche," in Dykema and Oberman (1993), 115-32.

23. Rolf Kiessling, *Bürgerliche Gesellschaft und Kirche in Augsburg im Spätmittelalter: Ein Beitrag zur Strukturanalyse der oberdeutschen Reichsstadt* (Augsburg, 1971).

24. John Van Engen, "Anticlericalism among the Lollards," in Dykema and Oberman (1993), 53-63.

25. Frantisek Smahel, *Jan Hus und die Hussiten in europäischen Aspekten* (Trier, 1987); Smahel (1985); Kaminsky (1967).

26. Klaus Arnold, *Niklashausen 1476* (Baden-Baden, 1980); Donald Weinstein, *Savonarola and Florence: Prophecy and Patriotism in the Renaissance* (Princeton, 1970).
27. Jürgen Miethke, "Die Konzilien als Forum der öffentlichen Meinung im 15. Jahrhundert," *Deutsches Archiv für Erforschung des Mittelalters* 37 (1981), 736-73.
28. Black (1979), 86-89.
29. Black (1979), 96-103; Nörr (1964).
30. Loomis (1961), 189-90.
31. Paul Arendt, *Die Predigten des Konstanzer Konzils* (Freiburg, 1933).
32. This point is made by Bäumer (1971) and Jedin (1957).
33. There is extensive bibliography to 1977 in Bäumer (1977) and to 1988 in *TRE*, vol. 19:534-35; and a narrative account now in Brandmüller (1991).
34. Debates over interpretation reviewed by Brandmüller (1991), 239-61, with references to earlier literature.
35. Heinrich Finke, "Die Nation in den spätmittelalterlichen allgemeinen Konzilien," *HJ* 57 (1937), 323-38; Lewry (1989); Brandmüller (1991), 198-210.
36. Joannes Domenicus Mansi, ed., *Sacrorum conciliorum nova et amplissima collectio*, 50 vols. (Florence, 1759-98; reprint, Paris, 1901-62), vol. 27:560ff.
37. Bibliographical guides in *TRE*, vol. 5:288-89, and Meuthen (1985).
38. These points are made respectively by Constantin Fasolt, *Council and Hierarchy: the Political Thought of William Durant the Younger* (Cambridge, 1991); and Tierny (1972).
39. For the Basel period, see Black (1979); for the period into the sixteenth century, see Bäumer (1971); for the enormous literature on "conciliarism," see Heribert Smolinsky in *TRE*, vol. 19:579-86.
40. Brian Tierney, *Religion, Law, and the Growth of Constitutional Thought, 1150-1650* (Cambridge, 1982).
41. See Swanson (1989), for England.
42. Schulze (1991).
43. Toussaert (1963).
44. Basic still is K. L. Wood-Leigh, *Perpetual Chantries in England* (Cambridge, 1965).
45. Roger S. Wieck, *Time Sanctified: the Book of Hours in Medieval Art and Life* (New York, 1988); H. L. M. Defoer, *The Golden Age of Dutch Manuscript Painting* (New York, 1990); and the forthcoming work of James Marrow.
46. Werner Williams-Krapp, *Die deutschen und niederländischen Legendare des Mittelalters* (Tübingen, 1986).
47. André Vauchez, *La sainteté en Occident aux derniers siècles du moyen âge, d'après les procès de canonisation et les documents hagiographiques* (Rome, 1981); Gabriella Zarri, *Le sante vive: profezie di corte e devozione femminile tra '400 e '500* (Turin, 1990).
48. See, for instance, P.S. Joliffe, *A Check-List of Middle English Prose Writings of Spiritual Guidance* (Toronto, 1974); or for the Dutch, Frits Pieter van Oostrom, *Court and Culture: Dutch Literature, 1350-1450* (Berkeley and Los Angeles, 1992), 172-218, treating Dirk of Delft's *Tafel vanden kersten ghelove*.
49. For a general appreciation (with bibliography), see Kaspar Elm, "Die Bedeutung Johannes Kapistrans und der Franziskanerobservanz für die Kirche des 15. Jahrhunderts," in: *Atti del Convegno storico internazionale Capestrano* (L'Aquila, 1989), 373-90.

50. Essential are Klaus Schreiner, "Laienbildung als Herausforderung für Kirche und Gesellschaft," *ZHF* 11 (1984), 257-354; and idem, "Laienfrömmigkeit: Frömmigkeit von Eliten oder Frömmigkeit des Volkes?" in *Laienfrömmigkeit im späten Mittelalter*, ed. Klaus Schreiner (Munich, 1992), 1-78.
51. Oakley (1979); Delaruelle (1964).

# BIBLIOGRAPHY

Bäumer, Remigius. *Nachwirkungen des konziliaren Gedankens in der Theologie und Kanonistik des frühen 16. Jahrhunderts.* Reformationsgeschichtliche Studien und Texte, 100. Münster, 1971.

Bäumer, Remigius, ed. *Das Konstanzer Konzil.* WdF, vol. 415. Darmstadt, 1977.

Binz, Louis. *Vie religieuse et réforme ecclésiastique dans Genéve pendant le grand schisme et la crise conciliare (1378-1450).* Geneva, 1973.

Black, Anthony. *Council and Commune; the Conciliar Movement and the Fifteenth-Century Heritage.* London, 1979.

Boockmann, Hartmut, Bernd Moeller, and Karl Stackmann, eds. *Lebenslehren und Weltentwürfe im Übergang vom Mittelalter zur Neuzeit: Politik—Bildung—Naturkunde—Theologie.* Abhandlungen der Akademie der Wissenschaften in Göttingen, philologisch-historische Klasse, 3d series, vol. 179. Göttingen, 1989.

Borthwick, R. N. *Universities, Academics and the Great Schism.* Cambridge Studies in Medieval Life and Thought, 3d series, vol. 12. London, 1979.

Bossy, John. *Christianity in the West 1400-1700.* Oxford, 1985.

Brandmüller, Walter. *Das Konzil von Konstanz 1414-1418.* Vol. 1. Paderborn, 1991.

Cameron, Euan. *The European Reformation.* Oxford, 1991.

Crowder, C. M. D. *Unity, Heresy and Reform, 1378-1460: the Conciliar Response to the Great Schism.* New York, 1978.

Delaruelle, E., E.-R. Labande, and Paul Ourliac. *L'Église au temps du Grand Schisme et de la crise conciliare (1378-1449).* Histoire de l'Église depuis les origines jusqu'à nos jours, vol. 14. Tournai, 1964.

Duffy, Eamon. *The Stripping of the Altars: Traditional Religion in England, 1400-1580.* New Haven, 1992.

Duggan, Lawrence G. "Fear and Confession on the Eve of the Reformation." *ARG* 75 (1984): 153-75.

Duggan, Lawrence G. "The Unresponsiveness of the Late Medieval Church." *SCJ* 9 (1978): 3-26.

Dykema, Peter A., and Heiko A. Oberman, eds. *Anticlericalism in Late Medieval & Early Modern Europe.* SMRT, vol. 51. Leiden, 1993.

Elm, Kaspar, ed. *Reformbemühungen und Observanzbestrebungen im Spätmittelalterlichen Ordenswesen.* Berliner Historische Studien, vol. 14. Berlin, 1989.

Fasolt, Constantin. *Council and Hierarchy: the Political Thought of William Durant the Younger.* Cambridge, 1991.

Finke, Heinrich, ed. *Acta concilii constanciensis.* 4 vols. Münster, 1896-1928.

Haller, Johannes, ed. *Concilium Basiliense.* 8 vols. Basel, 1896-1936. Reprint. New York, 1971.

Hay, Denys. *The Church in Italy in the Fifteenth Century.* Cambridge, 1977.

Hudson, Anne. *The Premature Reformation: Wycliffite Texts and Lollard History.* Oxford, 1988.

Huizinga, Johan. *The Waning of the Middle Ages.* Trans. F. Hopman. London, 1924.

Jedin, Hubert. *A History of the Council of Trent.* Vol. 1. Trans. Ernest Graf, O.S.B. St. Louis, 1957.

Jedin, Hubert, and John Dolan, eds. *Handbook of Church History.* Vol. 4, *From the High Middle Ages to the Eve of the Reformation.* New York, 1970.

Kaminsky, Howard. *A History of the Hussite Revolution.* Berkeley and Los Angeles, 1967.

Lewry, Osmund. "Corporate Life in the University of Paris, 1249-1418, and the Ending of Schism." *Journal of Ecclesiastical History* 40 (1989) 511-23.

Loomis, Louise Ropes. *The Council of Constance: the Unification of the Church.* New York, 1961.

Meuthen, Erich. *Das Basler Konzil als Forschungsproblem der europäischen Geschichte.* Rheinisch-Westfälische Akademie der Wissenschaften, Vorträge, G 274. Kleve, 1985.

Moeller, Bernd. "Frömmigkeit in Deutschland um 1500," *ARG* 56 (1965): 3-31. English: *Pre-Reformation Germany*, ed./trans. Gerald Strauss, 13-42. London, 1972.

Moeller, Bernd. *Spätmittelalter.* Die Kirche in ihrer Geschichte: Ein Handbuch. Göttingen, 1966.

Nörr, Knut. *Kirche und Konzil bei Nicholaus de Tudeschis (Panormitanus).* Forschungen zur kirchlichen Rechtsgeschichte und zum Kirchenrecht, vol. 4. Cologne, 1964.

Oakley, Francis W. *The Western Church in the Later Middle Ages.* Ithaca, 1979.

Oberman, Heiko A. *Forerunners of the Reformation: the Shape of Late Medieval Thought.* Philadelphia, 1981a [1966].

Oberman, Heiko A. *The Harvest of Medieval Theology: Gabriel Biel and Late Medieval Nominalism.* Durham, 1983 [1963].

Oberman, Heiko A. *Masters of the Reformation: the Emergence of a New Intellectual Climate in Europe.* Trans. Dennis F. Martin. Cambridge, 1981b.

O'Malley, John W., S.J. *Giles of Viterbo on Church and Reform: a Study in Renaissance Thought.* SMRT, vol. 5. Leiden, 1968.

Ozment, Steven. *The Age of Reform 1250-1550: an Intellectual and Religious History of Late Medieval and Reformation Europe.* New Haven, 1980.

Ozment, Steven. *The Reformation in the Cities: the Appeal of Protestantism to Sixteenth-Century Germany and Switzerland.* New Haven, 1975.

Post, R. R. *The Modern Devotion: Confrontation with Reformation and Humanism.* SMRT, vol. 3. Leiden, 1968.

Rapp, Francis. *L'église et la vie religieuse en occident à la fin du moyen âge.* Nouvelle Clio, vol. 25. 2d ed. Paris, 1980 [1971].

Rubin, Miri. *Corpus Christi: the Eucharist in Late Medieval Culture.* Cambridge, 1991.

Schulze, Manfred. *Fürsten und Reformation: Geistliche Reformpolitik weltlicher Fürsten vor der Reformation.* Spätmittelalter und Reformation, new series, vol. 2. Tübingen, 1991.

Smahel, Frantisek. *La révolution hussite: une anomalie historique.* Paris, 1985.

Stieber, Joachim W. *Pope Eugenius IV, the Council of Basel, and the Secular and Ecclesiastical Authorities in the Empire.* Leiden, 1978.

Swanson, R. N. *Church and Society in Late Medieval England.* Oxford, 1989.

Tanner, Norman P. *The Church in Late Medieval Norwich, 1370-1532.* Studies and Texts, vol. 66. Toronto, 1984.

Taylor, Larissa. *Soldiers of Christ: Preaching in Late Medieval and Reformation France.* New York and Oxford, 1992.

Tentler, Thomas. *Sin and Confession on the Eve of Reformation.* Princeton, 1977.

Thomson, John A. F. *Politics and Princes 1417-1517: Politics and Polity in the Late Medieval Church.* London, 1980.

Tierney, Brian. *Foundations of the Conciliar Theory.* Cambridge, 1955.

Tierney, Brian *Origins of Papal Infallibility: 1150-1350.* Leiden, 1972.

Toussaert, Jacques. *Le sentiment religieux en Flandre à la fin du Moyen Age.* Paris, 1963.

Trinkaus, Charles, and Heiko A. Oberman, eds. *The Pursuit of Holiness in Late Medieval and Renaissance Religion.* SMRT, vol. 10. Leiden, 1974

Van Engen, John. *Devotio Moderna: Basic Writings.* New York, 1988.

# THE ITALIAN STATES IN THE "LONG SIXTEENTH CENTURY"

John A. Marino
(University of California, San Diego)

On March 24, 1455, the Florentine-born Tommaso Parentucelli, Pope Nicholas V, summoned the whole college of cardinals to his deathbed to witness his oral testament. Recorded in the third of three books on the *Life of Nicholas V* by his humanist secretary, long-time friend, and fellow Florentine, Giannozzo Manetti, this rhetorically embellished, yet accurately transcribed oration self-consciously reflected upon the dying pope's spiritual and temporal legacy.[1] In this last will and testament, Nicholas chronicled his intentions, accomplishments, disappointments, and hopes for the Church, the papacy, secular states, and the city of Rome. Nicholas' speech from the grave emphasized his reforming policies on war and peace, both international politics and public order, on state finances and public administration, and on learning, architecture, and culture in order to urge his successors to complete his spiritual and building programs and his plans for a Turkish crusade. In Manetti's *vita*, Nicholas became the ideal humanist cleric and his eight-year pontificate the model for the union of classical antiquity with Christian culture.[2] Such humanist biography, artfully recapitulated in the pope's dying words, distilled in style and substance the themes that would come to define the transformations experienced in Italy during the two-century period of growth and decline that began in the mid fifteenth century. Nicholas' manifesto in theory, and his reign in fact can also stand today as an exhortation to create a truly comparative history that integrates Italian politics, society, and culture into the broad outline of European history over the next two centuries.

## 1. ITALY AND THE "LONG SIXTEENTH CENTURY"

That "long sixteenth century" in Italy, delimited roughly from 1450 to 1650, draws its parameters from economic history. An upward trend beginning in the mid-fifteenth century charted the slow recovery from the population loss and economic downturn of the fourteenth-century crisis, the 1348 plague and its aftermath. The upward conjuncture lasted until

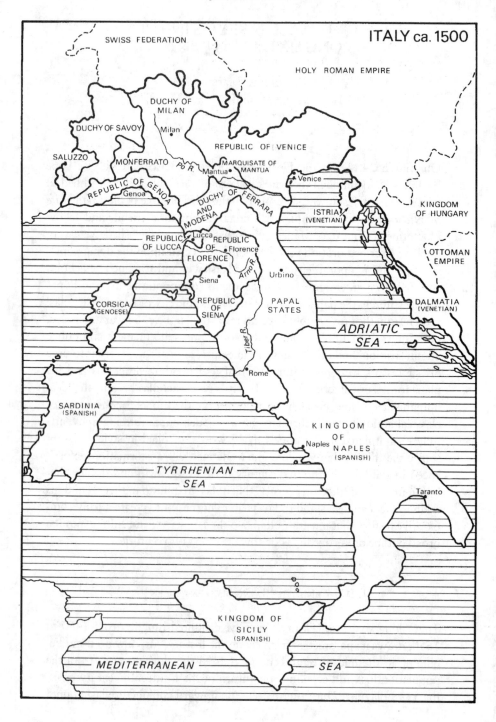

ITALY ca. 1500

SWISS FEDERATION

HOLY ROMAN EMPIRE

DUCHY OF MILAN

DUCHY OF SAVOY

Milan

SALUZZO

REPUBLIC OF VENICE

MONFERRATO

MARQUISATE OF MANTUA

Po R.

Mantua

DUCHY OF FERRARA AND MODENA

REPUBLIC OF GENOA

Genoa

Venice

ISTRIA (VENETIAN)

KINGDOM OF HUNGARY

REPUBLIC OF LUCCA

Lucca

REPUBLIC OF FLORENCE

Florence

Arno R.

Urbino

OTTOMAN EMPIRE

CORSICA (GENOESE)

Siena

REPUBLIC OF SIENA

PAPAL STATES

DALMATIA (VENETIAN)

Tiber R.

ADRIATIC SEA

SARDINIA (SPANISH)

Rome

KINGDOM OF NAPLES (SPANISH)

Naples

TYRRHENIAN SEA

Taranto

KINGDOM OF SICILY (SPANISH)

MEDITERRANEAN                    SEA

the crisis of the second decade of the seventeenth century, when, especially after 1619-22, a downward economic trend that continued into the 1680s reordered political economic relationships within the Italian states and among the European powers.[3] Such a periodization challenges the reigning paradigms about the relationship of politics and culture in Renaissance Italy, but it does not rest on demographic and economic evidence alone.

Historians of culture—political philosophers, literary critics, art historians, musicologists, and historians of religion—have long proposed a "second" or "late Renaissance" based upon their questioning of inherited categories.[4] Nineteenth century attempts at periodization had dated the end of the Italian Renaissance to the late 1520s, when military and political events brought the disruptions of the French invasions begun in 1494 to a close. But such periodization had devalued the High Renaissance as a doomed postscript and denigrated subsequent developments as decadent. Amputating the sixteenth and seventeenth centuries from Italy's preceding tradition had distorted the internal coherence and sense of continuity shared by political theorists from Machiavelli to Botero, by writers from Ariosto to Marino, or artists from Michelangelo to Bernini.[5]

### A New Historiography

The trajectory of Italian history, without doubt, has wider sweep than the nostalgia for lost liberty in Florence or the ignominy of the Spanish domination after 1530.[6] Similarly, schemes of periodization that dismiss "mannerist," Tridentine, or "baroque" Italy as uniformly negative after the last session of the Council of Trent in 1563 or after the 1633 trial of Galileo do not adequately capture the unifying themes and internal dynamism of early modern Italian history.[7] French romanticism, Victorian estheticism, German idealism, or Risorgimento nationalism no longer need impose their ideological preconceptions on the Italian past by constructing a seductive modernity of individualism, secularism, republicanism, realism, and capitalism.[8]

Instead, an evolving new historiography takes its starting point from the study of historical contingencies, especially from the innumerable local histories that combine the economic, political, social, and cultural realms to create the history of the peninsula. This approach, incompletely realized though it may be, has several advantages. It recovers the hard won victories of the philological method championed in that very period by Renaissance humanism's commitment to contextualize events. It can help us achieve a multicultural perspective that eschews the ethnocentric imperialism of Italian Renaissance studies, which sees in Renaissance Italy both the beginning of the modern age in politics, economics, learning, and the arts and the inspiration for personal credos of freedom and creativity.[9] Finally, this approach avoids the ambiguous hermeneutics of modernity. The mantle of modernism—whether draped on Renaissance Italy, Reformation Europe, seventeenth-century science, early modern crises and revolts, the rise of the bourgeoisie, capitalism and industrialization, or whatever design may become fashionable—covers a chimera conjured up by anachronistic readings of history. Such modernist self-fashioning and self-fascination manipulates the polyvalent distinctiveness of past events and the multi-causal processes of change.[10]

Structural analyses of Italy in terms of neat binary conflicts support such modernist theses. North versus South contrasts the heirs of the Italic Kingdoms with those of the Byzantine dependents. East versus West highlights Venetian and Genoese rivalries and their eastern and western Mediterranean contacts. City versus countryside pits an international economic profile against a feudal and agrarian one, as well as a dominant political center against a dominated periphery. And even if the older medieval allegiances to pro-papal Guelph and pro-imperial Ghibelline parties had lost their meaning by the fifteenth century, ecclesiastical jurisdiction continued to contest civil power as much as spiritual imperatives vied with temporal concerns. Tri-partite divisions push conceptualizations toward greater complexity and emphasize the range of variation up and down the peninsula. North, Central, and South divisions play upon distinctions between republics, the elected papal monarchy, and kingdoms as well as between industrial communes, bureaucratic consumers, and raw material exporters. French *géographie humaine* introduced landscape distinctions between plains, hills, and mountains, which Braudel coupled to history with a temporal analysis that divides change into long-term structures, medium-term conjunctures, and short-term, ephemeral events.[11] Not unlike the fanciful quest for the "Great American Novel," however, most writing on early modern Italy seeks to form a genuine synthesis that both accounts for regional diversity and shifts in cultural styles, on the one hand, and maintains the integrity of particular traditions and variant movements, on the other. This program remains largely unfulfilled and unfulfillable.[12]

The *memento mori* of Nicholas V, thus, cautions us against the facile interpretations of the propaganda of modernity at the same time as it initiates us into the more complex interaction among the Italian states and the rest of the world. Only a truly comparative perspective within and without the Italian peninsula will allow us to understand the problems surrounding Italy's part in the end of the schism and the coming reform, in the development of the modern state, in the growth of capitalist production and markets, in the increasing differentiation of society between elites and commoners, rich and poor, male and female, adults and minors and among livelihood groups within the city and the countryside, or in the changing cultural and intellectual currents that served, rationalized, and critiqued that world. The age of Nicholas V provides a vantage point to construct and deconstruct traditional arguments about the Italian Renaissance's self-styled modernity in terms of actual practices of Italian politics and culture.

## 2. THE AGE OF NICHOLAS V

Judgments on the preceding and succeeding periods necessarily structure the terms by which evaluations of Nicholas' reign are reached. Analyses of the causes and effects of the schism, of the transition from corporate (guild) dominated polities to elite mercantile oligarchies, of the increase in civic consciousness, of the socio-economic transformation of the countryside, and of the growth of regional states each suggest different ways of contextualizing Nicholas' achievements.[13]  Nicholas' conception of his own papal role as priest, builder, and governor allowed him to reassert the papacy's independent power and to jockey for position in the game of political fortune at home and abroad.[14]  Similarly, an understanding of the consequences of Nicholas' policies moderates the enthusiasm of the historians who continue to eulogize Nicholas in a humanist tradition. They tend to privilege Ludwig von Pastor's assessment of Nicholas' election as "mark[ing] one of the chief turning points in the History of the Papacy, for with him the Christian Renaissance ascended the Pontifical Throne."[15] The fact that the selling of indulgences to build the new St. Peter's sparked Luther's "Ninety-five Theses" in 1517 should remind us that humanism did not address the serious business of Church reform. Not until Protestantism had challenged the very nature of the Church would problematic issues be faced up to at the Council of Trent (1545-63).

### The New Rome
Instead of needed theological, sacramental, and institutional reform, Nicholas' program of renovation concentrated on the city of Rome, "to prefigure the Church Triumphant and to make Rome a heavenly city, the New Jerusalem of cosmic importance."[16]  And the new Rome that eventually emerged brought to fruition the first conscious Renaissance urban

plan, epitomized by the reorientation of the Campidoglio from looking down on the ruins of the ancient Roman forum to looking back over the densely inhabited quarters filling the Tiber-bend on to the pope's new residence in the Vatican. Manetti's *vita* sketched the plan: Rome's walls and station churches were repaired and restored, the Leonine *borgo* was to be reconstructed, the Vatican was to receive a new papal palace with a splendid library, and the basilica of St. Peter to be rebuilt. Nicholas employed the Renaissance architectural theory of Leon Battista Alberti to express his dominant theological principles on the sacramental vitality of the Church.[17] Rome's papal builder and governor, thus, made his guiding sacramental doctrine of the pope as chief-priest visible in urban space and stone.

This proposed urban renewal translated ideas into form and action, a cultural practice closely related to the age's so-called realism. But no new "realism"—whether defined in painting's use of linear perspective or identified with Machiavelli's later political insights—empowered Renaissance Italians to see things as they "really" were. Rather, a new aesthetic reordered their perceptions to depict and describe nature and politics according to new conventions. In art, two dimensional surfaces were geometrically manipulated to appear to be three dimensional, while ideal shapes, colors, and volumes subordinated their appearance in order to anchor pictorial details onto an invisible ideal grid. "Realistic" political analysis, for its part, resulted from the application of the practical concerns of policy-making in legal, administrative, military, and financial affairs to the wars, rebellions, and diplomatic conflicts of the fifteenth century.[18] In other words, the ongoing high culture debate between *fortuna* and *virtù* was not some abstract philosophical conundrum, but articulated the predicament of daily life to a practical calculus for determining individual action—what one could and could not do to achieve one's ends.[19] Machiavelli's oft-repeated injunction to princes to beat form onto matter literally reflected the common visual esthetic of putting theory into practice, just as the dictum of Baldessare Castiglione on *sprezzatura* (nonchalance) for the courtier applied to a way of seeing as well as being: "that art is true art which does not seem to be art."[20]

### Economic Stagnation and Renaissance Culture

The paradoxical inversion between seeming and being takes its most concrete form in the debate on the relationship between economy and culture in Renaissance Italy. Economic historians of the fifteenth century have disproved the thesis that hard times fostered investment in culture. But the so-called "economic depression" of the Renaissance did lead to a wide-spread economic reorganization that   accompanied the economic turn-around by mid century.[21]  Whether bricks and construction in Florence, Venetian salt imported from Cyprus and Ibiza into the Po Valley, or wool and silk production throughout the peninsula, hum-drum commodities and luxury goods led the recovery.[22]  Italy's favorable balance of payments, which resulted from its strong commercial and financial networks and its vibrant agricultural and industrial sectors, undoubtedly raised per-capita wealth and further fueled its luxury markets.  Commercial success was based upon profits gleaned from the price differentials in long-distance trade with the Near East and inland to France and Germany, from new manufactures (such as silk) and reexport, and from imperial conquest and investment.  Venice spread its dominion directly to the Italian mainland, the Dalmatian coast and Corfu on to Crete, Cyprus, and Constantinople; whereas the Genoese employed financial partnerships with the Portuguese for gold, sugar, and slaves in North Africa, the Atlantic islands, and along the West African coast on the way to bankrolling Portugal's and Spain's empires.  Nicholas V inserted the papacy into such imperial rivalries with the promulgation of four papal bulls between 1452 and 1454 that rationalized the Portuguese king's expanding African enterprise, which would reach the Cape Verde Islands by 1455, as part of a renewed crusading offensive against infidels.[23]

### The Italian Balance-of-Power

Nicholas' reign coincided with changes in political affairs as well as shifts in economic activity.  In Southern Italy, Alfonso V of Aragon, the Magnanimous, who ruled in Naples from 1442 to 1458, had defeated the Angevin successors of Giovanna II and reunited the Kingdom of Naples with Sicily in 1442.  In 1450, Francesco Sforza emerged victorious in the civil war in the duchy of Milan after the death of Filippo Maria Visconti. At the same time, the Italian states continued to enjoy a competitive advantage over their European rivals who extricated themselves from the Hundred Years' War only to become mired in civil wars.  England's War of the Roses, the French monarchy's efforts to extend the royal domain and especially the Burgundian wars under Louis XI, and Castile's and Catalonia's civil wars in the 1460s which culminated in the disputed succession (1475-79) of Henry IV of Castile, effectively kept foreign monarchs busy at home.  The greatest menace to Italy came from the East, for the Ottoman Turks conquered Constantinople in 1453 and Mehmed II the Conqueror began to threaten Italy directly.  Consequently, the five leading Italian states (Venice, Milan, Florence, the Papacy, and Naples) forged the Italian League after the Peace of Lodi in 1454 as a defensive alliance primarily against the Turks, but also against France and the Empire, to keep Italy free from foreign invasion, while the papacy consolidated its political dominance over its territorial state.[24]

This first international alliance system, an uneasy balance of power that gave rise to a new diplomatic structure with resident ambassadors, mediation of disputes, and a rough-and-ready political stability through the second half of the fifteenth century, contributed to the growing political "realism".[25] Six wars, nevertheless, fractured the forty-year peace in Italy while wars in Burgundy, ending in 1477, and between Venice and the Turks (1463-79) dragged on. The Ottomans invaded the Friuli in 1469 and the 1470s, and took advantage of the Venetian losses to capture and hold the Apulian town of Otranto for thirteen months (1480-81). *Condottieri*, the leaders of "contracted" or mercenary armies, such as Sigismondo Malatesta of Rimini, Bartolomeo Colleoni, who was captain-general of Venice from 1455-76, and Federico da Montefeltro of Urbino, were a permanent fixture in war diplomacy, further complicating the calculus of alliances with private armies and personal ambitions. Despite the simplification of Italy's political map after Lodi and the concentration of power in more centralized diplomatic services, fiscal offices, and professional bureaucracies, the core of politics remained violence and warfare.[26]

Two cases dramatize the contradictions between the Peace of Lodi's stated aims and political realism. The Pazzi Conspiracy of 1478 had the internecine character of a Florentine family rivalry between the Pazzi and the Medici, but its international dimensions were more sinister. Pope Sixtus IV had earlier substituted the Pazzi for the Medici as his bankers because Lorenzo de' Medici, "first citizen" of Florence (1469-92), had opposed the ambitions of the pope's nephew, Girolamo Riario, in the Papal States.[27] And if Sixtus played an indeterminate role in the failed assassination plot that only succeeded in killing Lorenzo's brother Giuliano, his involvement became unambiguous after he placed a papal interdict on Florence. A similar example of cynicism, duplicity, and deceit is the case of the Turkish pretender, Prince Jem. He was captured by the Knights of St. John at Rhodes during the war of succession following Mehmed's death, passed to France where he was held in captivity for seven years, and then turned over to the pope and maintained at the papal court from 1489 to 1495 as the nominal focus of crusading fervor. All the time that crusading fever was fanned, however, the sultan Bayezid II paid the grandmaster of the Knights of Rhodes and the pope indemnities to ensure that his half-brother Jem never left Italian soil.[28]    The new diplomatic order made Rome's papal court once again the center of international political intrigue.

The Florentine intervention in Rome at mid-century in the person of Nicholas V, his humanist cohort under Manetti, his patronage of Alberti's architectural theory, and his financial backing from Cosimo de' Medici ("first citizen" 1434-64), who served as the pope's banker, has often been described as clear evidence of the dissemination of Florentine Renaissance culture.  The Italian peninsula, however, already had a well established system open to circulation of products and ideas.  The easy flow of goods such as Abruzzesi wool and papal alum to Florence or Asian pepper and Black Sea grain to the Venetian market, as well as the exchange of personnel and advisers—Lorenzo Valla who went from a papal antagonist to a papal employee, Manetti himself from Florence to Rome and eventually to Naples, or later Leonardo da Vinci from Florence to Milan and beyond Italy to France—were symptomatic of a shared culture, both material and intellectual.  As symbolic as the election of a humanist pope or the creation of the Vatican Library may appear, their reception depended heavily on the diffusion of similar kinds of institutions and information in the pre-existing system.  The Library of San Marco (1444) and the Biblioteca Malatestiana (1447-52) had established the precedent for princely libraries, while the new learning flourished in a world where a shared Roman law defined the rules, Latin-speaking universities trained the professional elite, and both the beliefs and organization of a shared religion fostered universalism at the same time that it tempted rivalries over its power and property.[29]

### The New Learning: Humanism

The new learning, the *studia humanitatis*, itself became a program for the ruling class throughout Italy.  The case for Florentine origins of humanism remains strong, though not unchallengeable, and early humanism reflects a cultural milieu sympathetic to republican virtues in an urban, lay-oriented cosmopolitan world.[30]  As propagandists for that elite world, the Florentine humanists themselves pursued honored social position, which required honest wealth, service in public life, family tradition, and marriage connections with others in the elite.[31]  But Florence did not remain a unique venue for humanist careers or humanist programs, and once disseminated, new ideas need not have filtered through a Tuscan "monopoly" or been orchestrated by a Tuscan diaspora.

The diversity of humanist ideological emphases reflected the particular political system favored by the patron elites in the various Italian states. Venetian humanists comprising Margaret King's ninety-two-member core group from 1400-90 championed the ideal of unanimity, a mythic harmony born of aristocratic order and patrician rule in the island republic; Milanese humanists in the Visconti and Sforza courts, such as Antonio Loschi and the cousins Cicco and Giovanni Simonetta provided political apologies for princely regimes intent on military success and territorial legitimization; Neapolitan humanists in the Aragonese court, such as Antonio Beccadelli, known as Panormita, and Giovanni Pontano adapted their political reasoning to accommodate the feudal and agrarian kingdom ruled by conquering foreign monarchs; and Roman humanists such as Adriano Castellesi and Paolo Cortesi framed their arguments in the context of a clerical-curial society.[32] Whether in Florence, Venice, Milan, Naples, or Rome, humanists' employment as secretaries, diplomats, and advisors fostered a convergence of interests in language and history, political action and ethical conduct that reinforced the impression of an outsider like Erasmus that the Italians, despite their political fragmentation, formed a coherent group distinctive for their literature and civility.[33]

As the fifteenth-century humanists' writings are read and reread, however, new insights suggest that a far greater complexity should be assigned to their originality and independence of thought, albeit within limits tolerated by their patronage. Lorenzo Valla's *On the Falsely Credited Donation of Constantine* (1440), written under Alfonso of Aragon's patronage to disprove the temporal claims of the papacy in Italy, and in particular, the pope's feudal overlordship of the Kingdom of Naples, may appear to have closed the debate on the pope's temporal powers. Yet, Valla's own inaugural lecture at the University of Rome, when in papal service in 1455, held up the pope and curia as the unifying institutions linking Christianity, the Latin language and the ancient Roman *imperium*, as he sought to reestablish papal claims to secular leadership on a more scholarly foundation.[34] Similarly, Francesco Filelfo, another contentious personality often maligned for his opportunism and self-promotion, turns out to have been criticizing his patron, Francesco Sforza, rather than praising him in his first four books of the *Sforziad* (1453-54). Not only a critical eye on Renaissance carnage in war, but also a satiric tongue on the futile hope and painful betrayal inherent to the patronage system characterized Filelfo's works, which reflected the commitments of one who had internalized Plato's injunctions to philosopher-kings and their counselors.[35] And even the seemingly well-worn verities on the social function and meaning of Florence's Platonic Academy, founded by Cosimo in 1462 or 1463, must be reexamined in light of the fact that the central ideas of Marsiglio Ficino and the philosophical insights of Cristoforo Landino were already well developed in the 1450s and that such speculative philosophical studies found their matrix not in the reclusive villas of the so-called *pax medicea*, but during the collapse of the Medici party.[36] What emerges, then, is a much more politically engaged, if still classically inspired caste of philosophic literati whose observations and imperatives could transcend petty principalities and address the larger concerns of human values and cosmopolitan culture.

Humanist propaganda, including the self-promoting rewriting of history, has so captured the imagination of later scholars that categories and contemporary disputes of that era have often been distorted in favor of triumphal assertions about philological method and humanist learning. It should not be forgotten that the Catalan pope Calixtus III, a jurist by training, followed Nicholas V on the Papal throne and that legal learning and legalistic mentalities acted as a counter-weight to the inevitable victory of humanist rhetoric. The jurists provided an unbroken link with medieval traditions and forged an evolving body of norms and practices in a shared, organic language that provided the rational underpinning for institutions and power across the Italian states.[37] And even more deeply imbedded in the shared practices and mentalities of everyday life across Italy, one finds that elementary education in the liberal arts structured language and learning with moral imperatives and injunctions that inculcated and reinforced a normative code of common values.[38] Similarly, communication through and perception of gestures, conventional language/behavior, ceremonies, and rituals formed another level of regional and even peninsula-wide rules that structured personality formation and action both individual and collective.[39]

### Patronage and Politics

It is simply not accurate to postulate a Florentine or a humanist monopoly on power and culture. Rather, Nicholas' Florentine papacy exemplified micro-politics throughout the Italian states, namely, patron-client networks of reciprocal favors.[40] The papacy, the highest prize in ecclesiastical service, far from being captured by a particular prince, continued to be sought by noble families and contested by rival states as it had during the struggle to reestablish papal primacy after absenteeism and schism.[41] The politicking for votes knew no bounds and invaded even the privacy of the cardinals' privies, as the humanist Enea Silvio Piccolomini and future Pope Pius II noted in his description of the maneuverings that preceded his own election.[42] Relatives and supporters who backed a candidate's nomination inevitably received papal favors that could, as in the case of the Medici papal banking monopoly or the emergence of the power of the cardinal nephew (an unofficial position that made a pope's kinsman his unrivaled chief lieutenant), be sustained past the pontificate of their sponsor, incorporated as a cornerstone of their own power, and form the power base for contention in future disputes. Not by chance, the dynastic manipulations of papal families successfully promoted one of their members in eight of the thirteen papal elections in the century before Trent, with two Borgia, two Piccolomini, two della Rovere, and two Medici popes chosen. The extreme ambitions of Alexander VI and his son Cesare Borgia appear less aberrant in such a context.

Similar family politics determined the course of elitist consolidation of power as despotic rule reinforced itself around the Italian states in the fifteenth century. The Este of Ferrara and the Gonzaga of Mantua were among the few to survive the crisis of the Italian wars that eventually toppled the Bentivoglio of Bologna, the Malatesta of Rimini, the della Rovere of Urbino, as well as the Sforza in Milan and the Aragonese in Naples. At the same time, local politics continually moved to engage wider contacts and higher levels of power, such as the expansion of Venice on the *Terraferma*, the consolidation of the papal states, Milanese designs on Genoa, the growth of a territorial state in Tuscany, or in the incursions into Italy by the Angevin and Aragonese claimants to Naples.

## 3. The Age of Machiavelli and Guicciardini

The history of Italy in the "long sixteenth century," then, is a history of transition and transformation, as the precocious Italian towns of the medieval urban revolution, which had numbered twenty-two communes over 20,000 inhabitants by 1300, attempted to recover from the devastating losses of the century-long downturn. Feuding factions within the Italian polities and fighting among the states themselves gave way to a brief four decades of relative peace and prosperity after the Peace of Lodi. But as new territorial states with new centralized monarchies brought invading armies and foreign rule into Italy and new trade networks brought products direct to northwest Europe from Asia and America, the Italian states could no longer settle their disputes in isolation. The Italian states moved from independence to dependence, and the "industrial quadrilateral" of Venice, Milan, Genoa, and Florence moved from the core of a burgeoning world-economy to an area that has been called the semi-periphery.[43] Venetian power waned; the Genoese came to finance imperial Spain; Counter-Reformation Milan prided itself as a model reformed diocese; Medicean Florence entered its "forgotten centuries"; Spanish Naples swelled into Western Europe's largest city; and papal Rome emerged as Italy's cultural capital.

### The Shape of Italy

Such a list of the peninsula's leading cities raises the question once again of how to tell the history of Italy. Without the existence of a national political entity, the problem of the object of study, where to center one's inquiry, has perplexed historians from the time of the Renaissance itself. Humanist historiography began to grapple with the question of a unified "national" history and the periodization of a Christian "Middle Ages" with the influential *Decades* (1430s-50s) and other works of Flavio Biondo.[44] Although unsatisfactory as attempts to solve the problem of a unified Italian history, such histories helped firmly establish two long-standing historical tropes earlier championed by Petrarch and Leonardo Bruni—the decline and fall of Rome, and the Christian Middle Ages as an intermediary period between ancient Rome and the new beginning of modern times.

Petrarch's literary and sentimental Italy also stands behind the hard-boiled political analysis of Niccolò Machiavelli. The much debated Chapter 26 of *The Prince* (1513)—"Exhortation to Take Hold of Italy and Restore her to Liberty from the Barbarians"— concludes with a rousing nationalistic appeal taken from Petrarch's patriotic poem, *Italia mia* (1344-45):

> Ingenuity [*virtù*] will take up arms against rage;
> and the battle will be short
> For the ancient valor
> in Italian hearts is not yet dead.[45]

Petrarch's words, *virtù contro a furore*, are used to reiterate Machiavelli's passionate commitment to overthrow the immediate bondage of foreign invaders who had occupied Italy since 1494 and they are often cited as evidence for national rather than simply geographical consciousness. But just when Chapter 26 appears to provide the interpretive key to unlock the unity of *The Prince*, national pride gives way to personal action. The polysemous reading of Petrarch's poetic line,

Ingenuity/Virtue/Strength/Power/Action/Reason/Maleness
against
Rage/Fury/Anger/Love/Fate/Madness/Femaleness,

cautions us that the problem of war and peace involves all of the peninsula's states, and that the restoration of order through good arms and laws
can only be achieved by the action of a strong prince.

For Machiavelli, religion or religious spirit lies at the foundation of a
powerful polity.[46] He argues, however, that Christianity by its nature re-
jects worldly honor and material things in favor of humility and forbearance. Consequently, as a result of the Christian ethic, men in Machiavelli's
day were less bold or fierce than their ancient Roman forefathers. Moreover, Machiavelli condemns the corruption of the Roman Curia for causing
Italian ruin in two ways: bad example had made all the people irreligious
and political intrigue had kept the Italian states divided. Thus, both philosophical and historical examples make Machiavelli's case that the religion
of his times was the root cause of political disunion and moral weakness.
The papacy and curia, rather than drawing men closer to God, pushed
them farther apart from both God and each other.

Francesco Guicciardini, whose political acumen long served papal command, concurred in Machiavelli's judgments on the state of Roman religion in his unpublished *Ricordi*.[47] But for Guicciardini, generalizations
and classical allusions were less convincing proof than the rational analysis
of the minute details of the case at hand, the problem of Italian misfortune
after the 1494 invasions. Bringing his legal training to bear on the question
of the origins of the Italian wars, Guicciardini in his *History of Italy*
wished to disentangle the threads of responsibility from the chaos of the
calamities.[48] The vexed legal morass of Pisan indemnities and reparations,
for example, lies behind the long excursus on Florentine attempts to dominate its Arno neighbor.

Despite Guicciardini's famous opening description of a prosperous,
propitious and fortunate state of affairs in Italy with special credit due to
Lorenzo the Magnificent and the effects of renewing the Peace of Lodi in
1480 for another twenty-five years, the invocation of the Medici prince
and praise of his sagacity was only a nostalgic reverie. For Guicciardini in
Book I, the complications surrounding the death of Innocent VIII in 1492
provided the spark that set off the conflagration. Franceschetto Cibo, the
pope's illegitimate son, soon thereafter sold Anguillara, Cerveteri, and a
few other small castles near Rome to Virginio Orsini, a kinsman of Piero
de' Medici allied to Ferdinand of Naples. Ludovico Maria Sforza, called

"il Moro," concluded that Milan had been effectively isolated and, there-fore, had to seek aid from the French across the Alps. From such small in-cidents, Guicciardini's thesis on the caprice of princes gains its strength. What was at stake here, property, prestige, and power, were the preroga-tives of princely rule. Thus, for Guicciardini, the causes responsible for the so-called end of Italian history with the French invasions in 1494 began with native Italian rivalries over the papacy, with the papacy's own success in consolidating its secular holdings in its own territories and inserting it-self as a great temporal power in international affairs, and with the expul-sion of rivals as exiles out of their respective homelands. The incursion of foreign invaders newly revived as New Monarchies, then, was due as much to their own recovery from the war and economic setbacks of the long fourteenth-century crisis as to their being manipulated by dissident Italian exiles eager to turn the tables on their enemies.

### The Italian Wars: Habsburg vs. Valois

Two battles, their causes and consequences, must suffice to demonstrate Guicciardini's method and meaning. The Venetian defeat at Agnadello (14 August 1509) by the League of Cambrai (1508) depended on the per-suasive diplomatic hand of Julius II, who as the exiled Cardinal of San Pietro in Vincoli in 1494 had been similarly instrumental in fanning the ini-tial delusions of conquest of the young French king, Charles VIII. The re-percussions of the defeat at Agnadello of Italy's strongest power by the combined forces of all the great powers on both sides of the Alps was not only the turning point in Venetian history, but changed the course of Ital-ian political development.[49] Similarly, the battle of Pavia (23-24 February 1525) was not a critical event for its innovations in military technology (with the introduction of the musket and the solidification of tactics for more than a century) or for its aftermath in the Sack of Rome (with the ideological disillusion and physical dissolution of papal leadership).[50] Rather, for Guicciardini, Pavia provided the dramatic setting for the famous debate over the fate of Francis I upon his capture. Thus, Guicciardini's History of Italy, despite cavils that it concerned the history of the wars and not Italy, was indeed the first true history of Italy because its essential subject was not war, but the nature of politics—fortuna and virtù, chance and decision-making.

The capture of Francis I at Pavia in 1525, the Sack of Rome in 1527, the dispersal of the vicomte de Lautrec's French expeditionary force by plague in the Kingdom of Naples and the Genoese shifting of allegiance from France to Spain in 1528, the Treaties of Barcelona and of Cambrai in

1529, and the final loss of Florentine liberty in 1530 with the restoration of the Medici by Charles V who earlier that year had been crowned emperor in Bologna by the Medici pope, Clement VII—these events brought the Italian Wars to a preliminary close. Under Charles V, Spain had successfully dislodged Francis I from his Lombard victories, and control of Italy was no longer at issue in the Habsburg-Valois rivalry. The Piedmontese humanist Mercurino de Gattinara, Charles' chancellor from 1518 to 1530, saw in these events a providential design for Charles to be a new Charlemagne by forging a universal monarchy over his sprawling empires.[51] French opposition continued, both in Italy and elsewhere, until the treaty of Cateau Cambrésis (1559); Turkish power in the Mediterranean and North Africa flourished under Sultan Süleyman I; and Protestant resistance in Germany prevented the realization of Charles' greatest ambitions. By the accession of Philip II in 1556, Italy nonetheless assumed an integral place in the Spanish imperial system, under the newly formed Council of Italy in Madrid.

Naples (1503) and Milan (1535) were the two great prizes won by Spain in the Italian Wars and together anchored the Spanish hegemony in Italy. The rest of the Italian states—whether ruled by Genoese bankers, Medici dukes, Roman cardinals, or Savoy's military leaders—depended upon Spanish military power in the peninsula, save only Venice, which retained its independence in a delicate balancing act between the Spanish and Ottoman Empires. And this political stability remained in force in Italy until the War of the Mantuan Succession (or the Second War of Monferrat, 1627-31), with the long siege of Casale and the sack of Mantua (1630). That war resulted in a French victory, ruptured the peace, brought warfare back to Lombardy, sent Neapolitan taxes north for the defense of Milan, and only concluded the long sixteenth century with French ascendance over Spain in the Peace of the Pyrenees (1659).

## 4. ABSOLUTIST RULE IN THE LATER SIXTEENTH CENTURY

In the second half of the sixteenth century, greater rationalization and centralization of political administration and fiscal policy coupled with increased economic activity to create larger regional states. But this decisive restructuring of society and economy made the Italian states more hierarchical at home and less competitive in international markets. That new constellation of political stability established in the 1530s provides a convenient opportunity to review internal developments within the Italian states and to reconsider the history of Italy from those diverse regional perspectives.

### Absolutist Rule in Italy

Post-World War II Italian historiography attempted to use the problem of a national political history as a means to rethink the twentieth century's fanaticism for "nation" and "fatherland" so heavily implicated in the two decades of Fascist rule.[52]  Federico Chabod proposed three criteria to evaluate the distinctive style of absolutist power—armies, diplomacy, and state bureaucracies—and provided an example of such study in his research on Milanese administration under Charles V.[53]  Above all, a Weberian concentration on administrative centralization and rationality focused research on the growth of bureaucracy, institutions, the emerging nobility of the robe, and the relationship between monarchical/princely power and the hierarchy of councils and officials.

But scholars soon realized that such a conceptualization was not sufficiently responsive to the multiplicity of tensions pulling and pushing the new "absolutist" regimes.[54]  Administrative centralization was in fact enmeshed in constant conflict with resistant local entities.  This dynamic interaction between rulers and feudal aristocracy, cities and countryside, patricians and clerics, fiscal systems and economic entrepreneurs gave specificity to local variations and socio-political forces as it opened up an important new area of research into local power and the rapport between center and peripheries in the growth of the territorial state.[55]  Because no New Monarchy such as was established in England, France, or Spain imposed its unifying prerogatives on the Italian states, any integrated history of Italy must by necessity take into account "local knowledge" à la Geertz, "multinational" comparisons among the Italian states à la Galasso, and the wider Mediterranean context championed by Braudel.[56]  In other words, a true history of Italy must both incorporate the disparate interpretations assigned to contingent developments in the various states and avoid an antiquarian localization of problems into regional specificities without real synthesis.

Milan has been at the center of such historiographical debates because Lombardy's political trajectory—the continuity between Visconti and Sforza despotism in the fifteenth century and Spanish centralization in the sixteenth—provides a laboratory to test hypotheses on state formation and social change.  The Sforza seizure of power in the mid fifteenth century typified a century-long trend throughout Lombardy that saw the loss of municipal "liberty" as a result of a narrowing of power into the hands of a closed oligarchy and the formation of larger territorial states.[57] With the urban patriciate transforming itself into a territorial bureaucracy that wielded ever greater power from the center, the exploitive rationale of the territorial state allied itself with the feudal nobility. Economic historians have reinforced this model of "decadence" with evidence from the seventeenth-century crisis by pointing to the manufacturing losses in the cities and the collapse of agricultural production with concomitant aristocratization of the urban elites and reassertion of feudal pressures in the countryside.

Such descriptive generalizations are, however, somewhat superficial, since the real strength of the Milanese economy has been masked by scholarly concentration on the short term effects of the crisis.[58] From the late sixteenth century, Milanese government and fiscal policies underwent substantial reform that provided a restructured base for future economic strength. The reforms in the Milanese Senate that by 1584 reorganized its membership from twenty-eight feudal lords and clerics to fifteen professional lawyers directly undermined the old feudal nobility in favor of Spanish centralization. Fiscal reforms that equalized tax burdens on rural landowners after 1564 and taxed merchants after 1594 created the foundation for seventeenth and eighteenth-century economic expansion in the countryside.[59] This new investment in putting-out industries and agricultural innovation linked urban capital and rural production in a dynamic partnership that pointed to the long-term vitality of the Lombard economy and its divergence from the other Italian states thereafter.

### The South: Naples and the Islands

With recent exploitation of the archives of the Crown of Aragon in Barcelona, historians of the Kingdom of Naples have made invaluable strides in revising received wisdom about Alfonso's conquest, administration, and his Catalan empire.[60] As important as Naples was as an active international entrepôt and home of a vibrant cultural life, attempts to make Alfonso's regime a model of rationalization gives too much weight to the propagandistic intent of contemporary sources. What Aragonese Naples became for the subsequent Spanish viceroyalty, which was really founded by Pedro de Toledo (viceroy, 1532-53), was a referent to measure the regime's legitimacy and its subjects' loyalty.[61]

Despite the fact that monographic research into the history of Spanish Naples has been criticized for its fetishism for archival novelties in the quest to demonstrate variant interpretative models—a historiographical practice hardly unique to Naples—there has been a clear focus on three main problems: government organization and juridical controls, fiscal pressures and economic development, and noble cooptation and feudal involution.[62] A politics of compromise between monarchical and feudal authority, between the monarchy and the capital, between fiscal demands and economic resources, and among fisc, church, and state characterized Neapolitan political centralization.[63] The burgeoning population growth of the city of Naples by 1560 and the increase in fiscal pressures combined with low grain yields and famine after 1585 to precipitate the urban unrest that erupted in the insurrection of 1585 and established the preconditions for the revolt of 1647.[64] A sterile argument on the definition of terms—refeudalization or no—has not obscured the general consensus that this was a society imploding from imbalances between social orders and economic classes that favored urban and privileged elites at the expense of an ever-indebted countryside.

In Sicily and Sardinia, Spanish policy continued to support feudal monarchist regimes. The Sicilian viceroyalty remained an important export granary and, like Naples, a bulwark in Spanish Mediterranean defenses against the Turks. Spanish policy of divide and rule played off internal rivalries and regional interests against one another.[65] Neither Sardinia nor Sicily could resist the introduction of the Inquisition, as Naples did twice, but on both islands the independent jurisdiction of the Inquisition could also challenge viceregal power and further fracture the already divided feudal nobility.[66] Sardinia, alone among Spain's Italian possessions, remained under the jurisdiction of the Kingdom of Aragon and did not feel the brunt of Spanish fiscal demands until the Thirty Years' War (1618-48) and Olivares' Union of Arms exacerbated the already deteriorating economic climate of the 1620s.[67]

### Two Republics: Genoa and Florence

The old republics of Genoa and Florence were not directly under Spanish rule, but their sixteenth-century territorial states were directly dependent upon Spanish power. Genoa's unstable political history in the late medieval period reflected factious regimes divided between estates (nobles and *popolo*), classes (mercantile and artisanal), and among noble families (*alberghi* or clan/neighborhood associations), that gave way under strong rulers supported by Spanish arms. By the mid fifteenth century, the Genoese, caught between Levantine colonial losses from the advancing Ottoman Turks and the conflicts among the Genoese nobility, encouraged foreign intervention first from the French to avoid Aragonese domination in 1458, and then from Francesco Sforza's Milan in 1464 to escape the

French. Revolt against the Milanese in 1478 created an independent republic for ten years until Genoa fell once again under Milanese domination
from 1488-99. With the French conquest of Milan in 1499, Genoa returned to French control, until a 1505 insurrection by the artisanal class
created a popular republic that lasted only two years before French
reconquest. Thus, in the French-Spanish rivalry for Italy, Genoa became
an important prize, brutally sacked by Spanish-papal troops in 1522 and
fought over internally between its pro-French and pro-Imperial factions.
With ascendance of the Doria clan under Andrea Doria, the Genoese
switched sides from France to Spain in 1528, which gave Charles V a decisive naval advantage, and political compromise established a Doria hegemony to bring an end to the incessant feuding.[68] Civil war and institutional reform in 1575-76 further refined the reconstituted ruling class into
one, based on recognition that closing ranks among those with status and
wealth (with wealth slowly replacing status as the basis of social stratification and political alliance) would ensure their dominance over the non-noble, artisanal class.

Throughout this period, the economic intervention of the Bank of St.
George, founded in 1407 as Europe's first public bank, further complicated the game of alliances by acting as a supra-communal entity or alternative government.[69] If the period of Doria domination linked the
Genoese fleet inextricably with Spain from 1528, the Spanish Empire depended even more upon a century of Genoese financial expertise after the
Genoese bankers stepped in 1557 to refinance Philip II after his first
"bankruptcy." From Seville and the Atlantic to the war in Flanders, a
symbiotic relationship linked Genoese and Spanish fortunes. The Ligurian
republic reigned as the financial capital of Europe between the decline of
Antwerp and the rise of Amsterdam until the Spanish "bankruptcy" of
1627.

A similar chaotic political history could be constructed for Florence before the Spanish sponsored duchy of Cosimo I de' Medici (r. 1537-74).
The rise and fall of the Medici in the fifteenth century, the short-lived republic supported by Girolamo Savonarola, the 1498-1512 republic dominated by Piero Soderini through the Medici restoration of the 1510s and
1520s to the Last Republic of 1527-30 and the 1537 assassination of
Alessandro de' Medici gave way to the absolutist control of both city and
Tuscan countryside in Cosimo I's territorial state.[70] Rationalized bureaucracies helped stabilize the regime that benefitted from the economic recovery of the second half of the sixteenth century and whose forgotten centuries have only recently begun to be studied seriously.[71]

Florentine history, by reason of its artistic, literary, and political riches, has long attracted vibrant foreign scholarship. Two strands of recent research, one social-economic and the other cultural, have had strong influence inside and outside Florentine studies. Quantitative studies are less in vogue now, but David Herlihy and Christiane Klapisch-Zuber's computer-aided analysis of the Florentine *catasto* of 1427 reveals all that this rich documentation can tell us about demography—with much on taxation, economic activity, family and social structure—and offers the descriptive statistics for a base-line comparison of Tuscany in the city and country, both in earlier and later periods.[72] Similarly, Richard Trexler's controversial and challenging reconstruction of Florentine public life continues to stimulate anthropologically oriented inquiry into the relationship between public and private life.[73] Family history and women's history, especially, have been enriched from converging directions.[74] No other field of Renaissance Italian history in English offers the range of contentiousness and suggestiveness. But only when placed in the context of the histories of the other Italian states—research conducted by and large by Italians—can Florentine studies begin to transcend provincialism and provoke productive reflection on commonalities and differences, rather than sterile commonplaces.[75] And not only the historiographies of the six major states briefly reviewed here, but also those of the minor states of Piedmont and of the Po Valley (Mantua, Ferrara, and Bologna) must be integrated into the larger picture for what they tell us about courts, just as the minor Tuscan states (Siena, Lucca, and Pisa) supply comparative information about republics.[76]

### Late Renaissance Rome

Evidence from Nicholas V's reign and arguments from Machiavelli's ideas about solidarity and religion have already made a case for the papacy's claims as theoretical catalyst and practical crucible for the modern state. Paolo Prodi's study of the papal monarchy in early modern Europe (an elected, celibate monarchy of uncertain succession with spiritual and temporal prerogatives) has recently yielded a convincing formulation of this thesis.[77] Papal humanist rhetoric and the growth of papal bureaucracy make even greater sense in this context of state-building.[78]

Because of the cultural florescence of Renaissance Rome, research in art, literature, music, and religion has often superseded historiographical understanding of how the city worked.[79] Detailed investigation into the internal politics of the city has revealed the complex interrelationship among papal court, cardinal courts, noble families, foreign embassies, and the Ro-

man people, both elite and commoners.[80] Contests for power within the
city between overlapping jurisdictions that demonstrate the tension between cooperation and coercion at all levels of interaction—social, institutional, economic, and cultural—underline the problematic relationship between ruler and ruled in municipal government throughout the early
modern Italian states.

### The Republic of Venice

Venice, alone with Rome, could maintain claims of leadership in the long
sixteenth century. Venice's myth of peace and serenity, freedom and toleration, stability, justice, and good government masked its hierarchical
elitism at home and its imperial claims over the mainland and its overseas
empire.[81] Despite the erosion of its empire by the Ottoman Turks (with
Crete finally lost in 1669), Portugal's direct trade with Asia after 1498, and
Venice's resounding defeat in Italy at Agnadello, the Venetian republic recovered its mainland empire in Italy within a decade of its loss and its economic vitality after the Italian wars, acted as a major naval partner during
the defeat of the Turks at Lepanto (1571), and continued to present itself
as a model of maritime-commercial success and republican liberty.[82] Ships
and merchants crowding the docks in a Carpaccio city-scape or the haunt-
ing image of the Venetian arsenal evoked by Dante (*Inferno*, Canto XXI)
which captured the reality of some 2,000 guildsmen producing a ship per
day, allow us to visualize the economic dynamo that was Venice.[83] In human terms, Venetian apologists such as Gasparo Contarini and Paolo
Sarpi personify Venetian independence and resistance—Contarini in his
political writings on the Venetian constitution (*The Commonwealth and
Government of Venice* [1543]) or in his indefatigable efforts for religious
reform and rapprochement between Catholics and Protestants, and Sarpi
in his defense of Venetian liberty during the papal interdict of 1606-07 and
in his *History of the Council of Trent* (1619) aimed against papal pretensions to leadership.[84]

The Venetian model of republican government, above all, influenced
both Italian and non-Italian states alike.[85] But recent scholarship has
peeled away Venice's internal self-distortions and dismissed an earlier, cel-
ebratory historiography. Studies of public ritual and underground violence, factionalism and manipulation of constitutional procedures have
portrayed the "Serenissima" in terms more consonant with the deficiencies
of her sister Italian states not as a benevolent patriciate intent on domestic
tranquility.[86] With the myth of the good republic exploded as authoritarian, research in local and regional history must provide the building blocks

for new paradigms hopefully free of the mythical and anti-mythical polemics of an insular historiography.[87]

### Economic and Social Change

A second major area of research, social and economic history, like political history, has a rich heritage in Italy and, until it lost much of its vogue in the 1980s, played an important role in studies of the late medieval and early modern period both before and after World War II. Native historians such as Armando Sapori and Gino Luzzatto as well as foreign scholars such as Raymond De Roover, Frederic Lane, and Fernand Braudel set an inter-War agenda responsive to contemporary questions of economic depression, war, and finance, but always attentive to wider disciplinary theory in economics and sociology; their students broadened the enquiry to post-War questions on the relationship between city and country, economic development and decline.[88] Research followed regional sources according to the mature categories of economic history: demography, agriculture, industry and manufacturing, trade and transport, money and finance, prices and wages, wealth and social structure.[89] Works of synthesis have attempted to put the results together by emphasizing both the structural and institutional continuities favored by *Annaliste* historiography and the dynamic transformations that defined the beginning and end of the long sixteenth century.[90]

The vision of peace in the city and the country, as represented in Ambrogio Lorenzetti's frescos of *Good and Bad Government* (1338-39) in the Palazzo Pubblico at Siena, emphasizes security and prosperity, the inseparability of the political and the economic for the good commune/common good. The relationship between town and hinterland (where 87 percent of the population still resided in 1800) is a critical area for model-building aimed at Italy's "failed transition" to capitalism, whether the issue is the economic decline of Venice, to identify the motor of change in urban commerce and industry or agricultural production, or to disentangle the processes leading to the involution of the South.[91] The expansions and contractions within the Italian economic system depended upon a geographical division of labor not only between city and country, but also between North and South, upon the productivity of textile manufacture and its commercialization along with the supply of wheat and wool, upon the growing disparity between social classes and the increasing population that encouraged demand and capital formation.[92] The fiscal squeeze, competition from larger absolutist states across the Alps, urban regulations and restrictive legislation, rural manufacturing, clerical/noble

privileges and rural indebtedness, geographical constraints, climatic variation, and technological impasse all contributed to define limits or present
obstacles to the growth of regional economies in Italy. Those regional
economies, then, reacted to the crisis of the seventeenth century in diverse
ways, which led to the further differentiation and imbalances between rich
and poor, urban and rural, manufacturing and agriculture, silk and wool,
North and South.

### Late Renaissance Culture

Finally, a third area of research, the vast field of Italian thought and culture, has a similar distinguished genealogy, with Renaissance humanism,
as we have already seen, mapped out by Eugenio Garin, Paul Oskar
Kristeller, and Hans Baron, and religious themes of the late Renaissance
examined by Delio Cantimori and Hubert Jedin.[93] As in Italian political
and socio-economic history, attempts to draw a sharp dividing line between fifteenth and sixteenth centuries, Renaissance and Reformation,
pre-Tridentine and post-Tridentine thought and culture have missed both
the structural continuity and dynamic interplay of the changing context.[94]
Cantimori, who proposed a chronology to understand orthodoxy and het-
erodoxy in the sixteenth century, and Jedin, who formulated the question
of "Catholic Reformation" or "Counter-Reformation," redefined the field
of religious studies in early modern Italy. Continued research into religious beliefs and practices of local and regional churches and aggregate
groups of men and women, not just individuals, with correlation to social,
economic, and political developments, has shifted the Cantimori paradigm
and replaced a fictive "Evangelism" with actual ideas and movements.[95]
These movements of the Catholic Reformation era varied greatly and
spread widely—from dissimulation among the crypto-Lutheran
Nicodemites, the spectacular growth of new religious orders such as the
Capuchins (1528), the circle around the Spanish immigrant mystic theolo-
gian Juan de Valdés in Naples, to the Jesuit education system that by fifty
years after the death of Ignatius of Loyola saw more than 500 religious
houses and colleges throughout Europe and missionary activity from Peru
and Paraguay to India, Japan, and China. Thus, Cantimori's history of
ideas has blossomed into a more nuanced history of both high and popular
culture, which continues to bear rich fruit whether in the study of the Roman Inquisition and an architect of Catholic reform like Giovanni Cardinal Morone, or an obscure Friulian miller like Domenico Scandella.[96]

Carlo Ginzburg, whose anthropological "field work" in inquisitorial
archives, and Piero Camporesi, whose literary harvest of fears and fanta-

sies of daily bread and folkloric culture, have especially stimulated interest in narrative history, daily life, and popular mentalities, what has come to be called micro-history.[97] Ginzburg's history focuses on case studies and often insignificant details to illuminate not just the crannies of an individual mind, but also common mental habits of the age at large.[98] A close cousin to this methodological movement, but which has its roots in economic and intellectual history, can be seen in the new kinds of societal-based studies of scientific institutions and phenomena, from the plague-fighting institutions of early modern medicine, especially known from the devastating outbreaks of 1630-33 in the North and 1656-57 in Genoa, Naples, and Rome, to the scientific academies and court-sponsored investigations of mathematicians and astronomers.[99] One goal of such microscopic analysis is to create both emotive and intellectual recognition of what can often remain dry and undigested generalizations in macroscopic surveys. A parallel movement for humanism and the arts, "new historicism," attempts to dissolve the distinctions between high and low culture in the analysis of previously excluded sources and to integrate all writing and cultural artifacts in order to transcend artificial disciplinary boundaries.[100] The success of such methods *lies* in the telling, with the mendacious pun intended, for they return us to the conflation of fact and fiction in theater and *novelle* so popular in this period and make us confront atypical or contradictory examples to challenge otherwise comfortable historiographical categories and to rediscover the now forgotten assumptions of the past.

## 5. ITALY: AN ARRESTED DEVELOPMENT?

The history of late medieval, Renaissance, and early modern Italy claims precocious, yet arrested development. This dual identity of priority of place and failed transition has led to textbook simplifications and popular mythology that consign Italy to the role of being a mere transitional stage for a subsequent "triumph" of Western Civilization. In this untenable, ahistorical Anglo-American paradigm, Renaissance man—nary a woman—has become the central doctrine in a cultural catechism whose positivist credo glorifies creativity and change. Fully-actualized Italian heroes fill up a canonical litany of secular saints from Petrarch to Galileo, and high-priest historians of art, literature, music, science, society, economics and politics worship at the altar of a modernity defined by imagination (not imitation), genius (not expertise), risk-taking (not security), competition (not cooperation), and change (not continuity).[101]

In a post-colonial, post-Vatican II, post-Cold War, and post-modern cultural world, the conceptual problems of a common history without a unified state as seen from today's unified state without a common history must be grappled with anew, and scholars of Renaissance Italy—both natives and foreigners alike—are learning to free themselves from the historiographical posturing that their various ideologies, methodologies, and interpretations have spawned.[102] Rejecting canonical, long-term deterministic teleologies, they find themselves interrogating their subject matter to determine its internal logic and rules in language and perception, law and practice. A truly comparative history that connects politics, society, and culture remains the elusive goal.[103]

# NOTES

1. Giannozzo Manetti, *Vita Nicolai V Summi Pontificis* in *Rerum Italicarum Scriptores*, ed. Ludovico Antonio Muratori (Milan, 1734), vol. 3, pt. 2, cols. 907-960; Francesco Pagnotti, "La *Vita* di Niccolò V scrittta da Giannozzo Manetti: studio preparatorio alla nuova edizione critica," *Archivio della Società Romana di Storia Patria* 14 (1891): 411-436. See also another contemporary *vita*, Vespasiano da Bisticci, *Renaissance Princes, Popes, and Prelates*, trans. William George and Emily Waters (New York, 1963), pp. 31-58.
2. D'Amico (1983), 120-22.
3. Romano, (1971); and idem, in Romano and Vivanti (1972-76), vol. 2, pt. 2, 1811-1931.
4. Cochrane (1970), 7-20, and (1988), 1-6.
5. Garin (1991); Villari (1991), of which an English translation is in preparation.
6. A. Brown (1984), 285-300.
7. Braudel (1991) further divides the "long sixteenth century" into three periods—"three Italies in two centuries"—defined by war and peace: 1454-1494, equilibrium within the Italian states from the Peace of Lodi to the French invasions; 1494-1559, the ravages of the Italian Wars; and 1559-1648, prosperity and decline from the Treaty of Cateau Cambrèsis to the Peace of Westphalia.
8. Sergio Bertelli, "Il Cinquecento," in De Rosa (1989), 3-62. For the classic nineteenth-century historiographical tradition, see Jules Michelet, *La Renaissance*, vol. 7 of *Histoire de France*, (1855); John Ruskin, *The Stones of Venice*, 3 vols. (1851-53); Jacob Burkhardt, *The Civilization of the Renaissance in Italy* (1860); Francisco De Sanctis, *History of Italian Literature*, 2 vols. (1870-71); and Benedetto Croce, *Storia della età barocca in Italia* (Bari, 1929). For a useful annotated bibliography on the "problem" of the Renaissance, see Chabod (1967), 110-44.
9. Burke (1987); and Johan Huizinga, "The Problem of the Renaissance," in Huizinga (1959), 243-87.
10. Giuseppe Giarrizzo, "Il Seicento," in De Rosa (1989), 63-84.
11. Braudel (1972).
12. Brucker (1983), 616. Comparative history has been the theme of some recent conferences: *Florence and Venice. Comparisons and Relations*, 2 vols. (Florence, 1979-80) and *Florence and Milan: Comparisons and Relations*, 2 vols. (Florence, 1989).
13. Josef Macek, "La crisi ideologica del papato dal grande scisma al Rinascimento," in Cherubini, vol. 8 (1988): 65-86; Michael Knapton, "Dalla signoria allo stato regionale e all'equilibrio della pace di Lodi," in Cherubini, vol. 8 (1988): 87-122; Brucker (1977), 3-13; and "Bibliography of Philip Jones," in Dean and Wickham (1990), xiii-xv.

14. Westfall (1974), 17-34.
15. Ludwig von Pastor, *The History of the Popes*, trans. Frederick Ignatius Antrobus (St. Louis, 1898), vol. 2: 13.
16. Laura Onofri, "Sacralità, immaginazione e proposte politiche: La Vita di Niccolo V di Giannozzo Manetti," *Humanistica Lovaniensia* 28 (1979): 57. See also, Magnusson (1958).
17. Westfall (1974), 35-62 but see Manfredo Tafuri, *Ricerca del Rinascimento* (Turin, 1992), 33-84.
18. Bentley (1987), 138-94 mildly revises Gilbert (1965) and Skinner (1978). See also Burns (1991).
19. Struever (1992).
20. For English introductions to Machiavelli, *The Prince*, and Castiglione, *The Book of the Courtier*, see Pitkin (1984); Rebhorn (1978).
21. J. C. Brown (1989): 761-80; and Goldthwaite (1987): 15-39.
22. Goldthwaite (1980); Hocquet (1978-79); and Malanima (1982a).
23. Myron Gilmore, *The World of Humanism 1453-1517* (New York, 1952), 40-42. The best known case of papal arbitration is Alexander VI's Treaty of Tordesailles (1494).
24. Riccardo Fubini, "The Italic League and 'equilibrium politics' to Lorenzo de' Medici's coming to power," forthcoming in "The Origins of the State in Italy, 14th-16th Centuries," *Journal of Modern History* (1994).
25. Mattingly (1955).
26. Maria Ludovica Lenzi, "Le compagnie di ventura e le signorie militari," in Cherubini (1987-89), vol. 8: 123-67; Mallett (1974); and Mallett and Hale (1984).
27. Such papal-banker rivalries were common throughout the period. On Agostino Chigi (1466-1520), see Gilbert (1980); on Filippo Strozzi (1488-1538), see Bullard (1980).
28. Halil Inalcik, "Djem," in *The Encyclopaedia of Islam* (new ed.; Leiden/London, 1960), 2: 529-531.
29. Grafton (1993); and Ullman and Stadter (1972).
30. Fubini (1992): 541-74 reviews Baron (1988). Baron's classic work is Baron (1966). See also Kristeller (1984-85); Garin (1965); and Schmitt and Skinner (1988).
31. Martines (1963) and (1979), 191-217.
32. King (1986); Ianziti (1988); Bentley (1987); D'Amico (1983).
33. Erasmus, *The Praise of Folly*, trans. Hoyt Hopewell Hudson (Princeton, 1941), 61. See also, Seidel Menchi (1987).
34. D'Amico (1983), 118-19; Trinkhaus (1970), vol. 1: 103-70.
35. Robin (1991), 56-81.
36. Field (1988); and James Hankins, "Cosimo de' Medici as a Patron of Humanistic Literature," in Ames-Lewis (1992), 69-94.
37. Martines (1968); Costa (1969); Ascheri (1989); and Aldo Mazzacane, "The Juridical Foundations," forthcoming in "The Origins of the State."
38. Grendler (1989); Gehl (1993).
39. Burke (1987).
40. Kent and Simon (1987).
41. Hallman (1985).
42. Pius II, *Memoirs of a Renaissance Pope. The Commentaries of Pius II*, trans. Florence A. Gragg (New York, 1959), 79-87.

43. Immanuel Wallerstein, *The Modern World-System: Capitalist Agriculture and the Origins of the European World-Economy in the Sixteenth Century* (New York, 1974).
44. Cochrane (1981), 34-40; Riccardo Fubini, "Flavio Biondo," in *Dizionario Biografico degli Italiani*, 10: 536-59; and Hay (1977).
45. Francesco Petrarca, *Rime sparse*, ed. Giovanni Ponte (Milan, 1979), no. 128, ll. 93-96, 184-89, and Machiavelli, *The Prince*. See also the forthcoming analysis of *Italia mia* by Margaret Brose.
46. *The Discourses of Niccolò Machiavelli*, trans. Leslie J. Walker, 2 vols. (London, 1950), 1: 244-45 and 363-64 (Bk. I: 12, 5-8; Bk. II: 2, 6-7). See also, Gianfranco Berardi, "La riflessione storica e politica. Machiavelli e Guicciardini," in Cherubini (1987-89), vol. 8:237-67.
47. Francesco Guicciardini, *Maxims and Reflections of a Renaissance Statesman*, trans. Mario Domandi (New York, 1965), no. 28, p. 48.
48. Cavallar (1991) and (1993): 245-85.
49. Lane (1973), 241-49 explains the Venetian turning point as the 1503 decision to engage in land-based expansion, which culminated in the defeat at Agnadello.
50. Chastel (1983).
51. John M. Headley, *The Emperor and his Chancellor. A study of the imperial chancellery under Gattinara* (Cambridge, 1983).
52. Charles F. Delzell, "Italian Historical Scholarship: A Decade of Recovery and Development, 1945-1955," *Journal of Modern History* 28 (1956): 374-88.
53. Federico Chabod, "Esiste uno Stato del Rinascimento?" in Chabod (1967), 593-623.
54. Marino Berengo, "Il Cinquecento," in De Rosa (1989), vol. 1: 483-518, and Berengo (1965).
55. Elena Fasano Guarini, "Center and Periphery," forthcoming in "The Origins of the State."
56. For a critical view of Clifford Geertz, see Giovanni Levi, "I pericoli del geertzismo," *Quaderni storici* 58 (1985): 269-277; and Giuseppe Galasso in Galasso (1976- ). For a unique example of such a comparative approach over the long term, Giuseppe Galasso, *Potere e istituzioni in Italia della caduta dell'Impero romano ad oggi* (Turin, 1974).
57. Chittolini (1979); Patrizia Mainoni, "Lo stato milanese dei Visconti e degli Sforza," in Cherubini (1987-89), vol. 8: 169-201.
58. Domenico Sella, "Sotto il dominio della Spagna," in Galasso (1976- ), vol. 11; Gianvittorio Signorotto, "Milano e la Lombardia sotto gli spagnoli," in Cherubini, vol. 12: 189-223.
59. Sella (1979); De Maddelena (1982).
60. Ryder (1976) and (1990); and Giuseppe Galasso, in Galasso (1976- ), vol. 15, book 1.
61. Guido D'Agostino, "Napoli e il Sud dagli Angioini agli Aragonesi," in Cherubini (1987-89), 8: 437-64; Agostino (1979); and Giovanni Muto, "Il regno di Napoli sotto la dominazione spagnola," in Cherubini (1987-89), vol. 11: 225-316.
62. Cochrane (1986): 194-217; Calabria and Marino (1990); Astarita (1992).
63. Musi (1991).
64. Calabria (1991); Villari (1993); Aurelio Musi, "La rivolta antispagnola a Napoli e in Sicilia," in Cherubini (1987-89), vol. 11: 317-58; Musi (1989).

65. Koenigsberger (1971); Vincenzo d'Alessandro and Giuseppe Giarrizzo, *La Sicilia dal Vespro all'Unità d'Italia*, in Galasso (1976- ), vol. 16.
66. Monter (1990).
67. Bruno Anatra, "Dall'Unificazione Aragonese al Savoia," in John Day, et al., *La Sardegna medioevale e moderna*, in Galasso (1976- ), vol. 10: 191-663.
68. See Grendi (1987); Pacini (1990).
69. Claudio Costantini, *La Repubblica di Genova nell'età moderna*, in Galasso (1976- ), vol. 9; Gian Luigi Falabrino, "La repubblica di Genova nel XV secolo," in Cherubini (1987-89), vol. 8: 313-30; Carlo Bitossi, "La Genova di Andrea Doria," and "Il Banco di San Giorgio," in Cherubini (1987-89), vol. 10: 169-220.
70. Giovanni Cipriani, "Firenze, capitale dell'Umanesimo e dell'equilibrio italiano," in Cherubini, vol. 8: 331-71; Claudia Di Filippo Bareggi, "La Toscana dei Medici. Lo stato, l'economia, la cultura," in Cherubini (1987-89), vol. 10: 259-96; Fasano Guarini (1973); and Furio Diaz, *Il Granducato di Toscana. I Medici*, in Galasso (1976- ), vol. 13, Pt. 1. In English, D. Kent (1978); Rubinstein (1966); Weinstein (1970); Butters (1985); Stephens (1983).
71. Cochrane (1973); Dooley (1990): 519-50; Litchfield (1986); Waquet (1992); Malanima (1982b).
72. Herlihy and Klapisch-Zuber (1985); and on demography, Comba (1984).
73. Trexler (1980); and Giorgio Chittolini, "The Realm of the Private, the Public and the State" forthcoming in "The Origins of the State."
74. F. W. Kent (1977); Klapisch-Zuber (1985); Kuehn (1991); Strocchia (1992); and for an overview with excellent bibliography, King (1991).
75. On court culture, see Trevor Dean, "The Courts," forthcoming in "The Origins of the State."
76. Roberto Greci, "Gli stati minori della Padania: un anacronismo funzionale," in Cherubini (1987-89), vol. 8: 203-32; Michele Luzzati, "Siena, Lucca e Pisa fra Trecento e Cinquecento," in Cherubini (1987-89), vol. 8: 381-398; Lino Marini, et al., *I Ducati padani, Trento e Trieste*, in Galasso (1976- ), vol. 17.
77. Prodi (1987) and (1992).
78. Peter Partner, "Lo Stato della chiesa nel XV e nel XVI," in Cherubini (1987-89), vol. 8: 399-435; Partner (1990); O'Malley (1979); Mario Caravale and Alberto Caracciolo, in Galasso (1976-), vol. 14.
79. Stinger (1985).
80. Nussdorfer (1992).
81. Grubb (1986): 43-94.
82. Gaetano Cozzi, et al., *La Repubblica di Venezia nell'età moderna*, 2 vols., in Galasso (1976- ), vol. 12, Pts. 1-2.
83. P. F. Brown (1988), with a more theoretical examination of narrative painting in Greenstein (1992); Davis (1991); and Lane (1973) for an extensive bibliography on all aspects of Venetian history.
84. Bouwsma (1968); Gleason (1993).
85. Finlay (1980).
86. Pullan (1971); Muir (1981); Ruggiero (1980) and (1985).
87. John Law, "Il Quattrocento a Venezia," in Cherubini (1987-89), vol. 8: 233-311; Paolo Preto, "Venezia tra la Spagna e i turchi," in Cherubini (1987-89), vol. 10: 231-58; Michael Knapton, "Venezia e il Mediterraneo dalla guerra di Cipro alla pace di Passarowitz," in Cherubini (1987-89), vol. 11: 399-424; and Grubb (1988).

88. Luigi De Rosa, "Vent'anni di storiografia economica italiana (1945-1965)," in *La Storiografia italiana* (1970), vol. 2: 857-923; Antonio Di Vittorio, "La storia economica del mondo moderno," in *La Storiografia italiana* (1989), vol. 2: 235-308. Luzzato (1961); Sapori (1970); Lane (1966); De Roover (1974).

89. Felloni (1977), 1-36.

90. Carlo M. Cipolla, *Before the Industrial Revolution* (2d ed., New York, 1980); and Romano (1991). For a critique of the *Annaliste* method in Italy, see Mario Del Treppo, "La libertà della memoria," in Marina Cedronio, et al., *Storiografia Francese di ieri e di oggi* (Naples, 1977), VII-LI.

91. Van der Wee (1988); Pullan (1968); Aymard (1982); Quazza (1971); Epstein (1992); Marino (1988).

92. Franco Saba, "L'economia italiana del Cinquecento," in Cherubini (1987-89), vol. 9: 57-75; Franco Cazzola, "Il 'ritorno alla terra,'" in Cherubini (1987-89), vol. 10: 103-68; Paolo Malanima, "L'economia italiana nel Seicento," in Cherubini (1987-89), vol. 11: 149-88; Politi (1982).

93. Gaetano Cozzi, "Rinascimento, Riforma, Controriforma," in *La Storiografia italiana* (1970), vol. 2: 1191-1247; Cantimori (1979) and in Cochrane (1970), 211-24, 244-65; Jedin (1949-75) and (1957-61).

94. Albano Biondo, "Il primato culturale italiano," in Cherubini (1987-89), vol. 9: 77-112.

95. Gleason (1978): 4-25; Schutte (1989): 269-84.

96. Susanna Peyronel Rambaldi, "La Controriforma," in Cherubini (1987-89), vol. 11: 53-109; Gino Benzoni, "Intellettuali e Controriforma," in Cherubini (1987-89), vol. 11: 111-47; Firpo and Marcatto (1981-89); Ginzburg (1980).

97. Ginzburg (1983), (1989), and (1991); Camporesi (1988), (1989), (1991), and (1993).

98. Muir and Ruggiero (1990) and (1991); Muir (1993).

99. Cipolla (1973); Calvi (1989); Biagioli (1993).

100. For comparative literature, see Quint (1983) and (1993); for music history, see Tomlinson (1987) and (1993); and for art history, Starn and Partridge (1992).

101. Burke (1987); Molho (1981), 201-24.

102. Ruggiero Romano, *La Storiografia italiana oggi*, Espresso Strumenti 1, ed. Umberto Eco ([Rome], 1978).

103. Martines (1979) provides a brilliant model for a first approximation, albeit limited to the descendants of the old Italic Kingdoms of the North and ending with the High Renaissance.

# BIBLIOGRAPHY

*General Reference Works*

Braudel, Fernand. *The Mediterranean and the Mediterranean World in the Age of Philip II.* Trans. Sîan Reynolds. 2 vols. New York, 1972.
Braudel, Fernand. *Out of Italy, 1450-1650.* Trans. Sîan Reynolds. Paris, 1991.
Burke, Peter. *The Historical Anthropology of Early Modern Italy: Essays in Perception and Communication.* Cambridge, 1987.
Burke, Peter. *The Renaissance.* Houndmills and London, 1987.
Cherubini, Giovanni, et al., eds. *Storia della società italiana.* Vols. 8-12. Milan, 1987-89.
Cochrane, Eric. *Historians and Historiography in the Italian Renaissance.* Chicago, 1981.
Cochrane, Eric. *Italy 1539-1630.* Ed. Julius Kirshner. Longman History of Italy. London and New York, 1988.
Cochrane, Eric, ed. *The Late Italian Renaissance.* New York, 1970.
De Rosa, Luigi, ed. *La Storiografia italiana degli ultimi vent'anni.* Vol. 2, *Età moderna.* Bari, 1989.
Galasso, Giuseppe, ed. *Storia d'Italia.* 24 vols. planned. Milan, 1976- .
Garin, Eugenio, ed. *Renaissance Characters.* Trans. Lydia G. Cochrane. Chicago, 1991.
Hale, J. R., ed. *A Concise Encyclopaedia of the Italian Renaissance.* New York and Toronto, 1981.
Hay, Denys. *The Italian Renaissance in its Historical Background.* 2d ed. Cambridge, 1977.
Hay, Denys, and John Law. *Italy in the Age of the Renaissance 1380-1530.* Longman History of Italy. London and New York, 1989.
Huizinga, Johan. *Men and Ideas. History, the Middle Ages, the Renaissance.* Trans. James S. Holmes and Hans van Marle. New York, 1959.
Martines, Lauro. *Power and Imagination: City-States in Renaissance Italy.* New York, 1979.
Romano, Ruggiero, and Corrado Vivanti, eds. *Storia d'Italia.* 6 vols. Turin, 1972-76.
Romano, Ruggiero, and Corrado Vivanti, eds. *Storia d'Italia: Annali.* 9 vols. Turin, 1978-86.
*La Storiografia italiana negli ultimi vent'anni.* 2 vols. Milan, 1970.
Tranfaglia, Nicola, and Massimo Firpo, eds. *La Storia. I grandi problemi dal Medioevo all'età contemporanea.* Vols. 3-5, *L'Età moderna.* Turin, 1986-87.
Villari, Rosario, ed. *L'Uomo barocco.* Bari, 1991.


*Geo-Political Divisions*

*Milan*
De Maddelena, Aldo. *Della città al borgo: Avvio di una metamorfosi economica e sociale nella Lombardia Spagnola.* Milan, 1982.
Ianziti, Gary. *Humanistic Historiography under the Sforzas. Politics and Propaganda in Fifteenth-century Milan.* Oxford, 1988.
Robin, Diana. *Filelfo in Milan. Writings 1451-1477.* Princeton, 1991.
Sella, Domenico. *Crisis and Continuity: the Economy of Spanish Lombardy in the Seventeenth Century.* Cambridge, Mass., 1979.

*Venice*
Bouwsma, William J. *Venice and the Defense of Republican Liberty*. Berkeley and Los Angeles, 1968.
Davis, Robert C. *Shipbuilders of the Venetian Arsenal: Workers and Workplace in the Pre-industrial City*. Baltimore, 1991.
Finlay, Robert. *Politics in Renaissance Venice*. New Brunswick, N.J., 1980.
Grubb, James S. *Firstborn of Venice: Vicenza in the Early Renaissance State*. Baltimore, 1988.
Grubb, James S. "When Myths Lose Power: Four Decades of Venetian Historiography." *JMH* 58 (1986): 43-94.
Hocquet, Jean-Claude. *Le Sel et la fortune de Venise*. 2 vols. Villeneuve d'Ascq, 1978-79.
King, Margaret L. *Venetian Humanism in an Age of Patrician Dominance*. Princeton, 1986.
Lane, Frederic C. *Venice: a Maritime Republic*. Baltimore, 1973.
Lane, Frederic C. *Venice and History*. Baltimore, 1966.
Mallett, Michael E., and J. R. Hale. *The Military Organization of a Renaissance State. Venice c. 1400 to 1617)*. Cambridge, 1984.
Muir, Edward. *Civic Ritual in Renaissance Venice*. Princeton, 1981.
Muir, Edward. *Mad Blood Stirring. Vendetta and Factions in Friuli during the Renaissance*. Baltimore, 1993.
Pullan, Brian, ed. *Crisis and Change in the Venetian Economy in the Sixteenth and Seventeenth Centuries*. London, 1968.
Pullan, Brian, ed. *Rich and Poor in Renaissance Venice*. Oxford, 1971.
Ruggiero, Guido. *The Boundaries of Eros. Sex Crime and Sexuality in Renaissance Venice*. Oxford, 1985.
Ruggiero, Guido. *Violence in Early Renaissance Venice*. New Brunswick, N. J., 1980.

*Genoa*
Grendi, Edoardo. *La republica aristocratica dei genovesi*. Bologna, 1987.
Pacini, Arturo. *I presupposti politici del "secolo dei genovesi": La riforma del 1528*. Genoa, 1990.

*Florence*
Ames-Lewis, Francis, ed. *Cosimo 'il Vecchio' de' Medici, 1389-1464. Essays in Commemoration of the 600th Anniversary of Cosimo de' Medici's Birth*. Oxford, 1992.
Berengo, Marino. *Nobili e mercanti nella Lucca del '500*. Turin, 1965.
Brucker, Gene A. *The Civic World of Early Renaissance Florence*. Princeton, 1977.
Bullard, Melissa Meriam. *Filippo Strozzi and the Medici: Favor and Finance in Sixteenth-Century Florence and Rome*. Cambridge, 1980.
Butters, H. C. *Governors and Government in Early Sixteenth-Century Florence, 1502-1519*. Oxford, 1985.
Calvi, Giulia. *Histories of a Plague Year: the Social and the Imaginary in Baroque Florence*. Trans. Dario Biocca and Bryant T. Ragan, Jr. Berkeley and Los Angeles, 1989.
Cavallar, Osvaldo. "Francesco Guicciardini and the 'Pisan Crisis': Logic and Discourses." *JMH* 65 (1993): 245-85.
Cavallar, Osvaldo. *Francesco Guicciardini giurista. I ricordi degli onorari*. Milan, 1991.
Cochrane, Eric. *Florence in the Forgotten Centuries, 1527-1800*. Chicago, 1973.
Dooley, Brendan. "Revisiting the Forgotten Centuries: Recent Work on Early Modern Tuscany." *European History Quarterly* 20 (1990): 519-50.
Fasano Guarini, Elena. *Lo Stato mediceo di Cosimo I*. Florence, 1973.
Field, Arthur. *The Origins of the Platonic Academy of Florence*. Princeton, 1988.
Gilbert, Felix. *Machiavelli and Guicciardini: Politics and History in Sixteenth Century Florence*. Princeton, 1965.
Goldthwaite, Richard A. *The Building of Renaissance Florence: an Economic and Social History*. Baltimore, 1980.
Herlihy, David, and Christiane Klapisch-Zuber. *The Tuscans and their Families: a Study of the Florentine Catasto of 1427*. New Haven, 1985.

Kent, Francis William. *Household and Lineage in Renaissance Florence: the Family Life of the Capponi, Ginori, and Rucellai.* Princeton, 1977.

Kent, Francis William, and Patricia Simon, eds. *Patronage, Art and Society in Renaissance Italy.* Oxford, 1987.

Litchfield, R. Burr. *Emergence of a Bureaucracy: the Florentine Patricians 1530-1790.* Princeton, 1986.

Malanima, Paolo. *La decadenza di un'economia cittadina. L'industria di Firenze nei secoli XVI-XVII.* Bologna, 1982a.

Martines, Lauro. *The Social World of the Florentine Humanists 1390-1460.* Princeton, 1963.

Pitkin, Hanna Fenichel. *Fortune is a Woman: Gender and Politics in the Thought of Niccolò Machiavelli.* Berkeley and Los Angeles, 1984.

Rubinstein, Nicolai. *The Government of Florence under the Medici, 1434-94.* Oxford, 1966.

Stephens, J. N. *The Fall of the Florentine Republic 1512-1530.* Oxford, 1983.

Strocchia, Sharon. *Death and Ritual in Renaissance Florence.* Baltimore, 1992.

Trexler, Richard. *Public Life in Renaissance Florence.* New York, 1980.

Ullman, Berthold L., and P. A. Stadter. *The Public Library of Renaissance Florence: Niccolò Niccoli, Cosimo de' Medici and the Library of San Marco.* Padua, 1972.

Waquet, Jean-Claude. *Corruption: Ethics and Power in Florence, 1600-1770.* Trans. Linda McCall. University Park, Pa., 1992.

Weinstein, Donald. *Savonarola and Florence: Prophecy and Patriotism in the Renaissance.* Princeton, 1970.


*Rome*

Chastel, André. *The Sack of Rome, 1527.* Trans. Beth Archer. Princeton, 1983.

D'Amico, John. *Renaissance Humanism in Papal Rome: Humanists and Churchmen on the Eve of the Reformation.* Baltimore, 1983.

Gilbert, Felix. *The Pope, His Banker, and Venice.* Cambridge, Mass., 1980.

Grafton, Anthony J., ed. *Rome Reborn: the Vatican Library and Renaissance Culture.* New Haven, 1993.

Hallman, Barbara M. *Italian Cardinals, Reform, and the Church as Property, 1492-1563.* Berkeley and Los Angeles, 1985.

Magnusson, Torgil. *Studies in Roman Quattrocento Architecture.* Stockholm, 1958.

Nussdorfer, Laurie. *Civic Politics in the Rome of Urban VIII.* Princeton, 1992.

O'Malley, John W. *Praise and Blame in Renaissance Rome: Rhetoric, Doctrine and Reform in the Sacred Orators of the Papal Court, c. 1450-1521.* Durham, N. C., 1979.

Partner, Peter. *The Pope's Men: the Papal Civil Service in the Renaissance.* Oxford, 1990.

Prodi, Paolo. *The Papal Prince. One Body and Two Souls: the Papal Monarchy in Early Modern Europe.* Trans. Susan Haskins. Cambridge, 1987.

Stinger, Charles. *The Renaissance in Rome.* Bloomington, 1985.

Westfall, Carroll William. *In This Most Perfect Paradise: Alberti, Nicholas V, and the Invention of Conscious Urban Planning in Rome, 1447-55.* University Park, Pa., 1974.


*Naples and Sicily*

Astarita, Tommaso. *The Continuity of Feudal Power: the Caracciolo di Brienza in Spanish Naples.* Cambridge, 1992.

Bentley, Jerry H. *Politics and Culture in Renaissance Naples.* Princeton, 1987.

Calabria, Antonio. *The Cost of Empire.: the Finances of the Kingdom of Naples in the Time of Spanish Rule.* Cambridge, 1991.

Calabria, Antonio, and John A. Marino, eds. and trans. *Good Government in Spanish Naples.* New York and Bern, 1990.

Cochrane, Eric. "Southern Italy in the Age of the Spanish Viceroys: Some Recent Titles." *JMH* 58 (1986): 194-217.

D'Agostino, Guido. *La capitale ambigua: Napoli dal 1458 al 1580.* Naples, 1979.

Epstein, Stephan. *An Island for Itself: Economic Development and Social Change in Late Medieval Sicily.* Cambridge, 1992.

Koenigsberger, Helmut G. *The Practice of Empire.* Rev. ed. Ithaca, N.Y., 1971.

Marino, John A. *Pastoral Economics in the Kingdom of Naples.* Baltimore, 1988.

Monter, William. *Frontiers of Heresy: the Spanish Inquisition from the Basque Lands to Sicily.* Cambridge, 1990.

Musi, Aurelio. *Mezzogiorno Spagnolo: la via Napoletana allo stato moderno.* Naples, 1991.

Musi, Aurelio. *La Rivolta di Masaniello nella scena politica barocca.* Naples, 1989.

Ryder, Alan. *Alfonso the Magnanimous, King of Aragon, Naples and Sicily, 1396-1458.* Oxford, 1990.

Ryder, Alan. *The Kingdom of Naples under Alfonso the Magnanimous: the Making of a Modern State.* Oxford, 1976.

Villari, Rosario. *The Revolt of Naples.* Trans. James Newell. Oxford, 1993.


*Topics*

*Intellectual and Religious History*

Baron, Hans. *The Crisis of the Early Italian Renaissance: Civic Humanism and Republican Liberty in an Age of Classicism and Tyranny.* Rev. ed. Princeton, 1966.

Baron, Hans. *In Search of Florentine Civic Humanism: Essays on the Transition from Medieval to Modern Thought.* 2 vols. Princeton, 1988.

Biagioli, Mario. *Galileo, Courtier: the Practice of Science in the Culture of Absolutism.* Chicago, 1993.

Burns, J. H., ed. *The Cambridge History of Political Thought 1450-1700.* Cambridge, 1991.

Cantimori, Delio. *Italian Heretics of the Sixteenth Century.* Trans. Hilary A. Smith. Cambridge, Mass., 1979.

Firpo, Massimo, and Dario Marcatto. *Il processo inquisitoriale del cardinal Giovanni Morone.* 6 vols. Rome, 1981-89.

Fubini, Riccardo. "Renaissance Historian: the Career of Hans Baron." *JMH* 64 (1992): 541-74.

Garin, Eugenio. *Italian Humanism: Philosophy and Civic Life in the Renaissance.* Trans. Peter Munz. New York, 1965.

Gehl, Paul F. *A Moral Art: Grammar, Society and Culture in Trecento Florence.* Ithaca, N.Y., 1993.

Gleason, Elisabeth G. *Gasparo Contarini. Venice, Rome, and Reform.* Berkeley and Los Angeles, 1993.

Gleason, Elisabeth G. "On the Nature of Sixteenth-Century Italian Evangelism: Scholarship, 1953-1978." *SCJ* 9 (1978): 4-25.

Greenstein, Jack M. *Mantegna and Painting as Historical Narrative.* Chicago, 1992.

Grendler, Paul F. *Schooling in Renaissance Italy: Literacy and Learning.* Baltimore, 1989.

Jedin, Hubert. *Geschichte des Konzils von Trent.* 4 vols. Freiburg im Breisgau, Basel, and Vienna, 1949-75.

Jedin, Hubert. *A History of the Council of Trent.* Trans. Ernest Graf, O.S.B. 2 vols. St. Louis, 1957-61.

Kristeller, Paul Oskar. *Studies in Renaissance Thought and Letters.* 2 vols. Rome, 1984-85.

Schmitt, Charles B., and Quentin Skinner, eds. *The Cambridge History of Renaissance Philosophy.* Cambridge, 1988.

Schutte, Anne Jacobson. "Periodization of Sixteenth-Century Italian Religious History: the Post-Cantimori Paradigm Shift." *JMH* (1989): 269-84.

Seidel Menchi, Silvana. *Erasmo in Italia, 1520-1580.* Turin, 1987.

Skinner, Quentin. *The Foundations of Modern Political Thought.* 2 vols. Cambridge, 1978.

Struever, Nancy S. *Theory as Practice. Ethical Inquiry in the Renaissance.* Berkeley and Los Angeles, 1992.

Trinkhaus, Charles. *"In Our Image and Likeness."* Humanity and Divinity in Italian Humanist Thought. 2 vols. Chicago and London, 1970.


Political and Juridical History

Ascheri, Mario, *Tribunali, giuristi, e istituzioni dal medioevo all' età moderna.* Bologna, 1989.

Brown, Alison. "Florence, Renaissance and the Early Modern State: Reappraisals." *JMH* 56, no. 2 (1984): 285-300.

Brucker, Gene A. "Tales of Two Cities: Florence and Venice in the Renaissance." *AHR* 88 (1983): 599-616.

Chabod, Federico. *Scritti sul Rinascimento.* Turin, 1967.

Chittolini, Giorgio. *La formazione dello stato regionale e le istituzioni del contado, secoli XIV e XV.* Turin, 1979.

Costa, Pietro. *Iurisdictio. Semantica del potere politico nella pubblicistica medievale (1100-1433).* Milan, 1969.

Kuehn, Thomas. *Law, Family, and Women: Toward a Legal Anthropology of Renaissance Italy.* Chicago, 1991.

Martines, Lauro. *Lawyers and Statecraft in Renaissance Florence.* Princeton, 1968.

Mattingly, Garrett. *Renaissance Diplomacy.* London, 1955.

Molho, Anthony J. "Italian History in American Universities." In *Italia e Stati Uniti. Concordanze e dissonanze,* ed. A. Bartole and A. Dell'Omodarme, 201-24. Rome, 1981.

Prodi, Paolo. *Il sacramento del potere: il giuramento politico nella storia costituzionale dell'Occidente.* Bologna, 1992.

Quazza, Guido. *La decadenza italiana nella storia europea: saggi sul Sei-Settecento.* Turin, 1971.


Social and Economic History

Aymard, Maurice. "From Feudalism to Capitalism in Italy: the Case That Doesn't Fit." *Review* 6, no. 2 (1982): 131-208.

Brown, Judith C. "Prosperity or Hard Times in Renaissance Italy?" *RenQ* 42 (1989): 761-80.

Comba, Rinaldo, et al. *Strutture familiari epidemie migrazioni nell'Italia medievale.* Naples, 1984.

Dean, Trevor, and Chris Wickham, eds. *City and Countryside in Late Medieval and Renaissance Italy.* London, 1990.

De Roover, Raymond. *Business, Banking and Economic Thought in Late Medieval and Early Modern Europe.* Ed. Julius Kirshner. Chicago, 1974.

Felloni, Giuseppe. "Italy." In *An Introduction to The Sources of European Economic History 1500-1800,* eds. Charles Wilson and Geoffrey Parker, 1-36. London, 1977.

Goldthwaite, Richard A. "The Economy of Renaissance Italy: the Preconditions for Luxury Consumption." *I Tatti Studies* 2 (1987): 15-39.

Luzzatto, Gino. *An Economic History of Italy: From the Fall of the Roman Empire to the Beginning of the Sixteenth Century.* Trans. Philip Jones. New York, 1961.

Malanima Paolo. *L'economia italiana nell'età moderna.* Rome, 1982b.

Mallett, Michael E. *Mercenaries and their Masters. Warfare in Renaissance Italy.* London, 1974.

Politi, Giorgio, et al., eds. *Timore e carità: i poveri nell'Italia moderna.* Cremona, 1982.

Romano, Ruggiero, ed. *Storia dell'economia italiana.* Vol. 2, *L'età moderna verso la crisi.* Turin, 1991.

Romano, Ruggiero, ed. *Tra due crisi: l'Italia del Rinascimento.* Turin, 1971.

Sapori, Armando. *The Italian Merchant in the Middle Ages.* Trans. Patricia Ann Kennen. New York, 1970.

Van der Wee, Herman, ed. *The Rise and Decline of Urban Industries in Italy and in the Low Countries (Late Middle Ages-Early Modern Times).* Leuven, 1988.

*Art, Literature, Music, and Culture*
Brown, Patricia Fortini. *Venetian Narrative Painting in the Age of Carpaccio.* New Haven, 1988.
Burke, Peter. *The Italian Renaissance: Culture and Society in Italy.* Rev. ed. Princeton, 1987.
Camporesi, Piero. *The Bread of Dreams: Food and Fantasy in Early Modern Europe.* Trans. David Gentilcore. Chicago, 1989.
Camporesi, Piero. *The Fear of Hell: Images of Damnation and Salvation in Early Modern Europe.* Trans. Lucinda Byatt. University Park, Pa., 1991.
Camporesi, Piero. *The Incorruptible Flesh: Bodily Mutation and Mortification in Religion and Folklore.* Trans. Tania Croft-Murray. Cambridge, 1988.
Camporesi, Piero. *The Land of Hunger.* Trans. Tania Croft-Murray. Oxford, 1993.
Cipolla, Carlo M. *Cristofano and the Plague: a Study in the History of Public Health in the Age of Galileo.* Berkeley and Los Angeles, 1973.
Ginzburg, Carlo. *The Cheese and the Worms: the Cosmos of a Sixteenth-Century Miller.* Baltimore, 1980.
Ginzburg, Carlo. *Clues, Myths, and the Historical Method.* Trans. John A. Tedeschi and Anne Tedeschi. Baltimore, 1989.
Ginzburg, Carlo. *Ecstasies: Deciphering the Witches' Sabbath.* Trans. Raymond Rosenthal. New York, 1991.
Ginzburg, Carlo. *The Night Battles: Witchcraft and Agrarian Cults in the Sixteenth & Seventeenth Centuries.* Trans. John A. Tedeschi and Anne Tedeschi. Baltimore, 1983.
Kent, Dale. *The Rise of the Medici: Factions in Florence, 1426-1434.* Oxford, 1978.
King, Margaret L. *Women of the Renaissance.* Chicago, 1991.
Klapisch-Zuber, Christiane. *Women, Family, and Ritual in Renaissance Italy.* Trans. Lydia G. Cochrane. Chicago, 1985.
Muir, Edward, and Guido Ruggiero, eds. *Microhistory and the Lost Peoples of Europe.* Baltimore, 1991.
Muir, Edward, and Guido Ruggiero, eds. *Sex and Gender in Historical Perspective. Selections from Quaderni Storici.* Trans. Margaret A. Gallucci. Baltimore, 1990.
Quint, David. *Epic and Empire: Politics and Generic Forms from Virgil to Milton.* Princeton, 1993.
Quint, David. *Origin and Originality in Renaissance Literature: Versions of the Source.* New Haven, 1983.
Rebhorn, Wayne A. *Courtly Performances: Masking and Festivity in Castiglione's "Book of the Courtier".* Detroit, 1978.
Starn, Randolph, and Loren Partridge. *The Arts of Power, the Power of Arts.* Berkeley and Los Angeles, 1992.
Tomlinson, Gary. *Monteverdi and the End of the Renaissance.* Berkeley and Los Angeles, 1987.
Tomlinson, Gary. *Music in Renaissance Magic: Toward a Historiography of Others.* Chicago, 1993.

# FRANCE FROM CHARLES VII TO HENRY IV

Bernard Chevalier
(Université François-Rabelais, Tours)

Whether France in the fifteenth and sixteenth centuries remained medieval or had already become modern is *"une question mal posée"*—fruitless and largely obsolete. Indeed, it is now safe to say that the process which was leading France toward what we call the Old Regime, characterized by the power of an absolutist monarchy and a strong administration, had already begun by the early fourteenth century. This is not to view the outcome as predetermined. The main agent of this process was war: a foreign war conducted without respite for one hundred and fifty years and, beginning a century later, a series of internal conflicts, initially between the king and a group of semi-sovereign princes, later between crown and aristocracy within the bosom of the monarchy. These conflicts placed the state and the nation's cohesiveness constantly in question. In this sense, the boundaries of the era as a whole are marked by two crises of paroxysmal proportions: the first from 1422 to 1435, the second from 1559 to 1598. If we locate our narrative between these two moments of extreme tension, we will be able to describe a political and social system which possessed an originality and equilibrium of its own, one which cannot be assimilated to the paradigm of a transition between two worlds.

## 1. The Crisis of France from Origins to Apogee, 1422-1530

### The Crisis

The death on 21 October 1422 of Charles VI, the unfortunate French king who had been afflicted with dementia for more than thirty years, sparked an exceptionally serious crisis, because the late king had left not one, but two, claimants to the royal succession. The ensuing crisis was thus both dynastic and constitutional. When an infant of twelve months was proclaimed King at Paris, at Bourges the same was done for Charles VII. The infant Henry was the son of King Charles VI's daughter and her husband, King Henry V of England's only son; Charles was Charles VI's only surviving son. Their conflicting claims revived the issue of fundamental law that

FRANCE
IN THE 16th CENTURY

Brussels

Guines

ARTOIS

Cateau Combrésis

Picquiny  PICARDY
Montdidier
Noyon

Verdun
Metz

NORMANDY
Mont St.Michel

ISLE
DE  Paris
FRANCE

CHAMPAGNE

Vassy

BRITANNY

MAINE

ANJOU

Orléans

ORLÉANNAIS

BURGUNDY

Ponts
de Cé  TOURAINE

POITOU

BERRY

NIVERNAIS

Luçon

La Rochelle

MARCHE

BOURBONNAIS

Jarnac

LIMOUSIN

AUVERGNE

Lyons

PERIGORD

Bordeaux

GUIENNE

DAUPHINE

GASCONY

Toulouse
LANGUEDOC

PROVENCE

Marseilles

ROUSSILLON

CERDAGNE

had formed one cause of the Hundred Years' War. In 1328 King Edward III of England, whose rights derived solely from his mother, had seen his claim to the French throne blocked through an appeal to the custom of patrilineal succession to the throne, later called the "Salic Law." A century later, the recognition of King Henry VI, whose right to the throne descended solely through the female line, required a nullification of this ancient tradition and, therefore, a change in the very legal foundation of the French monarchy.

In the absence of a political crisis, the rule of succession dictated by the Salic Law could not have been called into question. The crisis arose from the fact that since 1415, King Henry V of England had won victory after victory in France, when the Treaty of Troyes (1420) forced the unfortunate Charles VI to recognize Henry as his son-in-law and heir. Henry aimed to unite the two kingdoms in his own person, thereby to end definitively the long-standing conflict between them, while at the same time the French king's unprecedented decision disinherited Charles, his son and legitimate heir. Already at this time, some writers held that the French crown was not subject to any contract or agreement and that, independently of questions of dignity or morality, it had to pass without question to the next male heir. The Treaty of Troyes, however, violated this principle, dispossessing the dauphin, the royal heir, because of "his horrible and enormous crimes and misdemeanors [*ses orribles et enormes crimes et deliz*]," that is, the murder of Duke John the Fearless of Burgundy in 1419.[1]

In order to understand the implications of this accusation of murder, one must take a few steps back in time. In France the Hundred Years' War precipitated the formation of vast principalities, sometimes incorrectly referred to as "feudal," since they were embryonic states modelled on the French royal state. Most of their rulers were princes of the royal blood, who generally also held lands and had interests outside the kingdom, which allowed them to develop genuine foreign policies of their own. The duke of Burgundy, who was a "peer of the realm [*pair de France*]," best illustrates this type. Within the French kingdom he had his duchy and the counties of Artois and Flanders, while in the Holy Roman Empire he ruled the Franche-Comté and the Netherlandish provinces of Brabant, Hainaut, Holland, and Zeeland. To protect his position, Duke John the Fearless had orchestrated, in 1407, the assassination of his chief rival, Duke Louis of Orleans, Charles VI's brother; since then the other great princes, who grouped around the count of Armagnac, had waged a merciless and implacable war to break John's power and avenge the murder. When the Burgundians took Paris in 1418, their foes, called "Armagnacs," sought refuge south of the Loire, taking the Dauphin Charles with them. Then, in 1419 they murdered Duke John with the dauphin's connivance. This act enabled John's son and heir, Duke Philip the Good, to ally himself with King Henry V of England and add his authority in 1420 to the Treaty of Troyes. Above and beyond the many sudden changes in these internecine struggles, there was a fundamental issue at stake. The king's authority would prevail, or France would be transformed, in the worst case into a confederation of principalities of the German type or, at best, into a system of princely control by an aristocratic great council of the English type.

### Victory over England

A crisis so acute could only be settled by a judgment of God, or by a trial of arms—and in the contemporary mind they amounted to the same thing. The war's initial operations, however, brought no clear decision. The government of King Charles VII, controlled by Armagnac extremists, relied on its Scottish alliance and sought a military solution, but its hopes were dashed by the disastrous defeat at Verneuil on 17 August 1424. King Henry VI's government, impatient to crown its tactical successes with a strategic victory, decided to capture Orleans in order to force passage of the Loire River and bring about the collapse of the rival party.

At this stage of the conflict, Joan of Arc appeared on the scene. This visionary young peasant woman from the depths of Lorraine made her way to Chinon in Touraine, where she declared to Charles VII in God's name that his was the cause not of a murderer, but of the only legitimate king of France, the only one worthy of the traditional coronation at Rheims. Everyone—king, soldiers, politicians—now regained confidence. Orleans was liberated on 8 May 1429, and following a remarkable passage through enemy-held territory, Charles was crowned as king of France. The English now began to lose the war, not on the ground, but in the hearts of the French. Hence the English insistence, following Joan of Arc's capture at Compiègne, that she be tried by French judges in an ecclesiastical trial to demonstrate that Joan was sent not by God, but by the Devil. She was burnt as a condemned heretic at Rouen on 31 May 1431.

Joan's execution was wasted effort, for in the court of public opinion it was believed that God had rendered judgment, though the verdict was still to be carried out. The duke of Burgundy still held the key to the military situation, and nothing decisive could be done against the English until Burgundy was reconciled to the French crown. This became possible in 1433, when power in the king's council passed to the princes of Anjou and Constable Arthur de Richemont, brother to the duke of Brittany. They wished to make peace with the duke of Burgundy, who, expecting no further benefit from the English alliance, hoped that he would be allowed to change sides and to recognize—saving his own honor—the royal legitimacy of his father's assassin.

The largest diplomatic congress yet held in Europe opened at Arras in Burgundian territory on 5 August 1435. When the English, who were in no mood for concessions, quickly withdrew, Duke Philip the Good was able to accept with honor the generous offer made to him by Charles VII. The French king, now obliged to accept the duke of Burgundy's near-total independence, nevertheless attained the one goal that was essential: no prince of the blood any longer recognized Henry VI of Lancaster as the legitimate king of France.

Over the long term, the Peace of Arras guaranteed to Charles VII a victory for the fruits of which he still had another twenty years to wait. His adversary remained strong, and the conflict continued under atrocious conditions: severe famines in 1438-39, the reappearance of the plague, and the ravages of the undisciplined troops, the worst of whom were dubbed "scorchers [écorcheurs]." It was nonetheless precisely during this era that the French kingdom regained its unity, and the state reestablished its authority. Paris, which had resolutely refused entry to Joan of Arc, opened its gates to the king without resistance on 13 April 1436. The unified Parlement and the Chamber of Accounts, hitherto divided between the rival claimants to the throne, was now reunited in Paris, though the king himself preferred to remain with his government on the banks of the Loire. So successful were his military efforts that by 1444 English power no longer extended beyond Calais, Normandy, and Aquitaine. These new conditions were recognized in a ten-year truce signed at Tours. The English would have been well advised to observe the truce, for a radical fiscal and military reform had now placed in Charles VII's hands the means to end the war. On 17 July 1449, alleging an English breach of the truce, the French king decided to reopen hostilities. His resounding victories at Formigny (15 April 1450) and Castillon (27 July 1453) paved the way for the rapid reconquest of Normandy and then of Aquitaine. The English had now lost all the French fiefs their kings had held since the twelfth century, plus all of their recent conquests, with the sole exception of Calais. God's judgment had been rendered. But only in fact, not in law, for the two kings signed no peace, nor even a simple truce. Only the extreme dislocation in England caused by the War of the Roses (1453-83) kept its king from seeking aid from French princes to reopen the unsettled quarrel.

*Victory over the Princes*

The disappearance of the great foreign menace had the immediate effect of sparking internal dissentions anew. Beginning in 1440, the dukes of Bourbon and Alençon under the Dauphin Louis led an insurgency (known as the *"praguerie"*)[2] which aimed to get control of the royal government. Although the rebellion failed, in 1442 the princely opposition regrouped and announced a program for the public good: control of the royal council, and consultation with the Estates General, the representative assembly for the entire realm. Although Charles VII gained the upper hand through skillful maneuvers, the debate continued over what form the state should take: an absolutist monarchy or one tempered by the aristocracy.

After Louis XI became king on 22 July 1461, he showed, despite his rebel past, no interest in sharing power, either with the princes, who had been his allies, or with his father's old retainers. His attitude explains why two princes, the Burgundian heir, Charles the Bold, and the royal heir, also named Charles, were able to assemble the most dangerous coalition of aristocratic malcontents the kingdom had ever known. The ensuing conflict, called the "War of the Public Good," brought the king to within a hair's breadth of losing his power to the princes. After the indecisive battle of Montlhéry (16 July 1465), Louis XI was able to escape only because his opponents' forces were so poorly coordinated, and because he had granted them—totally in bad faith—enormous concessions.

This affair left much bitterness in its wake, as a twelve-year struggle ensued between king and princes, filled with underground intrigues and treachery, political trials, and executions. Charles the Bold organized brief but cruel military operations, interspersed with tortuous negotiations, which sometimes went badly for the king, as at Peronne in 1468. These atrocious relations between king and princes were not due, as has so often been confidently alleged, to the Machiavellian scheming of Louis XI, who has been misleadingly dubbed "the Universal Spider." The source of the conflict was fear, on the parts both of the king, who knew he faced deposition or even assassination, and of the princes, who knew full well that the first false step might cost them their possessions and or even their lives.

Events came to a head in 1475, a serious crisis which is often overlooked. The conspiracy of the "king's malcontents" included almost all the princes of the blood, and, at court, the Constable himself—commander of the king's armies. After the Dauphin Charles of France conveniently died in 1472, Charles the Bold of Burgundy, the king's sworn enemy for the past ten years, led the revolt, this time in company with his brother-in-law, King Edward IV of England. Was the Hundred Years' War about to begin all over again? In fact, Louis XI was saved by his opponents' lack of coordination, for Edward IV, who found himself isolated when he landed at Calais, quickly lost heart and accepted a seven-year truce—the first since 1444—at Picquigny on 29 August. He was well paid for his decision.

Why had the allies failed? Charles the Bold missed this all-important rendezvous with Edward of England because of his commitments in the Empire, where he was trying to carve out a realm that stretched from Switzerland to the lower Rhineland. Louis XI had only a minor role in this grand European drama. Charles the Bold brought about his own downfall through his adventures against the Swiss and in Lorraine, where he fell in the Battle of Nancy (5 January 1477).

At one stroke, Charles' death transformed the European political game. Louis XI, not looking beyond the immediate situation, believed that the hour had come to break with one blow the princes' encirclement, the cause of all his worries. He immediately began a campaign designed to ruin the house of Burgundy and capture its inheritance. This proved a miscalculation. Duchess Mary, Charles the Bold's daughter and heir, found herself a defender—and a spouse—in Maximilian of Habsburg, archduke of Austria and de facto heir presumptive to the Imperial throne. The Treaty of Arras in 1482 left Louis XI his conquests—the duchy of Burgundy, the Franche-Comté, and the country of Artois, but the latter two only on condition of a marriage between the Dauphin Charles and Margaret of Austria, daughter of Mary and Maximilian and granddaughter of Charles the Bold. But since this arrangement was forced on Margaret's father, Archduke Maximilian, it did not settle the question of Burgundy or remove the continuing threat to France's northern and eastern borders.

Louis XI had better luck on other fronts. In the southeast he made good his claim to the inheritance of Anjou (1481), including Provence and an as yet dormant claim to the kingdom of Naples. In the southwest, with the suppression of the county of Armagnac and the placement of the lands of the house of Foix, including Béarn and Navarre, in the hands of one of his sisters, Louis had no fears. But further south, across the Pyrenees, Louis had made a formidable enemy in 1462, when he seized the county of Roussillon from Aragon, and he was unable to prevent the union through marriage of the crowns of Castile and Aragon in 1476. And, finally, in central France Louis XI sought to secure control of two great principalities, Orleans and Bourbon, by tying their heirs, Louis of Orleans and Pierre de Beaujeu, to himself as sons-in-law. In fact, however, the center could never be secure, so long as Brittany remained a semi-independent duchy in the west, to serve, with Burgundy, as the fulcrum for all the princely leagues formed against the king since 1465.

Louis XI died on 31 August 1483. The balance sheet for his policy of territorial consolidation is very favorable, although his long reign, riddled with deceit and treachery, could not help but encourage in those he left behind a violent appetite for revenge. And, since his son and successor, Charles VIII, was still an adolescent, power seemed ready for the taking. For example, by the prince next in line for the throne, Louis of Orléans, who demanded the reins of government for himself, and by Anne, the king's sister and wife of the future duke of Bourbon, Peter of Beaujeu, who refused to give them up. Thus conditions were ripe for a renewal of the great struggle between the monarchy and the princes. Albeit under different circumstances, the new struggle now unfolded within the aristocracy itself, where, excepting the house of Foix-Albret, Louis of Orléans had only one possible ally left against the Bourbons, namely, the duke of Brittany. But he found others outside of France who were willing to enter the fray in order to secure their own interests. One such ally was the house of Habsburg Austria, because of Burgundy; another was the Catholic kings of Spain, because of Roussillon; and a third was England, because of the crown.

This situation makes the ensuing events more understandable: Louis of Orleans' convocation in 1484 of the Estates-General, which turned to the advantage of the Beaujeus; the fruitless insurrection of 1485, called the "mad" war; and the flight of the rebel Louis in 1487 to Brittany, whither Pierre and Anne de Beaujeu had every intention of pursuing him. The war that now began at once became a European conflict, for Maximilian had already opened hostilities in the north and the east, while England and Spain supported Brittany with arms. A resounding French victory at Saint-Aubin-du-Cormier on 28 July 1488 placed Louis of Orleans in the hands of the Bourbons and left the duke of Brittany at their mercy, but it did nothing to break the triple alliance of Austria, Spain, and England. Then, in 1489 the duke of Brittany's death provoked a grave crisis of succession. Charles VIII, the young French king, entered into a contest with Duchess Anne, sole heiress of the late duke, who decided in 1490, like Mary of Burgundy before her, to acquire a foreign defender through a marriage-by-proxy to Maximilian of Austria. This tightened still further the alliance of Austria, Spain, and England around Brittany. But the French king's army proved stronger, taking Nantes and laying siege to Rennes. Rather than relinquish her duchy and join her husband in Flanders or Austria, Anne of Brittany decided to switch sides and become queen of France. Her marriage to Charles VIII on 6 December 1491 meant in effect Brittany's incorporation into the kingdom of France.

Who was responsible for pursuing this pitiless war, the Bourbons or King Charles VIII? Generally, historians do not even raise this question, for the policy of territorial consolidation, in imitation of Louis XI, seems like the only possible choice, because it enhanced both the unity and the grandeur of the state. Yet, was this so certain at the time? The young king, who understood the stakes of such an agenda, also saw its risks. The proof that he did so lies in the fact that when faced with a genuine coup d'état, he went of his own accord on 28 June 1491 to reconcile himself with Louis of Orleans, who had just been released from prison. By the same token, Charles would have preferred to marry Margaret of Austria rather than Anne of Burgundy—so long as he could still occupy Brittany—and thereby to settle the Burgundian question honorably and forever. The policy of his father and his sister had led to a mortal struggle within the kingdom and to the creation of a formidable foreign alliance against it. Charles wanted to change directions, to assemble the upper aristocracy around him and lead it into a war "of magnificence" in Italy, which would owe nothing either to internecine quarrels or a desire for vengeance.

This reasoning explains quite satisfactorily the three peace treaties that have long been vilified in the annals of French history, because of claims that the king had "let the prey escape and pursued its shadow [*lâcher la proie pour l'ombre*]."[3] The first agreement, the Treaty of Etaples (3 November 1492) with King Henry VII of England, arranged for a perpetual peace lined with French gold. The second pact, the Treaty of Barcelona with Spain (19 January 1493), made possible the restitution of Roussillon, while in the third, the Treaty of Senlis (23 May 1493), Maximilian of Austria renounced his claim to Burgundy and recognized Anne of Brittany's marriage to the king. For his part, the French king honorably restored to Maximilian the lands of Artois and Franche-Comté, the dowry of Maximilian's daughter, whom Charles had not married.

### France in the Italian Wars

Charles VIII's wish to go on campaign to Italy, therefore, did not lack reasons. The Italian states pleaded with him, as they had pleaded with his father, to intervene in their struggles; as heir to the Angevins, he possessed a claim to the throne of Naples; the reform of the Church, to which all of Christendom aspired, depended on the pope in Rome; and Italy, gateway to the east and the logical staging base for a new crusade, was threatened by the crusade's inevitable target, the Ottoman Turks. The expedition to Naples was thus for the king a just war, fought for the good of all Christendom.

Italy awaited Charles, literally, as a messiah. He traversed the peninsula without difficulty and entered Naples on 22 February 1495. Soon, however, a coalition formed against him, including Milan, Venice, the pope, and also Spain, which would not tolerate any competition either at Naples or in the leadership of a crusade. Charles VIII returned to France, jostling the enemy at Fornova on 6 July 1495, and died on 7 April 1498, having failed to take revenge on his foes.

Since Charles VIII and Anne of Brittany had produced no sons, Salic Law dictated the succession of Louis of Orleans, who reigned as Louis XII. The new king immediately took up his own house's claim to the duchy of Milan, allegedly usurped by the Sforza family, and took possession of it in 1499-1500, along with the city of Genoa, a one-time possession of the kings of France. In Lombardy, Louis found himself in Imperial territory and, therefore, in conflict with Emperor Maximilian I. Spain, meanwhile, had been an enemy of the French king since 1495, and England was ready to renew its enmity. The triple alliance of 1490 was virtually reconstructed. The conduct of what has been called a "war of prestige" in Italy, thus, produced the same baleful external consequences as had the royal policy of territorial consolidation, and Louis had either to abandon this policy or defend it in the field.

Though he never envisaged renouncing his rights at the expense of his honor, Louis XII did seek a diplomatic solution to this dilemma. At his accession he had broken his involuntary marriage contract with Louis XI's daughter, preferring to marry Anne of Brittany. Their daughter, Claude, could not ascend the throne, though she would one day inherit her mother's duchy and the properties and rights of her father's house of Orleans. As it happened, King Maximilian's son, who had married the heiress of both Spanish kingdoms, had a son, Charles of Ghent, who would one day succeed to the entire Burgundian heritage. The Treaty of Blois in 1504 prescribed the marriage of these two children, Claude of France and Charles of Ghent, who would share, with Spain's consent, rule of the duchies of Burgundy and Brittany, the Low Countries, Franche-Comté, Milan, and even Naples. This arrangement would have resolved all problems past and present and secured the peace, though at the cost of the past fifty years' progress toward the consolidation of the French state. The alternative policy, which Louis XI and the Beaujeus had pursued, required maintaining the unity of the kingdom and of the royal line by uniting Claude with Francis of Angoulême, the king's cousin and heir presumptive. This solution, which finally won out in 1506, meant the resumption of war.

Louis XII accepted the challenge. Chased out of Naples by 1504, he recaptured Genoa, which had revolted in 1507; he successfully defended Milan against the Venetians at the Battle of Agnadello in 1509, and against the pope's army at the Battle of Ravenna in 1512. His successes lent him a quasi-imperial stature, disturbing to that other Caesar, Pope Julius II, who assembled a "Holy League" against Louis. This league included not only the old triple alliance, but also the Swiss and a number of Italian princes. Beaten at Novara in 1513, France found itself threatened by invasion on all sides. Meanwhile, in 1512, Spain had taken from the Albret dynasty the portion of Navarre south of the Pyrenees. The new king, Francis I, unwilling to leave off war at such a point of failure, returned to the attack immediately upon his accession, and his great victory over the Swiss at Marignano before the gates of Milan on 14 September 1515 gave him control of Lombardy once again.

The brilliant victory at Marignano made an deep impression. The pope sought a treaty in 1516, obtaining also the concordat he desired, while King Charles of Spain followed suit in 1517, and the following year a crusade was proclaimed. More than any of his predecessors, the triumphant Francis I seemed a likely candidate for the Imperial throne until the German electors, their hands well greased, chose King Charles as emperor-elect on 28 June 1519. Theoretically, northern and central Italy were a part of the Empire, and Charles V, sole heir to Burgundy and both Spains, thus became the only representative of all those claims for which his various ancestors had fought France. This fact explains the very artificial convention of saying that the Italian wars ended in 1515, to be followed in 1521 by a perpetual rivalry between France and the house of Austria.

The notion of a lull between 1515 and 1521 is illusory, for the war resumed in 1521 because Francis I, like Louis XII, renounced neither the policy of territorial consolidation nor the "war of prestige" in Italy. Pursuing the former policy, he exploited unjustly a claim of inheritance against the duke of Bourbon, his own High Constable, whom he thereby pushed to revolt in 1523. The same policy led him to confiscate the Bourbonnais and the Auvergne. The latter policy, expansion in Italy, led Francis to try to secure Milan and regain Naples. In this he failed, however, and fell into Charles V's hands after the disastrous battle of Pavia (25 February 1525).

Having agreed as Charles' prisoner to observe the victor's conditions, as a free man Francis repudiated them and took up the conflict again, until the war was ended by the Treaty of Cambrai, also called the "Ladies' Peace," on 3 August 1529. The treaty may be seen as a settlement of the issue first broached in 1477, because Charles V renounced his claim to the duchy of Burgundy, and Francis I his rights of sovereignty over Artois and

Flanders. Did it also mark the end of the Italian Wars? Perhaps, for the king of France grudgingly agreed to yield his place in peninsular affairs to the emperor.

## 2. France in the Mid-Sixteenth Century

By 1530 the kingdom of France had taken a recognizable shape. It was enlarged and buttressed by the successful policy of territorial consolidation—of the great princely families there remained only the House of Albret, with its Navarrese claim in the southwest—but the kingdom had also been obliged to draw in on itself and desist from foreign adventures. The kingdom certainly had a solid base, for there was no longer any risk of its becoming a confederation of principalities in the German style. The king's sovereignty was unique, and it was in principle absolute, since, in order to win out over the princes, the king had been forced to resist all aristocratic control of a parliamentary type. The king's power, however, was definitely not absolute, for the king in no way claimed to impose his law at the expense of those social and local powers that ran parallel to his own. Moreover, until the middle of the sixteenth century there was no talk of "the state," but rather of "the estates of the kingdom," members of a body politic of which the king was the only head, but nothing more. The monarchy's very structure served to mitigate its power.

### The Shape of the French State

The sovereignty of the state, which resided in the sole person of the monarch, took a dual form. Indeed, the king was supposed to have two bodies. One of his bodies was immortal, its permanence guaranteed by the Salic Law. Following Charles VII's and Louis XI's victories, everything contributed to the exaltation of majesty of this body, from the treatises on law to the increasingly eloquent ceremonies marking the important moments in a reign. The king's other body was that of a mortal, but of no ordinary mortal, since this lieutenant of God in his kingdom, who was consecrated and invested with the miraculous power of healing, was also "most Christian," an old formula that first took on an official meaning in the diplomatic correspondence of Louis XI.

In point of fact these two bodies were really one, for they did not belong to a single individual, but to a family, symbolized by its blood, and chosen from the outset because of its sanctity. This fact had serious repercussions, for the king as sole legitimate heir incarnated in his own person the body of majesty, while as head of his family he was obliged to make place in his government for the princes of his blood line and for the first among them, his successor. Moreover, governing did not mean administering, but rather defending the kingdom and keeping its peace. This amounted to a moral as much as a political duty. The favors, pardons, privileges, and gifts, which the king was obliged to dispense to his subjects, contributed to his role as did his rigorous justice and his great legislative ordinances, which multiplied especially after 1490.

This enduring combination of juridical abstraction with the realities of family politics strongly influenced the structure of royal institutions. By the later fifteenth century, the old sovereign courts (*parlements, chambres des comptes, cours des aides*) coalesced into the great corporate bodies (*grand corps*) of the state, whose functioning alone they controlled. They embodied the king's majesty, but they did not govern. The men who did govern from day to day were recruited from among the princes of the blood, the high officers, prelates, and royal familiars, whom the king's favor admitted to his secret matters. They lived at court, as did the professional administrators such as the *maîtres des requêtes de l'hôtel*.

It is thus impossible to say whether the government resided more in the king's court or in his council. The court contained those close to him, his servants and his great officers, such as the chancellor, the admiral, and the constable, all of whom sat in the council as well. It is difficult to decide whether the little circle of intimates that dealt with the great questions, commonly called since Francis I's day the king's "privy council" or the "council of affairs," belonged to the royal council or to the court. In any case, from the reign of Charles VIII onward the chancellor acted more and more as the head of this very loosely structured machinery. Meanwhile, an administrative organization was also forming within the bosom of what was increasingly referred to in the sixteenth century as the council of state. This development was marked by the progressive appearance of units which specialized in dealing with judicial appeals or administrative disputes. In particular, four officers, had by 1547 emerged from the royal college of notaries and secretaries of the king to act as ministers; by 1559 they were called "secretaries of state."

Responsibility for executing the decisions emanating from these various courts and councils lay with the local judicial and financial officers, who presided over the bailiwicks (*bailliages*) and the smaller financial districts known as *élections*. There was not a great number of these officials—at most ten thousand or so by the beginning of the sixteenth century—but despite the kingdom's great size, they ensured that the king's presence was felt everywhere. Since 1467 each of them enjoyed an almost irrevocable tenure of office, and after 1521 the office-holder became a *de jure* rather than merely a *de facto* proprietor of his office, since he had to buy his office and could resell it. The officers, thus, came increasingly to serve the state, rather than the king in whose name they exercised their functions. Hence the venality of offices, initially a simple fiscal expedient, came eventually to limit the king's power.

The only aspects of central administration that experienced a precocious development were those which corresponded to the essential attributes of public authority, the army and finance, which may be examined together. The centuries-old royal fiscal system, was reorganized in 1436, and nine years later came the creation of a standing army that was supported by the new fiscal regime. This modern standing army, the first of its type in Europe, consisted of a corps of heavily armed cavalry, called "gens d'armes de l'ordonnance." The infantry of yeoman archers, created in 1448, constituted merely a reserve force. In order to maintain the standing army, the king relied not on the royal domain but on direct taxation (the *taille*) as well as indirect taxes, such as the *aides* and salt taxes (*gabelles*). The officers who presided over tax collection were granted autonomy vis-a-vis the council and henceforth functioned as a college. The four general officers of finance (*generaux des finances*), each of whom headed a "generality [*généralité*]," formed the keystone of the structure.

The reconstructed financial system and the modern army that emerged from the worst trials of the Hundred Years' War were perceived to be both an improvement and a necessity, so that those subjects who were required to contribute gave the king their consent once and for all. The king in this manner secured for himself not only the double monopoly of armed force and taxation, but also the power to exercise this monopoly without checks. This explains why already at this early date he was considered an absolute monarch by contemporary observers, notably the Italian ambassadors. They nonetheless failed to understand that the system had a moral basis, which also imposed certain limits on it.

Indeed, the direct tax was explicitly tied to the maintenance of a highly disciplined professional army. It was not a general tax, as it did not apply to the nobility, who supplied personal service, nor to the clergy, who were dedicated to the promotion of peace. Above all, the moralists and political theorists of the sixteenth century agreed that taxes, and in particular the hearth tax (*taille*)—in other words, what were called "extraordinary" finances—might only be employed for their primary purpose. All other uses, notably for defraying the expenses of the court or the state, were considered evidence of tyranny. The king of France thus collected not the taxes that his sovereignty might have permitted, but those that were sanctioned by his sense of morality.

These facts help to clarify the entire history of French taxation as it related to the army, since Charles VII's reign. In order to promote an arms race ruinous to the princes, Louis XI maintained a standing army of 40,000, men, plus some infantry on the Swiss model, supported by a powerful artillery. He thereby doubled the army's size and acquired his reputation as a tyrant. Upon his death, the estates-general of 1484 put a stop to this drift towards military expansion and reduced the standing army to the level of 1460. There were no significant changes for a long time thereafter, though the army did grow slowly during the sixteenth century until, under Henry II, it again attained the size of 1483. This growth involved a few innovations, notably the greater place given to light cavalry equipped with firearms. Since the establishment of yeoman-archers remained a failure despite all efforts to the contrary, short-term native levies and foreign mercenaries continued to make up the bulk of the infantry.

To finance this army, the king could not honorably multiply the sources of revenue, except for devices such as the sale of public offices, but he could improve the yield of those revenues already in existence. As of 1523, convinced that the oligarchy of the general officers of finances was constantly stealing from him, he put an end to their functions, indicted them, and attempted to centralize the flow of receipts under the control of a new official, the Treasurer of the *Epargne*. He also handed over the direction of finances to the council of state (*conseil d'État*), one of whose members became a sort of minister, assisted under Henry II by controllers-general and specialized intendants. In 1542 the four generalities created during Charles VII's reign were increased at one stroke to sixteen.

These reforms proved wasted effort, for the state continued to live beyond its means, and after 1483 it was forced constantly to resort to a line of credit that obeyed no principles of rational organization. Until their downfall, the oligarchy of the general officers of finance owed their influence more to their loans to the state than to their powers of office. Following the suppression of these offices, the crown had to rely increasingly on public credit. This took the form initially of annuities (*rentes*) issued in the king's name by the city of Paris, and later of loans negotiated on the Lyons market by financiers who were generally Italians. In 1555, the "great party [*grand parti*]" of Lyons even made a reasonable stab at consolidating the public debt. But war undercut this experiment. The king of France could neither pull out of the war nor pay for it, and by 1558 he, like his enemy, King Philip II of Spain, found himself on the edge of bankruptcy; he was forced to turn for help to the estates, with which he effectively shared his power.

### The Estates

The first estate of the realm was the Gallican Church. In 1438 Charles VII confirmed its liberties in the form of a charter called the "Pragmatic Sanction of Bourges." Yet, this guarantee proved something of an illusion, and Louis XI made it yet more uncertain; in fact, the French clergy escaped neither papal authority nor the royal control which the concordat of 1516 erected into a rule of law. The clergy was a fully integrated part of the kingdom's political order, though it retained the relative autonomy conferred by its privileges, its strong moral authority and its own distinct financial structure, which was regularized in 1561 in the form of an independent voluntary contribution to the king. Hence, the regular convening of general assemblies of the clergy, for which the assemblies of 1493 and 1510 provided a precedent.

The second estate was the nobility, a fraction of the population infinitesimal in size (2% at the most), but important in influence. At its head stood an aristocracy in which gentlemen of the court increasingly supplanted the princes of the blood. Well represented in the royal council, since the days of Louis XI the aristocracy monopolized the offices of lieutenants-general to the king and of governors in the new provincial commands. These commands began to replace the old principalities around 1450, and the aristocratic limitation of the king's power was acceptable to a monarchy that no longer feared direct aristocratic competition.

Below the great nobility, and often in the circle of its clients, were those whom one may call "the secondary nobility." Although as a group they continued to bear arms, only a small minority (5 to 6%) practised the military profession, and their real power lay in the possession of seigneurial rights of police and justice. This group ruled, as they always had done, at the local level.

Despite their strong ramparts and militia, and the considerable administrative autonomy exercised by their magistrates, the roughly 300 French towns of real size did not clearly form a third estate. They were nonetheless the focal points and centers of exchange, and they dominated the economies of the surrounding countryside. Local magistrates were the elite members of oligarchies of burghers and ennobled patricians, and they governed the cities with an authority which derived both from the towns themselves and, by delegation, from the state.

The distribution of power among the various social forces was complemented by the diversity of the different provinces, each with its own identity. In places, this identity was defended by provincial estates, and defined
by local customs. Far from wanting to modify these customs, the king decreed in 1456 that they were to be fixed in writing. Paradoxically, the
royal victory over the princes led to an increase in territorial decentralization. For example, Languedoc, because of its distance from the center, enjoyed its own particular regime. All of the areas reconquered or annexed
during the wars also retained their assemblies of estates, which were called
upon to approve taxation and to participate in tax collection. These regions also received governors and sovereign courts, which were created or
confirmed at the expense of their Parisian counterparts. Around the old
royal domain thus formed a circle of "lands," known as the "lands of the
estates [*pays d'états*]."

In sum, in the mid-sixteenth century the allegedly absolute monarchy of
France lacked any form of administrative centralization. Each estate and
each "land [*pays*]" possessed its privileges and by the same token its own
fiscal organization, which it was ready to defend by force, if necessary, as
the provinces of Guyenne and Saintonge did in 1541 and 1548.

### National Unity

Was the only unity in this splintered kingdom provided by the state? By no
means, for a French nation, as was becoming increasingly clear, was already forming. French art and rituals demonstrated it, and the writings of
the period provided it with a meaning. Humanism, which appeared in the
country in the course of the fifteenth century, contributed to the birth of
national consciousness by lending it the support of history. Following the
example of Julius Caesar, the humanists provided the nation with its ancestors, the Gauls, and thereby breathed new life into the old myth of
France's Trojan origins. The Gauls, the story went, returned to their native
soil after their passage through Troy, bearing with them a wisdom and
laws that owed nothing to either the Romans or the Germans. They had
accepted Christian baptism along with St. Clovis and his Franks. The holy
dynasty he founded had its emblematic figures in St. Louis and the saintly
Emperor Charlemagne. This dynasty had maintained the orthodoxy of the
people which had been chosen by providence to secure the defense of the
Church and the triumph of the spirit, under the leadership of a line of new
Davids, the "most Christian kings [*rex christianissimus*]." The ethos they
represented was expressed by a maxim about unity, which since Louis
XII's time was quoted to summarize this history and this mission: "One

king, one faith, one law [*un roi, une foi, une loi*]."[4]  One could even have added "one language," since that of the king, and by extension that of Paris and the banks of the Loire, imposed itself smoothly between 1450 and 1520 on the social elite of the kingdom from the north to the south, to the detriment both of the local languages and of Latin.  The edict of Villers-Cotterets in 1539 merely sanctioned this process after the fact.

The assemblies of the Estates General kingdom also manifested the nation's cohesion.  One must take them for what they were, that is to say, the great repositories of dynastic loyalty and national spirit.  The sovereign himself organized them and presided over them, either in order to give him ammunition against third parties, as in 1468, 1470, and 1527, or to close ranks at times of important decisions, as in 1484, 1506 and 1558.

The burgeoning national consciousness was thus not linked to a notion of parliamentarianism, but it was inseparable from a certain kind of messianism that lent it an imperial tinge.  It also mingled with Gallicanism.  The "most Christian king" had a holy mission to reform the Church by convoking a general council, a constant aspiration in this period.  The idea of the king's mission, repeatedly reaffirmed under Louis XI and Charles VIII, took full shape in Louis XII's day with the opening of the Council of Pisa on 1 November 1511, all the more so because of the confrontation between the king and Pope Julius II.  The affair ended abruptly, but it would be wrong to conclude from this that the council was a purely political calculation.

Failing to reform the Church Universal, it was the king's duty to proceed to a reform of the Gallican, or French, Church.  This mission was first proclaimed under Charles VII during the conciliarist crisis in the church, and by 1480 the reform movement had gathered force, as the number of individual attempts at reform multiplied.  Many brilliant minds, such as Jacques Lefevre d'Etaples, first distinguished themselves during this debate over reform.  When new ideas came to light, such as those of Martin Luther, which first arrived from Germany in 1520, King Francis I, and even more so his sister, Marguerite, future queen of Navarre, were very receptive to these developments.  It would take the "Affair of the Placards" in October of 1534, when violent tracts against the Mass were posted on the very doors to the king's chambers at Blois, to make him change his mind.  Henceforth, the extinction of heresy took precedence for Francis over the reform of the Church.

The king's decision against reform in 1534 was an ominous moment that ruptured a national consensus; fortuitously, it coincided with a reversal of the economic tendencies which, for nearly a century, had favored the growth of the state in France. Indeed, since 1450, following a period of deep demographic depression, the kingdom's population had begun to grow again, reaching the pre-plague level of 20 million around 1550. Agricultural production had followed this trend, further lightening the burden of taxation. The state, which took little or no hand in this agricultural reconstruction, did play an interventionist role in the subsequent restoration of large-scale commerce. It reestablished monetary stability in 1436, and the protectionist policy of Louis XI has sometimes, misleadingly, led to his being dubbed "the merchants' king [*le roi des marchands*]." The fairs at Lyons became a great center for European trade, monetary exchange in Marseilles doubled between 1520 and 1543, and the Normans and the inhabitants of Saint-Malo launched their great adventures into the Indian Ocean and up the St. Lawrence River.

The clear signs of economic dynamism nevertheless barely concealed a new stagnation in agricultural production, which since the winter of 1522-23 raised anew the specter of famine in France. A further reversal in economic conjuncture that became apparent around 1530 not only hampered the possibility of expansion but also undermined the possibilities for a French royal policy possessing truly imperial ambitions.

### 3. FROM DEFENSE AGAINST THE EMPIRE TO THE CIVIL WARS, 1530-1600

Was the Emperor Charles V truly convinced that it fell to him alone to direct Western Christendom? Scholars may argue about this point, but in fact he was never so close to realizing this claim as he was around 1530. It was at this very moment that his rival for this role, the French king, dropped out of the contest. The king's war against the Empire between 1536 and 1538, and again for fifteen years beginning in 1542, was a defensive struggle to end a new and formidable threat of encirclement.

*France Against the Empire, 1530-1557*
Francis I died on 31 March 1547, and though the royal council's composition changed under Henry II, its anti-Imperial policy did not. Depending on whether one took a conciliatory or a confrontational tack this policy could take two forms, giving rise to two distinct currents of thought. Their shifting fortunes at court depended on the various intrigues and struggles between the aristocratic factions. Opposing the Emperor meant supporting his enemies, notably in Italy, so that Milan and Naples remained as

central to the government's various political schemes as they had been thirty years before. The situation also suggested seeking an alliance with England, or at least an assurance of neutrality, to forestall a revival of the old Anglo-Burgundian collusion. Finally, it required forming alliances with the Emperor's new adversaries, the Protestant princes in Germany and the Turks in the Mediterranean. When France completed these new alliances in 1532 and 1535 respectively, the most Christian king, committed himself prudently but irresistibly to a wholly new path. He placed the interests of the kingdom and the maintenance of a European balance-of-power above all other considerations, even religion.

This momentous change explains why the various participants made such divergent choices, and why, beginning in the 1530s, their respective positions became progressively more radical. Anne of Montmorency, named Constable in 1537, took a public stand in favor of prudence, while the sons of Duke Claude of Guise, a younger brother of the duke of Lorraine who had come to court seeking his fortune, called for open war. Antoine de Bourbon, first prince of the blood, and king of Navarre by virtue of his marriage to Jeanne d'Albret, had not yet moved into the foreground of this conflict. During the later 1530s the war party had the upper hand. From 1536 to 1538, Francis I made war again to recapture Milan, and although he did not succeed, he was able to take Savoy and Piedmont, which he partially annexed. In 1542 he had the audacity to initiate hostilities against the emperor and his ally, Henry VIII of England. But the glory days of the Hundred Years' War were long past. Not one campaign brought any strategic results, neither in the district of Boulogne, nor in Champagne, nor in Piedmont, despite the French victory at Cerisole (14 April 1544). The Peace of Crépy demonstrated that the war had been pointless.

In 1552, five years after Francis' death, the conflict nonetheless resumed, this time in consequence of the new alliance of Henry II with German Protestant princes, who had offered him as pledge the "three bishoprics" of Lorraine (Metz, Toul, and Verdun). When Charles came westward to Metz, his counter-attack was broken by Francis of Guise, and his subsequent defeats in Italy led to the Truce of Vaucelles (5 February 1556).

Were these encounters merely a new phase of an endless cycle? No, for the situation had changed. On the one hand, the religious peace of 1555 in Germany meant a loss of support for France from the Protestant princes, but, on the other, a neutralization of Austria through the partition of Charles V's inheritance. From then on France's sole adversary was Philip

II, who had inherited all the lands which lay in contention between the houses of Valois and Habsburg—the Burgundian inheritance, Italy, and Navarre. On top of this, Philip married Queen Mary of England and espoused her claims to the crown of France. The war therefore resumed, more bitterly than ever. Although the rout of the Constable at Saint-Quentin on 10 August 1557 opened the way to Paris, the Spanish could not take the city, and when Francis of Guise took Calais from the English (9 January 1558), he swept away the last vestiges of the Hundred Year's War. After the fall of Calais the belligerents came to the peace table in earnest, and on 5 February 1559 they signed a peace treaty at the little village of Cateau-Cambrésis. Henry II ceded ground on all fronts, rights and lands his ancestors had struggled for in the north, in Italy, and even in Navarre. He kept nothing but Calais and the three bishoprics of Lorraine, that is to say, those lands that no longer concerned Philip II since Mary Tudor's death and the accession of Elizabeth.

Why did the king make this renunciation? Contemporaries asked themselves this question immediately after the peace. Traditional French history rejoices in the peace in the name of political realism and regrets only the French evacuation of Savoy. From this perspective the monarchy wisely abandoned its dreams in order to stick to a policy of territorial consolidation and expansion to its "natural" borders. At the time, a belief that putting an end to exterior warfare would better facilitate the crushing of heresy within the kingdom lay behind some of the diplomatic bargaining, though how important the issue was remains a subject of discussion.

There can be no doubt, however, that the Peace of Cateau-Cambrésis marked a notable moment in history, for it ended the great rivalries for the hegemony of Christian Europe. In the Empire, the Peace of Augsburg sanctioned the co-existence of the Catholic and Protestant churches, thereby reducing the immediate risk of a second German religious war. Other European rulers, however, threw themselves into religious conflicts in order to avoid solutions similar to the one reached in Germany. Philip II of Spain, for example, considered himself the bulwark of a militant Catholic Church, while Elizabeth of England viewed her relation to Protestantism in the same light. The era of wars of religion on a European scale was underway. In France it took the form of civil war.

### The Civil War of the Later Sixteenth Century

It is traditional to count eight wars of religion beginning in 1562, each concluded by an edict of pacification. There is little point in reiterating the traditional account of these wars. It would probably be more accurate to speak of thirty-six years of confrontations, of iconoclastic furor, of repeated massacres, of seizures and pillaging here and there by little bands, just as in the days of the Hundred Years' War. Instead of a day-by-day chronicle, which is in any case impossible to provide, it is doubtless a better strategy to review the dominant characteristics of this horrible explosion of violence that suffocated the entire kingdom.

To begin with, it consisted of a storm that arrived out of nowhere and surprised even contemporaries by its violence. It first manifested itself in the multiplication after 1555 of Calvinist reformed churches, which openly modelled themselves on that of Geneva. Since the "affair of the placards" in 1534, the hostility between Christians had hardened, a fact clearly demonstrated by the increasingly severe royal edicts of repression from 1551 to 1559. They had little effect, for the schism had penetrated to the heart of the Gallican Church, and by extension to the heart of the kingdom.

According to a recent interpretation by Denis Crouzet, the tension in this situation had the effect of creating another, deeper tension, similar to that which had exploded in Germany in 1520.[5] It was born of eschatological terrors and fear provoked by the conviction that the Day of Judgment and punishment by God were imminent. Calvinism saved its new adherents from this fear, but at the same time pushed them to violent acts of rupture in order to free themselves of the papal Antichrist, so that the destruction of idolatrous images and a persecution of the clergy raged in France between 1560 and 1570. These sacrilegious acts of violence exasperated the Catholics, who were strengthened, in turn, in their conviction that the social and ecclesiastical body had to be purified before the Day of Judgment.

These massive events spared no group, including notably the secondary nobility and the urban oligarchies, who held power at the local level. As a result, the religious tensions and the fear for individual salvation took on a political dimension. There is no need to seek a cause elsewhere. Indeed, it is clear today that the rallying of a part of the nobility to the Reformation owed nothing to a supposed social crisis, the very existence of which still begs to be proven. So, too, does the notion that the nobility's participation in the civil war linked to the idleness of the professional soldiery after the Peace of Cateau-Cambrésis, since noble membership within this group was very low.

The religious currents that were sweeping through this secondary nobility in no way spared the court aristocracy. Francis, duke of Guise, the hero of Calais, and his brother, the cardinal of Lorraine, identified their cause with that of the old religion, but the Montmorency family was divided: the

Constable's nephews, including Admiral Gaspard de Coligny, rallied to the Reformation. Antoine de Bourbon wavered between the two faiths, but his wife, Jeanne d'Albret, and his brother, Louis de Condé, became ardent Protestants. All of them, on either side and between the fronts, were firmly convinced of the old adage: "One king, one faith, one law." The old running battle over places on the council of state now took on a new dimension, as each aristocratic party, while respecting the king's majesty, became convinced that it could fulfill both political and religious missions by purging the king's entourage of all the enemies of the faith and of the kingdom. This duty was so self-evident that it justified armed revolt. Without any great pangs of conscience, the ousted party would call its friends and clients to rise, seek the aid of the fortified cities, and find the help abroad needed to mobilize and pay the indispensable mercenary forces. At its root this drama was of a religious nature, but it was the aristocratic structure of power that turned it into open civil war.

The one additional event needed to complete this rupture between the parties was supplied by Henry II's tragic death in a jousting accident on 10 July 1559. The king left behind four sons, all very young, of whom three— Francis II, Charles IX, and Henry III—gained the throne in rapid succession but produced no direct heirs. Power therefore remained almost uninterruptedly in the hands of their mother, Queen Catherine de' Medici, a capable and attentive woman who always sought to preserve the prestige of the royal dynasty, religious peace, and the public order, for the benefit of her sons. Lacking the means to pursue her policy, she felt herself forced to resort to cunning and to playing the aristocratic powers off against each other, which earned her the reputation for cynicism and perfidy, and the undeserved reproof of many contemporaries. Two, if not three parties existed therefore almost continuously at the court: the queen mother's, the reigning king's, and that of his younger brother, always impatient to reign. It was a situation highly conducive to intrigues and factional confrontations.

In 1559 the new king, Francis II, was entirely under the thumb of the Guise family, uncles of Mary Stuart, whose influence sparked the conspiracy of Amboise, hatched in 1560 by the Protestants—or "Huguenots," as they were beginning to be called—in order to oust the Guises from power by force. The coup failed, and the ferocious repression that followed did not even spare the prince of Condé, who was threatened with an ignominious death. The premature disappearance of the king returned power to Catherine de' Medici, who made a final effort to reconcile the parties by calling the realm's estates-general to Orleans and organizing a

theological colloquy at Poissy. Catherine thereby laid herself open to the
serious accusation of favoring the enemies of the true religion. A massacre
of Protestants in 1562 at Vassy, under the very eyes of Francis of Guise,
triggered the first religious war, which was followed by two more by 1570.
These wars were all calls to arms orchestrated by the prince of Condé, who
was intent on seizing power, but they also witnessed the eruption of "sacred" violence of a new kind: royal cities were conquered and immediately
purged of "papist" idolatry; popular furor led to massacres of Huguenots;
and there were political crimes, such as the assassination of Francis of
Guise beneath the walls of Orléans. The insurgent Huguenots leant on
England, even if this meant handing them Le Havre in place of lost Calais,
and on the support of mercenaries supplied by the German princes.
Against these forces, Catherine and her son, King Charles IX, sent the
royal army, which won battles at Dreux in 1562, at Saint-Denis in 1567,
and at Jarnac and Montcoutour in 1569. The government's chief objective, however, was always to reach a peace, if need be by substantial religious and political concessions of a type which exasperated Catholic public opinion and pushed it toward anarchic violence. An infernal cycle
developed, whereby the search for peace sustained the war.

The Massacre of Saint Bartholomew's Day (24 August 1572) represents
simultaneously the climax of this religious drama and a turning point in
the civil war. The affair embodied all the different elements of the crisis
through which France was passing: Admiral Coligny's ascendancy at the
court and his push for war against Spain, which was wrestling with a Protestant revolution in the Netherlands; the failed attempt against the admiral's life and the suspicion laid at the Queen Mother's door; King Charles
IX's order to slaughter all members of the Huguenot party on the rumor of
a supposed plot; and the blind massacres in which the Catholic crowd at
Paris and in many other cities engaged.

Saint Bartholomew's, the apogee of horror, was also a turning point.[6]
On the one hand, the Protestants of the south and the west seceded, so to
speak, and denounced through their polemicists not the monarchy, but the
criminal tyranny of the king, or rather that of "the Italian," i.e., the Queen
Mother. These publicists were described as "monarchomachs," and
François Hotman's *Franco-Gallia* is an important example of their work.
Many within the Protestant faction nevertheless began to doubt the
justifiability of iconoclastic violence. Meanwhile, many Catholics, denounced the barbarity of massacres that were odious in themselves and
had not even achieved the desired result. They, too, took a stand against
the alleged machiavellianism of the foreigner and called for a reform of the

government. These would-be reformers were dubbed the "malcontents," a term which had already been used in 1475, and were also called "politicals [*politiques*]." They placed themselves in the camp of the Montmorency clan, who did not forget its kinship to the slain admiral, and in the camp of "Monsieur," the young brother of the new king, Henry III. Henry's brother acted in concert with the nephew of Condé, the Protestant Duke Henry of Bourbon, who was also king of Navarre, or at least of its remaining part. The theoretician of this party was Jean Bodin, who in his *Six Books of the Republic* of 1576 set down as an absolute rule that the monarchy was sovereign, though he also insisted on the necessity of a moderate regime. Their program included religious peace in France and war against Spain in the Netherlands. In the wake of another clash of arms, this new alliance carried off its first success with the peace of "Monsieur" in 1576. This group's activities elicited a lively reaction from the Catholic party, which now began spontaneously to organize itself. The first Catholic League resulted when the local forces that had been forming and disintegrating here and there since 1561 finally regrouped. King Henry III, fearing that he would be overrun by both parties, decided to take a preemptive lead. He stole the "politicals'" program by submitting to the estates-general of Blois in 1576 a vast project for reforming the kingdom, and he waged war against the Huguenots from 1577 to 1580. These calculations, which might have had some chance of success, were ruined by the unexpected death of his brother and successor on 10 June 1584. Henry of Bourbon, who headed the Protestant party and was the hope of the "politicals," now became the legitimate heir to the throne. Suddenly, the crisis had attained its peak.

This crisis in which France found itself was, firstly, an economic one, still poorly understood but similar in scale to that of the years 1420-40. Its chief characteristics included the ravaging effects of the armies, a dizzying rise in prices, monetary devaluation, an epidemic, a fall in agricultural production and in trade, and a decline of population. The great victim of the crisis was the peasantry, deprived of its lands and crushed by debts and taxes. Desperation pushed the peasants to rebellions, called "jacqueries," which precipitated heavy bloodshed in a number of provinces from 1590 to 1600.

The crisis was also political. In order to escape the pressure being brought to bear on her by the armed aristocracy, Catherine de' Medici, all the while tacking back and forth between the factions, governed solely through her most faithful agents, who were almost all Italian, including the chancellor, the secretaries of state, and the financiers. She thereby drew the suspicion and anger of those supplanted. The king, for his part, used his mother's people, though he preferred his own faction led by his "mignons," that is, quite simply his own particular councillors, such as the duke of Epernon and the duke of Joyeuse, men who owed him everything. The hatred directed against these newcomers by the established aristocracy, whether Huguenot, Catholic, or "political," and the slanderous claims regarding their supposedly homosexual practices, were such that we are only just barely beginning to trace the role they played in the service of royal absolutism.

The crisis, finally, was constitutional. In the eyes of the Huguenots and the "politicals," the Salic Law, which had been in force as of 1422, designated Henry of Bourbon as the legitimate heir, whatever his profession of faith and all opposing claims. On the contrary, for a number of Catholics, this human law could not contradict the law of God. It could not happen that the most Christian king should be a heretic. Hence the resurgence of the Holy League, a sort of defensive reaction by the clergy and the people of the city of Paris and most of the other chartered cities. The pact concluded at Joinville on 31 December 1584 by Henry of Guise and his people with Spain was merely the League's political manifestation. The League proclaimed as heir to the throne the old cardinal of Bourbon, Henry's brother, and launched as its manifesto a program of reform (31 March 1585). Henry III was caught in the trap. Initially, he thought it clever to ally himself with the League, but the war that ensued only served to profit Henry of Bourbon, king of Navarre, who carried the day at Coutras (20 October 1587) and Henry of Guise. When he wanted to forbid this fearsome ally entry to Paris, the king ran afoul of the local population, which rose against him on the "day of the barricades" (13 May 1588). The king then retreated as far as Blois, where he had called together the estates-general, and decided to rid himself of the duke of Guise and his brother, the cardinal—whom he accused of lese-majesté—through political murder (22 December 1588).

*Henry IV's Conquest of the Kingdom*
This new royal political crime divided France into three parts: the south, held by the Protestants and the "politicals"; the north and the west, including Paris, held by the League; and the Loire area, the last zone loyal to the king. Wishing to recover Paris, Henry III reversed his alliances and recognized Henry of Bourbon, the king of Navarre, as his legitimate heir. Then, on 1 August 1589 a friar named Jacques Clément decided to punish the most Christian king for his treason by killing him. Such a baffling and ex-

traordinary act speaks volumes about the depth of the crisis France was undergoing.

Only his own partisans recognized Henry IV as king. The League, led by the duke of Mayenne, Henry of Guise's brother, wanted to present a rival candidate, but the cardinal of Bourbon was now dead. Should it then accept the candidate proposed by Spain, along with Spanish gold and military help? Extreme confusion prevailed throughout the kingdom, as members of the League and royalists faced off in every corner, and Spanish and Savoyard troops penetrated as far as Meaux and into Provence. Henry IV was victorious in combat at Arques and Ivry, but he failed twice before the walls of Paris, where the League, turned fanatical, had unleashed a reign of terror. Nevertheless, the estates-general, convoked by the League in 1593, dared not overthrow all of the laws of the country by electing a new king.

At this point, the situation abruptly resolved itself. Henry IV, at his own chosen moment, announced his decision to return (for the fifth time!) to the Catholic fold, which brought events rapidly to a head. Consecrated at Chartres on 25 February 1594, the king entered Paris in triumph on March 22, and then bought off the governors and the cities in the League more than he rallied them. On 13 April 1598 the Edict of Nantes set the terms of a religious peace by sanctioning the division of the kingdom according to faith. At the same time, Henry IV engaged in open warfare against Spain in 1595, and imposed his demands in the Peace of Vervins (1598). The duke of Savoy in turn agreed to negotiate, abandoning Bresse and Bugey to the east of the Saône (1601). The crisis had come to an end.

❊ ❊ ❊

The rapid return to civil peace and prosperity under Henry IV has created something of a mythic tradition in favor of this king, and one is quick to forget that he, too, was the victim of a regicide in 1610. Setting aside for the moment the personal qualities he brought to bear, what his brilliant victory demonstrated was the behind-the-scenes accomplishments of the servants of the state. Because of them, this creation held fast through the storm.

The king's victory also indicated, as the much maligned Henry III had understood, that only absolute royal power, existing on a higher plane than the factional strife and religious passions holding sway in the provincial parliamentary assemblies, could guarantee the peace and cohesion of the kingdom. Only this power could permit the king, while still Catholic, to carry out a national policy of resistance against the house of Austria and

Spain, which waited in the wings to revive the wars of religion in Europe.
France thus made a crucial contribution to the creation of the modern state
in the West, and it paid a heavy price for having done so.

Translated by Pegatha Taylor

# NOTES

1. Treaty of Troyes, art. 29, in E. Cosneau, ed., *Les grands traités de la guerre de Cent Ans* (Paris, 1889), 114.
2. An contemporary allusion to the Hussite revolt at Prague, for which see Jean Chartier, *Chronique de Charles VII*, ed. Vallet de Viriville (Paris, 1885), vol. 1:258.
3. Labande-Mailfert (1975), 117.
4. On the history of this formula, see R. W. Scheller, "French Royal Symbolism in the Age of Louis XII," *Simiolus* 13 (1983):122-23.
5. Crouzet (1990).
6. Estèbe (1968).

# BIBLIOGRAPHY

*Printed Sources*

Basin, Thomas. *Histoire de Louis XI.* Ed. Charles Samaran. 2 vols. Classiques de l'Histoire de France. Paris, 1963-66.

*Catalogue des actes de François Ier.* 10 vols. Paris, 1887-08.

Commynes, Philippe de. *Mémoires.* Ed. Joseph Calmette. Paris, 1924.

*Journal d'un bourgeois de Paris, 1405-1449.* Ed. A. Tutey. Paris, 1881. Ed. Colette Beaune. Paris, 1990.

Kendall, Paul Murray, and Vincent Illardi, eds. *Dispatches, with Related Documents of Milanese Ambassadors in France and Burgundy, 1450-1483.* 3 vols. Athens, O., 1970-81.

Laurent, Jean-Paul, Marie-Thérèse de Martel, and Marie-Noëlle Matuszek-Baudouin, eds. *Catalogue des actes de Henri II.* Vol. 1, *31 mars-31 décembre 1547.* Académie des sciences morales et politiques. Paris, 1979.

L'Estoile, P. de. *Journal pour le règne de Henri III.* Ed. L. R. Lefèvre. Paris, 1943.

Le Bouvier, Gilles. *Les Chroniques du roi Charles VII.* Ed. H. Courteault and L. Celier with M.-H. Jullien de Pommerol. Paris, 1979.

Lemaire des Belges, Jean. *Oeuvres.* Ed. A. J. Strecher. Paris, 1882-85. Reprint. Geneva, 1969.

*Lettres d'Henri III, roi de France.* Parts I-IV, *1557-1580.* Paris, 1959-84.

Machiavelli, Niccolò. "Rapport sur les choses de la France" (1510)." In *Oeuvres complète*, 135-49. Paris, 1952.

Mandrot, B., ed. *Dépêches des ambassadeurs milanais en France sous Louis XI et François Sforza.* Paris, 1916-23.

*Ordonnances des rois de France. Règne de François I.* 8 vols. Paris, 1902-89.

Seyssel, Claude de. *La Monarchie de France.* Ed. J. Poujol. Paris, 1961.


*Literature*

*General*

Favier, Jean, ed. *Histoire de France.* Paris, 1984.

Favier, Jean, ed. Vol. 2, *Le Temps des principautés de l'an mil à 1515*, by Jean Favier. Paris, 1984.

Favier, Jean, ed. Vol. 3, *La France modern de 1515 à 1789*, by Jean Meyer. Paris, 1985.

Imbart de La Tour, Pierre. *Les origines de la Réforme.* Vol. 1, *La France moderne.* 2d ed. Paris, 1948.

Lavisse, Ernest, ed. *Histoire de France illustrée depuis les origines jusqu'à la Révolution.* Paris, 1911-29.

Lavisse, Ernest, ed. Vol. 4, part 2, *1422-1492*, by Charles Petit-Dutaillis. Paris, 1911.

Lavisse, Ernest, ed. Vol. 5, parts 1-2, *1492-1559*, by H. Lemonnier. Paris, 1903-11.

Lavisse, Ernest, ed. Vol. 6, part 1, *1559-1598*, by J.-H. Mariéjol. Paris, 1911.

Le Roy Ladurie, Emmanuel. *Histoire de France: l'état royal, 1460-1610.* Paris, 1987.

Lewis, P. S. *Late Medieval France: the Polity.* London, 1968.

Mollat, Michel. *Genèse médiévale de la France moderne, XIVe-XVe siècle.* Paris, 1977.

Olland, Hélène. " La France de la fin du Moyen Age: l'état et la nation (bilan de recherches récentes)." *Médiévales*, 1986, 81-102.

*Biographies*
Autrand, F. *Charles VI*. Paris, 1986.
Baumgartner, Frederic J. *Henry II, King of France, 1547-1559*. Durham, N.C., 1980.
Champion, P. *Le roi Louis XI*. Paris, 1978 (1927).
Chevallier, Pierre. *Henri III*. Paris, 1985.
François, M. *Le Cardinal de Tournon, homme d'état diplomate, mécène et humaniste (1489-1562)*. Paris, 1951.
Gaussin, P. R. *Louis XI, un roi entre deux mondes*. Paris, 1976.
Heritier, Jean. *Catherine de Médicis*. Paris, 1984.
Jacquart, J. *François I*. Paris, 1981.
Kendall, Paul Murray. *Louis XI, "the Universal Spider"*. New York, 1971.
Knecht, R. J. *Francis I*. London, 1982.
Labande-Mailfert, Y. *Charles VIII et son milieu (1470-1498): la jeunesse au pouvoir*. Paris, 1975.
Mayer, D. M. *The Great Regent [Louise of Savoy]*. London, 1966.
Orieux, Jean. *Catherine de Médicis ou la Reine noire*. Paris, 1986.
Paravicini, Werner. *Karl der Kühne*. Göttingen, 1976.
Pradel, Pierre. *Anne de France, 1461-1522*. Paris, 1987.
Quilliet, Bernard. *Louis XII, père du peuple*. Paris, 1986.
Vale, M. G. A. *Charles VII*. Berkeley and Los Angeles, 1974.
Vaughn, Richard. *Charles the Bold, the Last Valois Duke of Burgundy*. London, 1973.
Vaughn, Richard. *Philip the Good, the Apogee of Burgundy*. London, 1970.

*Events*
Actes du colloque. *L'Amiral de Coligny et son temps. Société de l'histoire du protestantisme français, Paris 24-28 octobre 1972*. Paris, 1974.
Allmand, C. *The Hundred Years War. England and France at War, c. 1300-c. 1450*. Cambridge, 1988.
Barnavi, E. *La Ligue parisienne, 1585-1584*. Louvain, 1980.
Bercé, Yves-Marie. *Croquants et nu-pieds: le soulèvements paysans en France du XVIe au XIXe siècle*. Paris, 1974.
Chevalier, Bernard, and Philippe Contamine, eds. *La France de la fin du XVe siècle: renouveau et apogée. Colloque international, Tours, 1983*. Paris, 1985.
Constant, J.-M. *Les Guise*. Paris, 1984.
Crouzet, Denis. *Les Guerriers de Dieu: la violence au temps des troubles de religion, vers 1525-vers 1610*. 2 vols. Seyssel, 1990.
Demurger, A. *Temps de crises, temps d'espoir, XIVe-XVe siècle*. Paris, 1990.
Denis, A. *Charles VIII et les italiens: histoire et mythe*. Geneva and Paris, 1979.
Descimon, R. and E. Barnavi. "Débats sur la Ligue à Paris (1585-1594)." *AESC* 37 (1982): 72-128.
Duby, Georges, and A. Duby. *Le procès de Jeanne d'Arc*. Paris, 1973.
Estèbe, Janine. *Tocsin pour un massacre: la saison des Saint-Barthélémy*. Paris, 1968.
Famigliette, R. *Royal Intrigue: French Monarchy in Crisis*. New York, 1986.
Favier, Jean. *La guerre de Cent Ans*. Paris, 1980.
Gabory, E. *L'union de la Bretagne à la France: Anne de Bretagne, duchesse et reine*. Paris, 1941.
Garrison-Estèbe, Janine. *Protestants du midi (1559-1598)*. Toulouse, 1980.
Jouanna, Arlette. *Le devoir de révolte: la noblesse française et la gestation de l'Etat moderne, 1559-1661*. Paris, 1989.
*La France anglaise. Actes du 111e congrès des société savantes (Poitiers 1986)*. Paris, 1988.
Little, R. *The Parlement of Poitiers: War, Government and Politics in France, 1418-1436*. London, 1984.
Livet, B. *Les guerres de religion*. Paris, 1962.
Paravicini, Werner. "Peur, pratiques, Intelligences. Formes de l'opposition aristocratique à Louis XI d'après les interrogatoires du connétable de Saint-Pol." In *La France de la fin du XVe siècle. Renouveau et apogée, colloque int. Tours, 1983*, ed. Bernard Chevalier and Philippe Contamine, 183-96. Paris, 1985.

Richet, Denis. "Aspects socio-culturels des conflits à Paris dans la seconde moitié du XVIe siècle." *AESC* 32 (1977): 64-89.

Terrasse, C. *François Ier, le roi et le règne.* 3 vols. Paris, 1943-70.

Yardeni, M. *La conscience nationale en France pendant les guerres de religion.* Paris, 1971.

*The State, the Political Order, and the Estates*

Antoine, Michel. "Les gouverneurs de province en France (XVIe-XVIIIe s.)." *Prosopographie et genèse de l'Etat moderne, table ronde, Paris, 1984,* 1986, 185-94.

Barbey, J. *La Fonction royale: essence et légitimité d'après le Tractatus de Jean de Terre Vermeille.* Paris, 1983.

Brink, James Eastgate. "Royal power through provincial eyes: Languedoc, 1515-1560. " *Proceedings of the 10th annual Meeting of the Western Society for French History, Winnipeg, 1982,* 1984, 52-59.

Bulst, Neithard. "The Deputies at the French Estates General of 1468 and 1484: A Prosopographical Approach." *Medieval Prosopography* 5 (1984): 65-80.

Charbonnier, Pierre. *Une autre France: la seigneurie en Basse-Auvergne du XIVe au XVIe siècle.* Clermont-Ferrand, 1980.

Chaunu, Pierre. and Robert Gascon. "L'Etat et la ville." In *Histoire économique et sociale de la France,* vol. 1: *De 1450 à 1660.* Paris, 1977.

Chevalier, Bernard. *Les bonnes villes de France du XIVe au XVIe siècle.* Paris, 1982.

Chevalier, Bernard. "Gouverneurs et gouvernements en France entre 1450 et 1520." *Histoire comparée de l'administration, 14e colloque franco-allemand, Tours 1977,* 291-307. Munich and Zurich, 1980.

Constant, Jean-Marie. *Nobles et paysans en Beauce aux XVIe et XVIIe siècles.* Thèse Lettres, Paris IV, 1978. Lille, 1981.

Corvisier, André, ed. *Histoire militaire de la France.* Vol, 1, *Des origines à 1715,* ed. Philippe Contamine. Paris, 1992.

Dewald, Jonathan. *The Formation of a Provincial Nobility: the Magistrates of the Parlement of Rouen, 1499-1610.* Princeton, 1980.

Doucet, Robert. *Les Institutions de la France au XVIe siècle.* 2 vols. Paris, 1948.

Gaussin, Pierre-Roger. "Les conseillers de Charles VII (1418-1461). Essai de politologie historique." *Francia* 10 (1982): 67-130.

Guenée, Bernard. *L'Occident aux XIVe et XVe siècles. Les Etats.* Paris, 1971.

Guenée, Bernard. *Tribunaux et gens de justice dans le bailliage de Senlis à la fin du moyen âge (vers 1380-à 1550).* Strasbourg and Paris, 1963.

Guéry, Alain. "Le roi dépensier. le don, la contrainte et l'origine du système financier de la monarchie française d'Ancien Régime." *AESC* 39 (1984): 1241-69.

Kerhervé, Jean. *L'Etat breton aux XIVe-XVe siècles: les ducs, l'argent et les hommes.* 2 vols. Paris, 1987.

Leguai, A. "Les 'Etats princiers' en France à la fin du Moyen Age." *Annali della fondazione italiana per la storia amministrativa,* 1952, 133-67.

Lot, Ferdinand, and Robert Fawtier. *Histoire des institutions françaises au moyen âge.* 3 vols. Paris, 1958-62.

Major, J. Russell. *Representative Government in Early Modern France.* New Haven, 1980.

Mousnier, Roland, et al., *Le Conseil du Roi, de Louis XII à la Révolution.* Paris, 1970.

Petracchi, A. "I 'maître des requêtes'; genesi dell'amministrazione periferica di tipo moderno nella monarchi francese tardo medioevale e rinascimentale." *Annali della fondazione italiana per la storia amministrativa,* 1964, 190-241.

Richet, Denis. *La France moderne.* Paris, 1973.

Rosso, Claudio. "Stato e clientele nella Francia della prima età moderna." *Studi storici* 28 (1987): 37-81.

Sciacca, Enzo. "Les Etats géneraux dans la pensée politique française du XVIe siècle (1484-1571)." In *Assemblée di Stati e Istituzioni rappresentative, Convegno int. Perugia, 1982,* 1983, 73-84.

Spooner, F. C. *L'économie mondiale et les frappes monétaires en France, 1493-1680.* Paris, 1956.

Stocker, Christopher. "*Parti,* clientage and lineage in the XVth century Parlement of Paris." *Proceedings of the XIII Meeting of the Western Society for French History,* Edmonton 1985 (1986), 10-20.

Thomas, J. *Le Concordat de 1516, ses origines, son histoire au XVIe siècle.* Paris, 1910.

Viala, A. *Le Parlement de Toulouse et l'administration royale laïque, 1420-1525.* 2 vols. Albi, 1953.

Wolfe, Martin. *The Fiscal System of Renaissance France.* New Haven, 1972.

Zeller, Gaston. *Les institutions de la France au XVIe siècle.* Paris, 1948.


*Royal Idealogy, National Consciousness, and Mentalities*

Beaune, Colette. *Naissance de la nation France.* Paris, 1985.

Bloch, Marc. *Les rois thaumaturges.* Strasbourg, 1924. Reprint. Paris, 1983.

Boureau, Alain. *Les simple corps du roi: l'impossible sacralité des souverains français, XVe-XVIIIe siècle.* Paris, 1988.

Davis, Natalie Zemon. *Fiction in the Archives: Pardon Tales and their Tellers in the Sixteenth-Century France.* Stanford, 1987.

Davis, Natalie Zemon. *Society and Culture in Early Modern France.* Stanford, 1965.

Dupâquier, J., ed. *Histoire de la population française.* vol. 1 *Des origines à la Renaissance.* Paris, 1988.

Febvre, Lucien. *Le Problème de l'incroyance au XVIe siècle: la religion de Rabelais.* Paris, 1947.

Giesey, Ralph. *The Royal Funeral Ceremony in Renaissance France.* Geneva, 1960.

Guenée, Bernard. "Les entrées royales françaises à la fin du Moyen Age." *C. R. Académie Inscriptions et Belles-Lettres,* (1967): 210-12.

Hanley, Sarah. *The "lit de justice" of the Kings of France: Constitutional Ideology in Legend, Ritual and Discourse.* Princeton, 1983.

Jackson, R. *Vivat rex. Histoire des sacres et couronnements en France.* Strasbourg, 1984.

Jacquot, J., and E. Konigson, eds. *Les Fêtes de la Renaissance.* 3 vols. Paris, 1958-75.

Jouanna, Arlette. *L'idée de race en France au XVIe siècle et au début du XVIIe siècle.* Rev ed. Montpellier, 1981.

Jouanna, Arlette. *Ordre social: mythes et hiérarchies dans la France du XVIe siècle.* Paris, 1977.

Kantorowicz, Ernst. *The King's Two Bodies: a Study in Mediaeval Political Theology.* Princeton, 1957.

Krynen, Jacques. *Idéal du prince et pouvoir royal en France à la fin du Moyen Age (1340-1440): étude de la littérature politique du temps.* Paris, 1981.

Lecoq, A. M. *François I imaginaire: symbolique et politique à l'aube de la Renaissance française.* Paris, 1987.

Major, J. Russell. *The Monarchy, the Estates and the Aristocracy in Renaissance France.* London, 1988.

Mandrou, Robert. *Introduction à la France moderne: essai de psychologie historique (1500-1640).* Paris, 1961.

Marchello-Nizia, C. *Histoire de la langue française aux XIVe et XVe siècles.* Paris, 1979.

Muchembled, Robert. *Culture populaire et culture des élites dans la France moderne (XVe-XVIIIe siècles).* Paris, 1978.

Pange, J. de. *Le roi très crétien.* Paris, 1949.

Rossiaud, Jacques. "Fraternités de jeunesse et niveaux de culture dans les villes du Sud-Est à la fin du moyen âge." *AESC* 31 (1976): 289-325.

Valensise, Marina. "Le sacre du roi: stratégie politique de la monarchie française." *AESC* 41 (1986): 543-77.

Zeller, Gaston. "Les rois de France candidats à l'empire: essai sur l'idéologie impériale en France." *Revue historique* 173 (1934): 273-311, 497-534.

# ENGLAND UNDER THE TUDORS

David M. Loades
(University College of North Wales)

## 1. ENGLAND AT THE END OF THE MIDDLE AGES

In 1485 England was an agrarian society of about two million people. It had always been agrarian, but two centuries earlier had been much more populous. Before the famine of 1315-17 the population had numbered at least four million, and may have been as high as six million. After the major outbreak of bubonic plague known as the Black Death it had come down to about 2.5 million, and had continued to decline slowly for another hundred years as the plague remained endemic and harvest failures were numerous. By 1450 the population had stabilised, but a social pattern of late marriages and low fertility seems to have become established which would preclude any rapid recovery.[1] The reasons for this are obscure, and were not connected with either war or poverty. The mid-fifteenth century has been fairly described as a 'Golden Age' for the English peasantry, and yet it appears that between 1430 and 1480 some 24% of all males died unmarried, and almost 50% of those who did marry died without leaving a male heir. By the time that Henry Tudor came to the throne a slow recovery was under way. Fertility began to improve, so that by 1525 the total population of England and Wales was back to 2.5 million. Thereafter the demographic increase was rapid, hitting 3 million by about 1540, 3.5 million by 1570, and 4.5 million by 1603. The only check was provided by the influenza epidemic of 1557-59, which cost hundreds of thousands of lives and caused a short-term fall of about 2%.

There was no industrial revolution and 90% of this increased population continued to live in the countryside, supporting itself by agriculture. This caused a variety of social and economic problems which were very imperfectly understood and diagnosed at the time. For example, by about 1545 it was widely believed that the perceived increase in the number of landless labourers had been brought about mainly by the anti-social activity of grasping landowners who were seeking to maximise the profit of their estates by converting arable farms into sheep runs. However, it now seems certain that similar changes of land use had been going on, with

TUDOR
ENGLAND and WALES

Boundaries of the Shires ———

Edinburgh

Berwick on Tweed

R. Tweed

NORTHUMBERLAND

NORTH SEA

CUMBERLAND

DURHAM

WEST-
MORLAND

NORTH RIDING

ISLE OF MAN

LANCASTER

Y WEST RIDING

O R K

IRISH SEA

Liverpool

ANGLESEY

CARNARVON

FLINT

DENBIGH

CHESTER

DERBY

NOTTINGHAM

LINCOLN

MERIONETH

MONTGOMERY

SALOP

STAFFORD

LEICESTER

RUTLAND

NORFOLK

RADNOR

WORCESTER

WARWICK

NORTHAMPTON

HUNTINGDON

CAMBRIDGE

SUFFOLK

PEMBROKE

CARDIGAN

BRECKNOCK

HEREFORD

BEDFORD

CARMARTHEN

MONMOUTH

GLOUCESTER

OXFORD

BUCKINGHAM

HERTFORD

ESSEX

GLAMORGAN

Swansea

MIDDLESEX

London

BERKS

WILTS

SURREY

KENT

Dover

SOMERSET

HANTS

SUSSEX

Calais

DEVON

DORSET

Boulogne

ISLE OF WIGHT

CORNWALL

Plymouth

ENGLISH CHANNEL

sound economic justification, for upwards of a century, and the real reason for the outcry, which reached a crescendo in 1548 and 1549, was that the resources of the countryside could no longer provide for all those who sought their own holdings. Consequently the 'agrarian crisis' of Tudor England was social and legal rather than economic. By the end of the sixteenth century over-population was perceived to be a major problem, resulting in primitive welfare legislation on the one hand, and calls for colonial development on the other. Expanding domestic markets absorbed far more cloth and coal than was sold abroad, although cloth was the mainstay of England's international trade, and the granaries of Eastern and Southern England were sending over 60,000 quarters a year to less favoured parts of the country in the 1560s.[2] Demographic pressure was also relative Although in 1600 three-quarters of the population lived south and east of a line from the Severn to the Humber, malnutrition was more frequent and more serious in Cumberland or Merioneth in the 1590s than it was in Suffolk or Berkshire. Wales, with about 15% of the geographical area of England, had only about 8% of the population.

Although it did not often produce famine, demographic pressure did have a serious affect upon wages and prices. This is exceedingly difficult to quantify, because other factors, particularly the debasement of the coinage between 1545 and 1561 also played a major part. Inflation was common to the whole of western Europe, and one of the reasons was the increase in the quantity of coined bullion in circulation, the effects of which were spread through the international banking system by the military energies of the Habsburgs. However the chronology of English inflation, which was noticeable by 1530 and serious by 1549 does not suggest that American silver was a major contributor. Taking the average of the half century from 1450 to 1499 as the base (100), by 1549 the grain price index had risen to 187, and by 1559 to 348.[3] Other commodities had risen less dramatically – wool stood at 206 and animal products at 213 in the first year of Elizabeth's reign – but the hardship inflicted was severe in a society which had long been accustomed to stability. Much of the leap which occurred during the reigns of Edward VI and Mary can be attributed to the fact that the exchanges were unsettled by the action first of Henry VIII and then Protector Somerset in reducing the bullion content of the silver coinage, in some cases by as much as 70%. Elizabeth, however, called in these base issues in 1561, and the coinage for the remainder of the century was good, but the check to inflation lasted less than a decade. By 1579 the grain index stood at 370, and by 1600 at 590. At the same time as increasing demand was remorselessly pushing prices up, over supply was having the opposite effect upon labour costs – the opposite of the fifteenth century situation. By 1600 a building craftsman's wages were worth only 47% of what his great grandfather's would have been worth a century before, and an agricultural labourer was very little better off. Such a situation was only rendered tolerable at all by the fact that no one was wholly dependent upon wages, but even so in a bad year a large proportion of the average parish was partly sustained by the new and grudging system of poor relief.

At the same time, cheap labour encouraged the entrepreneur, and a variety of new manufactures began to appear in the second half of the sixteenth century; such as glass, soap, gunfounding and the 'new draperies'. More people meant a higher demand for clothing, shoes and houses, as well as food, and the increasing prosperity of the middle and upper classes led to a considerable boom in the building trade. The reign of Elizabeth was the era of the 'prodigy house', and of the Great Rebuilding, right across southern England. The largest industry, however, as well as the most highly regulated, continued to be cloth making. By the middle of the fifteenth century cloth had overtaken wool as the principle commodity of international trade, and the number of broadcloths exported rose steadily from 57,000 in 1450 to 150,000 a hundred years later.[4] However in 1551 the Antwerp market crashed, and although there was a brief recovery over the next few years, the annual rate throughout Elizabeth's reign was no more than 100,000. An increasing domestic market to some extent protected the industry from the effects of this decline, and increasingly adventurous merchants found a 'vent' for their commodity in Bokhara, Kiev or Santa Cruz to compensate for the loss of European markets. To the urban historians the period shows few clear trends or developments apart from the steady growth of London. The population of the capital increased far more rapidly than that of the country as a whole. Standing at about 70,000 in 1500, it had reached over 100,000 by 1550, and about 200,000 by the end of the century. London was the only English city to rank with the major European centres, such as Paris, Rome or Naples, and from about 1570 it was more than ten times the size of its nearest rivals such as Norwich and Bristol. London was also unique in attracting substantial immigration. By 1560 more than half the livery company members had been born elsewhere in the kingdom. Its taxation and customs revenues were among the chief props of the Exchequer, and its developing money market provided the Crown with a readily accessible source of credit and financial expertise.

Elsewhere the picture is much less clear. Norwich, which may have had as many as 25,000 inhabitants in 1300, and which had declined to 7,500 by 1377, had recovered to 9,500 by 1525 and to about 12,000 by 1550, making it the second largest city in England.[5] York, on the other hand, which had still housed nearly 14,000 people in 1377, had shrunk to about 6,000 by 1525 and did not reach 10,000 again until the following century. Among the smaller towns, Exeter, Crediton and Reading were growing substantially while Coventry, Beverley and Gloucester continued their late medieval decline. Local circumstances seem to have decided the fate of most towns, and only occasionally did government policy, such as the grant of a charter of incorporation, make very much difference to the economic condition of its crafts and trades. Many such charters were granted, particularly during the reigns of Edward VI and Mary, but these grants seem to have been determined more by the desire of the Council to maintain a level of social control than by any desire to encourage entrepreneurial activity.[6] Innovations in the relief of poverty, disease and unemployment, which were obvious both at the municipal and national levels, seem to have been fuelled by concern about crime and civil disorder to a similar extent. Protestantism was not as inimical to charity as is sometimes claimed. Although almshouses and hospitals were no longer founded out of a desire to secure saving spiritual merit, they were founded by pious laymen anxious to testify to the saving grace which had been bestowed upon them. No such considerations leavened the lump of economic self-interest, however, and both at the national and municipal level the stick triumphed over the carrot every time in attempts to breathe new life into stagnant urban trade and manufacture. The best received opinion is represented by the author of the *Discourse on the Common Weal*;

> ...another thing I reckon would much help to relieve our towns decayed, if they could take order that all wares made there should have a special mark, and the mark to be set on none but such as be truely wrought. And also that every artificer dwelling out of all towns...should be limited to be under the correction of one good town or another; and they to sell no wares but such as are first approved and sealed by the town that they are limited unto . . . .[7]

It is perhaps not surprising that, in spite of the rapidly growing domestic markets, urban recovery was slow and patchy throughout the period.

The natural inclination, both of government and people, was strongly conservative. Only dire necessity produced innovation, and made it acceptable. This can be demonstrated very clearly by the pattern of international trade. Throughout the late fifteenth and early sixteenth century the wool trade steadily declined, killed off very largely by over-taxation. From 35,000 sacks a year in 1350, it had shrunk to 10,000 by 1420 and 5,000 by 1530. Its place had been taken by the cloth trade, which expanded rapidly after 1500. However, this export became increasingly dominated by the merchant adventurers of London, who steadily concentrated it into a single great fleet which sailed from London to Antwerp once a year. In 1450 less than half the trade had gone by this route; a century later it was over 80%. And then the Antwerp market crashed. After a brief recovery, in the 1560s it was severely disrupted by war and political conflict. Without fresh thinking and new initiatives a prolonged economic crisis in England would have been inevitable, and the Crown stood to lose at least 10% of its annual revenue. Not only were the merchant adventurers constrained to find another staple port, they were also forced to seek more distant and less secure markets. At the same time the Crown was driven both to inspire and to assist. Since Henry VII had accorded limited and somewhat grudging patronage to John Cabot in 1497-98, there had been no interest in overseas enterprise from that quarter; but by 1552 the situation had changed. Led by the aged but still energetic Sebastian Cabot (son of John), a group of London merchants and courtiers put together a project for developing trade with the Far East via a new route, later to be known as the North East passage. Cabot had spent most of his adult life in Spain, in the service of Charles V, and his reappearance in England in 1547 is something of a mystery. Given the support which his ideas were soon to receive from several members of Edward VI's council, it is possible that they were responsible for tempting him, and Charles V's annoyance is a measure of their achievement. Cabot's expedition, led by Richard Chancellor and Sir Hugh Willoughby set out in 1553, Cabot himself being too old to take part. It did not reach China, and by the time that Chancellor returned in 1554 Edward was dead, and most of his council either dead also or out of favour. But the result was the establishment of the Muscovy Company in 1555, and the opening of a limited but lucrative trade with Russia, which was later extended to Persia. During Elizabeth's reign similar companies were established to trade with West Africa (Guinea), North Africa (Barbary), the Eastern Mediterranean (Levant), the Baltic (Eastland), and finally in 1600 the Far East (East India).

The queen's role in all this new enterprise was crucial. English monarchs had always been prepared to rent out their ships to merchants on a commercial basis, and some, such as Edward IV and Henry VII had even traded in a small way in their own right, but Elizabeth went much further. She became a shareholder in John Hawkins' risky and provocative voyages to the West Indies between 1562 and 1568, contributing both ships and money.  Later on she supported Drake and others in the same way, both trading and (after the outbreak of war with Spain in 1585), privateering.  Paradoxically a queen who was in most respects a model of caution, and a merchant community which had been a byword for conservatism, had by 1603 broken the traditional mould of England's overseas trade, and started to create a pattern which was to transform the wealth and international standing of the country during the following century.

## 2. GOVERNMENT: THE KING IN PARLIAMENT

Elizabeth, like her father and grandfather, was a personal ruler.  With the exception of a royal minority, no other form of government could be conceived.  However personal rule did not confer, or even imply, unlimited power.  All monarchs were responsible to God, although what that meant in practice depended very much on the circumstances.  They were also required by the terms of their coronation oaths to respect the laws and customs of their realms, to govern with equity and justice, and to protect the liberties of the church.  Late medieval England was what Sir John Fortescue called *dominium politicum et regale*, a balance between the unfettered authority of the Lord's anointed and the contractually limited superiority of a feudal overlord.[8]  The king of England made war and peace at his discretion, summoned whom he chose to council, distributed honours and rewards at his pleasure, and caused the law to be enforced in his name.  The machinery of English government was the most centralised and the longest established in Western Europe, rivalled only by that of the Venetian republic.  On the other hand the king of England could not raise taxation *mere moto suo*, nor did his will have the force of law.  For both these purposes a machinery of consent was necessary, reflecting the aristocratic commonwealth of the Germanic tribe rather than the authoritarianism of the Roman Empire.  The institution which had been created to give that consent a tangible and identifiable form was the parliament.  Similar representative bodies existed in most countries, but the English parliament was unusual in making no separate provision for the clergy, and in running the lesser nobility and the bourgeoisie together into a single House.  By the late fifteenth century the parliament had a defined and limited function.  It was called by the king essentially for his own convenience; either when he wanted to raise money and needed to be reassured that the relevant people would be willing to pay, or when he needed an exceptionally authoritative statement such as an Act of Resumption or an encroachment upon the church's rights of sanctuary.

The parliament had no autonomous authority, or even existence.[9] Nevertheless, when the monarchy was weak and the realm unsettled, as had been the case during the 1450s, it had functioned not only as a High Court (which was a part of its remit), but as a vehicle for expressions of discontent of a highly political nature, such as the attack upon the Duke of Suffolk for alleged misgovernment. To a strong king a parliament was an occasional tool, or weapon, to be used for specific purposes rather than a regular instrument of government, but at the beginning of the Tudor period it retained the potential to be a great deal more if circumstances so conspired. This potential was already being reflected in the desire of important gentlemen to secure seats for themselves and their sons in the House of Commons, often at the expense of the less wealthy and self-confident towns. Henry VII convened six parliaments for a total of ten sessions between November 1485 and January 1497, but after finally ridding himself of Perkin Warbeck called only one more, for a single session, in January 1504. Francis I of France, coming to the throne in 1514, never met his Estates-General in the 33 years of his reign. By contrast his almost exact contemporary Henry VIII convened ten parliaments, which ran for a total of 26 sessions; and only three of the last 18 years of his reign did not contain a meeting. By 1547 parliament was no longer an occasional expedient. It had proved to be so flexible and useful an instrument of royal policy that it had become one of the principal workhorses of Tudor government, and a symbol of the dynasty's *entente* with the political nation of England.

The reason for this transformation lay in Henry VIII's 'Great Matter' – his desire to free himself from his first wife, Catherine of Aragon, and remarry in order to secure a male heir. Henry had a case of a sort in canon law,[10] one which would probably have been strong enough for his purpose in normal circumstances. However, the circumstances were not normal. Not only did Catherine herself adamantly refuse to be cast off, her nephew was the powerful emperor, Charles V, whose interests she had assiduously promoted in England for the past fifteen years. Finding all routes to a canonical annulment blocked, and with his conscience and his obstinacy fully engaged, Henry was compelled to find another solution. By 1530 his specialist advisers, Nicholas de Burgo, Edward Fox and Thomas Cranmer had come up with a number of ingenious suggestions for circumventing an uncooperative papacy. Henry was willing, indeed anxious, to be persuaded, but at first he confined himself to bullying the English church in the hope that Clement would buy him off with concessions. Only when that failed and he began to listen to the more radical counsels of Thomas Cromwell, towards the end of 1553, did parliament become directly engaged with the issue of jurisdiction. What Cromwell suggested, in effect, was to use the highest recognised form of positive law – statute – to emancipate the realm from the traditional law of the church. A series of Acts, commencing with the conditional Restraint of Annates in 1532, and culminating in the Act of Supremacy two years later, effectively destroyed the authority of the Pope in England, and replaced it with that of the king. The full implications of this were not at first appreciated, which was one of the main reasons why opposition was initially so limited. English kings had quarrelled with popes before. Once Henry had a son he would renegotiate his relationship with Rome and the pretentious language of the Royal Supremacy would be quietly forgotten. However, the gentry and aristocracy were soon offered a massive inducement in the form of monastic lands, and the laity in general found attractions in being able to appeal to the king against ecclesiastical censures. So the royal Supremacy outlived its immediate inspiration; survived the deaths of both Catherine and Anne Boleyn in 1536, and had gained general acceptance by the end of the reign.

The consequences were far-reaching. From being a powerful but limited instrument, statute became virtually omnicompetent. In 1534 it was used to resolve the succession, a device which might have prevented the civil wars of the fifteenth century had it then been available; in 1536 to dissolve the lesser monasteries; and in 1549 to convert the doctrinal basis of the church from catholic to protestant. So entrenched had its authority become by 1553 that the conservative Mary felt obliged to use it for the purpose of restoring the pope's jurisdiction, a move which had neither logic nor principle to commend it, but only political common-sense. In 1565, when Sir Thomas Smith came to write *De Republica Anglorum*, he could declare

> The parliament abrogateth old laws, maketh new, giveth orders for things past and for things hereafter to be followed, changeth rights and possessions of private men, legitimateth bastards, establisheth forms of religion, altereth weights and measures, giveth forms of succession to the Crown...And the consent of parliament is taken to be every man's consent.[11]

It is not surprising that in 1543 Henry VIII felt constrained to announce that he never stood higher 'in his estate royal' than in time of parliament. However, from the Crown's point of view there was a price to be paid for the development of such an extremely useful instrument. Smith also wrote 'The most high and absolute power of the realm of England consisteth in the parliament'; and later in the same passage, with reference to statute 'That is the Prince's and the whole realm's deed... (and) is called firm, stable and *sanctum*, and is taken for law'. Kings of England had never claimed to be *legibus solutus*, but in encroaching upon other jurisdictions parliament had also encroached upon the royal prerogative, and by the end of the century the problem of demarcation was becoming urgent. Meanwhile the parliament itself had changed and developed. Many of its procedures were already established by 1500, but privileges such as freedom from arrest on a private suit, and above all freedom of speech, took on new meanings in the course of the century. The balance of power also slowly tilted from the Lords to the Commons. The latter did not even have their own debating chamber until they were granted St. Stephen's chapel in 1547, but in the arguments of James I's reign their spokesmen could claim, not only that they could buy out the Lords several times over, but also that they alone truly spoke for the realm 'their Lordships being but particular persons'. In fact the Lords probably continued to be the more powerful House down to the civil war, but the Commons had increased significantly in wealth, self-confidence, and numbers. From 296 in 1509 the Commons had increased to 460 by 1603, through the enfranchisement of Wales and the creation of numerous new boroughs.[12]

Nevertheless parliament was the legislature, not the executive. Executive power remained with the Crown and was implemented through a variety of instruments and institutions. The most visible and prestigious of these was the King's Council. The Council's competence was co-extensive with that of the monarch, but except during a royal minority it had no autonomous power to make decisions. In practice much routine administration was delegated to the Council, and in 1556 it was granted its own seal to facilitate that business, but in matters of policy its function was simply to advise the monarch. Unlike a modern cabinet, the Council had no collective responsibility. Its members were individually appointed by the monarch, and bound by oath to provide their advice and service in accordance with their individual consciences and aptitudes. The Council was automatically dissolved by the demise of the Crown, and each ruler had in theory complete freedom to call whoever he or she chose to consult. In practice there were numerous constraints, dictated by custom, purpose or sheer political common-sense. Henry VII's Council was large and somewhat amorphous. Over 200 councillors have been identified for the reign, and there seem to have been as many as 60 or 70 at any given time, but many of them appeared only occasionally, and their role was largely honorific. A number of these councillors were powerful nobles, who were not high in the king's confidence, but who expected that status as due to their lineage, and whose service it was important to retain. The main work of the Council was discharged by the officers, and by trusted senior officials, many of whom were clergy. This pattern was significantly modified during the later part of the reign of Henry VIII. Traditionally the Council had always exercised a judicial as well as an executive function, and during the Chancellorship of Cardinal Thomas Wolsey, this had been developed to the point at which a distinct institution became necessary. The Court of Star Chamber was a specialist aspect of the Council, exercising the king's prerogative of equity.[13] By 1526, partly as a result of Wolsey's style of management, Henry VIII was becoming dissatisfied with the organisation of his Council, and on his instructions the Chancellor drew up a plan of reform, known as the Eltham Ordinances. It took about a decade, and a change of chief minister, for these reforms to be implemented; but what had emerged by 1540 was a much smaller and more sharply defined group, known as the Privy Council.

This Council numbered about 20, was largely confined to senior office holders, and systematically differentiated its various types of business. Although the king reserved the right to refer particularly contentious issues to the Privy Council, the bulk of the judicial work was performed in Star Chamber, and separately recorded. Issues of policy continued to be discussed where and when the king chose, and no record was kept of such discussions, nor of who had participated in them. Regular administrative business, on the other hand, was now discharged at formal meetings, usually held at court, and minuted by a clerk appointed for that purpose. The king never attended such meetings, which were dominated by a small number of officers, and it was here that the routine work of government was carried on. Political circumstances during the reigns of Edward VI and Mary increased the size of the Privy Council to almost 50, and led to the re-appearance of specialised committees and commissions, but Elizabeth returned to the policy of 1540. At the beginning of her reign she named 19 councillors, and by 1601 that number had shrunk to 13.

The second institution through which the monarch operated was the household. The court was the theatre and context of royalty, and medieval kings had normally used their household servants as ambassadors, and specialised agents of all kinds. They were, by definition, personal dependents of the monarch, whose loyalty was unquestionable and undivided. Henry VII used his Chamber to build up an extensive gentry

clientage, particularly in Wales and the North, which injected a direct
royal presence into areas where authority had too often been mediated un-
satisfactorily through third parties. For a few years, from about 1520 to
1547, it looked as though Henry VIII's newly created Privy Chamber was
going to rival the Council as a channel of patronage and communication,[14]
and both Edward VI's regents, the Duke of Somerset and the Duke of
Northumberland, took pains to fill it with reliable dependents. However
that development was aborted by the succession of two female rulers. A
queen needed female familiars, and although the Privy Chamber continued
to be an important focus of patronage and intrigue after 1558, it ceased to
perform any function in the processes of government. Long before the end
of the century the Principal Secretary was clearly a key officer of state, and
the household no longer performed governmental functions.[15] The political importance of the court, as one of the main points of contact between
monarch and aristocracy, should not be underestimated either under Elizabeth or her immediate successors, but by 1603 it belonged to the culture of
politics rather than the machinery of state.

However the bureaucratic developments of the sixteenth century are
viewed, formal institutions of government had existed in England long before the Tudors. As early as the twelfth century the king's revenues had
been managed by the Exchequer, an accounting office whose archaic procedures remained substantially unchanged. From the 1460s to the 1550s
this inflexibility had caused the Exchequer to be bypassed for management
purposes, first by the Chamber and then by Cromwell's revenue courts,
but in 1554 it recovered its ancient control at the cost of a somewhat inadequate programme of reform, and Elizabeth allowed it to continue with
only slight modifications. Other aspects of government which had gone
'out of court' (that is, out of the monarch's personal control), had been the
central courts of common law – the King's Bench and Common Pleas –
and the Chancery. Originally the king's writing office, the latter had, before the fifteenth century, become largely concerned with the issuing of formal processes, mainly in the form of writs. Chancery also discharged important judicial functions, being the office through which the Lord
Chancellor discharged his equity responsibilities.

In 1470 the management of the royal estates could be represented as
similarly ossified, but first Edward IV and then Henry VII had introduced
new systems of accountability and stricter management, with the result
that the income from the Crown estates went up from about £3000 a year
in 1487 to £40,000 a year by 1505. Although the actual figure fluctuated
considerably thereafter, for the remainder of the century landed income

continued to account for about 30% of the Crown's ordinary revenue – which stood at about £120,000 in 1510 and £400,000 in 1600 – a decline in real terms of about 35%. Even a massive injection of over £1,000,000 from the sale of former monastic property between 1540 and 1560, and the retention of a significant proportion of it, could not make Henry VIII and his successors solvent. Neither the profits of justice nor the customs dues – those two other props of ordinary revenue – could be made to keep pace with inflation. This was partly a failure of political nerve. The customs rates were reassessed in 1504 and again in 1558. But thereafter, while prices were almost doubling, they were not touched for fear of conflict with the mercantile community. From about 1520 onwards, in order to have any semblance of a regal freedom of action, the Tudors needed extraordinary revenue. In order to attain this they devised a new system of direct taxation, the subsidy. The subsidy was a directly assessed tax on land and movable goods, from which the poorest members of the community were exempt. It was voted by parliament, and assessed and collected by specially appointed commissioners. In theory the subsidy was one of the fairest and most efficient taxes in Europe. It could be granted for any good reason – not just the traditional reasons of war or emergency – and was never refused. On the other hand it was afflicted by the same failure of nerve as undermined the customs revenues. After about 1560 realistic assessments were no longer insisted upon, and the yield of a standard subsidy (4 shillings in the £1 on land and 2s 8d on goods) which had stood at about £153,000 began to decline in absolute as well as relative terms.[16] The ascendancy of parliament also meant that it became increasingly difficult to raise money by other means. As early as 1525 Wolsey's attempt to raise a benevolence (non-parliamentary tax) hopefully entitled the 'Amicable Grant' was a total failure, and although Mary managed to raise a Privy Seal loan in 1557, the political price was normally too high. That left only the commercial money market, and there the financial price was too high. Elizabeth extricated herself from Antwerp by about 1565, after 20 years of heavy involvement, and thereafter preferred the genteel poverty of appealing to parliament. After a dramatic improvement in the late fifteenth century, Tudor government became progressively more under-funded, a situation which was eventually to undermine its political achievements.

The credit side of the Tudors' kid-gloved treatment of the gentry was the willingness with which that increasingly wealthy and numerous class co-operated in the processes of local government. At the beginning of the period, as for many years previously, there had been three types of regional jurisdiction; the corporate town, chartered by the Crown and largely self-governing; the shire, administered in the king's name by sheriffs, coroners and escheators; and the liberty or franchise, where the same laws applied, but were administered by the holder rather than by the king's officers. Unlike most parts of Western Europe there were no private or seigneurial jurisdictions. The common law was observed everywhere, although customary Welsh law survived in the Principality and the Marches, and outside the liberties was supervised by the King's Justices of Assize, travelling round upon their regular circuits. Since the late fourteenth century, however, another and more flexible jurisdictional instrument had been superimposed upon this traditional system – the royal commission. A commission was a specific delegation of the king's authority to a group of named persons. It might be occasional – to enable them to investigate or adjudicate upon a particular issue; or it might be standing, to enable them to exercise a certain type of jurisdiction within a defined area upon a regular basis. The most commonly used occasional commission was that of *oyer et terminer*, to hear and determine either a particular case or a particular type of case, at a given place and time. The commonest standing commission was that of the peace, whereby the commissioners were empowered to deal with certain types of crime and misdemeanour within a shire or other specified jurisdiction, meeting in regular sessions under the general supervision of the Justices of Assize. By 1485 commissions of the peace were established in every county, and in every town which had the status of a county. The arrangement was one of mutual convenience. The Crown made its local authority more effective by operating through men who had natural authority 'in their countries', and the gentlemen enhanced their own status by appearing as the king's agents and delegates. So well did this system work that the Tudors soon extended the responsibilities of the Justices of the Peace from crime to administration, and by the 1580s William Lambarde could complain of the 'stacks of statutes' which they were being called upon to enforce.[17] By then they were licensing ale houses, enforcing wage rates, supervising the poor law, and generally policing the countryside.

The advance of the commission was steady and unspectacular, but in 1536 a dramatic change was wrought in the pattern of local government by the familiar instrument of statute. Before 1530 there was no recognised means of terminating a franchise; even escheat for lack of heirs merely placed the franchise in the hands of the Crown, it did not bring it to an end. However in 1536, taking advantage of the newly extended competence of parliament, Thomas Cromwell implemented an Act for the abolition of all franchises and liberties. As a result the bishopric of Durham became a normal county for all purposes except parliamentary representation, and the government of Wales was completely reorganised. In place of the Principality and Marcher Lordships appeared twelve new shires on the English model, with sheriffs and commissions of the peace. The king's writ now ran uniformly throughout his realm, and the consolidation of the English state was complete. Only in one respect did the peripheries of the kingdom remain distinctive. In 1522 Cardinal Wolsey, concerned about the defence of the northern border, and dissatisfied with the progress which he was making to bring the region under control, revived the regional council which Richard III had instituted as Duke of Gloucester. By 1525 it was set up with wide civil and criminal jurisdiction, not replacing the county governments but overlapping with them. This Council failed in the face of the great northern rising of 1536, but the collapse of the Pilgrimage of Grace revived it in a strengthened form, and it continued to provide an additional and effective layer of government in the region, even after the union of the crowns in 1603.[18] A similar council in the marches of Wales had a continuous existence from the reign of Edward IV, but the act of 1536 extended its jurisdiction over the whole of the Principality as well as the English border shires. Like its northern partner, it had both administrative and judicial functions, being armed with a standing commission of *oyer et terminer*. It never had a defensive function, being entirely concerned with policing the area, a function which it was discharging with notable success by the reign of Elizabeth. In spite of these variations, by 1550 England had the most unified and centralised government of any European state.

### 3. Religion: The Shapes of the English Reformation

The establishment of the royal supremacy was the most important step in the English reformation. Unlike parts of Germany or Switzerland, there was no widespread or deeply rooted discontent with the traditional church in the later middle ages. There was an indigenous heretical movement, called Lollardy, which had been briefly important both intellectually and politically in the early fifteenth century. But the church and the Crown had combined to persecute it, and by the beginning of the Tudor period it survived only in certain areas, and at a relatively low social level. The Lollards were persistent, but they had no organisation, no leaders, and no theological cohesion.[19] However, the absence of organised dissent did not necessarily mean that all was well with the *Ecclesia Anglicana*. Like the church all over Europe, it had become heavily dependent upon the materialistic imagery of works salvation, and the answer to every spiritual problem seemed to be another ceremony to perform, or another donation to make. To the majority of the population for whom the church was a reassuring mechanism for coping with the terrors of the supernatural, this may not have mattered much; but it mattered to some, with more education or more spiritual sensitivity. At the same time the church, as a wealthy institution, found itself constantly at odds with the lay society which surrounded it over issues of jurisdiction, property and payments. Habits of piety had also shifted, spontaneously as far as can be seen. The *opus dei* had gone out of fashion before the rise of Lollardy, and the great monasteries of earlier days were attracting few vocations by the middle of the fifteenth century. The mendicants, on the other hand, were doing well. Similarly perpetual chantries became less favoured after about 1450, while specifically charitable and educational foundations moved in to take their place. This was not caused by a lack of faith in intercession, but probably by a growing conviction that the church should work in the world rather than withdraw from it. Later in the sixteenth century this conviction was to be shared by protestant and catholic reformers alike. Great theological themes and loyalties meant little to the average layman. Religion might be a very personal matter; more likely it was communal. The parish church, with its festivals, penances and acts of collective devotion, was the focus. Few Englishmen cared much about the papacy or the universal church, and when the king offered his own programme of reform, they were only too willing to embrace it.

Of anti-clericalism in the passionate German sense, there was probably very little, just as there was no organised dissent. Ordinations to the secular priesthood were holding up well, and foreign observers commented upon the devotion with which the English went to mass. Cardinal Wolsey, on the other hand, was generally unpopular, and when William Tyndale's English New Testament began to come in after 1526 it was an immediate best seller. There were very few heretics among the gentry and aristocracy, and those Englishmen who commented at all upon the early works of Luther were uniformly hostile – including the king.[20] However, when Henry announced that he was going to rule the church himself as Supreme Head, the general reaction was one of acquiescence. He had, after all, proved himself to be a Godly Prince, and if God disapproved of what he was doing, that was his own responsibility. His subjects had been taught that obedience was a matter of conscience, so obedience in this case absolved them of any possible sin. There were, of course, those who had a sharper eye for principles, or an inconveniently clear awareness of their duty to the Holy See – Sir Thomas More, Bishop John Fisher and the London Carthusians – but the king had enough general support to deal ruthlessly with them and get away with it. Some uneasy consciences, including that of Stephen Gardiner, the Bishop of Winchester and author of *De vera obedientia oratio*, were quietened by the thought that the Supremacy had nothing to do with doctrine. The king was in most respects a good catholic, being particularly devoted to the sacraments. Moreover, in 1537 God at last vouchsafed him a son, surely the seal of Divine approval upon his proceedings. Nevertheless, it soon became apparent that, in conceding the Royal Supremacy, the English Church had left itself no logical ground upon which to make a stand of principle. So when Thomas Cromwell (a layman) visited the church as the king's vicegerent, and issued royal injunctions in 1536, or when the archbishop of Canterbury, Thomas Cranmer, simplified the traditional calendar and introduced an official English Bible (1539), it had to be accepted that they were acting under Divine guidance.

The church which Henry VIII ruled from 1534 to his death in 1547 was not protestant. Lutheranism continued to be a capital offence, and the king's horror of sacramentarians was undiminished. On the other hand it was not catholic either. In dissolving the monasteries, forbidding pilgrimages and destroying shrines, the king removed aspects of the traditional faith which were of far more than cosmetic significance. Henry was undoubtedly a reformer, who saw himself as purging the church of superstition and corruption, and in his later years he surrounded himself with men, and women, who were later to emerge as protestants. His son, Prince Edward, was brought up by tutors such as John Cheke, Richard Cox and Jacques Belmain; his council was led by the Earl of Hertford; and his Privy Chamber by Sir Anthony Denny. Yet the king himself never accepted justification by faith alone, nor abandoned transubstantiation, and when he died in January 1547 he decreed 30,000 masses for the repose of his soul.

As soon as the old king was gone this reforming party moved swiftly and decisively to secure control of the minority government. There was virtually no opposition and within a few weeks the Earl of Hertford (Edward Seymour, the young king's uncle) had been created Duke of Somerset and Lord Protector, with quasi-regal powers. By the time that parliament met in November, the protestant orientation of the Protector's regime had become clear. Working closely with Archbishop Cranmer he had caused a series of Homilies to be issued in July, one of which taught justification by faith alone, and had permitted a flood of protestant polemic to appear, both in the form of sermons and of printed tracts and books.[21] How much active support they had for this religious policy is not clear.  Perhaps 20% of Londoners could be classed as protestants by this time, and a smaller but still appreciable proportion in the south east generally.  Outside that area, and among the gentry and aristocracy, there is very little evidence of positive reforming zeal,[22] yet within two years a protestant liturgy had been introduced, and within three years every vestige of traditional worship had in theory been removed.  The reason for this was not a spiritual revolution, but the nature of the royal supremacy.  Even those who most hated and opposed the changes could not deny that the king, with the consent of parliament, had the right to make them.  Stephen Gardiner, the conservative leader, claimed that it was unwise and inexpedient to carry out such a policy during a minority, but he did not challenge the king's authority.  Edward's youth was scarcely relevant, because each important step was carried out by statute; an Act for the dissolution of the chantries, an Act permitting clergy to marry, and two Uniformity Acts authorising the Books of Common Prayer.  By the time that Edward died (still a minor) in 1553 the personal authority which had been very noticeable in Henry's supremacy, had been almost entirely subsumed into the public responsibilities of the Crown.  Nevertheless, given the limitations of early modern government, it is legitimate to ask whether a lack of overt opposition actually implied effective enforcement.  If the great majority of people in all walks of life would have preferred 'religion as king Henry left it' – as seems to have been the case – was the conversion of England to protestantism largely theoretical?  Rather surprisingly, the answer must be no.  Genuine conversions may well have been few, but a very high level of outward conformity was achieved, even in regions like the South West and County Durham, where there was plenty of protest and reluctance.  By and large it seems clear that, in respect of religion, Englishmen did what they were told to do by lawful authority, and open dissent was rare.  It must also be borne in mind that this was a period of acute social tension, and the ruling classes were inclined to support the government strongly in the interest of discipline and control, irrespective of their private convictions.  Because of the manner in which the conversion had been carried out, by 1553 England had a church which retained its traditional structure almost intact, even to the canon law and the ecclesiastical courts, while using a liturgy and professing a set of doctrinal articles which were entirely protestant; not Lutheran, not Zwinglian, not Calvinist, but *sui generis*.

Edward's successor, Mary, had as Princess, resisted all these changes to the utmost of her power, ostensibly in defence of her father's settlement.  Consequently it surprised no one when, over the space of about six months, she swept away her brother's religious innovations, restoring the mass and many other traditional practices. Genuine protestants were dismayed but resigned, recognising in this reversal the will of a God whom they had insufficiently honoured.[23] Like the conservatives under Edward, the majority of them did not even contemplate resistance to the lawful authority of the Crown. Had Mary been satisfied with this achievement her whole subsequent reputation might have been very different. However, the queen had nursed many injuries and resentments through years of frustration, and was convinced that her accession had been decreed by God to put right all the wrongs which her father had perpetrated, particularly in the course of repudiating her mother, to whose memory she had remained fiercely loyal. She therefore determined to restore the whole catholic church 'even to the Pope's supremacy', and wedded a fanatically orthodox catholic prince, Philip of Spain, to help her achieve that goal. In some respects Philip turned out to be more pragmatic than his wife, and it was he who engineered the agreement whereby the pope conceded the loss of all those former monastic lands which had been transferred to the laity since 1536. Nevertheless he symbolised a foreign domination which was bitterly resented in England, and for the first time protestantism began to acquire a distinctively English identity. As Mary, assisted by the Cardinal Legate, Reginald Pole, turned from persuasion to force, and began to burn protestants for heresy, two things happened. It was soon conveniently forgotten that the papal jurisdiction had been restored, and the heresy laws re-enacted, by the English parliament. Philip and his Spanish councillors were blamed for a persecution far more severe than anything which Henry VIII had inflicted, and which never had much support from the English laity. Secondly the protestants, hitherto a not very popular minority who were seen as having seized power in a political coup, and who could be plausibly represented as time-servers, began to gain religious credibility. Their resolution, not to say heroism, under persecution, was quite unexpected by the council or the queen. The Lollards had not been made of the stuff of martyrs, but the 300 or so artisans, tradesmen and clergy who went to the stake between 1555 and 1558 not only found immediate fame in the polemical writings of their co-religionists, but also began to acquire an aura of having suffered for the freedom of their country. Far from having been suppressed, in 1558 the protestants were more vociferous, more confident, and more radical than they had been in 1553.

The conservative majority had welcomed Mary, but they did not welcome Philip, or the pope, or the persecution, and Pole found them recalcitrant material out of which to rebuild the catholic church. As an intellectual and an aristocrat he treated his flock with a patronising contempt, urging them to a dutiful obedience in place of the 'turbulent wits' which had afflicted them for the last twenty years.[24] Given time, his emphasis upon discipline, ceremony and good order might have restored the church of his youth, but in all probability too much had changed for such passive and negative methods to be successful. The dignity of the episcopate was refurbished, a few monasteries and friaries re-founded, and many traditional pieties resurrected. Edmund Bonner, the Bishop of London, wrote some admirable orthodox homilies, and the humanist spirituality of Richard Whitford prevailed at court; but of the evangelical fire of the contemporary counter-reformation there was no sign. Mary was undoubtedly unfortunate. Her marriage failed to produce an heir, and the bad harvests of 1555 and 1556 were followed by a devastating outbreak of influenza. Finally, having embarked upon a war with France to gratify Philip and against the advice of her council, she had the mortification of losing England's last continental possession, Calais. It is not surprising that when she died in November 1558 at the relatively early age of 43, the protestants both at home and abroad proclaimed a judgement of God, and the catholics were left as depressed and resigned as their enemies had been five years before.

Coming to the throne against her sister's wishes, and against a background of personal animosity, Elizabeth hastened to distance herself as far as possible from all that Mary had stood for. Prudence might have suggested a return to her father's settlement, but such a course was no longer practicable because no credible episcopate could have been found for such a church. Given her priorities, the queen's decision to call upon the protestants was neither daring nor foolhardy, but practically inevitable. When the parliament was convened in January 1559 there was no catholic party in the House of Commons, and although the bishops were able to make a tough fight of it in the Lords, lack of support from the Lower House proved fatal to their cause. By the summer of 1559 the Royal Supremacy was restored, and with it the Prayer Book of 1552 and the iconoclastic atmosphere of the Edwardian church. With one exception the Marian bishops were deprived. The refounded monasteries were again dissolved, and altars and images disappeared from the parish churches. For many years Elizabeth's enforcement of the Act of Uniformity was hesitant and patchy – the despair of her more zealous bishops – but her longevity guaranteed that her settlement would prevail, and long before she died in 1603 England was a protestant country. This was achieved less by high pressure evangelism and theological polemic than by shifting the basis of conformity. By the 1580s English national feeling had become unequivocally protestant, and the pamphleteer William Charke could write

He that smiteth our religion woundeth our commonwealth; because our
blessed estate of policie standeth in defence of religion, and our most
blessed religion laboureth in maintenance of the commonwealth.
Religion and policie are, through God's singular blessings, preserved
together in life as with one spirit; he that doth take away the life of the
one doth procure the death of the other.[25]

The connivance of successive popes in attempts to overthrow Elizabeth, or
to have her assassinated, and their support for Spanish enemies and Irish
rebels had by 1600 completely discredited the catholic church, even in the
eyes of the most conservative. The recusants were no longer survivors of
an earlier age, but a new and radical minority.

This was one of the reasons why Elizabeth was able to reconcile a conservative nation to a protestant settlement. Another was that she assiduously frustrated the ambitions of the more radical reformers, known by
this time as 'precisions' or 'puritans'. During their exile in Mary's reign,
many of these puritans had become converted to the doctrine and practice
of the church of Geneva, and upon their return had endeavoured to impose
conditions upon the Royal Supremacy. The queen, however, playing her
role as Godly Prince, refused to be either persuaded or coerced. As far as
she was concerned the settlement of 1559 was definitive. Her priority was
for unity and settlement rather than for ideological perfection. While she
was quite happy to use the puritans against the catholics when the latter
appeared to be a threat, she was unwilling to purchase that co-operation
with concessions to their demands, because she realised that, in the last
analysis, she did not have to.[26]

## 4. A SECOND-RANK POWER: ENGLAND AND HER NEIGHBOURS

Tudor England was not a great power. During the first half of the sixteenth century the great powers were France and the Empire of Charles V,
with England exploiting a strategic position and a balancing role to the
best of its ability. After 1559 there was only one great power (unless the
distant Ottoman Empire be included), and England was one of the elements in the constantly shifting coalitions which endeavoured to bridle
Spanish ambitions. Nor was England an island. The dominions of the Tudors included Calais (until 1558), the channel Islands, and part of Ireland
(the whole of Ireland in theory). They did not, however, include Scotland
until the Crowns were united by dynastic accident in 1603. Henry VII

dealt cautiously with all his neighbours, his main purpose being to secure recognition for his dynasty and security for his borders. Between 1492 and 1497 Perkin Warbeck travelled between Burgundy, France and Scotland, finding recognition and support in each in proportion to that ruler's temporary desire to embarrass the king of England. With dogged diplomacy Henry flushed him out from each refuge. The king's principal achievements (apart from 24 years of almost unbroken peace) were the marriage treaties which he secured with the Trastamara and the Stuarts. In 1499, after years of negotiation, Arthur, Prince of Wales, was finally married by proxy to Catherine, the third daughter of Ferdinand and Isabella of Spain; and in 1503 Margaret, Henry's elder daughter married James IV of Scotland. Both marriages were to prove, in quite different ways, highly significant for the subsequent history of England.

Unlike his father, Henry VIII regarded war as a proper and honourable instrument of policy. He fought three times against the French (1512-14, 1523-25, and 1543-46) spending vast sums of money and securing no permanent advantage. Where Henry was extremely successful, however, was in the somewhat intangible realm of honour and reputation. Although his resources were a fraction of those of Charles or Francis, he played in the same league, and was taken seriously. He was able to do this partly because of his 'larger than life' personality; partly because his only land frontier was with the much weaker state of Scotland; and partly because in the limited arena of naval warfare he was actually their equal.[27] The high watermark of his success was probably the Treaty of London in 1518, negotiated by Wolsey, which made him briefly the arbiter of Europe. After 1527 there followed a prolonged rapprochement with France, occasioned mainly by Henry's need for diplomatic support against the Emperor in Rome. There was even a brief and notional war against Charles V in 1528-29. Throughout the 1530s relations continued to be strained, and there was even a brief period in 1538-39 when it appeared that Charles and Francis were going to combine to enforce the papal sentence against him. This alarm not only occasioned a massive outlay on coastal defences, it also sent English diplomats scurrying around Europe looking for any alliance which could give Henry a little leverage. This resulted in the somewhat desperate and short lived expedient of the Cleves marriage, but the Franco-Habsburg *entente* had fallen apart by 1540, and Charles began to seek for a new English alliance as he prepared for another round against his traditional rival. Henry's last war was as much a part of his quest for renewed youth as it was responsible politics, but the side show against Scotland was more interesting and significant. A decisive victory at Solway Moss in 1542 appeared to give him an opportunity to dictate terms, and when King James V died only a few days later, he began to seek a union of the Crowns based upon a marriage between his young son Edward and James's even younger daughter, Mary, now Queen of Scotland in her own right. In a sense this was a visionary scheme which had much to commend it, but it is not surprising that the Scots saw themselves being absorbed by their more powerful neighbour. At first they were in no position to resist, but once Henry was fully engaged with France they began to retreat, and the king's furious reaction – which came to be known as 'the rough wooing' – drove them even more rapidly into the arms of Francis I.

Henry signed an inconclusive peace with France the year before he died, but the Scots war rumbled on into the following reign. Protector Somerset, continuing the policy which he had been executing for five years, invaded Scotland again in September 1547 and won a further victory at Pinkie Cleugh. The situation of 1542 was re-created with somewhat similar results. Somerset attempted to follow up his victory with the establishment of English garrisons, but these proved both vulnerable and expensive. Less than a year after Pinkie the French were again in the north in strength, and Mary was shipped out, to be betrothed to the Dauphin. Somerset's obstinate persistence in the face of this total failure was one of the prime reasons for his fall from power in the following year.[28] Meanwhile Henry II of France was anxious to take advantage of England's embarrassment to recover Boulogne, which he regarded as having been unnecessarily surrendered by his father in 1546. Somerset's successor, the Earl of Warwick, (John Dudley) plagued by financial crisis, was above all anxious to secure peace, and did so early in 1550 by selling Boulogne back to the French and by abandoning the remaining English positions in Scotland. Estranged from the Emperor by his protestant religious policies, he then began to seek improved relations with France, and was well on the way to success when Edward died in July 1553. However the succession of Mary dealt a heavy blow to Anglo-French relations. Henry tried everything short of open war to frustrate her marriage to Philip, and when he failed regarded hostilities as only a matter of time. In this frame of mind he made matters worse by harbouring English exiles and encouraging their piratical activities. No one was very surprised when Mary finally brought her reluctant subjects into the war in May 1557, but if she had been hoping to secure some advantage to England from Habsburg strength, then she was to be bitterly disappointed. The only outcome from the war from England's point of view was the loss of Calais in January 1558, a fiasco which resulted in long recriminations between the allies.[29] By the time the war was brought to an end at Cateau Cambrésis in March 1559 Mary was dead, and Elizabeth was again pursuing an independent foreign policy.

Cateau Cambrésis was a watershed in international relations. Charles V had died in 1558, and the two halves of the Habsburg Empire had separated. In the celebrations which followed the treaty Henry II had been killed, and within two years France was drifting into a civil war which was to last, on and off, until 1598. France's misfortune was Elizabeth's opportunity. A protestant rebellion in Scotland against the French-dominated Regency government gave her a chance to intervene, and the inability of Francis II to respond led to the establishment of a new Regency controlled by the so-called 'Lords of the Congregation', who retained power when the widowed Mary returned from France in 1561. Although Scotland gave Elizabeth occasional anxieties thereafter, particularly after Mary had fled from her realm in disgrace in 1568, the backdoor to England was effectively closed by the Treaty of Edinburgh. Success in the north was, however, tempered by failure in the south. Elizabeth's attempt to exploit France's divisions to secure the return of Calais foundered in the disastrous Le Havre campaign of 1563, and the queen retreated from active involvement in Europe for more than twenty years. There was no further war until 1585, but the intervening years were not without incident. Relations with Spain steadily deteriorated as Elizabeth became increasingly involved in the aggressive policies of her merchants and seamen, and regarded the repressive actions of the Duke of Alba in the Netherlands with mounting alarm. William Cecil's gamble in seizing the Genoese treasure bound for Alba's armies in 1568 provoked a long crisis, and in 1572 forty years of formal pro-Habsburg orientation was brought to an end by the signing of the Treaty of Blois with France. In the circumstances the value of this treaty was mainly symbolic, and Elizabeth continued to make periodic efforts to repair her fences with Philip, but the outbreak of open rebellion in the Netherlands in the same year, followed by large scale Spanish military activity in and around the Scheldt estuary, brought the prospect of open conflict ever closer. It came at last when the Dutch were faced with the prospect of total defeat after the assassination of William of Orange in 1584, and Elizabeth felt constrained in her own interests to go to their aid. In fact the army which she sent under the command of the Earl of Leicester (Robert Dudley) achieved little, and was probably more trouble than it was worth; but the debilitating sea war which Philip was then constrained to wage against the English distracted him, tied up resources, and took some pressure off the Netherlanders during a crucial period. The Armada campaign of 1588 was neither a beginning nor an end, but it was a severe psychological blow to Spain, and signalled that England had come of age as a naval power. This war outlasted Elizabeth, and the most dramatic events of the last decade of her reign were in Ireland rather than at sea. Thomas Cromwell had attempted to replace the old Anglo-Irish supremacy with direct rule from England after the rebellion of Silken Thomas in 1536, and the Royal Supremacy had been accepted there without demur. But protestantism had been seen as an English imposition, and Elizabeth's government had decided almost from the beginning to follow a policy of repression, marked by confiscations and re-settlement. In 1595 a combination of festering religious and political grievances caused a further major uprising, led by Hugh O'Neill, Earl of Tyrone, which in turn attracted Spanish intervention and it was not until 1601 that Lord Mountjoy was able to secure a decisive victory. Almost the last news that Elizabeth heard was of the final surrender of Tyrone, and of the securing of England's last open frontier. The Tudor state had survived a number of challenges nearer home, in 1497, 1536, 1554 and 1569, but none before had posed so serious a threat in time of war, or was ever to do so again.

# NOTES

1. Clay (1984), vol. 1:13.
2. Chartres (1977), 15.
3. Thirsk (1967), 861-62.
4. Dyer (1991), 15.
5. Guy (1988), 34-35; Dyer (1991), 72-74.
6. Tittler (1977): 24-42.
7. E. Lamond, ed., *A Discourse of the Common Weal of this Realm of England* (Cambridge, 1954), 130.
8. Sir John Fortescue, *The Governance of England*, ed. C. Plummer (Oxford, 1855).
9. There are a number of works discussing the functions of the Tudor parliaments, but the most succinct definition is in Elton (1982), 233-326.
10. There are full discussions of this issue in Scarisbrick (1968); Kelly (1976); Murphy and Surtz (1988).
11. Sir Thomas Smith, *De Republica Anglorum*, in Dewar (1982), 78.
12. C. Cook and J. Wroughton, *English Historical Facts*, 1603-1688 (London, 1980), 83-84.
13. Guy (1977).
14. David R. Starkey, 'Court and Government', in Coleman and Starkey (1986), 29-58; Starkey (1987).
15. Elton (1953).
16. Schofield (1988), 227-56.
17. William Lambarde, *Eirenarcha, or the Office of the Justice of the Peace* (London, 1602), but written in the 1580s.
18. Elton (1982), 199-217.
19. Thomson (1965); Aston (1964), 149-70.
20. Loades (1991a), 139-40.
21. Jordan (1968), 134-45.
22. Haigh (1987); Scarisbrick (1984).
23. Loades (1991b), 96-100.
24. Pogson (1975), 3-21.
25. Loades (1991a), 39.
26. Collinson (1967).
27. Loades (1992), 103-38.
28. Bush (1975).
29. Loades (1991b), 316-21.

# BIBLIOGRAPHY

*Bibliographies*
Elton, Geoffrey R., et al., eds. *Annual Bibliography of British and Irish History.* Royal Historical Society. Brighton, 1975- .
Levine, Mortimer, ed. *Tudor England, 1485-1603.* Conference of British Studies. Cambridge, 1968.
Milne, Alexander Taylor, et al., eds. *Writings on British History, 1901-1974.* 25 vols. Institute of Historical Research. London, 1937-75.
Read, Conyers, ed. *Bibliography of British History, Tudor Period, 1485-1603.* 2d ed. Oxford, 1959.
*Short Title Catalogue of Books printed in England, Scotland and Ireland and of English Books printed abroad.* Ed. Alfred William Pollard and Gilbert Richard Redgrave. Bibliographical Society. London, 1926. Rev. ed. by William A. Jackson and W. S. Ferguson. London, 1976, 1986.

*Comprehensive Surveys*
Cross, Claire. *Church and People, 1450-1660.* London, 1976.
Davies, C. S. L. *Peace, Print and Protestantism, 1450-1558.* London, 1976.
Elton, Geoffrey. R. *Reform and Reformation. England 1509-1558.* London, 1977.
Elton, Geoffrey. R. *The Tudor Constitution.* 2d ed. Cambridge, 1982.
Guy, John A. *Tudor England.* Oxford, 1988.
Loades, David M. *The Mid-Tudor Crisis.* London, 1992a.
Loades, David M. *Politics and the Nation, 1450-1660.* 4th ed. London, 1992b.
Smith, Alan Gordon Rae. *The Emergence of a Nation State: the Commonwealth of England 1529-1660.* London, 1984.
Thomson, John A. F. *The Transformation of Medieval England, 1370-1529.* London, 1983.
Williams, P. H. *The Tudor Regime.* Oxford, 1979.

*Literature*
Adams, Simon. "Eliza Enthroned? The Court and its Politics." In Haigh (1987), 55-77.
Alexander, G. "Bonner and the Marian Persecutions." *History* 60 (1975): 374-91.
Alsop, James D. "Innovation in Tudor Taxation." *EHR* 99 (1984): 83-93.
Alsop, James D. "The Theory and Practice of Tudor Taxation." *EHR* 97 (1982): 1-30.
Andrews, Kenneth R. *Trade, Plunder and Settlement: Maritime Enterprise and the Genesis of the British Empire, 1480-1630.* Cambridge, 1984.
Anglo, Sydney. *Images of Tudor Kingship.* London, 1992.
Anglo, Sydney. *Spectacle, Pageantry and Early Tudor Policy.* Oxford, 1969.
Aston, Margaret. *England's Iconoclasts.* London, 1988.
Aston, Margaret. "Lollardy and the Reformation: Survival or Revival?" *History* 49 (1964): 149-70.
Bartlett, Kenneth R. "The English Exile Community in Italy and the Political Opposition to Queen Mary I." *Albion* 13 (1981): 223-41.
Beer, Barrett L. *Northumberland: the Political Career of John Dudley, Earl of Warwick and Duke of Northumberland.* Kent, O., 1982
Beier, A. L. *Masterless Men: the Vagrancy Problem in England, 1560-1640.* London, 1985.

Beier, A. L. "Vagrants and the Social Order in Elizabethan England." *PaP*, no. 64 (1974): 3-29.

Bernard, G. W. *The Power of the Early Tudor Nobility: a Study of the Fourth and Fifth Earls of Shrewsbury*. Brighton, 1985.

Bernard, G. W. *War, Taxation and Rebellion in Early Tudor England: Henry VIII, Wolsey and the Amicable Grant of 1525*. Brighton, 1986.

Bindoff, Stanley Thomas, ed. *The House of Commons, 1509-1558*. 3 vols. London, 1982.

Braddock, R. C. "The Rewards of Office Holding in Tudor England." *JBS* 14 (1975): 29-47.

Bradshaw, Brendan. *The Irish Constitutional Revolution of the Sixteenth Century*. Cambridge, 1979.

Brigden Susan E. *The Reformation in London*. Oxford, 1989.

Brigden Susan E. "Youth and the English Reformation." In *Rebellion, Popular Protest and the Social Order in Early Modern England*, ed. Paul Slack, 77-107. Cambridge, 1984.

Bush, M. L. *The Government Policy of Protector Somerset*. London, 1975.

Canny, Nicholas. *The Elizabethan Conquest of Ireland: A Pattern Established, 1565-1576*. Brighton, 1976.

Challis, C. E. *The Tudor Coinage*. Manchester, 1978.

Chambers, David Sanderson. "Cardinal Wolsey and the Papal Tiara." *BIHR* 38 (1965): 20-30.

Chartres, J. A. *Internal Trade in England, 1500-1700*. London, 1977.

Chrimes, Stanley Bertram. *Henry VII*. London, 1972.

Clark, Peter, and Paul Slack, eds. *English Towns in Transition, 1500-1700*. Oxford, 1976.

Clay, C. G. A. *Economic Expansion and Social Change: England 1500-1700*. 2 vols. Cambridge, 1984.

Clebsch, William A. *England's Earliest Protestants, 1520-1535*. New Haven, 1964.

Cockburn, James S., ed. *Crime in England, 1550-1800*. London, 1977.

Coleman, Christopher, and David R. Starkey. *Revolution Reassessed: Revisions to the History of Tudor Government and Administration*. Oxford, 1986.

Collinson, Patrick. *Archbishop Grindal, 1519-1583: the Struggle for a Reformed Church*. London, 1980.

Collinson, Patrick. *The Elizabethan Puritan Movement*. London, 1967.

Collinson, Patrick. *Godly Rule: Essays on English Protestantism and Puritanism*. London, 1983.

Condon, M. M. "Ruling Elites in the Reign of Henry VII." In *Patronage, Pedigree and Power*, ed. C. Ross, 109-42. Gloucester, 1979.

Cooper, J. P. *Land, Men and Beliefs: Studies in Early Modern History*. London, 1983.

Cornwall, Julian. "English Population in the Early Sixteenth Century." *EconHR*, 2d ser., 23 (1970): 32-44.

Cornwall, Julian. *Revolt of the Peasantry, 1549*. London, 1977.

Cressy, David. *Literacy and the Social Order: Reading and Writing in Tudor and Stuart England*. Cambridge, 1980.

Cross, Claire, David M. Loades, and Joseph Scarisbrick, eds. *Law and Government under the Tudors*. Cambridge, 1988.

Davies, C. S. L. "England and the French War, 1557-9." In Loach and Tittler (1980), 159-85.

Davies, C. S. L. "The Pilgrimage of Grace Reconsidered." *PaP*, no. 41 (1968): 54-76.

Dewar, Mary, ed. *De Republica Anglorum* by Sir Thomas Smith. Cambridge, 1982.

Dickens, Arthur. G. *The English Reformation*. 2d ed. London, 1989.

Dickens, Arthur. G. *Lollards and Protestants in the Diocese of York, 1509-1558*. Oxford, 1959.

Dietz, Frederick C. *English Public Finance, 1485-1641*. 2 vols. 2d ed. London, 1964.

Dodds, Madeleine Hope, and Ruth Dodds. *The Pilgrimage of Grace and the Exeter Conspiracy*. 2 vols. Cambridge, 1915.

Dowling, Maria. *Humanism in the age of Henry VIII*. London, 1986.

Dyer, Alan. *Decline and Growth in English Towns, 1400-1640*. London, 1991.

Ellis, Steven G. *Tudor Ireland: Crown, Community and the Conflict of Cultures, 1470-1603*. London, 1985.

Elton, Geoffrey R. "Mid-Tudor Finance." *Historical Journal* 20 (1977): 737-40.

Elton, Geoffrey R. *The Parliament of England, 1559-1581*. Cambridge, 1986.

Elton, Geoffrey R. *Policy and Police: The Enforcement of the Reformation in the Age of Thomas Cromwell*. Cambridge, 1972.

Elton, Geoffrey R. *Studies in Tudor and Stuart Politics and Government*. 3 vols. Cambridge, 1974-83.

Elton, Geoffrey R. *The Tudor Revolution in Government*. Cambridge, 1953.

Emmison, Frederick George. *Tudor Secretary [Sir William Petre]*. London, 1961.

Fisher, F. J. "Influenza and the Inflation in Tudor England." *EconHR*, 2d ser., 18 (1965): 120-29.

Fox, Alistair G. *Thomas More: History and Providence*. Oxford, 1982.

Fox, Alistair G., and John A. Guy. *Reassessing the Henrician Age: Humanism, Politics and Reform, 1500-1550*. Oxford, 1986.

Garrett, Christina Hallowell. "The Legatine Register of Cardinal Pole." *JMH* 13 (1941): 189-91.

Glasgow, T. "The maturing of Naval Administration, 1556-1564." *Mariners Mirror* 56 (1970): 3-27.

Gleason, J. H. "The personnel of the Commissions of the Peace, 1554-1564." *Huntington Library Quarterly* 18 (1955): 169-77.

Gould, John Dennis. *The Great Debasement: Currency and the Economy in Mid-Tudor England*. Oxford, 1970.

Graves, Michael A. R. "The Management of the Elizabethan House of Commons: The Councils 'Men of Business'." *Parliamentary History* 2 (1983): 11-38.

Graves, Michael A. R. *The Tudor Parliaments: Crown, Lords and Commons, 1485-1603*. London, 1985.

Griffiths, Ralph A., and Roger S. Thomas. *The Making of the Tudor Dynasty*. Gloucester, 1985.

Gunn, Steven J. *Charles Brandon, Duke of Suffolk, 1484-1545*. Oxford, 1988.

Guth, DeLloyd J., and John W. McKenna, eds. *Tudor Rule and Revolution: Essays for G. R. Elton from his American Friends*. Cambridge, 1982.

Guy, John A. *The Cardinal's Court: the Impact of Thomas Wolsey on Star Chamber*. Brighton, 1977.

Guy, John A. "Henry VIII and the *Praemunire* Manoeuvres of 1530-31." *EHR* 97 (1982): 481-503.

Guy, John A. *The Public Career of Sir Thomas More*. Brighton, 1980.

Gwyn, Peter J. *The King's Cardinal: the Rise and Fall of Thomas Wolsey*. London, 1991.

Haigh, Christopher A. "Anticlericalism and the English Reformation." *History* 68 (1983): 391-407.

Haigh, Christopher A. "From Monopoly to Minority: Catholicism in Early Modern England." *TRHS*, 5th ser., 31 (1981): 129-47.

Haigh, Christopher A., ed. *The English Reformation Revised*. Cambridge, 1987.

Haigh, Christopher A. *Reformation and Resistance in Tudor Lancashire*. Cambridge, 1975.

Haigh, Christopher A., ed. *The Reign of Elizabeth I*. Cambridge, 1984.

Haller, William. *Foxe's Book of Martyrs and the Elect Nation*. London, 1963.

Harris, Barbara Jean. *Edward Stafford, Third Duke of Buckingham, 1478-1521*. Stanford, 1986.

Harriss, Gerard Leslie. "Thomas Cromwell's 'New Principle' of Taxation." *EHR* 93 (1978): 721-38.

Hasler, P. W., ed. *The House of Commons, 1558-1603*. 3 vols. London, 1981.

Haugaard, William P. *Elizabeth and the English Reformation: The Struggle for a Stable Settlement of Religion*. Cambridge, 1970.

Heal, Felicity. *Hospitality in Early Modern England*. Oxford, 1990.

Heal, Felicity. *Of Prelates and Princes: a Study of the Economic and Social Position of the Tudor Episcopate*. Cambridge, 1980.

Heinze, Rudolf W. *The Proclamations of the Tudor Kings*. Cambridge, 1976.

Hoak, D. E. *The King's Council in the Reign of Edward VI*. Cambridge, 1976.

Hoak, D. E. "The King's Privy Chamber, 1547-1553." In Guth and McKenna (1982), 87-108.

Hoak, D. E. "The Secret History of the Tudor Court: The King's Coffers and the King's Purse, 1542-1553." *JBS* 26 (1987): 208-31.

Holmes, P. J. "The Great Council in the reign of Henry VII." *EHR* 101 (1986): 840-62.

Hoskins, William George. *The Age of Plunder: the England of Henry VIII, 1500-1547*. London, 1976.

Houlbrooke, Ralph A. *The Church Courts and the People during the English Reformation, 1520-1570*. Oxford, 1979.

Hughes, Phillip. *The Reformation in England*. 3 vols. London, 1950-54.

Hurstfield, Joel. *Freedom, Corruption and Government in Elizabethan England*. London, 1973.

Hurstfield, Joel. *The Queen's Wards: Wardship and Marriage under Elizabeth I*. London, 1958.

Ives, Eric William. *Anne Boleyn*. Oxford, 1986.

James, Mervyn Evans. "The Concept of Order in the Northern Rising, 1569." *PaP*, 60 (1973): 49-83.

James, Mervyn Evans. "English Politics and the Concept of Honour." *PaP*, suppl. 3, 1978.

James, Mervyn Evans. *Family, Lineage and Society: a Study of Society, Politics and Mentality in the Durham Region, 1500-1640*. Oxford, 1974.

Jones, Norman Leslie. *Faith by Statute: Parliament and the Settlement of Religion, 1559*. London, 1982.

Jordan, William K. *Edward VI. The Threshold of Power: the Dominance of the Duke of Northumberland*. London, 1970.

Jordan, William K. *Edward VI. The Young King: the Protectorship of the Duke of Somerset*. London, 1968.

Kelly, Henry Ansgar. *The Matrimonial Trials of Henry VIII*. Stanford, 1976.

Kelly, M. J. "The Submission of the Clergy." *TRHS*, 5th ser., 15 (1965): 97-119.

Kerridge, Eric. *Agrarian Problems in the Sixteenth Century and After*. London, 1969.

King, John N. *English Reformation Literature*. Princeton, 1982.

Knowles, David C. *The Religious Orders in England*. Vol. 3, *The Tudor Age*. Cambridge, 1959.

Lake, Peter G. *Moderate Puritans and the Elizabethan Church*. Cambridge, 1982.

Lander, Jack Robert. *Government and Community: England 1450-1509*. London, 1980.

Lehmberg, Stanford E. *The Later Parliaments of Henry VIII, 1536-47*. Cambridge, 1977.

Lehmberg, Stanford E. *The Reformation Parliament*. Cambridge, 1970.

Levine, Mortimer. *Tudor Dynastic Problems, 1460-1571*. London, 1973.

Loach, Jennifer. "The Marian Establishment and the Printing Press." *EHR* 101 (1986): 135-48.

Loach, Jennifer. "Pamphlets and Politics, 1553-1558." *BIHR* 48 (1975): 31-44.

Loach, Jennifer. *Parliament and the Crown in the Reign of Mary Tudor*. Oxford, 1986.

Loach, Jennifer. *Parliament under the Tudors*. Oxford, 1991.

Loach, Jennifer, and Robert Tittler, eds. *The Mid-Tudor Polity, c. 1540-1560*. London, 1980.

Loades, David M. *Mary Tudor: a Life*. Oxford, 1989.

Loades, David M. *The Oxford Martyrs*. London, 1970.

Loades, David M. "Philip II and the Government of England." In Cross, Loades, and Scarisbrick (1988), 177-94.

Loades, David M. *Politics, Censorship and the English Reformation*. London, 1991a.

Loades, David M. *The Reign of Mary Tudor*. London, 1991b.

Loades, David M. *The Tudor Court*. London, 1986.

Loades, David M. *The Tudor Navy: a Military, Political and Administrative History*. London, 1992c.

MacCaffrey, Wallace T. *Queen Elizabeth and the Making of Policy, 1572-1588*. Princeton, 1981.

MacCaffrey, Wallace T. *The Shaping of the Elizabethan Regime: Elizabethan Politics, 1558-1572*. London, 1969.

McConica, James K. *English Humanists and Reformation Politics*. Oxford, 1965.

MacCulloch, Diarmaid. *Suffolk and the Tudors: Politics and Religion in an English County, 1500-1600*. Oxford, 1986.

Maltby, William S. *The Black Legend in England*. Durham, N.C., 1971.

Martin, John W. "The Marian Regime's Failure to Understand the Importance of Printing." *Huntington Library Quarterly* 44 (1980-81): 231-47.

Martin, John W. *Religious Radicals in Tudor England*. Oxford, 1989.

Mattingly, Garrett. *Catherine of Aragon*. Boston, 1941.

McGrath, Patrick. *Papists and Puritans under Elizabeth I*. London, 1967.

Miller, Helen. *Henry VIII and the English Nobility*. Oxford, 1986.

Miller, Helen. "London and Parliament in the Reign of Henry VIII." *BIHR* 35 (1962): 128-49.

Muller, James Arthur. *Stephen Gardiner and the Tudor Reaction*. New York, 1926.

Murphy, Virginia, and Edward Surtz, S.J. *The Divorce Tracts of Henry VIII*. Angers, 1988.

Neale, John Ernest. *Elizabeth I and her Parliaments*. 2 vols. London, 1953-57.

Neale, John Ernest. *The Elizabethan House of Commons*. 2d ed. London, 1963.

O'Day, Rosemary. *Education and Society, 1500-1800*. London, 1982.

Olsen, V. Norskov. *John Foxe and the Elizabethan Church*. Berkeley and Los Angeles, 1973.

Outhwaite, R. B. "The Trials of Foreign Borrowing." *EconHR*, 2d ser., 19 (1966): 289-305.

Oxley, James Edwin. *The Reformation in Essex to the Death of Mary*. Manchester, 1965.

Palliser, D. M. *The Age of Elizabeth: England under the later Tudors, 1547-1603*. London, 1983.

Parker, N.Geoffrey, and Colin Martin. *The Spanish Armada*. London, 1988.

Pettegree, Andrew. *Foreign Protestant Communities in Sixteenth Century London*. Oxford, 1986.

Pogson, R. H. "Reginal Pole and the Priorities of Government in Mary Tudor's Church." *Historical Journal* 18 (1975): 3-21.

Pogson, R. H. "Revival and Reform in Mary Tudor's Church: A question of Money." *Journal of Ecclesiastical History* 25 (1974): 249-65.

Porter, Harry Culverwell. *Reformation and Reaction in Tudor Cambridge*. Cambridge, 1958.

Potter, D. L. "The Duc de Guise and the Fall of Calais." *EHR* 98 (1983): 481-512.

Pound, John. *Poverty and Vagrancy in Tudor England*. London, 1971.

Pulman, Michael Barraclough. *The Elizabethan Privy Council in the 1570s*. Berkeley and Los Angeles, 1971.

Pythian-Adams, Charles. *Desolation of a City: Coventry and the Urban Crisis of the Late Middle Ages*. Cambridge, 1979.

Ramsay, George David. *The City of London in International Politics at the accession of Elizabethan Tudor*. Manchester 1975.

Ramsay, George David. *English Overseas Trade during the Centuries of Emergence*. London, 1957.

Read, Conyers. *Lord Burghley and Queen Elizabeth*. London, 1960.

Read, Conyers. *Mr. Secretary Cecil and Queen Elizabeth*. London, 1955.

Redworth, Glyn. *In Defence of the Church Catholic: a Life of Stephen Gardiner*. Oxford, 1990.

Richardson, Walter Cecil. *The History of the Court of Augmentations, 1536-1554*. Baton Rouge, La., 1961.

Richardson, Walter Cecil. *Tudor Chamber Administration.* Baton Rouge, La., 1952.

Ridley, Jasper. *Thomas Cranmer.* Oxford, 1962.

Rose-Troup, Frances. *The Western Rebellion of 1549.* London, 1913.

Rowse, Alfred Leslie. *The England of Elizabeth.* London, 1950.

Rowse, Alfred Leslie. *Tudor Cornwall.* London, 1941.

Scarisbrick, J. J. "Clerical Taxation in England, 1485-1547." *Journal of Ecclesiastical History* 11 (1960): 41-54.

Scarisbrick, J. J. *Henry VIII.* London, 1968.

Scarisbrick, J. J. *The Reformation and the English People.* Oxford, 1984.

Schofield, Roger S. "Taxation and the Political Limits of the Tudor State." In Cross, Loades, and J. J. Scarisbrick (1988), 227-54.

Simon, Joan. *Education and Society in Tudor England.* Cambridge, 1966.

Simpson, Alan. *The Wealth of the Gentry, 1540-1660.* London, 1961.

Slack, Paul. *The Impact of Plague in Tudor and Stuart England.* London, 1985.

Slack, Paul. "Social Policy and the Constraints of Government." In Loach and Tittler (1980), 94-115.

Slavin, Arthur J. "The Fall of Lord Chancellor Wriothesley: A Study in the Politics of Conspiracy." *Albion* 7 (1975): 265-86.

Smith, Alan Gordon Rae. *The Government of Elizabethan England.* London, 1967.

Smith, A. Hassell. *County and Court: Government and Politics in Norfolk, 1558-1603.* Oxford, 1974.

Smith, Lacey Baldwin. *Henry VIII: the Mask of Royalty.* London, 1971.

Smith, Lacey Baldwin. *Treason in Tudor England: Politics and Paranoia.* London, 1986.

Smith, Lacey Baldwin. *Tudor Prelates and Politics.* Princeton, 1953.

Starkey, David R., ed. *The English Court: from the Wars of the Roses to the Civil War.* London, 1987.

Starkey, David R., ed. *The Reign of Henry VIII: Personalities and Politics.* London, 1985.

Stone, Lawrence. *The Crisis of the Aristocracy, 1558-1641.* Oxford, 1965.

Stone, Lawrence. *Family and Fortune: Studies in Aristocratic Finance in the Sixteenth and Seventeenth Centuries.* Oxford, 1973.

Storey, R. L. *The Reign of Henry VII.* London, 1968.

Strong, Roy. *The Cult of Elizabeth: Elizabethan Portraiture and Pageantry.* London, 1977.

Thirsk, Joan, ed. *The Agrarian History of England and Wales.* Vol. 4, *1500-1640.* Cambridge, 1967.

Thomas, Keith. *Religion and the Decline of Magic.* London, 1971.

Thomson, John A. F. *The Later Lollards, 1414-1520.* Oxford, 1965.

Tittler, Robert. *Architecture and Power: the Town Hall and the English Urban Community, 1500-1640.* Oxford, 1991.

Tittler, Robert. "The Emergence of Urban Policy, 1536-58." In Loach and Tittler (1980), 74-93.

Tittler, Robert. "The Incorporation of Boroughs, 1540-1558." *History* 62 (1977): 24-42.

Tittler, Robert. *Nicholas Bacon.* London, 1976.

Walker, Greg. *John Skelton and the Politics of the 1520s.* Cambridge, 1988.

Warnicke, Retha M. *The Rise and Fall of Anne Boleyn.* Cambridge, 1989.

Wernham, Richard Bruce. *After the Armada: Elizabethan England and the Struggle for Western Europe, 1588-1595.* Oxford, 1984.

Wernham, Richard Bruce. *Before the Armada: the Emergence of the English Nation, 1485-1588.* New York, 1966.

White, Barrington Raymond. *The English Separatist Tradition.* Oxford, 1971.

Whiting, Robert. *The Blind Devotion of the People: Popular Religion and the English Reformation.* Cambridge, 1989.

Willen, D. *John Russell, First Earl of Bedford: One of the King's Men.* London, 1981.

Williams, G. *Wales and the Acts of Union.* Bangor, 1992.

Williams, Neville. *Thomas Howard, Fourth Duke of Norfolk.* London, 1964.

Williams, Penry. *The Council in the Marches of Wales under Elizabeth I.* Cardiff, 1958.

Williams, Penry. "Court and Polity under Elizabeth I." *Bulletin of the John Rylands Library* 65 (1983): 259-86.

Wolfe, Bertram Percy. *The Crown Lands, 1461-1536*. London, 1970.

Wolfe, Bertram Percy. "Henry VII's Land Revenues and Chamber Finance." *EHR* 79 (1964): 225-54.

Woodward, G. W. O. *The Dissolution of the Monasteries*. London, 1966.

Wrigley, Edward Anthony, and Roger S. Schofield. *The Population History of England, 1540-1871: A Reconstruction*. London, 1981.

Wyndham, K. S. H. "Crown Land and Royal Patronage in Mid-sixteenth Century England." *JBS* 19 (1980): 18-34.

Youings, Joyce. "The Council of the West." *TRHS*, 5th. ser., 10 (1960): 41-60.

Youings, Joyce. *The Dissolution of the Monasteries*. London, 1971.

Youings, Joyce. *Sixteenth Century England*. Harmondsworth, 1984.

Youngs, Frederic A. *The Proclamations of the Tudor Queens*. Cambridge, 1976.

Zeeveld, W. Gordon. *Foundations of Tudor Policy*. Cambridge, Mass., 1948.

Zell, M. L. "Early Tudor J. P.s at Work." *Archaeologia Cantiana*, 93 (1977): 125-43.

# THE HABSBURG LANDS:
# THE HOLY ROMAN EMPIRE, 1400-1555

Volker Press (†1993)
(Eberhard-Karls-Universität Tübingen)

## 1. THE THREE ROYAL DYNASTIES

Even after the fall of the Hohenstaufen dynasty in 1250, the Holy Roman Empire, with its generally open borders and its loosely attached periphery, remained the dominant political organization in Central Europe.[1] The decisive factor in this continuity was a shift in the Empire's political center of gravity toward the southeast. A shift of center in the contrary direction, to the rich Lower Rhenish lands of the northwest, remained a mere episode connected with the reigns of William of Holland (r. 1247-56) and, perhaps, Richard of Cornwall (1256-72).[2] Subsequently, Count Rudolph of Habsburg's (r. 1276-91) effort to establish a regional continuity with the Hohenstaufen power led to a certain embeddedness of the monarchy in southern Germany. Thereafter, their acquisition of Austria gave the Habsburgs a widened territorial basis in the more open regions of the Empire's southeast, where they could build a power base more easily than in the Empire's core, the political structures which were rigidly fixed by well established legal relations.[3]

The German princely dynasties' new self-confidence consolidated the practice of elective monarchy and frequent change of dynasty. Peter Moraw, the best historian of this era, has spoken of the "little kings,"[4] and, indeed, the effort to base the monarchy in the Empire's center met with no success. Adolph of Nassau (r. 1292-98), Rudolph I's successor, failed because he overreached his resources. The government of Henry VII, count of Luxemburg (r. 1308-13), could rely on the strong position of his brother, Archbishop Baldwin of Trier, but he, too, lacked a territorial basis for his rule. He did succeed nonetheless in returning Imperial presence to Italy, a move which his predecessors—Rudolph I, Adolph, and the second Habsburg king, Albert I, who was an especially successful expansionist— had already planned to make.[5] Even more important, however, was Henry VII's laying the foundations for the acquisition of an even larger group of lands, the Bohemian and Moravian complex of the Przemyslid dynasty, which was acquired by his son, John the Blind. The House of

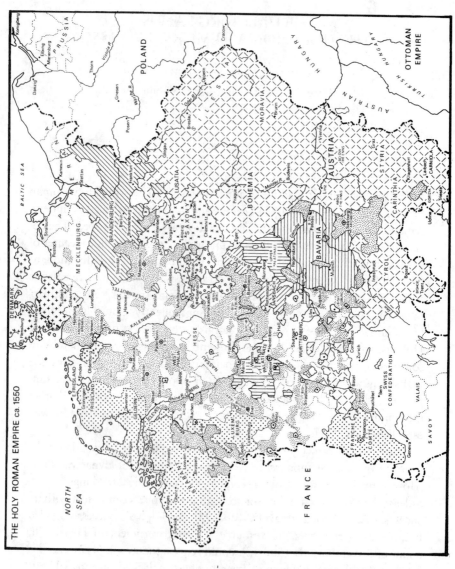

THE HOLY ROMAN EMPIRE ca. 1550

HABSBURG LANDS
  Austrian line
  Spanish line
WETTIN LANDS
  Albertine line
  Ernestine line
HOHENZOLLERN LANDS
  Brandenburg line
  Franconian line
WITTELSBACH LANDS
  Bavarian line
  Palatinate line
OLDENBURG DYNASTY
  Denmark - Schleswig-
            Holstein
  Oldenburg
  Ecclesiastical
    territories
  Imperial cities
  Boundary of the
    EMPIRE

Austria had also competed for this prize, and its success would have given the Empire's destiny a very different twist.[6]

Upon Henry VII's death in 1314, the Empire was divided between Luxemburg and Habsburg parties. In a disputed election the Habsburg candidate, Frederick the Handsome, gained four votes, which did not prevent the other four electors from following the Luxemburg plan to elect Duke Louis of Upper Bavaria, the first Wittelsbach king. In the ensuing military struggle, Louis held the upper hand against the Habsburg party, for the shared dual monarchy agreed upon in 1325 proved a brief episode. Once in office, Emperor Louis IV (r. 1314-47), called "the Bavarian," paid little heed to his Luxemburg patrons and sought to build up the power of his own dynasty instead through the acquisition of Brandenburg, Holland, and Tyrol.[7] His efforts demonstrate a basic phenomenon of the late medieval German monarchy, namely, that a strong base in family lands was the decisive prerequisite for a strong rule, because the royal demesne had been progressively diminished through mortgages, grants, and sales. In the beginning, the Wittelsbachs had enjoyed more respect than the Habsburgs or the Luxemburgs, but they had become too powerful to suit the German princes, and after the fall of the Hohenstaufen in the mid-thirteenth century, several Wittelsbach candidates had failed to gain election. The Welf dynasty, by contrast, had no chance at all, nor did the Ascanians or the Wettins—all of whom were pushed back into the second rank. Thus arose the triad of royal dynasties—Luxemburgs, Habsburgs, and Wittelsbachs— with the first two, because of their access to east central Europe, having the advantage over the Wittelsbachs.

Charles IV (r. 1347-78) seemed to give his dynasty, the Luxemburgs, a decisive lead over the other two.[8] He built his Bohemian lands into modern territorial state, added the lordship over the non-Imperial lands of Silesia and Lusatia, and expanded into the Empire as well. The old royal cities of Nuremberg and Frankfurt became pillars of his position. Charles tried to acquire the Upper Palatinate and was able to "succeed" the Wittelsbachs in Brandenburg, thereby bringing a second electorate into his dynastic possessions. With the Golden Bull of 1356, Charles tried to establish fixed rules for Imperial political life and to limit the number of electors to seven, excluding from their circle his dynastic rivals, Austria and Bavaria. The Bavarian Wittelsbachs were weakened by territorial divisions. Rudolph IV, the founder of the Austrian state, took drastic measures against the same dangerous practice. These measures brought Charles' power deep into the heart of the Empire, especially into Franconia, but also into northeastern Germany. Then, too, the securing of the Hungarian crown in 1384 by his second son, Sigmund, opened the prospect for an expansion into southeastern Europe.

By the late fourteenth century, the Empire seemed destined to live for a long period of Luxemburg rule from their base in a modernized Bohemian state. Soon, however, their position revealed its instability. To be sure, Charles was able to secure the succession of his eldest son, Wenceslaus IV, both in the Empire and in Bohemia, but the crisis of the Bohemian monarchy led rapidly to an Imperial crisis as well. Charles had reduced the Bohemian nobility's power, not destroyed it, and Wenceslaus' power was so circumscribed in Bohemia that he altogether lost his position in Empire.[9]

Around this time, the late fourteenth century, it was becoming evident that there could be no unitary royal lordship over the Holy Roman Empire. Times of crisis tended to make clear how the Empire was divided, at least from the royal point of view. It comprised the emperor's dynastic lands; the electoral territories, whose rulers' electoral function tied them closely to the monarchy; old zones of strong royal influence, such as Franconia, Swabia, the Rhineland, Thuringia, and the lands of the north, which were far removed from royal influence. The whole structure was overlain by zones of regional hegemonies of princely dynasties.[10] This is how things appeared, as the Luxemburg dynasty, which Charles IV had carefully constructed, collapsed.

King Wenceslaus (r. 1378-1411), a weak ruler, provoked the electors, especially the four Rhenish ones, into actions against him, as his conferral of Imperial rights on Duke Gian Galeazzo Visconti of Milan in 1400 provided the legal grounds for his deposition and the election of a new king from their own ranks, Elector Palatine Rupert III (r. 1400-10). Rupert's abortive Italian campaign, however, demonstrated his limits, leading to the remarkable situation of two competing but geographically quite distinct monarchies, Rupert's and Wenceslaus'. Not only was neither able to overcome the other, they did not even overlap. Rupert held sway in the old core region, though his power was based less on his Palatine dynastic lands—deeply fragmented, unlike Austria, Bavaria, or Bohemia—than on the region they dominated. He also possessed powerful rivals in the three ecclesiastical electors, who tended to hold him in check. Rupert's was the last attempt to build a monarchy based in the Empire's core.[11]

With Rupert's death in 1410, the situation shifted. The electors chose Wenceslaus' brother, Sigmund (r. 1410-37), who was king of Hungary.[12] At first he ruled from afar, as the later Hohenstaufens, Richard of Cornwall, and Alfonso of Castile had done, busying himself with the expansion of his royal power in the southeast and with his rivalry with Wenceslaus, whom he persuaded in 1411 to abdicate.

Sigmund, Wenceslaus' successor, did not return the seat of power to Prague but attempted instead to rebuild royal influence in the Empire's old core regions of Franconia, Swabia, and the Rhine Valley. Though he refrained from challenging the princes, he tried to mobilize the nobilities and the towns; he reactivated support in the old regions of loyalty to the monarchy; and he conducted an active ecclesiastical policy, chiefly as protector of the Council of Constance (1414-18).[13] Moreover, his territorial position was very widely extended, because he held on to his Hungarian crown. The most important development was the Bohemian crisis. When the Council of Constance ordered the execution of Jan Hus, a master of the University of Prague, Sigmund broke the safe conduct he had granted to Hus and his companion, Jerome of Prague. Then, at the death of Wenceslaus in 1419, Bohemia exploded.

The Hussite Wars robbed Bohemia of even the hope of regaining its old role as Empire's center, and the marginalization of Bohemia also tended to isolate Sigmund's Hungarian kingdom from the Empire. Sigmund, of course, did pacify the Bohemian kingdom in 1434, but even then he was faced by resistance on the parts of the Hussites and the Bohemian nobles.[14] In 1415 he also had given up the electorate of Brandenburg, an inherited land which had always been peripheral to his base of operations in Hungary. With this step began the long withdrawal of the royal authority from the Empire's northern lands. In Brandenburg he established a dynasty, the Hohenzollerns, who were able in the long run to exploit the fluid political landscape of the northeast, though as yet they posed no threat to the three competing royal dynasties.

## 2. THE SECOND RISE OF THE HOUSE OF HABSBURG AND THE CRISIS OF EMPEROR FREDERICK III

Emperor Sigmund sought reconciliation with the House of Habsburg. Since he had no male heir, the marriage of his daughter and heir, Elizabeth, became a political matter of the first rank. In 1421 she married Duke Albert V of Austria, so that, after eighty years of Luxemburg paramountcy, the Austrian dynasty came once more to the fore. After the failure of King Frederick the Handsome, the Habsburgs had devoted themselves to securing the duchies of Carinthia and Carniola, having already acquired Styria in 1282.[15]     Duke Rudolph IV (r. 1358-65), called "the Founder" of Austria, had tried to nullify the Golden Bull's exclusion of Austria from the electoral college by means of a series of forgeries that purported to document, by means of the *Privlegium maius*, the alleged special position of the House of Austria in the Empire[16]. Charles IV refused to confirm this privilege, which languished until its confirmation by Frederick III in 1453. Rudolph IV worked hard for the administrative consolidation of the Austrian lands and succeeded in 1364 in laying to rest the conflicts with Emperor Charles IV. He was able in 1363 to acquire title to Tyrol, which bridged Austria to his original dynastic lands in the west, though these were gradually falling prey to Swiss expansionism.[17] It was some compensation, therefore, that the House of Austria was also able to establish itself in Vorarlberg.

The House of Austria nonetheless also continued to weaken its position by means of partitions of the dynastic lands. The partition of 1379 gave Duke Albert III (r. 1379-95) Austria and Leopold III (1379-86) the larger share consisting of Carinthia, Carniola, Tyrol, and the western lands (*Vorlande*). The Leopoldine line split again into Styrian and Tyrolean branches. The entire dynasty nevertheless came to call itself "the House of Austria," while other names became established for the divided lands: "Lower Austria" for the lands above and below the River Enns; "Inner Austria" for the duchies Styria, Carinthia, and Carniola; and "Upper Austria" for Tyrol and the western lands.

Against these efforts at consolidation, centrifugal forces were also at work. When the energetic Leopold III tried to bring the Swiss once more under Austrian hegemony, he lost a battle, and his life, to them at Sempach in 1386. Then, too, strife between the various Austrian lines was not uncommon, and the strengthened position of the nobilities, constituted as estates of the lands, made for repeated conflict with the ruling dynasty. Finally, the city of Vienna maintained a relatively independent position.

New setbacks occurred under Duke Frederick IV (r. 1406-39), called "Empty-Pockets," who was severely beaten by the Swiss in the Appenzell War of 1405-8. Conflict arose between him and Emperor Sigmund on account of Frederick's unfortunate support for Pope John XXIII, who was deposed by the Council of Constance. The strife, in which Sigmund exploited the Tyrolean nobility's opposition to the duke, lasted until 1418.[18] More successful than Frederick was Duke Albert V of Lower Austria (1404/11-39), a capable ruler whose lands were badly damaged during the Hussite Wars. More than anyone else, Albert, through his marriage to Sigmund's daughter, Elizabeth, disrupted the three-way rivalry of royal dynasties, an important harbinger of future developments.

In fact, the triple rivalry for the crown was gradually being resolved. The Wittelsbachs, who were split into Palatine and Bavarian lines, dropped back, though they still hoped to redress their setback. Meanwhile, the Habsburg Albert II (r. 1438-39) succeeded his father-in-law in the Empire and as king in Bohemia and Hungary.[19] The untimely death of this capable ruler, who would surely have restructured the Imperial political order, made his an episodic reign. No similar constellation of forces favorable to consolidation would appear until 1526, when Archduke Ferdinand succeeded to the united crowns of Bohemia and Hungary. Albert's unexpected death proved a fateful event for the Habsburgs' lordship over the Empire, which could not be preserved for his posthumously born son, Ladislaus. When another Habsburg did come to the Imperial throne in 1440, the choice passed over the more centrally located Tyrolean line to fall on a representative of the Inner Austrian-Styrian line, Duke Frederick V, who became emperor as Frederick III. Once more, the Empire had a monarch from its periphery, and while Frederick's base was just as remote as Sigmund's had been, he possessed far fewer possibilities for expanding it.

The premature death of Ladislaus Postumus in 1457 posed a new threat in the form or revival of "national monarchies" in Bohemia and Hungary against Frederick III's opposition. The Hungarian crown passed in 1458 to Matthias Corvinus, son of János Hunyádi, who had been regent during his predecessor's minority. In Bohemia, meanwhile, a great noble, George of Podiebrady, came to the throne. Although he cast his eye for a while toward the German crown, his main task lay in Bohemia, where he began the reconciliation with the Hussites.[20] Fortunately for the Habsburgs, King George did not ally with Mathias Corvinus of Hungary, who gained control of the Bohemian satellite lands of Moravia, Silesia, and Lusatia, and who put growing pressure on Austria. Austria was always vulnerable to such external meddling because of its factionalized nobility, for the prominence of its great noble lineages made Austria very similar to the noble-dominated landscapes of east central Europe.

George of Podiebrady's reign in Bohemia remained episodic, and at his death the Bohemian nobles chose not a Habsburg but the king of Poland's son, Wladislaw (r. 1471-1516). This move enhanced, of course, Bohemia's trajectory away from the Empire, which the Hussites had begun. With the death of Matthias Corvinus in 1490, Wladislaw IV competed with the Habsburgs for the Hungarian succession and won the crown.

Duke Frederick V of Inner Austria (r. 1424-93) assumed in 1439 the guardianship of his cousins, Ladislaus Postumus and Sigmund (r. 1439/46-1490, d. 1496), who was a son of Frederick IV of Tyrol. It was therefore as undisputed head of the entire House of Austria that he was elected in 1440 to the Imperial throne as Frederick III.[21] Very soon, however, his dynastic lands came under pressure from all sides, and in 1446 he had to surrender his guardianship of Sigmund of Tyrol. He nevertheless made in 1451-52 a successful journey to Rome, where he was crowned emperor (the last to be crowned there). This did not protect him against his Hungarian and Bohemian rivals, who sought to seize his lands. As the situation deteriorated, Frederick grasped in 1458 for the Hungarian crown, but lost it to Matthias Corvinus and the House of Hunyádi. Meanwhile, Frederick conducted a violent feud with his brother, Albert VI (r. 1424-63), which lasted from 1458 to 1463. Their struggle, which arose over the partition of the Lower Austrian duchies, spread havoc and destruction through the lands. Albert VI conquered Vienna in 1461 and threatened to subdue his brother, who would thereby have lost the last territorial base for his monarchical regime. Albert's sudden death, however, brought all of Austria's Danubian lands into Frederick's hands, and in the Treaty of Sopron (1463) he was able to make peace with Matthias Corvinus. Finally, in 1471 he put down a new revolt by nobles under Andreas Baumkircher of Carinthia.

By the early 1470s, therefore, Frederick III had gotten his hands free for a more active royal policy in the Empire. He was nevertheless hindered by tense relations with Duke Sigmund of Tyrol, who had been excommunicated for his attack on the prince-bishopric of Brixen/Bressanone in 1460 and was then assaulted by the Swiss Confederates.[22] They seized from him the Thurgau, on the south shore of Lake Constance, leaving the Habsburgs no major possession south of the High Rhine (the Rhine above Lake Constance), where the dynasty's original seat of power lay. Sigmund, desperate for allies, sought help from the rising power of Burgundy and its duke, Charles the Bold, to whom he mortgaged the Habsburg possessions on both sides of the Upper Rhine (below Basel). In order to cement this tie, he offered the hand of Frederick III's son, Maximilian, to Charles for his daughter and heir, Duchess Mary of Burgundy. This project was dashed by Charles' attack on the prince-archbishopric of Cologne, which sparked an Imperial war against Burgundy. Sigmund now changed fronts, and in the "Perpetual Compact [*Ewige Richtung*]" of 1474, he renounced all claims against the Swiss Confederacy. The united former foes turned on the Burgundian, beat his armies at Grandson and Murten in 1476, and left him dead on the field of Nancy in January 1477.[23]

It was an important event when a desperate Charles the Bold renewed contacts to the Habsburgs and offered them Mary's hand in marriage. Not until after his death, however, did the wedding with Archduke Maximilian take place on 19 April 1477. This act at once unleashed the conflict with the king of France, which ended with the Peace of Arras in 1482.[24]  From the time of this marriage, the year 1477, people spoke of the "House of Austria and Burgundy."  Indeed, the young Austrian prince, Maximilian, established himself very well on this far northwestern edge of the Empire.  His father, meanwhile, was coming under new pressure from the east, for Matthias Corvinus, provoked by Frederick's clumsy actions, invaded Lower Austria and occupied Vienna in 1485 and Wiener Neustadt in 1487.[25]  The election of Maximilian 1486 as King of the Romans posed a counterweight to this Austrian disaster.  The election took place with little pressure from Frederick, who, hard-pressed by the Hungarian king, feared resistance from the electors.

By this time, Frederick III had revealed himself to be a skilled, if cautious, Imperial politician.  His dynastic pride carried him through the most difficult situations, and he defended fiercely the legal claims of emperor and Empire.  All in all, he exploited the possibilities of the Imperial office far better than the older scholarship was prone to acknowledge.  He tried repeatedly, for example, though without success, to establish a law of public peace (*Landfriede*) in the Empire.[26]  His ecclesiastical policy met with greater success, for by means of the Concordat of Vienna (1448) he secured a de facto right of nomination to church offices, which became an important step toward the revival of Imperial authority.

The Habsburg position nonetheless grew critical once more through the actions of Duke Sigmund of Tyrol, who had mountainous debts and no heir.  It all came to a dramatic head in 1486-87, when the Wittelsbach dukes in Landshut and Munich, backed by their Palatine kinsmen in Heidelberg, grabbed for the Habsburg lands in Swabia, and Duke Sigmund, called "Minter," supported them against his own kinsmen.  The situation was saved in the end by the young King Maximilian, who came to an agreement with the Tyrolean estates, expelled the pro-Bavarian "evil councilors [*böse Räte*]," and secured the Habsburg lands in Swabia and the succession in Tyrol.  Now the Habsburgs possessed a base of operations in the Empire, from which they could reassemble the old Imperial clientele in Swabia and alleviate, by means of the rich Tyrolean mines, the dynasty's chronic financial plight.[27]

The smaller rulers of southwestern Germany had watched with growing mistrust the westward expansion of the Bavarian dukes, fearing their growing territorial might.  This fear formed the background to the formation in 1488, at Emperor Frederick's initiative, of the Swabian League. The league was erected on the traditions of older noble federations, such as the Union of St. George ("*mit St. Jörgenschild*"), which had possessed

strong Habsburg ties. It embraced small and tiny rulers, all subject directly
to the Empire rather than to any territorial prince, especially the Swabian
nobles, prelates, counts, and free cities. The Swabian League was more
than a mere sworn league (*Einung*), for it formed a system of collective security which, on the one hand, united the small, vulnerable Imperial estates
of the southwestern region and, on the other, took up the tasks of securing
law and order and regulating conflicts. At the league's first renewal in
1500, membership was opened for the first time to the princes, who recognized the league's power by seeking voice in its councils. By this time the
Swabian League was becoming an important instrument of the Habsburg
dynasty's Imperial policy.[28] Maximilian extended this policy, too, to the
dynasty's most important rival in the southwest, Count Eberhard V, called
"the Bearded [*im Bart*]," of Württemberg, who was tied to the Habsburgs
through his elevation in 1495 to ducal rank.[29] All these moves doubtless
meant the return of Imperial authority to the Empire's core lands and to
Swabia, whence the emperor could make his will felt in many directions.
The Swabian League nonetheless remained a singular construction. Its
elder, Upper Rhenish counterpart, the "Lower Union [*Niedere
Vereinigung*]" established in 1474, never acquired any comparable significance.

## 3. THE MONARCHY OF MAXIMILIAN I

Maximilian I (r. 1486/93-1519) succeeded his father as emperor in 1493.[30]
His first Imperial Diet (*Reichstag*), at Worms in 1495, uncovered the deep-
est outstanding problems of the Imperial constitution. This dynamic ruler
was determined to counter the invasion of Italy by King Charles VIII of
France, which violated Imperial rights of rule over northern Italy, and his
demands for money touched off a dramatic discussion of the Empire's constitution. The common term for this discussion is "Imperial reform
[*Reichsreform*]," which probably suggests a more deliberate program of
reform than any of the participants possessed.[31] The estates, which had exploited Emperor Frederick III's difficulties to expand their own autonomy,
found themselves once again face-to-face with an activist emperor. And so
a compromise was reached and enshrined in the recess (*Reichsabschied*) of
Worms as a fundamental law of the Empire.

The core of the Imperial reform was the establishment of a law of public
peace (*Landfriede*). It was meant to supersede and abolish the right of
feud, which the nobles had long claimed and exercised as a procedure for

settling legal disputes. In its place was established a royal "Chamber Court [*Kammergericht*]," over which emperor had, however, to yield paramount influence to the electors and princes.[32]

A measure of reform concerned taxation. To finance the emperor's campaign in Italy, the Diet authorized the first general direct head- and property tax, called the "Common Penny [*der Gemeine Pfennig*]." This form of taxation, the Empire's first direct imposition on the subjects of the territorial princes, soon proved too antithetical to the Empire's territorial structure. It was replaced by a system of lump assessments on the Imperial estates (*Matrikularsteuer*) in 1521, when Emperor Charles V was planning his own Italian campaign.[33]

Just as important as these reforms was the fixing of the form of the Imperial Diet. This assembly of the emperor's direct subjects grew out of the royal assizes (*königliche Hoftage*), the assemblies of the electors, and the various kinds of meetings of the estates in the absence of the king—sometimes as emergency meetings during royal vacancies, sometimes as meetings directed against a ruling king.[34]

Taken together, these changes meant both an impressive intensification of the Empire's governance and an affirmation of the estates' role in it. The king, moreover seemed to have been driven on the defensive. The low point from his perspective may have come in 1500, when the Diet established an Imperial Governing Council (*Reichsregiment*) entirely divorced from the royal authority.[35] Maximilian nevertheless managed by 1502 to cripple, then to dissolve, this formation. The advantages he had were his unity of action against the divergent multiplicity of princely interests and the growth of his own royal government.

The king made his own contributions to the intensification of Imperial governance. His royal council (*Hofrat*), later the Imperial Council (*Reichshofrat*), developed into a court which competed with the Imperial Chamber Court (*Reichskammergericht*).[36] In 1507 he assumed the title of "elected Roman emperor," and he proved to be a ruler who managed to keep the estates under continuous pressure. Another change, which went back to the estates' initiative in 1500, was the division of the Empire into administrative districts, called "Circles [*Reichskreise*]," some of which represented simply regional hegemonies of great princes or groups of princes, although initially the Habsburg lands and electoral territorials were exempt from the system. Later, in 1512 were formed an Austrian and a Burgundian Circle, by means of which the House of Habsburg blocked outside intervention in its lands' affairs, though the same organization in Circles deprived the ruling dynasty of its traditional influence in neighboring circles, notably the Swabian Circle.[37]

Maximilian's activist policies ran against the invincible barrier posed by his perpetual financial difficulties. The Austrian lands and their estates contributed far more toward his expenses than did the fiscally sullen Imperial estates, but the two sources together never came close to covering his needs. Maximilian was nothing if not a master at managing Imperial and territorial estates, a skill he had perhaps acquired during his years in the Burgundian Netherlands. He was especially good with the lesser nobles and the burghers, though his position forced him to deal as well with the Imperial princes. And deal with them he did. He exploited internal crises in Württemberg and Hesse, and in the Landshut War (1503-5) he destroyed the position of the last of the rival royal dynasties, the Wittelsbachs. The war had begun when the last duke of Bavaria-Landshut violated dynastic law to leave his lands to his son-in-law, Rupert, who was the second son of Elector Palatine Philip. Maximilian then sided with the weaker side in the intra-Wittelsbach quarrel, the Munich line, and brought down on the Palatine Wittelsbachs a catastrophe that ended abruptly their great era of power during the previous century. From this blow, the line never recovered. The role of a rival semi-king, which Elector Frederick I (r. 1451-76), called "the Victorious," had played, was gone forever, and the fall of the Palatine Wittelsbachs formed a turning point for the future Habsburg position in the Empire.[38]

The process of political consolidation in the Empire, which Maximilian introduced, also led to a new definition of the periphery's relationship to the center. The long Venetian War (1508-16) brought territorial losses; in 1515 East Prussia had to recognize Polish feudal suzerainty; and under the Jagiellonian kings Bohemia drifted ever further from Imperial affairs. Indeed, since Bohemia took no part in the new constitutional consolidation, being represented neither in the Diet nor in the Chamber Court, only the old electoral right still bound the kingdom to the Empire.

Other lands on the Empire's margins were also drifting away. The Netherlands, despite their recent incorporation into the Burgundian Circle, maintained a very ambivalent relationship to the Empire. Their ruler, Philip the Handsome (d. 1506), Maximilian's son, preserved their distance from the Empire, which the Valois dukes of Burgundy had established.[39] Much nearer, of course, lay the Swiss Confederacy, which refused to recognize either the Chamber Court or the new Imperial taxes, and which in any case did not at all fit the feudal structure of the Imperial Diet. Maximilian had not forgotten, of course, that the original seat of his dynasty lay among the Swiss. In 1498-99 broke out a bloody war, called the "Swabian War" or the "Swiss War," which involved the Swabian League as well. The war dealt the king severe defeats and brought the de facto separation of the Confederacy from the Empire, though their legal relationship remained unsettled. After free cities of Basel and Schaffhausen joined the Confederacy in 1501, the border with the rest of the Empire assumed approximately the form it would maintain for centuries. This separation of the Swiss was to have important consequences for the German Reformation.[40]

Maximilian experienced many defeats. One of them was Duke Ulrich of Württemberg's exit from the system of Habsburg clientele.[41] Another was the failure of Maximilian's efforts to pacify the predatory nobles, such as Götz von Berlichingen and Franz von Sickingen.[42] The emperor's policies concentrated very much on the Empire's southern regions, so much so that the historian Georg Schmidt has written of a "South German Empire."[43] Maximilian's policy nevertheless did strengthen the Imperial political system as a whole, a fact illustrated by the very rapid succession of Imperial Diets during the first half of his reign. Later, it is true, the Diet met less frequently.

The last years of Maximilian's reign were occupied with securing the Imperial succession. At the "Congress of Vienna" in 1515, he negotiated an agreement with the Jagiellonian king of Bohemia and Hungary, which they sealed with a double marriage of the young Hungarian king, Louis II (r. 1516-26) to Mary of Austria, and of her brother, Ferdinand, Maximilian's grandson, to Anna of Bohemia-Hungary.[44] Maximilian also developed policy on a Europe-wide scale, which since 1495 involved him in the fateful alliance with the united houses of Castile and Aragon. This union brought to his son, Philip, the hand in marriage of Princess Juana, and to his grandson, Charles, the succession to both kingdoms. Philip, who as the son of Mary of Burgundy had inherited rule over the Netherlands, ruled the provinces in such a way as to magnify their independence from the Empire and its governance. This made the election of a German king to succeed Maximilian an issue of European rank, and the Imperial electors grew skeptical of another Burgundian on the throne. The growth of this Netherlandish problem also made Maximilian sensitive to the problematical character of tying the House of Austria and the Imperial crown to Spain, a distant Mediterranean power. The role of Charles of Ghent as heir to all three—the Empire, Burgundy, and Spain—encouraged him to reflect on an alternative plan, centered on Ferdinand, his second grandson, for whom he planned to create a kingdom out of Austria. He even declined to reject the idea of Ferdinand's succeeding him as Emperor. In the end, the intransigence of Charles, the elder grandson, who insisted on his own succession to the Imperial throne, ruled out any alternative.[45]

The disturbances that followed Maximilian's death in January 1519, both in the Austrian lands and in the Empire, show the importance of his consolidating work.  In the dynastic lands, the reactions ranged from revolt by the Austrian estates to the plundering of the archducal fishponds by his subjects, while in the Empire there were pogroms at Regensburg and Rothenburg ob der Tauber against the Jews, who stood directly under royal protection, and Duke Ulrich of Württemberg's attack on the free city of Reutlingen.  The central crisis attended the royal election itself, for the rival candidacies of Charles of Spain and Francis of France transformed the Imperial political structure into an object of European politics.  Understandably enough, for the election's consequences concerned all the European powers.  The electors thus moved to a "national solution," though not to the logical candidate—the new Elector Palatine, Louis V, whose lands had been wrecked by the war of 1504—but to Elector Frederick, called "the Wise," of Saxony.[46]  Frederick, unwilling to take on so great a risk, withdrew his candidacy, whereupon the "German blood" of the Habsburg candidate, Charles, won out over Francis I.  By virtue of his dynasty's royal tradition, of the strong pro-Habsburg party in the Empire, and, not least of all, of cash from the Fuggers, Charles of Spain became emperor as Charles V.[47]

## 4. CHARLES V AS THE EMPIRE'S "ABSENTEE RULER"

The electors tried to contain the risks inherent in their action by binding the new emperor-elect by means of an "election capitulation."  Their principal concern was to keep him from deploying his Spanish resources in the Empire, so as to block the formation of a court dominated by Spanish or Netherlandish interests.[48]  Yet, the German princes misread the plans of Charles V (r. 1519-56), who thought to draw on the Imperial office to strengthen his efforts to dominate Europe and Italy.  Germany lay quite on the periphery of his calculations, which centered on the Mediterranean lands.  This meant that the Empire became peripheral once more to royal policy, just as it had become under the Hohenstaufen emperors, under Sigmund of Luxemburg, and even under Frederick III.

In 1521-22 Charles came to Germany to be crowned and to preside over his first Imperial Diet, following which he turned to what appeared to him more important problems.[49]  Consequently, he had to leave the Empire's governance practically in the hands of the German princes, trusting to their solidarity with his dynasty.  The princes, for their part, wanted no interference in their territorial affairs by an absentee monarch. Judged in terms of Maximilian's system, this appeared to mean a shift in favor of the princes. Charles, however, also understood that he could not simply leave management of the Empire to the princes, nor could he himself rule the Austrian lands effectively. His solution was to install his brother, Archduke Ferdinand, as ruler of Austria, though the decision, made in 1521-22, was at first kept secret.[50] His revival in 1521 of the Imperial Governing Council was an act of trust in the princes, who chiefly staffed this body. A third pillar of Charles' regime in the Empire was the Swabian League.

Tensions between the Habsburg brothers were at first alleviated by Charles' foresight and Ferdinand's inexperience, also by the difficulties of communication. When Ferdinand received the dynastic lands, they included the duchy of Württemberg, from which Duke Ulrich had been expelled in 1519 on account of breach of the public peace (*Landfriedensbruch*). The acquisition of Württemberg seemed destined to crown Austria's position as the premier power of southwestern Germany.[51] The time seemed ripe, indeed, for an expansion of royal power on an expanded Austrian basis, since Ferdinand also became Charles' viceroy in the Empire.

This promise was never fulfilled. Ferdinand was soon confronted with the difficult problems connected with the beginnings of the religious reformation, as territorial princes, ever jealous of their territorial independence, began to support Luther in significant numbers. Ferdinand was not strong enough to oppose them.[52] Moreover, he tried and failed to protect the lesser nobles from the princes by means of the Governing Council, while the Swabian League, now under princely influence, set out to crush the free knights in a campaign of 1523. This was just a prelude, for beginning in the autumn of 1524, the great Peasants' War of 1525 enfolded right in the midst of the Habsburgs' South German-Austrian position. Indeed, this tremendous insurrection may be justly regarded as the wreck of Maximilian's system.[53] The countermeasures, when they came, were undertaken not by Archduke Ferdinand but by the Swabian League, spurred on by the Bavarian dukes, whose councilor, Dr. Leonhard von Eck, was to become a key figure in Imperial politics during the first half of the sixteenth century.[54]

For a long while, the Bavarians could not coin this situation into capital, even though the religious schism dealt them a central political position, once the dukes, meeting at Grünwald in 1522, decided to remain in the old church. In the following years, they played back and forth between insisting on their liberties as princes and keeping religious solidarity with the House of Austria and the emperor. The Habsburgs' own religious position never stood in question, for their European position permitted no other policy than support for the old church—even though the last word about Habsburg religious policy had by no means yet fallen. The Reformation it-self nonetheless became a peculiarly German movement, to which no princely dynasty, excepting Bavaria and Austria, remained immune. This religious split undermined Charles' German policy, which rested on coop-eration with the Imperial princes.

The Peasants' War had revealed Ferdinand's rule to be quite vulnerable to disruption. The wide geographic span of the Austrian territories made a power base in the center, in Swabia, a vital necessity. The Swabian League provided some qualified support, and so did the House of Waldburg in the persons of Jörg, called "Peasant George" for his actions against the rebels in 1525, and Wilhelm, his cousin.[55] When the Governing Council was translated in 1524 from Nuremberg to Esslingen in Swabia, close by the newly Austrian capital of Stuttgart, a new center of power seemed to be forming in this region. Just at this point, however, the death of the last Jagiellonian king of Hungary, Louis II, after the Battle of Mohács, turned Ferdinand's attention to securing—in keeping with an agreement of 1515—the crowns of St. Wenceslaus and St. Stephen. The Bohemian nobles elected Ferdinand over a rival, Duke William of Bavaria, while the Hungarian nobles tried to avoid this fate by backing their own man, János Zápolya. The ensuing struggle left Ferdinand with little time for his Swabian interests. Both for the prestige of the House of Austria and for his own position vis-a-vis Charles, the two eastern crowns were far weightier than Swabia, and Ferdinand's resources simply did not permit him to maintain his grip on both eastern and western policies at once. It was a fateful move, of course, for the Hungarian crown brought with it a long-standing struggle against the Ottoman Turks, who by 1529 stood at the gates of Vienna. At this point, neither Charles nor Ferdinand possessed much freedom of action in the Empire.

Very gradually, Ferdinand's position grew stronger. When Charles re-turned in 1530, the Empire had changed. His decision to leave its govern-ance in princely hands had favored the Reformation, which spread from electoral Saxon lands through the Empire chiefly by means of the major lay territorial states. Those of the north, where the emperor's writ hardly ran, lay far more open to religious innovation than did the southern zones of greater Habsburg influence. The advance of the Reformation doubtless weakened one basis of Habsburg power in the Empire, and from a great distance Charles could do little to influence the situation, and Ferdinand's resources were overtaxed. Thus, although Charles had acted decisively in the Edict of Worms of 1521 to ban Luther and his teachings, his reissuing of this edict in 1529 evoked protest (whence the name, "Protestants") from a number of German princes and a handful of free cities.

Since Charles had given Austria to Ferdinand, when he returned in 1530, his own dynastic lands in the Empire comprised only the Burgundian inheritance, that is, the Netherlands and Franche-Comté. This meant a shift of the center of his own power and policy to the Empire's northwestern corner, where Charles and his energetic sister, the regent Queen Mary of Hungary, were principally concerned to secure the approaches to the Netherlands. This movement provided a decisive support for the old church in the northwest. At the same time, with the growth of Ferdinand's prestige and ability, the House of Habsburg's Austrian base was growing in influence. This dual development produced a bifocal power system based on the Netherlands and Austria. Formally, the Austrian base was paramount, because of the Empire's long-standing southern-centeredness, and the royal election of Ferdinand as Charles successor-elect was supposed to stabilize the whole situation. The princes, seeing stabilization in a Habsburg sense as a threat to themselves, closed ranks to oppose it, led by the Bavarian dukes.[56]

When the Imperial Diet met at Augsburg in 1530, it produced both the formulation of an Evangelical (or "Protestant") statement of faith, the Confession of Augsburg by Philip Melanchthon, and a reinforcement of the Edict of Worms. There was, however, no bloody aftermath, for the Habsburgs' lack of power to change the situation meant a continuation of the princes' solidarity. During the 1520s a whole series of Imperial Diets had tried to deal, in the monarch's absence, with such pressing problems as the public peace, Imperial taxation, and the religious schism.[57] The frequency of these meetings tended to strengthen the Imperial governance as a whole, but after 1532 the whole process came to a halt. The emperor had already dissolved the Governing Council during his stay in the Empire in 1530, and in the following year the electors made Ferdinand King of the Romans and emperor-elect. The opposition party nonetheless remained strong, and in 1531 the Smalkaldic League was formed. This federation of Evangelical princes and free cities was not formally directed against the emperor and the Empire, but its confessional basis—the first in German history—contained great potential for disrupting the Imperial system of governance.[58] As early as 1532 the emperor had to back away from his Augsburg policy and concede to the Protestants the "Truce of Nuremberg." In 1534 the Swabian League fell victim to the new political situation, and its dissolution was swiftly followed by the collapse of the

Habsburg regime in Württemberg before an invasion by Landgrave Philip of Hesse to restore Duke Ulrich.[59] Every attempt to resurrect the Swabian League under Imperial and Catholic sponsorship—the Imperial League of 1535 and the Catholic League of 1538[60]—failed, although the Protestants did recognize Ferdinand's election as king in the treaty that ratified the Württemberg settlement.

The Reformation's advance had badly damaged the Habsburg position in the Empire. The loss of Württemberg in 1534, paradoxically, meant that Ferdinand's resources were not stretched so thin, and in any case the traditional Austrian clientele in southwestern Germany remained true to the old church. The chief exceptions were the free cities, which displayed a real affinity to the Reformation movement.[61] The Austro-Bavarian barrier to the Reformation nonetheless remained firm in the south, as did the Burgundian barrier in the northwest. And the Imperial church lived on, though hindered in its actions by its widespread colonization by the nobility. Later it would collapse in the zones most distant from Imperial governance. The European connections and position of the House of Habsburg both aided and hindered the Reformation's advance, which continued unimpeded during the 1530s. Gradually, however, there formed a middle group of German princes. Since the deadlock between the emperor and the estates could not be resolved from far away, Ferdinand gained weight as the Habsburg presence in the Empire and became the real counterpart of the German princes.[62]

## 5. Charles V's Return to the Empire

Charles V returned to the Empire in the first half of the 1540s. By now his position in the Netherlands exerted a strong influence over the northwestern parts of the Empire. In this region, Charles was able to prevent the shift of Archbishop Hermann von Wied of Cologne and Duke William V, called "the Rich," of Cleves-Jülich to Protestantism. Many smaller estates oriented their policies to the emperor's, and in a series of Diets Charles was able to push the religious question to the margin of Imperial politics. Yet, a new war against France and stronger Turkish pressure after the fall of Buda in 1541 tied the Habsburgs' hands. King Ferdinand's need of the Empire's aid to defend his dynastic lands from the Turks strengthened the Protestants' position in the Empire. In 1542 and 1544 the Diet even voted the Common Penny, a very promising sign, and Charles' plan to unite the confessions through talks, called "colloquys," drew strength both from humanist notions of reform and from Spanish experiences of religious reform. His plans nonetheless foundered on the situation, for not only had the Protestant movement already become too strong, but the Bavarian dukes still maintained their opposition.[63]

This deadlock led Charles to seek a military decision against the Smalkaldic League, once the Treaty of Crépy with France freed his hands in 1544. Following his skilled diplomatic preparations, Charles conducted a campaign of maneuver against the Protestants along the Danube, while King Ferdinand and Duke Moritz of Saxony, the Saxon elector's cousin, invaded the lands of Elector John Frederick of Saxony from Bohemia and ducal Saxony respectively. The Smalkaldic League's position in southern Germany simply collapsed, and the Protestant powers there had to surrender to the emperor, while after the emperor's victory over the Saxon elector near Mühlberg (April 1547), John Frederick and his co-commander, Philip of Hesse, also had to surrender.

Charles, now master of Germany except for a few unsubdued northern areas, moved to reform the Imperial political order. The religious question was to be settled by means of a step-by-step movement of the Protestants back to the old church through by means of an "Imperial transitional religion" defined by a document called the "Interim." In the southern free cities, this settlement would be secured by the overthrow of the guild regimes, to be replaced by the more loyal, politically more circumspect upper classes.[64] Above all, the victorious emperor sought to establish a new balance between himself and the Imperial estates through an "Emperor's League," which would embrace practically the whole Empire. The Swabian League stood as obvious godfather to this scheme, which also reflected the relatively new bipolarization of Habsburg power in Austria and the Netherlands. By means of this plan, Charles V sought to expand his position in the Empire, but the project shattered on the opposition of the leading estates, chiefly the electors and Bavaria, and on Charles' own inability to maintain the power he had won.[65] His one lasting achievement was to fix the special position of the Netherlands in the Empire in the "Burgundian Treaty" of 1548, which gave these hereditary lands few responsibilities and many rights vis-a-vis the Empire.

The failure of these federal plans, which marked the limits of the emperor's power, was to some degree the consequence of twenty-five years of absentee rule. It was Moritz of Saxony,[66] once again, now wearing the elector title Charles had in 1547 transferred from his cousin, John Frederick, who made the decisive move, placing himself at the end of a small group of Protestant princes against the emperor. Their bold strike into southern

Germany in 1552, carried out with quite limited resources, brought the emperor's position to collapse. Just like his plan for an Imperial settlement, Charles grand policy—to conduct his affairs on a European scale and leave the Empire to the German princes—ended in failure.

It now became quite apparent that the German Habsburg line had established its own position.[67] Ferdinand, as King of the Romans and designated successor to Charles V, had vetoed a plan to have the Imperial office alternate between the two lines of the House of Habsburg. Both Ferdinand and his son, the future Emperor Maximilian II, fought the idea of Philip of Spain succeeding Ferdinand as Holy Roman emperor. With Charles' defeat at the hands of the princes in 1552, Ferdinand moved into a key position, for he played a leading role, along with some German princes, in ending the revolt by means of the Treaty of Passau (1552). This action placed him in the role of an arbiter between the emperor and a group of German princes and displayed him as the true counterpart of the Imperial estates. He also realized that now there existed no alternative to a policy of compromise with the Protestants, a conclusion Charles could not accept.

Charles made one more attempt to recover his position after the princes' revolt of 1552, but neither his siege of Metz, taken by King Henry II of France, nor his attempt to punish one of the most violent princes, Margrave Albert Alcibiades of Brandenburg-Kulmbach, met with success. The margrave was crushed, but by Elector Moritz near Sievershausen in 1553. Charles now withdrew ever more, and in 1556 he abdicated. Already the year before, he left the conclusion of the Religious Peace of Augsburg (1555) to his brother, because he still could not accept the compromises needed to secure the peace. This treaty extended the provisions of the law for the public peace (*Landefriedensordnung*) of 1495 to cover the situation after 1548 and to protect both religions, Catholicism and Lutheranism, that is, Protestantism according to the Confession of Augsburg. It also preserved the ecclesiastical territories in Catholic hands. Other provisions guarded the existence of the Catholic Church in the Empire, while the decision about doctrine was put off into an indefinite future. The willingness of the German Protestants to trade their freedom to spread their religion for a legal guarantee of security, made this pacification possible.[68]

This settlement was principally Ferdinand's work. Although he was not recognized as emperor until 1558, he was de facto the Empire's monarch, and under him the center of Imperial governance shifted back to the Empire's southeastern regions. Under these conditions, Maximilian's southern German constellation of power began to revive. Meanwhile, the Netherlands drifted away.  For a time, between the Habsburgs' acquisition of the Burgundian Netherlands and Charles' use of these lands as his own dynastic base, they had become more tightly bound to the Empire, but his abdication loosed these bonds once more, as the Netherlands became part of the Italo-Spanish sector of Habsburg Europe.  Under Ferdinand's rule, on the other hand, Bohemia moved back into the main circuit of Imperial political life, as the events of 1526 had shifted the center of his power from Innsbruck, or even Stuttgart, to Vienna and Prague—even though Ferdinand himself continued to be a largely itinerant king.  To a certain degree, these events placed the House of Austria at last in a stable position, for, except for a brief interruption under the Wittelsbach Emperor Charles VII (r. 1742-45), the House of Austria wore the Roman-German Imperial crown until the end of the old Empire in 1806.

Translated by Thomas A. Brady, Jr.

# NOTES

1. On the late medieval monarchy, see Boockmann (1987); Krieger (1978); Krieger (1992); Moraw (1985); Moraw (1986); Moraw (1984); Thomas (1983).
2. Kempf (1893); Trautz (1961); Reisinger (1977); Hägermann (1977).
3. Redlich (1903); Rössler (1960); Martin (1976).
4. Moraw (1985), 211-28.
5. Lindner (1890-93); Fritz Trautz, "Studien zu Geschichte und Würdigung König Adolfs von Nassau," *Geschichtliche Landeskunde* 2 (1965): 1-45; Hessel (1931); Gerlich (1969).
6. Moraw (1993); Heyen and Mötsch (1985).
7. Stengel (1930); Schwöbel (1968); Heinz Angermeier, "Bayern in der Regierungszeit Kaiser Ludwigs IV., 1314-1347," in *Handbuch der bayerischen Geschichte*, ed. Max Spindler, vol. 2, 2d ed. (Munich, 1988): 149-95; Glaser (1980); Benker (1980).
8. Seibt (1978a); Seibt (1978b); Patze (1978); Moraw (1979); Stoob (1990).
9. Gerlich (1960); Hlavácek (1970); Klare (1990).
10. Moraw (1977); Volker Press, "Die Territorialstruktur des Reiches und die Reformation," in *Reformation und Revolution. Festschrift für Rainer Wohlfeil zum 60. Geburtstag*, ed. Rainer Postel and Franklin Kopitzsch (Stuttgart, 1989), 239-68.
11. Peter Moraw, "Beamtentum und Rat König Ruprechts," *ZGO* 116 (1968): 59-126; Seibt and Eberhard (1984); Ernst Schubert, "Probleme der Königsherrschaft im spätmittelalterlichen Reich: Das Beispiel Ruprechts von der Pfalz (1400-1410)," in Schneider (1987), 135-84.
12. Mályusz (1990); János M. Bak, *Königtum und Stände in Ungarn im 14. bis 16. Jahrhundert* (Wiesbaden, 1973); Mau (1941); Obenaus (1961); Isenmann (1988); Wefers (1989).
13. Angermeier (1961); Franzen and Müller (1964); Odilo Engels, "Der Reichsgedanke auf dem Konstanzer Konzil," *HJ* 86 (1966): 80-106.
14. Seibt (1965); Kaminsky (1967); Zeman (1977); Seibt (1984).
15. Zöllner (1988), 111-86; Huber (1885-88); Lhotsky (1967).
16. Winter (1934-36); Lhotsky (1957).
17. Mommsen (1958); La Roche (1971); Meyer (1972); Peyer (1978); Rück (1991).
18. Josef Riedmann, "Mittelalter," in *Geschichte des Landes Tirol*, ed. Josef Fontana, et al., vol. 1 (Bozen/Bolzano, Innsbruck, and Vienna, 1985), 430-59.
19. Hödl (1978).
20. Odlozilik (1965); Heymann (1965).
21. Kraus (1905); Paul-Joachim Heinig, "Kaiser Friedrich III. und Hessen," *Hessisches Jahrbuch für Landesgeschichte* 32 (1982): 63-101.

22. Baum (1987).
23. Vaughan (1973); Paravicini (1976).
24. Wiesflecker (1971-86), vol. 1:113-67.
25. Ràzso (1973); Nehring (1975).
26. Angermeier (1966); Brunner (1965); Karl-Friedrich Krieger, "Rechtliche Grundlagen und Möglichkeiten römisch-deutscher Königsherrschaft im 15. Jahrhundert," in Schneider (1987), 465-489.
27. Riedmann, "Mittelalter" (see note 18), 475-81; Press (1982); Volker Press, "Vorderösterreich in der habsburgischen Reichspolitik des späten Mittelalters und der frühen Neuzeit," in *Vorderösterreich in der frühen Neuzeit*, ed. Volker Press and Hans Meier (Sigmaringen, 1989), 1-41.
28. Bock (1927); Laufs (1971) Lutz ([1955]).
29. Ernst (1933).
30. Ulmann (1884-91); Wiesflecker (1971-86).
31. The fundamental discussion about the Imperial reform is taking place between Heinz Angermeier und Peter Moraw. See Angermeier (1984) and (1983); Moraw (1980b), (1983), and his review of Angermeier's book in *Göttingische Gelehrte Anzeigen* 44 (1993): 277-96. For a summary of this discussion, see Krieger (1992), 114-18.
32. Smend (1911); Press (1987).
33. Schmid (1989); Isenmann (1980).
34. Moraw (1980a).
35. Rainer Wolgarten, Das erste und zweite Nürnberger Reichsregiment, Unpublished dissertation (Cologne, 1957); Heinz Angermeier, "Die Reichsregimenter und ihre Staatsidee," HZ 211 (1970): 265-315; Wolf Römisch, Das Reichsregiment, Unpublished dissertation (Munich, 1970).
36. The thesis, that the Reichshofrat was founded in 1557, is false. See now the unpublished Habilitationsschrift of Heinz Noflatscher, Politische Führungsgruppen in den österreichischen Ländern (1480-1530) (Innsbruck, 1992).
37. Dotzauer (1989).
38. Ulmann (1884-91), vol. 2:178-254; Wiesflecker (1971-86), vol. 3:164-205.
39. Felix Rachfahl, "Die Trennung der Niederlande vom deutschen Reich," Westdeutsche Zeitschrift für Geschichte und Kunst 19 (1900): 79-119; R. Feenstra, "A quelle époque les Provences-Unies sont-elles devenues indépendantes en droit à l'égard du Saint-Empire?" Tijdschrift voor Rechtsgeschiedenis 20 (1952): 30-63, 182-218, 474-80; Volker Press, "Die Niederlande und das Reich in der frühen Neuzeit," in Etat et réligion aux XVe et XVIe siècle, ed. Willem P. Blockmans and Herman van Nuffel (Brussels, 1986), 321-39.
40. Horst Carl, "Eidgenossen und Schwäbischer Bund - feindliche Nachbarn?," in: Rück (1991), 215-65; Paul-Joachim Heinig, "Friedrich III., Maximilian I. und die Eidgenossen," in: Rück (1991), 267-93. For the broader ramifications in the Empire, see Brady (1985).
41. Volker Press, "Herzog Ulrich (1498-1550)," in *900 Jahre Haus Württemberg. Leben und Leistung für Land und Volk*, ed. Robert Uhland, 3d ed. (Stuttgart, 1985), 110-35.
42. Helgard Ulmschneider, *Götz von Berlichingen. Ein adeliges Leben der deutschen Renaissance* (Sigmaringen, 1974); Heinrich Ulmann, Franz von Sickingen (Leipzig, 1872); Volker Press, "Franz von Sickingen, Wortführer des Adels, Vorkämpfer der Reformation und Freund Huttens," in *Ulrich von Hutten, Ritter, Humanist, Publizist, 1488-1523* (Kassel, 1988), 293-306.

43. Georg Schmidt, "Integration und Konfessionalisierung. Die Region zwischen Weser und Ems im Deutschland des 16. Jahrhunderts," *ZHF* 20 (1993).
44. Wiesflecker (1971-86), vol. 1:181-204.
45. Wiesflecker (1971-86), vol. 1:405-6.
46. Ludolphy (1984).
47. Brandi (1937-41), vol. 1:85-98; Laubach (1971).
48. Kleinheyer (1968), 45-79.
49. On Charles V, see Brandi (1937-41); Fernández Alvárez (1977); Lutz (1982); Alfred Kohler, "Karl V.," in *Neue Deutsche Biographie*, vol. 11 (Berlin, 1977): 191-211. On the Empire under Charles V, see Lutz (1983); Schulze (1987); Schilling (1988).
50. Bucholtz (1831-33); Fichtner (1986); Alfred Kohler, "Kaiser Karl V., Ferdinand I. und das Reich. Bemerkungen zur Politik der habsburgischen Brüder," in *Europäische Herrscher. Ihre Rolle bei der Gestaltung von Politik und Gesellschaft vom 16. bis zum 18. Jahrhundert*, ed. Günter Vogler (Weimar, 1988), 58-70.
51. Puchta (1967).
52. Volker Press "Reformatorische Bewegung und Reichverfassung. Zum Durchbruch der Reformation - soziale, politische und religiöse Faktoren," in *Martin Luther. Probleme seiner Zeit*, ed. Volker Press and Dieter Stievermann (Stuttgart 1986), 11-42; Press (n.d.).
53. Press (1978). The fundamental works are Franz (1975); Blickle (1981).
54. Metzger (1980).
55. Joseph Vochezer, *Geschichte des fürstlichen Hauses Waldburg in Schwaben*, vol. 2 (Kempten, 1900).
56. Kohler (1982).
57. Schubert (1966); Aulinger (1980); Neuhaus (1982); Helmut Neuhaus, "Wandlungen der Reichstagsorganisation in der ersten Hälfte des 16. Jahrhunderts," *ZHF*, supplement 3 (1987): 113-40; Lutz and Kohler (1986); Press (1986b); G. Schmidt (1984).
58. Fabian (1962); Brady (1983).
59. Volker Press, "Die württembergische Restitution von 1534. Reichspolitische Voraussetzungen und Konsequenzen," *Blätter für württembergische Kirchen-geschichte* 87 (1987): 44-71; id., "Ein Epochenjahr der Württembergischen Geschichte. Restitution und Reformation 1534," ZWLG 47 (1988): 203-34.
60. Rudolf Endres, "Der kayserliche neunjährige Bund vom Jahr 1535 bis 1544," in *Bauer, Reich und Reformation. Festschrift für Günther Franz*, ed. Peter Blickle (Stuttgart, 1982), 85-103; Hermann Baumgarten, "Karl V. und der katholische Bund vom Jahre 1538," *Deutsche Zeitschrift für Geschichtswissenschaft* 6 (1891): 273-300.
61. Moeller (1987); Ozment (1975); G. Schmidt (1984); H. R. Schmidt (1986).
62. Luttenberger (1982).
63. Cardauns (1910); Müller (1980); Hollerbach (1982); Albrecht Pius Luttenberger, "Konfessionelle Parteilichkeit und Reichstagspolitik: Zur Verhandlungsführung des Kaisers und der Stände in Regensburg 1541," in *Fortschritte in der Geschichts-wissenschaft durch Reichstagsaktenforschung*, ed. Heinz Angermeier and Erich Meuthen (Göttingen, 1988), 65-101.
64. Naujoks (1958) and (1974); Fürstenwerth (1893).
65. Hartung (1910); Salomies (1953); Rabe (1971); Volker Press, "Die Bundespläne Kaiser Karls V. und die Reichsverfassung," in Lutz (1982), 55-106.

66. Simon Issleib, *Aufsätze und Beiträge zu Kurfürst Moritz von Sachsen (1877-1907)*, 2 vols. (Cologne and Vienna, 1989).

67. Lutz (1964); Ernst Laubach, "Karl V., Ferdinand I. und die Nachfolge im Reich," *Mitteilungen des Österreichischen Staatsarchivs* 29 (1976): 1-51.

68. Matthias Simon, *Der Augsburger Religionsfriede. Ergebnis und Aufgabe* (Augsburg, 1955); Hermann Tüchle, "Der Augsburger Religionsfriede. Neue Ordnung oder Kampfpause?" *ZHVS* 61 (1955): 323-40; Gerhard Pfeiffer, "Der Augsburger Religionsfriede und die Reichsstädte," *ZHVS* 62 (1955): 213-321; Martin Heckel, "Autonomia und Pacis Compositio. Der Augsburger Religionsfriede in der Deutung der Gegenreformation," *ZSRG, Kanonistische Abteilung* 34 (1959): 141-248.

# BIBLIOGRAPHY

*General*

Angermeier, Heinz. *Königtum und Landfriede im deutschen Spätmittelalter.* Munich, 1966.

Angermeier, Heinz. "Reichsreform und Reformation in der deutschen Geschichte." In *Säkulare Aspekte der Reformationszeit,* ed. Heinz Angermeier. Schriften des Historischen Kollegs, Kolloquien, vol. 5. Munich and Vienna, 1983.

Boockmann, Hartmut. *Stauferzeit und spätes Mittelalter: Deutschland 1125-1517.* Berlin, 1987.

Brunner, Otto. *Land and Lordship. Structures of Governance in Medieval Austria.* Trans. Howard Kaminsky and James Van Horn Melton. Philadelphia, 1992.

Brunner, Otto. *Land und Herrschaft.* 5th ed. Vienna, 1965. Reprint. Darmstadt, 1973.

Huber, Alfons. *Geschichte Österreichs.* Vols. 2-3. Gotha, 1885-88.

Isenmann, Eberhard. *Die deutsche Stadt im Spätmittelalter: 1250-1500.* Stuttgart, 1988.

Kleinheyer, Gerd. *Die kaiserlichen Wahlkapitulationen. Geschichte, Wesen und Funktion.* Karlsruhe, 1968.

Kraus, Viktor von. *Deutsche Geschichte im Ausgang des Mittelalters (1438-1486).* Vol. 1. Stuttgart, 1905.

Krieger, Karl-Friedrich. *König, Reich und Reichsreform im Spätmittelalter.* Munich, 1992.

Lhotsky, Alphons. *Geschichte Österreichs seit der Mitte des 13. Jahrhunderts (1281-1358).* Vienna, 1967.

Lindner, Theodor. *Deutsche Geschichte unter den Habsburgern und Luxemburgern (1273-1437).* 2 vols. Stuttgart, 1890-93.

Lutz, Heinrich. *Das Ringen um deutsche Einheit und kirchliche Erneuerung. Von Maximilian I. bis zum Westfälischen Frieden 1490-1648.* Frankfurt am Main, Berlin, and Vienna, 1983.

Meyer, Bruno. *Die Bildung der Eidgenossenschaft im 14. Jahrhundert. Vom Zugerbund zum Pfaffenbrief.* Zurich, 1972.

Moraw, Peter. "Fürstentum, Königtum und "Reichsreform" im deutschen Spätmittelalter." *BDLG* 122 (1986): 117-36.

Moraw, Peter. "Landesgeschichte und Reichsgeschichte im 14. Jahrhundert." *Jahrbuch für westdeutsche Landesgeschichte* 3 (1977): 175-91.

Moraw, Peter. "Das Mittelalter." In *Deutsche Geschichte im Osten Europas: Böhmen und Mähren,* 24-179. Berlin, 1993.

Moraw, Peter. "Reich." In *Geschichtliche Grundbegriffe,* ed. Otto Brunner, Werner Conze, and Reinhard Koselleck, vol. 5 (Stuttgart, 1984): 423-56.

Moraw, Peter. "Versuch über die Entstehung des Reichstages." In *Politische Ordnungen und soziale Kräfte im Alten Reich,* ed. Hermann Weber, 1-36. Wiesbaden, 1980a.

Moraw, Peter. "Die Verwaltung des Königtums und des Reiches und ihre Rahmenbedingungen." In *Deutsche Verwaltungsgeschichte,* vol. 1: *Vom Spätmittelalter bis zum Ende des Reiches,* ed. Kurt G. A. Jeserich, et al., 21-31. Stuttgart, 1983.

Moraw, Peter. *Von offener Verfassung zu gestalteter Verdichtung. Das Reich im späten Mittelalter 1250 bis 1490.* Berlin, 1985.

Moraw, Peter. "Wesenszüge der 'Regierung' und 'Verwaltung' des deutschen Königs im Reich (ca. 1350-1450)." In *Histoire comparée de l'administration (IVe-XVIIIe siècles),* ed. Werner Paravicini and Karl Ferdinand Werner, 149-67. Munich, 1980b.

Naujoks, Eberhard. "Obrigkeit und Zunftverfassung in den südwestdeutschen Reichsstädten." *ZWLG* 33 (1974): 53-93.

Naujoks, Eberhard. *Obrigkeitsgedanke, Zunftverfassung und Reformation. Studien zur Verfassungsgeschichte von Ulm, Esslingen und Schwäbisch Gmünd.* Stuttgart, 1958.

Peyer, Hans Conrad. *Verfassungsgeschichte der alten Schweiz.* Zurich, 1978.

Press, Volker. *Das Reichskammergericht in der deutschen Geschichte.* Wetzlar, 1987.

Press, Volker. "Schwaben zwischen Bayern, Österreich und dem Reich 1486-1805." In *Probleme der Integration Ostschwabens in den bayerischen Staat,* ed. Pankraz Fried, 17-78. Sigmaringen, 1982.

Rück, Peter, ed. *Die Eidgenossen und ihre Nachbarn im Deutschen Reich des Mittelalters.* Marburg an der Lahn, 1991.

Schilling, Heinz. *Aufbruch und Krise. Deutschland 1517-1648.* Berlin, 1988.

Schneider, Reinhard, ed. *Das spätmittelalterliche Königtum im europäischen Vergleich.* Sigmaringen, 1987.

Schubert, Friedrich Hermann. *Die deutschen Reichstage in der Staatslehre der frühen Neuzeit.* Göttingen, 1966.

Schulze, Winfried. *Deutsche Geschichte im 16. Jahrhundert. 1500-1618.* Frankfurt am Main, 1987.

Seibt, Ferdinand. *Revolutionen in Europa,* Munich, 1984.

Seibt, Ferdinand, and Winfried Eberhard, eds. *Europa 1400, Die Krise des Spätmittelalters.* Stuttgart, 1984.

Smend, Rudolf. *Das Reichskammergericht.* Part 1: *Geschichte und Verfassung.* Weimar 1911.

Thomas, Heinz. *Deutsche Geschichte des Spätmittelalters 1250-1500.* Stuttgart, 1983.

Zeman, Jarold Knox. *The Hussite Movement and the Reformation in Bohemia, Moravia and Slovakia, 1350-1650.* Ann Arbor, 1977.

Zöllner, Erich. *Geschichte Österreichs von den Anfängen bis zur Gegenwart.* 9th ed. Vienna, 1988.

*Three Royal Dynasties*

Angermeier, Heinz. "Das Reich und der Konziliarismus." *HZ* 192 (1961): 529-83.

Angermeier, Heinz. *Die Reichsreform 1410-1455. Die Staatsproblematik in Deutschland zwischen Mittelalter und Gegenwart.* Munich, 1984.

Benker, Gertrud. *Ludwig der Bayer: Ein Wittelsbacher auf dem Kaiserthron. 1282-1347.* Munich, 1980.

Franzen, August, and Wolfgang Müller, eds. *Das Konzil von Konstanz.* Basel, Vienna, and Freiburg im Breisgau, 1964.

Gerlich, Alois. *Habsburg-Luxemburg-Wittelsbach im Kampf um die deutsche Königskrone.* Wiesbaden, 1960.

Gerlich, Alois. "Königtum, rheinische Kurfürsten und Grafen in der Zeit Albrechts I. von Habsburg." *Geschichtliche Landeskunde* 5 (1969): 25-88.

Glaser Hubert, ed. *Wittelsbach und Bayern. Die Zeit der frühen Herzöge: Von Otto I. zu Ludwig dem Bayern.* Vols. 1/1 and 2. Munich and Zurich, 1980.

Hägermann, Dieter. *Studien zum Urkundenwesen Wilhelms von Holland.* Cologne and Vienna, 1977.

Hessel, Alfred. *Jahrbücher des Deutschen Reichs unter König Albrecht I. von Habsburg.* Munich, 1931.

Heyen, Franz-Josef, and Johannes Mötsch, eds. *Balduin von Luxemburg 1285-1354. Erzbischof von Trier—Kurfürst des Reiches.* Mainz, 1985.

Hlaváček, Ivan. *Das Urkunden- und Kanzleiwesen des böhmischen und römischen Königs Wenzel (IV.), 1376-1419.* Stuttgart, 1970.

Hödl, Günther. *Albrecht II. Königtum, Reichsregierung und Reichsreform, 1438-1439.* Vienna, 1978.

Kaminsky, Howard. *A History of the Hussite Revolution.* Berkeley and Los Angeles, 1967.

Kempf, Johannes. *Geschichte des Deutschen Reiches während des großen Interregnums, 1245-1273.* Würzburg, 1893.

Klare, Wilhelm. *Die Wahl Wenzels von Luxemburg zum Römischen König 1346.* Münster, 1990.
Krieger, Karl-Friedrich. *Die Lehnhoheit der deutschen Könige im Spätmittelalter (ca. 1200-1437).* Aalen, 1978.
La Roche, Emanuel Peter. *Das Interregnum und die Entstehung der Schweizerischen Eidgenossenschaft.* Bern and Frankfurt am Main, 1971.
Lhotsky, Alphons. *Privilegium Maius. Geschichte einer Urkunde.* Vienna, 1957.
Mályusz, Elemér. *Kaiser Sigismund in Ungarn: 1387-1437.* Budapest, 1990.
Martin, Thomas M. *Die Städtepolitik Rudolfs von Habsburg.* Göttingen 1976.
Mau, Hermann. *Die Rittergesellschaften mit St. Jörgenschild in Schwaben.* Part 1. Stuttgart 1941.
Moraw, Peter. "Kaiser Karl IV. im deutschen Spätmittelalter." *HZ* 229 (1979): 1-24.
Obenaus, Herbert. *Recht und Verfassung der Gesellschaft mit St. Jörgenschild in Schwaben.* Göttingen, 1961.
Patze, Hans, ed. *Kaiser Karl IV., 1316-1378. Forschungen über Kaiser und Reich* = BDLG, vol. 114. Neustadt an der Aisch, 1978.
Redlich, Oswald. *Rudolf von Habsburg.* Innsbruck, 1903.
Reisinger, Roswitha. *Die römisch-deutschen Könige und ihre Wähler, 1189-1273.* Aalen, 1977.
Rössler, Hellmuth. *Ein König für Deutschland.* Munich and Vienna, 1960.
Seibt, Ferdinand. *Hussitica. Zur Struktur einer Revolution.* Cologne and Graz, 1965.
Seibt, Ferdinand, ed. *Kaiser Karl IV., Staatsmann und Mäzen.* Munich, 1978b.
Seibt, Ferdinand. *Karl IV.: ein Kaiser in Europa, 1346-1378.* 3d ed. Munich, 1978a.
Schwöbel, Hermann-Otto. *Der diplomatische Kampf zwischen Ludwig dem Bayern und der römischen Kurie im Rahmen des kanonischen Absolutionsprozesses.* Weimar, 1968.
Stengel, Edmund Ernst. *Avignon und Rhens. Forschungen zur Geschichte des Kampfes um das Recht am Rhein in der ersten Hälfte des 14. Jahrhunderts.* Weimar, 1930.
Stoob, Heinz. *Kaiser Karl IV. und seine Zeit.* Graz, 1990.
Trautz, Fritz. *Die Könige von England und das Reich 1272-1377.* Heidelberg, 1961.
Winter, Ernst Karl. *Rudolf IV. von Österreich.* 2 vols. Vienna, 1934-36.
Wefers, Sabine. *Das politische System Kaiser Sigmunds.* Stuttgart, 1989.

*The House of Habsburg and Frederick III*
Baum, Wilhelm. *Siegmund der Münzreiche: Zur Geschichte Tirols und der habsburgischen Länder im Spätmittelalter.* Bozen/Bolzano, 1987.
Heymann, Frederick G. *George of Bohemia.* Princeton, 1965.
Isenmann, Eberhard. "Reichsfinanzen und Reichssteuern im 15. Jahrhundert." *ZHF* 7 (1980): 1-76, 129-218.
Nehring, Karl. *Matthias Corvinus, Kaiser Friedrich III. und das Reich.* Munich, 1975.
Odlozilik, Otokar. *The Hussite King.* New Brunswick, N.J., 1965.
Paravicini, Werner. *Karl der Kühne.* Göttingen, 1976.
Ràzso, Gyula. *Die Feldzüge des Königs Matthias Corvinus in Niederösterreich, 1477-1490.* Vienna, 1973.
Vaughan, Richard. *Charles the Bold. The Last Valois Duke of Burgundy.* London, 1973.

*The Monarchy of Maximilian I*
Bock, Ernst. *Der Schwäbische Bund und seine Verfassungen 1488-1534. Ein Beitrag zur Geschichte der Zeit der Reichsreform.* Breslau, 1927. Reprint. Aalen, 1968.
Brady, Thomas A., Jr. *Turning Swiss: Cities and Empire, 1450-1550.* Cambridge Studies in Early Modern History. Cambridge, 1985.
Ernst, Fritz. *Eberhard im Bart.* Stuttgart, 1933.
Laubach, Ernst. "Wahlpropaganda im Wahlkampf um die deutsche Königswürde 1519." *Archiv für Kulturgeschichte* 53 (1971): 207-48.
Ludolphy, Ingetraut. *Friedrich der Weise, Kurfürst von Sachsen 1463-1525.* Göttingen, 1984.

Mommsen, Karl. *Eidgenossen, Kaiser und Reich.* Basel and Stuttgart, 1958.

Schmid, Peter. *Der Gemeine Pfennig von 1495. Vorgeschichte und Entstehung, verfassungsgeschichtliche, politische und finanzielle Bedeutung.* Göttingen, 1989.

Ulmann, Heinrich. *Kaiser Maximilian I.* 2 vols. Stuttgart, 1884-91.

Wiesflecker, Hermann. *Kaiser Maximilian I.: Das Reich, Österreich und Europa an der Wende zur Neuzeit.* 5 vols. Munich, 1971-86.


*The Empire under Charles V*

Aulinger, Rosemarie. *Das Bild des Reichstages im 16. Jahrhundert. Beiträge zu einer typologischen Analyse schriftlicher und bildlicher Quellen.* SHKBA, vol. 26. Göttingen, 1980.

Blickle, Peter. *Die Revolution von 1525.* 2d ed. Munich and Vienna, 1981.

Brady, Thomas A., Jr. "Phases and Strategies of the Schmalkaldic League: a Perspective after 450 Years." *ARG* 74 (1983): 162-81.

Brandi, Karl. *The Emperor Charles V: the Growth and Destiny of a Man and of a World-Empire.* Trans. C. V. Wedgwood. London, 1939.

Brandi, Karl. *Kaiser Karl V. Werden und Schicksal einer Persönlichkeit und eines Weltreiches.* 2 vols. Munich, 1937-41.

Bucholtz, Franz Bernhard von. *Geschichte der Regierung Ferdinands des Ersten.* 9 vols. Vienna, 1831-33. Reprint. Graz, 1968-71

Cardauns, Ludwig. *Zur Geschichte der kirchlichen Unions- und Reformbestrebungen von 1538-1542.* Rome, 1910.

Dotzauer, Winfried. *Die deutschen Reichskreise in der Verfassung des Alten Reiches und ihr Eigenleben (1500-1806).* Darmstadt, 1989.

Fabian, Ekkehard. *Die Entstehung des Schmalkaldischen Bundes und seiner Verfassung 1524/29-1531/35.* 2d ed. SKRG, vol. 1. Tübingen, 1962.

Fernández Alvárez, Manuel. *Imperator mundi: Karl V., Kaiser des Hl. Römischen Reiches Deutscher Nation.* Trans. Ulrich Bracher. Stuttgart and Zurich, 1977.

Fichtner, Paula Sutter. *Ferdinand I of Austria: the Politics of Dynasticism in the Age of the Reformation.* New York, 1982.

Franz, Günther. *Der deutsche Bauernkrieg.* 10th ed. Darmstadt, 1975.

Fürstenwerth, Ludwig. *Die Verfassungsänderungen in den oberdeutschen Reichsstädten zur Zeit Karls V.* Göttingen, 1893.

Hartung, Fritz. *Karl V. und die deutschen Reichsstände von 1546-1555.* Halle, 1910.

Hollerbach, Marion. *Das Religionsgespräch als Mittel der konfessionellen und politischen Auseinandersetzung im Deutschland des 16. Jahrhunderts.* Frankfurt am Main and Bern, 1982.

Kohler, Alfred. *Antihabsburgische Politik in der Epoche Karls V. Die reichsständische Opposition gegen die Wahl Ferdinands I. zum römischen König und gegen die Anerkennung seines Königtums (1524-1534).* Göttingen, 1982.

Laufs, Adolf. *Der Schwäbische Kreis. Studien über Einungswesen und Reichsverfasung im deutschen Südwesten zu Beginn der Neuzeit.* Aalen, 1971.

Luttenberger, Albrecht Pius. *Glaubenseinheit und Reichsfriede. Konzeption und Wege konfessionsneutraler Reichspolitik 1530-1552 (Kurpfalz, Jülich, Kurbrandenburg).* Göttingen, 1982.

Lutz, Heinrich. *Christianitas afflicta. Europa, das Reich und die päpstliche Politik im Niedergang der Hegemonie Kaiser Karls V. (1552-1556).* Göttingen 1964.

Lutz, Heinrich. *Conrad Peutinger. Beiträge zu einer politischen Biographie.* Augsburg, n.d. [1955].

Lutz, Heinrich, ed. *Das römisch-deutsche Reich im politischen System Karls V.* Schriften des Historischen Kollegs, Kolloquien, vol. 1. Munich and Vienna, 1982.

Lutz, Heinrich, and Alfred Kohler, eds. *Aus der Arbeit an den Reichstagen unter Kaiser Karl V.* Göttingen, 1986.

Metzger, Edelgard. *Leonhard von Eck (1480-1550). Wegbereiter und Begründer des frühabsolutistischen Bayern.* Munich, 1980.

Moeller, Bernd. *Reichsstadt und Reformation.* Rev. ed. Berlin, 1987.

Müller, Gerhard. *Die Religionsgespräche der Reformationszeit.* Güterloh, 1980.
Neuhaus, Helmut. *Reichsständische Repräsentationsformen im 16. Jahrhundert. Reichstag-Reichskreistag-Reichsdeputationstag.* Berlin, 1982.
Ozment, Steven E. *The Reformation in the Cities: the Appeal of Protestantism to Sixteenth-Century Germany and Switzerland.* New Haven and London, 1975.
Press, Volker. "Der deutsche Bauernkrieg als Systemkrise." *Gießener Universitätsblätter* 11 (1978): 106-27.
Press, Volker. "Der Kaiser, das Reich und die Reformation." In *Martin Luther und die Reformation in Deutschland,* ed. Kurt Löcher, 61-94. Schweinfurt, n.d.
Press, Volker. "Die Reformation und der deutsche Reichstag." In *Martin Luther. Leistung und Erbe,* ed. Horst Bartel, et al., 202-15. Berlin, 1986b.
Puchta, Hans. *Die habsburgische Herrschaft in Württemberg 1520-1534.* Munich, 1967.
Rabe, Horst. *Reichsbund und Interim. Die Verfassungs- und Religionspolitik Karls V. und der Reichstag von Augsburg 1547/48.* Cologne and Vienna, 1971.
Salomies, Martti. *Die Pläne Karls V. für eine Reichsreform mit Hilfe eines allgemeinen Bundes.* Helsinki, 1953.
Schmidt, Georg. *Der Städtetag in der Reichsverfassung. Eine Untersuchung zur korporativen Politik der Freien und Reichsstädte in der ersten Hälfte des 16. Jahrhunderts.* VIEG, vol. 113. Stuttgart, 1984.
Schmidt, Heinrich R. *Reichsstädte, Reich und Reformation. Korporative Religionspolitik 1521-1529/30.* VIEG, vol. 122. Stuttgart, 1986.

# THE HABSBURG LANDS: IBERIA

Henry Kamen
(Higher Council for Scientific Research,
Barcelona)

The two central themes in the historiography of the Iberian peninsula during the fifteenth century are the unification of the kingdoms and the rise of world empire. During the following century attention moves to the evolution of monarchical power and the socio-economic problems within Spain. Portugal is the poor cousin in terms of scholarship: there are no good general surveys in Portuguese, and in English only a few research monographs. The classic study of the expansionist period by Charles R. Boxer must serve as the best introduction. For the Spanish kingdoms the best introduction to the century after 1410, divided up by theme and supported by a full bibliography, is that by J. H. Hillgarth; there is also a more general overview by Angus Mackay. For Spain the Habsburg centuries are amply served by two comprehensive and up-to-date books which supersede previous surveys: a student text by Henry Kamen, and an extended work by John Lynch, both with guidance on further reading, while Kamen has also a survey of recent views. Of older works the multi-volume survey by Merriman should be used with care but remains informative, while Elliott's aging *Imperial Spain* is thoroughly superseded.[1]

Over the last decades the work of many good scholars has made it possible to look with new eyes at peninsular history. The pioneers were historians of the *Annales* school: Fernand Braudel's masterpiece on the Mediterranean offered a whole new perspective. In Spain the formative influence was that of Jaime Vicens Vives, whose monumental study of Ferdinand the Catholic was unfortunately never completed. Of recent scholarship on the period particular influence has been exercised by Marcel Bataillon's now classic study of Erasmus, the pioneering studies of Ladero on the reign of the Catholic Kings, and the original examination of Philip II's government by I. A. A. Thompson. One of the most suggestive scholars on the period, Maravall, has produced major studies which are interdisciplinary rather than historical in approach; his two-volume work on the modern state is rich in ideas. The move to regional government in post-Franco Spain has encouraged a proliferation of studies at the provincial level: an outstanding pioneer was Bennassar's thesis on Valladolid.

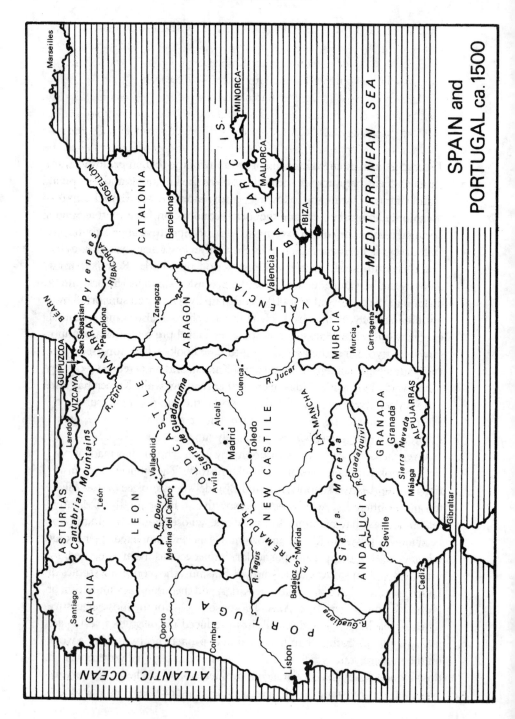

SPAIN and
PORTUGAL ca. 1500

The great number of regional studies has not always made it easy to stand back and obtain an overall perspective of the period, but they have served at least to dissuade most historians from referring to 'Spain' when they really mean to refer to only one area of it, namely Castile.[2]

Enormous gaps remain in our knowledge of the peninsula. Foreign policy has been virtually untouched, and the early work on diplomacy by Garrett Mattingly has been followed only by De Lamar Jensen's work on ambassador Mendoza. Despite a few small monographs, we still have no adequate idea of the external trade of the peninsula. Quite recently serious attention has been paid to demography, but for the early modern period family history is still in its infancy, and the role of women, though explored within the context of literature, has received no solid historical treatment beyond attention to religious visionaries. Many aspects of culture have never found their historian, and the social history of art in Iberia in the sixteenth century remains almost unwritten. Social implications of literature have been particularly well approached by French scholars, notably Maxime Chevalier and Noël Salomon, but in general the two disciplines of literature and history have, to their common disadvantage, been kept apart. Rather surprisingly, though ecclesiastical trivia have been exhaustively explored the Church has been little studied, and the social history of religion wholly neglected. Spanish sources for every aspect of the past are, however, particularly rich, and there is reason to hope that future generations of scholars will make up for the failings of their predecessors.[3]

## 1. THE RISE OF SPAIN

The continuing political confusion of the Iberian kingdoms in the early fifteenth century made it inevitable that historians should look to the order achieved under Ferdinand and Isabella, who commanded the attention of Europe for exceptional reasons: the merging of realms to produce a single crown; the defeat of the Muslims of Granada; the expulsion of the Jews; the discovery of the New World; the expansion of power; the sealing of dynastic alliances with England and the Holy Roman Empire. The world hegemony of the Habsburgs was prepared by their predecessors and they added little to it. Later Spanish commentators recognised this: Ferdinand 'began the greatness of this immense monarchy', claimed Fernández de Navarrete in 1626.[4]

But in three important respects this 'greatness' needs to be carefully defined. First, the centre of expansion was not 'Spain', which continued to be a moral concept rather than a political entity, but the Crown of Castile. The peninsular territories ruled by the crown of Castile made up two-thirds of the land surface of Spain and four-fifths of its population, and provided the dynamism and military personnel that took in hand the occupation of the Canary Islands, the wars of Granada, and the annexation of Navarre and of several Moorish towns in north Africa.[5] Castilian soldiers were likewise the main component of the forces that intervened in Naples. Foreign trade was predominantly Castilian, merchants in the north organising themselves through the Consulado of Burgos, and in Seville, when the trade to America opened up, through the monopoly House of Trade. Because the Crown of Aragon (consisting of the autonomous realms of Aragon, Catalonia and Valencia) by contrast played a more subdued role in both military and commercial terms, its different development cannot always be fitted into statements that claim to apply to 'Spain'.

Second, the 'monarchy' was not a world-wide dominion or empire under the direct rule of Spain, but a community of autonomous states. Contemporaries were conscious of the world-presence of Ferdinand and Isabella, the Castilian scholar Nebrija claiming that Spain rather than Germany deserved 'the title of Empire'.[6] But it was an empire unlike others. The kingdom of Naples, though confirmed to the Spanish crown in 1504, cannot be categorised as a 'conquest'. The king of Aragon had ruled Naples as recently as 1458, and when Spanish troops intruded into Naples into 1494 they were sent to fight not the Neapolitans but the invading French troops. Naples thus joined the Spanish realms as a sovereign state. Similarly when in 1512 troops took over Navarre the realm retained its full autonomy and privileges. The union of these territories with 'Spain' mirrored the terms which had created the union between Castile and Aragon. Apart from the true military conquests which had taken place in the Canary Islands and in north African settlements such as Orán, Spanish power in the sixteenth century, though usually affirmed through the use of an army (as in Navarre), arose through realms associating together on a basis of autonomy and equality. This arrangement was appropriately called by contemporaries a *monarquía* rather than an 'empire'. Later in the century when Charles V abdicated half his realms to Philip II the same principle of equality was observed with the link that bound the Netherlands and Milan to the Spanish crown; and the takeover of Portugal in 1580 followed the same lines.

As with the union of Castile and Aragon, the realms of the *monarquía* were linked only through the person of the sovereign and remained otherwise wholly autonomous, with their own laws and institutions. The exceptions were America, the Canaries, and Africa, treated as colonies of Castile and subject to its laws. To provide a system of control viceroys were appointed to each realm, and later on special councils for each territory were set up in Castile in order to facilitate control. Given its greater weight in resources and population, it was Castile, from which viceroys and troops normally came, that directed the *monarquía*. The Castilian presence, which always irritated native sensibilities in Aragon, Naples or wherever it was felt, could be tolerated indefinitely because of the fundamental autonomy of each realm, but led to explosions whenever Castile tried to increase its initiative in the areas of taxation and local privileges.

Third, the 'greatness' occurred not because of Spanish superior resources but thanks to the pooling of resources in the *monarquía*, enabling regional elites to participate with Castilians in the wider dimensions of a joint imperial adventure. The Italian states, for example, shared common interests in the Mediterranean and a common hostility to the Turk; Italians (such as Alexander Farnese) became generals and administrators elsewhere in the monarchy and even in Spain itself. Spain played only an auxiliary role in the wars of the emperor and was directly involved in none of them. Spanish troops were less than a fifth of the army that sacked Rome in 1527, less than a sixth of the 40,000 serving Charles in Germany in 1546. The country had no substantial naval forces in the Mediterranean until the Genoese fleet put itself under Charles's service in 1528, and thereafter the Italians were always the mainstay of 'Spanish' sea-power in southern Europe (at Lepanto in 1571 they supplied two-thirds of the ships and men). The great expedition that captured Tunis in 1535 was only one-third Spanish in composition. Castile came by stages to play a more significant role in imperial enterprises, its most significant contribution under the emperor being in personnel and in subsidies.[7]

## 2. FERDINAND AND ISABELLA: PACIFICATION AND 'UNITY'

After the civil wars which beset Castile (1464-1480) and Catalonia (1462-1472) peace came back to Christian Spain when Ferdinand succeeded his father in Aragon and Isabella her brother in Castile, but it was a peace based on compromises and not (as scholars once held) at the dictate of the crown. Compromise had to be reached with the nobles and with the cities, who between them constituted the political nation. In effect, the monarchs confirmed the privileges of the elites: both the Cortes of Toledo (1480) and the Catalan Sentence of Guadalupe (1486) confirmed the landed position of the elite, who in Castile were further gratified by the distribution of new noble titles. The cities in Castile were consulted through the Cortes, and made partners of the crown through the important Junta de Hermandad. In no respect was the crown's power over the ruling classes increased. The coming of peace, moreover, was only relative. From 1482 the campaigns against Muslim Granada gathered force, and the elites in Castile were actually encouraged to rearm rather than to disarm. Ferdinand put himself at the head of the troops, and gave the restless nobles a purpose to fight for: against the Moor rather than against each other. From this period a Castilian army, subsequently to distinguish itself in the Neapolitan wars, slowly took shape, and became an important factor in the emergence of a 'Spanish' identity.

Unification was as ambiguous an achievement as pacification. The sole link uniting Castile and Aragon was the marriage of their sovereigns. Even then the link was tenuous: when Philip I and Juana, called 'the Mad', ruled Castile after Isabella's death, Ferdinand was effectively excluded from any role; and had his marriage to Germaine de Foix produced surviving children these would have inherited a quite independent Aragon. The union of the realms was, fortunately, confirmed with Charles V's accession (1516) to both. But they remained separate countries in all vital respects: laws, government, currency, and language. Political unification was never on the cards. Nor, despite the views of some historians, was religious unification. Ferdinand and Isabella ended the legal status of Judaism in the peninsula and adjacent islands in 1492, but Islam continued to be legally permitted in Castile and Granada for another ten years, and was legally permitted in the Crown of Aragon throughout the reign of Ferdinand. In their overseas realms, moreover, in north Africa and Naples, they continued to tolerate both Islam and Judaism, a surprising attitude for rulers often presented as fanatical.

The Catholic Kings (a title granted by the pope in 1494 in return for services rendered against the French in Italy) cannot be regarded as 'modern' rulers bent on reforming their administration and their Church. All their acts merely followed medieval precedent. For example, the much vaunted reorganisation of the Council of Castile in 1480 was little more than a repeat of measures of 1459. The image of the reign given by a past generation of scholars is now wholly superseded, thanks largely to the researches of Ladero and others. For example, an argument offered in 1963—that 'Ferdinand and Isabella took no steps to encourage wheat production', that the Church was reformed and obtained 'new force and vigour', that 'the power of the *corregidor* extended to all the corners of Castile'—is now untenable, a measure of the important work done over the past generation.[8] Marvin Lunenfeld's short study of the *corregidores* reassesses the role of bureaucracy in Castile, and at the same time checks the exaggerations of previous historians over the alleged reforms of the Catholic Kings. Some changes certainly took place, but none with a view to establishing a new 'absolute' monarchy.[9]

The word 'absolutist' could be found in fourteenth-century Castile, and subsequent rulers down to Isabella claimed it as an attribute, but the word meant little more than a claim to derive power directly from God. The great nobility were happy to give more initiative to the crown as arbiter after the recent civil strife, but in return were confirmed in their privileges. The towns of Castile, sometimes represented as made subject, were in fact taken into partnership, by the Hermandad. Thus absolutism in the sense of ruling arbitrarily, did not occur. At least in Castile, the rule of the Catholic Kings was an impressive exercise in cooperation: the rulers administered the realm simply by travelling round it, an astonishing feat unparalleled in the history of any other nation. Though no innovations were made in the constitution, and no extra powers were created for themselves, the rulers initiated three key developments which were eventually to serve the monarchy well: they encouraged the growth of a state bureaucracy (in the new royal councils, and in the courts); they created a state debt through the system of *juros*; and they encouraged the concept of a state army (used first in Granada and then in Naples).

The early history of Spain's bureaucracy remains to be written, but an important aspect of it was considered in a recent study of the university background of officials.[10] Government preference for university-trained lawyers (*letrados*) boosted the study of laws in higher education, and in consequence boosted university expansion. The debt and finances before the Habsburg epoch were usefully analysed by Ladero, who has also shed important light on the organisation of Ferdinand's army for the war of Granada. In secular matters the image given of the Catholic Kings is of a diligent and highly efficient team, capable of bullying when there was no other way forward, but quick to accept compromise when it seemed best.

Their alleged fanaticism is more controversial. The foundation of the Inquisition (1478) was due to the monarchs' initiative alone, and its obvious excesses (the biggest organised holocaust of people of Jewish origin ever to have occurred in Europe till that date) never provoked them to intervene; on the contrary, at every step they reaffirmed their dedication to it. It is possible that they considered it only a temporary expedient, for they gave it no secure financial base; but the institution outlived them and survived for over three centuries more. Their expulsion of the Jews appears to confirm the image of religious extremism. The figure for Jews expelled is now much smaller than was once thought (possibly 40,000 rather than older figures of over 200,000), and it is certain that there were no negative economic consequences in Spain; but the question of the rulers' motives remains.[11] Both Inquisition and expulsion suggest a strain of antisemitism, yet at government level the position was more complex: Ferdinand and Isabella were well known for their close collaboration with both Jews and *conversos*, and Isabella's protective policy to Jews in Castile is well documented. It is certain that the antisemitism of the period must be explained on a broader social basis than simply in terms of the arbitrary actions of the rulers of Spain.[12]

## 3. The Spain that Awaited Charles V

Although Ferdinand and Isabella had laid the basis for a nation, it was far from being in existence when Charles V arrived in Spain in 1517. Political authority was highly regionalised, with each realm having its own estates or Cortes, themselves mere semblances of a power that rested effectively in the local communities and seigneurial lands. There was no national capital from which a king might attempt to impose policy; no effective tax-collecting personnel; and no armed forces. Each realm—and in lesser degree each political entity—had its own privileges (*fueros*), which the crown must not touch. The complete separation between the realms of Aragon and Castile was mirrored in the organisation of the Church, which likewise had no national character but was divided into several independent metropolitan areas. Spain's population of some 5.5 million in 1500 was weighted largely towards the Castilian realms (some 80%), and was denser on the coastal periphery than in the dry interior. Uniquely in western Europe, it included a substantial population (.25 million) of Muslims. Like western Europe it included several linguistic areas (possibly a quarter of all Spaniards did not normally use Castilian but instead spoke Arabic, Catalan, Basque and Galician). Spain was a poor nation which could not even feed itself, and relied heavily on imports of grain from Sicily; the only important exports were raw materials (notably wool). It was a society where population levels had been rising since the late fifteenth century, and in which women appear to have married at about 21 years (a bit younger in the Muslim areas), contributing to a demographic growth which in the course of the century increased the total of people in Castile by some 50%.

The new dynasty brought no significant changes to Spain. Shaken by the revolt of the Comuneros in 1520, Charles V seems to have done little to innovate and much to win the ruling classes to his side. A court circle (using newly-introduced Burgundian ceremonial) was created; new noble ranks were brought in ('*grandees*', a status created in 1520) and the orders of chivalry encouraged; concessions were made to the cities over tax-collection. Erasmian humanism entered the country and flourished under court patronage, but was rapidly eliminated by a conservative opposition in the 1530s after Charles V had left the country. Possibly the most important development of the reign was a rise in royal expenditure because of the king's active European policy. Logically, taxation rose and the funded debt of Castile grew in size. The mechanisms of finance were correspondingly boosted, and foreign bankers took an interest in Spain's economy, particularly in the trade of Seville to America.

Historians have not seen fit to study the internal history of Spain under Charles V, nor is there any biographical study of the king based on Spanish documentation: the entire reign, apart from the brief period of the Comuneros, remains a terra incognita. Only the important study on the emperor's chief Castilian adviser, Francisco de Los Cobos, fills the otherwise large gap on political history.[13] Attention falls, by default, on other aspects of the period, and on America. Given Spain's special role in the New World, the relevance of America is fundamental. Precisely in the reign of Charles, emigration to America introduced a major new dimension to the Iberian experience, and controversies over Spain's right to be there opened up new perspectives.[14] America changed the Spanish experience by offering new wealth and new mental horizons, and promoting social mobility.

New wealth took the form of imports of bullion which began to stimulate the economy but also to push prices upwards. There has been little change in the once controversial area of the 'price revolution', now accepted as having been set off in part by demographic expansion, in part by bullion imports.[15] Apart from bullion, America also came to offer other riches—sugar, hides, tobacco—that affected all levels of peninsular society. New mental horizons were opened up by the discoveries: for the historian Oviedo, America was the greatest intellectual adventure of all time: 'what I speak of cannot be learnt in Salamanca or Bologna or Paris'.[16] But the opportunity for advancement was the most cogent appeal, leading to a tide of emigration: it is likely that up to 150,000 Spaniards crossed to America before 1550, and for the whole century the figure could not have exceeded 250,000. To all this must be added the extensive racial experience of contact with American natives and black slavery: Portugal within a generation was inundated with blacks. By 1565 Seville was estimated to have 7.4% of its population as slaves, mostly black.[17]

The absence of great events in early sixteenth-century Spain is redeemed by the notable episode of the *Comunidades* (1520-1521).[18] Of limited significance as a political event, the episode has enabled historians to escape from the traditional romantic picture of a popular rebellion against royal power, in order to analyse the real forces that moved Castilian society. Scholars have fruitfully emphasised endemic regionalism, faction-fighting in the cities, grievances of the peasantry, the solid power of the aristocracy, the populist agitation of the clergy.[19] The conflict can validly be seen as an attempt at 'revolution', but also as a commentary on the inability of the Catholic Kings to stabilise political power.[20] By contrast, the unrelated Germanía insurrections in the Catalan lands seem to have been a simple conflict between social orders.[21]

After the defeat of the Comuneros the Spanish kingdoms lived through an impressive generation of peace, with no wars either abroad or at home, and only distant echoes from America. The reign was on balance satisfactory to all sections of the population: there were no major epidemics; there was (apart from isolated expeditions to Africa) peace; the heresy of the Reformation did not raise its head; the incidence of inflation had not yet left its mark. In this environment the economy of the peninsula went through a boom, as reports from travellers in 1526 and 1552 testify. Textile production at Segovia and Cuenca soared. The mid-sixteenth century was a boom period in which the success story of the Castilian trade fairs at Burgos overlapped with the new wealth of Seville and Andalusia.


## 4. A FRAGILE EMPIRE

In the reign of Charles the country was not yet plunged into a military role. The Spaniards who were beginning to subdue America were not royal troops but adventurers, 'conquistadors'. It is important to stress that in Europe Spain remained at peace throughout the reign; when Castilian troops took part in campaigns in Germany or Italy they featured merely as a small part of multi-national forces at the emperor's command. Charles's wars, in effect, did not commit any of his territories as belligerents.

Spain did not begin its career as an imperial power until the reign of Philip II. With its small population and weak economy, it did not have the resources to launch an imperial program. Yet the Turkish threat, surveyed brilliantly by Fernand Braudel, made defensive measures necessary; and the Granada rising of 1569 aggravated the urgency. 'The peace that has reigned here for so many years' was blamed by the Council of War in 1562 for Spain's defencelessness; in 1566 a leading military writer deplored 'the decline in our infantry'; four-fifths of the arms used to suppress the Granada revolt had to be imported.[22] Precisely from these years an immense effort was made to convert Spain into a super-power.

I. A. A. Thompson has shown how this program led to the building of a Mediterranean and then an Atlantic fleet, and the up-grading of the armed forces. Money was poured into the army of Flanders. Meanwhile the technology which all this required, was also upgraded. None of it was possible with Spain's resources alone. Spanish power became awesome because it drew not on Spain alone but on the naval expertise and military manpower of the Genoese and Neapolitans, the weaponry of the Milanese and Liègeois, and the financial backing of Antwerp. David C. Goodman has shown how technical experts were attracted to the peninsula from Germany and above all from Italy. Thanks to the multi-national *monarquía* Castile was able to draw on Europe's finest experts.[23] Spain's might, then, was the fruit of a collective effort rather than a product of its own capacities; a fundamental conclusion that saves us from exaggerating the nation's rise or postulating an illusory subsequent decline.

Surprisingly, there is no modern survey of Spain's army or navy in this imperial age, and little on resources, armament, training and officers. A highly important study on the part played by the Castilian government in preparing for war, however, offers a fundamental evaluation of the administrative background.[24] Great events such as Lepanto and the Spanish Armada have been examined in terms of tactics, but only Alba among the great commanders has received a modern biography.[25] This failure to examine closely the mechanics of Spanish 'imperialism' continues to prejudice a proper understanding of the nation's role in international politics, and leads inevitably to a distorted image of Spain's real potential. Even at the height of its imperial career Spain remained completely vulnerable, and the daring raids by Drake on Vigo (1585) and Essex on Cadiz (held by the English for an incredible three weeks in 1596) exposed constant weaknesses.

## 5. SPAIN AND THE REFORMATION

Defeated by the Lutheran Reformation in Germany, Charles V retired to Spain in 1556, trusting in its total orthodoxy. A few Protestants were nevertheless discovered in Seville and Valladolid from 1558 onwards, and on Charles's urging ruthlessly crushed. Protestantism did not surface again. The issue provokes a major problem of historical interpretation. Why were there no active cells of Protestants until a generation after the German Reformation? Why, when discovered, were they so easy to eliminate? The standard answer, that Spaniards (alone of all western Europeans) were too Catholic to be susceptible to the Reformation, is unconvincing and a measure of historians' neglect of the religious history of Spain. Though some aspects have been investigated, there are few well-rounded studies of the Church history of the peninsula and none on the social background, making it difficult to arrive at a balanced assessment. None of the existing evidence suggests that Spaniards were immovably Catholic or that they had a special immunity to heresy, and recent studies demonstrate that Spanish religion was not necessarily rooted in dogma, and that Spanish popular religion was much the same as elsewhere in Europe[26]. The alternative answer to the failure of a Reformation in Spain, that the nation was 'frozen into orthodoxy', in the phrase of John Lothrop Motley, by fear of the Inquisition, exaggerates the power of this tribunal to dictate the beliefs of Spaniards, and springs from a misapprehension of the nature of the Inquisition itself.

Important work has been done on the heterodox tendencies of the mid-sixteenth century, and only a handful of people, such as the Italian Carlos de Seso, can be identified as ideologically Protestant.[27] The inability of the Reformation to gain a hold is all the more inexplicable because there was no systematic exclusion of foreign influences, foreign presses had free contact with Spain, and only after 1558 were controls attempted.[28]

Not until the reign of Philip II, when the Council of Trent drew to its close in 1563, was there a systematic attempt to reform the Spanish Church, which suffered from all the vices associated with pre-Reformation Catholicism. Some reform was possible, and radical changes were made in the liturgy, but the impact was less significant than reformers hoped: the evidence suggests that popular and local religion put up strong resistance to officially approved forms of piety. Since the general presumption, fed by older historiography, has been that no Counter-Reformation was required in Spain, it has been assumed that none occurred and there are consequently no studies of one of the most important movements in peninsular history.[29]

By contrast, Spanish scholars have devoted much attention to the exterior and important role of Spain in the last stages of the Council of Trent.[30] The bishops of Spain, aided by leading Spanish theologians (who did not always agree with the bishops), helped to lay down the official belief of the Counter-Reformation Church, and attempted to carry out some reforms at home. The new Jesuit order, in its early days led mainly by Spaniards, played a decisive part in the aggressive anti-heresy campaign throughout the continent and scored notable successes in central Europe. Many studies on these themes are, however, permeated by an ecclesiastical triumphalism that severely reduces their historical value (the history of the Jesuits, for example, has been written exclusively by Jesuits); and the experience of the Catholic Church in the Spanish lands has yet to be written from a more detached viewpoint.

Some information on Iberian religion can be obtained from the papers of the Inquisition, which can be used to shed light on a broad spectrum of practices in religion and morals, ranging from Protestantism to bigamy. Ease of access to Inquisition papers has unleashed a chaotic flood of research which has at least provoked useful questions. There is now broad agreement that apart from the generation in which a holocaust was inflicted on Jewish *conversos* (1480-1520) the Inquisition was far from being the terrible instrument as it is featured in legend. For the greater part of its existence it was concerned not with heresy nor with Jews but with the dogmatic failings and moral attitudes of ordinary Spaniards, and the activity of ethnic minorities such as Moriscos and the French.[31] There remains some controversy over the overall impact of the tribunal: for some scholars its impact was 'marginal' to daily life, for others the tribunal was capable of controlling the thoughts of everyone from lord to peasant.[32]

The cultural history of sixteenth-century Spain has been dominated by Marcel Bataillon's survey of the growth of Erasmian influence and the Inquisition's role in suppressing it. Subsequent writers have tried to balance exaggeration of Erasmus's importance by giving due attention to indigenous influences, and particularly useful light has been shed on the important *alumbrado* movement in Castile.[33] It has also been argued that the Castilian mentality was not necessarily one given to religious persecution.[34] But the traditional image of Spain as a persecuting society has proved difficult to modify, largely because of the reputation of the Inquisition.

The emotive issue of the Inquisition's role in culture continues to provoke differences of opinion, despite apparent agreement on the facts. The tribunal did not control censorship, which was always in the hands of the state (the Council of Castile), but it exercised post-publication control.[35]

This has led past scholars to regard Spain as cut off by censorship from the civilised world and from its own creativity. Whatever the real impact of literary control, at least three considerations should be borne in mind. First, the famous censorship measures of 1558 were valid only for Castile, not for the rest of Spain, where censorship came in only a generation later and seems never to have operated effectively. Books in any case entered Castile without difficulty: between 1557 and 1564 one merchant alone, Andrés Ruiz, imported 1,012 bales of books from France. Second, apart from notorious cases where antisemitism was a motive (such as the trial of the Salamanca professors in the 1570s) only a tiny handful of Spaniards fell foul of censorship, and no evident harm resulted either to them or to literature.[36] Third, if Spaniards did not publish as much as they may have wished it was largely because of the poor state of publishing within the country.[37] Those who wished to publish abroad did so quite freely, either in Lyon or in Italy; indeed quite as many Spanish books were published outside as inside Spain during the sixteenth century. The Inquisition, in short, was not a benevolent institution, but its invariably negative impact on literature needs to be set in a broader context.

The so-called isolation of Spain, portrayed sometimes by older scholars as a 'fortress' society, was always a fiction. During the age of empire Spaniards were the most travelled nation in the world, including in their orbit not only the whole of Europe but also the New World and the Philippines (occupied 1571). Particularly active were the links with Italy (from which Spain drew its major influences in music, drama, poetry, art and religion) and the Netherlands (a link for commerce, art, spirituality and printing). The cultural creativity of the Golden Age would have been impossible without the continuing influence of these countries. Political thought in the period, stimulated precisely by empire, was particularly rich, with major contributions by Castilians to international law (Francisco Vitoria) and to monarchical theory (Francisco Suárez, Juan de Mariana): there is still no global survey of sixteenth-century writings, but specific thinkers have been surveyed in their contexts.[38]

## 6. WAR UNDER PHILIP II

It has recently been argued that there were differences of approach to foreign policy between Charles V and his son, but their objectives, both stated and implicit, were probably similar: peace among Christians, and war against the Turk.[39] The fact that both father and son never ceased to war against Christians was due to the need to defend themselves, mainly against France and England. The Venetian ambassador said in 1559 of Philip that he aimed 'not to wage war so he can add to his kingdoms, but to wage peace so that he can keep the lands he has.'[40] Habsburg Spain, certainly, was not an expansionist power, and is unique among all 'empires' in history in never adding permanently to its territory by conquest.

The crucial military danger came from Islam, both through the internal disorder caused by Morisco uprisings and banditry, and the external danger of piracy and invasion.[41] After the obligatory conversion of Muslims in the Crown of Aragon in 1526, Islam was theoretically abolished throughout the peninsula, but little attempt was made to bring about either conversion or integration. Some recent work has looked at the Moriscos themselves rather than simply at their alleged 'threat'. We know more about their society, and about their own ideological reaction to the unfavourable position within Christian society.[42] It is also clear that despite the constant tensions there were many Spaniards who refused to entertain the idea, which gathered force during the late century, of expelling the Moriscos. In Valencia, where Moriscos formed one-third of the population, even the inquisitors argued against expulsion, 'for after all they are Spaniards like ourselves'.[43]

There were military realities, however, which argued the other way. The rebellion of 1569 in Granada lasted nearly two years, and exposed Castile's weak position; nor was it entirely an internal matter, for 4,000 Turks and Berbers fought among the 25,000 insurgents in spring 1570.[44] It was arguably the most horrifying confrontation to take place in the Europe of its time: mass expulsions, death, and emigration, between them reduced the population of the kingdom of Granada by some 120,000 people. In a magnificent study Fernand Braudel has shown how the clash between Christian and Islamic civilisation culminated in the battle of Lepanto (1571). In Spain, though pressure on the Moriscos increased and the government itself decided in 1582 that expulsion was the only solution, there was no clear support for such a move.

In contrast to the peace of the early sixteenth century, the second half of the century was one of constant war, as we can see by the figures for the government's *juro* debt. *Juros*, or annuity payments on loans made largely for the war effort, absorbed by the end of the reign of Charles some 68% of normal Castilian revenue, and by the end of the reign of Philip the total *juro* debt was nearly eight times the annual revenue. As commitments increased, the government was forced to increase expenditure. Spain had not been a naval power, which necessitated some impressive new costs.

Between 1560 and 1574 Philip II had some 300 galleys built in the Mediterranean, at a total cost of over 3.5 million ducats.[45] The Armada campaign of 1588 cost 10 million ducats. In one generation, between 1566 and 1598, the total annual military expenditure of Castile increased fivefold, the biggest drain being the war in the Netherlands. Felipe Ruíz Martín has concluded that 'war in the sixteenth century cut short the positive evolution of Spain by absorbing resources which would normally have served to increase production.'[46] In the same way Thompson has shown that war had a powerful impact on administration and government, though it gave rise to no long-term changes. Castile's inadequate manpower and industrial resources made it ill-equipped to sustain an imperial program for long.[47] At most the country might manage to finance a program that was being serviced by its allies, with Castile paying the bills but its allies supplying the men and munitions. The periodic 'bankruptcies' of the treasury under Philip II, beginning with that of 1557, demonstrate that even before its imperial age had commenced Castile was in trouble.[48]

Peninsular unity was achieved by Philip II in 1580. It is easy to slip into talking of 'the conquest' of Portugal because force was used, but no conquest was implemented. The disappearance of the last king of the Avis dynasty, Sebastian, in an ill-fated expedition into Morocco, where he and the flower of Portugal's nobility perished at the battle of Alcazar-Kebir (1578) left Portugal without an obvious heir to the throne. Philip II's claim was the strongest, and he supported it with the use of force. But at the Cortes of Thomar he swore to observe the autonomy of Portugal, and did so; far from being conquered, the country retained its autonomy within Spain, its only link being through the crown.

Portugal was a realm in expansion. Its overseas territories fostered trade and economic activity. From its tiny population (some 1.25 million in 1527) thousands went to find their fortune in the empire, but the realm also attracted immigration and the commercial centres grew: Lisbon and Santarém doubled in population during the century, the Algarve expanded by 50%. The link with Castile, unfortunately, was no more beneficial to Portugal than it had been to the Crown of Aragon.


## 7. CROWN AND GOVERNMENT

Among the fundamental reassessments to have been done in recent years is that on the role of the crown. Without exception, older historians referred to Philip II as an 'absolutist' king, but the term had little justification. Over the greater part of the monarchy (Italy, the Netherlands, the Crown of Aragon, Portugal) the king was severely restricted by local laws, autonomy and privileges, and even in Aragon after the troubles of 1591 he took care to reaffirm the local laws (*fueros*). Recent discussion has centred on the mechanics of royal power in Castile and America. In the latter the crown created an impressive volume of legislation in the course of the century, but was in practice, almost from the beginning, defeated by the difficulty of controlling stubborn settlers who effectively enjoyed a practical freedom bestowed on them by their enormous distance from Spain.[49]

To some degree the power of the king could be defined by the evolution of 'state' power and bureaucracy. In pioneering essays Vicens Vives and Maravall looked at the emergent theory and mechanisms of the Renaissance state.[50] In Spain the starting point was Ferdinand and Isabella, who were completely medieval in their style of government but nevertheless moved inevitably, like their fellow monarchs, to the need for sedentary institutions, a reliable civil service of both Church and state, and a more organised army.[51] Under Charles the civil service came to include high officials such as the viceroys who acted for the king. The Inquisition was likewise part of the state bureaucracy. Enumeration of such officials, however, should not tempt us to conclude that a powerful state was in the making. In practice the bureaucracy helped to make the existing mechanisms function adequately, but there is no convincing evidence that they changed anything or that they extended royal power significantly.

In Madrid (official capital after 1561) the crown built up a complex and by no means inefficient machinery of consultative councils and executive officials. Viewed from the centre, the power of the crown was impressive. Philip II made his own decisions, though nearly always after close consultation with alternative views. A small number of his decisions were quite arbitrary (such as the decision to execute the Justiciar of Aragon in 1592) and undeniably 'absolutist'. The crown also had uncontested control over Castile's foreign policy. But away from the centre royal authority was tempered by other factors.

Recent historians of Spain have stressed the regional nature of early modern authority, and from this perspective the crown's role seems smaller. We know that in Castile the bulk of jurisdictions (over taxes, justice) were in the hands of the aristocracy: in Salamanca, largely controlled by the duke of Alba, two-thirds of territory and population were not under the king. In the kingdom of Aragon, the crown had jurisdiction over only 42% of towns; in Valencia over about 25%. Nor, at these regional levels, was crown authority strong. The *corregidores* in Castile (just over 60 towns had them in the sixteenth century) were linked with local elites and their salaries were paid locally, so their role as agents of the crown was limited. In the rest of Spain, even these officials were lacking. Moreover, office holders nominally in the pay of the crown were usually appointed from among the local elite, and it was with these elites that effective control and patronage lay.[52]  Government throughout the Habsburg period was typically regional and autonomous rather than national. At an even lower, day-to-day level, traditional structures were based on community authority, exercised through village councils which made the major decisions on all aspects of communal life.[53]  None of this implied a weak crown; in a federal monarchy such as the Spanish it is possible to view local autonomy as a strength rather than a weakness. It was also more economical, since it minimised the need to create a national bureaucracy.

A long-lasting orthodoxy was that the Habsburgs, starting with Charles V after the defeat of the Comuneros, crushed the cities and Cortes of Castile; under Philip II, we were once assured, they were 'little more than a rubber stamp'.[54]  The considerable increase in taxes voted by the Cortes, known as *servicios*, which rose from being about a quarter of royal income in the 1570s to over half early in the next century, meant however that the crown came to depend on the Cortes, which used the opportunity to criticise the war in the Netherlands, and to demand that certain conditions be met before *servicios* were granted. This has obliged historians to review the part played by the Cortes.[55]  In the closing years of Philip II there was a marked rise in constitutional feeling in Castile.

The hard-pressed crown also diminished its own authority by selling off lands, offices and towns in order to raise money. Charles V had begun the practice of selling royal possessions. From about 1557 Philip II began to sell communal lands (*baldíos*) to towns wishing to buy; in the same period he sold public offices both in Castile and in America, and numerous towns and their jurisdictions. Although the crown gained substantial cash, it was also alienating some of its power. It has recently been argued, however, that sales of jurisdiction were in fact beneficial to royal power, since many purchases were made by villages, which, having thereby gained autonomy from other towns, placed themselves in the service of the crown.[56]

## 8. SOCIAL CHANGE AND ECONOMIC CRISIS

Social change in sixteenth-century Spain has usually been identified with economic backwardness. In his *Mediterranean* Braudel proposed the thesis of a 'betrayal by the bourgeoisie', according to which the rising middle classes failed to re-invest their wealth and therefore prejudiced economic development. Scholars have been reluctant to follow this interpretation. Like other countries Spain had an active middle sector but paucity of urban trading centres and competition with foreign interests limited the success of the bourgeoisie.[57] Status in itself was no problem, since large-scale trade was deemed socially acceptable and only patience was required in order to obtain rank.[58] The claim that Castilians despised trade represents a persistent misreading of the evidence. There were enough Castilians in trade,[59]—in Burgos, Bruges, and Seville—to have put paid to the misconception, which however had an undeniable grain of truth in it, since in some commercial families a second generation took the money out of business and invested in houses and status. Among the Basques and Catalans there were by contrast no comparable doubts over the acceptability of trade.

Modifying yet another traditional image, it has been shown that the peninsular aristocracy played a key role in production, both agrarian and industrial; were among the biggest members of the sheep-raising syndicate known as the Mesta; and were important participants in foreign trade.[60] Survival of the documentation of noble houses such as the Osuna has shown the fairly efficient functioning of the great aristocratic estates and their struggle for solvency during the epoch of crisis.[61] Backwardness was not therefore a necessary consequence of a noble-dominated economy. The high cost of the noble style of life, nevertheless, was aggravated by economic difficulties, and by the end of the century many great houses (such as that of Alba) faced ruin.

Within their own spheres the social groups of the peninsula were active and successful, but Spaniards did not normally keep letter-books or diaries, and it has consequently been difficult to understand their thought processes. There are special studies of the rural nobles (*caballeros*) of Extremadura and the urban gentry (*ciutadans honrats*) of Barcelona, but except for a general introduction by Domínguez Ortiz, there has been no rounded examination of the attitudes and social role of the peninsular aristocracy.[62]

The great mass of the people remain virtually unstudied. The pioneering thesis on Valladolid by Bartolomé Bennassar touches on the urban population, and there are similar studies for other towns such as Murcia and Orihuela; but for most of the peninsula the picture is blank.[63] On the villages we have a splendid profile of the villages of New Castile, based on the census of 1575, and a study which broaches the important issue of

peasant communalism.[64] Apart from these studies, the social life of everyday Spain is virgin territory. Spanish scholars have preferred to approach
the question through the perspective of agrarian production, on which
there is a substantial bibliography, centered on subsequent centuries rather
than on the thinly-documented sixteenth.[65] Where historians have failed
to re-create the environment of Spanish society, literary scholars have
stepped in.[66]

The first three-quarters of the sixteenth century were years of comparative success for Spain, in which the economy developed tranquilly, the
riches of America were exploited, and there were few natural disasters (the
harvest crisis of 1560, common to all Europe, was a warning). From about
1580, over halfway into the reign of Philip, the situation changed in Castile. Of the three aspects which historians have noted—falling production,
rising inflation, population decay—the last was in the long run the most
crucial, though it would be naive to present the crisis in simplistic
Malthusian terms. Between 1530 and 1580 the population of Castile had
risen by about 50%, with even higher rates in the interior, where increases
of over 75% occurred.[67] In rounded terms the population of Spain (excluding the Canaries and Portugal) probably rose from about 5.25 million
in the 1480s to a ceiling of some eight million in the late sixteenth century.
From the 1580s, parish records show a downswing in births; population
levels fell so sharply in the subsequent generation that they were not regained till the middle years of the eighteenth century. In agrarian production it was a similar story. In the valley of Bureba, north of Burgos, output
between 1560 and 1580 had expanded by 26% in wheat and 51% in
wine; by contrast, between 1579 and 1595, production in wine fell by
30%, in cereals by 22%.[68] The continuing inflation can be best illustrated
through the likely impact on wages: it has been estimated that the living
costs of a building-worker in Valencia would have been comfortably covered by his wages in 1500, but only a third of his costs would have been
met in 1575. To make matters worse, the wool trade of Castile, the principal business of the great commercial centre at Burgos, now received a
deadly blow from the paralysis of the wool entrepot at Antwerp.

The wars abroad undoubtedly played a part in the change of fortunes:
rebellion in Flanders disrupted trade, and took away young men who
might have been procreating at home. For a historian the most obvious
impact of war was the heavier taxation. Philip II's annual income from
regular sources in Castile more than tripled between 1559 and 1598. Over
the same period the burden on the ordinary taxpayer in Castile increased
by some 430%, at a time when nominal wages had risen by only 80%. The

tax-rise may have been bearable up to the 1580s, because production kept apace, but it caused problems thereafter.

The literature makes it clear that an undeniable crisis was in the making, and continued into the early decades of the next century. No serious scholar now attempts to identify this as a 'decline of Spain'. For one thing, several aspects of the recession, both in demography and trade, were common to western Europe. Moreover, the impact was severe only in the heartland of Castile: in population, the whole north-west of the peninsula continued with uninterrupted growth, and Catalonia on the Mediterranean periphery now accelerated to a demographic increase of about 75% until the early decades of the seventeenth century.[69] In trade, it was precisely from the 1580s that the American commerce based on the Andalusian port of Seville expanded. There were negative consequences throughout the peninsula, but the regional crisis was at its most intense in central Castile, not on the periphery.

The crisis in agrarian production followed the same pattern. In New Castile cereal production had risen steadily from 1460 to 1560, reaching its zenith in the decades 1560-80; thereafter there was a decline. Since there were no technical improvements in agriculture, and yield ratios (at 4:1) remained among the lowest in Europe, the higher output came about solely from extension of arable. Even with this, many parts of Spain throughout the century relied on imports to survive. The crisis at the end of the century merely intensified an existing problem. Vassberg has drawn attention to the importance of the communitarian nature of much landholding in Castile, and suggests that 'poverty was the result of man-made institutions that were inefficient and did not permit the proper utilization of resources'.[70] Among factors he points to were inequitable land distribution, antiquated techniques and implements, and the burden of taxes. Recent scholars seem united in their pessimism about the state of Spain's peasantry. Even in Catalonia, where a past historiography used to suggest that peasants were freer, it has now been stressed that the 1486 Sentence of Guadalupe changed little and that the lot of the peasants worsened.[71] When the crisis came it could be seen in a shrinkage of arable and a fall in wheat production (by about a third); a decline in rentals; and a decline in livestock. The weakness of the rural sector has led to the suggestion of a basic structural weakness, in that 'Spain's peculiar failure was an inability to complete the transition to a more urbanised economy.'[72]

The crisis, in the case of the two great Castilian cities of Madrid and Seville, involved ironically a growth rather than a 'decline'. The expansion of these cities, the largest in Spain, seemed to be a sign of the country's success. In the wake of the trade with America, Seville grew from 10,000 households in 1533 to 24,000 in the 1590s and subsequent years; but much of this growth derived from the activity of foreign traders and their agents resident in the city. From the 1580s commentators in Castile began to denounce the mechanics of the monopoly system, which effectively worked in favour of foreign finance. Seville was no longer really a Spanish port: most of the goods traded out were foreign, and most of what came in from America went to foreigners. Seville's success was inimical to Castilian growth. Madrid offers a parallel example of the negative influence exercised by a city over its dependent regions. Adopted as his capital by Philip II in 1561, Madrid within half a century became the biggest city in Spain. David Ringrose sees the capital as a parasite, absorbing population and produce from its surrounding areas but in no real way aiding their growth. The capital, he suggests, 'could provide little stimulus for interior Spain, and may have functioned as a motor for regional economic stagnation'.[73]

Contemporaries (in particular those tract-writers who later came to be known as *arbitristas*) came to believe that the experience of empire beggared Castile. In the year that Philip II died one writer, Alamos de Barrientos, claimed to see 'our realms defenceless, infested, invaded; the Mediterranean and Atlantic lorded over by the enemy; the Spanish nation worn out, prostrate, discontented and disfavoured'.[74] The view was exaggerated, but there were disquieting signs that Castile, and with it Spain, may have become poorer rather than richer. Census figures show that between about 1530 and 1560 the proportion of registered poor in the cities of Castile increased from about 10% of the population to an average of 23%. Between 1561 and 1597 the census figures in many towns speak of an even sharper deterioration: at the latter date in the town of Arévalo 56% were registered poor. Studies of poor relief in Castile confirm the picture, commented upon by travellers, of poverty as a constant of the social scene in the peninsula.[75] Many attempted to escape from it. Over the same period emigration to America increased: symptomatic were the letters from the tailor in Mexico in 1576 pleading with his cousin in Castile to 'leave that wretched country', or from the mill-owner's wife from Puebla in 1589 asking her brother in Seville to come over from 'that poverty and need which people suffer in Spain'.[76]

At the very height of imperial power, then, doubt and disillusion were writ large in the thought processes of Spaniards. The most expensive imperial commitment, the war in the Netherlands, caused the most debate at home. A government committee in 1574, disagreeing with Alba's policy, said of the Dutch that 'to take away their liberties is difficult to justify'.[77] A French diplomat touring Spain in 1582 met many who 'felt that the cause of the Estates of the Netherlands could be justified'.[78] There was more discussion over such issues in the peninsula than historians have realised, and the image of a rigidly orthodox society, in which all freedom was repressed, is now beginning to be seen as implausible. One of the most persistent prejudices in Castilian society, the antisemitic stance of 'purity of blood (limpieza de sangre)', was by the 1580s being rejected not only by intellectuals but also by the king and by the Inquisition itself.[79] In political terms there was by 1580 a formidable movement of protest against war taxation, and a growing dissociation from imperial commitment. 'Why', protested a member of the Castilian Cortes in 1588, 'should we pay a tax here in order to stop heresy there?'[80]

The vision of sixteenth-century Habsburg Spain is both more vital and more complex than a previous generation of historians knew. Stereotyped images of great imperial power, of 'absolute' monarchy, of a 'fortress' Catholic dogmatism, of ineluctable 'decline', have all but vanished from the modern literature. In the process new debates and problems have arisen: on the function of the elite and organs of government, the stages of economic growth, the role of the Inquisition, the interrelation between the provinces and 'Spain'. Attention has moved away from the global to the detailed, in an effort to understand how things worked from the inside: recent studies on agrarian communalism, on village politics, and on community religion represent attempts to define the fundamental units within which Spaniards lived.[81] The people of Spain were part of a real world, not figures in an exotic landscape. There were evident variations between the regions of the peninsula, conditioned by centuries of coexistence with Judaism and Islam, but the problems of Iberia were not so very different from those of other European peoples.

# NOTES

1. Boxer (1969); Hillgarth (1978); Mackay (1977); Kamen (1991) and (1988); Lynch (1991); Elliott (1963).
2. Braudel (1972); Bataillon (1966); Ladero Quesada (1969) and (1973); Thompson (1976); Maravall (1972a); Bennassar (1967).
3. Mattingly (1955); Jensen (1964); Kagan (1990); Chevalier (1976); Salomon (1973).
4. Fernández de Navarrete, *Conservación de monarquías y discursos políticos* (Madrid, 1626), 218.
5. See Fernández-Armesto (1982); Ladero (1969).
6. Quoted by Highfield (1972), 201.
7. Carande Thobar (1949-67).
8. Elliott (1963), 97, 105, 118.
9. Lunenfeld (1970).
10. Kagan (1981).
11. Kamen (1988).
12. Mackay (1979) has shown the way on this subject.
13. Keniston (1980).
14. See Altman (1989); Hanke (1949). For a perspective of the impact of the New World on the Old some of the most useful information has been collected in the conference papers edited by Chiapelli (1976).
15. Hamilton (1934).
16. Quoted by Maravall (1966).
17. Mörner (1976); Saunders (1982).
18. Studied in depth by Pérez (1970).
19. Owens (1980); Gutiérrez Nieto (1973); Pérez (1970).
20. The views of Maravall (1972a) and Haliczer (1981) respectively.
21. Durán (1982).
22. Quoted by Thompson (1976), chap. 4.
23. Goodman (1988).
24. Parker's splendid analysis (1972) of the Army of Flanders can be supplemented by Quatrefages' study (1979) of the tercios. On administration, see Thompson (1976).
25. Maltby (1983).
26. See Christian (1981a) and (1981b), two studies which supply an interesting focus on local religion; and Kamen (1993b) on Catalonia.
27. See Tellechea Idigoras (1968), who concludes that the famous Catechism of archbishop Carranza was securely orthodox.
28. Such as Basel, studied by Gilly (1985).
29. An exception is Kamen (1993a).
30. García Villoslada (1980).
31. Monter (1991).

32. Nalle (1987).
33. Asensio (1952); Márquez (1972).
34. Kamen (1987).
35. Pinto Crespo (1983).
36. Márquez (1980).
37. Péligry (1981).
38. Fernández-Santamaría (1977).
39. The case for disagreement has been put by Rodríguez-Salgado (1989).
40. Quoted by L. P. Gachard, *Carlos V y Felipe II a través de sus contemporáneos* (Madrid, 1944), 92.
41. Hess (1978).
42. Caro Baroja (1957); Casey (1971); Cardaillac (1977); Chejne (1983).
43. Quoted by Kamen (1985), 113.
44. Domínguez Ortiz and Vincent (1978).
45. Thompson (1976).
46. Ruíz Martín (1978).
47. Thompson (1990).
48. Ruíz Martín (1968); Ulloa (1977).
49. Pérez-Prendes (1989).
50. Vicens Vives (1971); Maravall (1961).
51. Stewart (1969).
52. Studied by Pérez Picazo and Lemeunier (1988) for the province of Murcia.
53. Nader (1991).
54. Elliott (1963), 205.
55. Jago (1985); Thompson (1982).
56. Nader (1991).
57. Molas (1985); Maravall (1972a).
58. Maravall (1972a).
59. Lapeyre (1955); Phillips (1986); Pike (1972).
60. Pike (1972); and for the Osuna, see Atienza Hernández (1987).
61. Nader (1977).
62. Gerbert (1979); Amelang (1986); Domínguez Ortiz (1973).
63. Bennassar (1967). Weisser's (1976) brief study on the Toledo region is the only one to explore the social setting of the peasantry.
64. Salomon (1973); Vassberg (1984).
65. Anes Alvárez (1970); García Sanz (1977); Yun Casalilla (1987).
66. Perhaps the best-known example is Stephen Gilman's *The Spain of Fernando de Rojas*, an evocative work fatally weakened by its neglect of historical sources.
67. Molinié-Bertrand (1985).
68. Brumont (1984).
69. Nadal Oller (1984).
70. Vassberg (1984), 200.
71. Serra (1980).
72. Casey (1985), 224.
73. Studied in detail by Ringrose (1983), chap. 1.
74. Quoted in Ricardo del Arco y Garay, *La idea del imperio en la politica y la literatura españolas* (Madrid, 1944), 341.
75. Martz (1983); Flynn (1989).
76. Lockhart and Otte (1976), 119, 136.
77. Quoted in Kamen (1991), 137.

78. Kamen (1991), 138.
79. Kamen (1993a).
80. Kamen (1993a), chap. 7; and the Cortes of 1588 is quoted by P. Sainz
    Rodríguez, *Evolución de las ideas sobre la decadencia española* (Madrid,
    1962), 95.
81. Vassberg (1984); Nader (1991); Kamen (1993b).

# BIBLIOGRAPHY

Aldea Vaquero, Quintin. *Diccionario de historia eclesiástica de España.* 5 vols. Madrid, 1972-82.

Altman, Ida. *Emigrants and Society: Extremadura and America in the Sixteenth Century.* Berkeley and Los Angeles, 1989.

Amelang, James. *Honored Citizens of Barcelona: Patrician Culture and Class Relations, 1490-1714.* Princeton, 1986.

Anes Alvárez, Gonzalo. *Las crisis agrarias en la España Moderna.* Biblioteca política Taurus, vol. 16. Madrid, 1970.

Arnoldsson, Sverker. *La Leyenda Negra.* Göteborg, 1960.

Asensio, Eugenio. "El erasmismo y las corrientes espirituales afines." *Revista de Filología Española* 36 (1952): 31-99.

Atienza Hernández, Ignacio. *Aristocracia, poder y riqueza en la España moderna: La Casa de Osuna siglos XV-XIX.* Madrid, 1987.

Azcona, Tarsicio de. *La elección y reforma del Episcopado español en tiempo de los Reyes Católicos.* Madrid, 1960.

Azcona, Tarsicio de. *Isabel la Católica.* Biblioteca de autores cristianos, vol. 237. Madrid, 1964.

Bada, Joan. *Situació religiosa de Barcelona en el segle XVI.* Barcelona, 1970.

Baron, Salo W. *A Social and Religious History of the Jews.* 2d ed. Vol. 13. New York, 1983.

Bataillon, Marcel. *Erasmo y España.* Mexico, 1966.

Beinart, Haim. *Conversos on Trial: The Inquisition in Ciudad Real.* Trans. Yael Guiladi. Hispania Judaica, vol. 3. Jerusalem, 1981.

Belenguer Cebria, Ernest. *La corona de Aragón en la época de Felipe II.* Valladolid, 1986.

Bennassar, Bartolomé. *Recherches sur les grandes épidémies dans le Nord de l'Espagne à la fin du XVIe siècle.* Paris, 1969.

Bennassar, Bartolomé. *The Spanish Character: Attitudes and Mentalities from the Sixteenth to the Nineteenth Century.* Trans. Benjamin Keen. Berkeley and Los Angeles, 1979.

Bennassar, Bartolomé. *Valladolid au siècle d'or.* Civilisations et sociétés, vol. 4. Paris, 1967.

Boehmer, Edward. *Bibliotheca Wiffeniana: Spanish Reformers of Two Centuries, from 1520.* 3 vols. London, 1864-1904.

Boxer, Charles R. *The Portuguese Seaborne Empire.* London, 1969.

Boyd-Bowman, Peter. "Patterns of Spanish Emigration to the Indies until 1600." *HAHR* 56 (1976): 580-604.

Braudel, Fernand. *The Mediterranean and the Mediterranean World in the Age of Philip II.* Trans. Sían Reynolds. 2 vols. London, 1972.

Brumont, Francis. *Campo y campesinos de Castilla la Vieja en tiempos de Felipe II.* Madrid, 1984.

Bujanda, Jesus M. de. *Index de l'Inquisition espagnole, 1551, 1554, 1559.* Index des livres interdits, vol. 5. Sherbrooke and Geneva, 1984.

Carande Thobar, Ramón. *Carlos V y sus banqueros.* 3 vols. Madrid, 1949-67.

Cardaillac, Louis. *Moriscos y cristianos. Un enfrentamiento polémico (1492-1640).* Mexico, 1977.

Caro Baroja, Julio. *Los Moriscos del reino de Granada: ensayo de historia social.* Madrid, 1957.

Casey, James. "Moriscos and the Depopulation of Valencia." *PaP*, no. 50 (1971): 19-40.

Casey, James. "Spain: A Failed Transition." In *The European Crisis of the 1590s: Essays in Comparative History*, ed. Peter Clark, 209-28. London, 1985.

Chacón Jiménez, Francisco. *Murcia en la centuria del quinientos.* Murcia, 1979.

Chaunu, Pierre. *Sevilla y América (siglos XVI-XVII).* Seville, 1983.

Chejne, Anwar. *Islam and the West: The Moriscos.* Albany, 1983.

Chevalier, Maxime. *Lectura y Lectores en la España del siglo XVI y XVII.* Madrid, 1976.

Chiapelli, Fredi, ed. *First Images of America. The Impact of the New World on the Old.* 2 vols. Contributions of the UCLA Center for Medieval and Renaissance Studies, vol. 8. Berkeley and Los Angeles, 1976.

Christian, William. *Apparitions in Late Medieval and Renaissance Spain.* Princeton, 1981a.

Christian, William. *Local Religion in Sixteenth-Century Spain.* Princeton, 1981b.

Contreras, Jaime. *El Santo Oficio de la Inquisición de Galicia: poder, sociedad y cultura.* Akal universitaria. Serie Historia moderna, vol. 34. Madrid, 1982.

Crosby, Alfred. *The Columbian Exchange: Biological and Cultural Consequences of 1492.* Westport, Conn., 1972.

Cuartas Rivero, Margarita. "La venta de oficios públicos en Castilla-León en el siglo XVI." *Hispania* 44 (1984).

Dedieu, J. P. *L'Administration de la Foi. L'Inquisition de Tolède (XVIe-XVIIIe siècle).* Madrid, 1989.

Domínguez Ortiz, Antonio. *Las clases privilegiadas en la España del antiguo régimen.* Coleccion Fundamentos, vol. 31. Madrid, 1973.

Domínguez Ortiz, Antonio. *Los judeoconversos en España y América.* Coleccion Fundamentos, vol. 11. Madrid 1971.

Domínguez Ortiz, Antonio. "La venta de cargos y oficios públicos en Castilla." *Anuario de Historia Económica y Social* 3 (1970):105-37.

Domínguez Ortiz, Antonio, and Bernard Vincent. *Historia de los Moriscos.* Madrid, 1978.

Durán, Eulàlia. *Les Germanies als Països Catalans.* Barcelona, 1982.

Elliott, John H. *Imperial Spain, 1516-1714.* New York, 1963.

Fernández Alvarez, Manuel. *La España del Emperador Carlos V.* Vol. 18, *Historia de España*, ed. Ramon Menéndez Pidal. Madrid, 1966.

Fernández-Armesto, Felipe. *The Canary Islands after the Conquest: The Making of a Colonial Society in the Early Sixteenth Century.* Oxford, 1982.

Fernández-Armesto, Felipe. *The Spanish Armada.* Oxford, 1988.

Fernández Santamaría, J. A. *The State, War and Peace: Spanish Political Thought in the Renaissance, 1516-1559.* Cambridge, 1977.

Flynn, Maureen. *Sacred Charity: Confraternities and social Welfare in Spain 1400-1700.* London, 1989.

Fortea Pérez, José Ignacio. *Córdoba en el siglo XVI: las bases demográficas y económicas de una expansion urbana.* Córdoba, 1981.

García Oro, José. *Cisneros y la reforma del clero español en tiempo de los Reyes Católicos.* Biblioteca "Reyes Católicos." Estudios, no. 13. Madrid, 1971.

García Sanz, Angel. *Desarrollo y crisis del Antiguo Régimen en Castilla la Vieja: economía y sociedad en tierras de Segovia de 1500 a 1814.* Coleccion Manifiesto, vol. 63. Madrid, 1977.

García Villoslada, Ricardo . *Historia de la Iglesia en España.* Parts III-IV. Madrid, 1980.

Gelabert González, Juan Eloy. *Santiago y la tierra de Santiago de 1500 a 1640.* La Coruña, 1982.

Gerbert, Marie-Claude. *La noblesse de Castille. Etude sur ses structures sociales en Estrémadure de 1454 à 1516.* Paris, 1979.

Gilly, Carlos. "Juan de Valdés: Übersetzer und Bearbeiter von Luthers Schriften in seinem Diálogo de Doctrina." *ARG* 74 (1983): 257-305.

Gilly, Carlos. *Spanien und der Basler Buchdruck bis 1600.* Basler Beiträge zur Geschichtswissenschaft, 151. Basel and Frankfurt, 1985.

Goodman, David C. *Power and Penury: Government, Technology and Science in Philip II's Spain.* Cambridge, 1988.

Guiral-Hadziiossif, Jacqueline. *Valence, port méditerranéen au XVe siècle (1410-1525).* Publications de la Sorbonne. Série "Histoire moderne," no. 20. Paris, 1986.

Gutiérrez Nieto, Juan Ignacio, *Las Comunidades como movimiento antiseñorial: la formación del bando realista en la guerra civil castellana de 1520-1521.* Ensayos Planeta de historia y humanidades, no. 1. Barcelona, 1973.

Haliczer, Stephen. *The Comuneros of Castile: The Forging of a Revolution 1475-1521.* Madison, Wisc., 1981.

Halperin Donghi, Tulio. *Un conflicto nacional en el siglo de oro. Moriscos y cristianos viejos en Valencia.* Valencia, 1980.

Hamilton, Bernice. *Political Thought in Sixteenth-Century Spain.* Oxford, 1963.

Hamilton, Earl J. *American Treasure and the Price Revolution in Spain, 1501-1650.* Cambridge, Mass., 1934.

Hanke, Lewis. *The Spanish Struggle for Justice in the Conquest of America.* Philadelphia, 1949.

Henningsen, Gustav. *The Witches' Advocate: Basque Witchcraft and the Spanish Inquisition.* Reno, 1980.

Hess, Andrew C. *The Forgotten Frontier: A History of the Sixteenth-Century Ibero-African Frontier.* Chicago, 1978.

Highfield, Roger, ed. *Spain in the Fifteenth Century, 1369-1516.* London, 1972.

Hillgarth, J. H. *The Spanish Kingdoms, 1250-1516.* 2 vols. Oxford, 1978.

Hiltpold, Paul. "Noble Status and Urban privilege: Burgos, 1572." *SCJ* 12 (1981): 21-44.

Ibarra y Rodríguez, Eduardo. *El problema cerealista en España durante el reinado de los Reyes Católicos (1475-1516).* Madrid, 1944.

Iradiel Murugarren, Paulino. *Evolución de la industria textil castellana en los siglos XIII-XVI.* Salamanca, 1974.

Jago, Charles. "Philip II and the Cortes of 1576." *PaP*, no. 109 (1985): 24-43.

Jensen, De Lamar. *Diplomacy and Dogmatism: Bernardo de Mendoza and the French Catholic League.* Cambridge, Mass., 1964.

Kagan, Richard L. *Lawsuits and Litigants in Castile, 1500-1700.* Chapel Hill, 1981.

Kagan, Richard L. *Lucrecia's Dreams: Politics and Prophecy in Sixteenth-Century Spain.* Berkeley and Los Angeles, 1990.

Kagan, Richard L. *Students and Society in Early Modern Spain.* Baltimore, 1974.

Kamen, Henry. *Crisis and Change in Early Modern Spain.* London, 1993a.

Kamen, Henry. *Golden Age Spain.* London, 1986.

Kamen, Henry. *Inquisition and Society in Spain in the Sixteenth and Seventeenth Centuries.* Bloomington, 1985.

Kamen, Henry. "The Mediterranean and the Expulsion of Spanish Jews in 1492." *PaP*, no. 119 (1988): 3-55.

Kamen, Henry. *The Phoenix and the Flame: Catalonia and the Counter Reformation.* London, 1993b.

Kamen, Henry. *Spain 1469-1714: A Society of Conflict.* 2d ed. London, 1991.

Kamen, Henry. "Toleration and Dissent in Sixteenth-Century Spain: the Alternative Tradition." *SCJ* 19 (1988): 3-23.

Kedourie, Elie, ed. *Spain and the Jews.* London, 1992.

Keniston, Hayward. *Francisco de los Cobos, secretario de Carlos V.* Madrid, 1980.

Kinder, Gordon. *Spanish Protestants and Reformers in the Sixteenth Century.* London, 1983.

Klein, Julius. *The Mesta: A Study in Spanish Economic History 1273-1836.* Cambridge, Mass., 1920.

Koenigsberger, Helmut G. "The Statecraft of Philip II." *European Studies Review* 1 (1971): 1-21.

Kübler G., and M. Soria. *Art and Architecture in Spain and Portugal and their American Dominions 1500-1800.* Harmondsworth, 1959.

Ladero Quesada, Miguel Angel. "Les finances royales de Castille à la veille des temps modernes." Trans. Pierre Ponsot. *AESC* 25 (1970): 775-88.

Ladero Quesada, Miguel Angel. *Granada. Historia de un país islámico (1232-1571).* Madrid, 1969.

Ladero Quesada, Miguel Angel. *La hacienda real castellana en el siglo XV.* Estudios de Historia, no. 1. La Laguna, 1973.

Lapeyre, Henri. *Une famille de marchands: les Ruiz. Contribution a l'etude du commerce entre la France et l'Espagne au temps de Philippe II.* Affaires et gens d'affaires, vol. 8. Paris, 1955.

Lea, Henry Charles. *History of the Inquisition of Spain.* 4 vols. New York, 1906.

Lewy, Gunter. *Constitutionalism and Statecraft during the Golden Age in Spain.* Geneva, 1960.

Lockhart, James, and E. Otte. *Letters and People of the Spanish Indies. The Sixteenth Century.* Cambridge, 1976.

Longhurst, John E. *Erasmus and the Spanish Inquisition: The Case of Juan de Valdés.* Albuquerque, N.M., 1950.

Longhurst, John E. *Luther and the Spanish Inquisition: The Case of Diego de Uceda 1528-1529.* Albuquerque, N.M., 1953.

Longhurst, John E. "Luther in Spain 1520-1540." *Proceedings of the American Philosophical Society* 103 (1959).

López Piñero, J. M. *Ciencia y Técnica en la Sociedad española de los siglos XVI y XVII.* Barcelona, 1979.

Lorenzo Sanz, Eufemio. *Comercio de España con América en la época de Felipe II.* 2 vols. Valladolid, 1979.

Lunenfeld, Marvin. *The Council of the Santa Hermandad.* Miami, 1970.

Lunenfeld, Marvin. *Keepers of the City: The Corregidores of Isabella of Castile (1474-1504).* Cambridge, 1988.

Lynch, John. *Spain 1516-1598.* Oxford, 1991.

Mackay, Angus. "Popular Movements and Pogroms in Fifteenth-Century Castile." *PaP,* no. 55 (1979).

Mackay, Angus. *Spain in the Middle Ages: From Frontier to Empire, 1000-1500.* London, 1977.

Maltby, William S. *Alba: A Biography of Fernando Alvarez de Toledo, Third Duke of Alba 1507-1582.* Berkeley and Los Angeles, 1983.

Marañón, Gregorio. *Antonio Pérez, "Spanish Traitor."* London, 1954.

Maravall, José Antonio. *Antiguos y modernos. La idea de progreso en el desarrollo inicial de una sociedad.* Madrid, 1966.

Maravall, José Antonio. *Las Comunidades de Castilla: una primera revolución moderna.* Madrid, 1979.

Maravall, José Antonio. *Estado moderno y mentalidad social (siglos XV a XVII).* 2 vols. Madrid, 1972a.

Maravall, José Antonio. *La oposición política bajo los Austrias.* Barcelona, 1972b.

Maravall, José Antonio. "The Origins of the Modern State." *JWH* 6 (1961).

Marcos Martín, Alberto. *Economía, sociedad, pobreza en Castilla: Palencia 1500-1814.* 2 vols. Palencia, 1985.

Márquez, Antonio. *Los alumbrados. Orígenes y filosofía (1525-1559).* Madrid, 1972.

Márquez, Antonio. *Literatura e Inquisición en España 1478-1834.* Coleccio Persiles, no. 124. Madrid, 1980.

Martin, Colin, and N. Geoffrey Parker. *The Spanish Armada.* London, 1988.

Martz, Linda. *Poverty and Welfare in Habsburg Spain.* Cambridge, 1983.

Mattingly, Garrett. *Renaissance Diplomacy.* London, 1955.

Merriman, Roger B. *The Rise of the Spanish Empire in the Old World and in the New.* 4 vols. New York, 1918. Reprint, 1962.

Molas Ribalta, Pedro. *La burguesía mercantil en la España del Antiguo Régimen.* Madrid, 1985.

Molinié-Bertrand, Annie. *Au siècle d'or. L'Espagne et ses hommes. La population du royaume de Castille au XVIe siècle.* Paris, 1985.

Monter, William. *Frontiers of Heresy.* Cambridge, 1991.

Mörner, Magnus. "Spanish Migration to the New World prior to 1810: a Report on the State of Research." In *First Images of America: The Impact of the New World on the Old,* ed. Fredi Chiapelli, vol. 2: 737-82. Berkeley and Los Angeles, 1976.

Nadal Oller, Jordi. *La población española (siglos XVI a XX).* Coleccion de ciencia economica, economia y sociedad, vol. 7. Barcelona, 1984.

Nader, Helen. *Liberty in Absolutist Spain. The Habsburg Sale of Towns 1516-1700.* Baltimore, 1991.

Nader, Helen. *The Mendoza family in the Spanish Renaissance.* New Brunswick, N.J., 1979.

Nader, Helen. "Noble income in Sixteenth-Century Castile: the Case of the Marquises of Mondéjar." *EconHR* 30 (1977): 411-28.

Nalle, Sara T. "Inquisitors, Priests, and the People During the Catholic Reformation in Spain." *SCJ* 18 (1987): 557-87.

Nalle, Sara T. "Literacy and Culture in Early Modern Castile." *PaP,* no. 125 (1989): 65-96.

Notanyahu, Benzion. *The Marranos of Spain, from the Late Fourteenth to the Early Sixteenth Century.* New York, 1973.

Owens, John B. *Rebelión, monarquía y oligarquía Murciana en la época de Carlos V.* Murcia, 1980.

Parker, N. Geoffrey. *The Army of Flanders and the Spanish Road, 1567-1659.* Cambridge, 1972.

Parker, N. Geoffrey. *Philip II.* Boston, 1978.

Parker, N. Geoffrey. *Spain and the Netherlands.* London, 1979.

Péligry, Christian. "Les éditeurs lyonnais et le marché espagnol aux XVIe et XVIIe siècles." In *Livre et Lecture en Espagne et en France sous l'Ancien Régime. Colloque de la Casa de Velazquez, Madrid, 17-19 novembre 1980.* Paris, 1981.

Pérez, Joseph. *La Révolution des 'Comunidades' de Castille (1520-1521).* Bordeaux, 1970.

Pérez Moreda, Vicente. *Las crisis de mortalidad en la España interior (siglos XVI-XIX).* Madrid, 1980.

Pérez Picazo, Maria Teresa, and Guy Lemeunier. "Formes du pouvoir local dans l'Espagne moderne et contemporaine: des bandos au caciquisme au royaume de Murcie (XVe-XIX siècles)." In *Klientelsysteme im Europa der Frühen Neuzeit,* ed. Antoni Maczak, 315-41. Schriften des Historischen Kollegs. Kolloquien, vol. 9. Munich, 1988.

Pérez-Prendes, José Manuel. *La Monarquía Indiana y el Estado de Derecho.* Madrid, 1989.

Phillips, Carla Rahn. "Spanish Merchants and the Wool Trade in the Sixteenth Century." *SCJ* 14 (1983): 259-82.

Phillips, William D. "Local Integration and Long Distance Ties: the Castilian Community in Sixteenth-Century Bruges." *SCJ* 17 (1986): 33-49.

Pierson, Peter. *Commander of the Armada: The Seventh Duke of Medina Sidonia.* New Haven, 1989.

Pierson, Peter. *Philip II of Spain.* London, 1975.

Pike, Ruth. *Aristocrats and Traders: Sevillian Society in the Sixteenth Century.* Ithaca, N.Y., 1972.

Pinto Crespo, Virgilio. *Inquisición y control ideológico en la España del siglo XVI.* Madrid, 1983.

Prescott, W. H. *The Conquest of Mexico.* London, 1901.

Prescott, W. H. *The Conquest of Peru.* London, 1901.

Prescott, W. H. *History of the Reign of Ferdinand and Isabella.* London, 1837.

Quatrefages, René. *Los tercios españoles 1567-1577.* Madrid, 1979.

Redondo, Augustin. "Luther et l'Espagne de 1520 à 1536." In *Mélanges de la Casa de Velázquez* (1965), vol. 1:109-73.

Ringrose, David. *Madrid and the Spanish Economy 1560-1850*. Berkeley and Los Angeles, 1983.

Rodríguez-Salgado, M. J. *The Changing Face of Empire: Charles V, Philip II and Habsburg Authority, 1551-1559*. Cambridge, 1989.

Rodríguez Sánchez, Angel. *Cáceres: población y comportamientos demográficos en el siglo XVI*. Cáceres, 1977.

Ruíz Martín, Felipe. "Las finanzas españolas durante el reinado de Felipe II." *Cuadernos de Historia* 2 (anexos de Hispania). Madrid, 1968.

Ruíz Martín, Felipe. "Gastos ocasionados por la guerra: repercusiones en España." In *Domanda e Consumi. Livelli e strutture (s. XIII-XVIII)*, ed. Vera Barbagli Bagnoli. Florence, 1978.

Ruíz Martín, Felipe. "Rasgos estructurales de Castilla en tiempos de Carlos V." *Moneda y Crédito* 96 (1966): 91-108.

Rumeu de Armas, Antonio, ed. *Itinerario de los Reyes Católicos 1474-1516*. Biblioteca "Reyes Catolicos," Estudios, no. 15. Madrid, 1974.

Saavedra, Pegerto. *Economía, política y sociedad en Galicia. La provincia de Mondoñedo, 1480-1830*. La Coruña, 1985.

Salomon, Noël. *La vida rural castellana en tiempos de Felipe II*. Trans. Francesco Espinet Burunat. Ensayos Planeta de historia y humanidades, no. 5. Barcelona, 1973.

Saunders, A. C de C. M. *A Social History of Black Slaves and Freedmen in Portugal, 1441-1555*. Cambridge, 1982.

Serra, Eva. "El règim feudal català abans i després de la sentència arbitral de Guadalupe." *Recerques* 10 (1980): 17-32.

Stewart, Paul. "The Soldier, the Bureaucrat, and Fiscal Records in the Army of Ferdinand and Isabella." *HAHR* 49 (1969): 281-92.

Suárez Fernández, Luis, and Manuel Fernández Alvárez. *La España de los Reyes Católicos (1474-1516)*. 2 vols. Vol. 17, *Historia de España*, ed. Ramon Menéndez Pidal. Madrid, 1969.

Tellechea Idigoras, José Ignacio. *El arzobispo Carranza y su tiempo*. 2 vols. Coleccion Historia y pensamiento, vol. 9. Madrid, 1968.

Tellechea Idigoras, José Ignacio. *Tiempos recios. Inquisición y Heterodoxias*. Salamanca, 1977.

Thompson, I. A. A. In *Absolutism in Seventeenth-Century Europe*, ed. J. Miller. Basingstoke, 1990.

Thompson, I. A. A. "Crown and Cortes in Castile, 1590-1665." *Parliaments, Estates and Representation* 2 (1982): 29-45.

Thompson, I. A. A. "The Purchase of Nobility in Castile 1552-1700." *JEEH* 8 (1979): 313-60.

Thompson, I. A. A. "The Rule of the Law in Early Modern Castile." *European History Quarterly* 14 (1984).

Thompson, I. A. A. *War and Government in Habsburg Spain, 1560-1620*. London, 1976.

Ulloa, Modesto. *La Hacienda Real de Castilla en el reinado de Felipe II*. 2d ed. Madrid, 1977.

Vassberg, David. *Land and Society in Golden Age Castile*. Cambridge, 1984.

Vázquez de Prada, V. *Historia económica y social de España. vol.III. Los siglos XVI y XVII*. Madrid, 1978.

Vázquez de Prada, V., ed. *Historia General de España y América*. Vol. 6, *La época de plenitud 1517-1598*. Madrid, 1985.

Vicens Vives, Jaime. "The Administrative Structure of the State in the Sixteenth and Seventeenth Centuries." In *Government in Reformation Europe, 1520-1560*, ed. Henry J. Cohn. London, 1971.

Vicens Vives, Jaime. *Historia crítica de la vida y reinado de Fernando II de Aragón*. Saragossa, 1962.

Vicens Vives, Jaime, ed. *Historia Social de España y América*. 5 vols. Barcelona, 1957.

Weisser, Michael. *The Peasants of the Montes*. Chicago, 1976.

Yun Casalilla, Bartolomé. *Sobre la transición al capitalismo en Castilla: economía y sociedad en Tierra de Campos (1500-1830)*. Valladolid, 1987.

# THE BURGUNDIAN-HABSBURG NETHERLANDS

Hugo de Schepper
(University of Nijmegen)

The post-Carolingian disintegration of authority in the region of the Low Countries initiated a protracted struggle for power among the regions' authorities: on the one hand, the French and German crowns and the Church; on the other, the officials (*scabini*) of rural and (from 1200) urban communities, together with the lesser feudal local lords. In between stood the vassals of the German and the French crowns dukes, counts, and other territorial lords—who in the end emerged as the politically most active authorities.

In the parts of the Low Countries belonging to the German emperor, his suzerainty was reduced to merely symbolic significance by second half of the twelfth century.[1] By contrast, in the French fiefs of Crown-Flanders[2] and Artois, the royal presence endured until the early fifteenth century, and in judicial affairs even longer, while Tournai and the Tournaisis remained French until 1521.[3] The French king defended his rights in Flanders with force and he incorporated Walloon-Flanders (that is, the "governance" of Lille-Douai-Orchies) into the royal domain in 1312. In 1369, following the marriage of the king's youngest son, Duke Philip the Bold (d. 1404) of Burgundy, to Margaret of Male, sole heiress of the count of Flanders, the king restored Walloon-Flanders to the count.

From the thirteenth century onward, the territorial rulers also took advantage of the weakening of the Holy See and of the Western Schism to conclude concordats with each bishop in their respective domains, and gradually the Church's many jurisdictions passed into the hands of the temporal lords. Even earlier, these territorial rulers were expanding at the expense of local seigniories, Imperial or royal subvassals, rural communities, and cities within their lands. The process was enhanced, at least until the fourteenth century, by economic and demographic growth, which heightened the tensions between a relatively static rural society and the new, more dynamic, and rational order of cities and territorial principalities. The cities, for example, drew the surrounding countryside into their orbits, while territorial rulers strove to undermine the influence of the feudal nobility, allodial lords, and local vassals, and thus to increase their own

THE LOW COUNTRIES IN 1555

—————— Dutch provinces

------- Walloon provinces

············· Linguistic boundary

power. The territorial rulers exercised various kinds of power and influence over the cities, notwithstanding urban autonomies.

## 1. LAND AND CROWN

Working along the estuary of the Rhine, Meuse/Maas, and Scheldt rivers, the Low Countries' great axis of communications, during the fourteenth and fifteenth centuries the Burgundian dukes of the French royal house of Valois brought a large number of these territories, peripheral fiefs of France or the Empire, into a personal union which straddled state and linguistic borders.

### Territorial Formation of the Burgundian State

The process began with the marriage of Philip the Bold to Margaret of Male, through which the county of Flanders—including Walloon Flanders—the neighboring county of Artois, the seigniory of Mechelen and the counties of Burgundy (the Franche-Comté) and Nevers came to the duchy of Burgundy after the death in 1384 of Margaret's father, Lodewijk of Male. Three years later, Philip also acquired the usufruct of the duchy of Limbourg-on-the-Vesder and the Landen van Overmaas, of which he gained full possession in 1396. Through the marriage of Philip's daughter, Margaret, to the later count of Holland, Zeeland, and Hainaut these territories also become part of the Burgundian sphere of influence.

The political murder in 1419 of John the Fearless, Philip's son, prompted his son and successor, Philip the Good (d. 1467), to side openly with the English king against the king of France and to use the Anglo-Burgundian alliance to add new territories to his lands. In 1433 he forced his niece, Countess Jacoba of Bavaria, to cede to him the principalities of Holland, Zeeland and Hainaut. A few years earlier he had acquired Brabant upon the extinction of the Burgundian house's younger line in 1430. He also purchased right of succession to the childless ruler of Namur, who died in 1429. Finally, in 1441 Philip bought from the childless Elizabeth of Görlitz the succession to Luxembourg, which passed into his sovereignty in 1451. This remarkable achievement quite justifies the honorific title of "founder of the Netherlands" (conditor Belgii), which the historians have awarded to Philip the Good.

Philip's son and successor, Charles the Bold (d. 1477), sought to realize his father's dream of an independent middle kingdom between France and the Empire. He abandoned the cautious French policy, which his father had pursued after the Peace of Arras (1435), and renewed the anti-French alliance through his marriage in 1468 to Margaret of York, sister of England's King Edward IV. His conquest in 1475 of the duchy of Lorraine, an Imperial fief, supplied a convenient bridge between the Burgundian and Netherlandish parts of his patrimony, which were increasingly referred to as the "lands over there" ("Landen van derwaerts overe," "Païs de par dela") and the "lands over here" ("Landen van herwaerts overe," "Païs de par deça"), that is, the Netherlands. A few years earlier he secured recognition as heir to Arnold of Egmont, duke of Guelders and count of Zutphen, on whose death he succeeded to both lands. At the height of his power, however, Charles was slain fighting a hostile coalition in the Battle of Nancy (January 1477). The loss of Lorraine and the subsequent French conquest of the duchy of Burgundy definitely made the "Low Countries" ("Nyderlande," "Païs d'embas") the center of the Burgundian empire.

Charles the Bold's great-grandson, Charles of Ghent, succeeded to the rule (as Charles I) of the Spanish realms in 1516, along with their dependencies in Italy and in the New World, and (as Charles V) to that of Holy Roman Empire of the German Nation in 1519. Charles also continued his Burgundian ancestors' territorial policy in the Low Countries. Not only did he add the French fief of Tournai and the Tournaisis (1521), but he also incorporated the Imperial fiefs of Friesland (1524), Overijssel and Utrecht (1528), Drenthe, and Groningen and the Ommelanden (1536) into the Netherlandish patrimony. With his conquest of Guelders-Zutphen in 1543—the Burgundian occupations of 1473-74 and 1481-92 had not lasted—he completed what history knows as the unification of the Seventeen Provinces. The prince-bishopric of Liège (with the county of Loon), which cut off Luxembourg and Limbourg from the other provinces was never Netherlandish between 1477, when the Burgundian guardianship over Liège was revoked, and 1815.

### Independence and Unification

Duke Philip the Bold had been first and foremost "son of the king of France" ("filz de Roy de France"). He ruled from Paris with the aid of councillors drawn from the French royal administration. He seems to have envisaged not a permanent and separate union of his territories, but rather a dynastic power linked to that of France. His son and successor, John the Fearless, had great difficulties maintaining himself in the factional struggles in France, which culminated in his tragic murder on the bridge of Montereau. From that point onward, his successors, though legally still vassals of France, behaved more and more independently. Philip the Good was the first to view his lands as a power unto themselves and to put his regime on a solid financial footing. Since 1430 the duke of Burgundy had his titles preceded by the formula, "by the grace of God" ("Bi der gracien Gods," or "Par la grasce de Dieu"), presumably to express his independence. Philip the Good settled his differences with the French king in 1435 by recognizing Charles VII as his "souverain seigneur," while the king, in satisfaction for his father's assassination, freed Philip of his feudal obligations. This royal concession sealed the transition to a Burgundian state independent of France.[4]

Although the dukes held part of their lands from the Empire, they only rarely pledged fealty to its emperor. In practice they acted as free allodial proprietors, a stance which their provincial estates supported. In Brabant and Limburg-Overmaas the Burgundians indisputably possessed immunity, according to the Golden Bull of 1349, and only in Namur and Luxembourg did the emperor on occasion display some judicial activity.[5] The formal end of both French and Imperial jurisdiction over the Low Countries came under Charles V, who in 1521-22 declared all the sentences and ordinances of the French crown to be invalid in the Netherlands. The treaty of Madrid (1526) and the Peace of Cateau-Cambrésis (1529) removed any lingering doubt by forcing Francis I of France to renounce all his feudal rights and all claims of sovereignty over the former Netherlandish fiefs of France.

Concerning the Empire, in his capacity as "supreme lord of the Netherlands" Charles V declared that the Netherlandish provinces had been "free from Imperial practices and customs" since time immemorial. At Augsburg in 1548, with consent of the Imperial Diet he withdrew the Netherlands provinces from the Westphalian Circle and placed them in a new "Nedererflandse" or Burgundian Circle. The emperor thus lost the remainder of his judicial and regulatory authority over the Netherlands. By 1550, therefore, the Netherlandish rulers' old ties of vassalage to their respective liege lords in France and in the Empire had been completely transformed into bilateral relations between sovereigns.

The process of separation and consolidation of the Netherlands also affected the church. Apart from the rights over the church (iura circa sacra) that they inherited from their royal predecessors, the Burgundian and Habsburg rulers also acquired the right to nominate bishops and abbots in the Netherlands. Through their good relationship with the Holy See they often managed to fill neighboring episcopal sees with their own supporters. From the late fifteenth century onward ecclesiastical pronouncements were even subjected to the royal "placet." By agreement with Paul IV in

1559, the Netherlands acquired their own episcopal hierarchy with a primatial see.[6] The dukes nonetheless tried to maintain the Holy See's favor by not tampering with its jurisdiction. With respect to the prosecution of heretics, for example, a formal compromise was struck in 1524, according to which the church's inquisitors were to seek out and interrogate persons of suspect orthodoxy, while decisions about guilt and punishment were left to royal judges.

### The Idea of the Netherlands

Their pursuit of independence for the Low Countries notwithstanding, neither the Valois dukes of Burgundy nor their Habsburg successors ever acquired a common royal title for all the provinces. Initially the "Landen van herwaerts overe" were no more than a union of principalities under one sovereign, and for some time the separate lands could continue to conduct their own foreign policies, wage war, and conclude treaties, and each land retained its own legal systems. The ruler's separate titles for his principalities were listed one by one in the *suscriptio* of solemn acts: "Duke of Brabant, Count of Flanders, of Holland, etc.; Lord of Friesland, of Mechelen, etc." Although the idea was discussed, the Burgundian rulers never acquired a royal title. The closest they came was in the autumn 1473 at Trier, when Charles the Bold's expectation of being crowned king by Frederick III was frustrated by the emperor's mysteriously abrupt departure. In any case, Duke Charles could not accept the emperor's demand that territories of the Burgundian realm should remain Imperial fiefs. Moreover, his ambition to accede to the Imperial throne someday was considered dangerous.

Gradually the personal union was supplemented by a sense of Burgundian unity, an awareness of a commonwealth centered around the person of the duke. Since Philip the Good's time, this sense was promoted both by ducal propaganda and by the dukes' practice of consulting their provincial estates. They and their Habsburg successors succeeded in having themselves accepted as "natural prince" ("natuurlijcke prince," "prince naturel") and as the embodiment of the "chose publicque," which under Charles the Bold's daughter, Mary of Burgundy (d. 1482), came to be called the common fatherland ("gemeynen lande onser genediger Juffrouw herwerts over" and somewhat later "Patria"). Even though the Seventeen Provinces remained constitutionally a confederation, official documents called the Burgundian-Habsburg rulers "prince van herwertsovere," "prince de pardecha" and "princeps Belgii"—expressions of their sense of unity. The provincial parliamentary assemblies supported this sense by declaring ever and again their wish to continue collaborating with the other Netherlandish provinces. There were particularist reactions, to be sure, and even a few revolts (notably in Ghent), but no one involved in them renounced loyalty to the prince or his dynasty. Despite the wave of particularism which followed the death of Charles the Bold, for example, the States General immediately called for a general mobilization to defend the Burgundian dynasty against a French invasion. They also gave swift approval to Charles V's Pragmatic Sanction of 1549, which introduced a unified dynastic law of succession, declaring the Netherlandish territory "forever one and indivisible."

The persistence of various kinds of ideological, social, provincial, and local autonomies did not contradict the growing sense of "national" unity and solidarity in the Netherlands. During the early stages of the revolt against Philip II, when particularism was strong indeed, the States General offered the Duke of Anjou not the titles of duke and count of the various provinces, but that of "Prince et Seigneur des Païs Bas." In these years the Beggars of Brabant, Holland, Flanders and Zeeland sang with full voice about the Netherlands not in the plural but in the singular: "Netherland, watch your affairs" ("Nederlandt let op uw saeck") or about "Netherland, our earthly garden" ("Nederlant, ons aerts prieel"). Marnix van St. Aldegonde, the presumed composer of the "Wilhelmus Lied," has his fellow-Brabanter, William of Orange, utter the line, "Oh noble sweet Netherland" ("O edel Nederlant soet"). Political declarations and pamphlets appealed to "all patriots who love liberty and the preservation of their country" ("tous patriotes aymans la liberté et conservation de leur patrie"). Certainly from the mid-sixteenth century onward the terms "Nederlanden" and "'t Nederlan(d)t" were commonly used as alternatives. This usage also appeared in French. In 1558 a posthumously published French translation of "Historia de Statu Belgico deque Religione Hispanica" by Françoys du Chesne (a pseudonym for Francisco de Enzinas [d. 1552]) appeared under the title "Histoire de l'Estat *du* Païs Bas et de la Religion d'Espagne." Then, too, in the French version of his historical chronicle Gilbert Roy (1540-83/84) employed the term "Païs bas" both in the plural and in the singular but with a clear preference for singular forms: "le Païs bas", "au Païs bas" and "du Pays-bas." He and various other authors still used "Flandre(s)", "Provinces Belgiques" and "nostre païs Belgique" as synonyms. In cartography the singular forms were clearly preferred over plural ones, both in Netherlandish and in French. The cultivation of the native language by Renaissance poets and the writing of national histories by humanist historiographers also indicated an

emerging sense of belonging to the Netherlandish state of "Belgica" or
"Belgium." In sum, there was a growing identification with the state as
distinct from existing regional and local loyalties. Similar testimonies continue until the end of the seventeenth century and are so numerous and so
passionate that they can scarcely be called into question.[7]

## 2. Administrative and Judicial Organization and Methods

Although the courts (*curiae*) of the former principalities continued to function under the Burgundian regime, their personnel underwent an important transformation. Initially, they were staffed by feudal nobles and prelates, and few of their members possessed an academic training in Roman
and canon law. But the increasingly technical and complex task, of making sovereignty effective in a country undergoing enormous expansion required a professionally trained corps of judges and officials of a new, educated type. Legal education also promoted the spirit of obedience and
deference required by the new vertical relation of ruler to subject, so different from feudalism's contractual relationships. The recruitment of professional jurists from bourgeois and noble backgrounds by the Burgundian
dukes, and more consistently by their Habsburg successors, gradually
transformed the courts of the previously independent principalities in the
sense of a professionalization and rationalization.[8]

### Administrative Centralization

The more numerous the coordinating institutions became, the more the
various principalities were viewed as provinces of the new state, and the
more the old provincial *curiae* functioned as delegated departments and
extensions of the sovereign and his court. They became, in effect, provincial *consilia* holding an intermediate position in the pyramid of administrative and judicial bodies. Like all other princely officials, the members of his
councils could be transferred and dismissed at will, since they were appointed by or in name of the ruler "as long as it will please us" ("soo
langhe alst ons gelieven sal"). The result was a striking degree of mobility
for officials and magistrates, many of whom started in local government
and, via appointments in various provinces, worked their way up to the
highest levels of princely service, despite the privileges that restricted offices to natives of a given province. All officials were personally accountable to the prince for all the documents they drew up. By 1530 the older
elites, feudal nobles and prelates, had disappeared from such councils, at

least in the economically most developed provinces of Brabant, Holland, Flanders, and Zeeland. Such councillors naturally opposed the fragmentation of traditional law and promoted the incorporation of principles and rules from learned law into local customary laws.

### The Central Conciliar Regime

The creation of a central government organized on the conciliar principle proceeded more from practical considerations than from a deliberate policy of unification and centralization. After having governed for a time from Paris, the dukes of Burgundy gradually began to gather around themselves a chancellor for all the provinces and an informal itinerant Court Council of twelve councillors-chamberlains, whose composition depended on the circumstances. For reasons of *Realpolitik* the dukes selected their advisors from the ever-influential old Walloon, Luxembourg, Limbourg and Brabant feudal nobility. When these advisors resided at the court, they assisted the duke in the administration of justice and the formulation of his policy, in domestic, foreign, and military affairs. Since, the prince's council also had judicial functions, professional jurists, called "masters-of-requests," were added to the noble members. Because of its size the body came to be called the "Grand Council." Gradually, the duke restricted the nobles' influence by appointing urban patricians and bourgeois to the key positions of chancellor, president of the Court Council, and officials of the chancellery. The Burgundian and Habsburg rulers increasingly relied on these salaried officials, men from the new social, cultural, and political elites, who were highly ambitious and eager to make their career in princely service. They came, for the most part, from the economically and demographically most important provinces.

After 1440 the jurists began to form a separate and more-or-less permanent structure, called the "Council of Justice," within the Grand Council. Taking the French system as a model, Charles the Bold on 8 December 1473, elevated the Council of Justice into a sovereign Parlement of Mechelen with jurisdiction over all of his lands. The Parlement was the forerunner of the later Grand Council at Mechelen (*Grant Conseil arresté à Malines*), which in late 1501 was separated from the still itinerant Grand Council accompanying the prince (*Grant Conseil lez le Prince*). Originally, the central Council of Justice was a court for reserved cases which could not be tried by the benches of aldermen, feudal courts, or provincial councils of justice, as, for example, when foreigners were involved, or in case of denial of justice. From 1469 onward, it functioned also as the highest court of appeal against civil sentences from lower courts in lands of the

dukes of Burgundy, including the Franche-Comté. From the registers of
sentences, however, it is apparent that the Council also tried in the first instance suits for which other courts were competent.[9]

By an ordinance of 22 January 1504, Archduke Philip the Handsome
(d. 1506), Charles V's father, recognized the existence of two bodies
within the Court Council, the Grand Council at Mechelen and the Grand
Council accompanying the ruler. Meanwhile, overall government policy
("les grans et secres affaires") was more and more determined by an informal group of five nobles and jurists, who were summoned on an ad hoc
basis. Already under Philip the Good this group met sporadically and was
referred to in the sources as "le conseil secret et privé." Within the framework of the Prince's Grand Council (*Grant Conseil lez le Prince*) it was institutionalized into a permanent structure called the "Privy Council,"
which since 1517 was entitled to deal with "matters of favor (*matières de
grasce*)" and with "extraordinary justice" or matters "outside of the ordinary train of justice."

In practice, the Grand Council as Court Council and the Grand Council
following the ruler gradually lost their importance. They were superseded
by three independent "collateral councils," the Council of State, the Privy
Council, and the Council of Finance, all of which sat in the old palace of
the dukes of Brabant on the Koudenberg in Brussels, which was converted
into the permanent princely residence and seat of government. Noble
members of the Privy Council were from 1531 incorporated into a separate Council of State, which, according to protocol, as senior collateral
council had to advise the sovereign or his regent with regard to "les grans
et principaulx affaires," especially in matters concerning war and peace.[10]
The Privy Council continued to dispense "extraordinary justice," functioning as the highest court of revision for judgments of the Grand Council and
of the provincial courts, especially those of the Franche-Comté (Parlement
of Dole), Brabant, and Hainaut, whose sentences had been declared (1515)
to be "sovereign," meaning no further appeal was possible. When
Guelders-Zutphen was acquired in 1543, its court also received permission
to render judgments without appeal. The submission of these courts to revision ("propositie van erreur") by the Privy Council for procedural errors
was thus the last and only possibility for redress. The Privy Council was
also closely involved in the nomination of councillors, fiscal officers, and
procurators-general in the provincial councils; it could authorize, by virtue
of the princely right of "grace," all sorts of deviations from the common
law, and it could also interfere extra-judicially in any trial before any other
court. Finally, the Privy Council helped to formulate and then translate the

will of the sovereign or his regent into juridical language; in other words, it issued general regulations.

By means of this hierarchization of institutions, the Burgundian rulers and Charles V created favorable conditions for judicial unity. The more central governmental councils and officials were able to impose sentences and obligations on both natural and fictive persons, the more the Netherlands evolved from a confederate to a federal state, a stage which was reached in fact between 1517 and 1531. From then on Brussels truly was the "princely capital of the Netherland."

### The Unification of Law

Despite Renaissance political theories in which the "king as source of law" (*rex lex*) received great attention, the Burgundian and Habsburg rulers probably stimulated the formation of the Netherlandish state most strongly by exercising their prerogatives as "king-judge" (*rex iudex*) through councils and courts. To Charles the Bold proper justice was "the soul and spirit of the public weal" ("l'ame et l'esprit de la chose publicque"). Although the provincial and central courts accounted for the lion's share of sentences and administrative decisions, they derived their competencies from the sovereign, they represented him in the provinces, and they decided and administered justice in his name.

As supreme judge the sovereign penetrated into lower echelons of the law by introducing new procedures, which were more rational and sophisticated, and thus more uniform and efficient, than the traditional ones. Influenced by the procedural rules then in force in ecclesiastical courts and in the Parlement of Paris, the dukes of Burgundy from the outset promoted the introduction of appeal procedures which, following a new trial, permitted modification or cancellation of sentences pronounced by urban and rural aldermen, by local and regional feudal courts, and by other traditional law courts, all of which administered justice according to unwritten customary law. Appeals of this nature were in keeping with the traditional customary law procedures of arbitration and suit of court (*hoofdvaart*),[11] which they supplanted fairly smoothly.

Other new techniques, whereby Burgundian-Habsburg subjects could seek redress at princely courts, included evocation, whereby a case being tried by a lower court was transferred to a higher court, and a procedure analogous to the French legal institution of *prevention*, whereby the first court before which suit was brought was deemed to have competence in the first instance. Thus, princely courts not only had appellate jurisdiction in the realm of civil law, but as early as 1450 they also competed with the customary courts by trying cases in the first instance, the previously uncontested competence of other courts notwithstanding.  It is obvious that increasing resort to princely justice would permit both procedural principles and material law to find their way from learned jurisprudence into customary law, especially in cases of lacunae, ambiguities, or conflicts in the latter.  Lawyers would also appeal to learned law whenever it suited their clients' interests.  The increasing supplementary and explanatory use of learned law, which stemmed from the increasingly professionalized administration of justice, tended to create a growing legal uniformity.  The process was reinforced by the general transition from an oral to a scribal culture.

Initially, there was no thought of issuing common regulations for all the territories under Burgundian sovereignty.  As heirs of the pre-Burgundian *curiae*, the provincial councils continued to draw up and issue general regulations for their territories, in some cases in consultation with the provincial estates.  The councils themselves represented their territory in a more permanent way against the new sovereign than the estates did.  And though the prince could not yet claim to be supreme and sole legislator, he attempted by degrees to assume such powers.

Once he became *de facto* sovereign—and potentially a king—Philip the Good introduced since about 1440 a new dimension: the proclamation of statutory law valid for all of his possessions, giving precedence to matters involving domains, finances and mint ordinances.  In the matter of coinage, standard silver and gold units were introduced for all provinces, with parities fixed at the request of the estates and if necessary adjusted on a regular basis.  The procedure was to have identical ordinances and placards issued in each province by the provincial council, which also had to give its approval in the form of registration and attachment of its "briefven van attache."  Thus, the duke could impose a uniform law, while symbolically respecting provincial particularism.[12]  Clearly, the "general well-being," to which such ordinances refer, was being equated with the "sovereignty" of the monarch.

Before the end of the fifteenth century, the political functions of the provincial councils were taken over by central bodies.  The Court Council and after 1517 the Privy Council in particular formulated carefully considered and well-thought-out edicts, ordinances, and placards, plus other general administrative measures valid for all provinces.  In principle, the prince had the final decision, but as he was often abroad, he normally delegated this authority to his regent at the court of the Netherlands.[13]  Since customary law did not lend itself to dealing with relations crossing local or provincial boundaries, from the reign of Charles V onward the Habsburg monarch also intervened in its codification. In August and October 1531, Charles V issued his famous ordinances prescribing the systematic recording of local and regional customs in the whole country in order to create greater legal security by means of a written common law: from now on, the interpretation of legal customs was explicitly reserved to his councils.[14]

## 3. SUBJECTS

Around 1470 the territories that would later constitute the Seventeen Provinces contained 2.6 million souls, 34% of whom lived in the cities of Flanders, Brabant with Mechelen, and Holland. By this time they had nearly recovered from the collapse at the time of Black Death, which between 1350 and 1370 had probably reduced the population by about one-third. In the dynamic commercial and industrial cities, the collapse had been strongly countered by an influx of rural migrants and by the depopulation of some of the old-fashioned cloth towns. Meanwhile, the general fall of rural population—except where manufacturing had settled, led to a partial conversion of arable land into pasture. It also promoted a significant improvement in quality and greater diversity of agricultural production, as well as a fairly general rise in the standard of living. Over the long run wages showed a substantial increase. These trends continued until around 1470. Twenty years before, around 1450, the demographic level of 1350 had almost been restored, though thereafter a series of plagues and wars led to new demographic regressions until about 1485.

During the first half of the sixteenth century, the annual growth of Netherlandish populations ranged from 0.25% to 1.28%, depending on the region. The highest rates occurred in provinces deeply involved in the expanding maritime economy and intercontinental trade—Brabant, Holland, and Flanders, once again—where the urban proportion rose from an already high level of 34% during the fifteenth century to around 45%. The process of rapid growth, which Flanders had experienced during the thirteenth century, repeated itself in Holland and Brabant during the first half of the sixteenth, when population density and urbanization attained levels unparalleled in Europe, except for northern Italy. Around 1550 the lion's share of some 3 million Netherlanders lived within this expanding economic region, the boom provinces plus Zeeland, in which thirteen of the fifteen largest cities lay. Flanders, Brabant, and Holland alone accounted for 2 million people. Between 1400 and 1520 some cities in Holland, notably Haarlem, Delft, Gouda, Amsterdam, Rotterdam, and Leiden, were able to double their population. In Antwerp the population within the city walls increased from 15,000 in 1437 to 39,000 in 1526, when the city as a whole had between 57,000 and 63,000 inhabitants, and it rose further to 89,000 in 1566. In Europe north of the Alps, only Paris and London had larger populations at this time. Some cities owed their population growth to the opportunities offered by the expansion and bureaucratization of princely and urban officialdom. The population of Brussels and Mons doubled, for example, while that of The Hague, legally a village without urban privileges, quadrupled.[15]

### Core and Periphery

The urban merchants generally did well from this wave of economic expansion. In several cities, notably Antwerp and Amsterdam, foreign trade and shipping created an influential group of extremely affluent traders. Urban merchants controlled both their own city governments and the estates of the provinces most deeply involved in the burgeoning commerce and, therefore, politically most influential. These provinces, with their large concentrations of capital and production, often bolstered by rural areas having domestic linen industries, represented some two-thirds of Netherlandish capital. In manufacturing, small capitalist enterprises— usually under ten employees—were replacing the traditional structures, and although larger units were known, especially in textiles, brewing, and metals, they remained the exception.[16]

The upswing made some and ruined others, as formerly independent artisans were transformed into poor dependent workers to swell the industrial proletariat. This was so because wages lagged significantly behind grain prices and also behind rents, which rural emigration and higher natality were pushing upward. The rural folk found their incomes undermined by rising rents, though some found supplemental income in the new rural linen industry. The countryside also had all sorts of small domestic industries for local consumption, such as brickyards, potteries, and limekilns.[17]

Brabant, Holland, and Flanders led the way; the growth of cities in the Walloon provinces and in the eastern periphery from Friesland to Luxemburg was more modest, perhaps half the level of the richer provinces. In the peripheral provinces, cities were mostly small and widely dispersed, and, unlike the northwestern region, in such lands as Limburg-on-the-Vesder, Luxemburg, and the Walloon provinces, the clergy and the upper nobility were able to maintain their traditional social and political status. These regions, except for the pockets of mining, remained predominantly agricultural. Overall industrial production in Hainaut and Artois, for example, was six times lower than in Flanders and Brabant. The cheap, light draperies in centers such as Arras, Mons, Tournai, and Valenciennes sank into oblivion beside those of southwest Flanders. In Guelders, too, the feudal nobility managed to hold its own. In the sixteenth century three-quarters of rural Tournaisis was ecclesiastical property, while in Friesland and the Ommelanden of Groningen the church held a fifth to a quarter of the land. The five cathedral chapters of Utrecht occupied a strategic position in the economy and the politics of that province. In Guelders, Limburg, and Overmaas the old nobility and monasteries employed countless peasants. Some cities in Overijssel belonged to the Hanseatic League, but from about 1400 these towns lost out to the trading centers of Holland, because of the ever-deteriorating navigability of the IJssel River. Nobles were especially important in Salland and Twente, where they held about 30% of the land. The other eastern and far northern regions also had an agricultural character, though Friesland, Groningen, and Drenthe (unlike Guelders, Overijssel, Limburg-Overmaas, Luxembourg, and the Walloon provinces) had never been feudalized. In these regions, well-to-do farmers and monasteries were in control.[18]

Since there was great potential for conflict between the verdicts and regulations made by seigniorial and other local authorities and the judicial and administrative practice of the central government Burgundian and Habsburg princes had good reasons to seek to bring local courts under their control. This does not mean that the two levels, princely and local, were mutually incompatible, for often they complemented one another. The introduction of central and provincial courts and new legal procedures, for example, often served the subjects better than did the courts of customary law, for they provided a higher degree of professional competence, speedier settlement of law suits, more objectivity, security, and wider legal validity of judicial verdicts. The new central structure was also more transparent—easier to understand—than the labyrinth of traditional feudal, rural, and ecclesiastical courts, whose jurisdictions and procedures were often difficult to disentangle. For all such reasons, litigants increasingly resorted to princely courts of justice, especially as their trade relations increasingly crossed local, regional and even national borders. The explosive growth of princely justice during the sixteenth century, therefore, cannot be explained by population growth and territorial expansion alone, for the parties to a suit not only recognized princely competence to interpret legal customs and privileges, their very actions expanded his jurisdiction. Persons, both natural and fictive, brought their complaints as close as they could to the source of all law, and this not only on appeal but also in the first and last resorts as well. Litigants were not overly concerned about provincial or local privileges.[19]

A few exceptions aside, the hundreds of small allodial enclaves in the region's northwestern (and economically most highly developed) sector lost their autonomy quite early; they were accepting integration in the Burgundian-Habsburg regime. Vassals were no less obliged to execute the will of the sovereign than were the princes' own officials. In addition to judicial rights, local lords initially retained the right "de pooir faire et faire faire . . . toutes manières de status et ordonnances." The duke of Burgundy nonetheless reserved for himself the "declaracion et interpretacion" of disputes relating to the exercise of these prerogatives. In the end, seigniorial courts ceased issuing general ordinances or statutes, except to adapt—in consultation with local aldermen—regulations of the Habsburg sovereign to local circumstances.

Cities, too, failed to preserve the exceptional position they enjoyed in the pre-Burgundian period. According to the traditional common law, no further judicial appeal was possible against the verdicts of their aldermen. By means of their appellate functions, however, the princely provincial councils of justice were to end this state of affairs during the first half of the fifteenth century. It was the same all over, and by 1500 both the more important rural courts and urban benches of aldermen lost their competencies as "head courts of justice" to hear and determine appeals from rural benches of aldermen, polder and dike boards, and other lower tribunals. Thus, the new appellate procedure brought all local and regional magistracies in Brabant, Mechelen, Holland, Flemish Flanders, and Zeeland in civil and feudal affairs under direct review by jurisdiction of the sovereign. Although their criminal judgments continue to be unappealable ("confessus non appellat"), the prince was able to intervene in this sphere, too, through several forms of his right of grace. Subjects often petitioned for pardon, and the prince repeatedly granted such requests in order to establish his authority.

Urban courts of the pre-Burgundian period had developed their own written law in order to supplement legal customs and privileges and adjusted them to the circumstances of the time, generally under the license of the territorial lord or his local officer of justice, or sheriff. The latter was also responsible for the promulgation of urban legislation and made sure that the urban benches of aldermen did not violate princely prerogatives.

Indeed, urban ordinances were frequently published in the name of the ruler so as to make them more effective, so that after 1500 urban and rural aldermen imposed legal rules only in as far as they did not infringe on the law as ordered by the sovereign of the Netherlands or by his councils. The aldermen, in effect, conformed to the principle that the ruler was the supreme and sole legislator, who in the sixteenth century issued 76% of all legislative actions, while the provincial councils, whose law-making authority had been transferred to central bodies, accounted for a mere 5%, and all other authorities combined for 19%.[20] Local legislation, its role now reduced to adjusting general rules to local circumstances, thus came to contribute to the growth of the very centralization which it was intended to curb.

In Habsburg times, more than half of princely legislation concerned the institutional organization of the government, the preservation of public order and safety, the persecution of "heretics," and other areas of criminal law. Princely regulations dealt also with tax affairs, monetary policy and the maintenance of dikes, dunes, bridges and roads. Material private law received little attention, despite the fact that command law now took precedence over customary law in this sphere as well. Whole areas remained virtually neglected unless the matter involved had repercussions on public life, as in the case of letters of exchange, usurious practices, marital affairs, and possessory disputes.[21]

Yet, these developments were restricted to the urbanized provinces along the great rivers, while the sovereign's jurisdiction expanded very little in the Walloon and eastern provinces.[22] Here public authority remained fragmented, largely controlled by feudal nobles, allodial lords, large landowners, chapters and abbeys. In the periphery allodial lordships were numerous and they more or less preserved their independence, while maintaining their traditional, symbolic ties to the distant Empire or French crown. Customary fragmentation also remained in peripheral provinces, where the static agricultural societies had far less need of princely legislation and administration of justice than did the urbanized societies based on a monetary economy. Not only did local and regional courts continue to function as courts of appeal in feudal, civil, and criminal cases, but feudal and customary *curiae* of the previously independent territories displayed considerable activity, much as they had before the incorporation of these territories by the Burgundian and Habsburg rulers. Although these territories could not develop an independent foreign policy, they did not enter into a federal relationship with the Netherlands government.

*Participation of subjects*

The Burgundian dynasty's assumption of power also was associated with the appearance of parliamentary assemblies in several provinces: higher clergy, the upper nobility, and the representatives of the cities were held to represent the respective populations. This tripartite organization of estates obtained only in Brabant, Flemish Flanders, Zeeland, Utrecht, Artois, Hainaut, Namur, and Luxembourg. In Namur and Hainaut only the cities of Namur and Mons participated in the provincial estates, in which they carried little weight. In other principalities, such as Holland, the assemblies consisted of only two estates, the lesser nobles (seigniorial lords, banner lords, knights) or the large landowners (gentlemen-farmers) and the cities. In the provinces of the eastern and northern periphery from Guelders to Friesland, the parliamentary assemblies—called *Landdagen*— were organized on the basis of geographical quarters as well as on more familiar ideas of legal and social status.[23] The more the cities determined the relations of production and the economic order of the surrounding countryside, the more urban political influence in the parliamentary assemblies of the core provinces grew at the expense of the two other estates, the clergy and the nobility. In Flemish Flanders the tune was called by the "Four Members", that is, the cities of Ghent, Ypres, and Bruges and the large landowners of the rural district of the Franc of Bruges.[24]

Over the centuries, clergy, nobility, and cities had seized or acquired various "liberties and privileges" which were recognized by the Burgundian and Habsburg sovereigns at their accession, though they were gradually being undermined by the transition from a feudal society to the modern state. The estates attempted to preserve their rights and autonomy, causing tensions or even conflicts, in which they could turn to their advantage the ruler's inability to live from his domainial revenues. Whether privileges were respected depended less on the law than on fluctuations in the actual balance of power and/or the needs of the moment.[25] Privileges could also become less important over the course of time. Both the cities and the provincial estates, traditionally defenders of privileges and customary rights, respected or ignored them at their convenience. Privileges against appeals (*ius de non appellando et de non evocando*) notwithstanding, they repeatedly haled their own citizens before royal councils of justice in order to seek redress, for instance, when confronted themselves with defaulters, insolvent revenue collectors, or reluctant taxpayers.

The provincial estates were summoned by the Burgundian-Habsburg ruler in order to hear his requests (*beden*, *aides*) for financial assistance. From 1464 on they were also asked to send their delegates to the States

General, where the participants gradually realized their community of interests, though decisions continued to be made by the provincial estates
alone. The sovereign's financial need gave them a powerful means of leverage, not only for extracting political concessions, but also for gaining
participation in governmental decision-making. In exchange for their financial cooperation in the growth of the state, the government undertook
not to declare war, conclude peace, issue mint ordinances, or change the
existing customary law without their approval. Their financial dependence on the estates was the main reason that Burgundian-Habsburg rulers
never succeeded in acquiring the *plenitudo potestatis* of which learned jurists spoke. On the other hand, the estates never acquired the right to legis-
late. The Netherlands was thus quite unlike the classical mixed monarchies, in which legislation required the consent of a representative body.
The Netherlandish parliamentary assemblies nevertheless managed to develop into quasi-permanent deliberative bodies for the enactment of rules
of general import.[26]

Eighty per cent of all the general ordinances and placards issued by the
governments of Charles V and Philip II responded to request by subjects,
natural persons as well as cities, crafts, guilds, and even the provincial estates.[27] The growing preference for a written, more rational law of general
validity was bolstered by the humanist mentality that was diffused among
members of a relatively large educated stratum, and also by the economic
needs of the most active provinces. It comes as no surprise that the majority of petitions to the government came from the commercial and maritime
provinces, or that most ordinances of general import were issued on their
behalf. If the enforcement of royal decrees sometimes left much to be desired, it was because the decrees themselves sometimes showed little sense
of reality, for instance the placards against the Protestants, the mint ordinances and the ordinances prohibiting trade with the enemy despite economic necessities. Even in a post-medieval society, it was still difficult to
entrench an independent system of law in the practice of everyday life.

## 4. "Economy" and "Commerce"

Although the sovereignty of the Burgundian ruler was indivisible, a separate professional and specialized hierarchy of structures and offices was
gradually established for the "economy," independent of the official apparatus mainly concerned with "justice" and its derivatives, "police" and
"pardon." The separation was not absolute, and certain institutions and

officials in the area of "police" and "justice" were also accountable for the revenues from the administration of justice. "Economy" in this sense referred to the royal household, that is, the sovereign's personal fortune.

## The Princes' Revenues

It was only under Charles the Bold that the notion of "public finances" took a definite shape. Domainial revenues included the natural proceeds of landed properties dispersed over all provinces, plus their associated seigniorial rights and corvées, such as fishing and hunting rights. To the domain also pertained all revenues which were originally "regalia": revenues from Imperial and royal rights, including road and river tolls, ferry rights, mint prerogatives and rights deriving from feudal allegiance.

Domainial revenues were seriously affected by the steady deterioration of the agricultural economy, and by the devaluation of the money of account in which domainial rights were expressed. The mortgage of parts of the domain, rare during the fifteenth century, became common under Philip the Handsome and Charles V, who mortgaged their lands on a large scale to the big cities and to the Italian and South German merchant-bankers residing in the Netherlands. When credit became too expensive, sixteenth century rulers, especially Philip II, even resorted to the sale of domains. But such devices were not sufficient to cover increasing state expenditures on ceremony, palaces and court life, and military expeditions and the general armament of the country, nor to pay administrative expenses and official salaries.[28] Even in the pre-Burgundian period, territorial rulers had already looked to their vassals for an increasing share of their revenues. The steady growth of government expenditures caused by the expansion of the civil bureaucracy and the maintenance of a mercenary army equipped with ever-more sophisticated weapons forced the Burgundian-Habsburg rulers to turn time and again to their subjects. Fairly soon the subsidies, initially requested only on occasion, came to be levied on a routine basis; the estates could refuse "extraordinary" aides, but not what were now called "ordinary" aides. Thus, the "aides" evolved from an extraordinary into an ordinary source of income.

Exactly when revenues from subsidies came to surpass those from the prince's domains is difficult to say, but probably it was already the case under the later Burgundians and certainly under Charles V and Philip II. In 1394-96 the ordinary subsidies barely represent 20% (81,500 lb. t. [= Tournai pounds]) of the gross revenues (412,730 lb. t.), but a century later the volume of the ordinary subsidies granted had increased threefold, whereas nominal salaries increased a mere 20%. While just prior to 1400 the Crown domains accounted for three-quarters (248,540 lb. t.) of the ruler's ordinary revenues (330,040 lb. t.), after 1531 the subsidies sometimes constituted up to 85% of ordinary revenues.[29]

### Centralization of Finance

Centralization of domains and financial administration began early. Philip the Bold installed a receiver-general of all finances over the receivers-general for Flanders-Artois and Bourgogne-Franche Comté, and as new lands were acquired, their former receivers-general become provincial officials under the receiver-general of all finances, who centralized the balances of their revenues and expenditures and also kept account of the expenditures of the court and the central government. The receiver-general of all finances prepared an annual account for "domains and finances," but this did not include the extraordinary revenues collected (from 1445) by the "Secret Treasury," which gave the sovereign immediate access to liquid assets. For control of expenditures Philip the Good created a treasurer-(general), who had to initial each payment order, and who was assisted by three financial experts of bourgeois background serving as commissioners. Under Charles V and Philip II the Secret Treasury repeatedly came up with the disposable income that the heavily burdened ordinary revenues could not provide. In 1567 almost two-thirds of the net revenues of the ordinary treasury came from the "coffres du Roy," that is, from the treasurer of Castile.[30]

Separately from the Council of Justice, the treasurer-general and the commissioners of finance formed a kind of bureau within the Court Council for advisory and executive tasks relating to domains and finances, and for the initial control of receipts and expenditures. Out of the plenary Grand Council, initially responsible for financial policy, evolved an independent board of financial experts, called since 1487 the Council of Domains and Finances, who directed financial policy and managed final control of revenues and expenses. Two or three nobles were added, because of their expertise concerning domains, in 1507. In 1531 the Council of Finance was recognized as one of the Collateral Councils.

In pre-Burgundian times the hearing of the accounts of receivers was generally the task of the plenary *curia* or of some council members, sometimes accompanying of the ruler. In the Burgundian period central control of receipts and expenditures was considerably improved through the introduction of audits based on the Burgundian model at Dijon. In 1386 Philip the Bold established at Lille the "Chamber of the Council in Flanders," with a department for supervising the accounts of domains and justice. After the Four Members of Flanders demanded the use of the "mother tongue" rather than French, the Council's department of justice moved to Ghent in 1407, but the Chamber itself remained at Lille, where it gradually came to be known as the Chamber of Accounts. Its jurisdiction included all the then "Landen van herwaerts overe." An comparable audit office at Dijon, after 1493 at Dôle, heard the accounts in the "Landen van derwaerts overe," in both ducal Burgundy and the Franche Comté.

Expansion brought the creation of new audit offices with authority over various territories. The audit office at Lille, which was given responsibility for Namur and Hainaut as well as Flanders, remained the only audit office which had the right to examine the accounts of all other central receivers. From 1404 there was a "Camere vander rekeninghen" in Brabant, whose competency in 1465 was extended to Luxembourg-Chiny. After the incorporation of Holland and Zeeland in 1428 the supervision of the accountable officials was at first entrusted to "commissioners for the hearing of the accounts of officials and servants in Holland," but in 1446 Philip the Good founded a separate "chamber of Accounts for the Count's Domains in Holland." After the conquest of the northeastern regions the Audit Office in The Hague extended its jurisdiction to these provinces. In 1543 the incumbent controllers of the accounts in Guelders were initially confirmed. A proposal in 1549 to have all receivers in Guelders come under the audit office of Brussels, created so much inconvenience because of the distances involved that in 1559 a new audit office was established in Arnhem.

The creation of audit offices suited the Burgundian-Habsburg system of increasing government efficiency. It was more efficient, for example, when the sovereign could delegate the supervision of accounts to salaried auditors and masters of account. Presidents of audit boards were appointed by the sovereign, but auditors and masters of accounts were appointed by the Council of Finance in his name after consultation with the pertinent audit office. These men owed their expertise to the world of trade and finance or to their work as receiver of domains and finances. Because of the judicial competencies of audit offices, one of the members would often be a university-trained lawyer. They all belonged to the new class of bureaucrats drawn mostly from lesser nobility and especially from the urban patriciate. It is remarkable that the composition of the audit offices was interprovincial, underlining the fact that audit offices were central institutions. In a time of poor communications the efficient management of crown domains and finances was not well-served by concentration of supervision in the hands of distant central institutions. Hence, Charles the Bold's and Philip the Handsome's efforts to centralize all supervision in one General Chamber of Accounts at Mechelen came to nothing. The importance which the Burgundian-Habsburg sovereigns attached to the audit offices is apparent from the fact that during the frequent economy measures, when other government bureaus had to make sacrifices, the audit offices remained fully staffed, and even received salary increases.[31]

## Taxation

During the Burgundian period, once the provincial estates consented to a subsidy, everything from the levying of the sum to the supervision of receipts and expenditures was the business of the sovereign. The estates, who had to assess the taxes, in most provinces followed a system of repartition, by which the provincial receiver apportioned them among the rural districts and cities according to fixed formulae and without respect to changes in economy or population. The rural head-aldermen then divided their district's quota over the countryside, where assessors apportioned the share of each village in the form of a head-tax based on the *holding* of land, not on *ownership*, since the upper nobility and upper clergy were exempt. The cities paid mainly from their receipts from excise taxes on grain, meat, beer and wine, and by long-term borrowing through the sale of annuities (*renten*). Some cities also levied special indirect taxes ad hoc for this purpose. The tax system was as complex as it was unfair, chiefly to the commons, for consumption taxes hit heaviest people of modest means in town, and tenant farmers in the countryside. Quite apart from the time—sometimes months—required to negotiate taxes, their collection was arcane, impractical, and extremely time-consuming.[32]

For these reasons the central government would have preferred taxes assessed on everyone, rich and poor, according to their ability to pay. It also sought ways of raising money quickly. But the experiments with centrally collected imposts on consumption and on commercial profit and with import and export taxes proved disappointing. Wealthy merchants resisted taxes on trade, and the upper nobility defended its fiscal privileges. Forced into difficulty again and again, the governments of Charles V and Philip II negotiated advances on future subsidies and sought to relieve the most pressing problems through loans in money-market, for which future subsidies or domain revenues were pledged. The regime's shaky financial reputation pushed interest rates up to frightful levels. In 1556 the capital market demanded 23% on loans to the regime in Brussels, while they normally lent at 12-14%. The receiver in question obliged himself to repay the bankers directly, giving his bond as security. This faulty system contributed to several state bankruptcies under Philip II.

Regional collectors of subsidy revenue made payments to the provincial receiver-general, who were commissioned by the prince to keep accounts for each subsidy. The transfer of the funds to the central receiver-general, however, became more and more fictitious. Subsidy revenues were allocated to expenditure, documented by means of "briefven van deschargien" ("letters of *decharge*.")[33] The *decharge*, introduced in the Burgundian domains as early as the end of the fourteenth century after the example of Valois France, was a receipt from the central receiver-general, authenticated by *visum* of members of the Court Council, later the Council of Finance. It assigned payment to third parties from a specifically mentioned subordinate receiver of domains or subsidies. For the receiver himself, the *decharge* served both as a receipt for a sum fictitiously paid the receiver-general and as a payment order in favor of the third party.

This method of expending the income from provincial subsidies reflected rationalization of money transactions, but also the growing influence of the provincial estates, for the sovereign's growing needs eventually gave them a large degree of financial autonomy. Sales of *renten* by the estates, initially at the request of the ruler, raised their creditworthiness and increased the ruler's dependence on them. The estates of Flanders, for example, gained a say in the management of subsidy commitments probably in 1514, Brabant a bit later, and Holland and Zeeland later still. Income from sales of *renten* surpassed subsidy revenues in Flanders by 1543, in Holland by 1558.[34]

After 1540 the joint control of the subsidies by the sovereign and the estates became ever more common. The receivers of the subsidies in Brabant, Holland, Flanders and Zeeland were beginning to render their accounts to mixed audit commissions, equally divided between the estates' own deputies of the estates and the ruler's masters of accounts and auditors. In 1558 King Philip II negotiated a nine-year subsidy with the States General for an unprecedented sum of money, but under conditions which significantly increased the estates' financial independence. The king agreed among other things to give them complete control over the collection and expenditures of this "novenial" subsidy. It was to be collected by receivers appointed by the estates, who would no longer render their annual accounts to the audit offices of the sovereign, nor to a joint commission, but solely to a receiver-general of the subsidies appointed by the States General. This was the culmination of the long development whereby the collection of subsidies became more and more the affair of the estates and less and less that of the sovereign. The regime in Brussels was only mildly interested in the way in which the subsidies were collected, so long as the money kept flowing in to pay salaries and other obligations. Financial autonomy for the provinces also decentralized finance in a way that promoted an efficient organization of public finance. The time when money was transferred by horse and cart had long passed.

For the rest the princely right of supervision of urban accounts did not mean much in practice. As legal successors to the territorial lords, Burgundian and Habsburg rulers had the right to supervise urban finances, though some privileged had their own auditors and thus almost completely escaped princely financial control. In places where the annual renewal of aldermen provided an occasion for review of city accounts, audits by the princes' men became in practice a formality. The only real form of princely supervision was that cities had to apply for permission for any new tax or any sale of *renten* backed by the city treasury, even if it was for the purpose of raising the city's subsidy quota. To obtain such permission the cities had to submit a justifying petition to the Court Council and later the Council of Finance. Far from a threat, this kind of local fiscal autonomy actually contributed to the formation of the Netherlandish state.

### Trade and Commercial Policy

The Burgundian-Habsburg government had no systematic commercial policy. In general, what is now called the economy was subordinated to power politics and the financial interests of the sovereign. The merchants nonetheless had ways of profiting from the political constellation. Ambitious entrepreneurs, for example, could request from the government the temporary protection of monopolies and tax exemptions. The unification of the Netherlands, the dynastic ties with the Burgundians, and in particular with the Habsburg world-empire gave the country more prestige in diplomatic negotiations, which meant that international agreements contained a few plums for the merchants too. The government created a common Netherlandish money and the growing interprovincial monetary exchange indirectly fostered a kind of natural selection among the old provincial coins. Maritime trade and fisheries could obtain the protection of warships if they wanted it, and if they were willing to pay for it.[35] The regime also sometimes inconvenienced the merchants, of course, notably by prohibiting wartime trade with countries of an anti-Habsburg coalition, or by subjecting trade to the payment of license duties.

During the fifteenth and sixteenth centuries the provision of local economic needs was still very much a local affair. Gradually, however, despite interlocal and interprovincial rivalries, the provinces of Brabant, Holland, Flanders, and Zeeland were undergoing a process of economic integration. The Netherlands' relatively flat topography posed no barriers to transportation, and the extensive network of roads and inland water-ways—to which with the cooperation of the authorities still new ones were added—greatly promoted the unification of the domestic market. The proximity of the sea and the extensive coastline formed another important unifying element and made possible a lively waterborne traffic from coastal ports with England, France, Iberia, and the Baltic, as well as with Venice and Genoa. Netherlandish ports functioned as exchange points between northern and southern Europe. Trade in agricultural products from Holland ports, in particular in bread grains from the Baltic, the granary of Europe, expanded in order to supplement local agricultural production. In the sixteenth century 40.5% of the value of imports consisted of food products. After all, the agricultural sector represented only half of the overall value of production of the Netherlands, whereas it accounted for 80% of production in the Mediterranean lands. The fifteenth-century agricultural transformation had also freed arable to produce crops for the textile industry such as dyes and other products including flax, hemp, hops, cole- and rapeseed. In certain provinces moors were opened up for the cutting of peat. The consequence of these changes was that Netherlandish agriculture could not meet the local demand for food.[36]

The textile industry, traditionally the most important trade of Flanders, Brabant, and Holland, faced since around 1520 both growing competition from English woolens and rural textiles and rising prices of its traditional raw material, English wool. Under these conditions, the only urban firms able to hold their own were those in Antwerp, Mechelen, and Amsterdam that specialized in processing and finishing English woolens. Otherwise, the center of gravity of the Netherlandish textile industry shifted to the countryside, where wages were lower. Changes in clothing fashions greatly favored light draperies, which were made from Spanish wool in the countryside of Holland and southwestern Flanders and in certain Walloon towns.

Netherlandish manufacturers produced for both domestic and foreign markets. Their exports—some sixteen million guilders worth around 1550—were three times those of England, which had approximately the same population. Following a slump in the last decades of the fifteenth century, the Netherlands profited greatly from the sixteenth-century revival of intercontinental trade. The general upswing and the boom periods of 1494-1524 and 1540-65 benefitted Amsterdam and Antwerp most of all. The Amstel city, with its approximately five hundred ships, concentrated shipping and sea fisheries, while the Scheldt city and its hinterland throve on commercial capitalism. These two sectors fed one another's prosperity. Hollanders and Zeelanders, for example, traditionally active on the Brabant markets, profited from the shift of the major exchange point between northern and southern Europe from Bruges to Antwerp around 1500. They were deeply immersed in the expansion of long-distance trade and in the international transit trade of which the Scheldt city and its network of satellite ports became the axis. Flanders and Brabant, on the other hand, made extensive use of Holland's and Zeeland's cargo capacity, which accounted for the lion's share of Netherlandish shipping movements in the Scheldt delta, one of the busiest estuaries in Europe. The network of Flemish and Zeeland ports, which in the fifteenth century had served Bruges, shifted in the sixteenth century, as did Bruges itself, to serve Antwerp.[37]

This commercial and maritime boom ended rather abruptly in 1565. The depression had begun in the agricultural and industrial sectors around 1557, and in 1563 a trade conflict broke out with the Merchant Adventurers, which led Queen Elizabeth of England to withdraw the staple for English woolen from Antwerp. This not only caused the loss of the monopoly for the mass transit trade of English cloth to the rest of Europe, but also dealt a serious blow to the specialized cloth finishing industry and textile markets in the hinterland. At the same time products from the Netherlandish textile weaving mills and artistic crafts lost outlets on the English market. These setbacks were accompanied by a complete collapse of the traditional cloth manufacturing. Outputs of the textile industry and related finishing business dropped to one-third the level of fifteen years earlier. The metal industry was also past its prime. The falling exports had negative repercussions on the shipbuilding industry and its subsidiaries in Holland and Zeeland.

The conflict with England aside, the most important cause of the crisis was reduced demand from a dwindling domestic market, itself the result of the declining prosperity of the masses. Grain prices had soared in the aftermath of the Danish-Polish-Swedish War and the subsequent closure of the Sound by the Danish king in 1563. The Netherlands' chronic grain shortage could no longer be supplemented from the Baltic, and it became especially acute after the bad harvest of 1565 and the severe winter of 1565-66. All these things together produced an acute crisis, causing wages to decline even nominally and condemning many to lasting unemployment. According to some estimates, up to 40% of the urban population was now dependent on public and private charity. In the countryside poverty was widespread as well, especially since the market sales of linen and light woolen materials stagnated. The masses of the population were the first victims of the depression.[38]

In this atmosphere of crisis the announcement of Alva's tax proposal in 1569 made trading circles, who feared—probably without reason—that it would inflate domestic prices and undermine the Netherlandish ability to compete in foreign markets. By introducing a tenth penny on the sales of all consumer goods and other movable goods, and a twentieth penny on the sales of landed property, the Duke of Alva intended not to raise the burden of taxation, but merely to supplant the existing jumble of levies by uniform sales and transfer taxes. Yet a certain doom-mongering among the merchants concerning Alva's fixed levies may have added to the economic recession. The consequences of the All Saints' Flood of 1570, which caused enormous water damage from Friesland to Flanders, the quartering of Spanish troops, and a prevailing fear due to Alva's repression against those suspected of political opposition or Protestant sympathies, contributed to the economic upheaval.[39] In 1567-73 several tens of thousands of tradesmen and craftsmen left the country and migrated to France, England, East Friesland, and the Electorate of Cologne. The emigration, in which Protestant sympathies often reinforced the decision to seek a better living elsewhere helped to throw the whole country into a deep depression.[40]

❊ ❊ ❊

The economic crisis and social unrest since the 1560s formed the background of the Netherlandish revolt against the king of Spain. For a hundred and fifty years, the core provinces of the Netherlands had been developing together a system of governance balanced between centralizing princely power and local particularist pretensions. It was this Burgundian-Habsburg system that Philip II, king of Castile and sovereign of the Netherlands, disturbed through fiscal authoritarianism, a "Castilianization" of certain institutions, the presence of foreign troops under Spanish command, the dissolution of the States General in 1558 and the royal prohibition to summon them again, and the abrupt dismissal from the government of the influential remnants of the old military nobility. Taken together, these measures were seen to be an abandonment of the traditional model of cooperation between government and governed in political decision-making. Religious policy, seen to be both rigorous and centralist, and lacking any form of clemency or pardon, intruded on the everyday freedom of communities and individuals and was viewed as intolerant and inimical to freedom. In contrast to Charles V, who detached the Netherlands from the Empire and France, King Philip II and his "Consejo de Estado" believed that they could govern the Netherlands from Spain as a sort of dependency. Even so, loyalty to the dynasty, to princely sovereignty, and even to the person of the ruler remained undisputed. The struggle was mainly about the conditions of this sovereignty. All these elements, combined with the unfettered anti-Spanish and false propaganda, unleashed a nation-wide resistance, which after 1568 changed into a war of independence, and a provincial and even local overreaction to the perceived threat from the center.

Mutual financial, military, and political relations worked to split the country into two parts along arbitrary and whimsical lines. Religious polarization created an uncompromising atmosphere and caused the religious question to weigh more heavily during negotiations between the parties than anything else. But one also has to keep in mind the European and even the world-wide context. The Republic of the United Provinces eventually became a confederation with a parliamentary regime, in which the provincial estates—or rather their principals, by and large the patrician city regents—became the new sovereigns. It was only in the eyes of international law that sovereignty was vested in the States General. In the pacified Walloon provinces and in the provinces subsequently reconquered by the royal *terçios*—henceforth known as Royal or Spanish Netherlands—Philip II was forced to partially retrace his predecessors' footsteps toward a federal equilibrium.

Translated by Marcus Vink

# NOTES

1. That is: 1) on the right bank of the Scheldt river: Brabant with the marquisate of Antwerp, the seigniory of Mechelen with the Ressort of Heist-op-den-Berg, Guelders-Zutphen, Hainaut-Valenciennes, Holland, Zeeland, Limburg and Overmaas, Luxemburg-Chiny, Namur, part of Imperial Flanders (Overschelde [Bornem and surroundings], the Landen van Aalst and Dendermonde), part of Tournai-Tournaisis, Utrecht-Overijssel-Drenthe, Stad en Lande of Groningen, Friesland; 2) on the left bank of the Scheldt: the other part of Imperial Flanders (the Land van Waas and the Vier Ambachten [Hulst, Assenede, Axel, and Boekhoute]).
2. These comprise the remaining part of Flanders on the left bank of the Scheldt River.
3. With the exception of the ward Saint-Brice on the right bank of the Scheldt, which belonged to the Empire.
4. André Leguai, "Royauté française et État Bourguignon de 1435 à 1477," *Publication du Centre européen d'Études bourguignonnes (XIVe-XVe s.)* 32 (Neuchâtel, 1992), 65-67, 72-73.
5. Paul L. Nève, *Het Rijkskamergerecht en de Nederlanden* (Assen, 1972), passim; Filippo Rainieri, *Recht und Gesellschaft im Zeitalter der Rezeption. Eine rechts- und sozialgeschichtliche Analyse der Tätigkeit des Reichkammergerichts im 16. Jahrhundert* (Cologne and Vienna, 1985), 305-14, 318-19.
6. Dierickx (1950); Leopold Willaert, "Le placet royal aux Pays-Bas," *Belgisch Tijdschrift voor Filologie en Geschiedenis* 32 (1954), 466-506, 1075-1117; 33 (1955), 21-39; P. Gorissen, "De invoering van het vorstelijk benoemingsrecht in de Nederlandse abdijen onder Karel V," *Bijdragen betreffende de Geschiedenis der Nederlanden* 9 (1954-55), 190-237; 10 (1955-56), 25-57.
7. Jan Craeybeckx, "De val van Antwerpen en de scheuring der Nederlanden," in Jan Craeybeckx, et al., eds., *1585: Op gescheiden wegen* (Leuven, 1988), 124-125; De Schepper (1990), 222-23.
8. De Schepper (1990), 215-218, 220; Jean-Marie Cauchies, "La professionalisation dans les cours de justice princières aux Pays-Bas aux XIVe-XVe siècles," in Heinz Mohnhaupt and Dieter Simon, eds., *Vorträge zur Justifizforschung. Geschichte und Theorie* (Frankfurt am Main, 1992), 21-44.
9. Van Rompaey (1973), 3-60.
10. Baelde (1965), 4-25.
11. In case of a lacuna in the customary law, uncertainty about its interpretation or equal division of votes on a judicial bench, the rural courts from time immemorial would consult a court deemed more competent (depending on the subject matter); this could be the court of a feudal lord or of the rural district

or *kasselrij*. From the 13th century onwards rural courts made their *hoofd-vaart* to urban benches of aldermen. The verdict of the higher court was binding.

12. Cauchies (1981), 59-70.
13. Baelde (1965), 38-41; G. Martyn, "In de eeuwen der eeuwen, (t)amen: Over de edicten, eeuwige edicten en andere wetgevingsterminologie in de 16e en 17e eeuw," *Belgisch Tijdschrift voor Filologie en Geschiedenis* 70 (1992), 921-41.
14. Gilissen (1950), 49-66.
15. Prevenier and Blockmans (1986), 28-45.
16. Hugo Soly, *Urbanisme en kapitalisme in Antwerpen in de XVIe eeuw: De stedebouwkundige en industriële ondernemingen van Gilbert van Schoonbeke* (Brussels, 1977), 288-320, 401-30.
17. Van Uytven (1972), 60-93.
18. Arie Theodorus van Deursen, and Hugo de Schepper, *Willem van Oranje: Een strijd voor vrijheid en verdraagzaamheid* (Weesp/Tiel, 1984), 43-47.
19. De Schepper (1990), 218-22.
20. Gilissen (1981), 257-59, 280-83, 312-14; Arent H. Huussen, Jr., "Moderne staatsvorming en wetgeving aan het begin van de Nieuwe Tijd," in Willem P. Blockmans and Herman van Nuffel, eds., *Staat en religie in de 16de eeuw* (Brussels, 1986), 43-61.
21. Gilissen (1981), 316.
22. That is, for the northern and eastern periphery: Friesland, Groningen and the Ommelanden, Overijssel-Drenthe, Utrecht, Guelders-Zutphen, Limburg-Overmaas and Luxemburg-Chiny; and for the Walloon-Picard provinces: Namur, Hainaut-Valenciennes, Tournai-Tournaisis, Artois and Walloon Flanders (Lille-Douai, Orchies).
23. Cornelis Antonius van Kalveen, *Het bestuur van bisschop en staten in het Nedersticht, Overijssel en Drenthe, 1482-1520* (Groningen, 1974); Reitsma (1982); Koopmans (1990).
24. Willem P. Blockmans, "A Typology of Representative Institutions in Europe," *Journal of Medieval History* 4 (1978): 189-215.
25. Van Uytven and Blockmans (1969), 399-424; Woltjer (1975), 19-35.
26. Hugo de Schepper, "Ensayo sobre el modelo del proceso de decisión política en los Países Bajos de Felipe II, 1559-1598" in P. J. A. N. Rietbergen, et al., eds., *Tussen twee culturen: De Nederlanden en de Iberische wereld, 1550-1800* (Nijmegen, 1992), 173-98.
27. Gilissen (1981), 314.
28. Van Cauwenberghe (1982), 243-354.
29. Baelde (1963), 14-33; Van Nieuwenhuysen (1984), 52, 289.
30. Hugo de Schepper, "Las finanzas públicas en los Países Bajos Reales, 1480-1700. Una reseña," *Cuadernos de Investigación Histórica* 8 (1984), 14.
31. H. M. Brokken and Hugo de Schepper, "Beheer en controle van de overheidsfinanciën in de Nederlanden tot omstreeks 1600," in Peter Jan Margry, et al, eds., *Van Camere van der Rekeninghen tot Algemene Rekenkamer: Zes eeuwen Rekenkamer* (The Hague, 1989), 15-56, 477-81.
32. N. Maddens, *De beden in het graafschap Vlaanderen tijdens de regering van Karel V, 1515-1550* (Heule, 1978), 7-240; R. van Schaïk, *Belasting, bevolking en bezit in Gelre en Zutphen, 1350-1550* (Hilversum, 1987), 46-123; Blockmans (1986), 88-89.
33. Tracy (1985a), 72-117.

34. Tracy (1985b), 38-46, 57-69, 108-38.
35. James D. Tracy, "Herring Wars: the Habsburg Netherlands and the Struggle for Control of the North Sea, ca. 1520-1560," *SCJ* 24 (1993): 249-72.
36. Prevenier and Blockmans (1986), 12-27, 48-126; Van Houtte (1977), 59-190.
37. Wilfried Brulez, "De handelsbalans der Nederlanden in het midden van de 16e eeuw," *Bijdragen voor de Geschiedenis der Nederlanden* 21 (1966-67), 278-310; De Vries (1974), 22-245.
38. Herman van der Wee, "La Réforme protestante dans l'optique de la conjoncture économique et sociale des Pays-Bas méridionaux au XVIe siècle," in Jean Pieyns and Hugo de Schepper, eds., *Bronnen voor de religieuze geschiedenis van België. Middeleeuwen en Moderne Tijd* (Leuven, 1968), 303-15.
39. Ferdinand H. M. Grapperhaus, *Alva en de Tiende Penning* (Zutphen, 1982), 95-307.
40. Jan G. C. A. Briels, *Zuidnederlanders in de Republiek, 1572-1630* (Sint-Niklaas, 1985), 26-99, 218-21.

# BIBLIOGRAPHY

Arnould, Maurice A. *Les dénombrements de foyers dans le comté de Hainaut XIVe-XVIe siècle*. Brussels, 1956.

Baelde, Michel. *De Collaterale Raden Onder Karel V en Filip II, 1531-1578*.

Baelde, Michel. "Financiële politiek en domaniale evolutie in de Nederlanden onder Karel V en Filips II, 1530-1560." *Tijdschrift voor Geschiedenis* 76 (1963), 14-33.

Bartier, J. *Légistes et gens de finances au XVe siècle. Les consillers des ducs de Bourgogne*. Brussels, 1952.

*Bijdragen en Mededelingen betreffende de geschiedenis der Nederlanden* 95/2 (1980). Special number about Burgundy and the Netherlands.

Blockmans, Willem P., ed. *Estates or Powers*. Standen en Landen, vol. 69. Heule, 1977.

Blockmans, Willem P. "Finances publiques et inégalité sociale dans les Pays-Bas aux XIVe-XVIe siècles." In *Genèse de l'État moderne. Prélèvements et redistribution*, ed. Jean-Philippe Genet and Michel Le Mené. Paris, 1986, 77-90.

Blockmans, Willem P. *De Volksvertegenwoordiging in Vlaanderen in de Overgang van Middeleeuwen naar Nieuwe Tijd (1384-1506)*. Brussels, 1978.

Blok, Dirk Pieter, et al., eds. *Algemene Geschiedenis der Nederlanden*. Vols. 4-6. Haarlem, 1979-80.

De Boer, D. E. H., and J. W. Marsilje, eds. *De Nederlanden in de Late Middeleeuwen*. Utrecht, 1987.

Calmette, Joseph. *The Golden Age of Burgundy: the Magnificent Dukes and Their Courts*. London, 1952 [1959].

Cauchies, Jean-Marie. "L'essor d'une législation générale pour les Pays-Bas Bourguignons dans le dernier quart du XVe siècle." *Publication du Centre européen d'Études Burgundo-Médianes* 21 (1981), 59-70.

Cauchies, Jean-Marie. *La légalisation princière pour le comté de Hainaut. Ducs de Bourgogne et premiers Habsbourg (1427-1506)*. Brussels, 1982.

Van Cauwenberghe, Eddy. *Het vorstelijk domein en de overheidsfinanciën in de Nederlanden, 15de en 16e eeuw*. Brussels, 1982.

Chaunu, Pierre. "Séville et la Belgique 1555-1648." *Revue du Nord* 42 (1960), 259-92.

Cockshaw, Pierre. *Le personnel de la Chancellerie de Bourgogne-Flandre sous les ducs de Bourgogne de la maison de Valois, 1384-1477*. Standen en Landen, vol. 79. Heule, 1982.

Decavele, Johan. *De dageraad van de Reformatie in Vlaanderen 1520-1565*. Brussels, 1975.

Van Deursen, Arie Th., and De Schepper, Hugo. *Willem van Oranje. Een strijd voor Vrijheid en Verdraagzaamheid*. Weesp/Tiel, 1984.

Dhondt, Jan. "Les Assemblées d'État en Belgique avant 1795." In *Recueils de la Société Jean Bodin* 24 (1966), 325-400.

Dierickx, Michiel. *De oprichting der nieuwe bisdommen in de Nederlanden onder Filip II, 1559-1570*. Antwerp and Utrecht, 1950.

Van Dillen, Johannes Gerard. *Van Rijkdom en Regenten: Handboek tot de Economische en Sociale Geschiedenis der Nederlanden tijdens de Republiek*. The Hague, 1970.

Duke, Alistair C. *Reformation and Revolt in the Low Countries*. London and Ronceverte, 1990.

*Geschiedkunidge Atlas van Nederland*. 3 map vols. and 15 text vols. The Hague, 1913-38.

Gilissen, John. "Les États Généraux de pays de par deça, 1464-1632." *Standen en Landen* 33 (1965), 261-321.

Gilissen, John. *Historische inleiding tot het recht.* Antwerp, 1981.

Gilissen, John. "Les phases de la codification et l'homologation des coutumes dans les XVII provinces des Pays-Bas." *Legal History Review* 18 (1950), 49-66, 239-73.

Groenveld, Simon, and H. L. Ph. Leeuwenberg, eds. *De Unie van Utrecht. Wording en werking van een verbond en een verbondsacte.* The Hague, 1979.

Groenveld, Simon. "Image and Reality. The historiography of the Dutch Revolt against Philip II." In H. de Schepper, P.J.A.N. Rietbergen, eds., *España y Holanda. Ponencias de los colloquios Hispano-Holandeses de Historiadores.* Madrid/Nijmegen, 1993, 37-80.

Hirschauer, C. *Les États d'Artois de leur origines à l'occupation française, 1340-1640.* 2 vols. Paris, 1923.

Hommel, Luc. *Marie de Bourgogne ou le Grand Héritage.* Brussels, 1951.

Van Houtte, Jan A., et al., eds. *Algemene Geschiedenis der Nederlanden.* Vols. 3-5. Utrecht and Antwerp, 1941-52.

Van Houtte, Jan A. *An Economic History of the Low Countries, 800-1800.* New York, 1977.

Israel, Jonathan. *Dutch Primacy in World Trade 1585-1740.* Oxford, 1989.

Jansma, T. S. *Raad en Rekenkamer in Holland en Zeeland tijdens Philips van Bourgondië.* Utrecht, 1932.

Jongkees, A. G. *Burgundica et varia.* Hilversum, 1990.

Jongkees, A. G. *Staat en kerk in Holland en Zeeland onder de Bourgondische hertogen, 1425-1477.* Groningen, 1942.

Koenigsberger, Helmut G. "Composite States and Representative Institutions in Early Modern Europe and America." *BIHR* 62 (1989): 135-53.

Koenigsberger, Helmut G. *Estates and Revolutions: Essays in Early Modern European History.* Ithaca, 1971.

Koopmans, Johannes Wierd. *De Staten van Holland en de Opstand. De ontwikkeling van hun functies en organisatie in de periode 1544-1588.* Amsterdam, 1990.

Marshall, Sherrin. *The Dutch Gentry, 1500-1650: Family, Faith and Fortune.* New York and Westport, Conn., 1987.

Marsilje, J.W. *Het financiële beleid van Leiden in de laat-Beierse en Bourgondische periode c.1390-1477.* Hilversum, 1985.

Mollat, Michel. "Recherches sur les finances du ducs Valois de Bourgogne." *Revue historique* 219 (1958), 285-321.

Mollat, Michel, R. Favreau and F. Fawtier. *Comptes généraux de l'état bourguignon entre 1416 et 1420.* 4 vols. Paris, 1965-76.

De Moreau, Éduard. *Histoire de l'Église en Belgique.* Vol. 4: *1378-1559.* Brussels, 1949.

Munro, J. H. A. *Wool, Cloth and Gold: the Struggle for Bullion in Anglo-Burgundian Trade, 1340-1478.* Brussels and Toronto, 1974.

Van Nierop, Henk F. K. *Van Ridders tot Regenten. De Hollandse Adel in de Zestiende en de Eerste Helft van de Zeventiende Eeuw.* Dieren/Amsterdam, 1984.

Van Nieuwenhuysen, Andrée. *Les finances du duc de Bourgogne Philippe le Hardi, 1384-1404.* Brussels, 1984.

Paravicini, Werner. *Guy de Brimeu: Der burgundische Staat und seine adlige Führungs-schichte unter Karl dem Kühnen.* Bonn, 1973.

Paravicini, Werner. *Karl der Kühne. Das Ende des Hauses Burgund.* Göttingen, 1976.

Parker, Geoffrey [with coll of I. A. A. Thompson, and Hugo de Schepper]. *Spain and the Netherlands 1559-1659. Ten Studies.* London, 1979.

Peeters, J. P. *De financiën van de kleine en secundaire steden in Brabant van de 12de tot het midden der 16de eeuw.* Antwerp, 1980.

Pirenne, Henri. *Early Democracies in the Low Countries.* Trans. J. V. Saunders. New York, 1971.

Pirenne, Henri. "The Formation and Constitution of the Burgundian State." *AHR* 14 (1908-9), 477-502.

Pirenne, Henri. *Histoire de Belgique*. 7 vols. Brussels, 1902-32.

Prevenier, Walter. *De Leden en de Staten van Vlaanderen, 1384-1405*. Brussels, 1961.

Prevenier, Walter, and Willem P. Blockmans. *The Burgundian Netherlands*. Cambridge, 1986.

Reitsma, Reints. *Centrifugal and Centripetal Forces in the Early Dutch Republic: the States of Overijssel 1566-1600*. Amsterdam, 1982.

Renoz, P. *La chancellerie de Brabant sous Philippe le Bon, 1430-1467*. Brussels, 1955.

Van Rompaey, Jan. *Het grafelijk baljuwsambt in Vlaanderen tijdens de Boergondische periode*. Brussels, 1967.

Van Rompaey, Jan. *De Grote Raad van de Hertogen van Bourgondië en het Parlement van Mechelen*. Brussels, 1973.

De Schepper, Hugo. *Belgium Nostrum, 1500-1650. Over de Integratie en Desintegratie van het Nederland*. Antwerp, 1987.

De Schepper, Hugo. "De Grote Raad van Mechelen: Hoogste Rechtscollege van de Nederlanden?" In *Miscellanea Consilii Magni*. Amsterdam, 1980, 171-92.

De Schepper, Hugo. "Netherlandic Statemaking Through Princely Judicature in the Sixteenth Century." In *The Low Countries: Multidisciplinary Studies*, ed. Margriet Bruijn Lacy. Lanham, New York, and London, 1990, 211-26.

De Schepper, Hugo, and Jean-Marie Cauchies. *La genèse de l'état et ses moyens juridiques aux Pays-Bas, 1200-1600*. Brussels (forthcoming).

De Smidt, Johan Th. e.a., eds. *Fiscaliteit in Nederland. 50 Jaar Belastingmuseum "Prof.Dr. Van der Poel"*. Zutphen/Deventer, 1987.

Spufford, Peter. *Monetary Problems and Policies in the Burgundian Netherlands, 1433-1496*. Leiden, 1970.

Thielemans, M.-R. *Bourgogne et Angleterre. Relations politiques et économiques entre les Pays-Bas Bourguignons et l'Angleterre 1435-1467*. Brussels, 1966.

Tracy, James D. *A Financial Revolution in the Habsburg Netherlands*. Berkeley and Los Angeles, 1985b.

Tracy, James D. "Heresy Law and Centralization under Mary of Hungary: Conflict between the Council of Holland and the Central Government over the Enforcement of Charles V's Placcards." *ARG* 73 (1982): 284-308.

Tracy, James D. *Holland under Habsburg Rule 1505-1566: the Formation of a Body Politic*. Berkeley and Los Angeles, 1990.

Tracy, James D. "The Taxation System of the County of Holland, 1519-1566." *Economisch- en Sociaal-Historisch Jaarboek* 48 (1985a): 72-118.

Van Uytven, Raymond. "Sociaal-economische evoluties in de Nederlanden vóór de revoluties, 14e-16e eeuw." *Bijdragen en Mededelingen betreffende de Geschiedenis der Nederlanden* 87 (1972), 60-93.

Van Uytven, Raymond, and Willem P. Blockmans. "Constitutions and their Applications in the Netherlands During the Middle Ages." *Belgisch Tijdschrift voor Filologie en Geschiedenis* 47 (1969), 399-424.

Vaughan, Richard. *Charles the Bold, the Last Valois Duke of Burgundy*. London, 1973.

Vaughan, Richard. *John the Fearless: the Growth of Burgundian Power*. London, 1979.

Vaughan, Richard. *Philip the Good: the Apogee of Burgundy*. London, 1970.

Vaughan, Richard. *Valois Burgundy*. London, 1975.

Van der Wee, Herman. *The Growth of the Antwerp Market and the European Economy*. 3 vols. The Hague, 1963.

De Vries, Jan. *The Dutch Rural Economy in the Golden Age, 1500-1700*. New Haven, 1974.

De Win, Paul. "De adel in het hertogdom Brabant van de vijftiende eeuw. Een Terreinverkenning." *Tijdschrift voor Rechtsgeschiedenis* 93 (1980), 391-409.

Woltjer, Jan Juliaan. "Dutch Privileges, Real and Imaginary." In *Britain and the Netherlands* 5 (The Hague, 1975), 19-35.

Woltjer, Jan Juliaan. *Friesland in Hervormingstijd*. Leiden, 1962.

# THE ART OF WAR

Michael E. Mallett
(University of Warwick)

## 1. THE ERA OF 'MILITARY REVOLUTION'

Discussion of development in the art of war in the early modern period of European history has been dominated in recent years by a debate about 'military revolution'. To a large extent the debate falls outside the scope of this volume, being concerned with the seventeenth and eighteenth centuries. Nevertheless, the original thesis propounded by Michael Roberts focussed on the period 1560 - 1660, and at least a part of the subsequent discussion has tended to shift the first of these dates backwards towards 1500. The sixteenth century has become a century of military change and innovation rather than Charles Oman's 'most uninteresting period in military history'. But we also have to consider the fifteenth century and the contention of this chapter will be that any starting date for significant military change has to be placed earlier than 1500.[1]

The Roberts thesis proposed that dramatic changes in the nature and organisation of war in the fifty years after 1590 were crucial to the development of the early modern European state. The changes which he had in mind were the emergence of linear infantry tactics which allowed greater focus on firepower; this made battles more decisive, put a premium on control and discipline of troops in the new formations, and above all encouraged a considerable increase in numbers; effective infantry and guns gave a new ferocity to war, increased numbers required greater efforts and more logistical support to feed, supply and control them. Thus new, larger, permanent armies became the promoters and mainstays of absolutism.

Roberts was, of course, arguing that the Military Revolution around 1600 was 'a great divide separating medieval society from the modern world' and that our period is, therefore, dominated by essentially pre-revolutionary, traditional military practices and mechanisms. Geoffrey Parker and John Hale have responded to this challenge by emphasising that the problems of control and supply of large armies composed mainly of infantry were problems of the sixteenth century; that the growth in army size was itself a result of an earlier switch to infantry forces and of an emphasis on massive new fortifications to counter already effective guns. Hence, if there was a sense of break-out around 1600 it was a break-out from a particular sixteenth-century (not medieval) stalemate in a new area of Europe, central and northern Germany, which had been relatively little involved in sixteenth-century warfare.[2]

This debate focusses our attention on what constitutes significant military change. Are we really talking about changes in infantry tactics and formations which allowed for greater use of firepower, or are we not rather concerned with the change in balance of arms which produced a marked numerical superiority of infantry over cavalry? Are we looking for the first introduction of guns on the battlefield, or the moment at which their use was sufficiently effective to affect the conduct of war and the nature of military responses, or indeed the moment at which it could be said with confidence that they won battles? What is a standing army? Is continuous employment and organisation of troops in peace and war a sufficient criterion? Or are we to wait for the introduction of uniforms, formalised command structures, military academies, etc. before we recognise permanence? It will be the argument of this chapter that earlier rather than later dates are important for the identification of significant impact of changes in the relationship between war and society, and war and government. We are considering here not just war itself but also preparation for war; the perspective is therefore more gradual and inevitably less revolutionary.

## 2. EUROPEAN WARS OF THE FIFTEENTH CENTURY

In the first half of the fifteenth century there were three main areas of European warfare: the Hundred Years War between France and England was about to enter a new phase in which an increasingly independent Burgundy – together with substantial numbers of Scots and Italian troops – were to play a part; wars in Italy reached a new level of intensity and coherence; on the other hand the crusading endeavour of the *Reconquista* in the Iberian peninsula was going through a relatively quiet period.

### The Hundred Years' War
Already by 1400 the Hundred Years' War had seen the organisation of contract armies on both sides, and a degree of long-term service being generated both by the periodic experiences of the English *chevauchées*, and by

the sustained efforts of Charles V of France to create the nucleus of a royal army in the 1360s and 1370s.[3] The battles of Crecy and Poitiers had shown that well-trained archers and dismounted knights in a prepared position could repel a cavalry charge, but the crucial factor was the decision to accept battle in disadvantageous circumstances. Medieval leaders were always reluctant to do this, but on both these occasions the strategic situation seemed to demand that the opportunity to catch the English marauders be not lost. The cause of the French defeats was, therefore, less any new superiority of infantry over cavalry, than mistaken tactics and poor decision making. Undoubtedly the massed fire of the English archers was an innovation in continental warfare, but the knights soon turned to improved plate armour, longer lances and better discipline as counters to the new threat. As a result heavy cavalry continued to dominate warfare for much of the fifteenth century, and the nucleus of the first standing armies was always such cavalry.

Henry V's decision to invade and occupy Normandy in 1415 rather than just ravage the area was a turning point in the wars. The decision was dictated more by the ambitions and needs of a new dynasty seeking to consolidate itself and attract support, and by a clear realisation of the current factional disunity in France, than by any perception of military advantage. However, Henry did possess formidable artillery for the day and it was this that made possible the quick subjugation of towns and castles in Normandy after his initial victory at Agincourt in 1415. That battle, while it once again demonstrated the effectiveness of disciplined archers protected by dismounted knights, was not quite a carbon copy of Crecy and Poitiers. The larger French army on this occasion had the advantage of a prepared position astride the line of march of the English seeking to reach Calais and embarkation for the safety of England. It was Henry V's task to lure the French out of their position and incite them to attack and thus throw away their advantage. He achieved this by moving his archers forward and directing their fire on to the French from behind a hurriedly created stockade of stakes. The French, stung to action by the hail of arrows and not realising how effectively the archers had protected themselves, charged to their destruction. The cruel losses which they suffered at Agincourt, combined with the deep rifts which already existed between Burgundians and Armagnacs, left the French unable to prevent Henry's systematic occupation of Normandy over the next three years.[4]

However, the conquest of Normandy and the formal alliance with the Burgundians which followed, created an entirely new situation. England was now committed not just to the defence of the new possessions but to maintaining the assault on the position of the French crown. A permanent presence of standing forces in France now became necessary. Royal officials took on responsibility for the organising and paying of garrisons in Normandy in a more systematic way than had ever been necessary for the expeditions of Edward III and the Black Prince. At the same time the defence of Normandy and the exploitation of the new opportunities became the responsibility of a relatively small section of the English political class which had received estates there in the initial conquest. This situation would have applied even if Henry V had not died prematurely in 1422 leaving a child-heir and an increasingly divided baronage.[5]

The success of Charles VII of France in distancing himself from the factious Armagnacs and eventually healing the breach with Burgundy at Arras in 1435, and in giving the French nobility a new sense of purpose both to protect their lands from further English incursion, and recover what had been lost, was as important in turning the tide of war as the military reorganisation which he undertook. Initially in the 1420s he recruited large numbers of Piedmontese and Scots mercenaries to bolster the flagging morale of the Armagnac companies. But gradually a reorganisation of royal finances and the imposition of direct taxation through the *taille* made possible a return to the policy of creating a permanent royal army started in the middle years of the fourteenth century, particularly by Charles V. Through a series of *ordonnances*, initiated in 1439, a standing body of heavy cavalry made up of fifteen companies of 100 lances each was created. With captains chosen and appointed by the Crown, and troops paid individually by royal treasurers, the *compagnies d'ordonnance* became the standing core of the French army. At the same time recruiting without the royal licence was forbidden. The confirmation of this arrangement at the moment of the Truce of Tours in 1444, and at the end of the war in 1453, made it clear that such a permanent force was now regarded as essential. In 1448 a further *ordonnance* created a select militia system, set up to provide for the recruitment and training of supporting infantry, the *francs-archers*. Meanwhile the royal artillery had been steadily built up by the Bureau brothers and made a notable contribution to the gradual reduction of the English fortified places in Normandy and Gascony. On the other hand, Henry VI had shown little enthusiasm for the later stages of the war in France, and the central control of the defence force in Normandy tended to break down in the 1440s. Thus the initiative to maintain royal standing forces was not maintained even during the war, and certainly did not survive the return of the last troops in 1453. Therefore, unlike France, England did not emerge from the wars committed to a paid permanent army.

*Italy: Foundations of Mercenary Warfare*

The Italian states, however, played a major part in the development of permanent military institutions in this period. The admiration for things Italian, which beset Europe in the early Renaissance period, applied to military affairs no less than other spheres. Charles VII used Italian mercenaries and Charles the Bold of Burgundy relied on Italian troops and methods to a large extent. As always, however, the influences worked both ways; Charles V's military reforms in the 1360s and 1370s were undoubtedly noted in Italy and the English battle tactics of John Hawkwood were both effective and admired in Italy.

However, cross-fertilisation of ideas and outside influences are not the main explanation for the military developments in Italy. The emerging political structure of the peninsula exercised the greatest influence on the organisation of war. As long as that structure was dominated, at least in north and central Italy, by a myriad of small autonomous states, then impermanence, unreliability and treachery were the characteristics of the military system. Small, aggressive, expanding city states, often well-endowed with financial resources, sought professional military aid for their short-term enterprises. That aid was readily available from outside Italy in the fourteenth century – partly stimulated by the demand, partly by the wealth and climate of Italy, partly by breaks in fighting elsewhere in Europe. The practice of states hiring standing companies for short campaigning seasons and specific objectives satisfied both employers and employees. However, by the end of the fourteenth century the situation was changing; the successful consolidation of a small number of states at the expense of many others gave a new dimension to the problem of defence. Extended frontiers and large territorial areas required castles, garrisons and permanent bodies of cavalry to defend them, in a way that the walls of a single city did not. The new states, like the Duchy of Milan, had the resources to fund longer term contracts with companies, and soon discovered that this could actually reduce costs. The expansion of the Florentine state from the 1380s and that of Venice from 1404 completed the balance of major powers in northern Italy, while the ending of the Schism and the return of a single acknowledged Pope, Martin V, to Rome in 1420, and the Aragonese victory in Naples, confirmed in 1442, filled the power vacuums in the south. These states could no longer depend for their defence and their periodic aggressive enterprises on hastily hired mercenaries. At the same time they did not have the trust in their new subjects, or necessarily the domestic manpower available, to move towards self-dependence in this field. The answer, therefore, was extended contractual arrangements with established Italian captains, and increasingly sophisticated organisations for administering the standing companies.[6]

The fluid, piecemeal developments of the fourteenth century had encouraged an emphasis on mobility and professional skill in warfare. The inevitable dominance of cavalry had not been significantly challenged in Italy by archers, as it had been in France, nor had the traditions of the old communal infantry been maintained. Heavy cavalry dominated the scene in the early fifteenth century, and the two contrasting traditions which were to be influential throughout the century emerged in the 1420s. The Sforzeschi, led by Musio Attendolo Sforza and his son Francesco, originated in the Romagna and emphasised discipline and control in their training and manoeuvres; their rivals, the Bracceschi, led by Braccio da Montone from Umbria, relied more on speed and *élan* for their success. These are the age-old traditions of cavalry warfare; to some extent the techniques of the English and the French knights can be contrasted in the same way, and the pre-echo of Roundheads and Cavaliers in the English Civil War is obvious. But the emergence of the two schools in Italian warfare gave a new coherence and a new competitive edge to the fighting, they also ensured the continued dominance of cavalry through the first half of the fifteenth century.

Certainly the companies hired with the new long-term contracts tended to be heavy cavalry companies led by a *condottiere* (contractor), and made up of three-man lances. The size of the company depended initially on the prestige and resources of the *condottiere*, but increasingly the intentions and resources of the employing state began to dictate company size. The company, even in permanent service, had an internal life of its own; squadron and detachment leaders contracted themselves to the captain and pay mechanisms within the company became increasingly sophisticated. An outstanding example of a large, long-standing Italian company in the fifteenth century was that of Micheletto Attendolo, a cousin of Francesco Sforza, who served successively as Florentine, Papal and Venetian captain general in the years between 1425 and 1448. The accounts of the company were kept throughout this period by Ser Francesco Viviani, a notary from Arezzo, and these reveal a remarkable continuity of membership – and particularly of leadership – in Attendolo's force, which numbered 2,000 cavalry in the later years. During the twenty three years of the recorded life of the company Attendolo gave sub-contracts to 512 lieutenants, squadron and group leaders – of whom more than 100 served him for over ten years.[7]

The culmination of Micheletto Attendolo's career was a period of seven years as captain general of the Venetian army between 1441 and 1448. By that time Venice had extended its control over north eastern Italy to cover almost the entire area from Bergamo and the Adda frontier to the Istrian Alps. To defend this state from the envious Visconti and Sforza Dukes of Milan, from whom some of it had been taken, and to exploit possible opportunities for further expansion, Venice was bound to maintain a large permanent army. Warfare between 1424 and 1454 was almost continuous in northern and central Italy; some 50,000 men were kept under arms by states which, while promoting themselves as defenders of republicanism against tyranny, or stable princely rule against undisciplined popular forces, were in fact engaged in a vicious power struggle. This was a period in which non-Italian troops largely disappeared from the scene, as the retention in service of companies billetted in the country areas in times of truce and peace on reduced pay proved decreasingly attractive to fortune seeking Germans, Hungarians, Provencals and Catalans.

A notable feature of this new situation was the emergence, even more clearly than in France, of the bureaucratic and administrative framework required by the states to organise war in its novel guise. The preparation and supervision of contracts, recruiting, billetting, inspection, pay, and provisioning and supply became major preoccupations of state officials. Offices were established to carry out these functions, new taxes raised, armouries stocked, and merchants and horse dealers cajoled. The prospect of long term service and rewards together with the increased supervision of experienced officials gradually eroded the ambitions of the *condottieri*, and made infidelity and treachery less common.[8]

The traditional suspicions nurtured by civilians against hired soldiers did not, of course, disappear. Tensions remained, particularly over money and over the direction of war policy. Milan and Venice adapted more quickly to the exigencies of the new situation than did Florence which found it difficult to adapt to the idea of preparing for war, and indeed paying for war, in time of peace. Florence's backwardness in this respect, and the new pressures of the post 1494 period, were the background to the strictures of Machiavelli on Italian warfare. But war in Italy in the fifteenth century was not 'commenced without fear, continued without danger, and concluded without loss'.[9] From the viewpoint of 1513 and the aftermath of the battle of Ravenna it may have appeared less bloody and decisive, but compared to the situation in the fourteenth century, where Machiavelli's eyes seemed really to be focussed, it was infinitely more organised, sustained and fearsome. The battles in Italy in the first half of the fifteenth century, Aquila (1424), Maclodio (1427), Anghiari (1440),

Casalmaggiore (1446), Caravaggio (1448), were all more intense and involving larger numbers than any fought in France in the same period, except Agincourt. By the middle of the century when the Peace of Lodi (1454) led to an exhausted lull in the fighting, the standing forces of the Italian states included at least 25% infantry companies, many equipped with handguns; they included large artillery trains; they had the capacity to turn out large detachments of conscripted labour for field engineering works. The military world had already changed substantially since the beginning of the century.

### Tradition and Innovation in the Later Fifteenth Century

The period between 1453/4 and 1494 was, in contrast, to the first half of the century, a period of comparative peace in Europe. There were spasmodic outbreaks of fighting between England and France, and both countries experienced civil war, England for the extended period of the Wars of the Roses, France more briefly in the mid-1460s. Charles the Bold of Burgundy's campaigns in the 1470s particularly against the Swiss cantons, and the intensive, and eventually successful pressure exerted on the Moors of Granada by the newly united Spanish kingdoms, were obvious exceptions to the impression of peace. In Italy also a series of spasmodic outbreaks of vicious fighting between the states ensured that military preparedness was maintained. Indeed throughout western Europe in this half century, except in England, the importance of maintaining military preparedness in time of peace was a lesson that seemed to have been learnt.

Louis XI of France actually increased the numbers of the heavy cavalry *compagnies d'ordonnance* during the relatively peaceful 1470s, and began to organise large scale annual manoeuvres. Particular attention was given to building up the royal artillery train with an emphasis not just on more mobile guns but also on the training of gunners. In Venice also there was growing concern with how to maintain the standing forces effective in time of peace. Periodic training sessions supervised by Venetian officials, close attention to the maintenance of well-stocked armouries, and continual experimentation with artillery, for use both on land and at sea, were all part of a watchful policy of preparedness. In Milan a growing distinction emerged between a core of the army made up of a large ducal bodyguard and permanent companies of veterans, and the companies of the enfeoffed *condottieri* which were maintained on stand-by on their estates.[10]

Already there was a rather traditional look about these standing forces. The emphasis was still on heavy, armoured, lance cavalry drawn largely from the rural upper and middle classes. Doubt must be expressed about the extent of training of 'paper armies' particularly when perusing the archival records of the Duchy of Milan with their estimates of 42,000 men waiting under arms in the 1470s. The part-time nature of much of the infantry support was fully recognised. Both in France and in Venice considerable emphasis was placed on the periodic training of the militias, and Venice also maintained a large number of professional infantry constables on full pay with small followings in order to be ready for rapid mobilisation and recruiting of infantry. Even the Burgundian army, which was actually created in this period by Charles the Bold, showed this rather traditional appearance. Twelve standing companies of 100 nine-man lances were established in 1471 in imitation of the French companies, but with a larger infantry component of the lance formation, and in 1476 separate infantry and light cavalry companies were added. Charles's ordinances included meticulous instructions about training and discipline; large numbers of experienced Italian cavalry were recruited to fill the first companies alongside the Burgundian knights; great efforts were made to create an artillery train. Charles even proposed the use of linear tactics for the infantry to make more effective use of the new handguns with which many were armed. The newly created Order of the Golden Fleece, like other new military orders of the time, was intended to provide a national, patriotic framework for a resurgence of chivalric ideals linked to the new permanence being imparted to cavalry skills.[11]

### Innovations: the Swiss

But this new Burgundian army was to be shattered even before it was fully formed. The main agent in its destruction was the largely infantry army of the Swiss cantons created over the previous two centuries to defend the area against Austrian and imperial overlords. The main weapon of the Swiss was the long infantry pike wielded by men, largely from pastoral communities, who spent a considerable amount of their spare time training both to handle the weapon and to manoeuvre and fight in large formations. The Swiss pike square was not just an effective defensive formation against cavalry charges, but also, given the level of training and fitness of the infantry, was able to advance rapidly and become a fearsome offensive force against other infantry positions, and cavalry as they formed up. In defence of their independence the Swiss had already given warning of their potential in decisive victories over cavalry forces at Morgarten (1315) and Sempach (1386). A contingent of 500 Swiss played a part, and was widely admired, in the War of the Common Weal in France in the 1460s. However, it was in the mid 1470s that large Swiss armies, with the support of significant bodies of cavalry sent by their allies, succeeding in routing Charles the Bold's new army in three great battles. Grandson and Morat in 1476 were fought against an over-confident Burgundian army threatening the Swiss homeland, but Nancy in January, 1477, saw the Swiss on the offensive crushing a much smaller Burgundian force and killing its duke.

The victories of the Swiss in the 1470s were an important turning point. European rulers now became convinced that well trained infantry equipped with pikes and halberds had to be a component of their standing forces. Louis XI made arrangements to hire Swiss infantry whenever France needed them and began to disband the *francs archers*. In Germany and Italy princes began to raise and train their own infantry along the same lines; the German landsknechts soon emerged as rivals to the Swiss and almost equally sought after. Mercenary tendencies in European warfare were given a very considerable boost by the emergence and availability of new skills, as much as by new accretions of wealth or new foci of power.

However the military world did not change overnight as a result of the Swiss victories, any more than it had in the aftermath of the victories of archers at Crecy and Poitiers. The Burgundian army was newly formed and untried; it was made up of as many infantry as cavalry, and it was the Burgundian archers and militias which had been swept aside as much as the Italian and Burgundian cavalry; the defects of Charles the Bold's leadership on the battlefield were widely recognised. The limitations of the Swiss, the relative rigidity of their tactics, the lack of coherent leadership, the seasonal nature of their effectiveness, were not yet apparent, but European leaders were not about to abandon all else in order to employ Swiss or infantry trained in the same manner. Their presence had become indispensable in a large army but they did not yet form the core of a large army. The problems now were how many Swiss did a general need to create an effective force, how many could he afford, and how did he counter the effectiveness of such troops in the opposing army.

### Innovations: Iberia

Swiss-style pike infantry were not the only innovations on the international scene in the later fifteenth century. The sustained attack on the last Moorish strongholds in Granada launched by the united Spanish kingdoms of Ferdinand and Isabella, called for a new permanence and organisation of the Spanish armies and for the development of specific expertise. The last stages of the *Reconquista* were fought out in rough country and involved a series of fiercely contested sieges. To maintain the campaigns the Spanish crown organised the old guards of Castile into 25 companies of 100 men at arms in each, supervised and paid by royal treasurers. Five of the companies were made up of *jinetes*, light horse armed with round shields and short spears. Alongside this increasingly professional cavalry force a body of 40,000 infantry was maintained, recruited largely from the urban militias of the Hermandades, and made up to a considerable extent of the sword and buckler infantry used by the Aragonese kings. These were ideal troops for storming fortresses, and they were supported by large numbers of hand-gunners and arquebusiers, and by a formidable train of siege artillery largely manned by Germans.[12]

The Spanish light cavalry innovations owed something to Moorish and Arab precedents, but at the same moment the Venetians were using increasing numbers of Albanian stradiots, both in their wars against the advancing Turks and, from 1482, in Italy. The stradiots had similar characteristics to the jinetes; they were more mobile and flexible than the traditional heavy cavalry, they did not require followers and lance organisation, and they were therefore much cheaper to maintain. The Duke of Calabria, commander of the Neapolitan army in the 1480s, used captured Turkish *sipahis* in the same role.[13]

### Gunpowder Weapons

The large scale use of the hand-gun, and its successor the arquebus, in the second half of the fifteenth century, also has to be noted. This was a cumbersome and inaccurate weapon, but if large enough numbers of infantry were equipped with it very destructive firepower could be generated. Handgun shot could pierce plate armour in a way that arrows could not, and handgunners, ranging from companies of German professionals to the mass use of the weapon by Venetian militias, were increasingly respected and feared. They were, however, even more vulnerable on the battlefield than archers because of their slow rate of fire, and this led to a growing emphasis on collaboration between different types of troops in battle tactics, and on field fortifications.

The long debate on the effectiveness of gunpowder weapons and the development of counters to them in fortification techniques is now finally resolved in favour of a somewhat earlier chronology than used to be fashionable. Fourteenth century guns were indeed cumbersome and ineffective, relying on the looping trajectory of the catapult or the bombard, and massive weight of stone shot, to do their damage. However, improvements in the formula for the composition of gunpowder in the first half of the fifteenth century led to higher velocity firing by smaller guns using metal shot, and hence to the possibilities of greater mobility, lower costs and larger numbers.[14] All this was reflected not just in the highly organised artillery train of the French crown in the later fifteenth century, but in similar developments by other governments. Charles the Bold was said to have 400 guns for his army, and there were reports of 1,500 guns used by the Spanish crown in the *Reconquista*. Such figures undoubtedly included many hand-held weapons, but the numbers of effective cannon were increasing rapidly. The Venetian government ordered 100 wheeled 6-12 pounders in 1496, and four years later launched the basilisk, a 100 pounder mounted on a gun carriage, which began to be produced in large numbers.[15]

A considerable increase in the number of effective guns available was not necessarily reflected in the size of gun trains accompanying armies. A train of 40 or 50 guns like that of Charles VIII in 1494 was a formidable one, but the majority of the guns being cast at this time were for use in defending fortifications, and increasingly at sea. The need to site guns in fortifications was as important a factor in the changes in fortification techniques which accompanied these developments, as the new threat to the defences which guns posed. The changes, the arrival of solid angled bastions, low scarped walls, ravelins and extensive outer works, were apparent in the ideas of leading Italian military architects by the mid-fifteenth century and in practice in central Italy and in Rhodes by the 1480s.[16] This in itself is testimony to the increased effectiveness of the guns by this time; and that effectiveness was apparent on the battlefield as well as in siegecraft. The preparation of elaborate field fortifications to protect armies in the open became standard practice in Italian warfare and began to dictate the course of battle tactics.

By the end of the fifteenth century trained, professional infantry of various types had become essential components of every army. To a certain extent such troops were mercenaries, just as some of the new light cavalry companies were mercenaries. The availability of such skilled troops were key factors in periods of mercenary warfare. But the core of the increasingly permanent armies remained the heavy cavalry which was developing a strongly 'national' character. The army which Charles VIII led over the Alps in 1494 to invade Italy was a mixed army. The heavy cavalry and the gunners were largely French, the infantry was largely Swiss; all the elements, in their different ways, were largely professionals.

## 3. EUROPEAN WARFARE IN THE SIXTEENTH CENTURY

Warfare on a scale almost unimaginable for much of the fifteenth century dominated the three and a half decades which followed the French invasion of Italy in 1494. What started as Franco-Spanish confrontation for influence in the Mediterranean became, with the election of Charles I, king of the united kingdom of Aragon/Castile, as Holy Roman Emperor Charles V, a European power struggle which was to last throughout the sixteenth and seventeenth centuries. Italy was the focus of this struggle until 1529, initially as the key to Mediterranean predominance and wealth, eventually as the strategic lynch-pin of the Hapsburg empire. The Italian wars saw the peninsula occupied, dominated and fought over by large foreign armies, competing on neutral ground with extended communications and supply routes. This was a situation in which, quite apart from the great issues at stake, a more decisive, fearsome type of warfare was bound to emerge.[17]

### The Italian Wars

Italy, of course, had not been free from foreign intervention in the fifteenth century. An Aragonese dynasty had established itself in Naples by the middle of the century, and French armies had intervened in warfare between the Italian states three times during the second half of the century. The claims of Angevins to the throne of Naples and Orleanists to the Duchy of Milan were widely recognised and frequently invoked. The ambassadors of the Italian states at the French court kept their governments constantly informed of the rising aspirations of the French crown. On other fronts the Venetians fought the Austrians in the Trentino in 1487, and the Turks in Friuli and throughout their empire in the 1460s and 1470s. The kingdom of Naples also confronted Turkish invaders in 1480-81. All these were precedents for the events which took place at the end of the century, but none of them had really prepared the Italian states for the sustained onslaught which was to come.

Charles VIII's plans for his Italian expedition were prepared over a period of some five years. Frenzied diplomatic and military preparation started in the early summer of 1493. Charles's aims had a traditional and essentially Mediterranean focus to them. He claimed the crown of Naples on the basis of the rights of his Angevin forbears, he boasted of leading a crusade against the Turks from his new base in southern Italy, he offered his nobles visions of rich pickings in the treasure chests of Italy and the conquered estates of the Neapolitan kingdom. That success in Naples would lead to confrontation with Spain, newly released from preoccupation with the *Reconquista*, was inevitable; that it should be won and lost so easily without major intervention from Spain was more surprising. The French army of some 3,500 lances and 10,000 infantry, largely Swiss, entered Naples less than six months after crossing the Alps. It fought no battles on the way and scarcely fired a shot in anger. The disunity and political fragility of the Italian states made organised resistance difficult. However, the retreat from Naples in the spring of 1495 was almost as rapid. Charles escaped with difficulty from the Venetian-led army of the hastily formed Holy League at Fornovo, and the garrisons left in the Neapolitan kingdom were quickly overrun by a small Spanish army led into Italy by Gonsalvo de Cordoba, the Great Captain, with Venetian help.

Alliance with Milan had been essential to the first French invasion and provided Charles VIII with a friendly base for his operations. In 1499 Louis XII, his successor, used his Orleanist claims to that Duchy as an excuse for creating a more permanent base for French operations in Italy. He occupied Milan with the aid of the Venetians and evicted the Sforza Dukes. He then negotiated a partition of Naples with Spain at the Treaty of Granada in 1500. French troops moved south once more to occupy their part of the Kingdom, including Naples itself. But the inevitable tensions of the partition arrangement built up as both powers strengthened their armies in southern Italy. In 1503 the confrontation came; Gonsalvo de Cordoba inflicted two crushing defeats on the French at Cerignola and the Garigliano, with significant help from Italian captains and troops. French hopes of establishing themselves in the south were effectively at an end, and attention was now to shift to central and northern Italy.

Once again a pause in the conflict was to end with another partition project; the League of Cambrai was formed in 1508 to divide up the powerful Venetian state, and in the following year the first of the League's armies, that of France, crossed the Venetian frontier and crushed the Venetian army at the battle of Agnadello. The French success, although in fact not complete because of a determined Venetian rearguard action, quickly produced dissension within the League. Pope Julius II created a new Holy League with Spain and the Empire to drive the French out of Italy. Spanish troops began to move north in large numbers, and, although defeated at Ravenna in 1512, nevertheless maintained the initiative, reinstated the Medici in Florence and the Sforza in a reoccupied Milan.

The recovery of Milan and a renewal of the Italian enterprise became the first aim of the new French king, Francis I, in 1515. He attacked the Sforza duchy and the Swiss infantry which had been hired to guard it, and

destroyed both at Marignano. The next four years saw the gradual creation of the great empire of Charles of Hapsburg, uniting the Spanish kingdoms and Naples to the Burgundian Netherlands, the Hapsburg Austrian
lands and the Imperial title. In this context the Duchy of Milan, with its
control over Genoa and the western Alpine passes, became the key to the
Hapsburg system. Recovery and control of Milan assumed even more vital importance for Charles than for Francis. A surprise attack in 1520 secured that recovery and two attempts by the French to regain control were
stopped by victories at Bicocca (1521) and Pavia (1525). However, even
the capture of Francis I at Pavia and the death of many of the French leaders did not end the confrontation in Italy. Another French army set out in
1527 under Marshal Lautrec and even got as far as besieging Naples. But
the growing predominance of the Spanish in Italy could not be denied;
Pope Clement VII came to terms after the sack of Rome, the revived pro-
French Florentine republic surrendered to a Hapsburg army, and interest
gradually switched to other theatres of war—particularly the frontier
between France and the Netherlands.

### Tactics and Numbers

If the late 1520s, the Ladies Peace of Cambrai and the coronation of
Charles V as Emperor by the Pope at Bologna in 1530, seemed to mark a
turning point in international affairs and diplomatic alignments, there also
seemed to be a change of military mood. Up to this point in the wars there
had been a steady escalation in numbers committed to battle, in the proportion of infantry to cavalry, and in the fierceness and determination with
which the battles were fought. Pavia had been the culmination of this
process. The French army besieging Pavia in February 1525 numbered
8,000 cavalry and 23,000 infantry; the Marquis of Pescara attacked the
French camp with 5,000 cavalry and 20,000 infantry, and the vanguard of
the Spanish assault was made up of 7,000 arquebusiers, whose intensive
fire both disrupted the French cavalry charges and decimated the Swiss
pike squares. This was war of a very different kind even to that fought at
Fornovo thirty years earlier. On that occasion a French army of 9,000,
two thirds of which was cavalry, fought off a brilliant but unsustained attack by an Italian army of 22,000, of which less than half, nearly all cavalry, was effectively involved. A real turning point came with the first major encounter between French and Spanish armies at Cerignola in 1503. In
this encounter both armies numbered about 12,000. The Spanish had
4,500 arquebusiers in a force of which only one third was cavalry and
which was assembled in a prepared defensive position; the French, with a

slightly higher proportion of cavalry, attacked with the heavy cavalry in the van and the Swiss squares following up. At the heart of the Spanish defence were pikes to halt the impetus of the French advance; on the flanks were arquebuses to enfilade the mass of men and horses caught in front of them, in reserve was the main body of Spanish cavalry to sweep in and complete the rout. It was the classic battle scenario with firearms finally taking the place of bows, cavalry being more effective in counter attack than in the initial charge, and the triumphant march of the Swiss pikes halted and shattered by a combination of shot and shock. These were the battles in which the pike square gradually gave way to the tercio, a large flexible force of pikes, swordsmen and arquebusiers, and the dominance of infantry finally arrived. They were also battles in which, as Table 1 shows, the numbers involved quickly reached proportions similar to those engaged in the battles of the Thirty Years' War.[18]

Table 1

Numbers Engaged in Battles in the Italian Wars
and the Thirty Years' War

*The Italian Wars*
(cavalry:infantry)
French army invading Italy in 1494—31,000 (2:1)
Fornovo (1495)—French 9,000 (2:1); Italians 22,000 (1:1)
Cerignola (1503)—French 12,000 (5:7); Spanish 11,500 (1:2)
Carigliano (1503)—French 35,000 (1:1); Spanish 22,000 (4:7)
Agnadello (1509)—French 40,000 (3:5); Venetians 36,000 (2:5)
Ravenna (1512)—French 33,000 (2:3); Spanish 20,000 (1:2)
Marignano (1516)—French 48,000 (5:11); Swiss 22,000 (0:1)
Pavia (1525)—French 31,000 (1:3); Spanish 25,000 (1:4)

*The Thirty Years' War*
White Mountain (1620)—Catholic League 28,000; Bohemians 21,000
Breitenfeld (1631)—Hapsburgs 35,000; Swedes 42,000
Lützen (1632)—Hapsburgs 19,000; Swedes 19,000
Nördlingen (1634)—Catholics 34,000; Protestants 25,000
Rocroi (1643)—French 24,000; Spanish 17,000

But after Pavia the mood changed. The tempo of war slowed; attrition and manoeuvre returned, major battles became rare. The reasons for this will be discussed in more detail shortly, but one of them impinges immediately on the early decades of the sixteenth century. The campaigns in Italy stretched the military organisations of the combatants to their limit. Philippe de Commynes commented on the French expedition of 1494 that 'everything necessary for so great an enterprise was lacking', and what he meant by this was administrative, logistical and financial support.[19] A friendly base in Milan and the resources of the Milanese state were essential to the success of French ambitions in Italy. The fleet could provide only limited help in supplying and reinforcing the armies; living off the land was at best a temporary expedient which led quickly to bad discipline and resentment in the local population, and was eventually self-defeating. The French, like the Italian armies of the period, did have a sophisticated billeting system with quartermasters riding ahead of the army to requisition and allocate billets. But supply and regular pay were problems throughout the wars. An army of 30,000 men still had a large number of horses in the 1520s as artillery and baggage trains expanded; 90 tons of fodder a day were needed for such an army and this was the produce of 400 acres of forage.[20]

*Spanish Forces in the Sixteenth Century*

The Spanish army had developed a more innovative and centralised administrative structure during the *Reconquista*, and this was transferred to Italy by Gonsalvo de Cordoba. Aragonese Sicily was available as a supply base, and Neapolitan resources, both of finance and military supplies, were quickly harnessed to the exigencies of the campaigns. But as Spanish armies moved north after 1509 the supply lines and the organisation became stretched. The effect of these difficulties was bound to be limitation on the size of armies, on the duration of campaigns, on the discipline and determination of troops, and these factors gradually imposed themselves on a situation, i.e. fighting on foreign soil for great prizes, which had initially been conducive to expanded, permanent and ferocious armies.

The extent to which Spain wrestled with these problems throughout the sixteenth century as its lines of communications and supply extended northwards from Italy, and its commitments increased, has been admirably addressed by Geoffrey Parker.[21] The success achieved was a key factor in Spanish military dominance in the period and enabled the Spanish army to grow overall to 150,000 men under arms in the middle of the century. This was a considerably larger army than that maintained by any other Eu-

ropean power at this time and was made up of troops drawn from all over
the Hapsburg empire, Castilians, Aragonese, Italians, Netherlanders and
Germans. But numbers under arms increased generally in the middle years
of the sixteenth century. There were a variety of factors at work here: the
acceptance of the predominant role of infantry in war made recruiting
easier and cheaper; the spread of gunpowder fortifications outside Italy after 1520 placed a greater emphasis on numbers both to defend and assault
fortresses; demographic growth and the increasing resources available to
states were the external factors in the equation. The focus of conflict at
least until 1559 was the rivalry between the Hapsburg empire (after 1556,
and the accession of Philip II, particularly the Spanish Hapsburg empire)
and France. It was a conflict waged around all the frontiers of France, but
particularly on the north east frontier. It was a conflict that developed into
a sort of arms race but also into a balance of power, and eventually a stalemate. France with interior lines of communication, but more limited resources, was able to withstand Hapsburg pressure until Spanish preoccupation with Ottoman advance in the Mediterranean and religious civil war
in France distracted the rivals. Military stalemate cannot be fully explained in military terms. Undoubtedly the spread of the *trace italienne* did
slow down the tempo of war in certain theatres, particularly on France's
eastern frontier and on the Hapsburg frontier with the Ottomans. The
costs of fortress building, not just in these areas, but also round the English
coasts, and the coasts of Spain and Italy threatened by the Ottomans, diverted limited resources away from other forms of military expenditure.[22]
The emphasis on siege warfare, from the Ottoman siege of Vienna in 1529
to the siege of St. Quentin in 1557, dictated both the specialisms and the
numbers of the soldiery involved. All this is true, as it is equally true that
infantry armies march and manoeuvre more slowly than cavalry armies.
But in the last resort the interesting question is not how the stalemate developed but why it took so long to resolve it. The European powers in the
sixteenth century were not able to expand their military strength, the size
of their armies and their arsenals, the expertise of their troops, indefinitely.
Particularly were they not able to concentrate their forces in sufficient
strength, either on the battlefield or in a siege, to secure real success. Problems of supply, communications and command structures all contributed
to this, but even more fundamental was a basic limitation of resources as
economic tensions set in after about 1560, and the relative immaturity of
state organisation and control. Decentralised regular armies, poorly paid,
poorly supplied and poorly led, were at the heart of the problem in the second half of the sixteenth century.

*Innovations in Military Theory*

There were plenty of military theorists who sought the answers to these problems. From Diomede Carafa and Niccolò Machiavelli onwards, theorising about how to achieve success in war and the innovations necessary to bring that success became a major intellectual pastime. The advent of printing and the universal belief that the classical world, and in this case an intensively militaristic classical world, had the answers to all contemporary problems, fuelled the interest. The theorists correctly identified training and discipline as the key to improved warfare rather than technological innovation, but the mechanisms for such training, and the application of them to very large bodies of troops, emerged slowly. Genuine military academics, as opposed to schools of riding and fencing, only emerged in the last years of the century, despite much discussion for over fifty years previously. Drill manuals were gradually making an impact but on very large formations, like the 3,000-strong tercio, which performed their exercises in a mechanical way, drawing strength and comfort from numbers and the depth of their formations. Theory had outrun practice to a significant extent and this was all part of the stalemate.[23]

*The Quickening of Innovation around 1600*

That the last years of the sixteenth century saw something of a breakthrough, a quickening of the pace of innovation, a new possibility of dramatic military success, was due as much to new theatres of war as anything else. William Lewis and Maurice of Nassau succeeded, in the context of a relatively small and stable Dutch army, defending hearth and home, in instilling the necessary training to make linear tactics work, and hence maximising the fire power of their musket troops. The relatively new technology of making light cast iron guns was exploited by the Dutch, and even more by Gustavus Adolphus, to transform the role of artillery on the battlefield. The shift of the arena of war from the heavily fortified frontiers of France to the plains of central Germany in the early seventeenth century, gave a new impetus to exploiting mass and mobility on the battlefield. The innovatory nature of these developments has been much exaggerated, and the continued success of Spanish armies, and the eventual domination of French armies by the late seventeenth century, suggest the importance of continuities. Ideas spread very quickly because they had been long prepared for; Spanish commanders were reducing the size of the tercio and putting more emphasis on the musketeers throughout the last three decades of the sixteenth century. The Nassau cousins had read their Machiavelli as well as their Aelian.[24]

One of the intentions of this discussion of land warfare in the last medieval and early modern periods has been to push some of the key characteristics of the 'Military Revolution' back into the fifteenth century. Substantial permanent armies equipped with large numbers of reasonably effective guns and hand-held firearms were deployed by the second half of the century. At sea, however, permanent war fleets carrying large numbers of guns emerged somewhat later and, at least outside the Mediterranean, much more dramatically.[25]

## 4. DEVELOPMENTS IN NAVAL WARFARE

In the Middle Ages there were two quite distinct traditions of naval warfare. In the Atlantic and northern seas the standard vessel was the sailing ship or round ship, small, single-masted, cumbersome, manned by a tiny crew. Such a ship could be armed by putting fighting men aboard and even, by the fourteenth century, mounting two or three small breech-loaders. But its prime function was to transport goods. The sailing qualities and the potential fighting strength of such a ship precluded using it to command the sea, and indeed command of the sea was not a concept imagined by late medieval rulers and governments outside the Mediterranean. The rhythms of sea trade and the threats of large scale invasion were minimal, and standing fleets of royal ships could serve little purpose. Warships, when needed to carry armies or defend coasts, were created by hiring or requisitioning merchants' ships and arming them. Henry V of England built a few royal ships but to carry his troops to France, not to defend England, and his small royal fleet was soon rotting in the Solent. Ramming and boarding were the techniques of naval warfare, borrowed from the cavalry tactics of the land armies.

Within the Mediterranean more favourable sailing conditions and a greater intensity of commerce to be both defended and preyed upon, created very different conditions. Traditions of naval warfare, the maintenance of permanent war fleets, the concept of command of the sea, all went back to classical times. A specialist warship was developed, the trireme galley and its various offspring. In the Middle Ages the galley was used for the transport of small quantities of very high value goods, like spices, but its prime function was as a warship. Manned by free oarsmen, who could be used to fight the galley, and an additional complement of archers and swordsmen, it could carry as many as 400 men. With its oars it could maintain sailing schedules, keep watch on station for limited periods, and close with any sailing ship. With such a vehicle command of limited stretches of sea, and of specific trade routes, could be established. Venice was able to control the Adriatic and Genoa dominated the Tyrhennian sea with small permanent war fleets. The mounting of small groups of guns fore and aft on the galleys became common and effective practice in the Mediterranean in the fifteenth century. Such guns could even be quite large muzzle-loaders because their recoil was absorbed by the length of the galley. Thus permanent war fleets were being maintained by the Italian maritime states and by the Aragonese crown in the fifteenth century.[26]

The years round 1500 saw a real turning point in this situation. The development of much larger sailing ships with two masts and greater endurance improved the possibilities of using guns at sea, but still essentially off the top decks and castles. Improvements in gun founding and gunpowder had made relatively light guns more effective. The growth of international tension and aggressiveness, of standing armies operating at longer range, requiring supply and support, created a concern about standing war fleets which the fiscal resources of western European states could now begin to afford. In the 1490s Venice was experimenting with the construction of large sailing gunships of about 1,000 tons burden. Almost certainly these ships used gunports in the lower decks to make it possible to load more cannon on board. Two of such ships were used at the battle of the Zonchio against the Ottomans in 1499 to give greater fire power to the galley fleet. They were not a great success; they caught fire and blew up; their shot, directed mostly from well above the water level did little damage to the Turkish galleys; they were unable to manoeuvre with, and cooperate with, their own galleys.[27]

Following this experiment, the Venetians, and indeed all the Mediterranean powers, moved in a different direction. The now constant threat from the Ottomans required a major escalation in naval preparedness; a standing Venetian war fleet of 25 galleys became one of 100 within a few years; arsenals were expanded; merchant great galleys were converted into armed galeasses to provide greater firepower. Large fleets and major amphibious expeditions became commonplace. At the battle of Lepanto in 1571 over 400 galleys were engaged manned by 160,000 men. The Christian fleet, Venetians, Spanish and papal, had 1815 guns. The six Venetian galeasses which led the Christian fleet into battle were said to have destroyed 70 Turkish galleys with their guns.[28] But the costs of such warfare could not be sustained; other preoccupations were distracting both Spanish and Ottoman empires; the Mediterranean was gradually becoming less worth fighting over.

But outside the Mediterranean the developments which had started round 1500 were more sustained. Once again it was guns and permanent war fleets which were the key components but here new naval traditions were being decisively forged. The development of the gun port, either independently by Breton shipbuilders as tradition suggests, or possibly in imitation of the Venetians, created entirely new possibilities within a sailing ship tradition. For the first time it became possible to mount heavy muzzle-loaders in ships with a real possibility of inflicting severe damage near the waterline at relatively long range. The essential tactical shift from line abreast formation and bearing down on the enemy, to line ahead sailing in order to stand off and bombard the enemy with broadside, developed erratically. Portuguese fleets seem already to have been using this tactic in the Red Sea in the early years of the sixteenth century. But there is evidence that the Spanish Armada was still wedded to ram and board tactics in 1588.[29] What is clear, however, is that the emergence of sailing warships, specially constructed to carry guns and each equipped with more guns than were available to the average army siege train, meant inevitably that permanent war fleets had to be maintained. By 1547 Henry VIII's Royal Navy had 53 warships, and while the number of royal ships declined slightly in subsequent years the emphasis remained on well-maintained, large, gun carrying ships to defend the realm. Thirty-four royal ships confronted the Spanish Armada supported by large numbers of impressed and hired merchant ships, and these royal ships carried 678 guns. The Armada itself had a core of royal ships, both Spanish and Portuguese; in this case they were the galleons which had been developed for transatlantic trade protection; somewhat lighter and less heavily gunned than the English ships, but nevertheless specialist warships.[30]

The administrative and logistical implications of the establishment of permanent war fleets were considerable. Shipbuilding and munitions facilities were taken over or built by governments, navy boards set up, recruiting and impressment mechanisms established.[31] France lagged far behind the two major powers in the sixteenth century, but had the same problem as Spain of maintaining separate fleets for the Mediterranean and the Atlantic. By the end of the century the Dutch, already acknowledged masters of specialist shipbuilding, developed a war fleet which effectively confronted the dual task of defending the homeland and protecting long distance trade. Made up predominantly of 300-ton frigates, fast, medium-sized, 40-gun ships, this fleet was soon to show that it could outsail and outfight the more traditional Spanish and English fleets.

※ ※ ※

Once again, therefore, there is some justification for a view of dramatic military change around 1600.  The Dutch, at sea as on land, appeared to have introduced innovations which changed the nature and the course of warfare.  However, the warfare that was changed was sixteenth-century warfare, not medieval warfare.  It was a warfare that was already dominated by large permanent nuclei of ships and soldiers, heavily dependent upon guns.  It was a warfare in which infantry had already replaced cavalry as the predominant arm, and the full implications of this in terms of numbers, training, social and cultural realignments, had already been substantially explored and experienced.  Throughout the century, and indeed long before for land warfare and Mediterranean naval warfare, governments had been committed, often reluctantly and inconsistently, to financing and organising the military permanence.  While historians may still debate whether seventeenth-century military innovation fostered absolutism or was a product of absolutism, it is already clear that fifteenth and early sixteenth-century military innovation had a crucial inter-relationship with early modern European state building.

# NOTES

1. The 'Military Revolution' debate was initiated by Michael Roberts in Roberts (1956) and continued in the context of the sixteenth century by Geoffrey Parker in Parker (1976) and (1988), John R. Hale in Hale (1985), and Jeremy Black in Black (1991).
2. For Roberts' comment on the 'great divide', see Roberts (1956), 1. For the main points made by Parker and Hale, see Parker (1988), 6-44; and Hale (1985), 46-74.
3. Discussion of fourteenth-century military organisation is to be found in Contamine (1984), 12-204; Fowler (1968), 93-139; H. J. Hewitt, *The Organization of War under Edward III, 1338-62* (Manchester, 1966).
4. On Agincourt, see A. H. Burne, *The Agincourt War* (London, 1956); Delbrück (1982), 463-70; N. J. Keegan, *The Face of Battle*, 2d ed. (London, 1991), 79-116.
5. Christopher Allmand, *Lancastrian Normandy, 1415-50. The History of a Medieval Occupation* (Oxford, 1983); R. A. Newhall (1940); Anne Curry, 'The First English Standing Army? Military Organization in Lancastrian Normandy, 1420-50', in *Patronage, Pedigree and Power in Late Medieval England*, ed. C. D. Ross (Gloucester and Totowa, 1979), 193-214.
6. Mallett (1974); Pieri (1952), 257-319; Raffaele Puddu, 'Istituzioni militari, società e stato tra Medioevo e Rinascimento', *Rivista Storica Italiana* 87 (1975): 749-69.
7. Del Treppo (1973).
8. For the military organization of the Italian states, see particularly Mallett and Hale (1984), 101-52; E. C. Visconti, 'L'Ordine dell'esercito ducale sforzesco, 1472-4', *Archivio Storico Lombardo* 3 (1876): 448-513; A. Da Mosto, 'Ordinamenti militari delle soldatesche dello stato romano dal 1430 al 1470', *Quellen und Forschungen aus italienischen Archiven und Bibliotheken* 5 (1902).
9. Niccolò Machiavelli, *Istorie Fiorentine*, Bk. V, chap. 1. For an assessment of the protracted critique of Machiavelli's views on Italian warfare, see Gilbert (1943).
10. On the French army in the second half of the fifteenth century, see Contamine (1972), 277-50; on Venice, Mallett and Hale (1984), esp. 43-55; on Milan, Visconti, 'L'Ordine' (note 8).
11. In addition to Brusten (1953), see Richard Vaughan, *Charles the Bold* (London, 1973), 197-229. A considerable amount of useful information on the Burgundian army is also to be found in R. Taverneaux, ed., *Cinq-centième anniversaire de la bataille de Nancy (1477)* (Nancy, 1978).
12. J. H. Mariejol, *The Spain of Ferdinand and Isabella*, trans. Benjamin Keen (New Brunswick, N.J., 1961), 192-208; Stewart (1969); M. A. Ladéro Quesáda, *Castilla y la conquista del reino de Granada* (Valladolid, 1967).

13. On the Venetian use of stradiots and other light cavalry, see Mallett and Hale (1984), 71-74. For the Duke of Calabria's use of captured Turkish light horse, see Michael E. Mallett, 'Venice and the War of Ferrara', in *War, Culture and Society in Renaissance Venice. Essays in honour of John Hale*, eds. D. S. Chambers, C. H. Clough, and M. E. Mallett (London, 1993), 66.
14. Contamine (1984), 193-207; DeVries (1992), 143-68; Vale (1981), 129-46.
15. Mallett and Hale (1984), 81-87.
16. Hale (1983).
17. Specialist literature on the Italian Wars is sparse and often inadequate. Pieri (1952) remains the best general account, and Taylor (1921) has also not been superseded.
18. For the battle of Pavia, see Knecht (1982), 165-75; for an eye-witness account of Fornovo, see D. M. Schullian (ed.), *Diario de Bello Carolino di Alessandro Benedetti* (New York, 1967), passim; for Cerignola, see Pieri (1952), 407-14 and Taylor (1921), 116-17. The following table is based on Pieri (1952) and Black (1991), 12.
19. Philippe de Commynes, *The Memoires*, 2 vols., ed. Samuel Kinser, trans. Isabelle Cazeaux (Columbia, S.C., 1969-73), vol. 2:453.
20. Parker (1988), 77.
21. Parker (1972).
22. Parker (1988), 10-14; Pepper and Adams (1986) also give a vivid impression of the impact of even limited programmes of refortification on the nature of warfare.
23. For discussion of many of these issues, see Hale (1985), 127-52.
24. For remarks on the extended debate on the value of linear tactics, see ibid., 59-61, and on the impact of Machiavelli's ideas on sixteenth-century military thinking, see S. Anglo, 'Machiavelli as a Military Authority. Some Early Sources', in *Florence and Italy. Renaissance Studies in Honour of Nicolai Rubinstein*, ed. P. Denley and C. Elam (London, 1988), 321-34.
25. Parker (1988), 82-99, first introduced the naval dimension into the debate, but we still lack a comprehensive account of the emergence of permanent war fleets in early modern times.
26. Alongside the magisterial work of Frederick Lane (1934) on Venetian ships and naval institutions, see Jacques Heers, *Genès au XVe siècle* (Paris, 1961), 267-91; Michael E. Mallett, *The Florentine Galleys in the Fifteenth Century* (Oxford, 1967), 103-7; A. Guglielmotti, *Storia della marina pontificia nel Medioevo*, 2 vols. (Rome, 1886); L. Schiappoli, 'La marina aragonese di Napoli', *Archivio Storico delle Provincie Napoletane* (1940).
27. On the battle of the Zonchio, see Frederick C. Lane, 'Naval actions and fleet organization, 1499-1502', in *Renaissance Venice*, ed. J. R. Hale (London, 1973), 146-73; Guilmartin (1974), 85-88.
28. Alberto Tenenti, *Cristoforo da Canal: la marine venitiènne avant Lépante* (Paris, 1962); Guilmartin (1974), 221-52; Parker (1988), 87-89.
29. Parker (1988), 92-95.
30. Martin and Parker (1988), 23-66.
31. The growth of English naval administration and organization has been more studied than that of other sixteenth-century states; but there still remains a need for comprehensive works on this topic. Concina (1987) opens up some of the issues relating to the large scale construction of warships and the workforces involved.

# BIBLIOGRAPHY

Two general works seek to bridge the divide between medieval and modern warfare in the way that this chapter does:

Howard, Michael. *War in European History.* Oxford, 1976.
McNeill, William H. *The Pursuit of Power: Technology, Armed Force and Society since A.D. 1000.* Oxford, 1983.

The rest of this bibliography is divided into three sections on the fifteenth century, the sixteenth century and naval warfare.

## The Fifteenth Century

Allmand, Christopher. *The Hundred Years War: England and France at War, c.1300-c.1450.* Cambridge Medieval Texts. Cambridge, 1988.
Allmand, Christopher, ed. *War, Literature and Politics in the late Middle Ages.* Liverpool, 1976.
Brusten, Charles. *L'armée bourguignonne de 1465 à 1468.* Brussels, 1953.
Canestrini, Giuseppe, ed. *Documenti per servire alla storia della milizia italiana dal XIII secolo al XVI.* Archivio Storico Italiano, vol. 15. Florence, 1851.
Contamine, Philippe. *Guerre, état et société à la fin du moyen âge: Études sur les armées des rois de France, 1337-1494.* Paris, 1972.
Contamine, Philippe. *War in the Middle Ages.* Trans. Michael Jones. Oxford, 1984.
Curry, Anne E. *The Hundred Years War.* British History in Perspective series. London, 1992.
Del Treppo, Mario. "Gli aspetti organizzativi, economici e sociali di una compagnia di ventura." *Rivista Storica Italiana* 85 (1973): 253-75.
Delbrück, Hans. *History of the Art of War within the Framework of Political History.* Vol. 3, *The Middle Ages.* Trans. Walter J. Renfroe, Jr. Westport, Conn. and London, 1982.
DeVries, Kelly. *Medieval Military Technology.* Peterborough, Ontario, 1992.
Fowler, Kenneth. *The Age of Plantagenet and Valois.* London, 1968.
Fowler, Kenneth, ed. *The Hundred Years War.* London, 1971.
Goodman, Anthony. *The Wars of the Roses: Military Activity and English Society, 1452-97.* London, 1981.
Hale, John R. "The Development of the Bastion, 1440-1534." In *Europe the Late Middle Ages,* ed. John R. Hale, J. R. L. Highfield, and Beryl Smalley, 466-94. London, 1965. Reprinted in Hale (1983).
Hale, John R. "Gunpowder and the Renaissance: an Essay in the History of ideas." In *From the Renaissance to the Counter Reformation: Essays in Honor of Garrett Mattingly,* ed. Charles H. Carter, 113-44. New York, 1965: 113-44. Reprinted in Hale (1983).
Hale, John R. *Renaissance War Studies.* London, 1983.
Keen, Maurice. *Chivalry.* New Haven, 1984.
Keen, Maurice. *The Laws of War in the Late Middle Ages.* London, 1965.
Koch, H. W. *Medieval Warfare.* London, 1978.
Lot, Ferdinand. *L'art militaire et les armées au moyen âge en Europe et dans le Proche-Orient.* Paris, 1946.

Mallett, Michael E. *Mercenaries and their Masters: Warfare in Renaissance Italy.* London, 1974.

Mallett, Michael E., and John R. Hale. *The Military Organization of a Renaissance State: Venice, c.1400-1617.* Cambridge, 1984.

Newhall, R. A. *Muster and Review: a Problem of English Military Administration, 1420-40.* Cambridge, Mass., 1940.

Oman, Charles W. C. *The Art of War in the Middle Ages, 1378-1485.* 2d ed. rev. London, 1924.

O'Neil, B. H. St.J. *Castles and Cannon: a Study of Early Artillery Fortifications in England.* Oxford, 1960.

Pieri, Piero. *Il Rinascimento e la crisi militare italiana.* Turin, 1952.

Pollard, Anthony J. *John Talbot and the War in France, 1427-53.* Royal Historical Society Studies in History Series, no. 35. London, 1983.

Schaufelberger, Walter. *Der alte Schweizer und sein Krieg. Studien zur Kriegsführung vornehmlich im 15. Jahrhundert.* Zurich, 1966.

Stewart, Paul. "The Soldier, the Bureaucrat and Fiscal Records in the Army of Ferdinand and Isabella." *Hispanic American Historical Review* 49 (1969): 281-92.

Vale, Malcolm A. *War and Chivalry: Warfare and Aristocratic Culture in England, France and Burgundy, at the End of the Middle Ages.* London, 1981.

Vaughan, Richard. *Valois Burgundy.* London, 1975.

*Sixteenth Century*

Black, Jeremy. *A Military Revolution? Military Change and European Society, 1500-1800.* Studies in European History. London, 1991.

Corvisier, André. *Armies and Societies in Europe, 1494-1789.* Trans. Abigail T. Sidall. Bloomington, 1977.

Cruikshank, C. G. *Army Royal: an Account of Henry VIII's Invasion of France, 1513.* Oxford, 1969.

Cruikshank, C. G. *Elizabeth's Army.* Oxford, 1966.

Delbrück, Hans. *History of the Art of War Within the Framework of Political History.* Vol, 4, *The Modern Era.* Trans. Walter J. Renfroe Jr. Westport, Conn., 1985. Reprinted as *The Dawn of Modern Warfare* (Lincoln, Neb., 1990).

Feld, M.D. "Middle Class Society and the Rise of Military Professionalism: the Dutch Army, 1559-1609." *Armed Forces and Society* 1 (1975): 419-42.

Gilbert, Felix. "Machiavelli: the Renaissance of the Art of War." In *Makers of Modern Strategy,* ed. Edward Meade Earle, 3-25. Princeton, 1943.

Hale, John R. *Renaissance Fortification: Art or Engineering?* London, 1977.

Hale, John R. *Renaissance War Studies.* London, 1983.

Hale, John R. *War and Society in Renaissance Europe.* London and Baltimore, 1985.

Knecht, Robert. *Francis I.* Cambridge, 1982.

Lot, Ferdinand. *Recherches sur les effectifs des armées francaises des guerres d'Italie aux guerres de religion (1494-1562).* Paris, 1962.

Lynn, J.A. "Tactical Evolution in the French Army, 1560-1660." *French Historical Studies* 14 (1985): 176-91.

Mallett, Michael E., and John R. Hale. *The Military Organization of a Renaissance State: Venice c.1400-1617.* Cambridge, 1984.

Millar, G. J. *Tudor Mercenaries and Auxiliaries, 1485-1547.* Charlottesville, 1980.

Oman, Charles W. C. *The Art of War in the Sixteenth Century.* London, 1937. Reprinted. New York, 1979.

Parker, Geoffrey. *The Army of Flanders and the Spanish Road, 1567-1659.* Cambridge Studies in Early Modern History. Cambridge, 1972.

Parker, Geoffrey. "The Military Revolution, 1550-1660—a Myth?" *Journal of Modern History* 47 (1976): 195-214.

Parker, Geoffrey. *The Military Revolution: Military Innovation and the Rise of the West, 1500-1800.* Cambridge, 1988.

Pepper, Simon, and Nicholas Adams. *Firearms and Fortifications: Military Architecture and Siege Warfare in Sixteenth-Century Siena.* Chicago, 1986.

Pieri, Piero. *Il Rinascimento e la crisi militare italiana.* Turin, 1952.
Redlich, Fritz. *The German Military Enterpriser and his Workforce, 13th to 17th centu-ries.* Vierteljahrschrift für Sozial- und Wirtschaftsgeschichte, Beiheft 47. Wiesbaden, 1964.
Roberts, Michael. *The Military Revolution, 1560-1660.* Belfast, 1956. Reprinted in Michael Roberts, *Essays in Swedish History* (London, 1967), 195-225.
Taylor, F. L. *The Art of War in Italy, 1494-1521.* Cambridge, 1921. Reprint. Westport, Conn., 1973.
Thompson, I. A. A. *War and Government in Hapsburg Spain, 1560-1620.* London, 1976.
Webb, Henry J. *Elizabethan Military Science: the Books and the Practice.* Madison, 1965.

*Naval Warfare*
Carr-Laughton, L. G. "Early Tudor Ship-guns." *Mariner's Mirror* 46 (1960): 242-85.
Cipolla, Carlo M. *Guns and Sail in the Early Phase of European Expansion, 1400-1700.* London, 1965.
Concina, Ennio, ed. *Arsenali e città nell'Occidente europeo.* Studi Superiori NIS, vol. 28. Rome, 1987.
Guillerme, Alain. *La pierre et le vent. Fortifications et marine en Occident.* Paris, 1985.
Guilmartin, John R., Jr. *Gunpowder and Galleys: Changing Technology and Mediterra-nean Warfare at Sea in the Sixteenth Century.* Cambridge, 1974.
Hale, John R. "Men and Weapons: the Fighting Potential of Sixteenth-Century Venetian Galleys." In *War and Society. A Yearbook of Military History,* vol. 1, ed. B. Bond and I. Roy. London, 1975. Reprinted in Hale (1983).
Lane, Frederick C. *Venetian Ships and Shipbuilders in the Renaissance.* Baltimore, 1934.
Lesure, M. *Lépante: la crise de l'empire Ottomane.* Paris, 1972.
Martin, Colin J. M., and Geoffrey Parker. *The Spanish Armada.* London, 1988.
Padfield, Peter. *Tide of Empires: Decisive Naval Campaigns in the Rise of the West, 1481-1654.* London, 1979.
Pryor, J. H. *Geography, Technology and War: Studies in the Maritime History of the Mediterranean, 649-1571.* Cambridge, 1988.
Richmond, Colin P. "English Naval Power in the Fifteenth Century." *History* 52 (1967): 1-15.
Rose, Susan. *The Navy of the Lancastrian Kings: Accounts and Inventories of William Soper, Keeper of the King's Ships, 1422-7.* Publications of the Naval Records Society, vol. 123. London, 1982.

# TAXATION AND STATE DEBT

James D. Tracy
(University of Minnesota)

The "new fiscal history"[1] of recent decades treats taxation and state debt as points of intersection between the economic life of a given territory, its constitutional arrangements, its social structure, and the demands of war and of the new military technology. A brief survey cannot do justice to all of these themes, nor to the interplay between *histoire structurelle* and *histoire événementielle*.[2] Only the vicissitudes of personality and circumstance can explain how an assertive monarch could squeeze prodigious sums from his subjects without changing the rules under which they were taxed,[3] or how human ingenuity could summon forth huge amounts of borrowed funds for a government whose credit should by all rights have been exhausted.[4] But discussion here will focus on fiscal institutions, and on their constitutional and social implications. Insofar as there was a common pattern of development all across western and central Europe, it was based on the fact that revenue collection reflected negotiations of one sort or another between the central government and local elites (part 1). But control of revenue once collected was a different matter, and one of the more interesting regional variations is in the degree to which disbursement of state funds was accountable either to public bodies of some sort, or to the credit markets (part 2). Finally, there is an important *quaestio disputata* concerning the real burden of taxation during this period, especially given that most taxes struck hardest at persons of modest means (part 3).

## 1. No Taxation Without Negotiation

The idea that late medieval taxation occurred within an historically novel framework of legitimacy seems firmly established. England's Tudor monarchs could call upon some of their wealthier subjects for loans and benevolences, but, as Roger Schofield remarks, the conditions under which these extra-parliamentary revenues could be collected merely confirmed the basic principle of consent.[5] French scholars are now more willing to adopt "Anglo-American" models of political development that stress the

profound legal and institutional changes of the thirteenth century that
paved the way for a new form of revenue (taxation) and a new beneficiary
(the state). Thus the confiscatory practices of the Roman Emperors were
"the opposite of what is familiar from the Middle Ages and the modern
era, when sovereigns guaranteed the property of their subjects . . . but borrowed from them liberally."[6]  Other scholars working on the history of
France or Castile have endorsed the views of historians of Germany like
Otto Brunner and Gerhard Oestreich who would interpose between the
feudal era and the age of absolutism a state based on estates (*Ständestaat*)
or "finance state" based on a territorial community having a common
body of law and capable of acting as a corporate entity.[7]

In time of war, a late medieval prince could call upon his subjects to pay
taxes to supplement his domain revenue; usually the prince or his deputy
would briefly explain the extraordinary need at hand in a "proposition" to
the estates.[8] "Extraordinary" taxes had a way of becoming "ordinary,"
and by the fifteenth century most of a prince's revenue came from taxes introduced after about 1300.[9] But if few would now contend that western or
central European monarchies prior to the seventeenth century were "absolute" in practice, proponents of the constitutionalist thesis also no longer
claim all they once did for representative assemblies. Strictly speaking,
England's Parliament consented not to taxation itself, but "to the legitimacy of the king's demand," since no one disputed that the community of
the realm was obligated in any genuine military emergency.[10]  Moreover, it
has become hard to find any case of "redress before supply" that has stood
the test of scrutiny. Even in England the House of Commons did not use
its power of the purse in this way prior to the seventeenth century,[11] and
Spanish historians are now agreed that none of the regional parliaments
(*cortes*) under Habsburg rule in Spain—not even the famous *corts* of
Aragon—had anything more than the right of petition. Indeed, in Castile
proper, it is not even clear that the king had to have the consent of the
Cortes before levying a new tax.[12] In France, too, the creation during the
fourteenth century of provincial estates as well as the Estates General had
primarily to do with notions of consultation; formal consent of the estates
was deemed necessary for some things—such as treaties—but not for taxation.[13] In the Habsburg Netherlands, provincial states did have the habit
of attaching firm conditions to their consent to subsidies, but the sources of
Charles V's reign are full of rancorous disputes arising from the government's habitual evasion of these strictures.[14] Thus to show that a ruler
could levy or spend money as he pleased, heedless of the wishes of the representatives of the realm, does not in itself make the case for absolutism;[15]

it merely proves that parliamentary bodies were not able to stand between a determined prince and something that he really wanted.

At the same time, evidence for the dependence of princes on their estates for collection of their revenues continues to accumulate. J. Russell Major makes a persuasive case that the France of the *pays d'état*[16] remained a decentralized kingdom through the sixteenth century not because of the political role played by local assemblies, but because of their active involvement in the collection and disbursement of the king's taxes.[17] Similarly, José Ignacio Fortea Pérez argues for Castile that the decentralized character of royal government is evident from the ability of towns represented in the Cortes to insist on assuming responsibility for the collection of royal revenues for their districts, by means that they thought fit. After all, many of Castile's great nobles had long since received royal permission to continue collecting in their domains the royal taxes expropriated by their ancestors during the fifteenth century.[18] In some German territories, like Bavaria, collection of the prince's taxes by the estates dated from the fourteenth century.[19] In England, the "lay subsidies" introduced by the Tudors were assessed under the direction of gentlemen of the county who were commissioned by the crown, but not really under its control.[20] In the Habsburg Netherlands, especially after 1542, traditional tax revenues were collected by fiscal officials answerable to the provincial states, not the central government. The same development of a separate fiscal bureaucracy, capable also of raising funds for use by the estates (e.g. to bribe royal officials), can also be seen in France's more important *pays d'état* and in various German territories.[21]

### War Debts, Fiscal Guarantees, and Local Elites

If rulers acquiesced in the collection of some of their revenues through the estates, it was no doubt in the hope that more could be brought in by enlisting the collaboration of local elites represented in the estates.[22] But no government could fight a war without incurring debts well in excess of its revenues, and the insistent demands of creditors for better security were in some places a more compelling reason for the prince to seek the cooperation of his estates. The creditor's basic problem was that one could never be sure that a payment order, even if signed by the king himself, would be honored by the fiscal bureau on which it was drafted.[23] Not surprisingly, rates for short-term loans to the state could reach frightful levels: 30% for the French monarchy in the early decades of the seventeenth century, 34% for the Florentine republic during a military crisis of the 1430s, and over 50% for transfers to the Low Countries by Charles V and Philip II during the 1550s.[24] The only way to avoid insolvency was to roll short-term debt over into low-interest long-term debt, funded or consolidated by pledging stated revenues to the new debt in such a way as to offer lenders a reasonable assurance that interest would be paid regularly.[25] Some governments could offer the needed assurances without calling upon a parliamentary body to interpose its faith and credit to supplant their own. Beginning in 1526, the papacy created a form of long-term debt on which interest was so faithfully paid that shares regularly traded at rates as high as 120% to 150% of par on the secondary market.[26] In Castile Charles V and Philip II were able to quiet the anxieties of bankers for about half a century by converting their loans into *juros*, annuities funded by the crown's ordinary revenues.[27] In Spanish Naples, the reliability of interest payments on the *juros* issued in great amounts after 1550 remained "quite good" through the remainder of the sixteenth century.[28] In many other territories, however, potential investors had learned not to trust guarantees by the ruler or his officials. Thus, in a number of important lay principalities in Germany, the estates agreed during the sixteenth century to assume responsibility for the ruler's debts, in return for control of his revenues. After 1542, provincial states in the Low Countries raised funds for the Habsburg government by issuing bonds (*renten*) that were funded by new taxes levied and disbursed by their own officials.[29] In Castile, as crown revenues were one after another pledged to the limit for *juro* interest, Philip II agreed (1589) to transfer responsibility for his long-term debt to subsidies levied and disbursed by agents of the Cortes.[30] In France, too, provincial estates could be called upon to enter the credit markets on the king's behalf, although the chronology of this development is not clear from the literature.[31]

Thus by some point in the sixteenth century, many of Europe's rulers had come to depend on the collaboration of their estates, either for the collection of their taxes, or for the administration of their debts, or for both. This common pattern has an important corollary, already suggested by the case of Castile: the involvement of the estates in fiscal affairs meant in practice the involvement of localities. In England, the "tenths and fifteenths" granted by Parliament since the fourteenth century were fixed levies on towns and villages, to be collected by each locality as it saw fit. There were in any case important links between town finance and state finance, quite apart from the estates. For example, London's municipal corporation regularly served as guarantor for loans by Tudor and especially Stuart monarchs, using funds it controlled to make sure the crown's creditors were paid on time. In Piedmont-Savoy the important land tax was collected by local communities, and in the Venetian *terraferma*, taxes were assessed and collected under the direction of town councils, just as they had been before *la Serenissima* acquired a mainland empire. In France, as Bernard Chevalier shows, urban and royal taxation were both products of the same turbulent period. Just as urban deputies in the Estates General voted for new forms of taxation following the capture of King Jean II (battle of Poitiers, 1356), royal officials granted towns permission to levy excise taxes on their own citizens, primarily to finance the construction of new town walls. There would come a time when the demands of the fisc threatened urban solvency, but the two systems were at first mutually supportive; the king treated the favorable balances of his *bonnes villes* as a reserve treasury, and the towns in turn were rewarded with exemptions, or with a share of certain royal taxes. Indeed, the practice by which municipal governments sold *rentes* for the king in return for control of certain domain revenues seems to date from the early fifteenth century.[32] During the sixteenth century these so-called *rentes sur l'hotel de ville* were issued first by the city hall of Paris (1522), and later by such towns as Lyons, Marseille, Provins, Rennes, and Rouen.[33] Meanwhile, towns and other local entities represented in the estates often demanded a voice in the apportionment of royal taxes. In Languedoc, allotments were made first by the provincial *états*, then by assemblies of the three seneschalcies, then by those of the twenty-two civil dioceses, and finally by parish assemblies. Some of these consultative bodies survived longer than others. In Major's view the most favored regions were those mountain valleys, in the Alps and the Pyrenees, whose well-established representative assemblies long continued to send their own deputies to provincial *états*.[34]

The articulation between urban and princely finance that Chevalier finds for France appears as early as the twelfth century in the then separate provinces of the Low Countries, where local governments seeking funds to build town walls turned to the ruler, who then claimed for himself a share of the excise taxes he authorized.[35] At the turn of the fifteenth century, Philip the Bold, the first Burgundian ruler of the Low Countries, was still collecting a portion of the urban excises he renewed or approved. Like his nephew, the French king, Philip borrowed directly from the treasuries of his towns; in a region where the mechanisms of private credit were better developed, he could also have town governments act as guarantors for loans by third parties, or issue life annuities (*rentes viagères*) funded by ducal revenues placed under town control.[36] For purposes of the ducal subsidies or *aides*, dealing with towns and localities one by one was cumbersome, and, where such bodies did not already exist, Philip sought to form *états* through which he could present his fiscal needs to the representatives of an entire district or province. Here, too, one sees a parallel with France, where the crown fostered assemblies of this kind as a forum for the discussion of its financial needs.[37]

But the regional loyalties that parliamentary bodies helped to create did not extinguish the traditional desire of each town to protect its own interests. Thus when the provincial states of the Low Countries agreed in 1542 to fund *renten* issued for the benefit of Charles V, they set up a system in which each walled city would have its own collector for the new provincial excise taxes. Later in the century, as Holland and other northern provinces struggled to finance their rebellion against Philip II, each of the eighteen cities that now had voting rights in the States of Holland assumed responsibility for its share of the province's funded debt, and collected for its district the excises that were the main source of revenue.[38] One of history's small ironies is that Castile, which paid much of the cost for Philip II's wars in the Netherlands, was even then moving toward a similar fiscal decentralization.

Following his defeat of the rebellion of the *Comuneros* (1520-21), Charles V compelled the eighteen cities represented in the Cortes of Castile to give their deputies "full powers," so as to obviate the practice (common also in the Low Countries) by which the deputies had to refer all important questions back to their principals. It was, however, a hollow victory. Despite the crown's desire to treat the Cortes as if it were the kingdom, the "decisive vote" on all fiscal matters remained with the town halls of the "head-cities" of Castile's eighteen districts.[39] Collection of taxes by the municipalities had been a desideratum for the Cortes as early as the fourteenth century, and during the sixteenth century a series of decisions placed much of the king's revenue under urban management: beginning in 1500, subsidies granted by the Cortes were collected under the direction of the deputies for each head city; beginning in 1536, the important sales tax (*alcabala*) was transmuted into a fixed assessment for each district, again collected locally; and after 1589, as noted above, the crown's long-term debt (*juros*) was funded by the subsidies, not by revenues administered by the king's officials.[40]

### Local Elites and Indirect Taxation

Since local elites guided the administration of territorial revenue, their collective self-interest does much to explain the increasing reliance on indirect taxation after about 1300. Taxes on landed income were never a problem for Castile's landholders, but in most other parts of Europe levies on land or other forms of wealth were well known; in France the *taille* long continued to be the crown's principal tax revenue, and Piedmont-Savoy in time of war relied on temporary increases in direct taxation.[41] It could also happen that an ostensibly indirect tax (e.g., taxes on salt) was actually collected on the basis of population estimates. Yet the broad trend was toward a system in which hearth taxes and levies on wealth were overshadowed by sales taxes, especially on common items of food and drink, that were ultimately paid in one way or another by the consumer. For the major Italian city states, the transition from the land tax (*estimo*)of the thirteenth century to the indirect taxes (*gabelle*) of the fourteenth century is a familiar story. In Venice, as in Florence, it became customary to call upon wealthy citizens to contribute to the upkeep of the state not through direct taxation of their wealth, but through interest-bearing forced loans, funded in various ways by the *gabelle*. The *catasto*—a detailed assessment of real and property introduced by Florence in 1427—has sometimes been seen as a basis for taxation, but was in fact a basis for forced loans.[42] In the Low Countries, too, towns turned away from direct levies on wealth during the fourteenth century, and likewise in France, once the new circuit of town walls had been completed.[43] Where direct taxation remained important, it was often a sign of fiscal backwardness, as with the hearth tax in the kingdom of Naples; yet even here indirect taxation as a portion of government revenue rose from 9% in 1550 to 29% in 1605. Elsewhere direct taxation might carry, as in ancient times, the stigma of lower status. Thus Renaissance Florence retained the *estimo* not for her own citizens, but for persons living in the countryside and the subject towns of the Florentine state.[44]

The reasons why governments preferred indirect taxation are no doubt complex. In the towns it was easier to collect taxes on commercial transactions than to assess property, just as in the countryside land was the form of wealth that was hardest to conceal; hence new levies introduced in the sixteenth century could take the form of an excise in the towns and a land tax in the countryside.[45] The normal human greed and jealousy that made the assessment of property by town officials such a contentious issue[46] made it even more difficult to assess the wealth of a whole province or kingdom. In 1817, officials of one French *département* "found" some 2,500 hectares (about 6,250 acres) that had somehow never been included in the tax rolls. Even when large-scale assessments were done conscientiously, quota disputes among rival localities obstructed new assessments that would have captured for the fisc the benefits of ensuing economic growth. In Holland, the traditional assessment on real property, last done in 1515, was never again revised under Habsburg rule; under the Republic, it was revised but once between 1584 and 1729, and then only after five years of debate. In the Duchy of Milan the Spanish government struggled for nearly 60 years (1543-1600) before the towns could be induced to accept a new *estimo* that would make taxes on land more equitable; in the Grand Duchy of Tuscany, where (as Enrico Stumpo suggests) the Medici government lacked the legitimacy to attempt a reform of direct taxation, the assessment for the land tax went unchanged for over 150 years. In Tudor England, assessments for the lay subsidy voted by Parliament were "tolerably realistic" under Henry VIII, but property of all kinds—especially the personal property of the wealthy—was "ludicrously undervalued" by the end of the century.[47]

It does not follow as a matter of course that towns would favor excise taxes at the territorial level, especially if these new excises conflicted with those they collected from their own citizens, or curtailed exemptions that wealthy burghers shared with other privileged groups.[48] Yet indirect taxation was supported by the argument that it was one way of making the rich pay more than the poor (they consumed more).[49] In some territories representatives of the towns were willing to swallow new excises, provided that they be extended to everyone, and thus effect a breach in the exemptions hitherto enjoyed by nobles and clergy.[50] But surely the main point is that urban deputies represented the interests of their principals. Thus towns with voting rights swapped rebates on their own quotas for higher levels of taxation that would strike harder at towns and villages not represented in the estates,[51] and did not look with favor on proposals to extend the right of representation to towns or regions that did not already have it.[52] In the same way, the representative assemblies that endorsed and helped administer indirect taxes were shifting the burden to the peasants and urban workmen who (in most places) had no voice in fiscal negotiations.

In many cases locally collected excise revenue came to be used to make payments on taxes that were nominally in the form of levies based on an assessment of wealth, or on commercial transactions. In Castile, cities regularly used local excise taxes to pay their quotas in the subsidies voted by the Cortes. Moreover, after 1536 the *alcabala* or tax on sales was collected by "capitation" (*encabezamiento*); each locality had a fixed quota, and it seems municipalities often chose to raise the money from a combination of consumption taxes on residents and taxes on sales by non-residents.[53] In the kingdom of Naples, royal direct taxation was paid by local communities from a revenue base in which, during the sixteenth century, newer indirect taxes came to be more important than traditional levies on wealth. In the Low Countries, the more prosperous towns (like Amsterdam) could afford to pay their subsidy quotas from the surplus of urban excise revenues. In Genoa, the *Banco di San Giorgio*, which functioned as a holding company for the array of taxes that had been pledged to various consortia of creditors, preferred to maintain the *gabelle* on items of common consumption, and to retire those that burdened particular sectors of the city's trade.[54]

The Genoese example points to the fact that consumption taxes were also used to fund the growing mass of state debt.[55] When the estates of Bavaria approved a provincial tax on beverages (1542-43), it was to pay off ducal debts for which the estates agreed to assume responsibility. At about the same time, provincial states in the Low Countries funded new issues of *renten* by a combination of province-wide taxes on landed income (in the countryside) and on beverages (in the towns). In Castile after 1589, when each locality was free to decide how to collect its share in the subsidies by which the crown's long-term debt (*juros*) were now funded, the crown tried to promote the use of consumption taxes as a means of achieving some uniformity.[56] As a result of arrangements of this kind, towns with a large concentration of investors in state debt—like Valladolid, the residence of Castile's court before Philip II made Madrid his capital—might actually make a net gain on royal finances, except of course that those who paid out the money were not the same as those who got it back as interest. Apart from the occasional tax riot, ordinary folk had no means of making their views count, but they understood well enough the social implications of what one may call transfer payments to investors.[57] The issue would remain a focal point of debate in European political life down through the nineteenth century.

## 2. DISBURSEMENT AND ACCOUNTABILITY

If taxation was in interest of the realm, those who collected and disbursed the prince's revenue must somehow be accountable to the realm. Here, too, medieval practice differed from that of the ancient world, albeit less dramatically. Officials in classical Athens had to account for any public funds they spent, and there were similar accounts to the Roman Senate in the republican period, but only the medieval audit required bringing income and expenditure into balance.[58] If medieval fiscal accounts have survived in such profusion, it is in part because they were so carefully prepared (often on parchment), suggesting the seriousness of the enterprise in the minds of contemporaries. Paolo Prodi points to canonical theories of the *fiscus* as a fictive person, distinct from the person of the ruler, meaning that the property of the church (or the state, or the city) belongs in some sense to the entire community.[59] Audit bureaucracies had in any case an early and extensive development. Princely governments could differ greatly in the ways they collected taxes. France of the *pays d'élection* is notorious for its relatively dense network of fiscal officials, but in Castile the absence of such a bureaucracy left the government a choice between farming revenues out and having them collected by municipalities.[60] Yet in England, with its gentleman tax assessors, the Exchequer was of Anglo-Norman vintage, and changes in its methods of accounting may be the best indicator of real change in the nature of taxation. Castile, too, had its *contaduria mayor*.[61] No matter how taxes were collected there were auditors to check the books. As may be seen in Flanders, where in the 1290s the receiver-general began making annual accounts to a commission of auditors that soon became a separate Chamber of Accounts, the development of such bodies marked a conscious effort to make revenue agents answerable to the realm.[62] In France those who collected the prince's revenues and those who checked their accounts reported to distinct branches of officialdom.[63] To be sure, the accounting function of government did not always have a distinct and autonomous organization. Under a Medici regime of questionable legitimacy the Grand Duchy of Tuscany had neither a central chamber of accounts nor a clear distinction between state and household finance. More importantly, in towns all across Europe members of the same local elite served by turns as collectors and auditors. But one of the recurring features of late medieval urban history is the demand by commoners for better control of the city's books. At Leuven/Louvain, for example, a period of agitation among the craft guilds subsided only after the ruling oligarchy agreed to the creation of a new board of treasurers drawn from the guilds, who were to render their accounts in a room with open doors.[64]

A cynic might make the case that the financial records that fill so many shelves in Europe's town and state archives served mainly to provide gainful employment for legions of clerks and their well-paid supervisors. After all, scholars have yet to fathom all the possibilities for graft afforded by state revenue in the old regime, and it is fair to ask how much auditors really understood about where the prince's money went if they were still trying to close the books on accounts ten or twenty years old.[65] Yet no one can work with fiscal accounts from the late medieval or early modern period without forming a healthy respect for the auditing process for which such documents were intended. Any expenditure not documented by a receipt was stricken, and remained on the books as a charge against the revenue agent who had submitted the account.[66] The Leuven guildsmen had some definite ideas about accountability, and so did those who in many other settings struggled to gain access to fiscal records. They would not have done so had they not believed that auditing was a form of control.

### Control of Fiscal Information

Within a framework of broadly similar accounting practices there were important differences as to who was obliged to provide what kind of information to whom. At times, parliamentary control of finances was strong enough to keep the prince's auditors at bay: the Duke of Bavaria's men could not inspect accounts of how his revenue was spent, and Charles V's officials in Holland could look at, but not have copies of, records of a provincial tax on real property income. In the Rhineland duchies of Jülich and Berg, the estates more readily granted indirect than direct taxes, because indirect tax revenue flowed into the *Landeskasse* controlled by the estates, while monies from direct taxation were at the free disposal of the prince.[67] More often, it was the ruler who let his subjects have only as much information about his finances as was absolutely necessary to enlist their cooperation. When Philip II wanted Castile's town governments to accept a higher rate for the "capitation" of the *alcabala*, his commissioners had to let them see from accounts of crown revenues that more could have been raised by reverting to traditional methods of collection. In France, when deputies at the Estates General of Blois (1576) demanded access to the king's accounts but were shown only extracts, it confirmed their suspicion that the crown must be hopelessly in debt.[68]

There is a further question as to the extent to which the king's management of his revenue was open to the scrutiny of his own officials. Philip II's absentee manipulation of future crown revenues often infuriated his regency council in Castile, but the councillors at least knew what the king was doing, and were sometimes able to thwart the schemes of his Netherlands bankers.[69] In France, Catherine de Medici borrowed in Italy to get funds that would not appear on the budget estimates discussed in her council. Later, crown and council together tried to keep the *Chambre des Comptes* in the dark. Royal payment orders (summarized under expenditure items in the pertinent account) normally contained a reason for the payment, save for orders known as *acquits de comptant* in which no reason was given.[70] During the later sixteenth and early seventeenth centuries, the crown resorted more and more to this device, to avoid discussion of expenditures for war beyond the borders, or for loan contracts with syndicates of lenders. Conversely, the Chamber of Accounts always sought to rein in expenditures, and would have balked at interest rates and other conditions demanded by the financiers. But the Chamber's protests over the expanded use of *acquits de comptant*, though endorsed by the Estates General (1576, 1588, 1614), went unheeded.[71] Auditing procedures thus reflected a larger struggle for control of expenditures: parliamentary audit committees were at times paramount in the Low Countries, in some German territories and perhaps in some French *pays d'état*; in Castile the king had at least to consult with quasi-autonomous councils concerned for the solvency of the realm; and at the center of the French monarchy, the king and his most trusted advisers managed more and more to evade the watchful eye of the auditing branch of the royal bureaucracy.

### Accountability to Financial Markets

Accountability of a different sort came from the valuation by the credit markets of instruments of state debt. Although the phenomenon is not yet fully understood, there was at least from the fourteenth century an extraordinary demand for annuities.[72] The new state debt that resulted from rolling over short-term loans would find a ready market, provided only that buyers had satisfactory assurances that the government would indeed pay interest as due. Without a great deal of oversimplification, may one distinguish at least three different ways in which the market for state debt could be organized: by parliamentary sales to the public on behalf of the government, as in the Low Countries; by government sales to bankers who then sold to the public, as in Genoa, the Papal States, and (with a significant difference) Castile; and by government sales to speculators, as in France. Low Countries towns had a tradition of selling their own *rentes* to "foreigners," not just to their own citizens, and Burgundian and Habsburg rulers were likewise interested in attracting buyers from hither and yon for *rentes* based on domain revenue. When the provincial states began selling *rentes* for the account of the Habsburg government, they at first constrained wealthy individuals and institutions to subscribe to these novel instruments of debt. After about 1552, however, the practice of constraint was abandoned, and funds poured in as if floodgates had been opened. To be sure, it is possible to make too much of the free market for state debt in the Netherlands; in the dark days of the struggle against Spain, the provincial governments of the Dutch Republic had no compunction about compelling their citizens to buy *rentes*.[73]

If Venice and Florence had a state debt largely based on forced loans, Genoa's practice was to create a tax for the profit of a consortium of lenders, who then sold shares (*luoghi*) in their venture to the public. As noted earlier, the *Banco di San Giorgio* was formed as a holding company for these consortia. In the Papal States at the turn of the sixteenth century, it was possible to form a "society" for the purchase of a purely titular office, the annual salary for which was in fact a form of interest. Rome adopted the Genoese model (doubtless by way of Florence) under the Medici Pope, Clement VII: blocs of ownership shares in a new tax were sold to bankers, who then sold shares (*luoghi*) at a profit to third parties.[74] Meanwhile the *juros* issued by the crown of Castile were given a new twist, largely through the influence of Genoese bankers active in the peninsula. In the 1520s, holders of Charles V's burgeoning short-term debt received *juros* as a guarantee for repayment of their loans. Gradually, foreign bankers (especially the Genoese)[75] realized that strong market demand made it advantageous for them to liquidate their *juros* as soon as possible. Starting in 1542, lenders received *juros de resguardo* (security *juros*) which they could sell at once, on the understanding that the resale price would be deducted from any loan repayment that the lender eventually received. Students of Castile's finances are agreed that this maneuver had the effect of consolidating the crown's floating debt, while at the same time interposing the bankers as a permanent intermediary between the crown and the investing public. During the 1550s bankers induced the crown to suspend public sales until they had liquidated their *juros*, and after the 1560s evidence of further direct sales to the public is scarce.[76] One must note that the *juros de resguardo* differed from shares of state debt in Genoa or the Papal States in that Castile's bankers did not control the revenues by which the annuities were funded; had they done so, the *juros* (like papal *luoghi*) would have remained sound into the seventeenth century, but the kings of Castile could never have fought their foreign wars.

In France, there were from the outset questions about whether revenues alienated by the crown for the funding of debt were truly alienated; at Lyon, for example, the king repossessed in 1541 one of the revenues that had been granted under contract to the town council in 1536. Thus while the treasury raised modest sums through sales of *rentes sur l'hotel de ville* to the public under Francis I, the far larger sums raised under Francis II and Henry II were in effect forced loans. During the last phase of the religious wars neither Henry III nor (when it controlled royal finance) the Catholic League were able to keep up interest payments, so that by 1595 interest had not been paid for nine years. As in Castile, investors whose loyalty the crown could count on were treated worse than others, and by 1605 some *rente*-holders had received no interest for nineteen years. Meanwhile, Sully's retrenchments included such measures as unpledging all revenues by which payment of *rente* interest to foreigners was secured, and the cancellation of all arrears still due in 1604. Little wonder, then, that the public had long since lost interest. By the 1630s, when finance ministers were under orders to get funds at any cost for the war in Germany, royal *rentes* were sold at a steep discount to investors and financiers, who could count other royal paper at face value as part of the purchase price, and, at a later date, count the *rentes* themselves at face value in further loans to the crown.[77]

With some qualifications, one may conclude that the two kinds of accountability discussed here ran parallel to each other: the debts of those states whose finances were open to the scrutiny of public bodies (a parliament, or a well-established bureaucracy) fared better in the credit markets, and were thus better able to capture some of the private savings generated in periods of economic growth. But it must be noted that although available evidence supports the connection one would expect between debt management and investor confidence, there are for this period no comparative studies of the all-important secondary market for state debt.[78] Moreover, considering that even the Dutch Republic suspended payment of interest on old *rentes* for a time during the 1570s,[79] one must beware of presuming that parliamentary management of finances created the best of all environments for investors; the Genoese practice of alienating revenues directly into the hands of lenders afforded better a guarantee. In fact, what the most market-worthy forms of sixteenth-century state debt seem to have in common is that lenders controlled the revenues by which their investments were funded, either directly, in the Genoese manner, or indirectly, as deputies invested heavily in the annuities backed by their respective parliaments.[80] But to say that the most effective way to establish the credit of the state was to tie it to the interests of wealthy individuals is to raise once again the question of equity.

## 3. Disputed Questions: the Real Burden of Taxation

On all sides, sixteenth-century sources relating to military expenditures, tax revenue, and state debt report increases of a magnitude that would scarcely be credible were it not so well documented. To give but a few examples at random: owing to Charles V's foreign adventures, the average annual expenditures of the crown of Castile roughly doubled from the first to the second half of his reign; in the Netherlands, the cost of keeping an army in the field for a year's campaigning season rose by a factor of seven from the 1520s to the 1550s; income from the *taille* rose over 100% during the reign of Francis I (1515-47), and overall royal tax revenues were up nearly as much; interest payments by the crown on Castilian *juros* increased tenfold from 1505 to 1573; in 1575 Philip II sought to triple at one stroke the usual rate for "capitation" of the *alcabala*, but after the Cortes protested he had to settle for doubling it; total royal revenues in France were fifteen times higher in 1635 than in 1575; and the corporate debt of the city of Naples rose from 127,000 ducats in 1546 to 8,000,000 in 1607.[81] The problem is to know what such numbers meant in real terms, especially for the peasants and urban workers who paid most of the taxes.[82] Taking inflation into account, many scholars conclude that the real burden of taxation did not grow appreciably during the sixteenth century, the loud complaints of taxpayers notwithstanding. Major finds that taxation in Languedoc from 1474 to 1558 did not rise fast enough to keep up with inflation, and even refers to France before about 1600 as "a taxpayer's paradise." Citing Pierre Chaunu's figures for the silver equivalent of crown revenues, Chevalier finds a real increase of 30% to 40% from 1543 to the 1550s, but a relative lightening of the burden by 1588. Wolfe calculates that royal income rose by only 33% during a period when the purchasing power of the official money of account (*livres tournois*) declined by about 50% (1547-74).[83] For Castile, Fortea Pérez argues that the real burden of the *alcabala* was not greater at the end of the sixteenth century than at the beginning (despite the "doubling" of the 1570s), and that real totals for all tax revenue increased by a mere 10% even amid the din of all of Spain's wars during the last quarter of the sixteenth century.[84] In Spanish Milan, despite an imposing array of new taxes introduced during the sixteenth century, there was a real decline in state income, which had to be covered by an increase in state debt. In Spanish Naples, despite an economic decline visible already in the 1580s, it was not until 1610 that the real burden of taxation began to outpace the real increase in grain prices.[85] But one may come to very different conclusions for the sixteenth century by calculating into the equation the downward pressure on wages during an era of rising population, or the distorting effects of a privileged fiscal structure on investment decisions. Spanish historians see the opportunities offered by government debt draining large sums away from more productive investment. For Flanders, Wim Blockmans points out that while the real value of provincial subsidies increased by 163% between 1430/1450 and 1530/1550, the value of salaries for urban artisans increased by only 20%, making it substantially more difficult for townsfolk to bear their share of the burden. One wonders, too, about the joint burden of princely taxes and the urban excises that were used not only to pay the subsidies but for local expenses like interest on the town debt; as Chevalier notes, it was the combination of both forms of taxation that had "crushed" the townsfolk of northern France and provoked the tax rebellions of the 1380s.[86] The only point on which there seems to be agreement is that amid the religious wars and economic stagnation of the early seventeenth century there was in many areas a dramatic increase in the real incidence of taxation. For the district of Seville in Castile, the real burden of subsidies voted by the Cortes was three times higher in 1630 than it was in 1591. If, in terms of grain prices, France's total tax burden was eight times higher in 1635 than in 1575, three-quarters of the increase came between 1631 and 1635. It is to the France of Richelieu's wars that one can perhaps most properly apply the words of Yves-Marie Bercé: "The institutionalization of taxation in its modern form was the result of a veritable internal war carried out by the agents of the state against the resistance of subjects."[87]

At some point one must ask the inevitable question, *cui bono*? On the one hand, it was the participation of local elites in raising the prince's revenues that brought into being many if not all of the quasi-autonomous communities that are a distinctive feature of Europe's political landscape in the late medieval and early modern era: the rural federations of France's mountain valleys, or their counterparts in the Low Countries and northern Italy;[88] the provincial assemblies to which such bodies sent deputies, in Germany, the Low Countries, and parts of France; and those larger bodies, as in England and Castile, that claimed with more or less plausibility to be true communities of the realm.[89] Surely it is not possible to understand the force of modern conceptions of self-government without these deep historical roots. On the other hand the elites in question had an impressive variety of ways to enrich themselves from prince's revenues while making others pay the cost. Regardless of a territory's form of government, urban land-buyers knew how to shield their rural property from taxes on land: in Dauphiné, a classic *pays d'état*, they paid lower rates by having it listed as town property, leaving villagers with a reduced tax base but an unchanged quota; in the Venetian *terraferma* they kept it charged on the tax rolls (made up by obliging fellow-townsmen) to former peasant proprietors; in the kingdom of Naples, officials winked at fictive donations of land to a priest cousin or nephew. Indeed, systematic evasion of this sort led in Francesco Caracciolo's view to a massive overburdening of the Neapolitan peasantry, lending plausibility to the views of a Venetian ambassador who reported peasants tearing tiles from their roofs to pay taxes, and taking to the hills as bandits.[90] Meanwhile, those who could afford to bid for tax-farming contracts had abundant opportunities for profit, and the collective self-interest of such men was not so enlightened as to prevent them from squeezing revenue from a high-demand product to the point that it was priced out of the market.[91] Recent studies of financiers willing to extend short-term credit to princely governments (mainly for the seventeenth century) have emphasized the high risk that such men have incurred, while stressing the low risk and handsome gains for the silent partners who bought shares of these financial deals, often government officials and members of the old nobility.[92] Finally, those who chose the greater security of investing in long-term debt had not only the promise (more or less credible) of an assured income, but also the added liquidity of paper wealth that could for many purposes serve in the place of cash.[93]

One can look either to the larger interests that elites and their assemblies represented in theory, or to the narrower interests that they so often represented in practice. Advocates of a stronger princely power were not slow in noting this disparity. Absolutist or not, many early seventeenth century rulers managed to assert their prerogatives more strongly, like Maximilian II of Bavaria, who assumed control of ducal revenues that had long been administered by the estates, so as to pay off old debts quickly and build up a war treasury. If the French crown was able to convert Dauphiné from a *pays d'état* to a *pays d'élection*, it was because, owing to a bitter history of disputes over assessment of the *taille*, the claim of the privileged orders to act on behalf of the territory as a whole was no longer credible. In Castile, Philip IV met with little resistance when he took over administration of the subsidies by which the debt was funded, and forced the deputies of the Cortes to "vote decisively" instead of consulting their town councils.[94] But one ought not to think of European fiscal and political development as a march towards true representation of the realm along one path or the other, whether absolutist or constitutionalist. The point to keep in mind is that the framework of legitimacy by which taxation in this period was structured had three elements—the crown, the estates, and a realm that was somehow thought to be present in the interaction between the two. Each of the two active parties in this arrangement could wax eloquent on the other's shortcomings, but neither was capable of changing the ground rules for the venerable, almost ritual combat between crown and estates, or prerogative and privileges. In the long run, there could not be a more clearly focussed debate about the interests of the realm until the emergence of a new framework of legitimacy—roughly speaking, when the realm became a nation. Thus Joanna Fritschy can say about the fiscal system of the

Dutch Republic what Tocqueville said long ago about the French monarchy: centralization and reform were the work not of the old regime, but of governments issuing from a democratic revolution.[95]

# NOTES

1. The term is used by Hoffman and Norberg (1994), in their introduction.
2. For a good blend of both, see Bonney (1981).
3. Major (1980), 44-45: Louis XI (1460-80) nearly quadrupled income from the *taille*, but "although Louis XI is famous for his high-handed use of the fiscal system, he changed it hardly at all"; the quote is from Wolfe (1972).
4. Boyajian (1983), especially chap. 3.
5. Schofield (1988), 229; he cites the conspicuous failure of Wolsey's "Amicable Grant" of 1525, on which see Bernard (1986). I owe these and several other references on England to John Currin.
6. Genet and Le Men, (1987), "Introduction" by the editors, 7-9, and Mirélllé Corbier, "Prelèvement, redistributions et circulation monetaire dans l'Empire Romain (Ie-IIIe siecles)," 16.
7. Major (1980), 187; Fortea Pérez (1990), 13-15. See Brunner (1992); Oestreich (1982).
8. Henneman (1971).
9. Bulst, in Genet and Le Men (1987), 68, estimates the income of German territories (where taxation was less developed than in France or the Low Countries) as follows: 20% domain, 30% regalian rights, 50% taxation.
10. Harris (1978), 722. Harris disputes the contention of Elton (1975) that Cromwell was able to establish the principle that the ordinary running of the government justified taxation; Alsop (1982) offers a middle ground.
11. Stanford E. Lehmberg, *The Later Parliaments of Henry VIII, 1536-1547* (Cambridge, 1977), 95, 175-80; Elton (1975), 47.
12. Artola (1982), 28; Carretero Zamora (1988), 46-51; Fortea Pérez (1990), 13-19; Ladero Quesada, in Genet and Le Men (1987), 36-51; and Ulloa (1977), 84-85; Fernández Albaladeja (1992), 256.
13. Major (1980), 10-29.
14. Tracy (1990), 74-89; Van Nieuwenhuysen (1984), 320.
15. Carretero Zamora (1988).
16. Major (1980). Royal taxes were apportioned by the estates in the *pays d'état*, and in the *pays d'élection* by royal officials called *élus*.
17. Major (1980), esp. chap. 7.
18. Fortea Pérez (1990), 13-25; on the nobles, Yun (1991).
19. M. Fryde (1964): 246. For sixteenth century Hesse, Krüger (1980), 248-59, and id., "Public Finance and Modernization: The Change from Domain State to Tax State in Hesse during the Sixteenth and Seventeenth Centuries," in Witt (1987), 49-62.
20. Schofield (1988), 231, 255.
21. Tracy (1985), 87-89; Major (1980), 63-64 (Languedoc), 74-75 (Dauphiné), 84 (Burgundy); Wagner (1977), 91-92.
22. Major (1980), 38: levels of taxation were sometimes higher in the *pays d'état* than in the *pays d'élection*.

23. Examples: Bayard (1988), 66-67, 249-51; Rodríguez Salgado (1988), 71-72, 122-25; Ulloa (1977), 783-84.
24. Bonney (1981), 141-42; Molho (1987), 174-81; Rodríguez Salgado (1988), 67.
25. Tracy (1985), Chap. I.
26. Stumpo (1985), 219-27, 248-53; Reinhard, in Kellenbenz and Prodi (1989), 459-504; Delumeau (1957-59), vol. 2:783-824.
27. Toboso Sánchez (1987), 27-77, 86-92.
28. Calabria (1991), 105-6.
29. Tracy (1985), 20-21, and chap. 3. See Van Nieuwenhuysen (1984), 348: Dino Rapondi of Lucca, Philip the Bold's loan broker, recognized even in his day that subsidies granted by the provincial states would be the surest guarantee for the prince's loans.
30. On the so-called *servicios de millones* or million-ducat subsidies, Artola (1982), 109-13; Fortea Pérez (1990), 135-52.
31. For examples relating to Languedoc in the seventeenth and eighteenth centuries, see Philip T. Hoffman, in Hoffman and Norberg (1994), citing Beik (1985) and Dessert (1984), 23-25.
32. Schofield (1988), 231; Ashton (1960), 26-28; Stumpo, in de Maddelena and Kellenbenz (1984), 199; Del Torre (1986); Chevalier, in Genet and Le Men (1987), 137-51.
33. Bayard (1988), 15; Wolfe (1972), 115.
34. Major (1980), 60-64, 164, 174.
35. Van Uytven (1961), 5-9, and in Guarducci (1976), 533-35.
36. Van Nieuwenhuysen (1984), 273-78, 349-61.
37. Van Nieuwenhuysen (1984), 307-20; Henneman (1971) and (1976).
38. See the references given in Tracy (1985), 87. For Holland's finances in the early Republic, see the sole extant Receiver General's account for the period 1572-1630 (1581: Rijksarchief van Zuid Holland, The Hague, IIIe Afdeling, Inv. no. 3.01.29); Fritschy (1988), 34-37.
39. H. G. Koenigsberger, "The Powers of Deputies in Sixteenth-Century Assemblies," in his *Estates and Revolutions* (Ithaca, N.Y., 1971), 176-210; Fortea Pérez (1990), 46-61; Carretero Zamora (1988), 6-11.
40. Ladero Quesada ((1987), 46-47; Carretero Zamora (1988), 85-92; Fortea Pérez (1990), 55, 64, 87, 96-99, 104, 144, 463-70, 513.
41. Artola (1982), 22-23; on how the taille was collected, Bayard (1988), 60-64; Stumpo, in De Maddelena and Kellenbenz (1984), 192-96.
42. Luzzatto (1963), 6-29; Molho (1971), 85.
43. Van Uytven (1961), 105; Chevalier, in Genet and Le Men (1987), 144. Van Uytven notes that German towns were an exception to this common European pattern.
44. Stumpo (1985), 67-76; Calabria, (1991), 59-63; Molho (1987), 193; Webber and Wildavsky (1986), 108-9.
45. For the duchy of Milan after 1536, Sella and Capra (1984), 48-50; for the county of Holland after 1542, Tracy (1990), 143-44.
46. Brucker (1977), 444-46, 483-86 (disputes about the *catasto* of 1427); Del Torre (1986), 22-39.
47. Kathryn Norberg, in Hoffman and Norberg (1994); Tracy (1985), 51-56; Fritschy (1988), 34; Sella and Capra (1984), 50-52; Stumpo (1985), 219-33; Schofield (1988).
48. Tracy (1985), 76; Fortea Pérez (1990), 79-81.

49. Bonney (1981), 272.
50. Tracy (1985), 85-87; Fortea Pérez (1990), 49, 64, 103. "Derogation" from the privileges of nobles, clergy and crown officials was of course easier to obtain than to enforce.
51. Major (1980), 38; Tracy (1985), 36-37, 52-56, 84-85.
52. Major (1980), 44; Ulloa (1977), 76-77; Carretero Zamora (1988), 6, 15-17.
53. Fortea Pérez (1990), 24-25, 452-56, 463-70.
54. Carracciolo (1983), 19-29, 119-28, 282-84; Tracy (1990), 144; Heers (1961), 128-29.
55. I use "state debt" to avoid the controversy about when the king's private debts become "public." Are the *juros* of Castile a public debt (Artola [1982], 68-69, Toboso Sánchez [1987], but not the *rentes sur l'hotel de ville* in France (Wolfe [1972], 93)?
56. Dollinger (1968), 193, 475-79; Tracy (1985), chap. 3; Fortea Pérez (1990), 142-62.
57. Bennassar (1967), 250-59. For the political resonance of fluctuations in interest rates on the state debt in Florence, Brucker (1977), 53-54.
58. Webber and Wildavsky (1986), 96, 128, 136, 211-14.
59. Prodi, "Introduzione," in Kellenbenz and Prodi (1989), 10-13.
60. E. Fryde, in Guarducci (1976), 295-327; Wolfe (1972), 136; Fortea Pérez (1990), 93.
61. Alsop (1982), 16-17; Ulloa (1977), 60-68.
62. Kittell (1991), 81-84, 120-23; Carande Thobar (1949-68), vol. 2:7-70.
63. For the French distinction between *comptables* and *ordinateurs*, Bayard (1988), 52.
64. Van Uytven (1961), 23-26, 52.
65. Peck (1990); Thompson (1976), 76-80.
66. Tracy (1985), 74, photocopy of receipt for payment of annual interest on a States of Holland *rente*; these slips of paper are still occasionally to be found pressed between the appropriate pages of the receiver's account.
67. Dollinger (1968), 55; Tracy (1990), 122; Wagner (1977), 101.
68. Fortea Pérez (1990), 91-92; Wolfe (1972), 159-60.
69. Rodríguez Salgado (1988). Philip was in England, as Mary Tudor's husband. But see Yun (1991), 32-33, for Crown revenues in Castile that did not pass through the Contaduria.
70. Wolfe (1972), 114. See the rubric for payments by *mandement* of the prince in the accounts of the Habsburg Netherlands government.
71. Bonney (1981), 1, 19, 25-28, 82, 181; Bayard (1988), 67.
72. Rodríguez Salgado (1988), 63; van Nieuwenhuysen (1984), 369-71; Tracy (1985), 33.
73. Fritschy (1988), 36-39, partly as a corrective to the emphasis of my account in Tracy (1985).
74. Heers (1961), 97-147; Stumpo (1985).
75. The Genoese were also major investors in Naples, holding nearly a quarter of the state debt in 1596: Calabria (1991), 115-17.
76. Artola (1982), 87-89, 152; Fortea Pérez (1990), 63; Rodríguez Salgado (1988), 61-63; Toboso Sánchez (1987), 65-66, 85-89, 124; Ulloa (1977), 759-63, 770-71.
77. Doucet (1937), 19; Bonney (1981), 41, 46-58, 164-66; Ulloa (1977), 770-71; Wolfe (1972), 93, 115, 121-26; Schnapper (1957), 159-61; Dent (1973), 46-54.

78. Compare the fortunes of stock in Florence's *monte commune* during the political crisis of 1431-33 with that of papal luoghi in the early seventeenth century: Molho (1971), 157-62, and Stumpo (1985), 247-53. For the connection between juro rates and the soundness of the revenues by which particular issues were backed, Ulloa (1977), 847-48; Toboso Sánchez (1987), 147. For the organized capital markets of a later era, see James C. Riley, *International Government Finance and the Amsterdam Capital Market, 1740-1815* (Cambridge, 1980).
79. Houtzager (1950), 45-52.
80. The point is made for the provincial debt of Holland in Tracy (1985); but see the critique by Fritschy (1988).
81. Carande Thobar (1943-68), vol. 2:147, 191; Tracy (1990), 116; Wolfe (1972), 99; Artola (1982), 71; Fortea Pérez (1990), 96-100; Bayard (1988), 30; Caracciolo (1983), 231.
82. There are particularly useful discussions of this issue in Hoffman and Norberg (1994), esp. the contributions by Sacks, Thompson (first of two), and Hoffman.
83. Major (1980), 66, 171; Chevalier, "Fiscalité municipale et fiscalité d'état," 149; Wolfe (1972), 106.
84. Fortea Pérez (1990), 130-31, citing an article by Thompson, whose more recent views are giving in the article cited in note 76.
85. Guaro Coppola, in Kellenbenz and Prodi (1989), 298-301, citing Sella (1982); Calabria (1991), 57-58.
86. Fernández Albadeja (1992), 261-62; Blockmans, in Genet and Le Men (1987), 88-89; Chevalier, in ibid., 143-44.
87. Pulido Bueno (1984), 81; Bayard (1988), 28-29; Bercé in Genet and Le Men (1987), 165.
88. On the Franc of Bruges, W. Prevenier, *De Leden en de Staten van Vlaanderen, 1384-1405* (Brussels, 1961), 19-23, 57-84; on the corpo territoriale of rural Brescia, see Del Torre (1986), 27-30.
89. For the problematic character of the Cortes' claim to be the *reino* of Castile, see Carretero Zamora (1988), 6-17.
90. Hickey (1986), 19-32; Del Torre (1986), 22-39; Caracciolo (1983), 32-52, 128-29.
91. Bayard (1988), 146-62; Van Uytven, in Guarducci (1976), 551-52.
92. See especially Bayard (1988); Dessert (1984).
93. Ulloa (1977), 846; Molho (1987), 199-201.
94. Dollinger (1968); Hickey (1986); I. A. A. Thompson, "Castile: Absolutism, Constitutionalism, and Liberty," in Hoffman and Nordberg (1993).
95. Fritschy (1988), 11-19; Alexis de Tocqueville, *The Old Regime and the French Revolution* (Garden City, N.J., 1955).

# BIBLIOGRAPHY

*General and Comparative Works*
De Maddelena, Aldo, and Hermann Kellenbenz, eds. *Finanze e ragione di stato in Italia e Germanie nella prima età moderna.* Bologna, 1984.
Fryde, Edmund B. "The Financial Policies of the Royal Governments and Popular Resistance to Them in France and England." In Guarducci (1976), 295-327.
Genet, Jean-Philippe, and Hervé Le Men, eds. *Genèse de l'état moderne: prélèvement et distribution.* Paris, 1987.
Guarducci, Annalisa, ed. *Prodotto lordo e finanze pubblica, secoli XIII-XIX.* Prato, 1976.
Hoffman, Philip T., and Kathryn Norberg, eds. *Fiscal Crises and Political Development.* Stanford, 1994 (forthcoming).
Kellenbenz, Hermann, and Paolo Prodi, eds. *Fisco, religione, state nell'età confessionale.* Bologna, 1989.
Lyon, Bryce, and Adriaan Verhulst. *Medieval Finance: a Comparison of Financial Institutions in Northwestern Europe.* Bruges, 1967.
Parker, N. Geoffrey. "The Development of European Finance." In *Fontana Economic History of Europe*, ed. Carlo M. Cipolla, vol. 2. New York, 1977.
Reitsma, Richard. "Dutch Finance and English Taxes in the 17th Century." In *Bestuurders en Geleerden. Opstellen over onderwerpen uit de Nederlandse geschiedenis van de zestiende, zeventiende en achttiende eeuw, aangeboden aan Prog. Dr. J.J. Woltjer bij zijn afscheid als hoogleraar van de Rijksuniversiteit te Leiden*, ed. Simon Groenveld, M. E. H. N. Mout, and Ivo Schöffer, 107-12. Amsterdam, 1985.
Webber, Carolyn, and Adam Wildavsky. *A History of Taxation and Expenditure in the Western World.* New York, 1986.
Witt, Peter-Christian, ed. *Wealth and Taxation in Central Europe: the History and Sociology of Public Finance.* Leamington Spa, 1987.


*England*
Alsop, J. D. "The Theory and Practice of Tudor Taxation." *EHR* 97 (1982): 1-30.
Ashton, Robert. *The Crown and the Money Market, 1603-1640.* Oxford, 1960.
Bernard, G. W. *The City and the Court, 1601-1643.* Cambridge, 1979.
Bernard, G. W. *War, Taxation and Rebellion in Early Tudor England.* New York, 1986.
Dietz, F. C. *English Public Finance, 1558-1641.* 2 vols. London, 1964.
Elton, Geoffrey R. "Taxation for War and Peace in Early Tudor England." In *War and Economic Development*, ed. J. M. Winter, 33-48. Cambridge, 1975.
Harris, G. L. *King, Parliament and Public Finance in Medieval England to 1369.* Oxford, 1975.
Harris, G. L. "Thomas Cromwell's `New Principle' of Taxation." *EHR* 93 (1978): 721-38.
Peck, Linda Levy. *Court Patronage and Corruption in Early Stuart England.* Boston, 1990.
Schofield, Roger. "Taxation and the Political Limits of the Tudor State." In *Law and Government in Tudor England: Essays Presented to Sir Geoffrey Elton*, ed. Claire Cross, David M. Loades, and J. J. Scarisbrick, 227-56. Cambridge, 1988.
Wolffe, Bertram Percy. *The Royal Demesne in English History: the Crown Estate in the Governance of the Realm from the Conquest to 1509.* London, 1971.

*France*

Bayard, Françoise. *Le monde des financiers au XVIIe siècle.* Paris, 1988.

Beik, William. *Absolutism and Society in Seventeenth Century France: Aristocracy and State Institutions in Languedoc.* Cambridge, 1985.

Bercé, Yves-Marie. "Pour une étude institutionelle et psychologique de l'impot moderne." In Genet and Le Men (1987), 161-68.

Bonney, Richard. *The King's Debts: Finance and Politics in France 1589-1661.* Oxford, 1981.

Chaunu, Pierre. "L'état de finance." In *Histoire économique et sociale de France,* ed. Fernand Braudel, vol. 1:129-48. Paris, 1977.

Chevalier, Bernard. "Fiscalité municipale et fiscalité d'état en France du XIVe à la fin du XVIe siècle." In Genet and Le Men (1987), 137-51.

Dent, Julian. *Crisis in Finance: Crown, Financiers and Society in 17th Century France.* Newton Abbot, 1973.

Dessert, Daniel. *Argent, pouvoir et société au grand siècle.* Paris, 1984.

Doucet, Robert. *Finances municipales et crédit public à Lyon au XVIe siècle.* Paris, 1937.

Henneman, John B. *Royal Taxation in Fourteenth Century France.* Princeton, 1971.

Henneman, John B. *Royal Taxation in 14th Century France: the Captivity and Ransom of John II.* Philadelphia, 1976.

Hickey, Daniel. *The Coming of French Absolutism: the Struggle for Tax Reform in the Province of Dauphiné, 1540-1640.* Toronto, 1986.

Hocquet, Jean-Claude. "Qui la gabelle de sel du roi de France a-t-elle enrichi?" In Genet and Le Men (1987), 209-19.

Major, J. Russell. *Representative Government in Early Modern France.* New Haven, 1980.

Rey, Maurice. *La domaine du roi et les finances extraordinaires sous Charles VI, 1388-1413.* 2 vols. Paris, 1963.

Schnapper, Bernard. *Les rentes au XVIe siècle.* Paris, 1957.

Wolfe, Martin. *The Fiscal System of Renaissance France.* New Haven, 1972.

*The Holy Roman Empire*

Brunner, Otto. *Land and Lordship: Structures of Governance in Medieval Austria.* Trans. Howard Kaminsky and James Van Horn Melton. Philadelphia, 1992 (1939).

Bulst, Neithard. "Impots et Finances Publiques en Allemagne au XVe Siècle." In Genet and Le Men (1987), 65-76.

Dollinger, Heinz. *Studien zur Finanzreform Maximilians I. von Bayern in den Jahren 1598-1618.* Göttingen, 1968.

Fryde, Matthew M. "Studies in the History of the Public Credit of the German Principalities and Towns in the Late Middle Ages." *Studies in Medieval and Renaissance History* 1 (1964): 221-92.

Kellenbenz, Hermann, ed. *Öffentliche Finanzen und privates Kapital im späten Mittelalter und in der ersten Hälfte des 19. Jahrhunderts.* Stuttgart, 1971.

Krüger, Kersten. *Finanzstaat Hessen. Staatsbildung im Übergang vom Domänenstaat zum Steuerstaat.* Marburg, 1980.

Krüger, Kersten. "Public Finance and Modernization: The Change from Domain State to Tax State in Hesse during the 16th and 17th Centuries." In Witt (1987), 49-62.

Oestreich, Gerhard. *Neostoicism and the Early Modern State.* Cambridge, 1982.

Wagner, Stefan. *Staatssteuern in Jülich-Berg von der Schaffung der Staatsverfassung im 15. Jahrhundert bis zur Auflösung der Herzogtümer in den Jahren 1801 und 1806.* Cologne, 1977.

*Italy*

Bowsky, William. *The Finances of the Commune of Siena, 1287-1355.* Oxford, 1970.

Brucker, Gene A. *The Civic World of Early Renaissance Florence.* Princeton, 1977.

Bullard, Melissa M. *Filippo Strozzi and the Medici: Favor and Finance in 16th Century Florence and Rome.* Cambridge, 1980.

Calabria, Antonio. *Cost of Empire: the Finances of the Kingdom of Naples during the Time of Spanish Rule.* Cambridge, 1991.

Calabria, Antonio, and John Marino, eds., *Good Government in Spanish Naples.* New York, 1990.

Caracciolo, Francesco. *Sud, debiti e gabelle: gravami, potere e società nel Mezzogiorno in età moderna.* Naples, 1983.

Del Torre, Giuseppe. *Venezia e la Terraferma dopa la Guerra di Cambrai: fiscalita e amministrazione (1515-1530).* Milan, 1986.

Delumeau, Jean. *Vie économique et sociale de Rome dans la seconde moitié du XVIe siècle.* 2 vols. Paris, 1957-59.

Gilbert, Felix. *The Pope, his Banker and Venice.* Cambridge, Mass., 1980.

Heers, Jacques. *Gênes au XVe siècle: activité économique et problèmes sociaux.* Paris, 1961.

Kirshner, Julius. "The Moral Problem of Discounting Genoese *Paghe,* 1450-1550." *Archivum Fratrum Praedicatorum* (1977): 109-67.

Lane, Frederic C. "Public Debt and Private Wealth, particularly in 16th Century Venice." In *Melanges en honneur de Fernand Braudel,* vol. 1:317-25. Toulouse, 1973.

Luzzatto, Gino. *Il debito pubblico della Repubblica di Venezia (1200-1500).* Milan, 1963.

Meek, Christine. "Il debito pubblico nella otoria finanziaria di Lucca." *Actum Luce* 3 (1974): 7-46.

Molho, Anthony J. *Florentine Public Finance in the Early Renaissance, 1400-1433.* Cambridge, Mass., 1971.

Molho, Anthony J. "L'amministrazione del debito pubblico a Firenze nel quindicesimo secolo." In *I ceti dirigenti nella Toscana del Quattrocento,* 191-207. Impruneta, 1987.

Muto, Giovanni. *Le finanze pubbliche Napoletane tra riforma e restaurazione (1529-1634).* Naples, 1980.

Partner, Peter. "Papal Fiscal Policy in the Renaissance and Counter-Reformation." *PaP,* 78 (1980): 18-62.

Reinhard, Wolfgang. "Finanza pontificia, sistema beneficiale e finanza statale nell'eta confessionale." In Kellenbenz and Prodi (1989), 459-504.

Reinhard, Wolfgang. *Papstfinanz und Nepotismus unter Paul V.* 2 vols. Stuttgart, 1974.

Sella, Domenico. *L'economia lombarda durante la dominazione spagnola.* Bologna, 1982.

Sella, Domenico, and Carlo Capra. *Il Ducato di Milano dal 1535 al 1776.* Turin, 1984.

Stumpo, Enrico. *Il capitale finanziario a Roma fra Cinque e Seicento.* Milan, 1985.

Stumpo, Enrico. *Finanza e stato moderna nel Piemonte del Seicento.* Rome, 1979.

Stumpo, Enrico. "Finanze e ragione di stato nella prima età moderna. Due modelli diversi: Piemonte e Toscana, Savoia e Medici." In De Maddelena and Kellenbenz (1984), 181-233.

Vigo, Giovanni. *Finanza pubblica e pressione fiscale nello stato di Milano durante il secolo XVI.* Milan, 1977.

*Low Countries*

Blockmans, Willem P. "Finances Publiques et Inegalité Sociale dans les Pays-Bas au XIVe-XVIe Siècles." In Genet and Le Men (1987), 77-89.

Fritschy, Joanna Maria Francesca. *De Patriotten en de Financiën van de Bataafse Republiek (1795-1801).* The Hague, 1988.

Grapperhaus, Ferdinand H. M. *Alva en de Tiende Penning.* Zutphen, 1982.

Houtzager, Dirk. *Hollands Lijf- en Losrenten voor 1672.* Schiedam, 1950.

Kittell, Ellen E. *From Ad Hoc to Routine: a Case Study in Medieval Bureaucracy.* Philadelphia, 1991.

Klein, P. W. "De Heffing van de 100e en 200e Penning van het Vermogen te Gouda, 1599-1722." *Economisch- en Sociaal-Historisch Jaarboek* XXXI (1967): 41-62.

Maddens, N. *De Beden in het Graafschap Vlaanderen tijdens de Regering van Karel V (1515-1550) = Standen en Landen / Anciens Pays et Assemblées d'État,* vol. 72 (Heule, 1978).

Maddens, N. "De Invoering van de 'Nieuwe Middelen' in het Graafschap Vlaanderen tijdens de Regering van Keizer Karel." *Belgische Tijdschrift voor Filologie en Geschiedenis / Revue Belge de Philologie et d'Histoire* 57 (1979): 342-63, 861-98.

*Récherches sur les Finances Publiques en Belgique* = Acta Historica Bruxellensia, III. 2 vols. Brussels, 1967-70.

Tchistozvonov, Alexander N. "Le revenue global des exploitations paysannes et la politique fiscale en Hollande au debut du XVIe siecle." In Guarducci (1976), 369-84.

Tracy, James D. *A Financial Revolution in the Habsburg Netherlands: "Renten" and "Renteniers" in the County of Holland, 1515-1566.* Berkeley and Los Angeles, 1985.

Tracy, James D. *Holland under Habsburg Rule, 1506-1566: the Formation of a Body Politic.* Berkeley and Los Angeles, 1990.

Tracy, James D. "The Taxation System of the County of Holland under Charles V and Philip II, 1519-1566." *Economisch- en Sociaal-Historisch Jaarboek* 48 (1984): 72-117.

Van Nieuwenhuysen, A. *Les finances du duc de Bourgogne, Philippe le Hardi (1384-1404).* Brussels, 1984.

Van Uytven, Raymond. *Stadseconomie en Stadsfinanciën te Leuven van de XIIe tot het Einde van de XVIe Eeuw.* Brussels, 1961.

Van Uytven, Raymond. "Les Pays-Bas au XVe et XVIe siècle: finances publiques et industrie." In Guarducci (1976), 533-54.


*Spain*

Artola, Miguel. *La hacienda del Antiguo Regimen.* Madrid, 1982.

Bennassar, Bartolomé. *Valladolid au siècle d'or.* Paris, 1967.

Boyajian, James C. *Portuguese Bankers at the Court of Spain, 1626-1650.* New Brunswick, N. J., 1983.

Carande Thobar, Ramon. *Carlos V y sus banqueros.* 3 vols. Madrid, 1943-68.

Carretero Zamora, Juan Manuel. *Cortes, monarquia, ciudades: las cortes de Castilla a comienzos de la epoca moderna (1476-1515).* Madrid, 1988.

Fernández Albaladeja, Pablo. *Fragmentos de monarquia. Trabajos de historia politica.* Madrid, 1992.

Fortea Pérez, José Ignacio. *Fiscalidad en Cordoba 1513-1619.* Cordoba, 1986.

Fortea Pérez, José Ignacio. *Monarquia y cortes en la Corona de Castilla: las ciudades ante la politiica fiscal de Felipe II.* Salamanca, 1990.

Ladero Quesada, Miguel Angel. "De la `Reconquista' a la Fiscalite d'État dans la Couronne de Castile, 1268-1368." In Genet and Le Men (1987), 36-51.

Pulido Bueno, Ildefonso. *Consumo y fiscalidad en el reino de Sevilla: el servicio de millones en el siglo XVII.* Seville, 1984.

Rodríguez Salgado, M. J. *The Changing Face of Empire: Charles V, Philip II and Habsburg Authority, 1551-1559.* Cambridge, 1988.

Toboso Sánchez, Pilar. *La deuda publica castellana durante el Antiguo Regimen (juros) y su liquidacion en el siglo XIX.* Madrid, 1987.

Thompson, I. A. A. *War and Government in Habsburg Spain, 1560-1620.* London, 1976.

Ulloa, Modesto. *La hacienda real de Castilla en el reinado de Felipe II.* Madrid, 1977.

Yun Casalilla, Bartolomé. "Aristocracia, Corona y Oligarquias Urbanas en Castilla anies el problema fiscal." In *Historia de la hacienda en España (Siglos XVI-XX). Homenaje a Don Felipe Ruiz Martin* = Hacienda publica española, Monografias, No. 1. Madrid, 1991.

# THE OTTOMANS AND EUROPE

Cemal Kafadar
(Harvard University)*

In the summer of 1992, delegations from various cities were bidding for the right to host the Olympic games of the year 2000. The Turkish delegation, bidding for Istanbul, was astounded to hear their Central Asian cousins defend the case of Samarkand as the capital of Timur ("Tamerlane," 1336-1405), who "saved Europe from the Turkish menace" and made the Renaissance possible. So powerful has the European world hegemony rendered western public opinion, and so normative western historical experience, that such references are by now common. In reality, of course, Timur had no such thing in mind, for when he invaded western Asia in 1402, he aimed only to punish the upstart House of Osman.

## 1. FOUNDATIONS OF THE OTTOMAN POWER

The first large wave of Turkish tribesmen entered Anatolia while Byzantine defenses were crumbling after the Battle of Manzikert (1071). The modus vivendi, which subsequently arose between the (Seljuk) Turkish state and the Byzantine empire, was shattered after the 1220s, when Asian conquests of Chingis (1167-1227) sent a second wave of migrants westward into Anatolia. Most accounts of the House of Osman—none date before the fifteenth century—ascribe his ancestors' arrival in Anatolia to this wave. Chingisid armies followed, smashing the Seljuks in 1243 and turning western Anatolia into a political wilderness populated by chieftains who dreamed of becoming state-builders. The frontier ethos, as in contemporary Iberia, combined a drive for booty and personal glory with the championship of the faith, whose agents the Muslim Anatolians called "raiders for the faith" (*gazis*). Successful *gazis* attracted not only others of their own kind, but also disenchanted or dislocated Byzantines and scholar-bureaucrats from the former Seljuk provincial centers or the Islamic hinterland—all of whom helped to construct new institutions of governance.

The political enterprise of Osman (d. 1324), the eponymous founder of

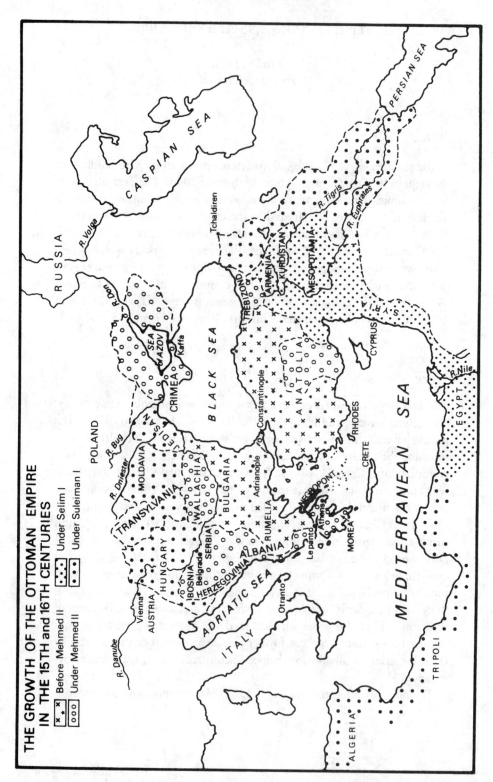

THE GROWTH OF THE OTTOMAN EMPIRE
IN THE 15TH and 16TH CENTURIES

Before Mehmed II   Under Selim I
Under Mehmed II   Under Suleiman I

the Ottoman dynasty, was one (relatively minor) among a pack of such *gazi* emirates (from "emir," prince or commander). He first appears in a Byzantine chronicle of 1301, and his principality, though less glamorous than those of some other *gazis*, sat auspiciously right next to Byzantine Bithynia (south of the Sea of Marmara) with its neglected defenses. As early as 1337, Osman's son transplanted *gazis* across the Sea of Marmara into southeastern Europe, and the narrow Thracian peninsula became the Ottoman gateway into the Balkans. Having gained a permanent foothold at Gelibolu (Gallipoli) in 1354, after an earthquake destroyed its Byzantine fortress, the Ottomans expanded across the Straits by means of political manipulation, raids, concessions, religious propaganda, and rigid centralization. The Serbian kingdom was reduced to vassalage after the Battle of Kossovo (1389), the Bulgarian one eliminated by 1394. By 1400 Ottoman power had established itself among the Slavic and Latin powers in southeastern Europe, the Turco-Muslim principalities in Asia Minor, and a much-diminished Byzantine empire still holding the region's natural center, Constantinople. By 1396, when Sultan Bayezid I (r. 1389-1402), called "the Lightning," crushed a Christian crusading army at Nicopolis, his lofty titles and style of life signalled that the Ottoman ruler was no longer primus inter pares among the raider lords.[1]

At this point, Timur issued a new challenge from the east. Claiming suzerainty as a son-in-law to the Ilkhanid branch of the Chingisids, he invaded Anatolia in 1402. Bayezid, who fancied himself transformer of the Ottoman emirate into an empire,[2] ignored Timur's warning and paid for this folly in the Battle of Ankara (20 July).

## 2. OTTOMAN RECONSTRUCTION IN THE FIFTEENTH CENTURY

When Timur, having shattered the work of four Ottoman generations, turned back eastward, the Ottoman lands fell into a fierce internecine struggle among three brothers. Süleyman (d. 1411), the eldest, ruled from Edirne (Adrianople) and initially looked to be the strongest, but his haughty sultanic style and his concessions to Christian neighbors alienated a good number of his veteran gazi commanders.[3] Such reactions nonetheless cannot be understood in the simplistic dichotomies—so beloved of modern scholars—of Turks vs. Greeks or Muslims vs. Christians. "In Gallipoli," runs one report, "we also learned that many Turks dwelt along Negroponte and did not wish to give up any of their land, and the Greeks there supported them."[4] Süleyman retained the upper hand so long as he remained in sole command of Rumelia, where the *gazis* had no alternative to his rule, but eventually his brother, Prince Mehmed, emerged from this confused time—the "Ottoman Interregnum" (1402-1413)—to rule over the entire Ottoman holdings.

Mehmed I (r. 1413-21) faced two major challenges in Europe, one from another brother, Mustafa, the other from Bedreddin, a religious mystic whose message of a proto-communist utopia crossed religious boundaries and fired an unsuccessful rebellion in western Anatolia. The movement of this *sheykh*, the son of a *gazi* and a Greek fortress commander's daughter from Thrace, was both the last gasp of the hybrid frontier society and the final test of the Ottomans' resolve to establish an orderly state and religious orthodoxy.

The small Christian powers of the region proved tougher, though by 1400 most had been reduced to vassals of the Ottomans, Hungary, or Venice. Only Mircea of Wallachia held out, but in 1417 Mehmed captured parts of southern Albania, including Valona, the first Ottoman outlet to the Adriatic, and the next year reduced Prince Mircea to a tributary vassal.

Toward the large Christian powers, Byzantium and Venice, Mehmed acted cautiously, for his brother and rival, Mustafa, was a hostage in Byzantine hands, and the Venetian navy threatened the Dardanelles. The holding hostage (or "hosting") of Ottoman princes by rival powers exploited a major fault line in Turkish political life, the legitimate right of all princes to compete for the throne. Byzantine and Venetian statesmen routinely encouraged bids by various Ottoman princes—not all hostages and not all authentic—which was sometimes a highly effective way to keep Ottoman aggression at bay. In this case, when the Byzantines released Mustafa, Murad II (r. 1421-51), Mehmed's son, beat him with the aid of the Genoese governor of New Phokaia, who ferried Ottoman troops across the Dardanelles in pursuit of Mustafa, and then brought the unruly *gazi* warlords to heel. Turning to the Venetians, Murad annexed all the Aegean principalities in 1424-25 and took Thessaloniki from its Venetian garrison in 1430, after an eight-year siege. Other threats—from Hungary and from Shahrukh—Timur's son, at Samarkand, failed to materialize.

Ottoman success in the Balkans during the 1430s depended partly on a harmonious relationship between state policy and the border raiders, a spontaneous but unpredictable force in a world ordered by treaties and borders.[5] The tireless *gazis* were nevertheless extremely useful, as they gnawed away at the resistance of frontier populations awaiting Ottoman conquest. Ultimately, of course, the state would transform most of them into cogs in the Ottoman prebendal system.

Having conquered Albania in the 1430s, and after a Hungarian peasant revolt in 1437, Murad launched a devastating expedition into Transylvania in 1438. His successes against Hungary put great pressure on the buffer states, Wallachia and especially Serbia, which lost ground even though its *despot* had only a few years earlier renewed his ties of vassalage and given his daughter in marriage to Murad. In 1441 came the turn of southern Serbia, as the sultan's forces captured Novo Brdo and its silver mines.

These years saw the assembly of the last serious crusading alliance, for the union of the Greek and Roman churches at the Council of Florence in 1439 and the end of a civil war in Hungary in 1442 produced a new situation in southern and central Europe. Several Christian powers now seemed willing to do more than pay lip service to the idea of pushing the Ottomans out of the Balkans. The Hungarians were to provide the main army of invasion, joined by the Serbian forces, while Venice and Burgundy undertook to close the Straits between Asia and Europe, and an alliance was also sought with the last major Turkish rival of the Ottomans in Anatolia, the Karaman principality. The advocates of crusade in these years had good reason to be skeptical of Ottoman invincibility. The Ottoman invasions of Hungary in 1441 and 1442 were cleverly thwarted by János Hunyádi, a Hungarian commander who apparently understood Ottoman military weaknesses. In Albania, too, the Ottoman power began to recede before the attacks of Scanderbeg.

Scanderbeg's story illustrates the complexities of Ottoman family politics. The Ottomans, like other rulers of the time, recognized that dynastic politics implied the strategizing of family relationships; while they conceived of hierarchies of power in the imagery of father/son/brother, they also cemented dynastic ties by means of arranged marriages. It was also common practice to "host"—i.e., hold hostage—the children of vassal nobilities in the court of their patron, so that the fifteenth-century Ottoman court hosted a number of princes and little lords from neighboring polities. Such children, if from Christian vassal families, were maintained in a Christian enclave at court. Such were the four sons of Carlo Tocco I, *despot* in the Epirus (r. 1417-30) and the two sons of Vlad Drakul, ruler of Wallachia (r. 1436-46). One of the latter, who became the famous Vlad the Impaler (known to later vampire lore as Dracula), spent many years in Murad II's palace. Nor were the princesses who married Ottoman princes necessarily expected to convert to Islam. Local nobilities, however, whose territories were earmarked for annexation and redistribution within the Ottoman system, were apparently expected or at least encouraged to convert to Islam. Some of these, too, had their children raised in the palace.

George Kastriota, son of the Albanian lord John Kastriota, came to the
Ottoman court following such an arrangement. Converted to Islam and
given the name Iskender, he graduated from palace training and received a
prebend in his native Albania. Called Iskender Beg (his Muslim name and
Ottoman title, hence "Scanderbeg"), he took up arms against the sultan,
reverted to Christianity, and defended his mountainous land for decades
against several Ottoman attempts to quash him. Although Scanderbeg
presented a stirring image as a "champion of Christendom," his real territorial challenge to the Ottomans was slight.

The same could not be said of János Hunyádi, who, following on his defensive successes, led a major strike into Ottoman territory in 1443. He attacked in the fall, when the normal campaigning season was over for the
sultan's army, especially the prebendal cavalry—by far the larger component in the Ottoman armies—which returned to supervise their *timars*.
The Hungarian-Serbian expedition of fall 1443 was able to penetrate deep
into the southern Balkans and was turned back only with great difficulty
and loss on the Ottoman side. The sultan's most important military force
turned out to be his standing ("Janissary") army of infantry and artillery,
whose star was now beginning to rise. Hunyádi's exploits were celebrated
across Europe. Yet, though he had indeed exposed the Ottomans' vulner-
ability and handed them some embarrassing losses, Murad had met his
challenge.

Murad's military exploits notwithstanding, contemporaries described
him as a man of peaceful disposition, which may be why in 1444, the year
after his truce with King Ladislaus/Vladislaw of Hungary, he abdicated in
favor of his twelve-year-old son, Mehmed. This act tempted Ladislaus to
begin land operations in cooperation with the blockading fleet organized
by Venice and the duke of Burgundy. The hindsight of later Balkan history
suggests that this successful crusade of the 1440s was based not on fantasy
but on real weaknesses—as perceived by both sides—of the Ottoman
power. When, for example, news came in the fall that the Hungarians had
once again crossed the Danube, trenches were dug as far south as Edirne.
Murad, recalled from retirement, forced a passage of the blockaded Straits
and defeated Ladislaus in the Battle of Varna (10 November 1444).
Murad returned to his withdrawal but could not remain for long. Grand
Vezir Chandarli (d. 1453) exploited a Janissary revolt to engineer Murad's
return to power in 1446[6]. The vezir's gamble paid off when Murad defeated another Hungarian army under János Hunyádi at Kossovo in 1448
(17 October). When the nineteen-year-old Mehmed returned to the
throne, he began to plan an all-out assault on Constantinople.

## 3. Mehmed the Conqueror and the Consolidation
## of the Ottoman State

The "imperial project" of Mehmed II (r. 1451-81) became the turning point in the Ottoman polity's evolution from principality to empire. Its hinge was the conquest of the Byzantine capital, an extremely prestigious feat which capped centuries of frontier warfare and fulfilled a venerable dream. The venture was facilitated by the withdrawal of the Timurids from Middle Eastern politics after the death of Shahrukh, Timur's son, in 1446. By the end of Mehmed's long reign, the Ottoman relationship to the House of Chingis was reversed, as the Chingisid khans of Crimea acknowledged Ottoman suzerainty.

*The Conquests of Mehmed II*

After the fall of Constantinople (1453), Mehmed absorbed all the powers he considered no more than reminders of Byzantine weakness: the Muslim emirates of western Anatolia, Slavic and Albanian powers in the Balkans, the Genoese and Venetian lands and the Latin legacies of the Fourth Crusade, the Greek offshoots of Byzantium, and the Wallachian and Moldavian principalities. Mehmed, who called himself "the ruler of the two seas and two continents," set out to create a seamless domain. Calling himself "Caesar," he imagined his empire to be a Byzantium restored. He took the Genoese holdings in the Aegean during the 1450s, the duchy of Athens, a remnant of the Fourth Crusade, from the Florentine House of Acciaiuoli in 1455, and the Genoese slave-trading towns Kaffa (Feodosiya) and Tana (Azov) on the Black Sea in 1475. The khans of the Crimea became Ottoman vassals, and the Peloponnese despots of the Palaeologue family lost their lands in 1458-60. The story of the two Palaeologue brothers encapsulates the desperate politics of late Byzantium, caught between the Turks and the Latins. When their lands were lost, Thomas took refuge with the pope, while Demetrios received the islands of Limni and Imbros from his son-in-law, Sultan Mehmed. Trabzon (Trebizond), the imperial seat of the Comneni dynasty since 1204, was captured in 1461.

In the Balkans, too, Mehmed moved the Ottoman power forward. The Serbian and the Bosnian kingdoms were overrun in 1457 and 1463 respectively. The local ruling family in Montenegro was coopted, though with a large degree of autonomy, as were many Albanian lords, whose rugged terrain was permanently incorporated into the sultan's realm after Scanderbeg's death in 1469. After the elimination of Vlad Drakul, Wallachia was more or less subdued, and though Moldavia held out longer, Mehmed reduced both principalities to tributary status.

Mehmed II's toughest opponent was Venice, against which he waged war from 1463 to 1479 in the Aegean and the Peloponnese, where the Most Serene Republic held several towns and forts. Venetian fleets also raided the Anatolian coasts, hoping to link up with eastern rivals to the Ottomans, such as the Karamanids, and, when they were reduced to Ottoman subjection, the Akkoyunlu (the White Sheep). But Mehmed defeated the Akkoyunlu in 1473, and in 1479 he forced Venice to make peace.

When in 1480 Mehmed's westward gaze extended beyond the Venetians' empire, his chief target was not Naples, whose king had backed Venice and Hungary against him, but Rome. The Ottomans were well aware of the papacy's central role and the emotive force of its rhetoric of Christian unity. The more so as the Ottomans, who employed a similar, Islamic, rhetoric of universal community, recognized the political potential of such ideas. Thus, the "Red Apple," the heart of Christendom which was an emotionally charged symbol enshrined in Ottoman military lore, was not a fixed target but a movable goal of Ottoman policy. Constantinople seems to have been the "Red Apple" until 1453, and, indeed, in the Byzantine capital there was a gilded orb held by a huge bronze statue, which was widely held to be a symbol of Roman-Christian world dominion, and which was one inspiration for the Ottoman counter-myths. Once Constantinople lay in Ottoman hands, and this great statue was cast into cannon, Rome became the "Red Apple," at least for a while.[7]

Mehmed's western venture stalled, as the Ottoman landing at Otranto in southern Italy in 1480 remained episodic, and the Knights of St. John repelled him from Rhodes in the same year. Mehmed, justly called "the Conqueror," died while on a mysterious campaign in the following year.

With the fall of Constantinople and the medieval principalities in Anatolia and the Balkans, Ottoman unitary rule was established in a region which for centuries had been fragmented. Something similar was concluded by the fall of Granada to Spain in 1492, so that by 1500 the long struggles for regional hegemony by powers, which claimed to represent respectively Islam and Christianity, concluded at both ends of the Mediterranean basin. During the following century, true, these two powers competed for what they regarded as world hegemony. That was "a time," wrote Leopold von Ranke, "when the power, and, in a great measure, the civilization of Europe, seemed to have their chief seat in the South; a time when the Ottoman empire and the Spanish monarchy had grown up, face to face, to an overtopping greatness, dangerous to neighboring and remote nations."[8]

*Mehmed II and the Ottoman State*

Not only a conqueror, Mehmed II also built a central administrative apparatus and invented an imperial style of rule. His "imperial project" doubtless completed Ottoman political development by means of a ruthless authoritarianism and unclouded vision, which bridled the tensions between the warlords and the bureaucrats that had bedeviled earlier efforts. The sultan's solution to this old problem was to create a new kind of elite to support a new kind of ruler. The frontier lords, for their part, understood that although Mehmed's aggressive militarism provided opportunities, his conquests also consolidated bureaucratic practices that undermined their way of life. A chronicler, sympathetic to the *gazis*, reports that they were not eager to attack Belgrade in 1456, since they "would have to take up farming if Belgrade were taken."⁹ They also resented making Constantinople the capital, or at least the kind of capital Mehmed had in mind, for, as a collection of frontier lore from around 1470 reports, the warlords wanted "the keys to Istanbul" kept at Edirne, "home of the warriors of the faith."¹⁰

Against *gazi* traditionalism, Mehmed preferred a "'Byzantine' style of government centered on the person of the emperor and based on the outright social [and economic] dominance of Constantinople over all other cities."¹¹ His vision emerged as a bricolage derived from a diverse heritage—Byzantine, Perso-Islamic, and Turco-Mongol—plus innovations drawn from fifteenth-century Mediterranean currents. Its central embodiment, a huge complex of buildings symmetrically organized around a mosque, announced the sultans' enhanced claims within the Islamic world by its unprecedented monumentality and its location on an important Byzantine site. Mehmed's Istanbul could also boast of a significant innovation in post-medieval fortification architecture, the first star-shaped fortress.¹²

In his design of a palace Mehmed's conception of imperial rule came fully to life. Three kiosks adorned the royal garden, each in the style of one of the traditions the Ottomans honored—Timurid-Persianate, Byzantine, and Ottoman—and there were Italianate elements as well. The palace defined not just an architectural style, but a new style of rule, for it emphasized the sultan's seclusion from all public functions except for a few carefully choreographed and ritualized appearances. Gone forever was the open court of a *gazi* chief.

The new bureaucratic Ottoman administration, for which Mehmed II laid the groundwork, came to maturity after 1550 under what historians have conventionally regarded as "weak sultans." Its cornerstone, legal codification, produced the first known written codes outside divine law in

Islamic history. There were, in fact, two codes, one to regulate fiscal-administrative practices throughout the empire, the other to regulate the court and the career paths of the ruling elite. The latter reveals Mehmed's vision in a singularly important way, for it offers a blueprint of the kind of ruling apparatus he had in mind. The code defines the terms of the sultan's seclusion, for in a government "centered on the person of the emperor," the very fact of codification made possible an impersonal system in which the royal personage could be an icon. Many of the "weak" sultans after Süleyman have been seen in just this light.

## 4. SOCIAL FOUNDATIONS OF CLASSICAL OTTOMAN CIVILIZATION

The mature empire's administrative heart, Constantinople/Istanbul, was also to be its cultural and commercial center. Soon after the conquest Mehmed set out to rebuild and repopulate the city, which had for years lain in some decay.[13] Rent-free property grants to the soldiers and dervish-mentors of the conquering army were rescinded, since this was not meant to be a city of the poor and of rentiers, and forced colonization brought in more desirable merchants and gifted artisans. Muslim and non-Muslim, many came from newly conquered territories (e.g., Karaman, Kaffa, Levkas), while the exiled and fugitive Greek population of the Byzantine city was pardoned and invited to resettle. Resentment of forced settlement notwithstanding, within a few decades Istanbul became a thriving metropolis. When Mehmed's court and the administrative elite settled in Istanbul as the permanent seat of government toward the end of his reign, the enormous scale of their consumption was bound to lure additional mercantile and artisanal communities. Many of the Iberian Jews, for example, chose to settle there after their expulsion from the Iberian kingdoms.

The city of Pera, across a narrow inlet from Constantinople, had been untouched by the conquest, since Mehmed had no desire to disrupt the brisk international trade of this famed commercial center and its European colonies, headed by the Genoese. The foreign communities' trading privileges under the Byzantines had been periodically renewed through charters, known as "capitulations," a policy which Mehmed continued. Relations with Venice, too, which had been briefly ruptured during the demise of the Byzantine empire, were restored by Mehmed's treaty with the Republic in 1454.

Meanwhile, as trade revived and grew, the typical elements of classical

Ottoman urban life were taking shape in the capital. One was the "charitable endowment" (*waqf*), an institution typical of Islamic urban life, though it also had Byzantine precedents. Mehmed II not only built his own imposing *waqf* complex, he apparently also encouraged his grandees to do the same. These acts set the model of charitable practice, and by 1546, Istanbul had 2,515 such institutions, which performed a whole range of educational, medical, charitable, and religious functions. The practice also spread to other cities.

Mehmed's reign laid the foundations of a new and stable urbanism. The lands now under Ottoman power possessed, of course, long traditions of urban life, and the Ottomans, by politically integrating a region long unstable, made possible a new flourishing of its cities, and not only of Istanbul. This *pax ottomana* promoted a relatively integrated regional economy which basically followed a "free trade" policy in the international sphere. Until the middle of the sixteenth century, when population growth began to have an impact, even the export of grain to Christian Europe—which the state by Islamic law had the right to prohibit—was often allowed, though some other exports—military equipment and horses—were forbidden.

The Ottoman economy developed as mixture of free and command elements, both of which were shaped primarily by political considerations. In general, international and transit commerce were left free, while internal trade and production were regulated. The victualling of Istanbul became a central concern of the regime, which carefully regulated the supply routes to and the sale of certain goods in the capital. To regulate prices and raw materials, the state worked increasingly through a guild system that drew on the medieval Islamic heritage of urban associations. Through these traditionally autonomous *futuwwa* or *akhi* brotherhoods, together, perhaps, with elements of Byzantine corporate tradition, the practitioners of specific crafts and trades were organized into strictly professional, sometimes multiconfessional, guilds, which gradually lost much of their earlier autonomy.

The extent of state control must nonetheless not be exaggerated. Outside the capital the guilds continued to enjoy a good deal of freedom, notably in the selection of their officials, and the state courts often simply verified and ordered enforcement of guild custom to settle disputes. Prices and disputes regarding market regulations were settled by negotiations among the state, representatives of guilds, and "people of expertise" among the townsfolk. The system functioned adequately until the late sixteenth century, when the Ottoman state could not maintain the stability of its coinage.

Although nomadic and pastoralist in origin, the Ottoman dynasty had come to rule an overwhelmingly sedentary and agricultural empire. Nomadism was increasingly circumscribed both directly, through forced settlements, and indirectly, by fiscal and social policies that encouraged settlement. The basic principle of the Ottoman land regime, except in tributary provinces such as Moldavia and Transylvania, was to keep as much arable land under the control of the public treasury as possible and to protect the exploitation of those lands by peasant families subject to taxation.[14] State ownership was not absolute but predominant, especially in the countryside, though even here the amount of privately owned arable was considerable—about 13% in 1528 and increasing thereafter.

The basic bureaucratic instrument for rationalizing the redistributive process was the cadastral survey. Surveys were normally conducted shortly after conquest, though in the fifteenth century they were undertaken for previously conquered, unsurveyed lands, and thereafter every 25 to 30 years until the end of the sixteenth century. They were discontinued in the seventeenth century, when the Ottoman fisc changed its methods. Once freehold and endowed lands were certified, and tax exemptions noted for those providing a variety of public or state services, revenues owed from state-owned lands were assessed, settlement by settlement, through negotiations that involved local officials, clergy, and peasants. Once assessed, the revenues were apportioned between members of the military-administrative class and the public (i.e., royal) treasury. Ledgers (*defter*) containing the information produced by these surveys were recognized as such an important instrument of the centralized power structure that a law forbade taking the imperial ("Janissary") army and the imperial *defters* on campaign, unless the sultan were personally present.[15]

The fundamental Ottoman unit of taxation was a peasant household (*chift-hane*), conventionally an adult male, his family, and a pair of oxen. To the *defters* were added lawcodes, which stipulated the categories, rates, and procedures of taxation and adjusted them to different regions, since the Ottoman fiscal arrangements partly continued pre-conquest local usages.[16] So long as the peasants paid their taxes, they were entitled to remain on their lands and pass them on to their descendants. If they left the land, they could be brought back by force, unless they agreed to pay a certain penalty, or unless they eluded the authorities for a number of years, normally fifteen.

## 5. Ottoman Elites in the Classical Age, 1400-1600

### Provincial Elites: Timars and Timar-holders

The Ottoman elites mediated between this tax-base and the state. During the classic age the preferred mode of exploitation was the *timar* system, which had clear affinities to both the Islamic *iqta* and the Byzantine *pronoia*. The *timar*-holder was assigned revenues from an area defined as his *timar*, in return for which he was expected to join the sultan's army when called, together with proper equipment and retainers in numbers depending on the *timar*'s size. There was a hierarchy of *timar*-holders, but no subinfeudation.

As an exchange of rights over territory for military service, the *timar* system has obvious similarities to medieval European feudalism. In fact, historians quite commonly wrote of "Ottoman feudalism" until the 1930s, when many Ottomanists began to emphasize the unique characteristics of the Ottoman land regime. The differences were truly significant: *timars* were not heritable; state ownership remained dominant; the peasantry was free; there was no subinfeudation; and the *timar*-holder, however high his position, lacked judicial power and full administrative autonomy. While some Marxist historians, especially of the formerly socialist Balkan and eastern European countries, continued to speak of an Ottoman "feudal mode of production," albeit of a lesser kind than in western Europe, during the 1960s and 1970s others preferred to see in the Ottoman empire an example of the Asian mode of production. In the main, however, historians continued to employ a political-judicial definition of feudalism but to shun the term itself.[17] In any case, the concentration of power in the hands of the central state—often associated with absolutism in Europe—was too strong in the Ottoman empire for the political definition of feudalism to be very useful.

The assignment of *timars* to Christians, not unusual in the fifteenth century, must have been one means to secure the cooperation of non-Muslim elites. The cadastral surveys of that era reveal Christian cavalrymen (*sipahis*), often ten and twenty percent of all *sipahis*—in several parts of the Balkans (and even in some parts of Anatolia).[18] While many Christians were evidently local aristocrats at the time of the conquests, others, probably of commoner backgrounds, were identified as retainers of this or that Ottoman commander. *Timar* revenues were also assigned to clergy or monasteries, possibly because of deals struck with them for their recognition of Ottoman rule. Various other Christian groups in southeastern Europe were expected to provide services to the state, such as auxiliary functions for the military, in return for full or partial exemptions from levies. That Christians of this era did not scorn service to the sultan, is shown by the biography of a Greek Orthodox martyr in which being a soldier in the Ottoman army was not seen as untoward; martyrdom arose from an unrelated incident.[19] In time, the Christian *sipahis* or their descendants probably converted to Islam, as fewer and fewer non-Muslims appear as *timar*-holders in the sixteenth-century surveys, though there were a few as late as the seventeenth century.

A *timar*, though granted as a reward for service or to coopt former adversaries, was not an unequivocal blessing. Some lesser *timar*-holders found it difficult to fulfill their commitments, while for those from landed families the acceptance of a *timar* was at best a way to retain some prerogatives and status within a new system. Their power was nonetheless diminished through integration into a tightly woven grid of checks and balances (the *kadi* courts, superior officers, and periodic cadastral surveys) or through outright transplantation. The Islamized son of Alexander Shishman, the last Bulgarian tsar, for example, received a large prebend in the early fifteenth century, but in western Anatolia, while Juneyd, a western Anatolian rival of the Ottomans, received a sizable *timar* in Bulgaria. Assignments to *timars* followed no hard-and-fast rules, though an attempt apparently was made to prevent families from holding the same land for generations, and in the long run dislocation, rotation, and reductions in size prevented challenges from prominent *sipahi* families.

Inherited status nonetheless remained an important part of the Ottoman system of *timars*. Sons of *sipahis* were entitled to a *timar*, even if it were not the same or as large as their father's, and there was even a limited number of heritable *timars*. Furthermore, registered freehold could be inherited, and an endowment could stipulate that its management would remain with the founder's descendants. Thus, even though no aristocracy arose to check Ottoman absolutism, there being no association of nobility and "blood"—except for descent from the Prophet—the Ottoman realm did evolve a form of gentry.

Whatever the ethnic, social, or religious backgrounds of its holder, the *timar* played a central role in the Ottoman state's redistribution of resources, for its logic discouraged the solidification of claims against the state. The state's undeniable control of resources, however, operated within limits set by the social consensus, which the state could never calculate with precision. Limits were negotiated not because of pressures from an entrenched, privileged aristocracy or because of a parliament, but because of the claims of groups which embodied "custom" as sanctioned by both religious and sultanic law.

The keys to the Ottoman success in preventing the parcellization of sovereignty during these centuries must be sought both in the intricacies of the land tenure arrangements and in other institutions that extended the reach of the central administration. Most important of the latter were the judiciary and the large body of the dynasty's slave-servants, known as the "*kuls* of the Porte."[20]

### The Sultan's Household: Kuls, Devshirme, and Harem

The *kuls* and the associated institution of the "gathering" (*devshirme*), more or less forced recruitment, formed one of the two central institutions—the other was the harem—that most attracted European curiosity. The *kul* was a fourteenth-century creation with Roman and Islamic roots. Medieval Anatolian rulers had converted captured slaves into pages, guards, and soldiers, and the Ottomans, following this precedent, created in the 1370s a whole new army, called the "new army" (*yeni cheri*, whence "janissary" and its variants in other European languages). This standing army, one of the earliest in late medieval Europe, consisted of salaried, hierarchically organized, professional infantry. Its emergence was followed, in the 1380's at the latest, by a uniquely Ottoman means of military recruitment, the "gathering" (*devshirme*), which supplied eight- to nineteen-year-old boys from the non-Muslim populations already under Ottoman rule. The boys were brought to the capital, converted to Islam, and screened to select the ablest for palace service, while the rest were sent off to work on the land. After several years of training and acculturation, they "graduated" to become "*kuls* of the Porte," whose ranks included others selected from among the slaves captured in wars or raids. The *kuls* served the central state in various military and administrative functions, rising through the ranks according, at least in principle, to their merit as determined by a fiercely competitive evaluation of their military or technical skills, but also of their literary abilities at times.

The literature on the *kul* institution and the *devshirme* has for centuries been freighted with misunderstandings. To begin with, the Janissaries were perhaps the largest and most significant part, but only a part, of the *kuls* of the Porte. The cavalry and the cannoneers "of the sublime threshold" were also *kuls* but not Janissaries. Moreover, while the *devshirme* came during the fifteenth century to supply most of the *kuls*, captives of wars and raids continued to be included, and some became *kuls* voluntarily. As for the *devshirme*, it apparently did not consist of regular levies, and its size depended on perceived needs, averaging in the classical age, perhaps, three thousand youths per year. Until about 1500, all were Balkan Christians (plus Bosnian converts to Islam who volunteered), though in later decades the Anatolian countryside was also combed for boys.[21]

While many of the *kuls* were of humble backgrounds, others came from the subdued aristocracies. Two of Mehmed's vezirs were of the Palaeologue family, and his longest-serving grand vezir, Mahmud Pasha (d. 1474), who acquired a saintly reputation among the Muslim subjects, was of the Serbian family of Angelovich and also related to the Byzantine imperial family. During the sixteenth century, after the conquered aristocracies had been absorbed, such noble-born *kuls* became a rarity, and the Ottoman system itself did not perpetuate noble lineages qua noble. Even so, the system occasionally contained enslaved Christian nobles, such as Cigala-zade Sinan Pasha (ca. 1545-1605), who as Scipione Cicala was born the son of a Genoese vicount.[22]

Nor was the uprooting of *devshirme* recruits from their families and native lands necessarily as total as it is often made out to have been. Most recruits were already teenagers when they were made into Ottomans, and although they became at least nominal Muslims and learned Turkish, their earlier memories and identities were not erased. Many are known to have kept, or re-established, relations with their original habitats. Some officials of *devshirme* background, for instance, undertook to construct public buildings in their hometowns, and others suggested the names of brothers and cousins for recruitment. This fostered cliques among the elites, though much more important was ethnic solidarity among, say, Albanians, Bosnians, Serbs, or (somewhat later) Circassians, and Georgians. Even some of the slaves whose homelands lay beyond Ottoman rule found ways, licit and illicit, to communicate with their kin and compatriots, as the numerous letters in Venetian and Genoese archives document.

Close ties to members of one's nuclear family outside the *kul* system were also not impossible. A powerful grand vezir of the early sixteenth century, for instance, Ibrahim Pasha (grand vezir, 1523-36) convinced his father to convert and secured him a large prebend, while he brought his mother, who kept her faith, to Istanbul and found her a residence convenient to the palace. Another grand vezir's brother became an archbishop in Montenegro, who had himself and his brother, the Ottoman grand vezir, depicted on stained glass windows in a church he had built. Naturally, more is known about the lives of those who rose to the top, but some of the lesser *kuls* are also known to have remained in touch with family and patrimony. A document from 1521 urges the *kadi* of Zichna (now in Greece) to make sure that local officials do not interfere with a piece of property inherited and jointly possessed by a Janissary (then a rank-and-file soldier in

Istanbul) and his brother who went back and forth between the estate and the capital city.[23]

These qualifications aside, the combination of Ottoman recruitment, training, and rewards and punishments created a large pool of individuals whose primary loyalty was to the House of Osman. While some recruits ran away, and many novices must have served begrudgingly, over the centuries the system successfully produced many accomplished statesmen and artists, as well as many thousands of able-bodied soldiers who loyally served the sultan. Not merely a standing army, but one whose members were relatively uprooted, this was the perfect centralizing instrument in a young state facing the quintessential Ibn Khaldunian dilemma of nomads-turned-rulers. Its purpose, as some of its pro-*gazi* critics saw, was to bolster at the center the cohesion that had formerly depended on the increasingly fickle ties of tribalism and war-band solidarity. This dimension of the *kul* system came to full fruition under Mehmed II, who enlarged the standing army, extended the *devshirme*, and, for the first time in Islamic history, regularly promoted individuals from this background to the highest administrative posts. Between 1450 and the late 1600s, a large majority of Ottoman vezirs belonged to this system.

The similarly myth-ridden *harem* was a female counterpart of the *kul*. A sultan's *harem* basically consisted of concubines and servants of slave background, whose lives and relationships with others, including the sultan, followed well-recognized codes of deportment.[24] The *kuls* and the *harem* received their architectural and institutional parameters under Mehmed II, though the *harem*'s great growth in size and political influence date to the later 1500s. Down to Mehmed's generation, Ottoman sultans and princes married either Christian or Muslim princesses; some of the Christian wives retained their faith and lived removed from their husbands' courts. This changed when the dynasty's style of rule changed, and since Mehmed no further marriages were contracted with women from Christian dynasties, nor, after the generation of Mehmed's grandson, with any neighbors, even Muslim ones. After 1520 for a dynast to marry was an exceptional event, while concubinage prevailed.

As for princesses of the Ottoman house, who as female Muslims could not marry Christians, during the fourteenth and fifteenth centuries their hands were given in marriage to Muslim emirs of neighboring principalities. Thereafter, there being no families whom the Ottomans deemed worthy of such a tie, ladies of the royal house were married off to *kul* vezirs, members of the extended artificial family.

While a large part of the Ottoman political elite during the classical age consisted of *kuls*, recruited through enslavement or the *devshirme*, there was considerable room for others, who are often neglected in depictions of the ruling institution. One might mention here members of the households of other grandees, further training pools to which the central administration had some access, or stray descendants of the leading families of extinct principalities or other reduced nobilities, but the most important alternative path to the elite was through the Islamic educational institutions (*medrese*), the colleges which had for centuries played such a role in Muslim states.

### Centralizing the Law and Property

The colleges produced the *ulema*, scholars of religious and legal sciences, and the judges, *kadis*, of the kadiships the empire was divided into, whose functions were reshaped by the Ottomans' centralizing logic.[25] The *kadis* as members of the *ulema* adjudicated on the basis both of the *sharia* (Islamic divine law) and the *kanun* (dynastic secular law). The recognition of custom had always furnished a kind of secular law, but under Mehmed II it was for the first time codified through the legislative (*kanun*- or canon-making) prerogative of the secular ruler. *Kanun*, like custom, was meant to supplement, never to oppose, *sharia*, and the supreme *ulema* was expected to interpret, in a highly politicized space, current practices on the basis of texts—sacred scriptures and a huge body of legal traditions—held to be authoritative. Many Ottoman political and fiscal practices, of course, newly introduced or simply codified local pre-Ottoman usages that were difficult to accommodate within the *sharia*. Mehmed's codification of fratricide, for example, which sanctioned the enthroned prince's execution of all his brothers, was difficult, if at all possible, to legitimate within the *sharia*. In this case, the notion of "public good" (i.e., the prevention of civil war) made the law sufficiently flexible.

Mehmed was most radical in extending the coverage of state property. Toward the end of his reign, nearly contemporaneous with the new palace and the legal codification, he transformed a large number of lands thus far recognized as allods or endowments (over 1,000 villages according to a fifteenth-century historian) into *timars*.[26] His high-handed action provoked widespread resentment, for he chose to disregard grants of early Ottoman rulers in favor of holy men and women, by means of which groups, sometimes whole tribes, had been integrated into the larger political community. The dervishes, who inherited the endowments as literal or spiritual heirs of the holy figures, held the allegiance of large numbers of persons.

Although future generations could not maintain Mehmed's absolutism in its full harsh rigor, the basic outlines remained normative for many centuries. It was not, however, nor was it meant to be, a frozen system inherently opposed to innovation, as it is often depicted. Both the desire to preserve and the will to change are simultaneously recognized in Mehmed's codebook, which offers no magic solution to the obvious tension between the two: "Let my descendants act accordingly generation after generation" is followed after a few pages by "Let my noble descendants work on reforming [or, improving] it."[27]

## 6. THE GROWTH OF OTTOMAN POWER

### The Reign of Bayezid II

Mehmed's son and successor, Bayezid II, could hardly afford to continue his father's disregard for public opinion. When his brother, Prince Jem, gathered support among the resentful Anatolian Turkish tribes, Gedik Ahmed Pasha, the general who landed in Otranto in 1480, was forced to give up further Adriatic designs.

Jem's story illustrates the intricacies of late fifteenth-century Mediterranean politics. Beaten by his brother's armies, Jem sought aid from the Mamluk sultan at Cairo, who had considerable influence in southern Anatolia and northern Syria, a buffer between the Mamluk and the Ottoman states. Unsuccessful, Jem tried to reach a Rumelian base but was taken hostage by the Knights Hospitaler. From 1482 until his death in 1495, he became the object of intense negotiations among the Knights, the pope, various European rulers, and the sultan. Jem was the perfect tool against Bayezid, who negotiated continuously to make sure that he was passed to neither King Matthias Corvinus of Hungary nor Sultan Qaitbay of Cairo. In 1489 Jem came into papal custody at Rome, where he became a regular presence at court, and then into that of King Charles VIII of France. His death in 1495—rumor whispered of Roman poison and Ottoman collusion—saved him from being used for Charles' projected crusade to Jerusalem. Jem, who never abjured his faith or accepted his role as a foreigners' tool against Bayezid, lived on as an exotic lover-prince in Renaissance culture: a novella told of his love affair with Philippine-Hélène Sassenage, a southern French baron's daughter; Pinturicchio painted him into several paintings; and Castiglione served him up as a stern counterweight to Cinquecento gaiety in the *Book of the Courtier*.

The story of Jem partly explains Bayezid's military inaction on the western front, though in diplomacy he was a regular player, especially in Italy, now the cauldron of European politics. Bayezid undertook only one important military expedition in Europe, against Moldavia in 1484. His main achievement was to conquer the important ports of Kilia and Akkirman, making the Black Sea the Ottoman lake it would remain until the end of the seventeenth century.

Internally, changes occurred under Bayezid II, notably continued codification of the law. New pious foundations helped to fuel the growth of cities, whose life was enriched by the skills and mercantile ties brought by Jewish refugees from Iberia. Better roads improved communications and transportation, both military and civilian. Through his attention to the navy and his patronage to privateers, Bayezid laid the foundations of Ottoman success in his only major confrontation with a European power, the war of 1499-1503 against Venice.

### Selim I and the Conquest of the East

His successes aside, Bayezid seemed weak to those of the political class who judged achievement in military terms. The more so, as a new challenge was arising in the east, where the *sheykh* of the Safavid Sufi order, Ismail (1486-1524), declared himself shah of Iran in 1501. His agents moved among the Anatolian tribes, rekindling old resentments against the Ottoman state.

At Istanbul the proponents of a more aggressive policy had hope in Prince Selim, who opposed his father's passivity toward the Safavids and losses with the Mamluks. When Selim became sultan in 1512, having disposed of his father and his brothers, he moved to meet these foes with a light foot and a heavy hand. Within five years, Selim, who spent more time on the move than any other Ottoman sultan, had blocked the Safavid advance, destroyed the Mamluk state in Syria and Egypt, and incorporated into the Ottoman realm most of the Arab world, including the twin jewels of the Hijaz, Mecca and Medina.

The Ottoman victories partly rested on the institutionalized use of artillery, tested with the Akkoyunlu in 1473 and in the Crimea in 1475. Ottoman guns blasted the traditional cavalry armies of Shah Ismail in 1514 and the Mamluks in 1516-17 and made the Ottoman state the superpower of the entire eastern Mediterranean region. Success breeds imitation, and right across the Islamic world, from Morocco to Atjeh in the East Indies, requests rolled in for guns and gunners, while the janissary system became possibly a source of inspiration for similar formations in sixteenth-century Iran, Morocco, and Muscovy.

The conquest of Egypt also opened a new era of Ottoman sea power, for the state now controlled the whole eastern Mediterranean shoreline and had access to the Indian Ocean as well. The origins of Ottoman seapower went back to Mehmed II. When his fleet sailed out into the Aegean in 1470, as a Venetian observed, "the sea looked like a forest."[28] During the following decades, the Ottoman navy swelled with the conquests of seafaring peoples, and when the Portuguese began to threaten the South Arabian coast and the Red Sea during the early years of the sixteenth century, the Mamluk sultan called on Ottoman help against them. With the conquest of Cairo, the Ottoman sultan assumed the role of protector of the holy cities and of the routes of pilgrimage to Islam's holiest sites.

The Ottoman protectorate over the holy cities symbolized their maturing representation of Islamic universalism. The office of caliph, of course, had long lost its prestige, though the title had still been held by an Abbasid line that lived, though with no real power, under the Mamluks at Cairo. The Ottoman sultans added this title to their others, plus that of "Servant of the Two Holy Cities," which was more meaningful than the caliphate until the latter's revival in the nineteenth century. The Ottomans could now boast of supremacy in the Muslim world.[29]

## 7. THE AGE OF SÜLEYMAN

With accession in 1520 of Süleyman, Selim's son, Ottoman universalism resumed a western orientation that had been marginalized in Ottoman policy since Mehmed II's death. For the remainder of the sixteenth century, Ottoman policy was shaped by a nearly continual rivalry with the Habsburg dynasty, which headed a Catholic universalism as the Ottomans headed a Muslim one. Süleyman's shifting, though occasionally effective, alliances with France, the relatively "warmer" attitude toward the "Lutheran" powers, and the wish to satisfy some of Venice's commercial demands, were all to some degree consequences of the Ottomans' underlying sense of themselves as heads of the Muslim world in a two-power system. Besides the competition of two universalist religions, the sultan opposed in his own name Charles V's project of a universal monarchy and claimed— oddly as it sounded to Europeans—for himself the imperial office. Süleyman called Charles "the king of Spain" and his brother, Ferdinand, "the king of Vienna."

The vigor with which Süleyman threw Ottoman weight westward brought ten of his thirteen campaigns, and all of the five during his first twelve years, against Christendom. His taking of Belgrade in 1521 and Rhodes the following year merely completed unfinished business, for Mehmed II had failed against both places. Belgrade opened central Europe to Süleyman, who campaigned up the Danube in 1526, 1529, and 1532. The first campaign was a smashing success, while opinion is divided about the other two. In 1526 his army crushed the Hungarians on the plain of Mohacs, and the subsequent death of King Louis II ended the Jagiellonian dynasty's rule in Hungary and brought their capital, Buda, into Ottoman hands. Through this kingdom the frontier between Ottoman and Habsburg power was to run for generations.

No more than his predecessors had with earlier conquests in the Balkans, Süleyman did not try to incorporate Hungary immediately into his realm. Instead, he cultivated patron-client relationships with the local aristocrats and encouraged King Jan Zapolya, leader of the Hungarian "patriotic" or anti-Habsburg party, who upon his defeat by King Ferdinand in 1528 threw himself under Ottoman protection.

Süleyman's forces conquered not only Buda but also the royal crown of Hungary, just as it was about to be smuggled off to Austria. The sultan personally crowned his Hungarian vassal with the Crown of St. Stephen, and in 1529, when Charles V was crowned by the pope at Bologna, Süleyman added to his titles that of "Distributor of Crowns to the Monarchs of the World." Although a crown was never, either before or since, part of Ottoman regalia, Süleyman carried the symbolism further on his next campaign, in 1532, when a bejeweled crown-like helmet was displayed during his processions, the sight of which, a Venetian reported, turned the Habsburg envoys into "speechless corpses."

The campaigns of 1529 and 1532 were tremendous logistical feats, in which huge numbers of troops were moved across vast spaces, fed, and kept in order for months at a time. They took a number of castles, including Esztergom, that secured Ottoman control over much of Hungary for 150 years. Yet, if Süleyman's aim was to deal the Habsburgs a mortal blow, he failed, for he could neither take Vienna—the primary target in 1529—nor draw the Imperial army into the field—apparently the main goal of the enigmatic campaign of 1532.

These magnificent enterprises also revealed the Ottoman state's incapacity for further expansion. By the time the Ottoman armies reached Vienna in 1529, for example, it was already late September, the usual time of return to winter quarters. When the armies did start back in mid-October, they were beset by many costly accidents due to bad weather and the great distances. It is not surprising, therefore, that although Süleyman's chroniclers portrayed the siege of 1529 as a grand show of might, the Ottoman public seems not to have agreed, and in the following year there was no campaign but a sumptuous public fête organized by the sultan and his vezirs. Thereafter, long, lavish theatrical displays became a standard part of Ottoman public ceremonial. The Ottoman elite, perhaps, had mastered the control of public opinion in early modern style.

Yet, not everything was for show. Between 1526 and 1529 Transylvania and Moldavia became Ottoman tributary states; Buda was taken; and in 1541 most of Hungary became an Ottoman province. King Ferdinand recognized this state of affairs in a treaty of 1547 and agreed to pay 30,000 ducats in annual tribute.

In this struggle, each power found a partner in the foe's enemy: the Habsburgs in Safavid Persia and the Ottomans in France. King Francis I first sought Ottoman help against Charles V in the terrible year of 1525, when he became the latter's prisoner, and the Franco-Ottoman coopera tion reached its peak in 1543, when the Ottoman navy, led by the grand admiral, Barbarossa, wintered at Toulon.

Its problems notwithstanding, in Süleyman's early years the Ottoman system was still capable of great expansion, as huge territories were absorbed in Hungary and in modern Iraq in the east. Even later, the empire grew by extending its power over parts of Yemen and the East African coast. Yet, if the sixteenth century was the age of Ottoman glory, it also brought the Ottomans face-to-face with the limits of their empire-building. Süleyman could do little to prevent the incorporation by Ivan IV of Muscovy of the Kazan Khanate. And later, after Süleyman's time, the great Ottoman project of a Don-Volga canal, begun in 1569, had to be abandoned for financial reasons.

By mid-century Süleyman seems to have become as tired of the struggle as had Charles V, who abdicated in 1556. The sultan was less dramatic, for his retreat was not a monastery but a more sober and more pious way of life. The syncretist ethos that made more of the sultan's role as emperor than of his leadership of Islam, slipped away, though sultans did retain the title of "world emperor."

### The Ottoman Empire after Süleyman

The central European frontier remained relatively quiet for about three decades following Süleyman's death in 1566, as the struggle against Christendom shifted to the Mediterranean front. The Ottoman conquest in 1570 of Cyprus, since 1489 a Venetian colony, was followed by a naval defeat at Lepanto—embarrassing, but not consequential in the long run, for when the allied Christian navy took to sea the next year, it was shocked to see a rebuilt Ottoman fleet. The navy bounced back, taking Tunis in 1574 and extending Ottoman control over the North African littoral from Libya to Algiers.[30] Soon, though briefly, the Ottomans were involved as well in Morocco, permanent control of which would have extended their rule to the Atlantic coast of Africa. This did not happen, partly because of a lack of Ottoman commitment but primarily because Moroccan political structures were far more firmly rooted than anything the Ottomans had encountered elsewhere in North Africa. Moreover, there was trouble in the east again, as the sultan's armies were bogged down in Iran from 1578 to 1590. In the long run, the Ottomans won out, gaining even more lands in eastern Anatolia, Azerbaijan, and the Caucasus. The costs of these wars, however, were staggering in money, human lives, military discipline, and Ottoman self-confidence.

The costly Iranian Wars heightened resistance at Istanbul to resuming war against the Habsburgs. Hodja Sadeddin Efendi (d. 1599), a major political and intellectual figure of the late sixteenth century, nearly finished with his chronicle, pleaded with the sultan not to be obliged to start a new chapter, now that he found such an appropriate ending; namely, that the sultan's wretched *kuls* had taken so much land from the Iranian shah.[31] Worried by a dream he recorded in a letter and anxiously sent for interpretation to his favorite *sheykh*, the sultan himself had misgivings. In this dream Murad III (r. 1574-95) engages in a wrestling bout with the Holy Roman emperor and falls flat on his back with the latter on top. The clever *sheykh*, however, saw a sign of strength in the sultan's shoulders touching the solid earth. Perhaps there was popular support for a western war.

When war did begin in 1593, the struggle against Austria turned out to be as protracted as the Persian Wars.[32] The Ottoman forces performed especially poorly during the war's first years. In 1596 Sultan Mehmed III (r. 1595-1603) personally took the field, yielding to heavy pressure from factions of the ruling class, and perhaps from a public who wanted to see the sultan lead his army. It had been thirty years since a sultan had commanded in person, a task long left to vezirs. This sign of the depersonalization of government was accompanied by others, as the sultanic presence in government became ever more an icon and ever less a force. It is clear from all accounts of the Austrian war in 1596, for example, that Mehmed III was just that, an icon, and not a field commander. His presence nonetheless helped to bring good results, Ottoman capture of the fortress of Eger and the last Ottoman victory in an old-fashioned field battle (at Meszökerestes). They were not enough, however, to persuade Mehmed to repeat his appearance, for though the war continued for another decade, no sultan appeared again at the front.

Finally, after thirteen years of struggle, the two sides felt exhausted enough to treat, and in 1606 they signed the Treaty of Szitvatorok. Neither side took major lasting achievements away from this war. Still, it was becoming clear that the balance of military might, which had for decades favored the Ottomans, was not so great as it formerly had been. The Habsburgs relieved themselves of the obligation to annual tribute, which they had paid since 1547, and the Holy Roman emperor now called the sultan his "brother" rather than his "father."

The Ottomans saved face by gaining some fortresses, taking back some castles, and reasserting control over the Danubian principalities. By this time domestic strife had grown very disruptive and disturbing to Ottoman self-confidence, so much so, that when the sultan had a grand royal mosque built (the Sultanahmet or Blue Mosque), it commemorated not the "victory" over the infidel but the suppression of Anatolian rebels in 1609.

### 8. THE "OTTOMAN DECLINE" IN COMPARATIVE PERSPECTIVE

There are several reasons why the year 1600 is an appropriate point to conclude this overview. For one thing, the two previous decades were a time of major unrest, beginning in the countryside and known as the "Jelali revolts." In 1589 a long series of *kul* uprisings began when soldiers objected to being paid in debased coins, and, with increasing participation by city people, they continued through the next two centuries. Then, too, after a century of fairly stable money and prices, in the 1570s began a monetary instability, fueled by debasements and since 1585 by rising prices. Many villages were abandoned, their people gone to the cities, and migrations led to problems of provisioning and disrupted guild discipline in the cities.

#### The End of the Classical Age
It is too early to say what lay behind these phenomena, and in particular too early to blame the "rise of the Atlantic economy" for the late sixteenth-century Ottoman downturn. Even if the influx of American silver could be blamed for monetary instability, it was not behind the rural disturbances. As for population, it is hardly clear that the countryside was overpopulated, though bachelor males are heavily represented in the late sixteenth-

century urban tax surveys. If there was excess labor in the countryside, why were so many villages abandoned? One possible answer is fiscal pressure from the growing state, the chronology of which is uncertain.

Although fiscal oppression must have played a role in rural unrest, as it did in early modern France, the disturbances in Asia Minor were not peasant revolts. The rebels recruited primarily from temporarily unemployed mercenaries and displaced or disenchanted soldiers, who became all the more dangerous, as the use of firearms spread. Behind their actions lay not population growth but declining opportunities for employment by the state. The end of expansion implied that there were no new *timars* to be distributed. The value of the *sipahi* cavalry, moreover, declined with the spread of lighter firearms, and the state, as in France, resorted to tax farming and in fact reduced the number of *timars* granted. It preferred to enlarge the *kul* forces, who, unlike the *timar*-holders, were paid in cash, and to hire mercenaries on a temporary basis. The latter, out of work at war's end, would in earlier times have become frontier warriors—like the Cossacks, Uskoks, and conquistadors in other lands. They now turned to banditry and rebellion.

It all added up to both a decline and a perception of decline. The leading statesmen did not react with despair, but their confidence—like the official coinage—was being debased, and "decline and reform" grew into one of the most fertile themes in contemporary Ottoman culture. The whole complex had much in common with what was happening in contemporary Spain, where, as Ranke wrote, there came a new era "in which the Spanish monarchy, far from asserting its force over friends and foes, was rent and sub-divided by foreign politics, . . . and in which the Ottomans ceased to be feared, and began themselves to fear. These changes, we know, constitute, in no small degree, the distinctive features that mark, respectively, two periods in modern history."[33]

### The Problem of the "Ottoman Decline"

Was this age, therefore, the beginning of an "Ottoman decline"? Until recently, it was taken for granted that this was so by Fernand Braudel, for example, whose *Mediterranean* describes an Ottoman empire in decline by the end of the sixteenth century. In *Civilization and Material Life*, written some years later, Braudel was ready to declare the same state "a viable entity until the nineteenth century." He thereby simply reflected the changing winds in Ottoman historiography, in which the notion of decline has become one of the most highly contested aspects of what increasingly looks like a dated paradigm. The revisionism has some obvious implications for the historiography of the era treated in this chapter.

For one thing, traditionally the course of Ottoman history from 1400 to 1600 has been conceived in terms of power and glory which masked a series of failures that led eventually to decline and ultimately to the underdevelopment of the entire Middle East. There was military grandeur, true, political stability, and some prosperity, but no capitalism, oceanic expansion, printing press (until 1721), Renaissance, or Reformation. The subjection of this perspective to critical revision nowadays is part of the much larger reassessment of the views associated with "orientalism," the viewing of the east in terms of what it is not, i.e., the west.

### New Perspectives on Ottoman and European History

The present state of revisionist research makes possible only tentative remarks, and it is important not to lapse into the apologetic position of "proving" that the Ottomans were just the same as the west, or just as advanced. Yet, some preliminary findings enable us to begin moving away from essentializing contrasts.

The European conceptualization of the Ottoman system as an "anti-Europe"—Braudel's term—is most deeply rooted in the sphere of politics: freedom vs. despotism, the rule of law vs. tyranny, and free property vs. state ownership. This vision of "Europe and the Orient" has been since the sixteenth century a most persistent conception, and it remains influential in the study of politics, economies, and histories. One well-received recent work on comparative politics, for example, convincingly develops the point that there existed a rule of law in late medieval and early modern Europe. The writer then adds:

> Many opponents of the prince were imprisoned or had property seized without due process. In speaking of the rule of law in this time, it is only meant that such trangressions, if routine, entailed the probability of noble and burgher opposition, from which monarchs and emperors of the Middle East and Orient had little to fear. The edifice of law was in effect an objective, structural restraint on the crown and other powerholders.[34]

The final point, about the Orient, is not developed or argued, it is simply a given of history. Another writer, Perry Anderson, deals with the Ottoman state as an "Asian colossus," whose "contours provide a strange contrast with those of the European Absolutism that was contemporary with it. The economic bedrock of the Osmanli despotism was the virtually complete absence of private property in land."[35] His evidence for this statement, it turns out, consists of disappointingly uncritical readings of early modern political writers: Niccolò Machiavelli ("they are all slaves"), Jean Bodin ("when [the timariots] die, their heirs can inherit only their movable goods"), and Francis Bacon ("nobility attempers sovereignty").

What European writers never appreciated was the presence of social institutions and practices that delineated a public sphere of political negotiation. Guilds represented their members before the *kadis*, market supervisors, and agents of the central government; Sufi orders, in the persons of influential *sheykhs*, spoke in the name of some sector of public opinion; and the spokesmen of the charitable institutions (*waqfs*) and non-Muslim communities did not just bow and comply. In this category, too, belong other institutions and practices, such as village headmen, whose roles are little understood. Enough is known, however, to make untenable facile references to a despotic apparatus which penetrated all levels of public and social life. There was a finely tuned legal machine with widely shared standards and symbols of justice, which totally escaped students of oriental politics from Machiavelli to Max Weber. Indeed, the Ottoman empire was not unlike the later Roman empire in that, although it is conventionally depicted in terms of corruption and tyranny, its upper classes and some of its subjects considered it to live under the rule of law.[36]

Limits on the practice of absolutism doubtless differed between the classical Ottoman state and, say, seventeenth-century France. Mehmed II, for example, the most "despotic" of the Ottoman sultans in this era, undertook an extensive program of confiscations justified by appeal to the public good, but his program had to be rescinded. His grandson, Selim, whose reputation is embodied in his epithet, "the Grim" or "the Terrible," could not return to Mehmed's policy but had to live with Bayezid II's compromise, since it was based on the law of the realm and the moral standards of his culture. Instead, Selim proclaimed an equally despotic program of converting Istanbul's remaining Greek churches into mosques. When he justified this step by the argument that the *sharia* permitted the confiscation of the properties of non-Muslims, his legal advisers said that his reading of the *sharia* was excessively literal.

The growth of Ottoman absolutism during the fifteenth and sixteenth centuries might well be seen in a larger context. It was characterized by such common early modern features as bureaucratization, legal codification, and the search for more efficient tax collection. Might the Ottoman and European trends have been linked by similar forces or even contacts?

*Contacts between the Ottomans and Europe*

Recent Ottoman historiography tends to emphasize the porosity of the boundaries between the eastern Mediterranean world and Europe and to reject essentialization of the contrast between the two worlds. Trade, migrations, diplomacy, and even war (and enslavement of prisoners) crossed the boundaries. Trade continued the late medieval pattern of Italian merchants enjoying charters and privileges in the Levantine port cities that connected to the caravan routes and kept growing. The sixteenth century brought new actors, from different European countries, onto this scene, who obtained similar charters. By the end of the era, the Ottoman state recognized the appearance of the early modern world's little tigers by extending trading privileges to Queen Elizabeth of England's subjects in 1581 and to the Dutch early in the next century. European traders, however, by no means displaced Ottoman merchants, nor were the latter exclusively non-Muslims (as nineteenth-century accounts alleged).

The sixteenth century also saw the revival of the land routes across the Balkans, traveled by European and Ottoman merchants, Muslim and non-Muslim, and by mid-century the Levant's connections to the Asian trade also revived from the initial shock from the Portuguese voyaging around Africa. This may be the reason why the Ottomans did not continue to challenge Portugal for control of the Arabian Sea and the Indian Ocean. Generally speaking, Ottoman trade policies centered on infrastructural support for trade, on the securing of ports and sea and land routes and on the construction of bazaars and caravansarais—naturally with expectations of profit to the treasury. Several governors thus endowed Aleppo for its role as a major entrepot of the silk trade; Sarajevo and Novi Bazar were created partly to serve the trans-Balkan carrying trade; and a Jewish merchant, an Ottoman district governor in Dalmatia, and the Venetian authorities cooperated to build up Split as a rival to Dubrovnik.

Beyond these contributions to the infrastructure of trade, plus provisioning which favored imports, we have as yet no larger picture of Ottoman commercial policy. Recent emphasis on early modern developments in world trade, plus the growing understanding of eventual western dominance as the outcome of an interactive process, makes urgent our need for comparative studies of commercial policies. We know little or nothing about the merchants' practices or about the legal institutions at their disposal, and the question of technological diffusion through commerce also remains to be explored. It is nonetheless already becoming clear that in the sixteenth or even the seventeenth century, the eventual supremacy of European merchants was by no means a forgone conclusion.

A closely related topic concerns science and technology. Sixteenth-century observers, certainly, would not have understood the modern orientalist depiction of the Ottomans as an essentially inward-looking society, which did not want to learn, and, but for a few enlightened statesman, would never have learned, from the west. Ogier Ghiselin de Busbecq, Charles V's envoy who visited the Ottoman realm in the mid-sixteenth century, wrote that

> no nation in the world has shown greater  readiness than the Turks to avail themselves of the useful inventions of the foreigners, as is proved by their employment of cannons and mortars, and many other things invented by Christians. They cannot, however, be induced as yet to use printing, or to establish public clocks, because they think that their scriptures would no longer be scriptures if they were printed, and that, if public clocks were introduced, the authority of their muezzins and their ancient rites would be thereby impaired.[37]

The inventions themselves aside, why did Busbecq write only of the Ottomans' readiness to borrow and adapt things invented by others? The question contains two issues, one about technological innovation and the other about openness to using the inventions of others. Was Busbecq biassed in that he failed to concede the former to the Ottomans? Probably not. However, the role of the craftsman, the technician, and the innovator in Ottoman society, and attitudes toward their skills, have hardly been investigated, and what is known does not support a categorical statement.

When did science and technology become "European" from an Ottoman point of view? The Ottomans do not, for instance, seem to have associated gunpowder and firearms with the Europeans during the fourteenth and fifteenth centuries. In oceanic discoveries, however, a European advantage was recognized. Piri Reis, the Ottoman sailor-cartographer who in 1513 drew, following a Columbus map, one of the earliest surviving pictures of the New World's coastline, observed that the infidels had recently scored some enviable advances in geographical knowledge. He then moved immediately to a type of argument later to appear repeatedly in Islamic westernization discourse, that the new discoveries were based on ancient learning from a book stolen from the Near East. In other words, to import infidel knowledge was really just to reappropriate one's own. Once again, the evidence suggests that the whole notion of "westernization," implying an essential difference between east and west, needs to be rethought for the whole period before the eighteenth century.

It is true, certainly, that Mehmed II was more interested in what the "Franks" were doing than most of his successors were, but this does not mean that the Ottoman court's interest in European culture can be reduced to a linear process of decline since his time. Piri Reis, for example, produced his map not on command but on his own initiative as a navigator, having acquired the necessary information from the fluid world of the Mediterranean sailors. He did present it to Sultan Selim upon the conquest of Egypt, which is why it is preserved in the palace library.

Some of the interest in things western was revived at court during the first third of Süleyman's reign. Under the grand vizirate of Ibrahim Pasha (1523-36) in particular, the links seem to have been active to various European artists, sources of luxury goods, and European mercantile communities at Istanbul. A son of a Venetian doge, for example, was one of the sultan's closest advisors and his appointee to oversee the most prestigious new conquest, Ottoman Hungary. The grand vezir himself, a native of the island of Parga in Venetian territory, was largely responsible for the good standing of this son of a doge and more generally for the links with European politics and culture. Ibrahim watched "ballet" performances with classical themes held in the Frankish quarter of Istanbul.

### The Ottoman Identity

Yet, to look at contacts and interaction is not enough, for the main point is to go beyond construing these relations in terms of two clearly delineated and separate entities—Europeans and Turks. We must reconstruct the Ottoman point of view, taking into account that inclusiveness was one of the most basic forces in the Ottoman identity.

Ottoman inclusiveness should not be attributed only to the *kuls* of the Porte, themselves of non-Turkish birth, for many who joined the Ottoman enterprise and acquired *timars* or other military or civil posts also came from non-Turkish, non-Muslim backgrounds. They all eventually became as Ottoman as anybody else. This fact is of vital significance for our interpretation of the political struggles within the Ottoman elite, which are often anachronistically seen in ethnic terms as conflicts between the *devshirme* and the old Turcoman families, that is, between non-Turks and Turks. Many *timar*-holders were also of non-Turkish origins, as were many members of the *ulema*, the ranks of which were not closed to those born to, say, Arabic-, Kurdish-, or Greek-speaking families.

The Ottomans, after all, did not call themselves "Turks," nor their land "Turkey," for these were European terms which ethnicized—much as the eastern use of "Franks" for Europeans did—what was basically a supra-ethnic identity. Indeed, the still current uses of "Ottoman" and "Turk" or "the Ottoman empire" and "Turkey" as interchangeable terms is comparable to the use of "Italy" for the Roman empire or "Italians" for the ancient Romans.[38]

The worst consequence of continuing this ethnicization of the Ottoman tradition is that it masks the imperial character of Ottoman history. One illustration must serve to support this point. Sinan Pasha, baptized "Scipione" as son of a Genoese nobleman and a Turkish woman, was captured by Muslim seamen and presented to the Ottoman court, where he grew up and graduated to a distinguished career as admiral and vezir. A loyal and successful Ottoman and a Muslim, he maintained a lively correspondence with family and friends in his native Genoa.

This does not mean that the problematic aspects of the relationships between Ottomans and Europeans disappear. For one thing, there is no Ottoman counterpart to the voluminous literature in various European languages about "the Turks." Although this difference is important to understanding the different roles of education and knowledge about the other in the age when the two worlds competed for hegemony, it cannot be reduced to an Ottoman lack of "curiosity" about foreign lands, as often is done. A Venetian or French diplomat may have needed to learn Turkish, but the Ottoman court was easily supplied with servants competent in European languages. For example, when the court interpreter Ferhad, a Hungarian by origin, died in 1576, his son was brought to Istanbul from his *timar* in northern Anatolia and given his father's position, because of his knowledge of Hungarian affairs and the pertinent languages.[39]

Focus on such examples, of course, makes it easy to confine the area of shared discourse to those who were of European origin, that is, to an "anomalous" stratum of renegades. The point is that the renegades could strike Ottoman roots so easily just because they were not anomalous, because they already had much in common with numerous others in this society, in which migration and conversion were common. There was a shared discourse even beyond the migrants and converts, because there were shared interests.[40]

*Shared Discourse of the Ottoman and European Worlds*
The roots of shared discourse and interests lay not only in interactions but in a complex of common traditions of the ancient Near Eastern/Mediterranean civilizations and of the Abrahamic religions. For example, the Jewish physicians who came into the Ottoman empire from Iberia after 1492, whatever their unique qualities, were also steeped in the familiar

humoralism of Galenic medicine. Emigrés and visitors from Europe would hardly feel totally lost, moreover, in an intellectual world that shared a respect for ancient Greek learning in general and Aristotle in particular. A late sixteenth-century wave of political pamphleteering, for example, included a Turkish translation (from Arabic) of Aristotle's *Politics*.

Ottoman scholars were not necessarily removed from the current scene of science in Europe either. When Taqi ad-Din arrived at Istanbul from Egypt in 1577, he not only brought a deep knowledge of medieval Muslim astronomy, which the Europeans also knew, but he was reputed to be aware of developments among the Franks. Does this make Ottoman astronomy as "advanced" as European astronomy? Not necessarily. Among other things, we must note that Istanbul's observatory was not, as other establishments of that nature were, turned to long-term astronomical observation—it was pulled down sometime after 1579. The efforts of Taqi ad-Din were up-to-date for his time—his measurements of the supernova of 1579 were as accurate as Tycho Brahe's, and they should not be judged by the standards of the subsequent Scientific Revolution in Europe.[41]

In religious thought and philosophy, too, some things were shared. Despite the differing traditions of Christian, Jewish, and Islamic piety, parallel developments occurred. For example, the neoplatonic revival of late medieval Europe has its counterpart in the Muslim world, where Sufi metaphysics, also imbued with neoplatonism, dominated intellectual life. Further, the waves of apocalypticism in Europe and in the Ottoman world during the late fifteenth and early sixteenth century were not only synchronous, they apparently were in contact with one another.[42] The heresies, too, had much in common, else how could Bedreddin have attracted such strong followings among the Christians of the Balkans?

### Shared Rhythms of the Ottoman and European Worlds

Beyond shared elements of culture, the shared rhythms of a number of Eurasian commonwealths lend some justification to the term, "the early modern world." The Ottoman empire partook of many of the changes generally thought of as characteristic of early modernity, including some of the most important economic and social ones. Population growth and urbanization, along with commercialization and inflation of prices, affected both the eastern and the western Mediterranean regions. The Middle East, which lay between different zones of the Old World, naturally felt the acceleration of world trade. One does not have to be a monetarist, for example, to acknowledge the impact of American silver via Europe on Ottoman markets in the later sixteenth century. Money flowed across all borders, and the German *groschen* lent its name to the *gurush*, which the Ottomans used for centuries.[43]   Curiously enough, these developments are seen as signs of both European growth and of Ottoman decline.

In Ottoman culture, too, there are clear signs of a "modern" mentality in the sixteenth century. New cultural forms deliberately departed from the past or sought competitive dialogues with the "classics."  A group of literati in early sixteenth-century Bursa, for example, decided not to continue reproducing new versions of the same old (Persian and Arabic) stories.  One member produced an amusing novella—a sort of tongue-in-cheek counterpart of Martin Guerre's story—in which the themes of love, communication, and identity are explored in the midst of an original narrative.  This "Bursan realism" also gave rise to new uses of a recently created Persian genre, the versified "city thrillers," of which dozens were set in western Anatolian and Balkan cities during the sixteenth century.  Often they open with descriptions of monuments, soon moving on to depictions of flirtatious young men and women.

The Ottoman imperial identity and ideology nonetheless found its principal expression not in literature but in monumental urban architecture. The Ottomans took pride in grand cityscapes, especially the internationally famous one of Istanbul, and dotted them with an architecture of "fresh idiom," as one Ottoman writer described the style of Mehmed II's complex at Istanbul.  Recent studies have begun revising the traditional judgment, that Ottoman architecture was a traditional and non-western style, through the study of its connections with contemporary building in Renaissance Italy.  The best Ottoman work, which was achieved around 1550 by an architect called Sinan, can be seen as part of broader Mediterranean architecture of the Renaissance era, which consciously departed from medieval traditions and looked for freshness of expression.  Sinan's autobiography leaves no doubt that he engaged in self-conscious dialogue and competition with the monumental traditions of late Antiquity and early Byzantium.

The sixteenth-century growth of schools, based on notably the charitable institution of the *waqf*, and the spread of written at the expense of oral culture, notably in histories and hagiographies, indicate a growth of literacy and suggest a secularization of culture.  The maxim, religion subsumes everything in Islam, is generally invalid, but particularly so for the Ottoman empire, which was built over a long period of experimentation in frontier circumstances.  The Ottomans emerged from this experience with a cultural bricolage of classical Islamic legal traditions with Inner Asian and Byzantine elements, and the syncretic nature of their achievement is especially clear in the realm of law, where the *kadis* were expected to adjudicate cases on the basis of the sacred *sharia*, local custom, and the written codes of *kanun*.

Elements of desacralization can also be observed in social life, notably in the transition from *ahi* confraternities to guilds, which combined traditional religious elements with a professional life which was trans-religious, at least in the trades practiced by adherents of more than one faith.

The most obviously desacralizing agent in Ottoman life of this period, however, was the coffeehouse.[44] The bright idea, according to Ottoman historians, came to two enterprising Syrian merchants, and the first coffeehouses appeared in Istanbul in the 1550s. They were soon all the rage, for reasons which remain little understood, but the initial reaction of the *ulema* allows no doubt that these new sites of sociability were considered dangerously beyond the control of the *sharia*. Women, of course, could not enter the coffeehouses, but they did use the public baths, which had similar social functions.

The sixteenth century also saw a widening gulf between elite and popular cultures, as the latter's beliefs and practices came under a new criticism from the former. Some of this criticism, perhaps, was related to the more structured orthodoxy required in the classical age, because of the challenge from dissents, especially the Safavid "heresy."

It remains now to ask whether the regional identities in the three Muslim empires of this era—Ottoman, Safavid, and Mughal—present us with a parallel to the emergence of proto-national identities in Europe. No unifier ever threatened this configuration, for the Muslim world knew no world conqueror after Timur. The changes between his time and the end of this era are revealed by the accounts of the two peerless travelers of the pre-industrial Muslim world, Ibn Battuta of the fourteenth century and Evliya Chelebi of the seventeenth. Their respective imaginations of "the world to be seen" display quite different sets of criteria. Ibn Battuta left his North African home to see the whole Muslim world and a bit more, going all the way to China. Evliya Chelebi spent even more time on the road and wrote an even longer account, but his horizons remained within the boundaries of the "well-protected Ottoman domains" (with side trips to Austria and Iran). When Chelebi wrote of imaginary journeys, they carried him not to other Islamic lands but to Europe and the Americas.

### Paths of Ottoman and European Divergence

The fact that, in reality, these regional-imperial identities were much less tightly woven than were the proto-nationalities of Europe leads us to recognize the divergent elements in the histories, both in- and outside the Islamic world. Among the three major Muslim empires, to begin with, only the Iranian state maintained its integrity of territory and identity during the era of nation-states. The Ottoman empire, by contrast, dissolved and was dissolved into more than twenty nation-states, a process of which no end is yet in sight.

The religious realm also displays important divergences. At first glance the sundering of Catholic Christendom and the splitting of Sunni Islamdom seem similar as well as being contemporaneous. The Protestant Reformation and Safavid Shi'ism could and were seen as backstabbing treason by the Habsburgs and the Ottomans respectively, who were comparably eager to lead an imagined universal community of the faithful. A closer look, however, reveals very important differences. While the Ottoman repression of heresy could turn very violent, it had no institutional counterpart to the Inquisition. Moreover, the nature of the Safavid challenge demonstrates that the tribal element was still very strong, if declining, in sixteenth-century Middle Eastern politics.[45]

If the survival of tribal nomadism rendered the Middle East less modern than Europe, the treatment of religious minorities apparently better accords with modern expectations of religious toleration. The Ottoman attitude in this respect, however, simply continued the ancient Islamic principle of *dhimma*, the covenant assumed to exist between rulers of the dominant Islamic faith and people of certain other religions. The covenant provided autonomy to different communities in the practice of their faith and in managing their educational and legal affairs, so long as they remained loyal to the state, paid a special head tax, and conformed to certain norms of public behavior.

Beyond these generalities, the historian of the non-Muslim communities in the Ottoman empire must treat gingerly this subject, since it is dangerously open to either abuse or romanticization of the Ottoman legacy. Thus, while Balkan nationalisms have in general tended to portray Ottoman rule as an unqualified yoke, Jewish history has lent itself to images of the Ottoman empire as a pluralist utopia. The truth, needless to say, lies somewhere in between, although, however harsh their experience, until the twentieth century the Ottoman Jews escaped forced conversion or ghettoization.

The place of women in the Ottoman order, one defined largely by Islamic tradition, always seemed strange to westerners. The comparison, explicit or implicit, often begins with the veiling of women and the segregation of genders. Restrictions on the appearance in public and the mobility of women were certainly much greater in Ottoman society, and in many other Islamic societies, than in Europe. While women may have played important roles in public life, they did so primarily from within the (sultanic or other) household, so that their activities were invisible except to family members and servants. Both Ottoman and European authors long regarded the "intrusion" of harem women in political life—beginning with Hürrem (Roxelana), Süleyman's slave-concubine and, later, wife—as illegitimate and a sign of decadence. Among European travelers, women's invisibility often turned into their sole or main mark of status in the Orient, a fascination not yet dead today. Yet, within the framework of legal inequality of genders, Muslim women did have access to property rights, divorce, conjugal rights, and although most of this lies beyond the scope of our treatment here, it might be noted that the comparison might look very different, if veiling and segregation were of lesser priority. On the other hand, it is true that, in Ottoman Muslim eyes, a social and religious life that brought the sexes face-to-face in a variety of ways clearly constituted a European peculiarity. Prince Jem, the royal hostage, expressed his astonishment at these liberties in a couplet: "Turned out to be strange, this town of Nice / One can get away with anything one commits." One wonders if, for all that, patriarchy was any less imposing among the Europeans.

❊ ❊ ❊

Many issues raised in these paragraphs remain to be studied, some for the first time. Some apparent parallels are bound to be found superficial on closer scrutiny, other, new ones may be yet discovered. There nevertheless remains the inescapable fact that the two worlds, western Christian and Ottoman Muslim, perceived each other as other, and that their historical trajectories display enough significant divergences to validate this perception. Yet, it also seems worthwhile to suggest that if the essentialized, bipolar view of the world—western and other—ought to be abandoned, if the unique qualities of modern European history are to be understood, rather than merely assumed, and if representations of otherness are to be studied as historical constructs, then Ottoman history can provide some of the most fruitful comparative agendas to historians of Europe.

# NOTES

[Editors' Note: Citations by author/date system in the notes refer to Part IIB of the Bibliography.]

* Dedicated to the brave people of Sarajevo—once Ottoman, always European.

1. For a thorough review of Ottoman political relations to 1520, see Halil Inalcik, "The Ottoman Turks and the Crusades, 1329-1451," and "The Ottoman Turks and the Crusades, 1451-1522," in *A History of the Crusades*, ed. Kenneth M. Setton, vol. 6: *The Impact of the Crusades on Europe*, ed. H. W. Hazard and Norman P. Zacour (Madison, Wisc., 1989), 222-75, 311-53. See also Imber (1990).

2. Whatever the validity of Ottoman genealogies that appear in sources only after the Timurid debacle, it is clear that their Anatolian rivals as well as the Timurids saw the Ottomans as upstarts. It is no coincidence that in Ottoman historical consciousness, the legitimacy of the dynasty, though buttressed by various and often contradictory genealogical claims, was ultimately based on their record as champions of the faith. On this issue, see Kafadar (forthcoming).

3. See the report of Pietro Zeno to the Venetian government from January-March, 1403, cited in George T. Dennis, "The Byzantine-Turkish Treaty of 1403," *Orientalia Christiana Perdiodica 33* (1967): 72-88.

4. Quoted in ibid., 86.

5. For pre-modern Islamic ideas on international relations, see J. T. Johnson and J. Kelsay, eds., *Just War and Jihad: Historical and Theoretical Perspectives on War and Peace in Western and Islamic Traditions* (New York, 1991). For historical examples, see Michael Köhler, *Allianzen und Verträge zwischen fränkischen und islamischen Herrschern im Vorderen Orient* (New York, 1991); Kissling (1974). For Ottoman practice, see Halil Inalcik, "Ottoman Methods of Conquest," *Studia Islamica 2* (1954): 103-29.

6. On Ottoman political life, including factions in the fifteenth century, see Halil Inalcik, *Fatih Devri Üzerine Tetkikler ve Vesikalar* (Ankara, 1954).

7. Ettore Rossi, "La leggenda turco-bizantina del Pomo Rosso," *Studi bizantini e neoellenici 5* (1937): 542-553; Karl Teply, "Der Goldene Apfel," in id., *Türkische Sagen und Legende um die Kaiserstadt Wien* (Vienna, 1980), 34-73.

8. Leopold von Ranke, *The Turkish and Spanish Empires in the Sixteenth Century and the Beginning of the Seventeenth*, trans. Walter K. Kelly (Philadelphia, 1845), 1.

9. See Ahmad ibn Yahya ibn Salman ibn 'Ashik Pasha, *Vom Hirtenzelt zur Hohen Pforte: Frühzeit und Aufstieg des Osmanenreiches nach der Chronik "Denkwürdigkeiten und Zeitläufte des Hauses Osman" vom Derwisch Ahmed, genannt 'Ashik-Pasha-Sohn*, trans. R. F. Kreutel (Graz, 1959), 206.

10. This text is analyzed by M. F. Köprülü, *Seljuks of Anatolia: their History and Culture According to Local Muslim Sources*, trans. G. Leiser (Salt Lake City, 1992), 47-48.

11. Peter Brown, *Power and Persuasion in Late Antiquity* (Madison, Wisc., 1992), 20.

12. See G. Necipoglu, *Architecture, Ceremonial and Power: the Topkapi Palace in the Fifteenth and Sixteenth Centuries* (Cambridge, Mass., 1991).

13. The Ottomans continued to use the Arabized form of Constantinople, Kostantiniyye, without inhibitions until the end of the empire, along with "Istanbul," which also derived from Greek. Only in the aftermath of the Turkish-Greek wars of 1919-21 did Turkish nationalists find the term offensive and make official the monopoly of Istanbul. See Halil Inalcik, "The Policy of Mehmed II toward the Greek Population of Istanbul and the Byzantine Buildings of the City," *Dumbarton Oaks Papers* 23/24 (1969/70): 231-49.

14. The works of Halil Inalcik are essential for understanding the Ottoman land system and related fiscal arrangements. His latest treatment of the subject will appear in a volume on Ottoman social and economic history edited by D. Quataert, to appear from Oxford University Press. I am grateful to Professor Inalcik for allowing me to read the parts that bring to light the fundamental role of small-holding peasant families in a comparative eastern Mediterranean perspective. The *timar* is studied by Beldiceanu (1980).

15. This rule had to be changed at the end of the sixteenth century, when the sultans no longer participated in campaigns. Feridun Emecen, "Sefere Götürülen Defterlerin Defteri," in *Prof. Dr. Bekir Kütükoglu'na Armagan* (Istanbul 1991), 241-68.

16. Halil Inalcik, "The Problem of the Relationship Between Byzantine and Ottoman Taxation," *Akten des XI. Internationalen Byzantinisten-Kongresses 1958* (Munich, 1960), 237-42. See also Heath Lowry, in Bryer and Lowry (1986).

17. Berktay (1987) and (1990).

18. Cvetkova (1978), 3-6.

19. E. A. Zacharaidou, "The Neomartyr's Message," *Bulletin of the Centre for Asia Minor Studies [Athens]* 8 (1990-91): 51-63.

20. "The [Sublime] Porte" refers in Ottoman usage to the central government and to its symbolic location just beyond the threshold of the sultan's residence. The notoriously difficult word *kul* encompasses the categories of slave, servant, and subject. Even though Ottoman historians have in general tended to restrict it to the first meaning ("slave"), the "*kuls* of the Porte" included many who cannot have been legally slaves of the sultan.

21. The inclusion of Bosnian Muslims in the *devshirme* and the incorporation of volunteers are two of the obvious reasons why all *kuls* should not be seen as slaves. The *devshirme* can be called enslavement for sociological (see Orlando Patterson, *Slavery and Social Death* [Cambridge, Mass., 1982]) and certainly moral reasons, but one can still note significant differences between their legal status and that of the slave formations in the armies of some other Islamic states (e.g., the Mamluks of Egypt).

22. The most detailed account of Sinan Pasha's life is in G. Benzoni, "Cicala, Scipione (Cigala-Zade Yusuf Sinan)," *Dizionario Biografico degli Italiani*, vol. 25: 320-40.

23. For a discussion of this official document and others that refer, without any hint of wrongdoing, to relations between *kuls* and their family as well as to *kuls* engaged in the economic sphere—both forms of conduct read as signs of later "corruption"—see Kafadar (1991b).

24. For a survey of Ottoman marriage policies, see Alderson (1956), 85-100.

25. For the training careers of the *ulema*, see Chapter 1 in Repp (1986).
26. The historian was Tursun Beg, for whose text see Halil Inalcik and Rhoads Murphey, *The History of Mehmed the Conqueror* (Minneapolis, 1978).
27. Ahmet Akgündüz, *Osmanli Kanunnameleri ve Hukuki Tahlilleri: Osmanli Hukukuna Giris ve Fatih Kanunnameleri*, vol. 1 (Istanbul, 1990), 317, 326. Though the original codification is now accepted to have been Mehmed's, the extant codebooks are not free of later embellishments and anachronisms.
28. Cited in Imber (1990): 201.
29. On competing claims to lordship of the entire Muslim world, see Farooqhi (1989).
30. See Hess (1972).
31. *Tarih-i Peçuyi*, 2 vols. in 1 (reprint, Istanbul, 1980), vol. 2:133.
32. For a concise narrative of the Ottoman-Habsburg wars of 1593-1606, see Finkel (1988).
33. Ranke, *Turkish and Spanish Empires*, 1.
34. Brian M. Downing, *The Military Revolution and Political Change: Origins of Democracy and Autocracy in Early Modern Europe* (Princeton, 1992), 34.
35. Perry Anderson, *Lineages of the Absolutist State* (London, 1974), 365; and there, too, the following quote.
36. Brown, *Power and Persuasion in Late Antiquity*, 8-9.
37. C. T. Forster and F. H. B. Daniell, trans., *The Life and Letters of Ogier Ghiselin de Busbecq*, 2 vols. (London, 1881), vol. 1:100-1.
38. The comparison is not far-fetched, for this is approximately what some of the Italian humanists did. Leonardo Bruni Aretino, for example, spoke of classical Latin and Tuscan as "our two languages" (editors' note).
39. The Ottomans seem to have received information from the Venetians of which no systematic written record was kept. See the instructions by the Senate to the *bailo* at Istanbul: "By the letters from England we understand that the most Serene King [Henry VIII], after beheading Queeen Anne . . . has taken to wife and proclaimed as Queen a gentlewoman by name Madame Jane. . . . Theyese advices we charge you to communicate as usual to the magnificos the Bashaws." From the Deliberazioni Senato (Segreta), vol. 57:35 (21 July 1536), in *Calendar of State Papers and Manuscripts relating to English Affairs, existing in the Archives and Collections of Venice and in Other Libraries of Northern Italy*, vol. 5: 1534-1552, ed. Rawdon Brown (London, 1873), 45-46, no. 112.
40. See, for instance, the interesting conversation about the end of the world between a Venetian diplomat and an Ottoman official; Venice, Archivio di Stato, Dispacci Costantinopoli, filza 20 (1584-85), fols. 426$^r$-433$^v$.
41. See A. Sayili, *The Observatory in Islam* (Ankara, 1960; reprint, New York, 1981).
42. See the forthcoming book by Cornell Fleischer.
43. Kafadar (1991a).
44. Hattox (1985).
45. Fletcher (1985): 37-57. He notes the "decline of nomadism" as one of the common dynamic elements of early modern history. While it is true that nomadism declined both as a way of life and as a pool of state-builders throughout early modern Asia, incuding the Middle East, its erosion occurred much later and slower than in Europe.

# BIBLIOGRAPHY

## I. Primary Sources

The most important collection by far is the Ottoman Archives, supplemented by the Topkapi Palace Archives, in Istanbul. See Bernard Lewis, "The Ottoman archives: Sources for European history," *Archives* 4 (1960): 226-31; S. Shaw, "Archival sources for Ottoman history: the archives of Turkey," *Journal of American Oriental Society* 80 (1960): 3-14. There are also important collections in former provincial centers (e.g. Cairo, Sofia, Thessalonike) of materials pertaining mostly to local-regional matters including, of course, trade with Europe. Except for a few 15th century examples in Balkan languages, all the documents are in the languages of the Islamic Middle East, mostly Turkish. European documents apparently survive only in Turkish translations that include such gems as Leonardo da Vinci's proposal for a bridge across the Golden Horn; see Franz Babinger and L. Heydenreich, *Vier Bauvorschläge Lionardo da Vincis an Sultan Bajezid II* (Göttingen, 1952). A good part of the thousands of court registers from different towns survive; for summary translations of cases from one city in 1600, see H. Duda and G. Galabov, *Die Protokollbücher des Kadiamtes Sofia* (Munich, 1960). For an introduction to the categories of Ottoman documents, along with archival lists, see J. Reychman and A. Zajaczkowski, *Handbook of Ottoman-Turkish Diplomatics*, trans. A. S. Ehrenkreutz, ed. Tibor Halasi-Kun (The Hague, 1968).

Several archives in Europe contain, in addition to some documents in Turkish or other Middle Eastern languages (see, for instance, N. Beldiceanu, *Les actes des premiers sultans conservés dans les manuscrits turcs de la Bibliothèque Nationale à Paris. I-Actes de Mehmed II et de Bayezid II du ms fonds turc ancien 39*, [Paris, 1960], which also includes summary translations), abundant materials in European languages. Among these, the Archivio di Stato of Venice is certainly the most important, in certain matters surpassing even the Istanbul archives, for the period covered in this survey. Venetian diplomats were well informed and insightful observers of Ottoman politics, institutions, finances and trade. Of their formal reports to the Senate, presented mostly at the end of a three-yearly term in Istanbul, the majority has been published. E. Alberi, ed., *Relazioni degli ambasciatori veneti durante il secolo XVI*, 3d ser., vols. 1-3 (Florence, 1842-55). On the other hand, reading the unpublished *Dispacci Constantinopoli* as a series, of which little use has been made by either Ottomanists or Europeanists, is the closest thing to reading a gazette from sixteenth-century Istanbul, including even some gossip about the private lives of the elite. The similar collection in Dubrovnik (in Latin and Italian) is almost totally uncharted terrain. No other city state is comparable to these two in terms of their relations with the Ottomans in the long run, but there are significant collections in many Italian cities such as Florence and Genoa as well as in the Vatican. There are also moments of intense relations that produced particularly noteworthy correspondence; for an interesting example, see H. J. Kissling, *Sultan Bajezid's II. Beziehungen zu Markgraf Francesco II. von Gonzaga* (Munich, 1965).

The Portuguese archives must be consulted for that relatively brief but significant moment in world history of Ottoman-Portuguese competition in and around the Indian Ocean; see S. Özbaran, "A Review of Portuguese and Turkish Sources for the Ottomans in Arabia and the Indian Ocean in the 16th Century," *Belleten* (1985): 64-78. The Spanish archives seem to contain mostly copies of Venetian materials, but no serious investigation has been conducted. Towards the middle of the 16th century, Austrian, French and Polish archives begin to acquire importance that would only grow in the next few centuries; only a portion is published in A. von Gevay, *Urkunden und Akenstücke zur Geschichte der Verhältnisse zwischen Österreich, Ungarn und der Pforte im 16. und 17. Jahrhundert*, 9 vols. (Vienna, 1840-42); E. Charrière, *Négociations de la France dans le Levant*, "Collection de documents inédits sur l'histoire de France," 1st series, 4 vols. (Paris, 1840-60). Towards the end of the century, traffic and correspondence begin in earnest with England; see S. Skilliter, *William Harborne and the Trade with Turkey, 1578-1582: a documentary study of the first Anglo-Ottoman relations* (Oxford, 1977).

In addition to archival documents, there are Ottoman manuscripts in libraries all across the former lands of the empire as well as western and eastern Europe. A good picture of Ottoman manuscript production and of their diffusion can be obtained from the excellent catalogues of the series, *Verzeichnis der orientalischen Handschriften in Deutschland* (5 vols. published so far of Turkish mss. [Wiesbaden, 1968-]). Many belong to genres of history- and biography-writing. An encyclopedic survey of the rich output of Ottoman historians can be found in Franz Babinger's *Die Geschichtsschreiber der Osmanen und Ihre Werke* (Leipzig, 1927). Very few of these works are translated into European languages despite the excellent beginnings made as early as around 1590 by Hans Löwenklau (Levenclavius) who translated an early Ottoman chronicle into Latin and German. For the beginnings of Ottoman historiography in the fifteenth century, see the articles by H. Inalcik and V. L. Ménage in B. Lewis and P. M. Holt, eds., *The Historians of the Middle East* (London, 1962). Some translated 15th-century chronicles, in addition to that of Ashikpashazade cited in the text above, are: Michael Kritovoulos, *History of Mehmed the Conqueror (1451-1467)*, trans. C. T. Riggs (Princeton, 1954); Tursun Beg, *The History of Mehmed the Conqueror*, facs. and summary trans. by H. Inalcik and R. Murphey (Minneapolis, 1978); *Der fromme Sultan Bayezid. Die Geschichte seiner Herrschaft (1481-1512) nach den altosmanischen Chroniken des Oruc und der Anonymous Hanivaldanus*, ed. and trans. R. F. Kreutel (Vienna, 1978). The rise of Ottoman naval power is recounted in Hajji Khalfa (=Katip Chelebi, 1609-57), *History of the Maritime Wars of the Turks*, trans. J. Mitchell (London, 1831). Süleyman's 1526 campaign is chronicled by the top scholar-jurisconsult of the time, Kemal Pachazadeh (=Ibn Kemal, d. 1534), *Histoire de la campagne de Mohacz*, trans. P. de Courteille (Paris, 1859); also see A. C. Schaendlinger, *Die Feldzugstagebücher des ersten und zweiten Feldzugs Süleyman I.* (Vienna, 1978). The voluminous chronicle of Hodja Sadeddin Efendi (1536-99), mentioned in the text above, is translated into Italian by V. Bratutti,in *Chronica dell'origine e progressi della casa ottomana* (Vienna, 1649). Many other translations of Ottoman sources were undertaken in the 17th and especially 18th centuries, but they remain by and large unpublished in European manuscript libraries (Bibliothèque Nationale in Paris, ms. occidentaux, may be the most important such collection).

The influential forerunner of the Ottoman decline and reform discourse is edited and translated by Andreas Tietze, in *Mustafa Ali's Counsel for Sultans of 1581*, 2 vols. (Vienna, 1979-82). Another early example, by Hasan Kafi, the Bosnian judge who observed Ottoman military flaws in the 1590's, is "Principes de Sagesse, touchant l'art de gouverner," trans. M. Garcin de Tassy in *Journal Asiatique* 4 (1824): 213-26 and 283-90.

Among the most important sources of Ottoman history are works written in European languages by those who relate their experiences in the Orient. Most of these are by travellers, but perhaps the best informed are the few that are penned by ex-slaves. The following authors served in the palace: Konstantin Mihailovic, *Memoirs of a Janissary*, trans. B. Stolz (Ann Arbor, 1975); G. Angiolello, *Historia Turchesca (1300-1514)*, ed. I. Ursu (who attributes the work to Donado da Lezze); (Bucharest, 1909); Giovantonio Menavino, *I cinque libri della legge, religione, et vita de' Turchi et della corte, e d'alcune guerre del Gran Turco* (Florence, 1548). For a different, non-courtly experience of captivity (between 1436 and 1458), see Georgius de Hungaria, *Tractatus de moribus, condicionibus et nequicia Turcorum* (Rome, 1480). A later example is Bartholomaeus Georgievic, *De Turcarum ritu et caeremoniis* (Antwerp, 1544). The travel literature is too huge to be covered here, but there is now an excellent guide to it all in S. Yerasimos, *Les voyageurs dans l'empire ottoman (XIVe-XVIe siècles): bibliographie, itinéraires et inventaire des lieux habités* (Ankara, 1991).

Not all the European materials on the Turks were produced by those with direct experience of the Orient. Ottoman history and customs were treated by authors in special works or general world histories to which there is no comprehensive guide in terms of our subject. The first English-language history is by Richard Knolles, *The General Historie of the Turkes* (London, 1610). For the voluminous "Zeitungen," or pamphlet literature of "news," sermons, prophecies, etc., on "the Turks," see Göllner, *Turcica: die europäischen Türkendrucke des XVI. Jahrhunderts* (Bucharest, 1961). Good bibliographic surveys of these sources are also provided by studies on the image of Turks (see next section).

II. Literature (in western languages)

*A. References, Surveys, and Historiography*
For bibliographic help, one could begin with G. Teich, "Bibliographie der Bibliographien Südosteuropas," *Wirtschaftswissenschaftliche Süd-osteuropa Forschung* (1963):177-213, or H. J. and J. Kornrumpf, *Osmanische Bibliographie, mit besonderer Berücksichtigung der Türkei in Europa* (Leiden, 1973). Since 1974, an annual publication, *Türkologischer Anzeiger* (ed. A. Tietze; first published as a supplement to *Wiener Zeitschrift für die Kunde des Morgenlandes*, later as individual volumes), has provided excellent coverage. For maps, see D. E. Pitcher, *An Historical Geography of the Ottoman Empire from the Earliest Times to the End of the Sixteenth Century* (Leiden, 1972).

Among the surveys, the magnum opus of Joseph von Hammer-Purgstall, an interpreter of Oriental languages for the Habsburg empire in the early 19th century, is unsurpassed as an old-fashioned narrative. The French edition of the work, authorized and revised by Hammer himself, should be preferred: *Histoire de l'empire ottoman depuis son origine jusqu'à nos jours*, trans. J. J. Hellert, 18 vols. (Paris, 1835-48). Still useful, particularly with regard to the Balkans, are J. W. Zinkeisen, *Geschichte des osmanischen Reiches in Europa*, 7 vols. (Gotha, 1840-63), and N. Iorga, *Geschichte des osmanischen Reiches*, 5 vols. (Gotha, 1908-13).

Of more recent surveys, the most authoritative one that covers the period studied in this book is Halil Inalcik, *The Ottoman Empire: The Classical Age 1300-1600*, trans. Colin Imber and Norman Itzkowitz (New York, 1973). Also see Stanford J. Shaw, *History of the Ottoman Empire and Modern Turkey*, 2 vols. (Cambridge, 1976-78), and R. Mantran, ed., *Histoire de l'empire ottoman* (Paris, 1989). The most accessible short introductions to Ottoman history before Westernization are Norman Itzkowitz, *Ottoman Empire and Islamic Tradition* (New York, 1972) and Bernard Lewis, *Istanbul and the Civilization of the Ottoman Empire* (Norman, Okla., 1963). Relevant articles from *The Cambridge History of Islam* are collected in M. A. Cook, ed., *Ottoman History to 1730* (Cambridge, 1976). For the Balkans, Leften S. Stavrianos, *The Balkans since 1453* (New York, 1958), and Peter F. Sugar, *Southeastern Europe under Ottoman Rule, 1354-1804* (Seattle, 1977) are useful introductions (though dated on Ottoman institutions and mentalities). For a more technical introduction to fiscal-administrative-military structures of Ottoman rule, with emphasis on the Balkans, see Bistra A. Cvetkova, *Les institutions ottomanes en Europe* (Wiesbaden, 1978).

Broad treatments of Ottoman cultural history are yet to appear; the closest thing to a general intellectual history is A. Adivar's dated but indispensable *La science chez les turcs ottomans* (Paris, 1939). E. J. W. Gibb's *History of Ottoman Poetry*, 6 vols. (London 1906-09), provides another entry through the most prestigous form of literary activity. A. Bombaci's *Histoire de la litterature turque*, trans. I. Melikoff (Paris, 1968), is shorter but more inclusive. M. And's *A History of Theatre and Popular Entertainment in Turkey* (Ankara, 1963) covers more popular genres and performance arts. For art and architecture, see: E. Alkurgal, ed., *The Art and Architecture of Turkey* (New York, 1980); and E. Atil, ed., *Turkish Art* (New York and Washington, D. C., 1980). See also the forthcoming work on Ottoman culture by Suraiya Faroqhi.

On the construction of "the Turk" in European consciousness, one now needs to be familiar with the growing critical literature on orientalism and "the other" which can not be covered here; for instances of its impact on current historiography, see the special issue of *PaP* 137 (Nov. 1992). For background in the old sense, see R. W. Southern, *Western*

*Views of Islam in the Middle Ages* (Cambridge, Mass., 1962); Norman Daniel, *The Arabs and Medieval Europe* (London, 1975) and Kenneth M. Setton, *Western Hostility to Islam and Prophecies of Turkish Doom* (Philadelphia, 1992). Earliest European literature on the Turks is studied, and some texts provided, in A. Pertusi, "I primi studi in Occidente sull'origine e la potenza dei Turchi," *Studi Veneziani* 12 (1970): 465-552. For an interesting motif mentioned by Pertusi, also see T. Spencer, "Turks and Trojans in the Renaissance," *Modern Language Review* 47 (1952): 330-33. For specific traditions, see C.D. Rouillard, *The Turk in French History, Thought, and Literature (1520-1660)* (Paris, 1938); C. A. Patrides, "'The Bloody and Cruell Turke': The Background of a Renaissance Commonplace," *Studies in the Renaissance* 10 (1963): 126-35; Albert Mas, *Les Turcs dans le litterature espagnole du siècle d'or, recherches sur l'evolution d'un theme litteraire* (Paris, 1967); Robert Schwoebel, *The Shadow of the Crescent: The Renaissance Image of the Turk (1453-1517)* (Nieuwkoop, 1967); M. J. Heath, *Crusading Commonplaces: La Noue, Lucinge, and Rhetoric Against the Turks* (Geneva, 1986). For the sixteenth-century evolution of European views on the Ottoman political system, in other words for the proto-history of the notion of "Oriental despotism," through an analysis of the Venetian relazioni, see L. Valensi, *Venise et la Sublime Porte: la naissance du despote* (Paris, 1987).

B. *Other Published Works (in Western Languages)*

Alderson, A. D. *The Structure of the Ottoman Dynasty.* Oxford, 1956.

Allen, W. E. D. *Problems of Turkish Power in the Sixteenth Century.* London, 1963.

Argenti, Philip P. *Chius vincta: The Occupation of Chios by the Turks (1566) and their Administration of the Island (1566-1912) Described in Contemporary Reports and Official Despatches.* Cambridge, 1941.

Babinger, Franz. *Mehmed the Conqueror and His Time.* Trans. Ralph Manheim. Ed. William C. Hickman. Princeton, 1978.

Barkan, Ömer L. "Essai sur les données statistiques des registres de recensement dans l'Empire Ottoman au XVe et XVIe siècles." *Journal of the Economic and Social History of the Orient* 1 (1957): 9-21.

Barkan, Ömer L. "The Price Revolution of the Sixteenth Century: A Turning Point in the Economic History of the Near East." *International Journal of Middle East Studies* 6 (1975): 3-28.

Barkan, Ömer L. "Research on the Ottoman Fiscal Surveys," pp. 163-71 in *Studies in the Economic History of the Middle East*, ed. M. A. Cook. London, 1970.

Bayerle, Gustav. *Ottoman Tributes in Hungary.* The Hague, 1973.

Beldiceanu, Nicoara. *La moldavie ottomane à la fin du XVe siècle et au début du XVIe siècle.* Paris, 1969.

Beldiceanu, Nicoara. *Le monde ottoman des Balkans, 1402-1566: institutions, société, économie.* London, 1976.

Beldiceanu, Nicoara. *Le timar dans l'état ottoman (début XIVe-début XVIe siècle).* Paris, 1980.

Berktay, Halil. "The Feudalism Debate: The Turkish End - Is Tax-vs.-Rent Necessarily the Product and Sign of a Modal Difference?" *Journal of Peasant Studies* (1987): 291-333.

Berktay, Halil. The "Other" Feudalism: a Critique of 20th-Century Turkish Historiography and Its Particularisation of Ottoman Society. Unpublished Ph.D. Dissertation, University of Birmingham, 1990.

Berktay, Halil, and Suraiya Faroqhi, eds. *New approaches to State and Peasant in Ottoman Society* [=*Journal of Peasant Studies* 18 (1992)]. London, 1992.

Braude, Benjamin, and Bernard Lewis, eds. *Christians and Jews in the Ottoman Empire: the Functioning of a Plural Society.* 2 vols. London, 1982.

Braudel, Fernand. *The Mediterranean and the Mediterranean World in the Age of Philip II.* Trans. Sián Reynolds. 2 vols. New York and London, 1972.

Bryer, A. and H. Lowry, eds. *Continuity and Change in Late Byzantine and Early Ottoman Society.* Washington, D. C., 1986.

Cook, M. A. *Population Pressure in Rural Anatolia, 1450-1600.* London, 1972.

Cvetkova, Bistra A. *Vie économique de villes et ports balkaniques au XVe et XVIe siècles.* Paris, 1978.

Epstein, M. *The Ottoman Jewish Communities and Their Role in the Fifteenth and Six-teenth Centuries.* Freiburg im Breisgau, 1980.

Erder, Leila. "The Measurement of Preindustrial Population Changes: the Ottoman Em-pire from the 15th to the 17th Century." *Middle Eastern Studies,* 11 (1975): 284-301.

Erder, Leila and Suraiya Faroqhi. "Population Rise and Fall in Anatolia, 1550-1620," *Middle East Studies* (1979).

Farooqhi, Naimur Rahman. *Mughal-Ottoman Relations: a Study of Political and Diplo-matic Relations between Mughal India and the Ottoman Empire, 1556-1748.* Delhi, 1989.

Faroqhi, Suraiya. *Peasants, Dervishes, and Traders in the Ottoman Empire.* London, 1986.

Faroqhi, Suraiya. *Towns and Townsmen of Ottoman Anatolia.* Cambridge, 1984.

Faroqhi, Suraiya. "Unrest" in *Türkische Miszellen. Robert Anhegger Festschrift.* Istanbul, 1987.

Fekete, Lajos. *Buda and Pest under Turkish Rule.* Studia Turco-Hungarica, vol. 3. Buda-pest, 1976.

Finkel, Caroline. *The Administration of Warfare: the Ottoman Military Campaigns in Hungary, 1593-1606.* Vienna, 1988.

Fischer-Galati, Stephen. *Ottoman Imperialism and German Protestantism, 1521-1555.* Cambridge, Mass., 1959.

Fisher, Sidney N. *The Foreign Relations of Turkey, 1481-1512.* Urbana, Ill., 1948.

Fleischer, Cornell H. *Bureaucrat and Intellectual in the Ottoman Empire: the historian Mustafa Ali (1541-1600).* Princeton, 1986.

Fletcher, Joseph. "Integrative History: Parallels and Interconnections in the Early Modern Period, 1500-1800." *Journal of Turkish Studies* 9 (1985): 37-57.

Fodor, Pál. "Ottoman Policy Toward Hungary, 1520-1541." *Acta Orientalia* [Budapest] 45 (1991): 271-345.

Frazee, Charles A. *Catholics and Sultans: the Church and the Ottoman Empire, 1453-1923.* Cambridge, 1983.

Gerber, Haim. "Anthropology and Family History: The Ottoman and Turkish Families." *Journal of Family History* 14 (1989): 409-421.

Gerber, Haim. "The Monetary System of the Ottoman Empire." *Journal of the Economic and Social History of the Orient* 25 (1982): 308-24.

Gibb, H. A. R., and H. Bowen. *Islamic Society and the West.* 2 vols. Oxford, 1950-57.

Goffman, Daniel. *Izmir and the Levantine World, 1550-1650.* Seattle, 1990.

Hasluck, F. W. *Christianity and Islam under the Sultans.* 2 vols. Oxford, 1929.

Hattox, Ralph. *Coffee and Coffeehouses: The Origins of a Social Beverage in the Medieval Near East.* Seattle, 1985.

Hess, Andrew C. "The Battle of Lepanto and Its Place in Mediterranean History." *PaP* 52 (1972): 53-73.

Hess, Andrew C. "The Evolution of the Ottoman Seaborne Empire in the Age of the Oce-anic Discoveries, 1453-1525." *AHR* 75 (1970): 1882-1919.

Hess, Andrew C. *The Forgotten Frontier: a History of the Sixteenth-century Ibero-African Frontier.* Chicago, 1978.

Heyd, Uriel. *Studies in Old Ottoman Criminal Law.* Ed. V. L. Ménage. Oxford, 1973.

Imber, Colin. *The Ottoman Empire 1300-1481.* Istanbul, 1990.

Inalcik, Halil. "Comments on 'Sultanism': Max Weber's Typification of the Ottoman Pol-ity." *Princeton Papers in Near Eastern Studies* 1 (1992): 49-72.

Inalcik, Halil. *The Ottoman Empire: Conquest, Organization and Economy.* Collected Studies. London, 1978.

Inalcik, Halil. *Studies in Ottoman Social and Economic History.* London, 1985.

Inalcik, Halil, and Cemal Kafadar, eds., *Süleymân the Second and His Time.* Istanbul, 1993.

Jennings, Ronald J. *Christians and Jews in Ottoman Cyprus and the Mediterranean World, 1517-1640.* New York, 1993.

Kafadar, Cemal. "A Death in Venice (1575): Anatolian Muslim Merchants Trading in the Serenissima." In *Raiyyet Rüsûmu: Essays presented to Halil Inalcik* [=*Journal of Turkish Studies* 10 (1986): 191-217].

Kafadar, Cemal. *At the Edge of the World of Islam: The Construction of the Ottoman State*. Berkeley and Los Angeles, forthcoming.

Kafadar, Cemal. "Les troubles monétaires de la fin du XVIe siècle et la prise de conscience ottomane du déclin." *Annales: ÉSC* (1991a).

Kafadar, Cemal. "On the Purity and Corruption of the Janissaries." *Turkish Studies Association Bulletin* 15 (1991b): 273-80.

Káldy-Nagy, Gyula. "The Administration of the *Sancak* Registrations in Hungary." *Acta Orientalia* [Budapest] 21 (1968): 181-223.

Káldy-Nagy, Gyula. "The Cash Book of the Ottoman Treasury in Buda in the Years 1558-1560." *Acta Orientalia* [Budapest] 15 (1962): 173-82.

Káldy-Nagy, Gyula. "The Effect of the *Timar*-System on Agricultural Production in Hungary." In *Studia Turcica*, ed. L. Ligeti, 241-48. Budapest, 1971.

Kiel, Machiel. *Studies on the Ottoman Architecture of the Balkans*. London, 1990.

Kissling, Hans J. *Rechtsproblematiken in den christlich-muslimischen Beziehungen, vorab im Zeitalter der Türkenkriege*. Graz, 1974.

Kortepeter, Max. *Ottoman Imperialism during the Reformation*. New York, 1972.

Kunt, I. M. *The Sultan's Servants: the Tranformation of Ottoman Provincial Government, 1550-1650*. New York, 1983.

Kurz, Otto. *European Clocks and Watches in the Near East*. Leiden, 1975.

Labib, S. Y. *Handelsgeschichte Ägyptens im Spätmittelalter (1171-1517)*. Wiesbaden, 1965.

Lewis, Bernard. *The Muslim Discovery of Europe*. New York, 1982.

Lewis, Raphaela. *Everyday Life in Ottoman Turkey*. London and New York, 1971.

Lifchez, Raymond. *The Dervish Lodge: Architecture, Art, and Sufism in Ottoman Turkey*. Comparative Studies on Muslim Societies, vol. 10. Berkeley and Los Angeles, 1992.

Mantran, R. *La vie quotidienne à Constantinople au temps de Soliman le Magnifique et des ses successeurs*. Paris, 1965.

Mas, Albert. *Les Turcs dans la litterature espagnole du siècle d'or, recherches sur l'évolution d'un theme littéraire*. Paris, 1967.

Maxim, Mihai. "L'autonomie de la Moldavie et de la Valachie dans les actes officiels de la Porte Ottomane de la seconde moitié du XVIe siècle." *Revue des études sud-est européennes* 15 (1977): 207-32.

Miller, B. *The Palace School of Muhammad the Conqueror*. Cambridge, Mass., 1941.

Moutafchieva, V. P. *Agrarian Relations in the Ottoman Empire in the 15th and 16th Centuries*. New York, 1988.

Murphey, Rhoads. "Ottoman Census Methods in the Mid-Sixteenth Century: Three Case Histories." *Studia Islamica* 71 (1990): 115-26.

Necipoglu, Gülru. *Architecture, Power, and Ceremonial: The Topkapi Palace in the Fifteenth and Sixteenth Centuries*. Cambridge, Mass., 1991.

Pachi, P. "The Shifting of International Trade Routes in the 15th-17th Centuries." *Acta Historica* 14 (1968): 287-321.

Pantazopoulos, N. J. *Church and Law in the Balkan Peninsula During the Ottoman Rule*. Salonica, 1967.

Peirce, Leslie. *The Imperial Harem: Women and Sovereignty in the Ottoman Empire*. Oxford, 1993.

Preto, Paolo. *Venezia e i Turchi*. Florence, 1975.

Repp, R. *The Müfti of Istanbul*. London, 1986.

Runciman, Stephen. *The Fall of Constantinople*. Cambridge, 1965.

Runciman, Stephen. *The Great Church in Captivity*. London, 1968.

Shaw, Stanford J. *The Financial and Administrative Organization and Development of Ottoman Egypt, 1517-1798*. Princeton Oriental Studies, no. 19. Princeton, 1958.

Shaw, Stanford J. *The Jews of the Ottoman Empire and the Turkish Republic*. New York, 1991.

*Soliman le Magnifique et son temps: Actes du Colloque de Paris, Galeries nationales du Grand Palais, 7-10 mars 1990.* Paris, 1992.

Sugar, Peter F. *Southeastern Europe under Ottoman Rule, 1354-1804.* Seattle, 1977.

Tietze, Andreas, ed. *Habsburgische-osmanische Beziehungen.* Vienna, 1985.

Todorov, Nikolai. *The Balkan City, 1400-1900.* Seattle, 1983.

Vacalopoulos, Apostolos. *The Greek Nation, 1453-1669: the Cultural and Economic Background of Modern Greek Society.* New Brunswick, N. J., 1976.

Vaughan, Dorothy M. *Europe and the Turk: a Pattern of Alliances 1350-1700.* Liverpool, 1954.

Veinstein, Gilles. "Some Views on Provisioning in the Hungarian Campaigns of Süleyman the Magnificent." In *Osmanistische Studien zur Wirtschafts- und Socialgeschichte*, ed. H. G. Majer. Wiesbaden, 1986.

Vryonis, Spiros. *The Decline of Medieval Hellenism in Asia Minor.* Berkeley and Los Angeles, 1971.

Werner, Ernst. *Sultan Mehmed der Eroberer und die Epochenwende im 15. Jahrhundert.* Sitzungsberichte der Sächsischen Akademie der Wissenschaften zu Leipzig, Philologisch-Historische Klasse, vol. 123, no. 2. Berlin, 1982.

# THE SEABORNE EMPIRES

Wolfgang Reinhard
(Albert-Ludwigs-Universität Freiburg)


## 1. The Mediterranean Tradition of Expansion

The "discovery of America" by a Genoese in Spanish service, far from being a coincidence, reflected the convergence of Italian and Spanish traditions of maritime expansion. Already in 1291 the Genoese were sailing westward, with the aim of perhaps reaching India.

*Trade and Colonial Commerce in the Mediterranean Sea*
The Mediterranean peoples had obtained spices, silks, and other valuable goods from Asia since Antiquity, generally paying for them with precious metals, since their own products evoked little demand in Asia. Some centuries later, long after the profitable wholesale trade in Asian goods passed into the hands of Muslims, retail trade in such goods in Christendom passed into the hands of merchants from the Italian coastal cities, who were permitted to build trading bases in Muslim and Christian ports. Then, during the age of the Crusades, their grip on seaborne transport gave them an added incentive to gain control over the western termini of the trans-Asian trade routes on the Syro-Palestinian coast. Entire city districts in Acre and Tyre belonged to Genoa, Pisa, and Venice. When Acre, the last Latin Christian city in the Levant, fell to the Muslims in 1291, the Vivaldi brothers of Genoa sought for a new route westward. By then, admittedly, the western Asian trade routes had already shifted northward, because of the "Mongol peace [*pax mongolica*]," to reach new western termini on the coasts of the Black Sea. Meanwhile, after the Latin conquest of Constantinople in 1204, the Venetians, who had maneuvered the Fourth Crusade there, had temporarily transformed the city into the center of their trading empire. The Genoese responded in 1261, forming an alliance with the revived Byzantine Empire, which gave them predominance in the Black Sea markets. During the following century, when political changes in Central Asia led to the breaking off of direct trading contacts, the Black Sea region remained important for the supply of slaves, a branch of trade in which the Genoese maintained the upper hand in Europe over

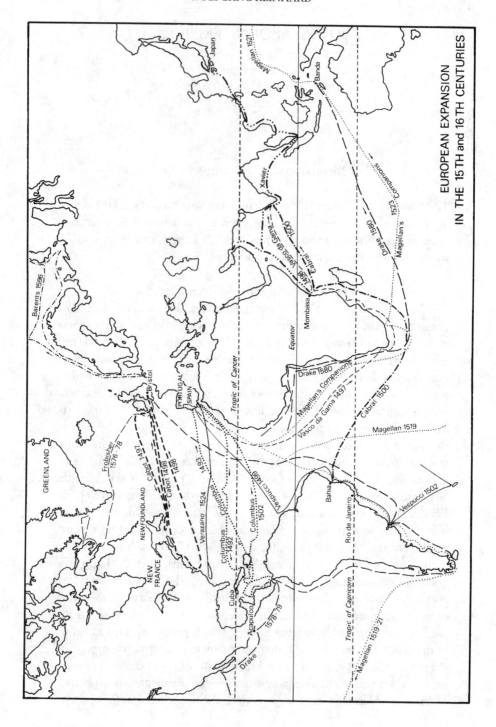

EUROPEAN EXPANSION
IN THE 15TH and 16TH CENTURIES

the Venetians. Besides the trading bases, some of which developed into independent communities, the great Italian coastal cities also acquired territorial empires in the East: Venice took Crete and other islands in the Aegean, capping the process with the acquisition of Cyprus in 1489; Genoa got Chios in 1346 and Phocaea in Asia Minor in 1351. In these possessions trade goods were produced under monopolistic conditions, such as mastic on Chios and alum in Phocaea, while on Crete and Cyprus sugar was produced in the manner well established in Palestine, on plantations worked by slaves.

The rise of the Italian maritime powers via the seaborne trade has been called a "commercial revolution,"[1] by which phrase is meant economic expansion in terms which were not only quantitative, but also qualitative. The Italians proved creative, for example, in the organization of trade, conquest and colonial rule. The Venetian empire developed under close governmental supervision, while the Genoese expansion occurred via the private form of the business company (*societas*). The expansion was promoted, too, by improvements in shipbuilding, notably the further development, alongside the traditional galley, of the round ship. By the fifteenth century, this commercial workhorse had a straight keel, a stern rudder, and complex rigging with square sails forward and amidships and a lateen sail aft—a combination which allowed both efficient running before the wind and tacking into it. Coastal navigation, an art based entirely on experience, was gradually complemented by the art of oceanic navigation of the high seas, which relied on the compass, on instruments for taking the position of sun and stars, and on mathematical tables that enabled the sights to be converted into determinations of latitude.

The two chief Italian maritime powers used their mastery of the navigational arts, their capital, and their desire for profits in different directions. The Venetians dominated the trade with Egypt, the entrepot of the Asian trade following the fourteenth-century crisis, while the expanding power of the Ottoman Turks crept toward the old trading stations on the Black Sea's coast. The Genoese, meanwhile, were shifting westward, toward Iberia, a change symbolized by the Portuguese king's appointment in 1317 of a Genoese to the hereditary position of admiral.

### The Iberian Reconquista

The European expansion in the fifteenth and sixteenth centuries formed an extension not only of the Italian system of maritime commerce, but also of the Iberian *reconquista*, the retaking of the peninsula from the Muslims. The *reconquista*, which had begun in the eighth century, had by the mid-thirteenth achieved its goals, except for Granada, which would not fall until 1492. The institutions of the *reconquista*, honed during this process, were to shape decisively the overseas expansion of the subsequent age. An important force, both in Europe and later overseas, for example, was the lower nobility (Sp. *hidalgos*, Port. *fidalgos*), who aspired to glory and wealth through plunder, conquest, and the founding and settlement of cities in the service of God and the king. Also, "bourgeois" acquisitiveness —even without Italian influence—and extensive transhumance practices in Castile played positive roles as inducements for opportunity–minded Castilians to migrate. In Castile the Crown stood at the center of the great enterprises and the distribution of the conquests: it awarded the conquerors and their new establishments with privileges regarding legal status. The feudal language employed in such charters is deceptive, for the Castilian and Portuguese monarchies were not feudal but absolutist, and they drew support from the cities and from the rising class of lawyers in their efforts to tame the higher aristocracy. The church was also subject to extensive royal control.

If the *reconquista* had taken on the character of a crusade, then only in part. The decisive principle in this struggle had been religion, of course, but the *reconquista* was also an affair of plunder and conquest in which changing sides was a common enough occurrence. This phenomenon does not imply a recognition of equality of religions, although initially the Christians did respect their Muslim subjects' way of life as, conversely, the Muslims respected that of the Christians, and both respected the Jews'. But the Christians continued this practice only with reservation and on condition of the Muslims' continued good behavior. This practice of limited toleration may be regarded as a form of colonialism coupled with an early form of racial apartheid.[2] The situation changed again toward the end of the Middle Ages through a process which at the end of the fifteenth century led to the expulsion of Jews and Muslims and the subsequent persecution of converts suspected of relapsing into their former religions. Although, when necessary, the Iberian powers remembered the toleration that had once been possible, the rule in the sixteenth century was a Christianization policy heedless of all other considerations.

### Overseas Expansion in the Late Middle Ages

The overseas expansion of the Iberian kingdoms did not begin in the fifteenth century but already in the thirteenth. In addition to the Aragonese Mediterranean empire and the Castilian and Portuguese voyages to Flanders, Portugal and Castile extended their grasps toward Africa and the Atlantic islands, partly with the aid of Italians. At that time, through the application of the achievements of Mediterranean shipbuilding, the Portuguese developed from older Iberian models a very seaworthy ship known as the caravel, which became especially useful for the exploration of unknown coasts. That the Portuguese Prince Henry the Navigator actually planned the expansion is uncertain, though he certainly was the undisputed promoter of Portuguese oceanic quests during first half of the fifteenth century.

The Canary Islands, which had been rediscovered by a Genoese at the beginning of the fourteenth century, were not occupied until after the competing claims of Portugal and Castile were settled in the latter's favor in 1474. During the first half of the fifteenth century the Portuguese settled the Madeira Islands and the Azores, which lay further out in the Atlantic. Their advance further south down the African coast went hand-in-hand with the conquest of the North African port of Ceuta, and in 1437 the Portuguese ships rounded the dreaded Cape Bojador. Their motives here were the same as in the Iberian *reconquista*: fame and plunder, conquests and conversions in the struggle against the Muslims.[3] They also searched for a Christian ally against the Muslims, though this motif was much older than the Portuguese voyages of the fifteenth century. As yet, they hardly discussed India itself, nor was there much talk at this time of commercial possibilities. Nor did overpopulation at home play any role, no more than it had in the Iberian reconquista or would in the conquest of the Americas. We deduce from later developments that these early voyages also arose from an interest in access to the sources of African gold, in the slave trade, and in new possibilities for agriculture, especially sugar, the production of which had moved westward from the Levant via Sicily and Valencia to Madeira.

## 2. DISCOVERY AND CONQUEST

Concepts such as "discovery," "conquest" and "conversion," and names such as "The New World," "America," even "India" and, accordingly, "Indians" as well are purely European creations and express a eurocentric point of view. From the viewpoint of European history, however, they are legitimate, for at issue here is a process which began in Europe and derives its historical unity only from this source.

*The Portuguese Quest for Gold and Slaves*

When a Portuguese sailor brought slaves from West Africa back to Portugal in 1441, the interest of investors was peaked, and not only in Portugal. Their interest increased when, as a result of further advances during the following two decades, gold and pepper were brought from Guinea. In 1443 the Portuguese Crown declared a "national" monopoly over this trade, for which papal approbation would be sought in 1452-56. More important was the Treaty of Alcáçovas in 1479, by which Castile recognized the Portuguese monopoly south of the Canary Islands. In 1481 Fort São Jorge da Mina (Elmina) was built out of pre-fabricated parts in what is now Ghana, designed to be a center of the gold trade. The new king, John II, pushed expansion systematically, and at this point there began to be talk of reaching India and the sources of the spice trade. What was meant by "India" at this point is unclear, since the term could have referred to Christian Ethiopia.

After he had become acquainted with other Atlantic routes, the Genoese Christopher Columbus came to Elmina as a Portuguese captain about 1483. In 1484 he presented his plan to King John to reach India by sailing westward, but it was rejected by the king's scientific experts. Of course, because of several errors, Columbus had miscalculated the globe's circumference, which led him to suppose that Japan lay where in fact North America was. The errors, however, became an important basis for his success. In 1485 he went to Spain, but the experts were skeptical here too, and the Catholic Kings, Ferdinand and Isabella, were concentrating their resources on the conquest of Granada.

Between 1482 and 1484 the Portuguese discovered the kingdom of the Congo, whose ruler wished to institute, with Portuguese help, a policy of promoting Christianization and trade. But the interests of the slave traders and the sugar planters, who had in the meantime settled on the island of São Tomé, proved to be stronger.[4] In 1487 John II's agents searched for a passage to India not only along the African coast but also through the interior of Guinea and by means of dispatching spies disguised as Muslims to explore the East. The king displayed interest as well in a new offer by the frustrated Columbus, only to turn him down again when the news arrived in 1488 that the southern tip of Africa had been rounded.

*The India in the West*

After the conquest of Granada, Spanish and Italian businessmen were able to win the Spanish monarchs over to an attempt to catch up to their Portuguese rivals by means of Columbus' project. The way south was closed to the Spanish by the Treaty of Alcáçovas (1479), whereas the possession of the Canary Islands offered them a base in the trade winds zone, from which one could sail westward with little difficulty. Columbus was given credit, three ships and a contract which promised him an hereditary title, the position of Admiral and Governor, as well as a fixed share of the profits. After thirty-six days of quiet crossing, he reached one of the Bahamas on 12 October 1492. Having explored the north coasts of Cuba and Haiti he returned to Spain after a stormy crossing by way of the Azores and Portugal. His log speaks not only of the "magic" of the New World and the conversion of its inhabitants, but also of their willingness to help, trade goods, and especially gold—words that very likely reflect the Portuguese experience in Africa.

Because the newly discovered islands lay south of the line stipulated by the Treaty of Alcáçovas, Columbus' claims threatened a conflict with Portugal. The Spanish monarchs met this threat by obtaining a papal bull whereby Pope Alexander VI, an Aragonese, gave them all the land west of the 38th longitude in 1493. The Treaty of Tordesillas with Portugal in 1494 shifted the line westward to 46° 30'W. In three subsequent voyages between 1493 and 1504, Columbus explored the Greater and Lesser Antilles, the South American coastline north of the mouth of the Orinoco River, and the Central American coast between Honduras and Panama, always with the belief that he was in some unknown part of East Asia. A very good navigator, as a colonizer Columbus was not particularly successful. The settlement on Haiti, where the oldest Spanish-American city, Santo Domingo, was established in 1496, slipped from his control. In 1500 he was replaced by a representative of the court. The slave trade that he began failed as well, because of the unsuitability of the Indians and the Crown's resistance.

In view of Columbus' limited success, the Crown began already in 1499 to authorize contracts (*capitulaciónes*) with other entrepreneurs and explorers. At the same time Portuguese expeditions arrived in Brazil, which a Portuguese captain had discovered by chance in 1500 on a voyage to the East Indies, and England and France had made various voyages in the North. In 1513 Vasco Núñez de Balboa crossed the Isthmus of Panama and reached the "South Sea," the Pacific Ocean. The eastern coastlines of both continents were extensively explored during the following decade. Italians were always to be found among the discoverers, with the result that the continent was finally named for one of them, Amerigo Vespucci of Florence. Vespucci, who remains a controversial figure to the present day, was the first to promote successfully in writing the idea that this was a

"New World."⁵ Consequently, in 1507 two German geographers proposed naming the fourth continent "America" after him.

### The India in the East

The coincidental discovery of Brazil by the Portuguese arose from the experience that for optimal navigation ships should stick as much as possible to the zones of trade and westerly winds created by the clockwise movement of the wind and currents in the North Atlantic and the counterclockwise movement in the South Atlantic. Columbus used this knowledge already on his first voyage, and Vasco da Gama's first voyage to the East Indies in 1497-99 exploited it through a maneuver know as the *volta do mar*, which took him far west from the Cape Verde Islands to steer for the Cape of Good Hope in the westerly wind zone after three months with no sight of land. The return trip at the time followed the African coast. Da Gama's men met with resistance from the Muslim cities on the coast of East Africa until Malindi, a rival of Mombasa, gave them a pilot who took advantage of the monsoon wind to bring them to Calicut on the Malabar coast. Despite initial misunderstandings, the Portuguese entered into business dealings with Hindus there, though it soon became clear that the control of the spice trade to which they aspired was only to be gained through violence. Pepper came from the Malabar coasts, cinnamon from Ceylon, nutmeg from the Banda Islands, and cloves from the Molucca Islands. The last two items were transshipped in Malacca. Muslim traders from Arabia and Gujarat handled the movement westward across the Arabian Sea to Egypt, where the Mamluke Sultan of Egypt, and after 1517 the Ottoman Sultan, made money from the duties on the re-export trade. The movement further westward toward Europe lay in Venetian hands. It is no wonder that the middlemen resisted the incursion of the Portuguese. Both a combined Egyptian-Gujarati fleet (1507) and an Ottoman fleet (1538) were sent against the Portuguese in the Indian Ocean, and Italian artillerymen, said to have been sent by Venice, aided Portugal's enemies.

Beginning in 1500 a whole series of Portuguese fleets sought to destroy the Muslim trade through violence and terror and to impose a Portuguese monopoly in India. From 1505 a viceroy, appointed for three years, undertook to establish a lasting Portuguese presence through a system of fortified bases. Though not viceroy, Afonso de Albuquerque became the chief Portuguese "empire builder" in Asia during the years from 1509 to 1515. Beginning with existing control over East African ports, in 1509-10 Albuquerque took the island port of Goa on the Indian coast, which would remain the capital of Portuguese India until 1960. Malacca, the hub of the Eastern trade, followed in 1511, and Hormuz, the gateway to the Persian Gulf, in 1515. Albuquerque failed only at Aden in 1513, which would have given the Portuguese control of all the western termini of the trans-oceanic trade from India. Contact with the Christian Ethiopians also formed part of this strategy. Portuguese control over Ceylon began in 1518 with a trading post in Colombo; in 1513 the first Portuguese ship arrived at the Moluccas; a fort was built on Ternate in 1522; and trading posts on Amboina and the Banda Islands followed. In China things progressed more slowly, and initial relations were rather poor. Gradually however, the city of Macão, which was not built until 1557, gained a monopoly of sorts on Chinese trade with the West. The Portuguese landed in Japan in 1543 and opened the next year regular trade, which was concentrated at Nagasaki after 1569.

How was it possible that so few people from a small country could attain such success among great empires and advanced cultures with their own sense of identity? The daring of the Portuguese fighters and their ships' superior artillery does not fully answer the question. They profited from the quarrels of opposing sides in India and Japan, and from the fact that most Asian kingdoms had little interest in maritime trade. In China, where they encountered a unified empire that armed its fleets with artillery, they had few successes to report.

*From "Reconquista" to "Conquista": The Invasion of the Americas*
In the beginning Columbus and the Spanish Crown intended to imitate the Portuguese system of trading stations. But when they discovered that Columbus had reached not Asia but a hitherto unknown land, where trade goods were not in regular supply, they reverted to the familiar pattern of conquest, subjection, and exploitation they had first employed against the heathen Guanches of the Canary Islands. The Greater Antilles were occupied by such methods by 1511. Since the Spanish Crown, unlike the Portuguese, did not invest very much, the *conquista* had to finance itself, proceeding outward step-by-step from central points, where the resources for further advances had to be accumulated. By 1509 Panama had developed into a second center, from which Nicaragua in the north and Peru in the south were conquered. In 1519 Hernán Cortés (1485-1547) organized an armed trading expedition, at the head of which he conquered the Aztec empire; once he became aware of the divisions within this loosely structured empire, Cortés made skillful use of parties opposed to Aztec rule.[6] The *conquista* then spread to Guatemala, Yucatan, and Honduras, bring-

ing into Spanish hands the Americas from Panama to Nicaragua. The
southern part of what is today the United States was explored, but, since
there was little promise of return, it was not occupied. Then, with resources he gathered at Panama, in 1531-34 Francisco Pizarro (ca. 1478-
1541) defeated the enormous and well-organized Inca empire in Peru by
means of skillfully-led attacks against its centers of power. From their base
in Peru, the conquistadors next turned to Ecuador and then Columbia,
where expeditions from the south, the north coast, and Venezuela met in
1538. Chile was also conquered from Peru, beginning with the settlement
of Santiago in 1541. From Peru conquistadors also entered the jungles to
the east and followed the Amazon to its mouth in 1541-42. Finally, although the initial colonization of the Rio de la Plata, and Buenos Aires,
first settled in 1543, had to be abandoned, this region was settled, this time
successfully, from Peru in 1580.

The first step in such an expedition (*entrada*) was the organization of
capital, often through the formation of a commercial company
(*compañia*). By means of a charter (*capitulación*) granted to the company's leader, the Crown appointed him commander of the expedition and
governor of territories claimed and stipulated limitations on his authority.
When soldiers were being recruited, the wealth of the destination area and
its similarity in landscape to Spain were advertised in the best possible
light. Native allies and loyal concubines proved helpful to such enterprises. Columbus, like Cortés and Pizarro later on, engaged in the practice
of taking princes as hostages, the execution of whom served like other cru-
elties to intimidate the enemy through terror. The desecration of holy
shrines not only yielded plunder but also demonstrated the power of the
Christians and their God. The Spaniards were superior to their opponents,
not only organizationally, as harsh, professional soldiers with horses and
firearms, but also psychologically. The cosmological fatalism of many Indians was no match for the Castilians' sense of their own superiority,
rooted in their religion, and their pursuit of rationally chosen goals. The
quintessential act of Spanish colonization was the establishment of a city
under Spanish law with the allocation of properties and Indians to the conquerors. To be sure, the pioneer generation was soon deprived of power
by royal bureaucrats, and contracts with the conquistadors were framed in
such a way as to make clear their subordination to the crown.[7]

*Via the West Indies to the East Indies*
One can see the participation of large European commercial interests not
only in the involvement of the German trading firm of Welser in Venezuela

but also in the attempt, following in Columbus' footsteps, to enter the spice trade by sailing westward from Europe. In 1519 a Hispanicized Portuguese, Fernando de Magellan, began a circumnavigation of the globe with his five ships. Passing through the straits later named after him, he met his death in battle in what were later to be called the Philippines, though one of his ships returned in 1522 with a rich load of spices. Because a repeat voyage was not possible, not even from Mexico, the emperor Charles V, by means of an agreement made at Zaragoza in 1529, sold his highly attractive claims to the Moluccas to Portugal for 350,000 ducats.

The Philippines became a sub-colony of Mexico only in the 1560s, when prices for spices were rising, and when the ideal path for a return voyage to Mexico across the North Pacific was discovered. The islands thus opened a back door to the Asian trade for Spanish America, although less for spices than for silks and other luxury articles from China. For centuries a convoy of "Manila Galleons" made an annual return voyage from Acapulco to Manila.

### 3. "THE LORD OF GUINEA AND INDIA": PORTUGUESE DOMINATION OF THE EASTERN TRADE

#### *Portuguese Power and the Asian Trade*

With the expansion of the king's title to "Lord of Guinea and of the conquest of the navigation and commerce of Ethiopia, Arabia, Persia, and India,"[8] Portugal asserted its claim to the control of traffic in the Indian Ocean and the monopoly on the European supply of spices, all legitimized by the right of conquest in the struggle against the archenemy, the Muslims (*mouros*). The system was based on strings of fortified trading posts between Mozambique and Nagasaki, especially numerous in East Africa, at the entrance to the Persian Gulf, and on the Indian west coast. At Goa, Cochin, Colombo, Malacca, and Macâo, the Portuguese population was sufficiently numerous to be given rights of municipal self-government. At the mouth of the Zambesi River, on the Indian west coast, and in Ceylon, the Portuguese acquired limited territorial possessions, while Goa housed the fiscal bureaucracy and the superior court as well as the nearly omnipotent viceroy. In their other Asian outposts, the Portuguese establishments lived under a "captain [*capitâo*]" as governor, a "factor [*feitor*]" for business operations, and a "judge [*ouvidor*]" for justice. East of Malacca, the commander (*capitâo mor*) of the current royal convoy to the Moluccan Islands, the Banda Islands, and Japan possessed an authority that competed with that of local governors. The Portuguese attempted to impose a system of passes (*cartazas*) that obligated foreign ships to put in at Portuguese ports and pay tolls. Prior to the advent of the ground rent and taxes, these tolls formed an important contribution to the self-financing of the system. More important still was the trade between places within Asia, later known as the "country trade." The Portuguese traded Japanese gold and copper, later also Persian silver, for spices, Indian cotton goods, and Chinese silks, and they also sold Persian horses to the Hindu kingdom of Vijayanagar. In addition, gold from southeast Africa flowed through Portuguese commerce in the Indian Ocean. Hence the value of goods brought from Portugal by the great convoys, constituted only a fraction of the turnover of this trading system.

An outward-bound voyage, known as a *carreira da India*, was organized and financed chiefly by the Crown, through the *Casa da India* in Lisbon and through royal "factors [*feitores*]" in Africa and Asia. The Crown monopoly of the India trade lasted from 1506 to 1570. From 1570 to 1597 there were monopoly contracts with German-Italian consortia that operated within the royal system but assumed the financing and risks. When large-scale private investment was no longer to be found, the Crown had to rely on compulsory contributions by the Portuguese cities. During the sixteenth century four to eight ships of 400 to 2,000 tons made annual voyages to India on a schedule dictated by the monsoons on the Indian Ocean. A voyage in one direction could last as long as nine months, with average losses of 10% to 20% for ships, and 40% to 50% for the crews. The compensation for such losses was paid by the cargoes, which the factors collected for the convoys: a calculation in 1558 estimated a profit of 152% for pepper, after deducting costs of 88.8%.[9] Since revenues and profits from the *Estado da India* in Asia could not cover the purchase price of trade goods, the fleets from Portugal brought gold coins and copper, and, from the second half of the century, silver from Spanish America.

### Colonial Society and Religion

The adult male population of Portuguese descent in Portuguese Asia probably never exceeded 14,000 persons. Since Portuguese women seldom came to India, relations with baptized Indian women were promoted, giving rise to a Eurasian population and culture, which helped to make Portuguese the *lingua franca* of the Orient. Admittedly, women of light color were especially esteemed; in contrast to attitudes still prevalent at the beginning of the sixteenth century, darker women came to be considered inferior. Color lines also established themselves among the clergy of the Portuguese colonial world.

The financing and control of local ecclesiastical institutions as well as missionary enterprises formed a part of the Crown's rights of patronage over the Church. The Inquisition, which also stood under royal authority, enforced orthodoxy and sound morals, but also the royal prerogative. Goa became an archdiocese with three or four suffragan dioceses in India and others at Macâo in China and Funai in Japan. The missions, which extended widely beyond the Portuguese sphere of influence, were the concern of the Jesuits since Francis Xavier. He was a Spaniard, and many of the other "Portuguese" Jesuits were in fact of Italian, German, or Dutch origin. Their attempts to adapt their message to the Japanese, Chinese, and Hindu cultures are noteworthy, for in China and India their efforts produced an intensive encounter with native thought. In Japan their efforts were ultimately blocked by a political reaction in 1639, which almost completely closed the country to foreigners. In China and India, on the other hand, the Jesuits' undertaking was eventually frustrated by the cultural ethnocentrism of their own church.

### 4. SPANISH COLONIAL DOMINION

*Spanish Dominion and the Church*

The Castilian Crown, like its Portuguese counterpart, originally based its claims to dominion on papal authority, the bull of 1493, and then, as time went by, on a more general appeal to its duty to spread the Christian faith. Indeed, the *conquista* in the Americas provided the Catholic Church with the greatest growth in its history. Spanish America was officially not a colony, for "las Indias" were dependencies of the monarchy enjoying Spanish rights and governed by viceroys, much like Aragon or Naples. The Indian subjects, of course, did not enjoy rights equal to those of Spaniards, but this situation—a uniformity of rights among kingdoms, but not among their subjects—was an old story in the Iberian *reconquista*. The administrative and legal basis of Spanish America consisted of about 200 municipalities, plus the corresponding communities of Christianized Indians, for, as in Castile, the "city"—the city and its district—formed the primary unit of organization. And, again as in Castile, the municipal oligarchies enjoyed a measure of self-government under the authority of royal bailiffs (*corregidores*). On this municipal basis arose the five pillars of the Spanish colonial system: thirty-to-forty governors (*gobernadores*); ten collegial courts (*audencias*) of justice; the regional military commands (*capitanes generales*); the royal treasury offices (*cajas reales*) in the principal cities; and the thirty-to-forty bishops, whose dioceses were organized into five ecclesiastical provinces. The system was less orderly than this description suggests, for the boundaries of the different administrative districts did not coincide. Some coordination of the five institutions nevertheless was possible, for the viceroys and some governors simultaneously served as presidents of *audiencias* and as military commanders (*capitanes generales*). Yet the viceroys had no authority over any other sector or institution, since the heads of each sector of colonial administration reported directly to the Council of the Indies in Madrid, the supreme authority for all sectors of administration.

The Church was also subordinate to the Crown, a condition confirmed by the papal grant of "royal patronage [*patronado real*]" to the Catholic Kings. The Crown created dioceses and parishes and levied the church tithe, and in return it assumed responsibility to support the hierarchy and the Christian missions. Thousands of Franciscans, Dominicans, Jesuits, and members of other orders came to America at royal expense as missionaries to the Indians. Missions served not least of all to secure the empire's borders, and the chains of missions in California and Paraguay are only the best known frontier establishments of this type.

### Society and the Indians

As defenders of the Indians, the missionaries always attempted to influence royal policy toward them. The great polemic poured forth by Bartolomé de las Casas, a Dominican, has defined until the present day the negative image—called "the Black Legend"—of Spanish colonial domination and exploitation.[10] Spanish policy toward the Indians suffered from an insurmountable contradiction, for though the Crown displayed, on the one hand, a sincere interest in the welfare of its Indian subjects and sought to promote their Christianization and Hispanization, both its ability and its willingness to undertake these tasks depended on royal profits from the American colonies. This situation forced the Crown to place the Spanish settlers' interests above those of the Indians and resulted in discrimination against and exploitation of the Indians.

During the sixteenth century about 300,000 Spaniards emigrated to America, a considerable number of whom were women. Many settlers, the bulk of whom came from the southern and western parts of Castile, were unprepared to perform manual labor, and none of them wanted to be farmers, so despicable had the status of the farmer become in Castile itself.

Consequently, Indian labor became perforce the basis of agriculture and mining. Rather than allow the Indians to be made chattel slaves, the Crown introduced the *encomienda*, the allotment to a Spaniard of groups of Indian laborers forcibly recruited in exchange for a livelihood, wages, and education in Christianity. Because this system was brutally exploitative, and because the Crown wished to avoid the rise of a new feudal system in America, allocation of the *encomiendas* was divorced from the allocation of land, on the holding of which the Crown initially placed limits. Finally, the *encomienda* was transformed into a temporary transfer of the tribute owed the Crown by specific groups of native subjects, whom the *encomiendero* was forbidden personally to visit.

These changes were consistent with a policy of "separate development," which arose in the sixteenth century out of the negative consequences of permitting Spaniards and Indians to live alongside each other, and for the purpose of better control. Thorough Hispanization was reduced to a long-term aim. The Indians were resettled in *reducciones*, planned along the lines of the Spanish colonial cities, to which no Spaniard, apart from officials and priests, was admitted. There was, in fact, no Indian clergy. Once the authorities became aware of how easily the Indians combined Christianity with their traditional beliefs, they deprived the Indians of some of the rights of "normal" Christians. The compensation for this "weakness of faith," on the other hand, was the Indians' exemption from the Inquisition, which dealt with heretics and *conversos*, as in Spain, though there since the mid-sixteenth century it concentrated increasingly on moral offenders.

The resettlement measures were made easier by the catastrophic dying off, that succeeded the Spanish *conquista*. Precise information about this is, to be sure, unobtainable, for the population levels previous to the arrival of the Spanish are unknown. On Haiti the Indians died out after a few years, while in central Mexico during the period 1519-1605 their numbers decreased from some 25 million to about 1 million and in Peru between 1520 and 1620 from 9 million to 670,000. At a minimum, the losses may be estimated at two-thirds of the pre-contact population.[11] Deaths during the *conquista* from killing and disruption aside, the great agents of death were the contagious diseases of the Old World, against which the Indians had no built-up immunity.[12]

The ultimate result of the process of conquista was a racially stratified society, though the idea of race was not, as in modern times, based on biological descent but on color and culture, primarily language. On the highest rung stood the European-born Spaniards, followed by whites who had been born in America (*creoles*), people of mixed race (*mestizos*), and In-

dian chieftains. Next came the bulk of the Indian population, and finally
the imported Africans.

### Economic Policy and Development in Spanish America

The goal of Spanish economic policy was to supply the royal government
with income to support its projects in Europe, a policy which has been
called "fiscalist." Part of this policy consisted of the leasing of royal monopolies, especially the regalian mining prerogative and the mercury monopoly, the royal salt prerogative, and the tobacco monopoly. The Crown
also attempted to prevent production in the colonies of finished goods produced in the mother country, for instance, in the wine and liquor and textile industries, though with only limited success. All this served purely fiscal purposes and lacked any hint of the policy of centrally steered
development, known as "mercantilism," which was later to become common among European states.

Spanish America imported wine, liquor, textiles, and metalwares from
Europe, but it also developed colonial industries, not only to supply domestic needs but also to supply an intense interregional trade. Much of the
demand developed from the capital cities, Mexico City and Lima, and especially from the great mining centers of Zacatecas and Potosí, a city almost 4,000 meters above sea level. Large textile factories (*obrajes*) arose in
Ecuador and Mexico, whose laborers, as well as those in the mines, were
obtained in Mexico through the free market, but in Peru under the Inca
system of forced labor (*mita*) and through the *encomienda*.

The pivot points of the system lay in the mines for precious metals in the
highlands of Peru and Mexico. They, in turn, depended on mercury from
Peru and Europe, which was used to extract silver through the amalgamation process. The Crown leased its mining prerogative to entrepreneurs for
whom, in addition, they obtained forced labor in Peru. The miners
worked and lived in terrible conditions, though some of them were able to
free themselves from forced labor or to become mining entrepreneurs
themselves. The Crown's share of the silver and the tax revenues, so far as
they were not required to pay for the expenses of government in America,
flowed to Spain as "crown silver," together with the "private silver," payments for imports, and other transfers. By comparison with this river of
silver, Spanish America's other exports were of little economic consequence.

The Spanish voyages to America took the form of royal convoys, which
were organized monopolistically by the royal trade organization, the *Casa
de la Contratación* at Seville, which lay in the hands of privileged Castilian

merchants. Once a year the Mexico fleet sailed under escort for Veracruz and the Peru fleet for Nombre de Dios on the Isthmus of Panama. The voyage westward took eighty days, the return trip one hundred-twenty. Averaged over the long term, seventy-three ships per year sailed for America, and fifty per year sailed for home—silver was less bulky than the European commodities. The scale of smuggling, however, was so large —the mouth of the La Plata was especially notorious—that all figures about the American trade must be regarded as incomplete.

### 5. Europe, Africa, America—The Beginnings of the Triangular Trade

The supply of labor formed the central problem of the colonial economy in Spanish America, since most of the European settlers would not do heavy labor in the mines and in agriculture. In the highland regions, where the indigenous civilizations had employed forced labor, the Spanish had success with the same methods, but hardly any with the "savages" of the islands and the tropical lowlands. Las Casas had already given the advice, which he later regretted, that the demand for labor should be satisfied by importation of African slaves, who were better suited for heavy labor in a tropical climate. In fact, a few areas of Spanish America, plus many of the American regions seized by other European powers, first entered the world market by means of enslaved Africans, who produced agricultural goods of high quality on American plantations. Although this "plantation America" reached its peak in the eighteenth century, its beginnings lay in the sixteenth and its roots in the Mediterranean of the Middle Ages.

Brazil received its name from a red dye-wood found there, which was exported to Portugal under a royal chartered monopoly. Because Brazil's longitude could not be determined precisely, Portugal could maintain its claims to the land in spite of the fact that much of the hinterland lay in the Spanish zone of acquisition. French activity on the coast induced the Portuguese Crown to engage in a not particularly successful attempt to open the interior to private development by leasing territory. Although an official colony was founded at Bahia with capital city of Bahia (1548) and a diocese (1551), Brazil remained in the shadow of the East Indian empire until the end of the sixteenth century. Then, however, as Portuguese Asia declined, Brazil became the more valuable imperial sector, since it had meanwhile developed its sugar industry. Because the growing of sugar cane quickly exhausted the soils, it paid to transfer the production of sugar from the Atlantic Islands to Brazil, where enough land was available in a favorable climate. The first sugar mill was built in 1533, and by 1610 there were already 210, concentrated primarily in the area of Pernambuco. By this time Brazil's sugar exports had reached the level of 8,050 metric tons.[13]

The growth of the sugar industry would have been impossible without the labor of Africans, who had been imported to Brazil since about 1570. At the beginning of the seventeenth century 10,000 to 15,000 Africans were being brought annually from Africa to Brazil. At first Portugal maintained a monopolistic hold on the African slave trade, the centers of which shifted from the Guinea coast and the Congo to Angola where Luanda, founded in 1575, developed into the chief slave market. The symbiosis of sugar and African labor was so close that Angola developed into a subcolony of Brazil.

## 6. Markets and Monarchs in Europe

### European Politics and the Spanish Economy

The Iberian monarchs were interested in commerce not for its own sake but only to fill their own coffers, and the Spanish kings' main goal, the expansion of their power in Europe, eventually exercised a ruinous effect on the Spanish economy. In spite of the flow of American silver, state fiscal crises followed one another regularly in 1557, 1575, 1596, 1607. On the other hand, if politics took little notice of commerce, commerce could also undermine politics. The Spanish merchants at Seville became purely front men for foreign suppliers of trade goods for America, especially the Netherlanders, who continued to supply Spain with guns and materials for shipbuilding, the Dutch revolt against the Crown notwithstanding. The Netherlands needed the Spanish silver not only to lubricate their flourishing commerce but also to finance their war precisely against Spain. But when King Philip II of Spain personally united Portugal and its colonies with Spain in 1580, Indian spices and Brazilian sugar, in the marketing of which the Dutch long had been involved, came under the control of their enemy.

### Marketing Asian Spices in Europe

The Portuguese initially marketed their spices at Antwerp, later at Lisbon itself. After 1570 the same foreign cartels that had contracted with the Crown to deliver the spices from India, committed themselves via further contracts to purchase the spices in Lisbon at a fixed price. They thus had to speculate on the prices on the wider European market, since they could recoup their outlays and protect themselves against risks only by the resale of spices to other European merchants. In any case, in addition to the newer market sector based on Antwerp and Lisbon, the traditional spice trade via the Levant stabilized by the middle of the sixteenth century, when it was not much troubled by conflicts between Venice and the Ottomans. The Portuguese kept the Strait of Hormuz and the Persian Gulf open and engaged in extensive smuggling of spices to Egypt. If Lisbon dropped out of the market, northern European buyers could also fill their needs in the Levant.

### American Silver and the European "Price Revolution"

Already in the sixteenth century, thoughtful observers noted a connection between rising silver imports from America and inflation of prices in Europe, especially Spain. They identified the growth in the supply of money as a cause of the inflation. Modern scholars have pointed to the decrease in the production of silver in Potosí and, especially to the decrease of the silver imports registered in Spain, as causes of the "Crisis of the Seventeenth Century." Still more recently, it has been shown that the silver imports were not so much decreased as disguised, and that inflation in Europe had already begun before silver was exported from America. It also appears probable that price movements depended not only on the quantity of money, but, above all, on the increase in population and the consequent growth of demand. There was also an indirect increase in the money supply, of course, because of an increased speed in the circulation of money and expansion of the volume of credit.

Because the Spanish Crown spent so much on war, American treasure flowed quickly out of Spain during the second half of the sixteenth century, mainly to the Genoese, whose banking institutions had developed into Spanish Crown's most important creditors. It then flowed more and more toward the hostile city of Amsterdam, which in the seventeenth century became the hub and financial capital of international commerce. So much Crown and private silver was paid out in Spain that the rate of inflation increased, the closer one came to the starting point of the flow of silver at Seville. Because costs in Spain were affected by this inflation, it was both cheaper for the Spanish and more profitable for the Dutch, French, and others to export to America goods manufactured outside Spain. This economic mechanism, together with the strains of power politics and the excessive taxation of agriculture in Spain, the population losses caused by

epidemics, and the aristocratic military mentality, contributed to the economic stagnation of a country that was apparently privileged by its possession of great colonial wealth. The silver which flowed out of Spain did not
remain in the receiving lands but was used to compensate for their trade
deficit with Eastern Europe, on the one hand, and India and East Asia, on
the other. Like the Portuguese had done, the Dutch and the English paid
for Asian goods mainly with Spanish silver. A global system of payment
emerged, in which silver moved from Latin America via the Philippines
and Europe to India and China, where silver commanded the highest
prices. Given these facts, it is worth considering to what extent cheap
money in northwestern Europe depressed the rate of interest there and thus
contributed to economic and political growth through favorable terms of
credit.

## 7. Competition from the North

*Beyond the Iberian Monopoly: the French, the English, and the Dutch*
Iberia's connection with the commerce of the Mediterranean basin, the
*reconquista*, and the peninsula's favorable geographical situations probably do not wholly suffice to explain why sixteenth-century Spain and Portugal took the lead in seaborne imperial expansion. The roles of the respective monarchies were, of course, very important. By contrast, the
monarchy in France was long paralyzed by the religious wars, and in England by the weakness of English financial institutions. Thus, successes
achieved by the numerous French and English monopoly breakers and
"freebooters," however spectacular, could not be turned to permanent advantage for those countries. This applied to the French establishment in
1555-60 in Rio de Janeiro and the French foot-holds in Florida from 1562-
65, as well as to such enterprises as Drake's raids, Hawkins' slave trade,
and Raleigh's conquistador-like behavior. From such operations emerged
the maxim "no peace beyond the line," according to which the constant
guerilla war south of the Tropic of Cancer and west of the Line of
Tordesillas would not become a *casus belli* in Europe. The Dutch, on the
other hand, profited indirectly as subjects, and later as business partners,
from the Spanish empire, just as they had through direct trade with Portugal. Why should they have ventured their own oceanic expansion under
such favorable circumstances? Admittedly, the confessional conflict played
a role, but seldom was it decisive.

*Founding of the East India Companies*

But after the personal union of the Portuguese and Spanish crowns in 1580, when Philip II threatened to force the Dutch out of the spice trade not through an embargo but through his contracts with the Germans and Italians, the Dutch sought a direct access to the sites of spice production. Because of their effective commercial espionage, the Dutch were able to concentrate the voyages they began in 1595 on spice markets in Java, where the lack of a Portuguese presence enabled them to avoid costly conflicts. Since the different Dutch companies competed against one another, they were amalgamated into the "United East India Company" (V.O.C.) in 1602 with over fifteen hundred shareholders and an equity of 6.4 million guilders.

English merchants were more rigidly excluded from the Iberian markets. Nevertheless, the chartered Levant Company could cover its demand for spices and other Asian goods at Aleppo, until the first Dutch voyages to the East Indies destabilized this market. The London merchants of the Levant Company then decided to undertake their own voyages to India, and in 1600 the English East India Company (later E.I.C.) received a royal charter. Their equity, however, amounted to an eighth of that of their Dutch counterpart, and the English company's success during the seventeenth century was much more modest than that of the V.O.C. Conflicts between the two companies, such as those on Amboina in 1623, always ended in Dutch victories. In keeping with northern European commercial traditions, the English company was initially only a temporary formation, but in time, as it came to possess monopolistic rights, such as exercising dominion, building forts, conducting wars, and concluding treaties, it too became a permanent joint-stock company of a modern type, like the V.O.C. These novel organizations brought forth a new type of colonial policy with capital accumulated on a previously unknown scale and of a strict commercial rationality that directed all activities toward the increase of profit. In contrast to the Iberian *fidalgos* and *hidalgos*, fame, conquest, and religious conversion counted next to nothing for these merchants. Discoveries which could not be exploited, such as Australia and New Zealand, were ignored.

*Dutch Domination of the Asian Trade*

Before the twelve-year truce with Spain began in 1609, the Dutch drove the Portuguese out of the Moluccas, Amboina, and the Banda Islands, which gave them a monopoly on nutmeg and cloves. In 1619 they began building their trading center in Jakarta, called Batavia, on the island of

Java, and established trading posts for textiles on the Indian coast and for coffee in Yemen. The Dutch also took over permanently the role of exclusive foreign trading partner to Japan, now closing itself in isolation. Then, when the truce with Spain expired in 1621, a European war of global extent began. The Spanish fought the Dutch at sea and in the European markets, where at first they were quite successful. The Dutch counterattacked by seizing the overseas possessions not of Spain, but of Portugal, which were poorly defended and were of much greater commercial interest. Characteristically, they did not cease this campaign at the separation of Portugal from Spain in 1640. In the period from 1636 to 1658 they conquered the coast of Ceylon. Malacca fell in 1641. Macâo, attacked in 1622, held its ground but remained isolated, especially after the Dutch occupied Formosa (Taiwan) in 1624-61. From 1647 to 1663 all the important Portuguese possessions in the Indian Peninsula were seized by the Dutch, except for Goa, which was isolated by a naval blockade. The Portuguese domination of the sea and trade in the East was replaced by power of the Dutch.

### Settlers in America

With a Dutch "West India Company," (W.I.C.) established for this purpose, the Dutch also carried the offensive in 1621 to the Americas, where the Portuguese, again, were the main target. With the conquest of Brazil the Dutch aimed to seize complete control of the sugar trade, in which they were already involved. From 1630 to 1652 a Dutch colony existed in the northern part of Brazil around Recife, but it could not be maintained any more than could Dutch Luanda, which had been conquered in 1644 for the purpose of controlling the supply of slaves. On the other hand, the Dutch did maintain themselves on the coast of Guinea, where they had seized Elmina in 1637. From Brazil, where they had learned the operation of sugar production, the Dutch spread the monoculture of sugar with slave labor to various islands in the West Indies, which they, the English, and the French had seized since 1623 in the wake of the European war. Now, as sugar and slave traders, the Dutch could develop the West Indian triangular trade in competition with Brazil, where they had lost their foothold. This trade triangle was taken to its peak by the French and English in the eighteenth century: European goods to Africa, black slaves to the West Indies, and sugar to Europe.

The situation in North America was very different, for the major trade involved beaver pelts to make hats for European gentlemen. Since the beginning of the seventeenth century a colony of the Dutch W.I.C. existed in the Hudson valley, later New York, and a French colony in New France on the St. Lawrence River. Supplying this trade led to bloody wars among the native peoples, and the numbers of European settlers in these colonies grew slowly. Around 1645 New France had around 300 inhabitants, while on the Hudson there were at least 4,000 Europeans.

These Dutch and French establishments were trading stations, quite unlike the settler colonies established by the English in North America in this era (Virginia in 1607, Plymouth in 1620 as the forerunner of Massachusetts). Indeed, in English North America the initiative came not from the penurious Crown but from chartered commercial companies. That they survived and became powerful, unlike their predecessors, is to be traced primarily to a tobacco boom that gave Virginia a large clientele, whereas New England became a place of refuge for radical Protestants fleeing religious persecution in England. In 1650 these colonies together numbered 42,000 whites and 1,100 blacks. Nevertheless, if one compares this number with the 10 million in Spanish America, or the commercial intentions of the English colonists with the huge profits of the Dutch trading empire, one could hardly have predicted that the future lay more with these settler colonies than with the vast trade empires.

Translated by Henry Jansen and Thomas A. Brady, Jr.

# NOTES

1.  Lopez (1971); Abu Lughod (1989).
2.  Burns (1973); Goss (1986).
3.  The classic analysis of motives is by the Portuguese royal historiographer, Gomes Eanes de Zurara (1410?-73/4), in *The Chronicle of the Discovery and Conquest of Guinea*, trans. Charles Raymond Beazley and Edgar Prestage, 2 vols., Hakluyt Society, Works, vols. 95, 100 (London, 1896-99; Reprint, New York, 1963), vol. 1:7. Gomes Eanes Zurara, *Crónica do descobrimento e conquista da Guiné*, ed. José de Braganza, 2 vols. (Oporto, 1937), provides the text in Portuguese.
4.  Jadin and Dicorato (1974).
5.  *Mundus novus* (Paris, 1503/4).
6.  Todorov (1984).
7.  Pietschmann (1987), 249-62.
8.  Boxer (1969 [1977]), 37.
9.  Godinho (1984-86), vol.2: 47. Much of the Portuguese archives was destroyed in 1755.
10. See Maltby (1971).
11. McAlister (1984), 83-85, 118-21.
12. Because the Spanish, despite their atrocities during the *conquista*, never intended to exterminate the Indians, the use of the term "genocide," with its echoes of the twentieth-century Holocaust, seems inappropriate.
13. Phillips (1990), 56.

# BIBLIOGRAPHY

Abu Lughod, Janet L. *Before European Hegemony: the World System, A.D. 1250-1350*. New York, 1989.

Albuquerque, Affonso de. *Cartas de Affonso de Albuquerque seguidas de documentos que as elucidam. Collecçâo de monumentos ineditos para a historia das conquistas dos portuguezes*, I. *História da Asia*, vols. 10, 12-17. Lisbon, 1884-1935. Reprinted, 1976.

Andrews, Charles. *The Colonial Period of American History*. 4 vols. New Haven, 1934-38.

Andrews, Kenneth R. *Trade, Plunder and Settlement: Maritime Enterprise and the Genesis of the British Empire, 1480-1630*. Cambridge, 1984.

Bakewell, Peter. *Silver Mining and Society in Colonial Mexico: Zacatecas 1546-1700*. Cambridge, 1971.

Barros, Joâo de. *Asia. Dos feitos que os Portuguezes fizerem no descubrimento e conquista dos mares e terras de Oriente*. 4 vols. Ed. Hernani Cidade and Manuel Múrias. Lisbon, 1945.

Bitterli, Urs. *Die Entdeckung Amerikas von Kolumbus bis Alexander von Humboldt*. Munich, 1991.

Boxer, Charles R. *The Christian Century in Japan, 1549-1650*. Berkeley and Los Angeles, 1951. Reprint, 1974.

Boxer, Charles R. *The Dutch in Brazil, 1624-1654*. Oxford, 1957. Reprint, 1973.

Boxer, Charles R. *The Dutch Seaborne Empire, 1600-1800*. London, 1965.

Boxer, Charles R. *The Portuguese Seaborne Empire, 1415-1825*. London, 1969. Reprint, 1977.

Boxer, Charles R. *Portuguese Society in the Tropics: the Municipal Councils of Goa, Macao, Bahia and Luanda, 1510-1800*. Madison, Wisc., 1965.

Boxer, Charles R. *Race Relations in the Portuguese Empire, 1415-1825*. New York, 1963.

Brading, David A., and Harry E. Cross. "Colonial Silver Mining: Mexico and Peru." *HAHR* 52 (1972): 545-79.

Bridenbaugh, Carl. *Vexed and Troubled Englishmen, 1590 to 1642*. 2d ed. New York, 1967.

Burns, Robert I., S.J. *Islam under the Crusaders: Colonial Survival in the Thirteenth-Century Kingdom of Valencia*. Princeton, 1973.

*Calendar of State Papers. Colonial Series*. 8 vols. London, 1860-1892. Reprint, 1964.

*The Cambridge History of India*. Vol. 5, *British India, 1497-1858*. Cambridge, 1929. Reprint, 1968.

*The Cambridge History of Latin America*. Vols. 1-2. Cambridge, 1988-89.

Chaudhuri, Kirti N. *The English East India Company: the Study of an Early Joint-Stock Company, 1600-1640*. London, 1965.

Chaudhuri, Kirti N. *Trade and Civilization in the Indian Ocean: an Economic History from the Rise of Islam to 1750*. Cambridge, 1985.

Chaunu, Pierre. *Les Philippines et le Pacifique des Ibériques (XVIe-XVIIe siècle)*. 2 vols. Paris, 1960-66.

Chaunu, Pierre. *Séville et l'Amérique aux XVIe et XVIIe siècles*. Paris, 1977.

Chaunu, Pierre, and Huguette Chaunu. *Séville et l'Atlantique (1504-1650)*. 11 vols. Paris, 1955-60.

Correia-Afonso, John, ed. *Indo-Portuguese History. Sources and Problems.* Bombay, 1981.

Cortés, Fernando. "Cartas de relación de Fernando Cortés sobre el descubrimiento y conquista de la Nueva España." In *Historiadores primitivos de Indias.* ed. Enrique de Vedia, vol. 1:1-153. Biblioteca de Autores españoles, vol. 22. Madrid, 1918.

Crosby, Alfred W. *Ecological Imperialism: the Biological Expansion of Europe, 900-1900.* Cambridge, 1986.

Danvers, Frederick C. *The Portuguese in India.* Vols. 1-2. London, 1894. Reprint, 1966.

Diaz del Castillo, Bernal. "Verdadera Historia de los Sucesos de la Conquista de la Nueva-España." In *Historiadores primitivos de Indias,* ed. Enrique de Vedia, vol. 2:1-317. Biblioteca de Autores españoles vol. 26. Madrid, 1923.

Diffie, Bailey W., and George D. Winius. *Foundations of the Portuguese Empire, 1415-1580.* Europe and the World in the Age of Expansion, vol. 1. Minneapolis, 1977.

*Dutch Asiatic Shipping in the 17th and 18th Centuries.* 3 vols. Rijks geschiedkundigepublicatiën, grote serie, ed. Femme S. Gaastra, J. R. Bruijn, and Ivo Schöffer, vols. 165-167. The Hague, 1979-87.

Fernández-Armesto, Felipe. *Before Columbus: Exploration and Colonization from the Mediterranean to the Atlantic, 1229-1492.* Basingstoke and London, 1987.

Friede, Juan and Benjamin Keen, eds. *Bartolomé de las Casas in History.* Dekalb, Ill., 1971.

Furber, Holden. *Rival Empires of Trade in the Orient, 1600-1800.* Europe and the World in the Age of Expansion, vol. 2. Minneapolis, 1976.

Gaastra, Femme S. "Die Vereinigte Ostindische Compagnie der Niederlande. Ein Abriß ihrer Geschichte." In *Kaufleute als Kolonialherren: Die Handelswelt der Niederländer vom Kap der Guten Hoffnung bis Nagasaki, 1600-1800,* ed. Eberhard Schmitt, Thomas Schleich, and Thomas Beck, 1-89. Bamberg, 1988.

Garcia, Albert. *La découverte et la conquête du Pérou d'après les sources originales.* Paris, 1975.

*Generale Missiven van Gouverneurs-General en Raaden aan Heren XVII der Verenigde Oostindische Compagnie.* Vol. 1. Ed. Willem P. Coolhaas. Rijks geschiedkundige publicatiën, grote serie, vol. 104. The Hague, 1960.

Gibson, Charles. *The Aztecs under Spanish Rule: a History of the Indians of the Valley of Mexico, 1519-1810.* Stanford, 1964.

Glamann, Kristof. *Dutch Asiatic Trade, 1620-1740.* Copenhagen and The Hague, 1958.

Godinho, Vitorino Magalhaes. *Os descobrimentos e a economia mundial.* Vols. 1-4. 2d ed. Lisbon, 1984-86.

Goslinga, Cornelis C. *The Dutch in the Caribbean and on the Wild Coast, 1580-1680.* Assen, 1971.

Goss, Vladimir P., ed. *The Meeting of Two Worlds: Cultural Exchange between East and West during the Period of the Crusades.* Kalamazoo, Mich., 1986.

Hamilton, Earl J. *American Treasure and the Price Revolution in Spain, 1501-1650.* Cambridge, Mass., 1934.

Henze, Dietmar. *Enzyklopädie der Entdecker und Erforscher der Erde.* Vol. 1. Graz, 1978- .

*Historia de América y de los Pueblos Américanos.* 28 vols. Barcelona, 1945-65.

Israel, Jonathan I. *Dutch Primacy in World Trade 1585-1740.* Oxford, 1989.

Israel, Jonathan I. *The Dutch Republic and the Hispanic World, 1606-1661.* Oxford, 1982.

Israel, Jonathan I. *Empire and Entrepots: the Dutch, the Spanish Monarchy and the Jews, 1585-1713.* London, 1990.

Jadin, Louis, and Mireille Dicorato, eds. *Correspondance de Dom Afonso, roi du Congo, 1506-1534.* Brussels, 1974.

Jensen, Merrill, ed. *American Colonial Documents.* English Historical Documents, vol. 9. London, 1955.

Kellenbenz, Hermann, ed. *Precious Metals in the Age of Expansion.* Beiträge zur Wirtschaftsgeschichte, vol. 2. Stuttgart, 1981.

Kernkamp, J. H. *De handel op den vijand.* 2 vols. Utrecht, 1931-34.
Konetzke, Richard, ed. *Colección de documentos para la historia de la formación social de Hispanoamerica 1493-1810.* Vols. 1-2. Madrid, 1958.
Lach, Donald F. *Asia in the Making of Europe.* Chicago, 1965- .
Lockhart, James. *The Men of Cajamarca: a Social and Biographical Study of the First Conquerors of Peru.* Austin, Tex., 1972.
Lockhart, James. *Spanish Peru, 1532-1560: a Colonial Society.* Madison, Wisc., 1974.
Lockhart, James, and Stuart Schwartz. *Early Latin America: a Short History of Colonial Spanish America and Brazil.* Cambridge, 1983.
Lopetegui, León, Felix Zubillaga, and Antonio de Egaña. *Historia de la Iglesia en la América española. Desde el descubrimiento hasta comienzas del siglo XIX.* Vols. 1-2. Madrid, 1965-66.
Lopez, Robert S. *The Commercial Revolution of the Middle Ages, 950-1350.* London, 1971.
Lorenzo Sanz, Eufemio. *Comercio de España con América en la época de Felipe II.* 2 vols. Valladolid, 1979-80.
McAlister, Lyle N. *Spain and Portugal in the New World, 1492-1700.* Europe and the World in the Age of Expansion, vol. 3. Minneapolis, 1984.
Maltby, William S. *The Black Legend in England.* Durham, N.C., 1971.
Masselman, George. *The Cradle of Colonialism.* New Haven, 1963.
Mauro, Frédéric. *Le Portugal et l'Atlantique au XVIIe siècle, 1570-1670: étude économique.* 2d ed. Paris, 1983.
Meilink-Roelofsz, Maria A. P. *Asian Trade and European Influence in the Malay Archipelago between 1500 and about 1630.* The Hague, 1962.
Morales Padrón, Francisco. *Historia del descubrimiento y conquista de América.* 5th ed. Madrid, 1990.
Morison, Samuel E. *The European Discovery of America.* Vol. 1, *The Northern Voyages, A.D. 500-1600.* Vol. 2, *The Southern Voyages A.D. 1492-1616.* New York, 1971-74.
Phelan, John L. *The Hispanization of the Philippines, 1565-1700.* 2d ed. Madison, Wisc., 1967.
Phelan, John L. *The Millenial Kingdom of the Franciscans in the New World.* 2d ed. Berkeley and Los Angeles, 1970.
Phillips, Carla Rahn. "The Growth and Composition of Trade in the Iberian Empires, 1450-1750." *The Rise of Merchant Empires: Long Distance Trade in the Early Modern World, 1350-1750,* ed. James D. Tracy, 34-101. Cambridge, 1990.
Pieper, Renate. "The Volume of African and American Exports of Precious Metals and Its Effects in Europe, 1500-1800." In: *The European Discovery of the World and Its Economic Effects on Pre-Industrial Society, 1500-1800. Papers of the Tenth International Economic History Congress,* ed. Hans Pohl, 97-117. Vierteljahrsschrift für Sozial- und Wirtschaftsgeschichte, supplement 89. Stuttgart, 1990.
Pietschmann, Horst. "Estado y conquistadores: las capitulaciones." *Historia,* no. 22 ((Santiago de Chile, 1987): 249-62.
Pietschmann, Horst. *Die staatliche Organisation des kolonialen Iberoamerika.* Stuttgart, 1980.
Porras Barrenechea, Raoul. *Los cronistas del Perú, 1528-1650.* Lima, 1962.
Quinn, David B. *North America from the Earliest Discovery to the First Settlements: the Norse Voyages to 1612.* New York, 1978.
Quinn, David B., and A. N. Ryan. *England's Sea Empire, 1550-1642.* London, 1983.
*Recopilación de las Leyes de los Reynos de las Indias.* Madrid, 1681. Reprint. Madrid, 1973.
Reinhard, Wolfgang. *Geschichte der europäischen Expansion.* Vol. 1, *Die alte Welt bis 1818.* Vol. 2, *Die Neue Welt.* Stuttgart, 1983-85.
Schwartzberg, Joseph E. *A Historical Atlas of South Asia.* Chicago, 1978.
Simmons, R. C. *The American Colonies: From Settlement to Independence.* London, 1976.
Stapel, Frederic W. *Geschiedenis van Nederlandsch Indië.* 5 vols. Amsterdam, 1938-40.

TePaske, John J., and Herbert S. Klein. "The 17th-Century Crisis in New Spain: Myth or Reality?" *PaP*, no.90 (1981): 116-35.

Todorov, Tzvetan. *The Conquest of America: the Question of the Other.* New York, 1984.

Tracy, James D., ed. *The Political Economy of Merchant Empires, 1450-1750.* Cambridge, 1991.

Tracy, James D., ed. *The Rise of Merchant Empires: Long Distance Trade in the Early Modern World, 1350-1750.* Cambridge, 1990.

Trigger, Bruce G. *Natives and Newcomers: Canada's "Heroic Age" Reconsidered.* Kingston, Ontario, 1985.

Trudel, Marcel. *The Beginnings of New France, 1524-1663.* Canadian Centenary Series, vol. 2. Toronto, 1973.

Van Dam, Pieter. *Beschryvinge van de Oostindische Compagnie.* Vols. 1-7. Ed. Frederic W. Stapel, et al. Rijks geschiedkundige publicatiën, grote serie, vols. 63, 68, 74, 76, 83, 87, 96. The Hague, 1927-54.

Van Klaveren, Jacob. *Europäische Wirtschaftsgeschichte Spaniens im 16. und 17. Jahrhundert.* Stuttgart, 1960.

Whiteway, Richard S. *The Rise of Portuguese Power in India, 1497-1550.* London, 1899. Reprint, 1967.

Wills, John E. *Pepper, Guns and Parleys: the Dutch East India Company and China, 1622-1681.* Cambridge, Mass., 1974.

Wolff, Inge. *Regierung und Verwaltung der kolonialspanischen Städte in Hochperu 1538-1650.* Cologne and Vienna, 1970.

# CONCLUSION:
## STRUCTURES AND ASSERTIONS

If the fact of being caught up in historical time means anything at all, it means that no generation can judge the validity of its own premises. As historians we cannot function without categories of analysis that give our work a certain focus and direction, but one may always ask whether a given set of polarities should be surmounted in the interest of a unified vision of the past, or retained as valid but separate approaches to an object of study that cannot possibly be grasped from any single perspective. Ultimately this is a judgment to be made not by the editors of this volume, nor by its contributors, but by our readers, especially those who represent the coming scholarly generation. Here it may be useful to offer a comment on two such polarities, one that governed the organization of this volume, and another that has emerged from the state-of-the art contributions of our authors.

Readers will recognize that Parts 1 and 2 roughly correspond to the distinction between *histoire structurelle* and *histoire évenementielle* that was made current in the years following World War II by scholars working in the French *annaliste* tradition.[1] Part 2 deals not with "events" in general but with the concatenations of events we call "assertions"—especially the assertion by national monarchies and terriorial states of new and greater control over their respective lands and subjects. By guiding the discussion in this direction we have intended both to do justice to the central importance of the state for early modern Europe, and to take advantage of the rich traditions of national historiography that remain a constant feature of historical writing about Europe. But this editorial decision has also meant that the "event history" described in many of these essays has a definite "structure," one that is closely tied to the incremental growth of state power and its characteristic instruments, such as law codes, taxation, and armies. Thus Bernard Chevalier shows how a king's choice to go to war could have the effect of preserving "progress towards the consolidation of the French state." David Loades explains that Parliament's role in the king's divorce enabled it to become not just an occasional instrument of royal policy, but "a symbol of the dynastic entente with the political nation of England." Hugo de Schepper makes clear that the network of legal and administrative decisions by which the Netherlands provinces were brought into a closer unity "responded to the requests of subjects, natural persons as well as cities crafts and guilds, and even the provincial estates." Michael Mallett traces the emergence in this period of "a warfare in which infantry had already replaced cavalry as the predominant arm, and the full implications of this in terms of numbers, training, social and cultural realignments, had already been substantially explored." To this development the growing capacity of states to borrow against future revenues, building and servicing sizeable debts, was a necessary precondition (Chapter 17). Cemal Kafadar presents the new empire of Mehmed II—with its "ruthless authoritarianism," its condification of law, and its creation of a new elite—as the foundation upon which subsequent Ottoman conquerors were able to build. Finally, Wolfgang Reinhard illustrates how the Iberian monarchies promoted and in some ways determined the course of overseas economic expansion: the *carreira da India* was for much of the sixteenth century "organized and financed chiefly by the Crown," while the Spanish monarchy's desire to prevent the rise of a new feudalism in America transformed the *encomienda* into a "temporary transfer of the tribute owed the Crown by specific groups of native subjects, whom the *ecomiendero* was forbidden personally to visit."

Conversely, although the notion of "structural history" as originally formulated was often associated with evolutionary models of the development of human societies, or with efforts to identify timeless "substrata" in human culture that were thought to perdure "beneath" more superficial changes, several of the authors in Part 1 present a particularist view of history that is decidedly skeptical of grand theories of whatever ilk. Thus for Merry Wiesner there is little that remains of Le Play's interpretative schema concerning stages of development in the history of the family. Research results do confirm the existence of a "European marriage pattern" in northwestern Europe as early as the fourteenth century, but it is uncertain whether different findings about "individualism" in England and the importance of "das ganze Haus" in Germany reflect actual regional differences, or the assumptions of differing historiographical traditions. For Thomas Robisheaux there has not been a clear resolution of the famous debate about whether capitalistic agriculture can only emerge through the appropriation of peasant land by upper-class land-holders, or whether peasants themselves can make the transition, as they seem to have done in regions with an expanding economic infrastructure. Similarly, the village commune was a strong presence in rural Europe, but not strong enough to prevent the growing violence of village elites against their social inferiors in the later sixteenth century. As for the better known urban communes, Steven Rowan finds that "the organically developed constititions of the High Middle Ages" were undermined both by the fact that princely governments deemed guild representatives not "sufficiently wealthy or sad (sober)" to lend the required dignity to town governments, and by the rise of professional functionaries who themselves "molded" the support they enjoyed from elected officials. Robert Bonfil outlines interesting Jewish variants both on the formation of communal institutions and on the internal tensions that marked the course of their history. The well-organized Jewish communities of Italy had their General Assembly, sometimes a Great Council and a Small Council (as in Venice, paralleling the Senate and the Council of Ten), and registers show the efforts to balance to goals of keeping elections to such bodies "democratic" or popular, while prolonging the "staying power of restricted oligarchies made up of richer and more influential members." Finally, Robert Scribner's caution against thinking that the Reformation brought a radical rupture in folk beliefs is in keeping with a "structuralist" historian's stress on continuity, but he has little patience with the notion of a hard and fast separation between an unchanging folk mentality and the fluid mental world of the elite: "What arises spontaneously can be appropriated officially, while officially created norms and practices can be internalised to the point that they may appear unofficial."

Thus to judge from these essays, it seems that the dichotomy between structure history and event history has been overcome by scholars working from both directions toward a fusion of the strengths of both approaches. Jan de Vries comes closest to making this point explicitly, when he says that "historical demography is a discipline with a hard mathematical core and a soft socio-economic rind;" For example, the cultural norms that governed breast-feeding practices were "far more important than economics, medicine, or social class in determining whether 650 or 450 of every 1000 births would survive childhood." At the same time, the essays presented here also show the importance for scholars of this generation of a more subtle dichotomy, dividing those who choose to emphasize the uniqueness of discrete processes from those who choose to emphasize larger patterns in which discrete processes acquire a greater coherence. The issue seems to be whether the interepretative patterns that are proposed for a particular topic are themselves dependent on a modernization hypothesis that separates peoples and cultures of the past into winners and losers, in a manner that no truly historical sensibility can accept. Thus in the essays by John

Marino and Henry Kamen, the common generalizations about (respectively) Italy and Spain that fall to the ground one after another are in many cases tied to the notion that these two nations were at some point relegated to the rear in the forward march of civilization. Noting that scholars have sometimes seen their own values reflected in a secular and republican Renaissance projected onto a very diverse Italian peninsula, Marino finds in the "local contingencies" of regional history the antidote to a "modernist self-fashioning" that has manipulated "the polyvalent distinctiveness of past events." As for Spain, Kamen concludes that Ferdinand and Isabella were not "modern" rulers bent on reform, that apart from the initial holocaust of Jewish *conversos* "the Inquisition was far from being the terrible instrument" featured in legend, and that the Cortes of Castile under Philip II was a body strongly conscious of its constitutional role, not a rubber stamp. Similarly, in Part 1, Bartolomé Yun and John Munro each deal with trade against a broader economic background, but from quite different perspectives. Munro takes as it were the high road of economic history, focussed on the pattern of events by which trade networks and financial innovations were knitted together, first in Antwerp and then in Amsterdam, giving these Low Countries entrepots each in turn a commercial and banking hegemony that would in the following century pass to London. Yun acknowledges that Amsterdam's economic position during the Dutch Revolt represented "a panorama quite different from that of polynuclear growth" in the late fifteenth century, but even then one cannot speak of "marginalization" of areas outside the favored zone; regional variation is the key, and it cannot be reduced to a single evolution.

The two perspectives might conveniently be labelled "developmentalist" and "polycentrist." To present a developmental view of, for instance, state formation or merchant capitalism is to express an implicit preference for those strands of the story that are more "central," consonant with the fact that in all things human some set a pace that others follow; at a given period, it might be the French monarchy, or the Amsterdam market, or the British Parliament. Conversely, to insist on the autonomy of regional processes—their capacity not to be determined from the center—is also to adopt a relativistic stance consonant with the ebb and flow of all things human: because of its peculiar organization the Amsterdam market may now be dominant, but in time its strengths may seem weaknesses. Thus we began with the belief that a rounded view of early modern Europe required the collaboration of scholars working on the somewhat distinct terrains of event history and structure history, and our collaborators have now shown us, quite without any editorial prompting, that the collaboration of historians representing the complementary perspectives of "development" and "polycentrism" is equally vital.

But collaboration is not the same as integration. Readers will find in these essays hints as to how one might conceive the relation between the general and the particular, including two that seem worth stressing here. First, just as we learn from John Van Engen that it was only the decisive intervention of Emperor Sigismund that enabled the Council to convene at Constance, we learn from Volker Press that Sigismund's presence in that particular corner of the Empire had something to do with his attempts to "rebuild royal influence in the Empire's old core regions of Franconia, Swabia, and the Rhine Valley," rather than making Prague (Kingdom of Bohemia) the seat of his power. It thus becomes necessary to see the Council of Constance a) as in some degree a by-product of political calculations in which the "structure" of the medieval Holy Roman Empire was a given, and b) as a consequence of the papal schism of 1378 and of the failure of previous efforts to overcome it. In fact, any historical conjuncture on which we may choose to focus our attention represents, like the Council of Constance, a layering of structures, strands of development, and particular histories, each of which has its own origins, and all of which are necessary for comprehension of the whole. In terms of scholarly strategies, one may choose to present a rounded picture of the event or process in question, which means sounding the various layers as they impinge on a common point, or to isolate one of the layers amd work out as it were its horizontal connections. The only strategy that is not legitimate is to presume that one layer alone is spun gold, the others mere dross; on such premises one may write fairy tales of the intellect, but not history.

The second interesting suggestion is contained in Van Engen's description of the Council of Constance as the "tone-setting event" in a "drive towards participation" or greater consultative procedures that characterized the fifteenth century Church. A moment's reflection will bring to mind "tone-setting events" touched on by other contributors, like Joan of Arc hailing Charles VII as France's rightful king ("everyone—king, soldiers, politicans—now regained confidence"), or Nicholas V's rebuilding of Rome, "to make Rome a heavenly city, the New Jerusalem of cosmic importance." But even the most dramatic events can only be tone-setting within the framework of a universe of meaning, the formation of which is a matter of centuries rather than of years. Thus a "structure" in the rather loose sense in which historians use the term can also signify a context that gives events their meaning, as well as an instrument within which important events can reverberate. Conversely, there is perhaps no kind of historical event that is more momentous than one that involves a challenge to a long established universe of meaning that is both radical and at least in some degree successful. This judgment expresses in a nutshell the principle the editors have employed in sorting our material out into two volumes. The present volume, *Structures and Assertions*, is intended to describe the reality of late medieval and early modern European life. The forthcoming vol. 2, *Visions, Programs and Outcomes*, is meant to describe efforts to reshape that reality into something quite different.

1. For a programmatic statement, Fernand Braudel, *La Méditerranée et le Monde Méditerranéen a l'époque de Philippe II* (2 vols., 1st édition Paris, 1947-1949), preface to the third part.

# APPENDIX 1: THE COINAGES
# OF RENAISSANCE EUROPE,
# CA. 1500

Before the more widespread diffusion of negotiable credit instruments, early-modern European economies utilized primarily commodity moneys in the form of metallic coinages: gold, silver, and copper. Both the gold and silver coinages were alloyed, in varying degrees, with some copper as a base-metal hardening agent. Alloys with proportionately more copper were also used, rather than just smaller size, to distinguish lower from higher denomination coins.[1] Thus most petty coinages were predominantly copper (hence *base* coinage), some with virtually no silver; but not until 1543 was Europe's first all-copper petty coinage issued, in the Habsburg Netherlands, to mark an important step towards fiat money, i.e. money whose exchange value is established solely by government decree.

European governments, however, also played a crucial role in determining the domestic values of their gold and silver coins, so long as they were able to enforce a monopoly on domestic minting. Through their mint indentures and monetary ordinances, they stipulated the three essential components of all coins struck: the weight or the *taille*, as the number of coins struck from the legal mint-weight; the fineness or alloy; and the exchange rate or "nominal value", expressed in the domestic money-of-account. That nominal money-of-account value had to be greater than the current market value for the coin's bullion contents (its commodity value), in order to cover the costs of minting, in the form of the mint-master's *brassage* fee and the government's *seigniorage* fee. Normally, coins did command such a premium over bullion, because the transaction costs in effecting exchanges were much lower with legal-tender coins, bearing the government's stamp to certify its value, than with raw bullion (especially when trading in bullion was prohibited by law). Most governments also permitted the circulation of certain good-quality foreign gold coins (*not* silver), though at rates that accorded a smaller premium than those enjoyed by domestic coins. If, for any reason, the public lost confidence in the domestic coinage, that coinage would lose its essential premium and the domestic mints would no longer receive any bullion. For then the market values of both bullion and foreign coins would rise proportionally above the values assigned to domestic coins, as expressed in the domestic money-of-account.

Most early-modern moneys-of-account, an accounting system for reckoning and recording coin values, prices, wages, rents, etc., were based on the current domestic silver penny: with 12 pence to the shilling and 20 shillings to the pound (£1 = 20s = 240d). Thus a sum expressed as 6s 8d was always worth 80 currently circulating pennies. When Carolingian officials established this system, c.800, the "pound" was in fact the pound weight of silver, from which 240 pence were meant to be struck; but subsequent changes in coin weights, alloys, and nominal values forever severed that original relationship. Any increase in the coin's *taille* (reducing its weight), nominal value, or its copper alloy (reducing its fineness) constituted a *debasement* that proportionally increased the total money-of-account value of coinage struck from the *pound*, *marc*, or other mint-weight of fine metal. Conversely, any reduction in the *taille* (increasing the coin's weight), its face value, or its copper alloy (increasing the fineness) constituted a *renforcement* (strengthening) that proportionally reduced the total money-of-account value of coinage struck from the *pound*, *marc*, etc. of fine metal. Those relationships, which indicate the total money-of-account or "tale" value of the coinage struck from the legal mint-weight of fine gold or silver (*pound*, *marc*), can be expressed by this formula:[2]

TALE VALUE =

TAILLE (NUMBER STRUCK PER POUND) X COIN'S FACE VALUE/PERCENTAGE FINENESS

The following tables on the leading west European coins in 1500 provide their weights and fineness in modern metric terms, and their official values in terms of three moneys-of-account: the English pound sterling, the Flemish *livre gros* (*pond groot*), and the French *livre tournois*. They also indicate the relative purchasing power of these coins in 1500, expressed in terms of: (1) major consumer goods in the Antwerp-Mechelen-Brussels region of Brabant; and (2) the summer daily wage of an Antwerp master mason. Self-evident from this table is the fact that an Antwerp mason would then have consumed far more North Sea herring than luxury woolens from Ghent, and that gold coins were usually reserved for just very high-value transactions.

1.  England was an exception in doing so by weight alone, so that a farthing weighed 25% of the penny.

2.  The proportional changes in these relationships involve reciprocal values that are expressed by the formula $\Delta$ TV = [1/(1-$\chi$]-1. TV represents the total money-of-account value of coinage struck from the mint-weight of pure metal (silver or gold): $\Delta$ represents percentage change; and $\chi$ represents the percentage reduction of silver (or gold) in the money-of-account unit. As late as 1278, only 242d were being struck to the English Tower Pound (12 oz), which weighed 349.914 grams; in 1500, however, almost double that amount, 450d (though of the same sterling fineness), was struck from the Tower Pound. The mint-weight for both France and the Netherlands was de *marc de Troyes* (8 onces), weighing 244.753 grams. The Cologne *Mark* weighed 233.856 grams; the Florentine *libbra* (12 oncie), 339.542 grams; and the Venetian *marco* (8 oncie), 238.50 grams.

Table 1. A Selection of Gold and Silver Coins Circulating in Western Europe in 1500: Weight, Percentage Fineness and Intrinsic Fine Metal Contents, and their Nominal Values in Flemish (Habsburg Netherlands'), French, and English Moneys-of-Account.

| COIN | Place of Issue | Struck (in this form) during or since | Weight in Grams | Percent Fineness | Grams Fine Metal (Gold or Silver) | Value in pence gros of Flanders[a] | Value in sous tournois of France | Value in pence sterling of England |
|---|---|---|---|---|---|---|---|---|
| **GOLD** | | | | | | | | |
| florin | Florence | 1252 | 3.528 | 97.90[b] | 3.454[b] | 79 | 38.76 | 55 |
| ducat | Venice | 1284 | 3.560 | [99.50[c]] | 3.542[c] | 79 | 38.76 | 55 |
| genovino | Genoa | 1252 | 3.560 | [97.90[b]] | 3.485[b] | 79 | 38.76 | 55 |
| ducat | Hungary | 1308 | 3.536 | [97.90[b]] | 3.462[b] | 79 | 38.76 | 55 |
| Rhenish florin | Germany: Four Electors | 1490 | 3.278 | 77.08 | 2.527 | 58 | 28.76 | 41 |
| postulaat de Bourbon | Liège | 1456-1482 | 2.331 | 62.50 | 1.457 | 32 | 15.28 | 22 |
| cavalier (rijder) | Burgundian Netherlands | 1433-1454 | 3.626 | 99.22 | 3.598 | 79 | 38.76 | 54 |
| lion (leeuw) | Burgundian Netherlands | 1454-1466 | 4.257 | 95.83 | 4.079 | 92 | 45.00 | 63 |
| florin of St Andrew | Burgundian Netherlands | 1466-1496 | 3.399 | 79.17 | 2.691 | 61 | 30.00 | 42 |
| florin of St Philip | Habsburg Netherlands | 1496-1500 | 3.300 | 66.67 | 2.200 | 50 | 24.50 | 36 |
| toison d'or | Habsburg Netherlands | 1496-1500 | 4.490 | 99.17 | 4.453 | 100 | 49.06 | 72 |
| florin of St Philip | Habsburg Netherlands | 1500 | 3.300 | 66.33 | 2.189 | 50 | 24.50 | 36 |
| écu à la couronne | France | 1474 | 3.399 | 96.35 | 3.275 | 71 | 35.00 | 50 |
| écu au soleil | France | 1475 | 3.496 | 96.35 | 3.368 | 74 | 36.26 | 51 |
| Henricus noble | England | 1412-1464 | 6.998 | 99.48 | 6.962 | 153 | 75.00 | 108 |
| angel-noble | England | 1465 | 5.184 | 99.48 | 5.157 | 116 | 56.88 | 80 |
| ryal or rose noble | England | 1465 | 7.776 | 99.48 | 7.736 | 173 | 85.00 | 120 |
| sovereign | England | 1489 | 15.552 | 99.48 | 15.471 | 346 | 170.00 | 240 |
| cruzado | Portugal | 1457 | 3.780 | 98.90 | 3.738 | 84 | 41.00 | 58 |
| florin | Aragon | 1346-1476 | 3.480 | 75.00 | 2.610 | 58 | 28.75 | 40 |
| excelente | Spain | 1497 | 3.780 | 98.90 | 3.738 | 84 | 41.00 | 58 |

| COIN | Place of Issue | Struck (in this form) during or since | Weight in Grams | Percent Fineness | Grams Fine Metal (Gold or Silver) | Value in pence gros of Flanders | Value in sous tournois of France | Value in pence sterling of England |
|---|---|---|---|---|---|---|---|---|
| | | | | | | in d gros | in d tournois | in d sterling |
| **SILVER** | | | | | | | | |
| toison d'argent | Habsburg Netherlands | 1496-1521 | 3.399 | 87.85 | 2.986 | 6.00 | 34.88* | 4.12* |
| stuiver or patard | Habsburg Netherlands | 1496-1521 | 3.098 | 31.94 | 0.990 | 2.00 | 11.63* | 1.38* |
| gros or groot | Habsburg Netherlands | 1496-1521 | 1.827 | 25.95 | 0.474 | 1.00 | 5.81* | 0.69* |
| courte or double mite | Habsburg Netherlands | 1496-1521 | 1.078 | 2.66 | 0.029 | 0.083 (2 mites = 1/12d) | 0.48* | 0.06* |
| groat | England | 1464-1526 | 3.110 | 92.50 | 2.877 | 5.82* | 33.82* | 4.00 |
| penny | England | 1464-1526 | 0.778 | 92.50 | 0.720 | 1.45* | 8.45* | 1.00 |
| halfpenny | England | 1464-1526 | 0.389 | 92.50 | 0.360 | 0.73* | 4.23* | 0.50 |
| gros de roi | France | 1488-1519 | 3.547 | 91.84 | 3.258 | 6.19* | 36.00 | 4.22* |
| grand blanc à la couronne (douzain) | France | 1488-1519 | 2.846 | 35.94 | 1.023 | 2.06* | 12.00 | 1.41* |
| demi-blanc (sizain) | France | 1488-1519 | 1.423 | 35.94 | 0.511 | 1.03* | 6.00 | 0.70* |
| denier tournois | France | 1488-1519 | 0.971 | 8.00 | 0.078 | 0.17* | 1.00 | 0.12* |
| grosso or matapan (= 32 denari piccoli) | Venice | 1421 | 1.600 | 95.20 | 1.523 | 3.07* | 17.87* | 2.12* |
| soldino (= 8 denari piccoli) | Venice | 1421 | 0.400 | 95.20 | 0.381 | 0.77* | 4.47* | 0.53* |
| grosso (of 6s 8d in denaro picciolo) | Florence | 1489 | 2.310 | 95.83 | 2.214 | 4.46* | 26.00* | 3.08* |
| quattrino (4 denari piccioli) | Florence | 1490 | 0.786 | 16.67 | 0.131 | 0.26* | 1.54* | 0.18* |

\* Money-of-account values of silver coins estimated on the basis of relative silver contents.

a. The *livre gros* (*pond groot*) of Flanders was the common money-of-account for the Burgundian and then Habsburg Netherlands (from 1433-34). £1 *livre gros* (= 20s = 240d = 5760 mites) = £1.50 *groot* of Brabant = £12.0 *parisis* (of Flanders). From c.1460 the *gulden* money-of-account (or guilder, based on the 1460 value of the Rhenish florin) = 20 stuivers = 40d gros Flemish = £1.0 Artois.

b. Nominally the Florentine florin was 24 carats fine, i.e. 100% pure gold; but no gold coins were finer than 99.7%. The fineness (and also the weight) of the Florentine florin in this table is taken as the mean fineness of those coins actually struck from 1496 to 1507; and that fineness has been arbitrarily assigned to the Genoese and Hungarian gold coins.

c. The Venetian mint accepted bullion that was 23.5 carats (23 carats 2 grains) or 97.92% fine and further refined it, but probably not beyond 99.5%- 99.7% pure.

Table 2. The Purchasing Power of Selected Gold and Silver Coins and of a Master Mason's Daily Summer Wage in the Antwerp-Mechelen-Brussels Region in 1500.

Relative Quantities of Selected Goods Purchased by the following coins:

| Commodity and Unit (Metric) | Price per Unit in Flemish d gros | Flemish Stuiver (2d gros) | Flemish Florin of St Philip (50d gros) | French écu à la couronne (74d gros) | Italian florin or ducat (79d gros) | English angel-noble (116d gros) | Purchasing Power of Antwerp Masons' Daily Summer Wage (8.33d gros) |
|---|---|---|---|---|---|---|---|
| Rhine Wine, red: liter | 2.46d | 0.81 | 20.29 | 28.80 | 32.05 | 47.06 | 3.38 |
| Butter: kilogram | 2.97d | 0.67 | 16.82 | 23.89 | 26.58 | 39.03 | 2.80 |
| Rye: liter | 0.17d | 11.94 | 298.60 | 424.01 | 471.79 | 692.75 | 49.76 |
| Wheat: liter | 0.25d | 8.00 | 199.86 | 283.80 | 315.78 | 463.68 | 33.31 |
| Peas: liter | 0.25d | 7.86 | 196.59 | 279.16 | 310.61 | 456.09 | 32.76 |
| Beef, salted: kilogram | 1.86d | 1.07 | 26.81 | 38.08 | 42.37 | 62.21 | 4.47 |
| Herrings, smoked red: number | 0.19d | 10.42 | 260.42 | 369.80 | 411.46 | 604.17 | 43.40 |
| Eggs: by number | 0.10d | 20.88 | 521.92 | 741.12 | 824.63 | 1,210.86 | 87.00 |
| Sugar-loaf: kilogram | 8.51d | 0.24 | 5.88 | 8.35 | 9.29 | 13.63 | 0.98 |
| Pepper: kilogram | 78.70d | 0.03 | 0.64 | 0.90 | 1.00 | 1.47 | 0.11 |
| Ginger: kilogram | 36.16d | 0.06 | 1.38 | 1.96 | 2.18 | 3.21 | 0.23 |
| Candles, tallow: kilogram | 4.00d | 0.50 | 12.51 | 17.76 | 19.76 | 29.02 | 2.08 |
| Flax, combed: kilogram | 4.08d | 0.49 | 12.26 | 17.42 | 19.67 | 28.45 | 2.04 |
| Linen sail-cloth: 1 meter long | 4.71d | 0.42 | 10.61 | 15.07 | 16.77 | 24.62 | 1.77 |
| Wool/worsted Cloth, coarse grey, from Weert/Maaseik: 1 meter | 17.27d | 0.12 | 2.90 | 4.11 | 4.58 | 6.72 | 0.48 |

| Commodity and Unit (Metric) | Price per Unit in Flemish d gros | Flemish Stuiver (2d gros) | Flemish Florin of St Philip (50d gros) | French écu à la couronne (74d gros) | Italian florin or ducat (79d gros) | English angel-noble (116d gros) | Purchasing Power of Antwerp Masons' Daily Summer Wage (8.33d gros) |
|---|---|---|---|---|---|---|---|
| Woolen Cloth:* Ghent *Dickedinnen* fine black: 1 meter long by 1.75 m. | 167.62d | 0.01 | 0.30 | 0.42 | 0.47 | 0.69 | 0.05 |
| Woolen Cloth:* Mechelen black *Rooslaken* fine: 1 meter long by 1.75 m. | 110.55d | 0.02 | 0.45 | 0.64 | 0.71 | 1.05 | 0.08 |

\* The Ghent *dickedinnen* woolen broadcloths (made from English Staple wools), fully finished, measured 21.0 by 1.75 meters (30 by 2.5 ells) and cost £14 13 4d gros Flemish. Mechelen's black *Rooslaken* woolen broadcloths, also made from fine English wools, measured 20.67 by 1.75 meters, fully finished, and cost £9 10s 5d gros Flemish.

*Sources*

Bernocchi, Mario, *Le monete della repubblica fiorentina*, Vol. III: *documentazione* (Florence, 1976).

Blanchet, A., and Dieudonné, A., *Manuel de numismatique française*, 2 vols. (Paris, 1916).

Lane, Frederic, and Mueller, Reinhold, *Money and Banking in Medieval and Renaissance Venice*, Vol. I: *Coins and Moneys of Account* (Baltimore and London, 1985).

Munro, John, "Money and Coinage of the Age of Erasmus," in R.A.B. Mynors, D.F.S. Thomson, and W.K. Ferguson, eds., *The Correspondence of Erasmus*, Vol. I: *Letters 1 to 141, 1484 to 1500* (Toronto, 1974), pp. 311-47.

Spufford, Peter, "Coinage and Currency," in M.M. Postan and E.E. Rich, eds., *The Cambridge Economic History of Europe*, Vol. III (Cambridge, 1963), pp. 576-602.

Spufford, Peter, *Handbook of Medieval Exchange* (London, 1986).

Van der Wee, Herman, *The Growth of the Antwerp Market and the European Economy, Fourteenth-Sixteenth Centuries*, Vol. I: *Statistics* (The Hague, 1963).

# APPENDIX 2: EUROPEAN RULERS, 1400-1650

The years given are those of the reign or regency.

## POPES

Martin V (1417-1431) (Oddone Colonna)
Eugenius IV (1431-1447) (Gabriele Condulmer)
Nicholas V (1447-1455) (Tommaso Parentucelli)
Calixtus III (1455-1458) (Alonso de Borja)
Pius II (1458-1464) (Enea Silvio Piccolomini)
Paul II (1464-1471) (Pietro Barbo)
Sixtus IV (1471-1484) (Francesco della Rovere)
Innocent VIII (1484-1492) (Giovanni Battista Cibo)
Alexander VI (1492-1503) (Rodrigo de Borja)
Pius II (1503) (Francesco Todeschini-Piccolomini)
Julius II (1503-1513) (Giuliano della Rovere)
Leo X (1513-1521) (Giovanni de' Medici)
Adrian VI (1522-1523) (Adriaan Floriszn)
Clement VII (1523-1534) (Giulio de' Medici)
Paul III (1534-1549) (Alessandro Farnese)
Julius III (1550-1555) (Giovanni Maria Ciocchi del Monte)
Marcellus II (1555) (Marcello Cervini)
Paul IV (1555-1559) (Gian Pietro Caraffa)
Pius IV (1559-1565) (Giovanni Angelo de' Medici)
St. Pius V (1566-1572) (Antonio Michele Ghisleri)
Gregory XIII (1572-1585) (Ugo Buoncampagni)
Sixtus V (1585-1590) (Felice Peretti)
Urban VII (1590) (Giambattista Castagni)
Gregory XIV (1590-1591) (Niccolò Sfondrati)
Innocent IX (1591) (Gian Antonio Facchinetti)
Clement VIII (1592-1605) (Ippolito Aldobrandini)
Leo XI (1605) (Alessandro de' Medici)
Paul V (1605-1621) (Camillo Borghese)
Gregory XV (1621-1623) (Alessandro Ludovisi)
Urban VIII (1634-1644) (Maffeo Barberini)
Innocent X (1644-1655) (Giambattista Pamfili)

❈ ❈ ❈

## KINGS OF GERMANY AND HOLY ROMAN EMPERORS

*House of Luxemburg*
Sigmund (1410-1437)

*House of Habsburg-Trastámara*
Albert II (1438-1439)
Frederick III (1440-1493)
Maximilian I (1493-1519)
Charles V (1519-1556)
Ferdinand I (1556-1564)
Maximilian II (1564-1576)
Rudolph II (1576-1612)
Matthias (1612-1619)
Ferdinand II (1619-1637)
Ferdinand III (1639-1657)

❈ ❈ ❈

## DUKES OF BURGUNDY

*House of Valois*
Philip "the Bold" (1364-1404)
John "the Fearless" (1404-1419)
Philip "the Good" (1419-1467)
Charles "the Bold" (1467-1477)

*House of Habsburg*
Maximilian I (regent, 1477-1482)
Philip "the Handsome" (1482-1506)
Charles V (1506-1556)
Philip II (1556-1598)
Philip III (1598-1621)
Philip IV (1621-1655)

❈ ❈ ❈

## KINGS OF DENMARK AND NORWAY (UNION OF KALMAR, 1397-1523)

*House of Estrith*
Margaret (1387-1412)
Eric VII (1412-1439)
Christopher III "of Bavaria" (1439-1448)

*House of Oldenbourg*
Christian I (1448-1481)
John (1481-1513)
Christian II "the Cruel" (1513-1523)
Frederick I (1523-1533)
Christian III "Father of the People" (1534-1558)
Frederick II (1558-1588)
Christian IV (1588-1648)
Christian V (1646-1699)

❈ ❈ ❈

## KINGS OF ENGLAND

*House of Lancaster*
Henry IV (1399-1413)
Henry V (1413-1422)
Henry VI (1422-1461)

*House of York*
Edward IV (1461-1483)
Edward V (1483)
Richard III (1483-1485)

*House of Tudor*
Henry VII (1485-1509)
Henry VIII (1509-1547)
Edward VI (1547-1553)
Mary (1553-1558)
Elizabeth I (1558-1603)

*House of Stuart*
James I (1603-1625)
Charles I (1625-1649)

❊ ❊ ❊

KINGS OF FRANCE

*House of Valois*
Charles VI (1380-1422)
Charles VII (1422-1461)
Louis XI (1461-1483)
Charles VIII (1483-1498)
Louis XII (1498-1512)
Francis I (1515-1547)
Henry II (1547-1559)
Francis II (1559-1560)
Charles IX (1560-1574)
Henry III (1574-1589)

*House of Bourbon*
Henry IV (1589-1610)
Louis XIII (1610-1643)
Louis XIV (1643-1715)

❊ ❊ ❊

KINGS OF HUNGARY AND BOHEMIA

*House of Luxemburg*
Sigmund (Hungary 1387-1437, Bohemia 1410-1437)

*House of Habsburg*
Albert (1437-1439)
Ladislaus I "Posthumus" (Hungary 1440-1444, Bohemia 1439-1457)

George Podiebrady (Bohemia 1459-1471)

*House of Hunyádi*
Mathias Corvinus (Hungary 1458-1490, Bohemia 1465-1490)

*House of Jagiello*
Ladislas II (Hungary 1490-1516, Bohemia 1471-1516)
Louis II (1516-1526)

*House of Habsburg-Trastámara*
Ferdinand I (1526-1564)
Maximilian (1564-1576)
Rudolph (1576-1608)
Matthias II (1608-1619)
Ferdinand II (1619-1637)
Ferdinand III (1637-1657)

❧ ❧ ❧

OTTOMAN SULTANS

*House of Osman*
Bayezid I "the Lightning" (1389-1403)
Mehmed I "the Restorer" (1413-1421)
Murad II (1421-1451)
Mehmed II "the Conqueror" (1451-1481)
Bayezid II (1481-1512)
Selim I "the Terrible" (1512-1520)
Suleiman I "the Magnificent" or "the Lawgiver" (1520-1566)
Selim II "the Sot" (1566-1574)
Murad III (1574-1595)
Mehmed III (1595-1603)
Ahmed I (1603-1617)
Mustapha I (1617-1618)
Osman II (1618-1622)
  Interregnum (1622-1623)
Murad IV (1623-1640)
Ibrahim I (1640-1648)
Mehmed IV (1648-1687)

❈ ❈ ❈

KINGS OF POLAND

*House of Jagiello*
Wladyslaw V (1386-1434)
Wladyslaw VI (1434-1444)
Casimir IV (1447-1492)
John Albert (1492-1501)
Alexander (1501-1506)
Sigmund I (1506-1548)
Sigmund II (1548-1572)
 Interregnum (1572-1573)

*House of Valois*
Henry (1573-1574)
 Interregnum (1575-1576)

*House of Báthory*
Stephen (1575-1586)
 Interregnum (1586-1587)

*House of Vasa*
Sigmund III (1587-1632)
Wladislaw IV (1632-1648)
John Casimir (1648-1668)

❈ ❈ ❈

KINGS OF PORTUGAL

*House of Avis*
John I "the Great" (1385-1433)
Edward (1433-1438)
Afonso V "the African" (1438-1481)
John II "the Perfect Prince" (1481-1495)
Emanuel "the Fortunate" (1495-1521)
John III (1521-1557)
Sebastian I (1557-1578)

*House of Trastámara-Habsburg*
Philip I (1580-1598)
Philip II (1598-1621)

*House of Braganza*
John IV "the Fortunate" (1640-1656)

❈ ❈ ❈

RULERS OF MUSCOVY

*House of Riúrik*
Basil I Dmitrievich (1389-1425)
Basil II "the Blind" (1425-1462)
Ivan III "the Great" (1462-1505)
Basil III (1505-1533)
Ivan IV "the Terrible" (1533-1584)
Theodore I (1584-1598)

*House of Godunov*
Boris Godunov (1598-1605)
Theodore (1605)

*House of Romanov*
Michael (1613-1645)
Alexis I (1645-1676)

❈ ❈ ❈

KINGS OF SCOTLAND

*House of Stuart*
Robert III (1390-1424)
James I (1424-1437)
James II (1437-1460)
James III (1460-1488)
James IV (1488-1513)
James V (1513-1542)
Mary of Guise (regent, 1543-1560)
Mary, "Queen of Scots" (1561-1567)

James VI (1567-1625)
Charles I (1625-1649)

＊＊＊

## KINGS OF SPAIN

*House of Trastámara (Castile)*
Henry III (1390-1406)
John II (1406-1454)
Henry IV (1454-1474)
Isabella "the Catholic" (1474-1504)

*House of Aragon*
Martin (1395-1410)
Ferdinand I "the Just" (1412-1416)
Alfonso V "the Magnanimous" (1416-1458)
John II (1458-1479)
Ferdinand II "the Catholic" (1479-1516)

*House of Trastámara-Habsburg*
Philip I "the Handsome" (1504-1506)
Charles I (Castile 1506-1516, Aragon 1516-1556)
Philip II (1556-1598)
Philip III (1598-1621)
Philip IV (1621-1665)

＊＊＊

## KINGS OF SWEDEN

*House of Vasa*
Gustavus I (1523-1560)
Eric XIV (1560-1568)
John III (1568-1592)
Charles IX (1604-1611)
Gustavus Adolphus (1611-1632)
Christina (1632-1654)
Charles X (1654-1660)

⬚ ⬚ ⬚

## SOVEREIGNS AND REGENTS OF THE HABSBURG NETHERLANDS

*House of Valois*
Mary of Burgundy (1477-1482)

*House of Habsburg*
Maximilian I (1482-1494)
Philip "the Handsome" (1494-1506)
Maximilian I (1506-1514)
*Regent:*  Margaret of Austria (1507-1515)

*House of Habsburg-Trastámara*
Charles V (1514-1556)
*Regents:*  Margaret of Austria (1517-1530)
        Mary of Hungary (1531-1555)
Philip II (1556-1598)
*Regents:*  Emmanuel Philibert of Savoy, Gov. General (1556-1559)
        Margaret of Parma (1559-1566)
        Fernándo Alvárez de Toledo, Duke of Alba (1566-1573)

⬚ ⬚ ⬚

## SOVEREIGNS AND REGENTS OF THE SPANISH NETHERLANDS AFTER 1572

*House of Habsburg-Trastámara*
Philip II (1556-1598)
*Regents:*  Luis de Requesens y Zuniga (1573-1576)
        Don Juan of Austria (1576-1578)
        Alexander of Parma (1578-1592)
        Peter Ernst von Mansfeld (1592-1594)
        Archduke Ernst of Austria (1593-1595)
        Archduke Albert of Austria (1596-1598)
Archduke Albert and Infante Isabella (1598-1621)

❈ ❈ ❈

RULERS FOR THE UNITED PROVINCES AFTER 1572

*Stadtholders of Holland and Zeeland*
  *House of Orange-Nassau*
William I "the Silent" (1572-1584)
Maurice of Nassau (1585-1621)
Frederick Henry (1625-1647)
William II (1647-1650)

*Grand Pensionaries of the States of Holland*
Paulus Buys (1572-1584)
Johan van Oldenbarnevelt (1586-1618)

# INDEX OF PERSONS

# INDEX OF PLACES